THE FABULOUS LUNTS

JARED BROWN

THE FABULOUS LUNTS

A Biography of

ALFRED LUNT *and* LYNN FONTANNE

Foreword by HELEN HAYES

ATHENEUM

New York

1986

The written and recorded words of Alfred Lunt and Lynn Fontanne on tape, on records, or in letters, used with permission of George Bugbee, Executor of Lynn Fontanne's estate and heir of Alfred Lunt and Lynn Fontanne.

Material from the tapes, interviews, and notes of Maurice Zolotow used and quoted with the permission of Mr. Zolotow.

Lunt/Fontanne material from the William G. B. Carson Papers, Washington University Libraries, St. Louis, Missouri, used with permission.

Material from the Behrman, Lindsay/Crouse, and Lunt/Fontanne collections of The State Historical Society of Wisconsin used with permission.

Material from the Maxwell Anderson and Stark Young collections of the Harry Ransom Humanities Research Center, The University of Texas at Austin, used with permission.

Material from the Barnouw, Somerville, Belmont, Salisbury, Norton, Random House, and Rose Franken collections of the Rare Book and Manuscript Library, Columbia University, used with permission.

Alfred Lunt's responses to questions asked and answered at Carroll College, Waukesha, Wisconsin, used with permission.

Page 510 constitutes a continuation of this copyright page

Library of Congress Cataloging-in-Publication Data

Brown, Jared.
    The fabulous Lunts.

    Bibliography: p.
    Includes index.
    1. Lunt, Alfred. 2. Fontanne, Lynn. 3. Actors—
United States—Biography. I. Title.
PN2287.L8B76   1986   792'.028'0922 [B]   85-43249
ISBN 0-689-11648-9

For J U D Y, *my wife,*
with love and gratitude

Foreword by HELEN HAYES

I have nothing but very happy recollections of the Lunts. One of the earliest and most pleasant memories dates from 1919, when, on September 20, Booth Tarkington's *Clarence* opened at the Hudson Theatre in New York. Alfred Lunt played Clarence. The cast included Glenn Hunter, Mary Boland and a starry-eyed teenager: me. Alfred and Lynn were "going together" at the time, but had not yet gotten married.

In that engagement Alfred taught me the meaning of genius, which, I remember someone said, is "the infinite capacity for taking pains." Alfred had that capacity. In *Clarence* he was supposed to win all the women in the cast by playing the saxophone superbly at the end of the first act. The managers wanted to have an offstage saxophone, of course. Not Alfred. Long before we even went into rehearsal, he began saxophone lessons, probably driving Lynn mad with his practicing. He practiced diligently, though, and when the play went into performance, he played the saxophone creditably.

But occasionally the saxophone would get out of hand and a great high-shrilled note would come forth unexpectedly. As the curtain would fall on the first act, Alfred would say, "Damn, this saxophone is under the influence of Adelina Patti!"

I learned—not only from that saxophone, but from everything else Alfred did in that play—that you never leave a stone unturned or an effort unmade to do your best in everything you try in the theatre. That was a very important lesson for a nineteen-year-old.

We played for a long time because we were a great success. During the run every woman in the company fell in love with Alfred. Each night, as the last act was in progress, the whole company would be lined up on a row of chairs provided backstage, waiting for our entrance cues. Along about the middle of the act, as Alfred and the leading lady were playing a scene on stage together, we would see a rather shy and discouraged-looking young woman, her head down, slip through the dark and tiptoe to Alfred's dressing room. This, of course, was dear Lynn, arriving to wait for Alfred and take him home after the performance. But we hardly knew her then; we only knew that we were in love with Alfred and that she wasn't worthy of our hero. So we looked at her with daggers as she went by. Mary Boland, who had more courage than the rest of us, even tried to talk him out of marrying Lynn Fontanne.

Many years later, when I repeated that story in an interview, Lynn told me, "I could feel it, you know, I could feel the daggers right between my shoulder blades." But it wasn't until I was in my late seventies that I first heard that Lynn was jealous of me, that she had been afraid I might take Alfred away from her. That was probably the most glowing, glorious moment in life. To think that I—who so often had been given the care of husbands by their wives when they had to go away, leaving them confidently in my hands—had had Lynn Fontanne worried about *me*.

I think today of all the years of beauty and joy and inspiration that Lynn and Alfred gave to me and to so many other young actors. They had a most amazing career in that respect, starting so many wonderful people in the theatre. I couldn't begin to name them all or this foreword would be longer than the book it accompanies.

As much as I valued the Lunts as theatrical colleagues, for me our personal relationship was most memorable. Lynn was a gentle, dear and, as someone once said about her (I think it was Noël Coward in his recollections), a *comfortable* person. It may be difficult to imagine that comfortable quality with someone who was so glamorous, but she was that. She was the only woman I ever knew who could actually tame a chipmunk. She had a pet chipmunk in Genesee Depot who came and ate out of her fingers. Nobody can do that, of course, not even the most fabulous animal trainer—but Lynn did.

Lynn cared for Alfred with infinite love and patience. He was a very nervous man, as all perfectionists are. But she encouraged him when he would tighten up, cared for him, watched out that he didn't get too frightened. She was, in some respects, like his nurse or his nanny.

After the Lunts retired and moved permanently to their farm in Wisconsin, someone asked me, "What does she *do* with her life out there?" I said that it was the busiest life you ever saw. She had so many pets—her poodle, who adored her, her pet goose, all the things she loved; her life was very contented and very quiet after all the years of excitement in the theatre.

The last conversation I particularly remember having with Alfred was when he called me one day and said, "I called because I can't see anymore. I can't watch the television. I can't read. So," he said, "I just sit and remember. And I had a long session of remembering you. I began to laugh as I thought of all the things I remembered about us over the years. I laughed for a good hour or two, just remembering and remembering." Then he asked, "Do you remember the time in *Clarence* when Mary Boland made her entrance in a chiffon negligee and the costume caught on a great urn that was supposedly made of cement? The urn fell on stage without making a sound. And Mary quietly, without a thought, picked it up with two fingers, replaced it on its base and exited, leaving us on stage to see ourselves through the rest of the scene." I remembered it well. Mary got a large hand from the audience, but I was so stunned that I forgot every word of Booth

Tarkington's dialogue. "Do you remember that you never spoke another word in the scene after that?" Alfred asked me. "You just stood there and couldn't speak, and we had to say your lines. I made up some extraordinary lines in your place."

God bless Alfred for remembering such things. The bitterness of fate is that his eyes—which he used better than anyone I ever knew—failed him late in life. But neither his head nor his heart failed him.

The Lunts were my friends. They were my idols, my teachers, my mentors. I think, of all the lucky things that happened to me in my life in the theatre, the Lunts were the luckiest.

Author's Note

Noël Coward once wrote that he "burst out into a kind of spiritual sweat" whenever he contemplated writing a biography of Alfred Lunt and Lynn Fontanne. Comparing them to an Oscar Hammerstein lyric, Coward said, "Catching a moonbeam in your hand would be falling off a log compared with catching and holding the truth about the Lunts between the covers of a book. Neither I nor anyone in this world could do it entirely successfully." Duly warned, I embarked on this project nevertheless, determined to capture and convey as much of the Lunts' characters and careers as my abilities would allow.

The Lunts did not wish to have books written about them during their lifetimes and were indifferent at best to the idea of a biography appearing after their deaths. They made no attempt to record their memories systematically or to compile materials that would assist a writer who wished to chronicle their lives. Consequently, considerable digging on my part has been required to unearth the information that appears in this book. I am particularly grateful to George Bugbee and Suzanne Knapp, Lunt's brother-in-law and niece, who, as his heirs, permitted me to have access to the Lunts' correspondence. They also gave me a tour of Ten Chimneys in Genesee Depot and allowed me to interview them on several occasions. Another invaluable source was a series of audio-taped interviews of the Lunts, Noël Coward and S. N. Behrman, recorded by Maurice Zolotow in the early 1960s when he was preparing his biography, *Stagestruck: The Romance of Alfred Lunt and Lynn Fontanne*. For Mr. Zolotow's generous permission to quote from the tapes (and from notes and correspondence) I am deeply appreciative.

Among those who permitted me to interview them at length, I wish particularly to thank John Randolph (who also allowed me the use of his letters to his wife, which constituted a diary of his experiences in *The Visit*), Alan Hewitt, whose many kindnesses to me were of invaluable help, George Schaefer (who also gave me access to many hours of videotaped—but never telecast—interview material with the Lunts), William Le Massena (who also made his letters from the Lunts available), Carolyn Every, who shared clippings and other documents with me as well as her reminiscences, Mr. and Mrs. Donald Seawell (Eugenia Rawls), and Renée Orsell, who gave me a great deal of information, allowed me to quote from her correspondence and permitted me to reprint several photographs of the Lunts from her personal collection.

To the following friends and colleagues of the Lunts who were also interviewed by this writer, I wish to express my gratitude: Anna Jane (Williams) Berg, Adaline (Butchart) Hoag, Gwen Davies, Harriet Owens, Dick Van Patten, Carol Channing, Charles Lowe, Armina Marshall, Uta Hagen, Julie Harris, Peg Murray, Maurice Valency, Phyllis Thaxter, Dr. Edward Bigg, Mary Sargent, George Burns, Charles Bowden, Roger Stevens and Robert Whitehead.

Research material came primarily from the Wisconsin State Historical Society in Madison and the Performing Arts Research Center of the New York Public Library. Additionally, I found valuable information at the Carroll College Library, the Waukesha County Historical Society, the Washington University Library, the Rare Book and Manuscript Library of Columbia University, the Manuscript Library of the New York Public Library, the Wisconsin Center for Film and Theater Research, the Players Library, the University of Texas Humanities Research Center, the Department of Rare Books and Special Collections at the University of Michigan and the Library of Congress. Two people who assisted my researches materially and have my thanks are Barbara Kaiser, archivist at the Wisconsin State Historical Society, and Kathryn L. Beam, Manuscript Librarian of the Department of Rare Books and Special Collections at the University of Michigan. To those few librarians whose officiousness made life difficult at times, I grant forgiveness.

The following individuals graciously allowed me to peruse and quote from the letters the Lunts wrote to them: Dr. Edward Bigg, William Le Massena, Mrs. Richard (Tinx) Whorf and Helen Hayes. I am also grateful to Mrs. Robert E. Sherwood for permitting me to quote from her husband's letters and diary, as well as from a letter of her own; Mrs. Russel Crouse and Mrs. Howard Lindsay for allowing me to quote from their husbands' correspondence; Brooke Hayward for permission to quote from a letter of Margaret Sullavan's; Irene C. Windust and Penelope Windust for permission to quote from the correspondence of Bretaigne Windust; and the estates of Edna Ferber, S. N. Behrman, Noël Coward and Alexander Woollcott for allowing me to quote from the letters of Miss Ferber and Messrs. Behrman, Coward and Woollcott.

Financial support for this book was provided by many sources at Western Illinois University. Special mention should be made of the College of Fine Arts (Forrest Suycott, Dean; Titus Karlowicz, Assistant Dean), the Research Office (Shirley Myers, Acting Director), the Department of Theatre (Gene Kozlowski, chairman), the Graduate School and the Office of Faculty Development. Without the funding and the encouragement provided by these offices and individuals, this book might not have been completed.

Valuable research was undertaken in London at my request by Mim Canny and David McCordick, for whose labors I am extremely appreciative. For assistance of various kinds, I wish to thank Julian Bach, June Brown, Charles and Susan Calhoun Moss, Jo Farwell, Jonathan Farwell, Mark Landis, Philip M. Runkel, Ellen Langill, Lauren Brown, Sam Parker, Becky Parker, Barbara Ridenour, Egla Birmingham, Royanna Benjamin and my editors at Atheneum. Several graduate and undergraduate students helped make written transcripts of the many hours of tape-recorded interviews I conducted, and I am grateful to them for their labors.

Special thanks are due Professor Dean O'Brien, who located and permitted me to use several photographs taken by his father, Warren S. O'Brien. The senior O'Brien, whose studio was located in Waukesha, Wisconsin, was often referred to as "the Lunts' favorite photographer."

George Bugbee and Alan Hewitt read the manuscript before publication, maintaining watchful eyes for factual errors. The emendations they suggested to me were invariably helpful, and for their assistance I am most appreciative. Alan Hewitt, who participated in many of the events chronicled in this book, called upon his encyclopedic knowledge and remarkable memory to discover several items that were not completely accurate and to offer much additional material. When his memory could not supply the information he wanted, he consulted his diaries as well as his superb collection of books and theatrical memorabilia. He also spent many hours checking microfilm of old newspapers in various libraries in New York City. Surely his uncanny eye for detail, combined with his reverence for the memories of Alfred Lunt and Lynn Fontanne, made him the ideal reader for this manuscript.

Above all, I am grateful beyond words to my wife, Judy. Far beyond good-naturedly enduring my obsession with this biography for several years and providing continual encouragement, she served as my editorial assistant, reviewing each chapter as it emerged from the typewriter (or, more often, from the word processor's printer), offering thousands of suggestions for revisions, organizational and stylistic, major and minor. Whatever quality this book may possess is due in great part to her valued assistance.

Preface

We live in an electronic age. An actor who appears on a network soap opera, in a major film or a prime-time television series becomes an instantaneous celebrity, not necessarily because of the quality of his performance, but because he has appeared in a glamorous medium.

Despite the status of the electronic media, many actors prefer to work on the stage because of the spontaneous and immediate audience response. Most good actors also enjoy the challenges that only the stage can provide. There is almost no margin for error in the theatre; a performance must be carefully built because each moment is a finished product; a scene cannot be repeated if the timing misfires or a line is misread or an accident occurs. A performer must expend his energies wisely on the stage. If his "big scene" occurs in the third act, he must plan his performance so that he has sufficient reserves of physical and emotional intensity for the climactic scene, regardless of how grueling earlier scenes may have been. Finally, the stage actor must be able to project one emotion immediately after another, as the play requires. A comic scene may be followed by an intensely dramatic one, and the actor must be capable of playing both with equal skill and conviction. The same demand is placed on the television and film actor, but with this difference: he may be given time between takes to make whatever internal and external adjustments are necessary for him to project each succeeding emotion.

Although many performers enjoy these challenges, very few prominent actors in the twentieth century have chosen to work exclusively, or even primarily, in the theatre. The financial reward is not nearly as great as that provided by the electronic media, and the celebrity status the stage can confer does not begin to compare with the kind of fame created by exposure in film and television.

Many prominent actors ignore the stage entirely. It is too risky: lack of technique or the inability to project emotions and attitudes believably are all too clearly apparent in the theatre. A few present-day actors have chosen to balance film and stage careers; George C. Scott and Jason Robards, Jr., are examples. Fewer yet have selected the theatre as their primary means of expression. Helen Hayes is one. Mary Martin is also in that category, as were Tallulah Bankhead and Ethel Merman. Even in their cases, however, each appeared in films occasionally in order to keep themselves in the eye of the vast public that neither attends the theatre nor follows its history.

At the head of the short list of those who have concentrated upon stage careers are the names of Alfred Lunt and Lynn Fontanne, who, virtually alone among prominent American actors of this century, almost completely ignored the electronic media during their most active years. They made one talking picture together, then rejected all further offers—and there were many—to appear in films. They never appeared on television until he was sixty-five and she was seventy, by which time they were nearing retirement from the physical demands of the stage. They did perform on the radio when radio was a mass medium in America, but generally as an adjunct to their stage performances, giving abridged versions of their plays. Yet Lunt and Fontanne achieved an international prominence that far exceeded the fame accorded to many actors in the electronic media. An audience of hundreds of thousands awaited their productions throughout the United States and in England. The opening of a Lunt-Fontanne play was an occasion that no other entertainment could rival.

The Lunt-Fontanne Theatre in New York was named in their honor, and the event took place during their lifetimes. One could count such occasions on the fingers of one hand. Their contributions to culture were recognized by several presidents of the United States and by many colleges and universities, which awarded them honorary doctorates. Their efforts on behalf of the Allied forces in World War II were of such significance that the armed services of America and England acknowledged themselves to be deeply in the Lunts' debt.

Many performers who worked for and with Lunt and Fontanne are still active in the entertainment world today. Without exception, the actors who worked with the Lunts have expressed their gratitude in the most effusive terms. To have acted with the Lunts, they all insist, was a privilege, an unforgettable experience and an everlasting lesson in theatrical discipline and technique. Many of those who knew or acted with the Lunts continue to be deeply affected by their memory. Their qualities as generous, compassionate human beings, as well as their artistic brilliance, won them the undying admiration of nearly all who knew them.

Who were these extraordinary individuals who chose to merge their separate (and compelling) personalities into a single unit? who chose the rigors of the stage over the comparative ease of film and television acting? who consciously rejected the financial rewards (as well as the greater fame) the electronic media could bring them? who maintained a fifty-five-year marriage based on mutual love and respect in a profession known for its infidelities and volatility? who inspired the love and loyalty of hundreds of professionals in the theatre? whose names still conjure up images of greatness long after their careers have come to an end? Those are some of the questions this biography will attempt to answer.

Contents

Illustrations

The Lunts with their friend Noël Coward at Genesee Depot
(Photograph by Clifford O'Brien)

in *Design for Living,* 1933
(Theatre Collection: N.Y.P.L. at Lincoln Center)

after the Tony Award presentations in 1970
(State Historical Society of Wisconsin)

Lunt in *Idiot's Delight* with Les Blondes
(Theatre Collection: N.Y.P.L. at Lincoln Center)

Following page 302

As Petruchio and Katharine in *The Taming of the Shrew*
(Theatre Collection: N.Y.P.L. at Lincoln Center)

Reunion in Vienna, 1931
(Theatre Collection: N.Y.P.L. at Lincoln Center)

Quadrille, 1954
(Theatre Collection: N.Y.P.L. at Lincoln Center)

The Lunts enjoying the role of simple farmers: Three variations on a
favorite pose over a fourteen-year period
(Photographs by Warren S. O'Brien)

With Montgomery Clift in *There Shall Be No Night*
(Theatre Collection: N.Y.P.L. at Lincoln Center)

With the USO in Germany at the end of World War II
(State Historical Society of Wisconsin)

Lunt posing with some of his prized toy theatres
(Theatre Collection: N.Y.P.L. at Lincoln Center)

and in the kitchen at Genesee Depot
(Photograph by Warren S. O'Brien)

Some of the murals that cover the walls and ceilings at Ten Chimneys
(Photograph by George Karger, reprinted with the permission of George Bugbee)

Lunt and Fontanne as they appeared in *The Visit*
(Theatre Collection: N.Y.P.L. at Lincoln Center)

A portrait of the Lunts in their later years
(Wisconsin Center for Film and Theater Research)

Lynn with Donald Seawell at Alfred's funeral
(Courtesy of Donald Seawell)

THE FABULOUS LUNTS

Chapter One

GETTING STARTED

"[Ellen Terry] taught me one invaluable thing. . . . It was this: always think the thought behind the words. Pay no attention to the diction or the reading, she told me, but fill your mind with the thought and let the words pour out of your mouth."

Lynn Fontanne, 1938

"[May Nickell Rankin] showed me how to make something of my capabilities. . . . Her method was just as modern as the studios in New York. She was way ahead of Stanislavski in this country. He could have learned an awful lot from Miss Rankin."

Alfred Lunt, 1962

1887–1905

There were four Fontanne sisters: Mai, born in 1882, Antoinette, born in 1883, Frances Emma, born in 1884, and Lillie Louise, born in 1887. Lynn, who was acutely sensitive about her age, claimed that she was a fifth sister who had been born several years afterward and whose birth certificate had been lost. But she made two separate admissions that, taken together, disproved her claim. The first was that she had been born on December 6 (which just happens to be the date of Lillie Louise's birth in 1887), and the second was remarking to her niece on one occasion that her real name was Lillie Louise. There can be no doubt, then, that Lynn Fontanne was born on December 6, 1887, to Jules and Ellen Fontanne.

Jules Pierre Antoine Fontanne, a first-generation Englishman whose parents had come from France, was educated both in France and in England, where he attended Charterhouse, a public school, but, as Lynn said of him, "his milieu was France." On August 1, 1881, when he was twenty-six, Jules Fontanne married twenty-two-year-old Frances Ellen Thornley Barnett, who had emigrated from Ireland to England, in the parish church of Woodford Bridge in the county of Essex.

The Fontannes' first daughter was born only a year after their marriage, the others coming along at regular intervals. Frances Emma did not survive to maturity, but the other children all enjoyed long lives. "Lillie Louise" became "Lynn" immediately after she was born, according to her niece, Suzanne Knapp. As soon as Frances Ellen brought the infant home from the hospital, she told her husband she disliked the name they had given the child, and that she would thereafter be known as Lynn.

Jules Fontanne's father, Antoine, owned a printing foundry in the Clerkenwell Road. Jules took over his father's occupation and inherited the factory as well, shortly before Lynn was born. He seems to have been a talented type-designer—Lynn claimed that her father had designed the type that was adopted for use by the *Times* of London—but a dreadful businessman. The foundry's fortunes declined steadily under his management, and after eight years the factory failed and Fontanne was forced to sell it. The family went through a period of considerable economic difficulty as he drifted from one occupation to another.

Jules was "very inventive, clever at making things," Lynn said of her father; "he could do anything with his hands." But, skilled as Fontanne may have been, his lack of business sense dogged him. For a time he thought of himself as an inventor; each morning he would bid his wife goodbye and walk the few steps to a shed in his garden, where, as Lynn said, "he'd go and invent. He was trying to solve the secret of perpetual motion." Unfortunately, Fontanne failed to solve that secret. He was also convinced that he could invent a flying machine, but that attempt, like all of his attempts at invention, met with failure.

Still, even though Jules Fontanne was unable to provide for his family or to achieve professional success, he seems to have been a man of considerable charm. His daughter Antoinette said, "Father was wonderful." He had the ability to make the apt remark at the right time. On one occasion the Fontanne children were being looked after by a governess who boasted that she had once worked for a titled Englishwoman. According to Antoinette, Lynn went to her father and asked, "Where is our title?" Fontanne responded, "Your ancestors once trod the courts of Versailles." And, Antoinette said, after her father's comment "we all felt like princesses."

Lynn, recalling her father's remark, remembered the circumstances differently. "He said it because I had shoes on that were very worn and full of holes," she said. "The children laughed and made fun of me, and he said, 'Never mind those common little children. Your ancestors walked the courts of Versailles.'"

Still, Lynn's memories of her father were not all happy ones. "He was a strange sort of man," she said many years later, "reading all the time." Although Fontanne's constant reading was a source of annoyance to his youngest daughter, it also resulted in her initial exposure to good literature, including Shakespeare, Dickens and Jules Verne. Antoinette described their father as "a natural actor; he'd recite Shakespeare by the yard. A large, dignified man with a handlebar mustache, vivacious, amusing, with a fine diction." But Lynn's clearest memory was of the economic difficulties into which he plunged his family. Because of him, she said, "we went through some very hard times."

Antoinette remembered her mother as the divisive force in the family. "Mother was a witty woman with a sharp tongue and malicious," she said. "He [her father] and Mother were bitter and unhappy with each other." The usual family situation, she recalled, found "three girls and him in an armed camp against Mother." Antoinette felt that it was because of her mother that the Fontanne children moved so far from home. "She had something in her that drove us all away," Antoinette said, "Mai to New Zealand, I to Paris when I was twenty" and Lynn to America.

Lynn had many vivid memories of her mother. "My mother would be having people in to tea," she recalled, "and I'd go into the room, and once I remember going in and stumbling over a chair, and she'd say sharply, 'Go out and come in again!'" But Lynn also thought of her mother with some tenderness and understanding. "I was her favorite, really, her baby. She loved me, showed great favoritism towards me. I think she wasn't well. That's what made her irritable and high-strung."

As the Fontannes' fortunes declined, the family moved from Essex to London, and soon afterward to the south of France, where, unable to afford any housing of their own, they stayed with Jules Fontanne's aunt. When his aunt died, she left what little money she had—just "enough to live without starving," according to Lynn—to Jules, who thereupon took his family back to England, this time to a village near Windsor.

When Lynn was three, Antoinette asked her, "What will you be when you're a grownup woman?" Lynn replied promptly and haughtily, "I will be a mother and have four children and twelve nursemaids for each one." She loved to invent stories about her family, her favorite being that they were of noble blood and immensely wealthy, and that her father was a famous man.

Lynn was a tall, thin child with big eyes and long brown hair with a hint of red in it; at Buckstill School in Essex her teachers and classmates had thought her quite unattractive, lacking in femininity. She developed into an athletic girl who walked with long, masculine strides. At school in Windsor she became a runner, easily outdistancing her classmates in most races. When Antoinette recalled Lynn as a child, her image was of a swift and agile little girl, her toes turned in—and running, always running.

From earliest childhood Lynn was independent and unafraid. Once when she was three years old and with her family in Brighton on a holiday, she decided to wander down the beach in search of adventure. When the family discovered that she was gone, they proceeded to the local police station, where she was found perched on a table reciting a poem to an audience of policemen. Her curiosity frequently led her to wander off alone, and whenever she found she was lost, she would simply ask the way to the nearest police station and a policeman would escort her home.

Lynn revealed a theatrical aptitude at an early age. Antoinette remembered her as both observant and imitative. Whenever Mrs. Fontanne had guests, Lynn would sneak off to her mother's bedroom, rummage through her closets for clothes similar to those the guests were wearing, and emerge in "costume" to join the company. On some occasions she added a regal touch by making a dramatic appearance with a tablecloth tied around her waist, the bulk of it trailing behind her.

Lynn's poetry recitals—whether given for policemen, for the family or for guests—were delivered in a clear and beautiful voice and were always accompanied by graceful gestures. When she was three, her favorite piece was about a little girl who took her dolls to the seaside. Lynn later recalled that "in the last verse there was a long word, and all through the first part I was getting ready for it. Finally, with my face red and my whole body tense, I brought it out: 'She *dis-lo-cated* her shoulder.' And then I finished in a breathless rush, to the accompaniment of uncontrollable laughter on the part of the audience."

Soon she was participating in oratorical contests in church and at school. "My popularity as a reciter," she said, "was simply because I was funny and didn't know it." Whatever the source of her success, it led her into amateur theatricals.

At the age of five, she was reciting Shakespeare with perfect diction, according to Antoinette. And from the time she was six or seven, her future had become clear to her: she would go on the stage; no other life was possible for her.

Lynn was not the only one who saw her future clearly. Although her mother may have meant it as a joke, she often said, "Lynn will be a second Ellen Terry. Someday she'll be earning twenty pounds a week." But it was no joke to Lynn. "I believed every word of it. And since, as I thought, it was my destiny to be a second Ellen Terry and to earn twenty pounds a week, I proceeded to plan my life accordingly."

With each successive financial reversal, the children were transferred from one school to another. Lynn went to a succession of them until she was fifteen or sixteen, but she was then withdrawn from school (as her sisters had been) in the hope that she would be able to find a job and contribute to the minuscule family treasury. "There were no teens for us," Antoinette said, "we had to grow up overnight and go to work." As far as

Lynn was concerned, there was no question in her mind what sort of job she should have: it had to be as an actress.

On one occasion Lynn dragged Antoinette, who was working as a stenographer, to a theatre in London and insisted they audition together for the theatre's manager. "It'll be such fun," she said. But Antoinette had no theatrical ambitions whatever. "I didn't want to go on the stage and be with such horrible people—ill-mannered, rude," she said years later. When the manager appeared, he confirmed Antoinette's opinion of theatre people by keeping his hat on in the girls' presence and continuing to smoke his cigarette. "Ah," said the manager when he saw them, "just the two girls I need." Whatever it was that he needed them for, he didn't give them a job, and Lynn stalked out of the theatre. "I'm going to be an actress," she told Antoinette defiantly, "a great actress. No matter how rude these people are, the day will come when they're polite to me."

Despite her vow, however, Lynn's prospects of getting a job in the theatre were slim. She had no experience, she was still regarded as awkward and unattractive, and she had had no training in the technique of acting. Moreover, the extroversion that had characterized her as a child had somehow vanished, replaced by a painful shyness. But Lynn was fortunate. A family friend named Sophie Kean, who knew of Lynn's theatrical aspirations, happened to be an acquaintance of Ellen Terry, the rival of Eleonora Duse and Sarah Bernhardt. Lynn, who undoubtedly recalled her mother's frequent references to England's foremost actress, badgered Sophie Kean until she agreed to give Lynn a note of introduction.

Few performers have been as beloved as Ellen Terry was by the English people, and never was idolatry better deserved. Together, Ellen Terry and Henry Irving had created not only the finest theatrical company in England but one of the finest in the world. Each was an incomparable performer, and Irving's outstanding direction added immeasurably to the success of their productions. Beyond her brilliance as an actress, Ellen Terry was also known for her generosity. She had begun to train young actresses, endeavoring to pass on to them the knowledge she had gained in her long and distinguished career.* It would clearly be the opportunity of a lifetime to be given lessons by her, and any young actress would have been rapturous at the prospect.

Lynn Fontanne was fifteen or sixteen when she was given Sophie Kean's letter of introduction to Ellen Terry.** "Off I went to 315 King's Road with my little letter," Lynn remembered years later. At her knock,

---

*Among the few students she had accepted were Lena Ashwell, Ellaline Terriss and Violet Vanbrugh, actresses who were well established on the British stage several years before Lynn Fontanne met Ellen Terry.

**Or so it seems. When Fontanne told the story, she generally said that she was eleven years old at the time. But she didn't tell of her training with Ellen Terry until after she had become a successful actress in New York, by which time she had taken to deducting several years from her age. It seems most likely that the meeting occurred in early 1904.

the door was opened by Terry's maid, also named Ellen, who said, "Miss Terry is expecting you—go on up." Lynn climbed the stairs, turned left and knocked on the door. Behind it, a low, husky voice said, "Come in." Lynn opened the door and shyly introduced herself. "I'm Lynn Fontanne," she said.

"I know," said the renowned actress; "come here." Lynn described the scene: "She was sitting up in bed with a tray on her lap having breakfast. So I went forward very timidly, and she pulled me to her and kissed me. I was absolutely stunned. She smelled divine; such a scent. And so I suddenly found myself absolutely speechless with shyness, and she said, 'Now don't waste any time. You go over there and do something. Do anything you like. I'll be having my breakfast.' So she sat having her scrambled eggs and bacon, and this awkward, gawky child—and what do you think I did? I did the 'quality of mercy' speech. I thought she'd like to hear it."

Ellen Terry was flabbergasted, and with good reason. She had often played Portia in *The Merchant of Venice* and was esteemed for her performance of that particular speech. That a young girl with no theatrical experience would choose to perform it on that occasion might have been thought to be remarkably arrogant. For Lynn Fontanne, however, there was no arrogant intention, simply a naïveté so complete that she chose to read the speech because "I thought she'd like to hear it."

When Lynn was no more than nine or ten years old, she had been taken to see Terry and Irving act together in a matinee performance of *The Merchant of Venice*. On that occasion Lynn, who had memorized portions of the play for one of her recitals, stood up when Terry began to speak the "quality of mercy" speech and delivered it along with her. "I had to be sat down," Lynn said about the incident, "and I thought it would amuse her [Ellen Terry] if I did the mercy speech. So I did it for her."

Despite Terry's initial reaction—she couldn't suppress an exclamation of "Oh, my God!"—Lynn proceeded confidently. After a moment's silence, during which Terry must have wondered whether the aspiring young actress was slightly mad, she gave her verdict on Lynn's audition. "Well, now," she said, "I think you have talent, and I will give you lessons, but you have to come promptly when I call for you, and there will be no dates for you," making it plain that nothing was to interfere with Lynn's focus on a theatrical career and upon the lessons Terry would give her.

Ellen Terry warned Lynn that the lessons might have no positive result. "My family say that all my swans are geese," Terry said, "so don't expect anything from this. I may be wrong about your talent, but we'll see, we'll see."

Despite her warning, Terry must have sensed great talent in this young, naïve and painfully shy girl, for when she discovered the state of the Fontannes' finances, she volunteered to give lessons to Lynn at no charge. And the lessons began immediately. "I believe you learn most about acting from big parts," she said, "and so I'll give you a big part to learn. I want you to learn Cordelia from *King Lear.*" Terry handed Lynn a copy of the play on which she had written comments on the role of Cordelia, and told her to study the play and the role thoroughly.* She also wrote a special note for Lynn in the margin. "Don't worry about the words," it said, "but rather the significance of the words—the meaning of the words. Get the character of Cordelia through her words and the words spoken about her."

At their next meeting the instruction in acting became more specific, as Terry guided Fontanne through several possible approaches to a single line of dialogue, demonstrating to her how a line in a play can be reinforced or contradicted by its subtextual meaning, and how an actress can give shape and color to every word she speaks, depending upon its interpretation and delivery. After a thorough examination of the line in question, Terry said, "I won't tell you another reading, but from that you must get the sense of the part, and everything you say must be said with your whole heart and mind behind it."

Then Terry gave Lynn what Lynn would later describe as "the key of acting": Terry said, "Think of the *meaning* of what you are saying and let the words pour out of your mouth." This one bit of advice, given when Lynn was only sixteen, formed the basis of Fontanne's technique for her entire career. Her method was to learn the words so thoroughly that no effort of memory was needed to speak them; instead, all her concentration was focused upon the meaning—not necessarily the literal meaning of the words, but the inner meaning the character wished to express. She would later say that Ellen Terry had "taught me one invaluable thing. . . . It was this: always think the thought behind the words. Pay no attention to the diction or the reading, she told me, but fill your mind with the thought and let the words pour out of your mouth."

Terry's training also concentrated on the technical aspects of acting. She trained Lynn to enunciate every word clearly and taught her the art of vocal projection so thoroughly that she was soon able to fill a theatre effortlessly with the sound of her voice. Terry instructed Lynn to speak naturally, without the artificial and exaggerated manner that many British performers of the time cultivated. And she worked to develop Lynn's natural flair for dialect.

Ellen Terry also taught Lynn how to move gracefully and elegantly in long dresses by the simple expedient of pinning bedsheets to her—"yards and yards wrapped around my legs," Lynn recounted, with the excess trailing on the floor. Terry commanded: "Now walk for me."

"I can't," Lynn said, "I'll fall over."

* More than fifty years later Alfred Lunt spoke of his admiration of Terry's notes. The prompt script "is a model of not only 'readings' but of stage business as well," he said. "It is still ahead of its day!"

"No you won't, no you won't," said Terry. "Go on. Walk. Have confidence. Walk!"

So, Lynn recalled years later, "I walked boldly and the sheet flew out in front of me. The trick was to do it very boldly. In that way, the sheets blew away from the legs and you could move."

Fontanne's studies with Terry continued intermittently for considerably more than a year, during which time she was coached in a number of Shakespearean roles. According to an account in the New York *Times* of 1916, Terry actually played opposite Lynn in scores of scenes enacted in the drawing room of Terry's home for an audience of one: Ellen, the maid. The lessons were demanding and unfailingly helpful. "Having gone through a hard, practical school herself," Lynn later said of Terry, "she was not one to pamper a pupil, or to let you off with scamped work."

Ellen Terry became quite fond of her pupil. On several occasions she invited Lynn to her cottage in Kent. At other times Lynn stayed in Terry's house in the King's Road. And she saw to it that Lynn would not go hungry by giving her odd jobs, one of which was to read her to sleep in the afternoons. At such times Terry gave her explicit instructions that she must not read with expression; a monotone was much better suited for putting her to sleep.

Still, Terry fretted that Lynn needed a more secure source of income. "Must get Lynn more money," she noted in her diary. "It's wicked. . . . She is so intelligent."

And Lynn was equally fond of her mentor. They spoke for hours on end about Terry's career. "She had a lot of charm," Lynn said years later, and added: "She was highly intelligent and was practical-minded—no fantasies—full of fun, tremendous humor."

At last, Terry decided it was time for Lynn to strike out on her own. She herself was going on tour, and she must have felt that Lynn needed to be made aware that she could not depend upon her teacher for help in the future. So Terry handed Lynn two letters of introduction, one to the manager of the Drury Lane Theatre and another to the renowned actor-manager Beerbohm Tree, and said, "That's all I'm going to do for you, my dear. You must make your own career. The race is run by one, and if I helped you any more, it wouldn't be good for you. So run along now and don't ever ask me for any more letters or any more puffs. They'd hurt you more than they'd help you."

If Ellen Terry (with an assist from Sophie Kean) was Fontanne's fairy godmother, it is fitting that the first professional job she got was in the play *Cinderella*. The story would be complete if, while performing in that production, Fontanne had lived through a Cinderella story of her own; if she were to be hired for a nonspeaking part, perhaps, only to go on in a major role when the actress who generally played it became too ill to perform. Of course, that would too closely resemble a young actress's typical fantasy—but it is exactly what happened.

Fontanne took Ellen Terry's letter of introduction to the manager of the famous Theatre Royal, Drury Lane, where a Christmas pantomime of *Cinderella* was scheduled to go into rehearsal.* She stood in line with the other aspirants until she was finally permitted to see the manager, Arthur Collins. When she presented her letter, "an amused smile came on his face," Fontanne later said, "and I didn't know what was in the letter because it was a sealed letter."

Collins put her through a brief audition and then informed her that she could have a job as a member of the chorus; she would have no lines to speak. Fontanne accepted the offer without hesitation. She would now be able to call herself a professional—not a professional *actress* exactly, but a professional nonetheless.

She was lucky not to be let go after the first rehearsals of *Cinderella*. The line of chorus girls was supposed to move in unison during one of the dances in the production, and, as she said, "I wasn't very good because I kept going the wrong way, and I was told that if I did that again I'd be fired." At the next rehearsal she again began to move in the wrong direction, but a kindly soul behind her pushed her the right way and enabled her to keep her job. Seventy years later Fontanne said, "Saved my life and I don't know who it was. I wouldn't be here if it wasn't for that girl."

The first performance of *Cinderella* was given on December 26, 1905. Lynn could barely believe that she had made it so far. As she marched on stage for her first entrance, she kept repeating to herself in time to the music, "I'm on the stage, I'm on the stage!"

Lynn was also paid to understudy the actress who played the Fairy Queen. Understudies often never get the opportunity to perform the roles they have learned, but this particular Cinderella story would not be complete if the actress playing the Fairy Queen had not been unable to go on one evening. Lynn was elated, but the management of Drury Lane was apprehensive. After all, this was an eighteen-year-old novice who had never spoken a word on the professional stage. Would she even be heard in the large theatre? To put her to the test, the manager stationed listeners throughout the house during a hastily called rehearsal, and to his surprise they reported that every word she said could be heard with perfect clarity. Ellen Terry's lessons had made the difference.

Lynn's sister Antoinette attended one of the few performances in which Lynn played the Fairy Queen. "I sat in the dress circle [the balcony] and I could hear her clearly," she recalled; "I heard a manager say, 'Her voice is like a bell.' "

---

*Christmas pantomimes are a long-standing tradition in the English theatre. Although the word "pantomime" originally referred to a performance in which no words were spoken, Christmas pantomimes in England have for many years connoted musical entertainments, including dialogue, specifically designed for children. In 1905, as now, many such entertainments were presented during the holiday season.

1892–1912

Alfred David Lunt, Jr., was born on August 12, 1892, at 1701 Grand Avenue (now Wisconsin Avenue) in Milwaukee, Wisconsin. After he had become famous, stories circulated that Lunt had been born in Scandinavia, perhaps because his stepfather was Swedish, and, as Lunt said when he was in his late twenties, "I went through a fatuous stage when I used to mention my Middlewestern birthplace with a slight feeling of shame. But I got over that when I reached the age of reason."

Most of the biographical material later written about Lunt indicated that he was born on August 19 rather than on the 12th—undoubtedly because, for some reason, his mother always insisted he was born on the 19th—and often the year of his birth was said to be 1893. But his birth certificate is clearly marked August 12, 1892, and that was the date Lunt gave whenever he was asked when he was born.

His father, a lumberman and land agent from Orono, Maine, one of five sons of Nathaniel and Sallie Lunt, was born in 1830 and moved to Wisconsin around 1855, where he achieved great success in the lumber business. He must have been popular as well as successful because he belonged to seven lodges. He was also known as a kind and generous man who, according to Alfred, "built houses and furnished them for all of his brothers—Paid for his nieces' and nephews' education, etc.—Smothered them in seal skin coats, etc."

Will Briggs, a timber estimator, was the foreman of the senior Lunt's lumber mill. Briggs's sister, a schoolteacher from Hortonville, Wisconsin, named Harriet Washburn Briggs, met and fell in love with Alfred Lunt and, despite the great difference in age—she was thirty-two years younger than he—they were married in 1882.

A daughter, Inez, was born on April 1, 1887, but died four years later of pneumonia. Inez's death was a terrible blow, especially to Mrs. Lunt, who had adored her. For many years afterward, pictures of Inez—which showed her to be an unusually beautiful child—continued to be displayed in the Lunts' home. Mrs. Lunt was so devastated by Inez's death that she was inconsolable for months. When Alfred, Jr., their only son, was born soon after his sister's death, she was understandably terrified by the notion that he, too, might die. As a result, Alfred was coddled, even spoiled by his mother.

In one of Alfred's scrapbooks there is a photograph of his father and himself, painstakingly labeled by the boy: "Alfred Lunt, Sr. and Alfred Lunt, Jr." Alfred's scrapbooks also contain pictures of his father's brothers, David—who looked a good deal like Abraham Lincoln—and Jonathan. Pictures of Alfred show him at eighteen months, at two years (wearing a dress, as was customary for young boys in the 1890s), at four years (with long blond hair) and at six years (in boy's clothes, and with short hair parted in the middle).

Alfred barely knew his father, who died in 1894 after a series of strokes. Mr. Lunt left a considerable fortune: $500,000 to his wife, an inheritance of $30,000 to Alfred (the bulk of it to be held in trust for him until he was twenty-one) and still more to relatives. The wealth that Mr. Lunt had amassed permitted Alfred and his mother to spend several years in luxury. The Grand Avenue home was a large and beautifully decorated mansion.

Alfred's religious upbringing might best be characterized as "varied." Sallie Lunt, Alfred's paternal grandmother, was a deeply religious woman whose obituary noted that "she was a positive, earnest, conscientious, be-lieving Christian. To her, the Bible meant what it says; to her, Christ was real." Hattie Lunt, Alfred's mother, was a Presbyterian, but the first reli-gion that her son knew was Catholicism, the faith of Cathy McNellis, his nurse when he was a young child. She took him to early mass at Gesu Church in Milwaukee before he went to Sunday school at the Presbyterian church. "I was so small I used to play with the holy water in the fountain," he said later. Cathy McNellis hoped that Alfred would one day become a Catholic. Many years later, after he was married, she visited him and said, "It's not too late yet." But religion was never a significant factor in Alfred's life, either as a child or as an adult.

If Alfred was not spiritually moved by religion, he did respond to the theatricality of the rituals in the Catholic church, and his imagination was equally stimulated by literature. His mother read poetry and novels—es-pecially *Oliver Twist, David Copperfield* and *Great Expectations*—aloud to him until he was seven years old, creating in him a lifelong enthusiasm for Dickens. As an adult, he made it a habit to read one of Dickens's novels every year. "I find them simply entrancing," he said, "and I can read them over and over and over again."

But the most vital force in Alfred's life, almost from the beginning, was the theatre. His first theatregoing experience occurred in 1895, when he was three years old. His mother took him to see the Royal Lilliputians, a company of midgets performing in a musical extravaganza called *The Golden Horseshoe* at the Davidson Theatre in Milwaukee, and the effect upon him was immediate and electric. At one moment in the play, a dancer performed in an authentic-looking fire, and Alfred was terrified. He screamed so loudly that his mother had to take him from the auditorium. But he was given a chance to return after spending some time in the lobby, and when he did, his enjoyment was unalloyed. To the end of his life he could remember the excitement of that performance in remarkable detail. In the finale, he recalled, "the scenery rose up and one felt the entire com-pany was descending into the sea."

Hattie herself loved theatregoing and found in Alfred an eager companion. And there were many theatres to choose from: the Bijou, where blood-and-thunder melodramas held the stage; the Davidson, where touring productions from New York often played; the Alhambra, where vaudeville shows were performed; he saw Sarah Bernhardt and vaudeville's Sliding Billy Watson and was equally taken by both. "They were as good as any circus," he said later, "and I've always been crazy about the circus." After the show Alfred could usually look forward to a visit to Martini's for coffee and cakes.

Alfred's theatrical instinct could not, however, be satisfied solely by watching others perform, and one afternoon while his mother was having a tea party, the urge to play a role was too great to resist. Alfred was not yet four; he looked under a window seat where a pile of magazines was kept, and on the top was a copy of *Puck,* with a figure of Puck on the cover, wearing only a sash. As Alfred later described the incident, "I descended the stairs as Puck. I hadn't bothered about the sash. For some time this incident was looked upon as a family disgrace."

Hattie Lunt remarried when Alfred was seven. Her new husband was Dr. Carl Sederholm, who had been born in Sweden and still had many relatives there and in Finland. Dr. Sederholm was a charming man and, like his new wife and stepson, an avid theatregoer. He also loved music and played the piano skillfully, singing Swedish, German and Finnish songs in a high baritone voice. At first Alfred was broken-hearted when his mother married Dr. Sederholm. Buffalo Bill was his hero, and he fantasized that Buffalo Bill would one day become his father. (Alfred spoke of Buffalo Bill so often that his friends took to calling him "Bill," a nickname that continued to be used by some until he was in his thirties.)

Within a few months Alfred came to admire his stepfather and to share his love of music. Still, he seems never to have reconciled himself entirely to his mother's remarriage. Years later, his relatives recalled, when Alfred spoke of his childhood he never mentioned his stepfather.

Hattie Briggs Lunt was a charming but impractical woman whose flamboyant dress and behavior occasionally embarrassed her children. Because of increasing deafness, she dominated every discussion by speaking emphatically and ignoring questions or interruptions. Fortunately, her conversation was sprightly and sparkled with wit. Later on, such noted raconteurs as Robert Benchley and Alexander Woollcott enjoyed hearing her anecdotes and observations. She loved luxury, always insisting on having breakfast in bed. She smoked, but only so that she could use a long cigarette holder as a prop. She loved to be the center of attention and never failed to achieve that aim. Regarded as "the most entertaining character" in town, she evidently deserved that reputation. One spring a friend named Dr. Sharp forgot to take his overcoat home with him after a visit to the Lunts'. He would not need the overcoat again until the weather turned cold, so he did not attempt to recover it until the following fall. But he had not considered Hattie's penchant for eccentricity. When he returned to the house and asked for his coat, Hattie said, "Doctor, you're standing on it." She had had strips torn from the overcoat worn into an oval rag carpet.

Hattie's capacity for peculiar albeit often endearing behavior blossomed when she became Mrs. Sederholm. For example, she refused to let the doctor send bills to his patients. Perhaps she reasoned that her family was already sufficiently wealthy from the inheritance Mr. Lunt had left them and that no further income was necessary. If that was her belief, it proved to be incorrect. Dr. Sederholm gambled away much of the inheritance on horse races and prize fights. Alfred described his stepfather years later as "extravagant, a bad business man [who] loved luxury." Half a million dollars was a great deal of money, the equivalent of many millions today, but, in a curious parallel to Lynn Fontanne's history, Alfred's family lost its wealth over several years and was reduced to straitened circumstances.

Dr. and Mrs. Sederholm had three children: Louise, Karin and Carl. Carl revealed an eccentric streak to rival his mother's. When Hattie gave him a rifle as a gift, Carl terrorized his sisters by pretending to be a big-game hunter and shooting at them as they cowered behind a tree. He also used the rifle indoors on occasion, shooting at targets at the end of a long hallway. One day he missed the targets and destroyed a piece of Hattie's Dresden china, after which he was forbidden to shoot in the house.

While the money lasted, the family's mode of living remained luxurious. Alfred (who continued to use the surname Lunt) was given an extended vacation nearly every summer. He was bundled off to visit his aunt's farm, where he was awakened every morning at 5:30 and put to work. Surprisingly, perhaps, for a city child accustomed to luxury, Alfred loved the farm and the hard work it entailed. As an adult, he would buy his own Wisconsin farm and spend every summer there; and when he was on his farm, he worked as hard as when he was a boy.

Alfred's appetite for theatrical entertainment continued to grow. Eventually it even outstripped his mother's. At least once a week he pleaded to be taken to see a play or a vaudeville show, and that was more entertainment than Hattie wanted. By the time he was seven, Alfred claimed, he was attending matinees by himself, an arrangement to which his mother and stepfather had no objections. He saw a prodigious number of productions, for which he paid as little as ten cents for a balcony seat and as much as fifty cents for a seat in the orchestra. He carefully preserved the programs and handbills in a series of scrapbooks, and to these he added newspaper photographs and drawings of the visiting actors who appeared in Milwaukee, along with reviews and information on the theatrical scene.

One of his scrapbooks is dated August 19, 1901. Presumably the scrapbook was a ninth birthday gift, presented on the date that Hattie insisted he had been born. Alfred pasted clippings of productions from 1900 to 1910 in the scrapbook, with a catalogue of each photograph and clipping printed in his handwriting inside the front cover. The scrapbook contains pictures of all of the leading American actors of the day: E. H. Sothern and Julia Marlowe, who toured the country in productions of Shakespeare; Minnie Maddern Fiske, the most progressive actress in America; Adele Ritchie, Annie Russell, Blanche Bates, Maxine Elliott, Ada Rehan and the great Edwin Booth. There is also a portrait of Shakespeare, another one of Ellen Terry's acting partner, Sir Henry Irving, drawings of scenes from Shakespeare's plays—and a prized autograph of Sarah Bernhardt, who signed his program for *L'Aiglon* when she appeared in Milwaukee in 1910.

Alfred's scrapbooks also contain a large collection of theatre caricatures by Briggs of the Chicago *Tribune*. It seems that any reference to the theatre, no matter how trivial, sent Alfred running for scissors and paste.

Milwaukee was graced by the presence of many visiting actors, performing in Shakespeare and in nineteenth-century melodrama, but it also had theatrical companies of its own. The Pabst Theatre featured "The Pabst English Stock Company," and there Alfred saw *Old Heidelberg, The Fires of St. John, The Princess and the Butterfly,* and *Trelawny of the "Wells."* There was also the Tannhauser Stock Company on Milwaukee Street, which at one time included in its company both Pauline Lord and Ruth Chatterton, who were later to become famous actresses in New York.

On several occasions, Alfred said, he went by himself to see the burlesque show at the Star Theatre. Burlesque in 1900 did not include nude women or the degree of vulgarity with which it later became associated, but it was still not the type of entertainment to which children generally went by themselves. Nonetheless, Alfred sat in the cheap seats in the balcony among a much older clientele, and when he came home his clothes smelled so strongly of cigar and cigarette smoke that his mother told him to hang them out the window.

Burlesque and vaudeville, musical extravaganzas and Shakespeare, Alfred loved them all. "I knew what I wanted to do when I was four years old," he said many years later. After only a few visits to the theatre, he was so beguiled that he could think of no other life. Indeed, he pursued a theatrical career with remarkable singlemindedness. By the time he was eight, he was writing and producing plays. A typed program from 1900 is still in existence; it announces the premiere of *Rip Van Winkle* to be given at the "Lunt Stock Company's Wisconsin Theatre, A. D. Lunt, Manager." The production was given in a miniature toy theatre, designed to resemble a British stage, which was set up in a house across the street that belonged to Alfred's friends and fellow theatre-lovers, the Alexanders.

The Lunt Stock Company also gave performances of *Parsifal* (for which Alfred wrote a three-act libretto) in 1901. The miniature theatre had been given to him for Christmas, equipped with little cardboard figures, but the set designs were his own. During a period of illness Alfred devoted many hours to the making of miniature sets for *Parsifal*. "I drew all my own characters and scenery," he said. "My God, I was fearless—and even tossed a few of King Arthur's knights into *Parsifal,* just to give my talent range." Kenneth Conant, Alfred's friend and nextdoor neighbor (who later became a distinguished professor of architecture at Harvard), helped out by designing a cardboard curtain with the word "asbestos" on it; the curtain hung just behind the proscenium of the toy theatre.

Alfred also manipulated his cardboard characters by hand in minia-ture-theatre performances of *Twelfth Night, A Midsummer Night's Dream, Julius Caesar, The Mikado* and *Der Freischütz* for an audience that included neighborhood children and adults, but never—despite her love of the-atre—his mother. Hattie had her own life to live and, although she cared fiercely for Alfred and her other children, she rarely became involved in their activities.

The room in the Alexanders' house where Alfred gave his plays was reserved for his use only. In the enormous house a room on the top floor was vacant, and it became the home of Alfred's stock company. The Alex-anders "built a theatre for me to give plays in—footlights and all," Lunt said years afterward. "But Mrs. Alexander did find it trying when for a production of *The Count of Monte Cristo* I brought up rolls of sod. I wanted real grass. I carried all the sod up to the third floor and dirtied all the steps. It was the only time she ever said anything. But very gently she said, 'No, Alfred, you mustn't.'" Mrs. Alexander's children, Pauline and John, were Alfred's closest childhood friends, and Pauline was the only girl, other than Lynn Fontanne, with whom he ever fell in love—although this was a love of the ten-year-old variety. Pauline, a beautiful child with long blond hair who seemed destined to become a beautiful woman, died in a tragic acci-dent when she was sixteen. She was riding in a motor launch on Lake Oconomowoc when it caught fire. She leaped into the water and was drowned.

Alfred's consuming passion was for the theatre, but he maintained other enthusiasms, foremost among which was good food. He loved to be taken to Whitefish Bay for a fish dinner. "That was a long day's excursion," he said, "but it was worth it." He also enjoyed visits to his aunt's farm in Neenah, Wisconsin, and never forgot the delicious odor of baking bread that filled the house. Alfred always retained a vivid picture of his aunt's house, lit with kerosene lamps, and especially of the kitchen with its wood-fired stove. His aunt was an excellent cook who gave Alfred his first taste of finely prepared food. Later in life he became an accomplished gourmet cook.

Alfred attended the 17th District Number 1 School at 18th and Wells streets in Milwaukee, and his second-grade teacher, May Massee, recalled him clearly in a Columbia Oral History Interview in 1964. "He was a little . . . boy—well, he wasn't little; he was a big boy," she said. "Alfred always stood up very straight—he was the first one the children would choose to read to them when they were reading out loud. [Dr. Sederholm] had taught him to keep one arm behind his back, and the other one held the book up. Alfred would bow, first to one side of the class and then to the other," before he began to read.

In the third grade Alfred's mother transferred him to the private Milwaukee Academy, where, just as Lynn Fontanne had done in England, he began to give recitations in declamation contests. A medal was awarded each year at the contest held at the Milwaukee Academy, and Alfred was an annual entrant. Hattie and Dr. Sederholm worked with him in an attempt to improve his articulation, but they were only moderately successful. "I wasn't very good," he said later. "I wasn't good at all and I knew it. I was so ashamed of losing I once hid inside a cupboard for a whole day. I went through agonies, but I would do it every year, with the opposite of flying colors."

Alfred may not have been an accomplished performer as a child, but, as he said, he was "the most persistent. If lack of encouragement could have held me down, I'd never have seen the footlights, except from the audience.

"Not a soul ever hinted that I would be a second Irving, or would even earn twenty cents a week as an actor. Yet I never was so happy as when I was trying to speak a piece, mumbling the words, and waving my arms, apparently under the impression that I was a windmill."

He did not experience success until the age of twelve, when he came upon a speech of Cardinal Wolsey's from *Henry VIII* and decided to ask a family friend for coaching. The friend, a lawyer named Chevannes, had established a local reputation as a talented speaker and had impressed Alfred with his prowess. Mr. Chevannes was pleased to help, and he must have done a good job. "I recited Wolsey's farewell," Lunt later recalled. "Well, I walked away with it, and I won the medal, and my nurse, Cathy McNellis, rose to her feet and applauded wildly: 'And he's only twelve, he's only twelve!'" Alfred's victory in the contest brought him his first recognition as a performer. "The contest was attended by a large audience," a local newspaper stated, and "the John C. Spencer medal was awarded to Master Alfred Davis Lunt."*

Soon after that success Alfred suffered an attack of acute appendicitis complicated by peritonitis. He further contracted scarlet fever while in the hospital. The attending physician decided the case was hopeless and sent him home to die. Hattie refused to accept that verdict, however, and she persuaded a local surgeon to operate on her son on the kitchen table of the Grand Avenue home. The surgeon removed not only Alfred's appendix but one of his kidneys as well. After a long period of recuperation, Alfred was able to return to school, but the legacy of that operation caused health problems for the rest of his life.

---

*Alfred tended to alternate "Davis" and "David" as his middle name, apparently depending on his mood.

When he began school in the fall of 1906, it was at the Carroll College Academy in Waukesha. The Sederholms had moved from Milwaukee to the small village of Genesee Depot, where Dr. Sederholm practiced medicine but was still prevented by his wife from charging for his services. Alfred commuted from his home to Waukesha (seven miles to the east) each school day by steam train.

In the summer of 1907, Dr. and Mrs. Sederholm discovered that their once ample supply of money had all but disappeared. Dr. Sederholm's gambling, poor investments and his (along with Hattie's) habitual extravagance had depleted Mr. Lunt's legacy; nor had there been any income for several years because of Hattie's benevolent nature. As a result, the home in Genesee Depot became a luxury the Sederholms could no longer afford.

Dr. and Mrs. Sederholm, increasingly concerned about money, attempted to persuade Alfred to turn some of the income from his father's trust fund over to them. The fund was arranged so that Alfred had complete control over its income, however, and, resenting the pressure, he resisted most of their requests. The Sederholms thus decided to move to Finland, where they could live with Dr. Sederholm's relatives in the Swedish colony. That fall, however, Alfred returned to Wisconsin so that he could continue school at the Carroll College Academy. For the next several years, he spent his summers in Finland and the remainder of the year in Waukesha, living with friends.

As a boy on vacation in Finland, Alfred acted in several productions of Ibsen's plays given at a folk theatre on an estate near Helsingfors (now Helsinki). Depending on the account, the performances were given either in Swedish, Finnish, English or the original Norwegian. In any case, they were the first plays (other than those performed in his toy theatre in the Alexanders' house) in which Alfred Lunt ever appeared.

For Alfred, the visits to Finland were joyous occasions. He developed a deep attachment to the Swedish and Finnish people, one that would remain constant throughout his life. As an adult, he made several trips to Finland where he always felt very much at home.

During the summer of 1909, Alfred and his stepfather were sharing a hotel room in Helsingfors when, one morning after he awoke, Alfred became aware that Dr. Sederholm was unusually quiet. Fearing that something was terribly wrong, Alfred called out to his stepfather. When he got no response, he gave the bed a violent shake. But there was no movement, and Alfred soon realized that Dr. Sederholm was dead. Whether the death was attributable to natural causes or whether the Doctor had committed suicide by taking an overdose of sleeping pills—perhaps in anguish over the loss of $500,000—remains unresolved, although Alfred always maintained that his stepfather had simply died in his sleep.

When the family returned to Wisconsin that summer, they were forced to confront the fact that the family fortune had been entirely lost. Only the meager income from Alfred's trust fund remained. Hattie and her children, unable to afford a house, moved in with friends in Milwaukee.

Alfred, now seventeen, was regarded as "the man of the family." In their straitened circumstances, the normal course of events would have found him taken from school and put to work to support his mother and her children. But Alfred and Mrs. Sederholm, whose conscience may have been troubled by her part in the loss of Mr. Lunt's inheritance, formulated a plan. Hattie would provide for the family by renting a large home in Waukesha and turning it into a boardinghouse. Alfred would thus be enabled to finish high school at the Academy and then proceed to Carroll College itself.

Waukesha in 1909 was a small town of about 7,000 people. However, it was connected to Milwaukee by interurban electric railway, and three other railroads serviced the city. In many respects, Waukesha represented an ideal community for Alfred: most residents knew one another by their first names, an environment he thoroughly enjoyed; culturally, however, it was more advanced than most towns its size because of the existence of Carroll College; and its proximity to Milwaukee, about twenty miles east, meant that the advantages of living in a large metropolis—including the opportunity to see resident professional theatre and visiting actors in touring productions—were available to him. Waukesha and Milwaukee thus represented two ends of a spectrum—the small town and the big city—both of which Alfred found highly attractive. But there are towns much smaller than Waukesha and cities much larger than Milwaukee. Eventually, the life Alfred made for himself was one in which he spent most of his time either in the tiny hamlet of Genesee Depot, Wisconsin, or in the country's largest city, New York.

Waukesha, in the words of an article in the Waukesha *Journal* in 1891, was "embowered in foliage, cooled by the moisture-laden breezes blowing across Lake Michigan, rich in springs, whose medicinal properties have won for it a world-wide reputation." It was, the article went on to say in its lavish chamber-of-commerce style, "the ideal summer home for the tourist and traveler, and the fountain of health for all the world. . . . All the larger springs are further rendered attractive by handsomely laid out parks, brilliant with flowers, and provided with seats and games for the amusement of the guests. Bands of music spend the whole [summer] season in these pleasant spots, and open air concerts are given daily."

Waukesha's medicinal springs had made it something of a tourist attraction, and the summer visitors tended to swell the population considerably. Alfred and Hattie believed that a boardinghouse would be an attractive alternative to expensive hotels for summer guests, and that the family would thrive on the profits.

One of the many jobs Alfred had to take on at the boardinghouse was the cooking, a skill his mother entirely lacked at first, although she became quite proficient eventually. In many respects, his mother depended upon him to run the boardinghouse, and without his efforts it would surely have failed. Alfred had truly become "the man of the family," responsible for taking care of his mother and his half-brother and -sisters. Indeed, what with his studies, looking after the children (another job which Hattie tended to pass on to him) and the work he had to do to keep the board-inghouse running, he often drove himself to the point of exhaustion. "In God's name, please don't have any more children," he cried to his mother after one particularly tiring day.

Hattie's lack of practicality and orderliness was a source of continuing frustration to Alfred. Having inherited those qualities from his father, he knew how much more effectively the boardinghouse could be run. But Hattie was incapable of altering her behavior. She continued to insist upon having breakfast served to her in bed; she could not concern herself with such mundane notions as cleaning the house and seeing that there was sufficient food on hand for the day's meals. Such tasks had always been performed by servants, and Hattie could not accept the fact that servants were a luxury the family could no longer afford. She spent money lavishly despite her impoverished state. At last Alfred restricted her to a weekly allowance. Blithely, however, she continued to exceed her allocation. Alfred's attempts to persuade his mother to see the Sederholms' financial predicament more realistically became a recurrent theme in family discussions and a constant source of irritation to him.

Despite his best efforts, the income produced by the boardinghouse was meager at best, and the family faced a constant economic struggle. But in spite of his own difficulties, Alfred developed a compassion for others whose circumstances were more severe than his. One example concerns the "town character," a woman named Susie who lived in a tiny house without plumbing or electricity. Susie occasionally did some sewing for Hattie Sederholm. In payment, the Sederholms gave her furniture so that she would be able to live a bit more comfortably. Alfred took a particular interest in Susie, whom he admired as a nonconformist, and whose behavior, dress and appearance set her apart from the solid citizens of Waukesha. Some years later, when he owned property in Genesee Depot, he hired Susie to hand-braid rugs for the house. This was a luxury he could ill afford, as there was still very little money in the family, but he wanted to help Susie. Still later, after he became established in the theatre, he periodically sent china, glassware and valuable antiques to her, and never forgot to send her cards on her birthday and at Christmas.

Carroll College was established in 1846 as a nonsectarian Protestant school, but within four years it became affiliated with the Presbyterian synod. In 1866, Walter Lowrie Rankin became the president of the small College and its preparatory school, the Academy. Rankin's daughter, May Nickell Rankin, was to become one of the strongest influences on young Alfred Lunt. Miss Rankin had herself attended the Academy, graduating as valedictorian in 1887. After attending the Emerson College of Oratory at Boston (but not completing her degree), she was invited by her father to return to Carroll and teach courses at the Academy and at the College, where she became a specialist in elocution and physical culture.

May Rankin's passion was for the theatre, and she was determined to mount theatrical productions at Carroll. This was a novel and radical idea. No college or university in the United States—and certainly no preparatory school—had a Department of Theatre at the time; to offer instruction in theatrical technique would have been thought absurd. (Not until the 1920s did the establishment of theatre departments begin to gain acceptance in American colleges and universities.) Schools that did present occasional productions did so strictly as an extracurricular activity. But Miss Rankin believed that dramatic literature could be taught satisfactorily only if her students were permitted to produce some of the plays they studied. Moreover, she felt that the students needed expert guidance; therefore, she herself proposed to direct the plays. And the productions would not simply be classroom projects; they would be presented before an audience. In 1895, when she was appointed to the Voorhees Chair of Oratory,* she expanded her curriculum to include the first dramatic program in any school in the history of the state of Wisconsin. Her dramatic organization, which came to be known as the Carroll Players, lasted nearly forty years. The members of the Players underwent a rigorous training in theatre, designing and building costumes and scenery for most of the productions in which they acted.

The curriculum established by May Rankin offered her students an opportunity to explore all facets of dramatic art. The course work in her department—initially known as the Department of Oratory and Physical Culture, but renamed the Department of Oratory and Dramatic Literature by the time Alfred Lunt enrolled in the Academy—was described in the catalogue of 1894–95 as including "class work in oratory, steps in the evolution of expression, physical culture, voice culture, articulation, inflection, quality of tone, pitch, force, time, power, abandonment in rendering, elementary gesture, declamation [and] recitation." There were also courses in literary interpretation, Shakespearean drama and play production. Her classes in dramatic literature focused on contemporary European playwrights such as Hauptmann, Sudermann, Wilde, Ibsen and Strindberg—playwrights whose work was often ignored in other colleges' courses because their plays were regarded as scandalous.

* Ralph Voorhees was Carroll College's principal financial benefactor.

Miss Rankin continued to develop her program from year to year. In 1910, courses in set construction were added to the curriculum. And Miss Rankin often took her students to Milwaukee to see dramatic productions. There were times when Waukesha itself was home to a visiting professional company. Such an occasion occurred in 1909 when the Ben Greet Players visited Waukesha, and it must have been an exciting time for Miss Rankin and her students. Included in this professional aggregation was Sydney Greenstreet, who often appeared with Lunt and Fontanne in the 1930s and '40s before going on to become a favorite in Hollywood. The company gave performances of *The Comedy of Errors, A Midsummer Night's Dream, As You Like It* and *The Tempest;* the Rosalind in *As You Like It* was Adela Rankin of Waukesha, May Rankin's younger sister. Adela was an amateur, about whom the local newspaper said that it was "no easy task . . . to take the heroine's role in a good professional company, but she did it and did it well."

By the time Alfred entered the Carroll College Academy in 1906, Miss Rankin's program was well established. But the program flourished as never before during the time that Alfred was in attendance, largely because of his contributions. He first came to her notice because he was able to recite the whole of *Twelfth Night* from memory—a legacy from the time he had presented the play in his miniature theatre. While he was still an Academy student, Alfred began playing the leading roles in many of Miss Rankin's productions. His talent was obvious from the beginning, so obvious that word quickly spread beyond the campus that an extraordinary young performer was enrolled in the Academy. And, indeed, his performances on and off campus made his name known throughout the state. After he played the role of Benjamin Goldfinch in *A Pair of Spectacles,* the school newspaper, the *Carroll College Echo,* paid tribute to his prowess. The paper said, "Mr. Lunt is too well-known to require words of praise from us. He has an enviable reputation in Waukesha and throughout the State of Wisconsin. [He] brings to this part a breadth of sympathy which makes the character real and living."

His fellow students were quick to recognize his brilliance. A friend and classmate, Ray Weaver, later said, "We who played with him knew he was already the leading actor in America; we knew that long before the Broadway critics."

Alfred attended the Carroll Academy for four years and spent two more years at Carroll College. He acted in twelve plays under Miss Rankin's direction and never failed to acknowledge his debt to her afterward. It was Miss Rankin, he later said, "who showed me how to make something of my capabilities. She was the substance of my education. . . .

"Miss Rankin was a disciplinarian who never showed it. She was an encourager—she inspired us. She also instilled excitement in what you were doing. What she did with all the small town and country boys was unbelievable, simply unbelievable. Her method was just as modern as the studios in New York," he said in 1962. She was not at all typical of the elocutionary school of the time, abjuring artificial speech and unmotivated gesture. "Broad, free gestures that came from inside" was the method she taught to her students. "She was way ahead of Stanislavski in this country," Lunt said, and added, perhaps hyperbolically, "He could have learned an awful lot from Miss Rankin."

At Carroll, Alfred went through the process of auditioning for the first time—an ordeal for any actor. To be admitted to the Carroll Players, a candidate had to try out with a memorized scene from one of Shakespeare's plays. Miss Rankin also insisted on a lengthy period of rehearsal for her productions, refusing to accord any play a shoddy presentation. From her, Lunt learned discipline and the value of striving for perfection.

One of her most outstanding characteristics as a director was that she encouraged her student actors to experiment. Lunt, for example, had the novel idea of playing occasional scenes with his back to the audience, something that, to his knowledge, had never been done before. Rather than telling him to adopt a more conventional approach to acting, May Rankin encouraged him to perform in whatever relation to the audience seemed most natural and effective. This tolerance for his interest in experimentation was not often repeated. Throughout his early professional career, directors and critics often questioned his unconventional approach, especially in regard to playing scenes with his back to the audience. But he continued to be enthusiastic about the technique and used it throughout his life. Eventually the technique became so associated with him that a song in a London musical revue was entitled "Alfred Lunt's Back."

Among the productions in which Alfred appeared was Bernard Shaw's *You Never Can Tell*, which was reviewed by the Waukesha *Freeman*, whose critic said, "Alfred Lunt, whose talent for comedy has been often demonstrated, never had a part which fitted him better nor which he carried out with more delicious humor." Years later, Lunt recalled that the college paid no royalties to Shaw or to any of the other dramatists whose plays they produced. "If Shaw found out now," he said, "he'd jump right out of his grave."

The Carroll newspaper, the *Echo,* said of Alfred's performance in *The Young Mrs. Winthrop* in 1911, "Alfred Lunt has always delighted his audiences by his clever art and splendid sense of humor in character roles, and it was interesting to them to discover that he has the ability, also, to portray with dignity and strength a serious character." For *The Cricket on the Hearth* in March 1912, Alfred designed the scenery as well as playing the role of Caleb Plummer.

Although Henrik Ibsen's plays were considered too daring for most commercial theatres, May Rankin produced *The Pillars of Society* in 1912, with Alfred playing Karsten Bernick. (He designed the scenery for this production as well, and received credit for it on the program. This was a unique arrangement because designers of scenery, costumes and lighting were rarely acknowledged.) Miss Rankin's willingness to challenge the tastes of her audience in the plays she chose was, like so many other things, a lesson and an inspiration to Alfred Lunt. In this production Carl Sederholm, Alfred's half-brother, was brought into the cast to play Consul Bernick's son Olaf.

During the time Alfred attended Carroll, most plays were given in the chapel of the main building. Because the stage was extremely small, plays were chosen with scenic requirements in mind: the fewer changes of set, the better. Some of the productions were mounted entirely without scenery. Occasionally, productions were given off-campus at an old theatre called the Colonial, behind the Soo Railroad station. According to Lunt, the productions were invariably sold out.

Alfred's education was a well-rounded one. In addition to his theatre work, he took a variety of courses including dramatic literature, English, French, German, history, mathematics, oratory, Bible (the class read the Old Testament, and Alfred said that this completed his religious education; he had become and would forever afterward remain a "Catholic-Jewish-Presbyterian-Atheist"), anatomy and public speaking. He performed capably in all of them, receiving the numerical equivalent of A or B. But Dr. Rankin, the president of the college, who also taught Latin, once said to Alfred in the midst of a Latin class, "What a piece of ignorance we have here!" Still, Alfred plugged away at the subject and emerged from the course with an above-average grade.

Lunt was active in the social life of the Academy and, later on, the College. His Academy classmates elected him Director of Social Affairs. He also evidently had an eye for the girls on campus. He was taken to task in the 1910 yearbook, which noted that he was seen in class "actually reciting in French, conjugating the verb *Fusser*"—which meant, in campus slang, to flirt. And he participated in other activities of the Academy and the College besides acting in Miss Rankin's productions, although most of them were related to the theatre in one way or another. He gave interpretative readings at commencement recitals, read poetry for English classes and joined the Philomathean Literary Society. He appeared with the Carroll College Minstrels and participated in the "Carroll Carnival," for which he wrote and appeared in *Follies of 1911*.

Alfred's college experience was of the profoundest importance to him. "You will never know the kind of peace we had when I was in college," he said fifty years after he left Carroll. "We had no radio or television. We had telephones, but we never used them. We tried to make our own recreation—perhaps that's why we were so happy."

Adaline Butchart Hoag, Alfred's classmate, recalled him as an extremely popular young man. "He always seemed very happy," she said. "Everyone liked him. Many girls had crushes on him at school—he was talented, friendly and very good-looking. But he was too busy to have time for girls. I don't remember that he ever had a date while he was going to Carroll."

Ray Weaver, who boarded with the Sederholms for three years, was Alfred's closest friend. He, too, was active in Miss Rankin's productions, along with his brother Andrew. Ray, who (as Bennett R. Weaver) became chairman of the Speech Department at the University of Michigan, recalled that Lunt "never dated any girls. Neither did I," he said. "We were a world unto ourselves. We were completely absorbed by the theatre, by literature, by artistic problems. In those days . . . he had a serious philosophy of the theatre. He believed it had a profound, humanist function in a democratic society and was to replace organized religion. It was to uplift and purify man. . . . Alfred was 'called' as much as any priest. He was a man dedicated, a man obsessed by a vision, by something out of his control or conscious choice." Weaver also claimed that Lunt "was born for the theatre. It was all he was interested in from the time he was four or five years old. Why, when we did plays at Carroll, Alfred would go to the oratory room and take three hours to make up. He painted the character on his face as if he were a Rembrandt. . . . Anything that did not relate to the theatre bored him. I sat next to him in a trigonometry class. All he did was draw stage settings."

Even before Alfred graduated from the·Academy, it was evident to May Rankin that he had the potential to become a professional actor. She suggested that Alfred attend the Emerson College of Oratory in Boston, as she had done. Together, they evolved a plan for him to spend one or two years at Carroll College and then transfer to Emerson.

Hattie was less than enthusiastic about the fact that Alfred's ambition was pointing toward a career in the professional theatre. She reminded him that his participation in the declamation contests in Milwaukee had been generally unsuccessful, that he continued to have difficulty in speaking with clear articulation, and that it was unlikely he would ever be able to make his living as an actor. But Hattie's advice failed to take into account the improvement Alfred was making as a performer, and, fortunately for the future of the American theatre, he elected to ignore it. Later, when Alfred began to demonstrate that he could make a living in the professional theatre, Hattie quickly revised her attitude and delighted in his success.

Just before he graduated from the Academy, Alfred was inspired to collaborate on a play with Ray and Andrew Weaver (who also boarded at the Sederholms' house). The play was taken from a short story which was in turn based upon an incident that occurred at Gethsemane, a Trappist monastery near Bardstown, Kentucky. Brother Huber discovered that the monastery and adjoining college were on fire, but, sworn to a vow of silence, he was unable to tell the brothers or the students of the blaze. Instead, he threw stones through a window in order to alert them to the danger. All the monks and students escaped unharmed, but the monastery burned to the ground.

From this incident and the short story based upon it, the boys wrote a three-act play, originally called *The White Cowl* and eventually retitled *The Greater Love*. Miss Rankin encouraged their efforts and wrote to her sister, "I think it will be a success." Both versions of the play were written out by hand, and nearly all of the handwriting was Alfred's. Anticipating a production at Carroll, Alfred also copied out "sides" (the dialogue of each speaking role preceded by the last few words of the cue line) for each character in the play.

Lunt and the Weavers did a prodigious amount of work on their play. Alfred designed props, ground plans, sets and costumes, all based upon meticulous research from such sources as *Footprints of the World's History;* and the young authors learned about the daily routine of monastery life in Huysmans's *En Route!* Lunt's designs, which also included at least twenty-five suggested poster layouts, are striking and impressive. He had no formal training in drawing or painting, but he was clearly a talented artist. At this time and for several years afterward, he thought seriously of becoming an architect or a scene designer, although his preference for acting gradually asserted itself.*

Despite the sophistication of Alfred's designs, the depth of the boys' research and the earnestness with which they approached the project, they were defeated by their inability to write dialogue that bore the slightest resemblance to the language of human beings. A speech by one of the characters in Act I of *The Greater Love* is all too typical: "Elaine, in all verity, the task is not an easy one. You know, I go, I see, I feel sensations—I study, I delve—and the more I do it, the thicker becomes the veil of mystification. Somehow I cannot but feel that the basis of the whole unpardonable institution, is mystification."

But Alfred and the Weaver brothers were evidently unaware of the deficiencies of the dialogue. Alfred wrote to the Office of Patents and Copyrights on November 10, 1910, asking "what rights a person has in dramatizing a story that has 'all rights reserved'—Is it absolutely necessary to have permission of the author of that story before the play may be produced?" The Copyright Office responded by sending him a booklet on copyright law and a series of forms. Perhaps the information in the booklet proved discouraging; at any rate, the boys apparently made no attempt to contact the author of the original story.

Alfred's success as an actor and interpretative reader led him to an association with the College's Men's Glee and Mandolin Club, a group comprised of twenty-nine members. While still an Academy student, he

*Many years later, when Lunt was in retirement, his friend Donald Seawell suggested to him that he should assemble the scene designs he had created over the years and publish or exhibit them. Lunt, who had not looked at them in years, promised to peruse them that night. The next morning he told Seawell that they had proved disappointing to him, and that he had burned all of them. Seawell, of course, regretted that he had ever brought the subject up. Lunt's poster designs for *The Greater Love* are among the few designs that survived.

joined the Club, not as one of its singers but primarily as a nonmusical performer. Sandwiched between the songs were Alfred's recitations, usually comic in nature. His readings were extremely popular, often to the point of being the highlight of the evening's entertainment. The Glee Club's reputation had already been good before Alfred joined it; now it became one of the most highly praised entertainments in the area. Indeed, its reputation was not limited to Waukesha because, beginning in the spring of 1908, it traveled throughout Wisconsin, driving in a bus on muddy dirt roads. People took special note of the young man whose readings so enhanced the presentations, and a number of Wisconsin newspapers praised him lavishly. The Racine *Journal*, for example, said that "Alfred D. Lunt was easily the main attraction on the Program and the audience could not get enough of him." The Madison *Democrat* agreed: "Mr. Lunt, the irrepressibly funny impersonator, made a decided hit with his interpretation of Scotch life." The Reedsburg *Times* went further: "For versatility of impersonation and pantomimic power Mr. Lunt is remarkable."

The success of the tour in 1908 was repeated the following year. Soon the Glee Club began performing outside the borders of Wisconsin. In Menominee, Michigan, the *Herald-Leader* wrote, "One of the big hits of real, rare talent were the offerings of Alfred Lunt. His dialect songs, stories and impersonations exceeded anything that has ever been heard in the twin cities. The hall rocked with encoring applause."

Alfred achieved such notoriety with the Carroll Glee Club that in 1909 he was asked by Beloit College to appear with its glee club as well. He did so, and once again his contributions proved to be the highlight of the performances.

Before Alfred's freshman year as a Carroll College student, he received a significant amount of money from the trust his father had left him ("twice as much as I thought I had," he said), so he and his family dipped into his inheritance and took another of their periodic trips abroad, this time to visit Canada, England and Finland. They also bought a house, arranging to move into it when they returned from their trip in September. While on board the *Empress of Ireland*, Alfred gave readings for the amusement of the passengers. The voyage also gave him an opportunity to observe and study the manners and speech of foreigners. He wrote to Ray Weaver on June 20, 1910, "All the stewards are so English & am trying my best to be able to talk like them." And after he reached Finland, he made it a point to watch the behavior of the Finns closely. The ability to observe actively and to store the observations for future use is essential to an actor, and Alfred made full use of his opportunities.

While on shipboard, Alfred was hard put to maintain his usual intense concentration on the theatre, although he did send Ray several suggestions for rewrites and poster designs for *The Greater Love,* as well as some ideas for one-act plays he was intending to write. As there was no one on the ship with whom to share his ideas, he took interest instead in his female sailing companions. "Have been 'fussing' that is sort of fussing with a Montreal girl all evening," he told Ray; "she's terribly cute and pretty too, piles of life and good at 'shooting the breeze.'"

Alfred, his mother and his sister Karin arrived in Finland on June 30, after spending several days in England. He saw Franz Lehár's new light opera, *The Count of Luxembourg*, in Helsingfors on July 9. But the highlight of his trip occurred when, on his mother's instructions, he went to Vyborg where a friend was to meet him and take him to [St.] Petersburg. The friend was not there when Alfred arrived, so he ventured forth himself for a trip around Finland. "Don't know how long it's going to last or anything," he wrote to Ray, "but will go where I like & do what I feel like."

His wanderings took him through various Finnish cities, where he saw medieval castles and other architectural delights. He shot the rapids from Kajaani to Uleaborg, only seventy-five miles from the Arctic Circle, and he was enchanted by the scenic beauty of the country.

He was, in fact, far more at home wandering the country by himself than he was in the company of others. When he returned to Jarvela to be with his mother and sister, he once again found it necessary to assume a social pose, and felt as if "somebody wanted to make a social monkey or jumping jack out of me. . . . I always feel weary when I am out and do not breathe a natural breath til I get back to my room. It's worse than nightmare! Mother often insists on 'dragging' me around to various 'homes of friends' but if she knew the inside torture I go thru I'm sure she would stop that habit."

On August 16, Alfred learned that Dr. Rankin, the president of Carroll College, had died. He immediately wrote a letter of condolence to May Rankin. He also described to her the work he and Ray Weaver were doing on *The Greater Love*. Andrew Weaver, the third coauthor, had graduated at the end of the previous term, but Alfred and Ray hoped to produce the play at Carroll during the next academic year.

The plan was to return to Waukesha by mid-September. But something happened to interfere with that plan and to ruin the Sederholms' trip. Evidently they learned that their new house would not be ready when expected, and at the same time their Finnish hosts decided that the Sederholms were no longer welcome to stay with them. Alfred's letters to Ray took on a despairing tone, beginning with his message of August 25: "When we are obliged to leave Eriksholm the first of September and with no roof that we know of to shelter us after that time you can well imagine how I hope and pray that letters to mother will come soon from America 'saying' we may leave these horrible people 'for ever and ever.'" On August 27 the situation had further deteriorated: "Well old boy, 'it has happened'! Matilda [Dr. Sederholm's mother] told Mother to leave Sat. or she would have the police . . . the children & I are still here [in Jarvela] while Mother is in Helsingfors looking for a 'home' to stay at until she can leave for the States." And on September 1: "Well if it isn't just one d—— thing after another! Now this is the first time I have used that expression and naughty word this summer. . . . The latest is, that there is no place on any line to America before Sept. 17th! Isn't that awful? You cannot imagine how discouraged we are." His main concern was that his arrival in Waukesha would now be delayed until at least the 6th of October, after the fall term had begun, and that he might have to wait until the second semester before beginning college.

But he and his family were also worried about where they would stay until passage to America became available. "Haven't found anyone who can take us all yet," Alfred wrote to Ray, "so expect I shall have to sleep in the barn. . . . Oh this has been a great experience for me and have lots of business for a 'melerdramer' especially one in which the heroine is turned out into the street on Xmas eve. . . ."

Still another of Alfred's concerns was that the money he had saved to buy props and costumes for the production of *The Greater Love* was being eroded by the longer-than-expected stay in Finland. In order to ensure that some of the money would still be available, Alfred decided that he would return to America in steerage class. "Don't you dare say a word," he cautioned Ray, "Mother would be wild if she knew this but I can . . . save a dollar or so."

By September 1 the emergency was over. Alfred wrote to tell Ray "the joyful news. . . . Mother came home to-night & told me, we could go Saturday after all and every last one of us at that!" And since only third-class tickets were available, some savings would be possible without Alfred's having to travel steerage. "I was sure the thing would come out all right & my belief in God has grown a little stronger," he said. "Expect us about Sept. 20th." The family returned home in time for Alfred to register for his freshman year without penalty.

Alfred was disappointed that *The Greater Love* was never produced at Carroll College, but he was exhilarated by the success of the Glee Club. In 1911 the club tour took the group to Reedsburg, Madison, Marshfield, Chippewa Falls, Beaver Dam, North Prairie, Lake Mills and other cities and towns in Wisconsin. Alfred performed such pieces as "The Missionary," "Barbara Frietchie," "Mother Hubbard," "Yiddish Theatre," "The Silent Retreat," "The Fate of Yim Yohnson" and "Prunes." But one evening he became irate because during his readings the Glee Club's singers "were making piles of noise back of the stage," he wrote to Ray Weaver, "so much noise you'd have thought 'Bedlam' was truly let loose. When I 'came off' & went back I naturally was furious & for the first time on any glee club trip I said something like this (in a loud, quivering voice full of pathos) 'See here young people if you ever do that again, I'll quit on the spot, I mean it.'" But the offending members of the Club apologized and the tour continued without further incident.

Alfred was so successful in his appearances with the glee clubs that, even before graduating from the Academy, he began to be asked to perform by himself. In May 1909 he had appeared at the First Congregational Church in Oshkosh, reading from "The Kalevala, the Epic Poem of Finland," and in August 1911 he was engaged to perform at the Racine Country Club. To capitalize on the success he was achieving, he distributed a handbill headed "Alfred Davis Lunt, Character Artist," which went on to say:

> MR. LUNT has for several years been one of the most successful Impersonators on the platform. He has appeared with both the Carroll College and Beloit College Glee Clubs and his work has always met with unstinted praise wherever he has gone. Now for the first time he announces himself in complete programs which will satisfy the demand for high class amusement. He will please any audience who is fortunate enough to hear him.
>
> Those who enjoy real rollicking fun of the most wholesome kind will find their demand satisfied in the artistic and inimitable impersonations of the greatest fun maker known to the stage— the great Scotch Comedian who has the hearts of two continents—Harry Lauder. MR. LUNT is without a peer in his representations of the songs and dances that have given Lauder such high place among artists of our time.

The Carroll Glee Club tour went further afield than ever in the spring of 1912. Venturing west for the first time, it played in Missouri, Kansas, Colorado, New Mexico, Nevada, Arizona and California. Until then Alfred had been thrilled with his ability to hold and fascinate an audience, but for the first time he began to be dissatisfied with his performances. He realized that he was barely tapping his potential skill, and there was a great gap between the performances he actually gave and the effects he intended to achieve. The standards of the amateur were no longer his standards. "I never did such poor work in my life as I'm doing on this trip," he told Ray Weaver.

The desire to improve and the dissatisfaction with his current level of ability would characterize Alfred Lunt for the rest of his career. Long after others had come to regard him as one of the world's foremost actors, he was unable to accept their judgment. Consequently, he never settled into a comfortable niche; instead, he continually drove himself to greater heights.

After Alfred's second year at Carroll College, he made the long-anticipated transfer to Emerson,* moving to Boston in September 1912. Two other students from Carroll—Juliet Weeks and Mia Stanton—also transferred to Emerson that year, so Alfred was not entirely on his own. For Juliet, the move was permanent. Her parents went to Boston with her, where they settled in a large new home. Alfred lived in an attic room in the Weekses' house, where he found the atmosphere congenial and invigorating. It was also awkward at times, for both Juliet and Mia (who also lived in the house) were in love with him.

"Tomorrow," Alfred wrote to Ray on September 23, "I register at Emerson. Ye Gods! I shake when I think of it." But Emerson would see little of him. After attending classes for only a few days, he was less than enthusiastic. "The fellows at school aren't particularly interesting in fact they are 'neither here nor there.' . . . The girls are 'not much' either but I may become 'used to 'em' after a little," he told Ray. As it turned out, there was no time for Alfred to become "used to 'em." On September 30, on his way to school, he passed the Castle Square Theatre, where a year-round stock company employed local actors as well as importing performers from New York. Alfred came to the abrupt decision that the real reason he had come East was to begin his career as a professional actor, and that his enrollment at Emerson was merely a step in that direction. Perhaps he could eliminate that step by getting a professional job immediately.

He entered the theatre and asked to see John Craig, the company's actor-manager. When Craig found out that Alfred was looking for a job, he introduced him to the director, George Henry Trader, who had at one time directed at the Pabst Stock Company in Milwaukee. During his tenure there, Trader had received a letter asking him to send Alfred a play the director had written. Alfred now inquired if Trader remembered that young man's letter. Trader replied that he certainly did; he also recalled that the young man had said afterward that he had read the play four times, and, Trader said, "Any man who can stand to read my play four times certainly has a place in my heart."

Once the ice was broken, Alfred told Trader that the reason for his visit was to try to secure a position as an actor with the Castle Square Company. Remarkably, Trader did not lecture him on the difficulties of the theatrical profession or tell him to return after he had gained several years' experience. Instead, the director simply asked, "Will you take five dollars a week?" Alfred accepted the offer without hesitation, and, as he wrote to Ray Weaver, "I play a part in next week's production of *The Aviator*—Play a country sheriff who attempts to correct the struggling hero, in the last

* After Lunt began to make a name for himself in the professional theatre, he often told interviewers that the college to which he transferred was Harvard, and that his intention was to study architecture there. This account was totally fictional and also totally unlike Alfred Lunt. He was a remarkably truthful man who rarely embroidered upon reality in order to impress others. In this instance, however, he did indeed invent circumstances that he must have felt would seem more impressive.

of the third act, but am kicked out by the crowd. Not a particularly satisfying & grateful role but it is an actual beginning & I shall 'go on' now if I die in the act. . . . So here goes—Good luck to you Alfred—May heaven protect you. This may interest Miss Rankin & you may tell her, concerning my first appearance, if you so wish—I'm quite tickled."

Lynn Fontanne's career had begun inauspiciously in England as a chorus girl in *Cinderella* in 1905. Now, several thousand miles away and seven years later, Alfred Lunt was about to make his professional debut in an equally unspectacular role. Neither of them would rocket to success. Both would have to serve long apprenticeships in minor roles, but both had achieved the first rung on the ladder: they were now professional performers.

Chapter Two

THE FONTANNE OF YOUTH

> "While acting with [Lynn Fontanne in
> 1916–23] I forgot we were actresses. We
> lost our identities completely and be-
> came the people of the play."
> *Laurette Taylor*

L ike many other British actors of her generation, Lynn Fontanne disliked discussions of the intricacies of acting, perhaps feeling that her
performances would somehow suffer if she tried to analyze them too
closely. Rather, she went to the other extreme, maintaining that there was
no mystery to great acting, that it was simply a matter of hard work. Trial-
and-error was the only method she would acknowledge. As an actress, she
would try one approach unless and until it proved to be profitless; then
she would try another, and then still another. The secret, if it can be called
a secret, was that she never stopped trying to improve, never settled for
the second-rate.

In part because of her reticence to discuss her techniques, in part because so many of the plays she acted in while she was a young performer
in England have faded into total obscurity, and in part because the roles
she played were generally minor ones, it is difficult to trace the gradual
steps she took in achieving mastery of theatrical technique. We know the
names of the plays in which she appeared, when they were given and the
names of the roles she played, but all too often information concerning her
development is tantalizingly out of reach.

1905–19

Even young women living Cinderella stories have to return to reality
sometime. When the production of *Cinderella* closed (like all Christmas

pantomimes, it had only a limited run), Lynn Fontanne was cast in a small role in a touring production of *Alice Sit-by-the-Fire,* but a period of unemployment followed. She lived for a time in a small flat in Down Street, paying six shillings per week. The nature of the flat can be surmised from the fact that there were no cooking facilities other than a gas ring and no plumbing facilities at all. In order to take a bath, Lynn had to carry water to her room and heat it on the gas ring. Another item missing from the flat was a telephone. Then, as now, actresses needed to have a telephone number to give to producers in case a job should become available. Lynn asked a neighborhood plumber if she could give out his number. He agreed to take her calls and to leave a message at her flat whenever anyone telephoned her.

In March 1906 a call came offering Lynn a job at the Savoy Theatre, where she would play a series of walk-on roles in various productions, beginning with *The Bond of Ninon* in April. The play featured Lena Ashwell, another of Ellen Terry's protégées.

The salary Lynn was paid at the Savoy was hardly munificent, but it did allow her to move into a larger flat in Victoria Street, which she shared with two other young actresses. Since Lynn was employed and the others were not, she found herself picking up the check whenever the three of them went out together. As they walked down Victoria Street, Lynn's roommates would shout in chorus, "Rich Lynnie will pay!" (That story never failed to amuse Alfred Lunt, who often referred affectionately to his wife as "Rich Lynnie.") The money also allowed her an occasional visit to her family in their cottage near Windsor.

Still later Lynn and her sister Antoinette lived together in a small flat in Chelsea. Throughout this period, as Lynn looked for employment in the theatre, she also worked to rid herself of the shyness that she felt was holding her back, both socially and professionally. "I thought to myself, 'Why are you so shy? What makes you stiffen up as soon as you meet anyone?' I said, 'It is because you are wondering what it is they think about you. Now, don't think that any more. Wonder what it is *you* think about *them*. And when you go into a restaurant, instead of dying when you go in, just look about you and see who's there that's interesting. You have a look, Lynnie, and see who's there instead of bothering whether they're looking at you.' And so I began curing myself," she said.

At eighteen Lynn found herself becoming interested in men and to her initial surprise, men began paying attention to her. When Antoinette took Lynn to parties, she said Lynn "kept these men in their thirties in fits of laughter." Although none of her infatuations proved serious, Lynn developed crushes on several young men, and would caution her sisters, "Please be nice to them," an injunction difficult for Mai and Antoinette to follow because they detested most of Lynn's suitors.

One evening Antoinette—whom Lynn described as "a raving beauty" and who attracted men in great numbers—was invited to dinner by three young men, among them an apprentice lawyer named Edmund Byrne. Antoinette "thought these three men were too much for her to handle," Lynn said, "so she brought little sister along for protection." Lynn immediately developed a crush on Byrne, and when it came time for the men to take the girls home, Lynn managed to arrange it so that the other two were in one hansom cab with Antoinette while Byrne and Lynn shared another. As soon as the ride began, Teddy (as his friends called him) tried to kiss Lynn, and she kicked him in the shins. Her reaction only fueled his interest in her. How to win over an impressionable, naïve girl of eighteen? Byrne found the way: he wrote a poem to Lynn and gave it to one of his friends, who gave it to Antoinette, who in turn passed it on to Lynn. "That was the beginning," Lynn said. "It was the poem that got me, a romantic kid like me. I was so excited having somebody write a poem to me."

On one occasion both Lynn and Antoinette were out of work and their funds were almost completely gone. Despite their circumstances, the girls had all the optimism of youth and they refused to worry. They decided that their choice was whether to buy a loaf of bread with the little money they had or to call Edmund Byrne in the hope that he would take them out to dinner. The toss of a coin was used to reach a decision, and the result was that the girls telephoned Byrne at his office. Fortunately for them, he was free for the evening and willing to buy them dinner, so the three of them ended by having an elegant meal at the Savoy.

As a little girl, Lynn had designed and sewn clothing for her dolls, and she now found another use for her talents. She made a party dress for herself that she hoped would impress Teddy Byrne. "Oh, he had a beautiful baritone voice," she told George Schaefer seventy-five years afterward, "and he stole my heart away."

Antoinette worried that Lynn had become too seriously infatuated, and that she was not yet capable of handling such an emotionally demanding relationship. She asked Byrne to stop seeing Lynn, which, for a time, he did. But Lynn was so desperately unhappy that Antoinette returned to Byrne, asking him to call on Lynn once again. Byrne said, "I wish you'd make up your mind." But he needed little prodding.

After her appearances at the Savoy Theatre in 1906, Lynn continued to alternate short periods of employment in the theatre with uncomfortably long periods of joblessness. Not until July 1907 was she offered another role: she was seen briefly in a short-lived revival of Booth Tarkington's *Monsieur Beaucaire* at the Lyric Theatre (where her pleasure at being employed must have been tempered by the fact that her name was misprinted in the program as Viva Fontanne). Lynn was given little to do in the production beyond wearing a little white wig and a long dress and dancing a minuet.

Until this time Lynn had been reluctant to use the letter of introduction Ellen Terry had given her to Beerbohm Tree. Now, however, her sit-

uation was bordering on desperation and she forced herself to attend an
audition for *The Mystery of Edwin Drood* at His Majesty's Theatre. Tree was
looking for a dozen or so girls to play minor roles. He could not have failed
to be impressed by Lynn's letter, but he was looking for girls with experience, he told her, and the few productions in which she had appeared
simply weren't enough. In an uncharacteristic act of bravado, Lynn replied
to him: "How will you get girls this young who have experience?" Tree
answered that such actresses were in plentiful supply. She responded indignantly, "But where am *I* to get experience if you don't give me work?" And,
as she said later, Tree "was so pleased with that remark from so young a
girl that he gave me the job. So I walked on and I got experience."

Lynn found a way to supplement her meager income by becoming an
artist's model. She posed frequently for Wilfred and Jane de Glehn. The
painting of "The Blue Coat" by Jane de Glehn, which hangs in the Royal
Academy in London, is one of many for which Lynn was the model. After
her modeling sessions Teddy Byrne would usually be waiting for her on
the Battersea Bridge. He would accompany her to her room in Mayfair
(the increased income from her modeling had allowed her to get a room
of her own), where she would change into another dress, "and off we'd
go, out for the evening," Lynn said. "We'd have dinner—lovely places. He
had money. We used to go to the Café Royal, the Savoy, the Carlton—very
often to a place called Hatchett's in Piccadilly."

Establishing a foothold in the theatrical world was, however, proving
difficult. She might have preferred staying in London, where managers
from the city's theatres would have an opportunity to see her if she was
appearing in a play, where she could attend casting calls, and where she
would be close to Teddy and Antoinette, the two people who were more
important to her than anyone else. But what she needed most of all were
some speaking roles in which she could develop her talent and gain experience. So she enthusiastically accepted the opportunity to play the role of
Rose Carlisle, the ingenue, in a touring production of Somerset Maugham's *Lady Frederick*. It opened in Bristol on January 4, 1909, with Lynn
also playing a role in the curtain-raiser, *The Peacemaker* by E. M. Bryant.
The tour offered her a period of assured employment, and it resulted in an
offer to appear in London once again.

However, her new play, *Where Children Rule,* ran only a short time
and Lynn was unemployed again. Unpleasant as unemployment was, it is
a condition any actor is likely to face periodically. What must have been
more discouraging for Lynn was that the jobs she was offered did not seem
to be advancing her career. Occasionally she would be given a speaking
role, but then, as in *Where Children Rule,* she would find herself once again
back in the chorus. Jobs, however, did continue to be offered, and she
accepted them gratefully, as they allowed her to broaden her acquaintance
with producers.

Somewhere along the line Lynn attracted the attention of Weedon Grossmith, who engaged her to play the maid in his touring production of *Mr. Preedy and the Countess,* beginning in March 1910. Grossmith was pleased with her work and next offered her the small role of Lady Mulberry in a play called *Billy's Bargain,* which he had written under the pseudonym Robert Lascelles. It opened at the Garrick Theatre in London on June 23 of that same year. For Lynn, the opportunity to expand her range from maids and ingenues to a titled lady (even though the role was minuscule) must have been gratifying. Nor did Grossmith forget Lynn when he decided to bring *Mr. Preedy and the Countess* to North America. Playing first in Montreal and then in Washington, D.C., the production arrived at Nazimova's 39th Street Theatre in New York on November 7, 1910. However, it did poorly in New York, playing for only 24 performances. Grossmith took his actors, including Lynn Fontanne, back to London immediately after the play closed.

She acted in two other plays directed by Grossmith in 1911. And in January 1912 a touring company of one of the plays, *Baby Mine,* was organized, with Lynn traveling as an understudy. It had now been more than six years since she had made her debut in the professional theatre. She was twenty-four, still a struggling actress who had achieved only modest successes in a series of highly forgettable plays, and was now relegated to understudying in a touring company. A performer of less determination might have been tempted to give up, but Fontanne was driven by an ambition and a confidence in her own abilities that could not be crushed.

Her good friend Teddy Byrne was, however, less certain that she was a talented actress. Although he had never seen her perform in a sizable speaking role, he felt that her lack of progress spoke for itself. But he decided to help her if he could. He offered to introduce her to Lady Higson, a prominent socialite who was acquainted with many people important in the English theatre. Lynn called upon Lady Higson, who, apparently impressed, introduced her to the producer J. E. Vedrenne and his partner, actor-manager Dennis Eadie. These men, finally, would be responsible for giving Lynn her first real opportunity to make her mark.

Vedrenne and Eadie offered her a leading role in *Milestones* by Arnold Bennett and Edward Knoblock. It was for a tour rather than a London production, and she was not to be in the principal touring company but in the least important of three that were being sent on the road. The Red company would play in the most prominent provincial centers in England, the Blue company in less significant cities and the White company in the most obscure locales. Lynn was hired to travel with the White company, but the fact that she would be playing one of the principal roles indicated at last that her confidence in herself was justified. Lynn would be playing the challenging role of Gertrude Rhead, which required her to age from a twenty-one-year-old to a woman in her seventies. The role would stretch her abilities and give her—for the first time—an opportunity to display her talents to the fullest.

Fontanne was warned by her director that she would probably have little difficulty in playing the young Gertrude, for she was reasonably near that age herself. And he doubted that playing the elderly Gertrude would be unduly troublesome. The real challenge, he suggested, would be in playing middle age convincingly, for that is the age that is invariably the most difficult for young actors to portray. Fontanne later commented that she "worked very hard" on that role, adding proudly, "I pulled it off." She studied the attitudes and mannerisms of every middle-aged woman with whom she came in contact, "and it turned out to be my best act," she said, "which shows the advantage of hard work in acting."

Asked by George Schaefer in 1978 what techniques she had used, Fontanne answered, "Very simple. I learned the words, hard. I really worked with them to the mat. I learned them. And when I learned the words I put the book down and began to act." This is a good example of Fontanne's characteristic response when asked about her approach to a role. Obviously, the process was far more complex than she let on, involving a thorough understanding of her character, analysis of the character's interrelationships with the other characters in the play, a determination of how to project her character's personality and attitudes in terms of rhythm, timing, the pitch of her voice, the manner of her walk and a hundred other details—but she would invariably assert that there was no mystery to it. She simply learned the words and proceeded to do what she was being paid to do: go onto the stage and act.

Teddy Byrne saw Lynn perform while she was on the road with *Milestones* and after the performance he came backstage and said to her with astonishment, "My dear, but you're good!" This belated recognition of her talent by the man with whom she had fallen in love must have been enormously gratifying. Gradually, Lynn's friendship with Edmund Byrne had blossomed into a romance. Byrne invited her to visit him and his parents in the London suburb of Walthamstow, and shortly afterward they were engaged. But with the World War approaching, they decided to postpone their wedding until the fighting was over.

Fontanne toured in the White company from January until May of 1913 and, after a summer layoff, from August until December. Afterward, in the greatest confirmation of her talent to date, it was Lynn, rather than the actresses who had been featured in the Red and Blue companies, who was asked to play Gertrude Rhead when *Milestones* was revived in London in the fall of 1914.

In the interim she was featured in two roles in another play by Edward Knoblock, *My Lady's Dress,* which opened at the Royalty Theatre in London in April. Two other young actresses who were on their way to outstanding careers were also in the cast: Edith Evans and Gladys Cooper. The play, a series of nine sketches, gave Fontanne the chance to develop two diverse characterizations. One was in the brief role of Mrs. Collison, a flirtatious woman in a dress shop. The second and more significant was that of Liza, a thoughtless young woman who despairs that she will never be able to marry the man she loves because they cannot afford it; her older sister, a hunchback who earns her meager living by selling flowers, sacrifices her long golden hair to get enough money to give Liza a fine wedding. Cooper and Fontanne were praised for their performances in this piece, one critic noting that Gladys Cooper "gives a pathetic study of a hump-backed girl with a selfish sister whom Miss Lynn Fontanne enacts to the life."

Milestones began its London run on October 31, 1914. This was Lynn Fontanne's first major role in a play in London, but it was not an auspicious time for an actress to make an impression upon the public. The World War had begun, and neither the British press nor the public could work up much enthusiasm about the theatre. Only a fraction of the West End theatres were open, and the November 2 issue of the *Times* of London, which included a brief and perfunctory review of *Milestones,* gave most of its space to war news. The *Milestones* notice was favorable ("an agreeable revival") and Lynn was singled out for mention ("Miss Lynn Fontanne, who takes up the old-maid part [originally played by] Miss Haidee Wright, achieves the miracle of making as beautiful a thing of it as her predecessor"), but Fontanne would have to wait for another occasion to attract the undivided interest of the public.

As a result, despite her success in *Milestones,* Fontanne's career was no more advanced than it had been a year or two before. In her next play she was once more cast in a minor role, acting the part of a nurse in Horace Annesley Vachell's *Searchlights* at the Savoy Theatre in February 1915. But if the play offered little else, it did give her the opportunity to act in the same company as H. B. Irving, the son of the great Henry Irving, Ellen Terry's longtime acting partner.

Her next appearances, in *The Terrorist, A War Committee* and *How To Get On,* were no more significant. About the best that could be said for these engagements was that they kept Fontanne busy. Finally, in the musical extravaganza *The Starlight Express* (with music by Edward Elgar) she had returned to the point from which her career had been launched: once again she was only a member of the chorus. But this time she could receive no consolation from Teddy Byrne, who was off in France fighting with the British army.

The significant role in *Milestones* had been the vehicle that should have given impetus to her career. But more than a year later she was still waiting for a decisive breakthrough. At last the opportunity for which she had been hoping did occur, and in the least expected way.

One of the biggest hits in the London theatre that season had been the appearance of the American actress Laurette Taylor in *Peg o' My Heart.*

Taylor and the production had been a great success wherever it played. Opening in Los Angeles in 1912, it established a new record for long-running stock-company productions in that city. Then it moved to Broadway, where it ran for 604 performances, closing only because Laurette Taylor had become weary of acting in it. As in Los Angeles, the play drew packed houses, primarily to see Taylor, who, as a result of the production, became one of America's foremost stars. Taylor brought the play to London in 1914, where it repeated its American success, running for more than a year, finally closing in November 1915.

A society tea was given in Taylor's honor after the play closed, and one of the guests—invited at the suggestion of Lady Higson—was Lynn Fontanne, who was "terrified at the posh doings," she said. Others at the party were standing in line to meet Taylor, but Lynn hung back shyly. "She doesn't want to meet me. I'm much too unimportant," she whispered to a friend. However, as she sat drinking tea in a chair across the room, she watched Taylor closely and came to the realization that the guest of honor was feeling as nervous and insecure as she was. Perfectly at home on the stage, Laurette Taylor was out of her element at a British society function. Fontanne thought that she might be able to salvage the afternoon for both of them. She walked over to Taylor and sat down beside her. "When I saw Laurette sitting there terrified—there is no other word—I forgot my own terror in sympathy," she said.

Taylor feared that the intruder, whom she described as "a slender young thing, with black velvet streamers hanging down her back . . . attached to a very prim hat," was another socialite. But Fontanne told her not to worry. "I'm an actress," she said. Taylor was immensely relieved; at last she could speak to someone with whom she had something in common.

Taylor asked Fontanne what plays she had appeared in, and Lynn mentioned *Milestones*. Taylor looked at her skeptically; she had seen *Milestones* in its revival at the Royalty, and she couldn't recall anyone in the cast who looked like Lynn. "What part did you play?" she asked. Fontanne identified herself as the actress who had played Gertrude. Taylor was astonished. She later said that Fontanne "had captured each age so completely [in acting the role of Gertrude] that I didn't know whether she was a slender thing of eighteen or a skinny woman of eighty." "You were wonderful!" she cried and asked what else Lynn had done. *"My Lady's Dress,"* came the answer. Taylor had also seen that play and had been equally impressed by Fontanne's performances.

Taylor called to her husband to come and meet the young actress. J. Hartley Manners was the English-born author of *Peg o' My Heart* and a prominent director as well. Manners had also admired Lynn's performances and immediately asked if she would be interested in coming to America as a member of their company.

Fontanne could hardly believe her good fortune. After a hiatus of ten years, it seemed that her Cinderella story was being enacted once again. "Yes, Mr. Manners," she said, "oh—yes—indeed—yes!" Still, actors are not unused to receiving offers of employment one day and having them forgotten the next. Fontanne fully expected this would be one of those occasions.

As Taylor was leaving the tea, she invited Lynn to a party she was giving at the Grafton Club the next night. Fontanne wanted to go, but she literally had nothing appropriate to wear and her savings at that point consisted of a mere three pounds. She spent the next day searching London for an evening dress that she could afford, but found none. Then she thought of one other possibility; perhaps a theatrical costume could be rented for three pounds. She entered a costume-rental store, emerged with the evening dress she wanted and went to the party. There, she and Taylor cemented the friendship that had begun the day before, and Taylor invited Lynn to visit her again. "We talked parts and plays," Fontanne said; "she was very, very kind to me in every way. But when she returned to America [in December 1915] I never expected to hear from her again."

With no acting job on the horizon, Lynn volunteered for special war service and was given a job driving an army vehicle in Devonshire, as chauffeur to Captain Sir Louis Mendl. Soon after the job began, however, she was handed a cablegram from Laurette Taylor in America. The cable offered her a role in the New York production of Hartley Manners's *The Wooing of Eve* at a salary of $100 a week. She turned to Captain Mendl seated beside her and asked, "How much is one hundred dollars a week in English money?" He answered that it was the equivalent of about twenty pounds. Twenty pounds a week! Lynn had never made so much money in her life.

She handed the cablegram to Captain Mendl and asked him to read it. "Does that say what I think it does?" she asked.

Mendl read the cablegram aloud and confirmed the message. He was just as astonished as she was. Twenty pounds a week was indeed a fortune in England during the war.

This must have seemed like the fulfillment of a prophecy to Fontanne. Years before, her mother had blithely predicted that Lynn would one day be earning the queenly sum of twenty pounds a week as an actress, and the prediction had at last come true.

When a friend of Fontanne's was told of the offer, he asked skeptically, "Are you worth twenty pounds a week?" She said, "I didn't know I was," but immediately began arranging for a passport. This was no easy matter, for wartime restrictions normally dictated a wait of several months. But Fontanne was not about to be stopped by red tape. "I had to make friends with all sorts of officials," she said, but she was riding a wave of good fortune and within a matter of days the passport came through. The only remaining snag was that George C. Tyler, the manager of the Taylor-Manners company, refused to pay her passage to the United States. "God

Almighty!" he said. "We have hundreds of girls in America who can play that part."

"Not the way this one can," Manners answered. "I wrote it with her in mind."

Still, Tyler was adamant. Manners, knowing that Lynn had no way of raising the money, sent it to her from his own funds. Within ten days from the time she had received the original cablegram, she was sailing on a cargo ship for America.

Tyler was predisposed against Fontanne, and his puzzlement as to why Taylor and Manners had invited her to join their company increased tenfold the first time he saw her. That first meeting occurred at a rehearsal hall in New York in the middle of winter, only days after she had arrived. Lynn, unused to such cold weather, came dressed in an oversized sweater that did nothing whatever to enhance her appearance. "It hung from her thin frame like a coat on a scarecrow," Laurette Taylor said. Tyler took one look at her, sighed deeply and, spluttering with rage, muttered "God Almighty!" to anyone who might be listening.

For her part, Lynn was frightened by his outburst. Despite his short stature and his plumpness, Tyler was an imposing figure, regarded by all who knew him as a tyrant, and his employees were in awe of him. Helen Hayes admired Tyler, but, like Lynn, she was terrified of him. "His word was law," she said, "his slightest suggestion an edict. His disfavor was too terrible to contemplate, much less incur."

Although J. Hartley Manners had been greatly impressed by Lynn's performances in London, he felt that she needed some basic stage technique. In particular, he believed that her walk—slightly pigeon-toed and awkward—had to be corrected. But because he thought that giving her instructions on how to walk would only make her more self-conscious, he recommended dancing lessons instead. The suggestion was taken, and it accomplished the desired end. The elegant carriage for which Lynn Fontanne became famous was, at least in part, a result of the dancing lessons she took at Hartley Manners's suggestion.

Lynn experienced all of the usual problems one normally suffers when moving to another country. She found America puzzling at first. She would venture into shops and find that she knew only the British name for the item she wanted. Consequently, she said, "I was shy of going into shops because I couldn't speak American yet. The girls, the assistants, were very impolite." As time went by, however, she began to feel comfortable in the United States and to think of making the move a permanent one. And whatever loneliness she may have felt at first was alleviated by the presence of two other British actors in the Taylor-Manners company, Frank Kemble Cooper and Philip Merivale, both of whom had been recruited during the English run of *Peg o' My Heart*.

The Wooing of Eve opened in Rochester, New York, in March 1916, with Laurette Taylor in the leading role and Lynn playing Winifred, a weepy ingenue who bursts into tears at the slightest provocation. The production moved to Philadelphia on April 10, but it did poorly there, and Manners decided that the play needed rewriting. Consequently, the Broadway opening was postponed, and another play by Manners—*The Harp of Life*—was rushed into rehearsal and immediately went on tour.

On November 27, 1916, a warm and cloudy evening, *The Harp of Life* was first presented in New York. Both the play and the production were enthusiastically acclaimed. J. Hartley Manners was regarded as one of the leading dramatists of his day, and the New York *Times* commented, "There is more real substance, thought and philosophy in *The Harp of Life* than in any other play of this year." Of course, the American theatre had not yet produced its first outstanding playwright (Eugene O'Neill would make his Broadway debut several years later) and few plays from 1916 are remembered today.*

Fontanne played Olive Hood, an eighteen-year-old innocent whose world is shattered when both the man she loves and her mother disappoint her brutally. The dramatic confrontation scene between Olive and her mother was played by Fontanne with intensity and poignancy. And the critical response to her performance could not have been more encouraging. The New York *Times* said that "next to Miss Taylor's the outstanding performance of the evening is given by Lynn Fontanne . . . it is a notably direct, eloquent, and moving performance." The critic for the *World* went further: "Despite the delicate shading and fine resourcefulness of Miss Taylor's acting, the performance of a fresh ingenuous young girl—the slave of her mother's tyrannical protection—by Lynn Fontanne, an English actress . . . stood out as one of the bright spots of the night."

One member of the audience on the opening night of *The Harp of Life* was Guthrie McClintic, who would later become famous for the series of plays he produced and directed for his wife, Katharine Cornell. McClintic went to the theatre that night primarily to see Laurette Taylor, but he was captivated by Fontanne. "She was a young woman, tall—dark—very thin and angular," he wrote. "She was also English, and she riveted your attention from the moment of her first entrance. Somewhere in the middle of the second act she had a brief emotional scene and so true was she—so touching and so vivid—that on her exit she brought the house down. During the entr'acte her name was on everybody's lips. The following day all the critics echoed the verdict of the opening-nighters. A new star was in the firmament."

---

* Some of the productions running on Broadway on the night *The Harp of Life* opened were *The Thirteenth Chair, The Man Who Came Back, Getting Married, Our Little Wife* and *Old Lady 31* (advertised in the newspaper as containing "306 laughs in 2½ hours"). All of those plays have long been forgotten and all probably deserved their fate. But great performers were active on Broadway in 1916: E. H. Sothern, Alla Nazimova, Pauline Frederick, Anna Held, Henrietta Crosman, Ruth Chatterton; and Sarah Bernhardt was soon to open in a repertory of plays.

Taylor and Fontanne became close friends during their professional association, which lasted (with interruptions) for more than seven years. Taylor's acting style also influenced Lynn enormously. Her timing and the unique way she spaced her words within a speech were picked up by Fontanne; for several years the similarity in approach was obvious to anyone familiar with their performances. Ultimately, of course, Fontanne came to realize that she needed to develop her own style and she stopped imitating Taylor's mannerisms and speech. But the work they did together was remarkable for the rapport the two actresses developed while on stage. "While acting with her I forgot we were actresses," Taylor said. "We lost our identities completely and became the people of the play."

Years later the team of Lunt and Fontanne developed the technique of overlapping one another's lines in such a way that the audience would miss the dialogue of neither. This technique had its genesis in the work Lynn did with Laurette Taylor, although they never perfected it to the degree that Lunt and Fontanne would later achieve. Another technique on which Fontanne and Taylor worked was improvisation. Often they would improvise their dialogue together during rehearsals in order to get a stronger feeling for their characters and the relationship between them. On occasion, with Manners's blessing, they carried the improvisation into the performance itself.

Fontanne's professional career was progressing splendidly at last, but her participation in *The Harp of Life* was marred by personal tragedy. While the play was in rehearsal, she received a cablegram from a friend of Edmund Byrne's in London, informing her that her fiancé had been killed while fighting in France. The will he left stipulated that she was to be the sole beneficiary of his estate, but she arranged to have it given instead to Byrne's sister in London. "I never knew his sister, and she never knew where it [the money] came from," she said.

One wonders how committed Lynn was to marrying Edmund Byrne. They met in 1906 and almost immediately became romantically involved. They did not become engaged until 1913, after which they postponed plans for a wedding because of the impending war. And Fontanne's engagement did not prevent her from coming to America during the war. There can be no doubt that they were in love, but the slow pace of the romance leads one to question whether it would have culminated in marriage had Byrne lived beyond 1916.

Nevertheless, the death of "the first man I loved seriously," as Fontanne called Teddy Byrne, served to increase her dependence on Laurette Taylor, who became her mentor, her guide, her spiritual advisor. Although only three years older than Lynn, Taylor told her what to eat, which parties to go to, what clothes to wear, which men she should go out with. And later, when Lynn became involved with Alfred Lunt, it was Laurette Taylor who stage-managed the romance, advising Lynn on every aspect of the relationship.

The Harp of Life was a personal triumph for Lynn Fontanne. Night after night she was given an ovation at her curtain call, and the consensus was that an actress of great talent had emerged. Immediately after the opening night, Lynn was approached by several managers who offered her contracts to work in their productions as a leading performer. Fontanne told Taylor about the offers, and Taylor cautioned her against accepting them. It was all very well to be "a star," Taylor told her, but an actress can maintain that position only if she is given superior roles in first-rate plays. The managers who had contacted Lynn had no particular roles in mind, only promises of stardom. Taylor recommended that Lynn remain with Manners and herself as a supporting player as long as they could provide her with good roles. When a manager could promise Lynn better, she would have Taylor's blessing to accept the offer.

In order to keep Fontanne in the company, Manners created roles especially for her in all the plays he wrote during the next two years. And Lynn's performances amply repaid his efforts on her behalf.

The next production on which they all collaborated was *Out There,* a sentimental war play that opened on March 27, 1917, just two days before the United States became an active participant in the war. Fontanne played "Princess" Lizzie, the Cockney sister of 'aunted Annie (Taylor), a sort of British Joan of Arc whose visions call upon her to get "out there" and help England win the war, which she does by going to France as a nurse.

Lynn received second billing to Laurette Taylor in this play, and she was favorably reviewed once more. "Again Lynn Fontanne strikes thirteen," said the *Times. Town Topics* commented upon her "astoundingly finished character study of a slangy Cockney," and Harold Clurman, who like Guthrie McClintic would become a famous director, was equally impressed by Fontanne's "unforgettable comic acuity" in the production.

Like her other roles in Hartley Manners's plays, Fontanne's part in *Out There* was limited, allowing her only to develop one aspect of a character. But in each case the personality trait she was called upon to play was different from any she had portrayed before. An observer who saw her only once might have believed that her talent was limited; but anyone who saw the gallery of portraits she was presenting would have been impressed by the variety of her characterizations. A feature magazine article took note of Fontanne's versatility, saying that her role in *Out There* was "as far removed from the little girl in *The Harp of Life* as the imagination could possibly conceive."

The coincidence of America's entry into the war and the opening of this play undoubtedly prolonged its run on Broadway. *Out There* became a symbol of the Allied fighting spirit to Broadway audiences, and the mayor of New York asked Laurette Taylor to pose for an enlistment poster in her character of 'aunted Annie.

Out There closed for the summer, but reopened at the Liberty Theatre in September 1917. In all, the production ran for 80 performances, a moderately successful run in those days.*

Now that Lynn Fontanne's name was becoming known to the public and the press, she had an important decision to make. Interviewers and compilers of theatrical biographies asked for details about her past, including the date of her birth. Fontanne was nearly thirty, but the characters she was playing were girls in their teens or early twenties. She may well have calculated (perhaps with Laurette Taylor's assistance) that it would be theatrically disadvantageous for her to reveal her real age. Actresses in America tend to be cast according to type, as she would have discovered by 1917. Had she admitted to being nearly thirty, she would have faced the probability that managers other than Hartley Manners would not have offered her younger women's roles—roles that she was perfectly able to play convincingly—or that the public would refuse to accept her in those roles.

Moreover, Fontanne did not look her age. Even in her fifties and sixties, her appearance was so miraculously youthful that she was dubbed "the Fontanne of youth." So remarkably young did she seem that she was often asked the secret of her seeming immunity to age.

Whatever the reason may have been, Fontanne refused to be specific about the date of her birth, but hinted that she had been born in 1892, five years later than her actual birth date. From that time until shortly before her death, she was extremely sensitive on the subject and gave out false or misleading information when asked directly for her date of birth.

After Alfred Lunt had died, she maintained that the only reason she had not openly divulged her age was that she had been determined to keep the truth from her husband. Soon after they met, she explained, Lunt had told her how old he was and had asked her age. But she feared to tell him the truth—that she was five years older than he—because she thought he would lose his romantic interest in her. So, according to her account, she reduced her age by five years and spent the rest of her life trying to maintain that fiction.

But that version seems unlikely. Alfred Lunt might conceivably have been disturbed by the knowledge that she was five years older than he when he was twenty-seven and falling in love, but surely after thirty or forty years of happily married life he would not have been traumatized by the knowledge that he had married an older woman. It seems much more likely that her wish to conceal her age was based upon the perfectly reasonable desire to further her career.

---

*A year later the American Red Cross revived the play with an all-star cast including Taylor, George Arliss, H. B. Warner, Chauncey Olcott, James K. Hackett and George M. Cohan. The cast—which did not include Lynn Fontanne—then went on tour for three weeks, donating their salaries to the war effort and raising a total of $680,000 for the Red Cross.

* * *

Hartley Manners completed his revision of *The Wooing of Eve,* the play for which Fontanne had first been hired, in time for a November 9 opening at the Liberty Theatre on Broadway. She had made some interesting adjustments in her approach to the role since the original production. At first, she had played Winifred (who is required to break into tears nineteen times in a single scene) with all seriousness, at Hartley Manners's insistence. But she had felt strongly all along that the role would be better played with a comic touch, and after the play's initial failure she was able to persuade Manners to allow her to approach the role comically. Her instincts were correct, as the reviews confirmed. "As the weeping and willowy bride, Lynn Fontaine [*sic*] also decked herself in laurels," the *Times* critic wrote. "Miss Fontaine's instinct is so true and her methods so sure that she is endlessly delightful—really an extraordinary performance."

The revisions that Hartley Manners made in *The Wooing of Eve* were not, however, sufficient to turn the play into a success. For the first time there was general agreement by the fickle critical fraternity that Laurette Taylor's talents surpassed those of her husband and that she would be well advised to present those talents in the work of another playwright.*

Before the run of *The Wooing of Eve* came to an end, the next Hartley Manners play was already in rehearsal. The plan was to open the new play immediately after the old one closed, which, it was hoped, would suggest that *The Wooing of Eve* had not been a failure but that the change from one to the other had been planned in advance. In the event, there was a one-week interval before the new play, entitled *Happiness,* opened at the Criterion Theatre on December 31, 1917. As the curtain went up, the temperature outside was two degrees above zero. Inside, the reception for Manners's new effort was not much warmer. John Corbin of the New York *Times* wrote that Manners's plays had long been flawed by ramshackle construction, but that the most recent of them were especially faulty because they were so obviously written as vehicles for his wife. Manners's failure lay in the fact that, whereas he was creating multifaceted characters for Laurette Taylor to play, he was surrounding her with stereotypes, as indicated by the roles Fontanne was called upon to perform.

Fontanne herself may well have begun to wonder whether there would be many meaningful opportunities for her in a company that was devoted to showcasing the talents of Laurette Taylor. She began to listen to the offers of other managements, and at the end of the run of *Happiness* she left the Taylor-Manners company for the first time since her arrival in America.

Her decision must have been a difficult one, because the relationship

---

*On the night after the opening of *The Wooing of Eve,* "the Great White Way" was dimmed by an edict signed by Dr. H. A. Garfield, the government's Fuel Administrator. The edict declared that the electric signs on Broadway must be turned on no earlier than 7:45 in the evening and must be extinguished no later than 11:00. Dr. Garfield was conserving coal for industries that were regarded as essential to the war effort.

of Fontanne and Taylor was as close as ever. The two of them spent as much time together outside the theatre as they spent within it. They shopped together, ate together, joked together, shared secrets, spoke to one another in Cockney accents and flirted with the same men, later to compare notes on them. In many ways they behaved like adolescents, giggling and gossiping.

But Lynn, who was unfailingly polite, could not have failed to be distressed by Taylor's rudeness to some of the other actors in her company. Taylor had no patience with actors she considered to be inferior. After a rehearsal a group of actors might be invited to the Taylor-Manners home for a party, but if Manners suggested an actor whose ability Taylor disdained should be invited, she would loudly and tactlessly shout, "My God, I have to suffer with him for three hours on the stage, isn't that enough?" Lynn was never the object of such rudeness during this period—that would come later.

Taylor also had a habit of taking over Manners's directorial function during rehearsals, using her position as "star" to criticize her supporting performers. She would demand that they change their approach to their roles or their reading of lines to conform with her expectations. "Bad actors could not take it at all, and even the good ones quailed," observed Taylor's daughter, Marguerite Courtney. Manners was as upset by Taylor's behavior on these occasions as the actors were, threatening to dismiss the rehearsal—or to dismiss Taylor from the rehearsal—if she did not stop interfering with his direction.

Of course, the battles within the Taylor company paled in comparison to the state of the world outside the theatre. The World War was about to enter its final phase, as Sir David Beatty, Commander of the Grand Fleet, predicted. "The United States is destined to be the deciding factor in the world war," he said. "We enter the year 1918 full of confidence and in the firm belief that victory will be secured by our combined efforts." Germany and its allies were making their first offers of peace, lending support to Sir David's claim.

For those whose lives were spent in the theatre, however, the outside world was secondary. Laurette Taylor's thoughts were not on the war but on her career, and the last two plays in which she had appeared had been pronounced unworthy of her by the critics. She arrived at what seemed to her to be an intelligent decision: she would prove that she was more than an actress who required tailor-made vehicles by acting in scenes from Shakespearean plays at special matinees.

Taylor's first job was to convince her producer, George C. Tyler, of the wisdom of her decision. That done, she presented her plan to Manners, who disagreed vehemently on the grounds that she had had no training or experience in Elizabethan drama. So much the better, she countered. Most productions of Shakespeare's plays, she said, were buried under a mountain of tradition—traditional approaches to character, line readings, business and so on. She, with no allegiance to the traditional approach, would offer completely new interpretations; furthermore, she would ensure freshness of approach by using only actors who had never before performed in Shakespeare's plays.

Manners remained highly skeptical, but he ultimately agreed to direct the production, which would include scenes from *The Taming of the Shrew*, *Romeo and Juliet* and *The Merchant of Venice*. As a result, Lynn Fontanne was cast as Bianca in *Taming of the Shrew* and Nerissa in *Merchant of Venice*. At the rehearsals, which began while *Happiness* was still running, Manners found it impossible to establish his authority. Taylor continually contradicted or ignored his instructions, not only with regard to her own performance but in respect of the other actors as well. She made it clear that this was to be *her* production, in every sense. But her ignorance of Shakespeare, so proudly flaunted, was woeful, and the choices she made, as actress and as *de facto* director, were invariably foolish ones.

The first matinee was given on April 5. The scene from *Taming of the Shrew* was greeted with polite applause, but the *Romeo and Juliet* scene can only be characterized as an unmitigated disaster. The audience found it so ludicrous that they howled with laughter. Helen Hayes, who was present, called the occasion "absolutely unforgettable. When she did the balcony scene . . . and Romeo revealed himself beneath the balcony, our Laurette actually met his eye and whispered, 'Hello, Romeo.' It was goodbye, Juliet, from that moment on."

So convulsed was the audience that Taylor allowed them an unusually long time to compose themselves before beginning the next scene, which was from *The Merchant of Venice*. It began with dialogue between Portia and Nerissa—Taylor and Fontanne—and that part of the scene was well received. Then, however, the process of disintegration set in once again, and the remainder of the scene was the object of more derisive laughter.

After the performance Taylor went before the front curtain to speak to the audience. This was not an uncommon practice, and Taylor was an accomplished speaker. She told the audience that she was aware how poorly the afternoon's entertainment had gone, but if she was to become the great actress she hoped to be, it was necessary for her to perform in Shakespeare's plays. She hoped the audience would understand that this was only a first attempt and that she would improve with time.

Her speech helped to contain the damage. Burns Mantle's review, for example, said that although the performance had been woeful, Taylor's courage was worthy of praise. "How many of our allegedly fine actresses would have dared so much," he asked, "or would have worked so hard and risked so much for the mere satisfaction of doing something worthwhile?"

Taylor's response to the disastrous evening was to continue to rehearse the scenes and to increase the number of performances. But there was little improvement, and most of the actors felt that they had been humiliated. Taylor never attempted to act Shakespeare again, and neither did anyone else in the company except Lynn Fontanne, whose scenes had been singled out for praise.

The offer of a leading role in *A Pair of Petticoats,* a comedy by Cyril Harcourt produced by the Shubert Brothers, finally provided an opportunity for Fontanne to leave Taylor and Manners's company, at least temporarily. Harcourt, who was directing, had developed a ferocious crush on Lynn, which undoubtedly had something to do with his offer. *A Pair of Petticoats* had been running for two months, with Laura Hope Crews in the lead, when Fontanne replaced her on May 20. This was what Lynn had been waiting for: a leading role of her own. True, she would not be reviewed, since the play was already running, but the opportunity was nevertheless too great to turn down. And when the production went on tour shortly afterward, Fontanne went along with it.

Before she left Laurette Taylor's company, Fontanne informed the producer, George C. Tyler, of her decision. Tyler, who had been so opposed to hiring Lynn in the first place, was now determined not to let her get away. He had a well-deserved reputation as a producer of hit plays and as a "star-maker," and was not in the habit of seeing one of "his" performers become a star under anyone else's banner—especially when that performer had shown the skill that Lynn Fontanne had demonstrated. Later, after she had joined the *Pair of Petticoats* company, he telegraphed to Lynn in Chicago that he hoped she was not about to do anything foolish, such as marrying Cyril Harcourt and signing a long-term contract to appear in his plays. Lynn responded that she had no intention of marrying Harcourt and that she resented Tyler's implication that she would become Harcourt's wife in order to further her career.

Buoyed by her answer and undaunted by her criticism, Tyler set out to win Fontanne back. Consequently, he offered her what he described as a wonderful part in a wonderful play. It would not be a lead, he told her, but the role was so good that she would be sure to steal the show. Fontanne agreed to terms and arranged to return to New York to appear in Tyler's production after the Chicago engagement of *A Pair of Petticoats* concluded.

One of the secrets of Tyler's success in the theatre was that, rather than wait for good plays to be submitted to him, he actively sought out such plays and the playwrights who could write them. In December 1917, Tyler invited George S. Kaufman, an obscure young journalist who worked on the drama desk of the New York *Times,* to visit his office at 10:00 at night. When Kaufman arrived, he was informed that Tyler was looking for someone to rewrite a comedy-melodrama by Larry Evans and Walter Percival called *Among Those Present.* Tyler had presented the play in Richmond, Virginia, and in Philadelphia, but it had not done good business. The play still seemed to have potential, however, and Tyler felt that the best approach was to build up the comedy at the expense of the melodrama. The difficulty was that Evans had been taken seriously ill, and Percival alone was not up to the job. Would Kaufman like to make the attempt? Tyler asked.

Kaufman, who had been trying for years to break into the theatre, replied that he would love to try his hand at it. Tyler then suggested that the comic element he wanted to emphasize was potentially present in the role of the wife of the play's main character. The role, however, would have to be developed and expanded. Furthermore, he already had an actress in mind: Lynn Fontanne. If Kaufman could supply the necessary scenes, Tyler said, success would be assured. How soon would you need the rewrites? Kaufman asked. You have twelve hours, Tyler replied. Rehearsals were scheduled to begin at 10:00 the next morning.

Kaufman was aghast. The likelihood of doing a satisfactory job in twelve hours seemed slim, but he was far too grateful for the chance to turn it down. Fortunately, when Tyler described the role he wanted Fontanne to play—the scatterbrained, socially prominent wife of J. Percival Glendenning—Kaufman thought immediately of a character, created by Franklin P. Adams, whose fictional platitudes were quoted regularly in Adams's column in the New York *Tribune*. The character was Dulcinea, who possessed a degree of innate wisdom but whose vocabulary consisted entirely of clichés. Kaufman believed that he could take Adams's character, call her Mrs. Glendenning and insert her into the play. But there was no time to contact Adams for permission; Kaufman needed every moment of the next twelve hours to write the new scenes.

The next morning Kaufman presented his material to Tyler, who burst out laughing as he read it. Kaufman did not tell the producer that he had neglected to secure Adams's permission to use the character of Dulcinea. He hoped and believed that his friendship with Adams would be sufficient to overcome any difficulties.

When *Among Those Present* opened in Chicago, *A Pair of Petticoats* was still on tour. Consequently, Fontanne's role was played by another actress. But Tyler was ready to delay the Broadway opening until she was available. In the late summer of 1918, Lynn began rehearsing for the play, which opened on September 9 in New York.

Now titled *Someone in the House,* it was a modest critical success for its authors and a triumph for Fontanne and for Hassard Short, who played her husband. John Corbin's feature article in the New York *Times* said that "Lynn Fontanne's performance . . . marks a step forward in the career of a notable young actress. That she has extraordinary power of personality has been obvious from the start. It would be a brilliant scene indeed that her entrance did not lift and inspire." Corbin went on to praise Fontanne's range. "With each succeeding part, it is more evident that Miss Fontanne possesses [versatility] in an unusual measure. Her present character is totally different from anything she has done hitherto. . . . With all her smiling, impromptu platitudes of culture and uplift, she is a real person. . . . It is a sound and true impersonation, avoiding all temptations to caricature. Fortunately her spouse is the no less admirable comedian, Hassard Short; and between them, with the aid of lines of unusual brilliancy and humor, they keep the audience in a gale of sympathetic laughter."

More than a few of those lines had been written by the actors. Fontanne and Short, believing that their roles were insufficiently developed, would "go off while the rest were rehearsing and sort of build their little scenes up," Alfred Lunt later revealed.

Someone in the House appeared to be ready to settle in for a long run. But once again Fontanne's success was limited by a force she could not control. New York was attacked by a dreadful flu epidemic in the fall of 1918 that caused numerous fatalities. Many people chose to avoid congregating in theatres or other public places, and attendance at most Broadway plays dropped precipitously. Some productions, those already established as hits, were able to continue, but *Someone in the House* did not fall into that category. Kaufman sardonically recommended to Tyler that the name of the play be changed to *No One in the House*. And just in case he had missed the point, Kaufman sent along copy for several suggested advertisements. One ad read: "Avoid crowds! See *Someone in the House* at the Knickerbocker Theatre." Another read: "Do you want to be alone with your girl? See *Someone in the House* at the Knickerbocker."

Bowing to the inevitable, Tyler closed the play after a disappointing five-week run. But the production made him more certain than ever that Fontanne would eventually become an important name in the theatre, and he was determined to keep her under his management. In order to keep her working while he looked for the vehicle in which she would play her first starring role, he sent her back on the road in *Happiness,* and then persuaded her to join the George C. Tyler Stock Company in Washington, D.C., where she agreed to appear in two plays during the summer of 1919.

Someone in the House had seemed, even to Kaufman, to be an abject failure. But it was significant for having established Lynn Fontanne as a formidable actress in her own right, one who no longer needed the sponsorship of Laurette Taylor and Hartley Manners. In addition, it marked the Broadway theatrical debut of George S. Kaufman, who was to be one of America's leading playwrights for the next four decades; and the role that Kaufman wrote for Fontanne became the basis for *Dulcy,* the play and the role that finally established her as one of the leading comic actresses in America.

Chapter Three

AN ONION IS AN ONION

> "Make no mistake, Lindsay—that boy has
> quality. I like him."
>
> *Margaret Anglin*

1912–15

The first professional play in which Alfred Lunt appeared was *The Avia-tor,* which opened at the Castle Square Theatre in Boston on October 7, 1912. He was originally assigned a role with only nine lines, but was given additional business during the rehearsals. His nervousness and ex-citement about being a professional actor caused him to lose his voice at each rehearsal, but, he wrote to Ray Weaver, "I've learned more in this last week than I have in months."

Lunt's enthusiasm was to be expected; he was being paid to do exactly what he had always dreamed of doing, and he was doing it in the company of some well-known performers. John Craig and his wife, Mary Young, were the company's mainstays, acting most of the leading roles, and gen-erally playing them quite well. Other members of the company included Henry Hull and Donald Meek, both of whom went on to enjoy successful careers on the stage as well as in films.

The Castle Square was also a well-equipped theatre, generally held in high regard. It was inexpensive: ticket prices ranged from fifteen cents to fifty cents for matinees and fifteen cents to seventy-five cents for evening performances. And it was thought to offer first-class entertainment: Ruth Gordon, who grew up in Boston seeing many productions at the Castle Square, said, "It was a wonderful stock company. For people who wanted to learn to act, it was heaven. . . . It was very first-class repertory theatre. It had great stature in Boston." Periodically during Lunt's three years at the Castle Square, he told Ray, "One couldn't have better training than in stock & Mr. Craig is really unusual. . . . I don't need to tell you how much I like [the director, George Henry] Trader."

But Lunt's enthusiasm was tempered by his recognition of the draw-backs inherent in the stock system. It is, in fact, astonishing that he became disenchanted with the routine so quickly. On October 7, just three days after *The Aviator* opened, a letter to Ray Weaver betrayed his reservations. "I've passed through seven performances & I guess I can stand the other five—I'm learning a lot (some good much bad) and maybe it will be valuable later on."

The reasons for his abrupt change of attitude are not difficult to discover. The Castle Square, like most stock theatres of the time, operated on a back-breaking schedule. The company normally offered a different play each week (although a popular production might run two weeks or more); matinee and evening performances were given on six days every week. While the current play was running, a new play was being rehearsed in the mornings. But that gave the actors only about twenty hours' rehearsal, which was insufficient for them even to learn their lines, much less to polish their performances. The actors had to spend their late nights and early mornings and whatever other time might be available to them—the interval between the matinee and evening performance, perhaps—memorizing dialogue. Such a schedule would obviously be onerous for any performer, but for Lunt it was particularly so, for he was trying to attend classes at Emerson College at the same time.

Lunt described his typical day to Ray on October 10: "I rise at 7:30 get my breakfast shave—clean up the dishes & then read my mail—Juliet knocks, we meet Mia & all walk to school (six blocks)—Chapel is out at 9:35 & I hurry over to the theatre (another six blocks) & stand around until sometimes eleven & twelve (it is impossible to study or write there) and then hie me to lunch—I go to class (at school) at one fifteen & am out at two—Again hike to the theatre & make-up & read Kipling . . . until the third act call bell rings—go through my performance & am out at five o'clock or so—Hurry home (12 blocks or so—I hate to spend a nickel for car fare) wash up & then we all have supper. . . . I leave here at about eight—by the clock—for the theatre & return & have my door locked at about eleven."

When Lunt told his friend he was "learning a lot (some good much bad)," he was referring to the frustrations of inadequate rehearsal time. At Carroll College, May Rankin had rehearsed every production until it had reached the highest level of quality she could achieve. As an actor in one of her productions, Lunt had felt secure in the knowledge that he was being given sufficient time to work on every detail of characterization and interreaction. To Lunt, who had already become a perfectionist in his approach to the theatre, the rehearsal procedure at the Castle Square seemed chaotic and inartistic. He was learning that the speed demanded of professional actors in stock (an analogy could be drawn to actors in television sixty and seventy years later) was calculated to produce only a superficial performance with none of the detail that can result in great acting. At the Castle Square, rehearsals were devoted to the basics: learn the lines, learn the blocking and the business, go over them a time or two and then open the play. Years later, when Lunt was in a position to establish the rehearsal schedules for his own productions, he saw to it that every actor had all the time that Actors' Equity would permit to develop his performance.

But, despite its drawbacks, the regimen at the theatre had considerable value to Lunt. The experience quickly demonstrated to him that he had yet to master the skills required of a professional performer, and it revealed what he would have to do in order to become more proficient. On October 18 he was rehearsing the role of Richard P. Roberts in *The Man of the Hour,* and he wrote:

> Honestly Ray—I don't know what ails me but I simply can't do a thing at the theatre—Never have I had the need of *repose* thrust upon me as I have in the last two weeks—I simply can't say one line without becoming tense in every part of my body, extremely nervous & you know what the effect is—and the worst of it is that I realize I've always been that way—I tried standing still, this morning, for five minutes & tried to give my lines naturally & easily but I couldn't. . . . I just abhor seeing a person on the stage—prance & twitch around as most amateurs do (there are two other young fellows at the C. Sq. & I act just like 'em—so inexperienced you know) but I do love to see a man who can go thru a part with *ease,* grace—intelligence back of it all—one who does not pretend to do anything, but who truly accomplishes a great deal. . . .
>
> I don't know why I never thought of these things before—Miss Rankin has spoken about them but I never realy [*sic*]* *felt* it before this fall—Trader said this morning "Now Lunt—remember the man in the last row in the gallery wants to hear—Keep your hands still! They'll look at them & miss what your saying—now lean up against this table—then put one hand on it—now go on with your lines—big—out" etc.—and all the while I have a pulse of about 212—Draw a moral from this poor struggling soul in Boston—"Take things easy" and in the name of all that is good be natural. I have learned . . . it doesn't pay to work one's self up to a bursting point before going out before an audience.

Although Lunt was tall, young and quite handsome, Trader invariably cast him as a middle-aged or elderly man. "It was unheard of [at the time]

*The spelling and punctuation of all letters are reproduced exactly as in the originals.

for tall actors to play young men," Lunt said later; "the juvenile was always short, curly-haired, rather plump." Nevertheless, Trader's insistence on casting Lunt as fathers and uncles and grandfathers was a source of continual irritation to him. "You can't imagine how very difficult it is to play a middle aged man *to* a middle aged man," he wrote to Ray; "I feel like a little boy—actually—and then that everlasting baby face—Have a frightful time making up my eyes and mouth." And he found himself the possessor of enough wigs to fill several shelves. Time and again he begged to be given a role he believed himself to be physically and psychologically equipped to play, but time and again his request was denied.

Lunt was mentioned in a review for the first time for his performance in *The Man of the Hour,* and the review was not favorable. Lunt told Ray, "It made me feel pretty blue—and I honestly am rotten in the part," but he said that he felt he was improving week by week. One reason for the improvement, he wrote on October 25, was that he and Juliet Weeks had had a good dinner that night at the Wellington. "It doesn't pay to skimp on food & try to 'play' (even tho it is only four lines). . . . I noticed a great difference tonight in my 'performance' after eating a decent meal." Normally, Lunt ate at Smith's Basement Dining Room, which served twenty-one meals a week for $4.50; the food there was adequate and "you get more for your money at Smiths than anywhere else around here," but, Lunt said, "one grows dreadfully tired of 'essence of beef' (soup) roast beef & apple pie & . . . very, very weak coffee."*

In addition to rehearsals and performances at the Castle Square and the lectures at the College, Lunt also tried to see as many plays in Boston as he possibly could. He saw the musicals *The Quaker Girl* and *The Woman Haters Club* in September, George Arliss in *Disraeli* and Henry Miller in *The Rainbow* in November. In January 1913, Annie Russell appeared in *She Stoops to Conquer* ("Annie Russell has completely won my heart," he said) and Mary Nash played *The Woman.* He also saw productions of *The Rivals, Milestones*—the play in which Lynn Fontanne was touring England—and he saw Mrs. Fiske at every opportunity.

Minnie Maddern Fiske was an actress of great stature who also managed her own repertory company. She was without doubt the most innovative performer of her time, having pioneered a style of subtle, realistic American acting founded on a system much like that of Constantin Stanislavski in Russia. "She is unquestionably the finest actress on the American stage & anyone interested in acting can't afford to miss her," Lunt commented in a letter to Ray. "In no place is there any 'acting'—they [Mrs. Fiske and the members of her company] all just live it & the 'fewness' of the gestures would startle you. Such an example of repressed emotion you never saw before & you are just fairly swept off your feet, by it." All in all, Lunt managed to see a remarkable number of plays during his three years

---

*Lunt's meager salary was supplemented by money from his trust fund. However, he regularly sent money home to his family.

in Boston. Although the theatregoing cut still further into his time and his budget, it was an essential part of his theatrical education.

Boston also provided a social education for Lunt. For the first time in his life, he began to contemplate the problems of American society. One day after rehearsal he, Mia and Juliet walked "to one of the 'slummy' parts of the city and oh such sights as we did see . . . the place is horribly congested." The poverty and misery they witnessed exceeded anything they had been aware of in Milwaukee. They stopped in a medical dispensary and spoke to the woman in charge, who told them that "the great touring-cars often run over the children & pass right on, the owners never stopping to help the little kids." They went on to see a settlement house on the southeast side of Boston, where volunteers were asked to provide whatever help they could. "If I had the time, nothing could make me happier than to take some kind of class to teach for an hour or so each week," he said, "but the best I could do was to offer my services as entertainer. The girls did too."

Lunt also found time to read widely, going considerably beyond what he was required to study for his courses at Emerson. He read *Shakespeare on the Stage* by the eminent critic William Winter; Hugo's *Les Misérables;* Thoreau's *Walden; The Master Builder, Hedda Gabler, The Lady from the Sea* and other plays by Ibsen. The books and plays he read represented a standard of literature that far outstripped the farces and melodramas that provided the usual fare at the Castle Square Theatre. He wanted desperately to act in *good* plays that would challenge the taste of the audience, rather than simply cater to it. Every once in a while, the Castle Square gave him that opportunity, but for the most part it was necessary for him to defer the realization of his hopes until the following decade, when he would join the Theatre Guild, an organization whose views paralleled his own.

He also began to read the works of Gordon Craig for the first time. Craig, the illegitimate son of Ellen Terry, was a visionary who rejected the notion of the realistic stage and called for a poetic theatre that would encompass the beauty and significance of religious ritual. "He's a great man," Lunt said in 1912, "about fifty years ahead of his time and one to 'be reckoned with'—a bit eccentric perhaps but he's after the right thing." A year later he repeated this opinion when he wrote to May Rankin that he was "wildly enthusiastic" about Craig's notion that the audience should be encouraged to let its imagination take the place of realistic detail in the theatre.

The most exciting production Lunt worked on in 1912 was *Othello,* which began its run on November 25. Trader gave him the job of copying business for the production out of Edwin Booth's original promptbook. The opportunity to study the notes and business of America's greatest actor of the nineteenth century was one Lunt relished. "I never read a play in such a pleasant way," he said, "& Trader will never know what a good old time he gave me." The production of *Othello* was "terrific," according

to Lunt (who played Lodovico), although he found Craig's performance
as the Moor lacking in richness. "Not that he wasn't pretty good, for he
really was," he said, "but such lines as 'this look of thine will hurl my soul
from heaven & fiends will snatch at it' . . . are far beyond comprehension
or understanding without years of study."

Having done a thoroughly satisfactory job with Booth's promptbook,
Lunt was entrusted with other important assignments. For a production
of *Damon and Pythias,* he assisted the director by researching ancient Greek
dress, armor and weapons. These jobs fascinated Lunt and added greatly
to his enjoyment.

Lunt looked forward to returning home for Christmas as most of his
classmates at Emerson were planning to do. He missed his family terribly
and was especially eager to see Ray Weaver. He had not yet been fully accepted by the members of the stock company, and his attendance at Emerson was so infrequent that he had had no opportunity to make friends
there. He did spend considerable time with Juliet and Mia, "but they are
so very very feminine," he complained, "and I realy can't talk to them about
the things I want to." He was certain that a visit to his family and friends
at home would be wonderfully invigorating. But one of the Castle Square's
most profitable productions every year was the Christmas musical, and
Craig and Trader told Lunt that his absence would be out of the question.
So he remained in Boston to play the Fiery Dragon in *The Gingerbread
Man* and barely avoided disaster when the lacopodeium powder he ignited
in order to produce flashes of flame coming out of his dragon's mouth set
the costume on fire.

Alfred Lunt, Sr., had come from New England and some of his de-
scendants lived in the Boston area. On holidays Alfred's loneliness was alleviated by visiting one or another of his cousins for a family get-together.
Although he was barely acquainted with these cousins, they were important to him, as were his contacts with Juliet and Mia and the occasional
visits of Ray's brother, Andrew, who had graduated from the Carroll College Academy in 1909 and was now attending college in the East.

The Castle Square actors got together for New Year's Eve at the
Craigs' house in Brookline, and for the first time Lunt was invited to one
of the company's parties. The acceptance that was implied by the invitation
made him feel less of an outsider. As to the party itself, Lunt disapproved
of the amount of liquor the other performers consumed, but he clearly
enjoyed the camaraderie.

Two months after having begun at the Castle Square, Lunt was still
attending classes occasionally—but only occasionally—at Emerson. In late
October, he had realized that he would be unable to derive as much benefit
from his classes at Emerson as he had hoped ("I've only gone to classes on
the average of one a week so far, altho I've kept up on the reading," he
said), so he had gone to see President Southwick to ask that his tuition be
refunded. To Lunt's dismay, Southwick refused to discuss even a partial

reimbursement, so Alfred decided to attend that semester's classes whenever possible in order "to get my money's worth."

He clearly had reservations about the quality of the training he was receiving at the Castle Square, and he frequently questioned his own commitment to the professional theatre. Nonetheless, he was pulled more and more in the direction of an acting career. He often asked Ray for details about May Rankin's current productions at Carroll College. On one occasion he wrote, "I long for the 'good ole days' as the professional ones are long & far from pleasant—why Ray, the more I see of it the less I want people, decent young people & girls in particular, to go into it—it is *cruel* & tho' I *thought* I knew of its trials & tribulations, still those thoughts were *ideal* compared to the *reality* of the life. . . . More than once I want to give up & go back to school . . . which realy in many ways is far more satisfactory." But the letter ends, "And yet—and yet—all I can do is wait—"

But he could not wait too long. He was already being asked whether he intended to finish out the season at the Castle Square. Two weeks later he was still undecided. "I don't know what to think or do," he said. "Some days I think this, some days that, some moments it's Lyceum, other moments theatre—just like a clock pendulum, forever swinging & with an alarum buzzing up at the top of my head most of the time besides—day in day out—and the worst of it is the thing never runs down except at night & even then I'm winding it up for the next day."

Lunt's exposure to theatre at Emerson helped him to make up his mind. He discovered that his enthusiasm for academic theatre was based solely upon his experiences at Carroll College and that other programs did not necessarily measure up to that standard. He saw a postgraduate production at Emerson and described it as "the rottenest & most disgusting affair I ever saw"; he attended some senior readings and concluded that they "can't compare to our old Friday recitals"; and he decided that Juliet and Mia would "have been better off if they'd stayed at home as far as school work is concerned . . . personally I think the girls have gained little except thru the wonderful advantages that Boston itself has afforded them." He told Ray to "thank your lucky stars for a Miss Rankin, old boy, for I doubt very much if you'll ever find another that can teach in the way she does."

On the night of December 29, Lunt met George Henry Trader on the street and revealed his doubts concerning a career in professional theatre. Trader told him that he would not advise anyone to remain in the theatre unless he "just *had* to become an actor, [that] if it wasn't just absolutely necessary to do it—stop." But Trader told Lunt that he thought the young man possessed talent, a strong voice and good looks, and that he wouldn't be surprised if Lunt were one day to make a good living as an actor. Still, he tempered his encouragement by reminding Lunt, "It isn't always the ability that counts, I'm sorry to say; it's often the circumstances."

At last, on January 8, 1913, Lunt told Ray excitedly: "Yes! I have decided to remain on the stage—I battled & stormed & tore my little brain to pieces, wondering & worrying & debating & 'handed my decision in' late last week." Not that his doubts about his own ability had been resolved. "I may not be alto-gether fitted for it," he said; "I have no voice, I have little brilliance & force & worse of all that hellish 'lack of confidence' which is oh so weak—but I do believe there is a great field to work in, unlimited when once the muck & grime is gone & tho' it will without doubt take years to get there I shall keep on."

Lunt's inexperience and lack of technique were brought home to him again and again. He wrote to Ray, "If you only realize how much we young ones need control & command—Playing with older & experienced people makes one realize this keenly." Later he added, "I seem to lack all self confidence—I never felt the need of any one to help, teach, correct & argue points with me, in my life as I do now. Someone who would really tell you the truth & criticize for your good, some one to give you points to build upon—I've had little or no direction & one's powers of observation can only go 'so far' & no further. . . . I do believe there is something in me but how to draw it out I do not know."

Lunt was given a new responsibility in February 1913, when John Craig asked him to serve as assistant stage manager. He would continue to perform in most of the productions as well, and his salary would be raised to $20 per week. Lunt was enthusiastic: "No finer training could be had," he said. "Hold the book, ring the bells, help see that the props are in their places, &c &c." He began his career as assistant stage manager with a production of *Believe Me, Xantippe,* in which he also played William the Butler and understudied two of the leading actors. The play was one of the biggest hits the Castle Square Theatre ever had, running for well over 100 performances.

As assistant stage manager, Lunt was occasionally called upon to step before the curtain and deliver messages to members of the audience. This proved to be one of his most difficult challenges, as on the night he was told to announce that if a Dr. Brown was in the audience he was wanted in his office. Alfred, who was able to speak the most intricate dialogue as long as he could hide behind the mask of the character he was playing, became utterly flustered at having to speak for himself. "If Dr. Brown is in his office," he said, "he is wanted in the audience."

Lunt's attitude toward his fellow performers seemed to change weekly. In his job as assistant stage manager, he found that he was the object of many of the actors' frustrations—they yelled at him if a prop was missing or a sound cue was late—and he resented it, describing their behavior as "childish" and "ridiculous." " 'Much work, little thanks' is the motto of the A.S. Mgr.," he lamented. But in his next letter he would express admiration for them both as actors and as people.

As the 1912–13 season at the Castle Square Theatre drew to a close in June, Lunt was both excited about returning home for the summer and apprehensive about whether he would be offered a contract for the following season. He was relieved when Craig asked him to return in 1913–14 for thirty-two weeks. He was to receive the same pay, but, he said, "I need the money & experience so 'to he— with the rest'—That's just the way I feel about it."

So, refreshed by a relaxing summer at home and several stimulating conversations with May Rankin, Lunt returned to Boston with renewed enthusiasm in late August. His second season was highlighted by the company's production of *Hamlet* in January 1914, which he described as "the best classic done at the C. Sq. so far," although it had to be mounted in a mere nineteen hours of rehearsal. Lunt played the First Player and "tho' scared to death I love it—it's the best thing I've done so far," he said, adding characteristically, "but that's not saying much." Craig as Hamlet was "really good," and "Mrs. Craig's mad scene (as Ophelia) . . . is really a beautiful piece of work."

But *Hamlet* was a departure for the company. More typical were the productions of such forgettable melodramas and farces as *Under Two Flags, Bachelors and Benedicts, A Butterfly on the Wheel, A Temperance Town, Monte Cristo, Miss Pocahontas, The Girl of the Golden West* (in which Lunt played an Indian and spent hours applying his makeup and another hour removing it), *Mrs. Wiggs of the Cabbage Patch, Rip Van Winkle* and *The Mind the Paint Girl.*

Lunt's roles at the Castle Square Theatre in 1913–14 were more significant than those he played in his first year, and, although he was never offered a lead, he had become a valuable member of the company—so much so that the scene designer offered to get him a job in a stock company in Quincy, Massachusetts, for the summer. Lunt turned down the job, however, because he and his mother were planning a trip to Europe with the $30,000 inheritance that had finally come to him on his twenty-first birthday. Lunt rationalized the expensive trip by convincing himself that his mother needed to get away from the smaller children for a time and that "I'll never have an 8 weeks vacation again so I feel I ought to take advantage of it."

His only regret was that a trip abroad would not allow him to spend time with Ray Weaver, whom he called in his letters "dearest boy," "honey," "my darling boy" and "my hero of delight." The relationship between the two young men does not appear to have been grounded in sexuality, only an intense emotional closeness, expressed in a florid rhetorical style typical of the period. Lunt's letters to Weaver are remarkable in that respect, especially in light of his tendency to be somewhat perfunctory in all his later correspondence, speaking freely about his activities but being careful to maintain an emotional distance.

It seems likely that Lunt did have a sexual encounter—perhaps his first—with a girl named Anne whom he met in Boston. Anne came, he said, "from a very fine old Cambridge family, . . . educated in France & Boston, in fact graduated from Radcliffe with some honors, brilliant, extremely well read & is one of the few women who dresses in elegant taste—extremely refined & aristocratic." He described her appearance to Ray in the greatest detail. "It was the privilege of this young lady to teach me a good deal," he confided, "& this knowledge I hope some day I may impart to you—that you may use it to your best advantage."

Lunt had no worries about a job for the following year, as Craig had offered him a contract for 1914–15 at a slight raise in pay. His salary would climb to $25 per week, and in addition to his performing he would graduate from assistant to full-fledged stage manager.

Hattie Sederholm visited Lunt in Boston in May 1914, just prior to their trip abroad.* From the R.M.S. *Laconia,* Lunt wrote Ray, "We are having such a good time. . . . I haven't seen mother so happy for years & years—I doubt if I ever did." The ship took them to England, where they spent two days in Stratford-on-Avon and a week in London. There, Lunt delighted in the British theatre and other attractions. He saw Beerbohm Tree and Mrs. Patrick Campbell in *Pygmalion* and George Alexander in *An Ideal Husband*. He toured Westminster Abbey, and, most thrilling of all, he saw Diaghilev's Russian ballet featuring Nijinsky, with scenery and costumes by Bakst; "wanted to die then & there," Lunt reported. The ballet was given at the Theatre Royal, Drury Lane, where, in 1905, Lynn Fontanne had made her professional debut as a chorus girl in *Cinderella*.

From London, Lunt and his mother sailed to France, where they visited Versailles and Fontainebleau and saw *Cyrano de Bergerac* at the Comédie Française. "An ideal performance," Lunt reported. "Wept 'copiously' during the last act."

They then journeyed to Brussels, Germany and Russia, where he found the churches "gorgeous in the extreme" and the art galleries the "finest ever." Lunt was moved and elated by his visit to Russia, although he was perplexed by its contradictory character. "Such confusion, such dirt, such misery, such wealth, such ignorance, such rotten systems of business & government, such intelligence, such artistic temperament all messed up together . . . the people have more 'character' in their faces than any other country we've been in."

They arrived in Finland, where they saw their relatives once again, just in time for the outbreak of the World War. "It came with frightful suddenness to us," Lunt told a newspaperman after returning to Boston, "because all papers in Finland are censored even in normal times, and we

---

* Karin, Louise and Carl remained at home. A Waukesha friend looked in on them occasionally, but for the most part the children—who ranged in age from nine to fourteen—were left on their own.

had no idea that Europe was on the verge of war." When Lunt left his hotel in Helsingfors on the morning of July 31, he felt an apprehension that something was terribly wrong. The banks and most of the stores were closed, and the people on the streets "were running about aimlessly, talking for a few seconds and then running off again, just like ants in an ant-hill that has been turned up."

Lunt walked down to the sea front and found it blocked off by armed Cossacks mounted upon their horses and heading for the arsenal. He immediately returned to his hotel, where he learned that all Americans had been advised to leave Finland at once. He and his mother attempted to cash in their traveler's checks, but found that their value was almost nil. Using what little cash they had, they managed to get places on a train for the frontier town of Tornea. The train was delayed for seventeen hours, and when it departed it was crowded to overflowing, primarily with Swedish refugees but also with a large complement of Russian officers returning to their garrisons in the west of Finland. The passengers tried to get information from the officers, but the Russians refused to talk about what was happening.

Lunt described the rest of the harrowing journey to the Boston reporter:

> We got to Tornea . . . on the 2d of August, and after waiting for hours in the dark, managed to get our baggage piled on a handcart and started across to Haparanta on the other side [i.e., in Sweden]. No railways are allowed so near the frontier, but we found automobiles and hired one to take us to Boden, 150 miles away for 90 kroner, about $24. This was really the worst part of the journey, as two of the women of the party became violently ill, either from fatigue or the terribly bad food we had had to eat.
>
> Conditions at Boden were nearly as bad as in Finland, for mobilization had begun in Sweden. Food had gone up three times its value in three days. The town was crowded with Russian refugees, who seemed to have quite lost their heads and had evidently been driven out of Germany with nothing but the clothes they were wearing. They were almost starving. One woman, evidently of a noble family, was offering a necklace of beautiful diamonds for 200 kroner, less than the value of the settings.

From Boden, Lunt and his mother took a train to Stockholm and then traveled steerage class on the Scandinavian-American ship *United States* to America. The voyage was crowded, uncomfortable, "terribly rough, and, to make matters worse, there seemed to be nobody on board who could cook, all the cooks and stewards having had to join their regiments or ships in Norway."

After his return from Europe, Lunt decided to spend more of his inheritance on a plot of land where he could build a house for his family to live in while he pursued his career. He recalled the brief time he and they had lived in Genesee Depot (and where they often drove for picnics after having moved to Waukesha) and determined that that would be the perfect location. Fortunately, three acres in Genesee Depot were for sale. Lunt bought the land and designed a small house similar to those he had seen in Finland. As he returned to Boston two weeks later, his family made plans to move into the new house as soon as the builder could have it ready for them.

Lunt's last season at the Castle Square Theatre began in late August 1914. His salary now permitted him to take a room of his own near the home of the new director, Al Roberts. In September, Roberts relieved Alfred of his job as stage manager so that he could devote full time to acting. Lunt's talent was finally beginning to prove itself, and he drew special attention from the Boston critics. Of his appearance in *Paid in Full*, a critic wrote: "Mr. Lunt, as Jim Smith, again demonstrated his versatility . . . his tone and his manners were those of a skillful actor, who made the most of an excellent part."

His performance in a melodrama entitled *The Ne'er Do Well* was even more highly praised. "Mr. Lunt was particularly effective as the jealous husband," said the critic. "The part is a difficult one; it can be easily botched; it can be dully played or coarsely played, but Mr. Lunt made none of these mistakes. Instead he showed us the semblance of a man whose careful bearing is an attempt to veil the fires that increasingly smoulder beneath. He showed us how this man could not conceal his rage at last, how it had burned so hot from its smouldering that no veil could hide its searing. His man shaken, inarticulate, yet suppressed his jealousy until it burst forth and consumed him." And when the Boston *Sunday Herald* ran photographs of the leading theatrical lights of the city in 1914, Alfred Lunt's picture was among them.

The makeup of the company had changed significantly, Lunt told Ray, and "The Castle is rather a sorry place this year. . . . We actually have only 3 experienced men, besides Mr. Craig (who seldom plays) & the rest of us are nearly kids with but one to 2 years of real stage life behind us." One thing that had not changed, Lunt found to his consternation, was that he was still assigned to play characters who were twenty to fifty years older than he was. At last, however, in *Ready Money* he was given the opportunity to play a juvenile. Ironically, he told Ray during the rehearsals for that play, "Am really uncomfortable—Long to put on a beard again."

A great success of that season was the world premiere of *Common Clay* by Cleves Kinkead, in which Lunt played the leading man's father. Kin-

kead was a Harvard undergraduate, and his play was chosen for performance because John Craig offered $500 and the assurance of a production
for the best play written by a Harvard man. *Common Clay* was no masterpiece, but, unlike many of the plays presented at the Castle Square, it expressed a point of view, and, as Lunt told Ray Weaver, the author expressed
it "naturally & with startling force. If the police will only keep away we
ought to run seven or eight weeks at the least—You see said piece contains
some 'broad' situations & frank honest speeches as to sex relationships &
our celestial Mayor Curley is apt to look scornfully down on 'truth in the
theatre.'" But the police evidently kept their distance because *Common
Clay* ran for several months to standing-room-only houses. Eventually the
play was purchased for a Broadway production and was given in New York
with an entirely different set of actors.

The Castle Square Theatre had clearly offered Alfred Lunt all that it
was capable of offering. Well before the end of his third year there, Lunt
was "sick unto death of it all." He determined that he would not return for
a fourth season. In fact, he nearly failed to complete his third. Gertrude
Kingston offered him a contract to play with her in *The Cherry Orchard* in
New York for a salary of $60. She could only guarantee him one week's
employment, but the chance to be seen in New York was not to be dismissed. However, when Lunt told John Craig about his opportunity,
Craig "flew up in the air." The two of them argued for the better part of
an hour before Craig offered Lunt a $10-per-week raise if he would finish
out the season. Lunt agreed and decided that "things have not come out
so badly after all."

In fact, Lunt was not seriously disappointed that he had to postpone
his New York debut. He felt that he still lacked skill and experience and
that he would be best served by learning more about his profession before
attempting to perform for a New York audience and New York critics,
both of whom were likely to be more demanding than their Boston counterparts. Livingston Platt, who occasionally designed scenery for the
Castle Square Theatre, told him about the possibility of an acting job in
the touring company of Margaret Anglin, one of America's most respected
actresses, that would begin in the summer of 1915. This would offer him
a perfect opportunity to develop his talent and to further his career. Platt
had worked with Anglin and knew that she needed an actor to replace
William Boyd, her leading man in *Beverly's Balance,* then playing in Chicago. Boyd had given notice that he would have to leave the production
shortly before it closed, giving Anglin plenty of time to look for the best
possible replacement for the last two weeks of performances. Platt gave
Lunt a letter of introduction to Anglin and encouraged him to get in touch
with her.

In June 1915, Alfred Lunt left the Castle Square Theatre permanently.
During his tenure there, he had endured many unpleasant times, and on
several occasions he had derided the work of the company and the train-

ing—or the lack of it—that he was receiving. But his unhappy memories faded with time, and in later years he would look back fondly on his days at the Castle Square, recalling everyone there with affection and admiration, and telling one and all that the theatre had provided him with some of the happiest times of his life.

1915–16

After contacting Margaret Anglin by letter and being told to meet her in Chicago for an audition in late June, Lunt returned to Wisconsin to visit his family. A considerable amount of painting and wallpapering needed to be done in the Genesee Depot house, so Lunt spent much of his two weeks at home helping with those jobs. He also revisited Carroll College, where he watched several rehearsals for Miss Rankin's current production. To his surprise, he discovered that the level of quality was not nearly as high as he had remembered. The many professional plays he had seen since he attended Carroll had undoubtedly instilled in him a higher standard.

By June 20 he was in Chicago. Livingston Platt advised him to watch as many performances of *Beverly's Balance* as he could before his audition, and he took the advice gratefully. Once the audition date was set, Lunt's self-confidence—never high at the best of times—began to erode. "Shades of Edwin Booth!!" he wrote to Ray Weaver. "A *lead* with America's foremost actress! I can't believe my ears."

When Lunt appeared at the theatre for the tryout, he discovered that he would not actually be reading a scene with Miss Anglin. She would sit in the auditorium and watch while the stage manager read her lines in several scenes with Lunt. The stage manager was a young man named Howard Lindsay, who later wrote (with Russel Crouse) some of the most successful plays in the American theatre, including one for the Lunts. At this time, however, Lunt and Lindsay were not acquainted, and it cannot be said that either made a good impression on the other.

In reading with Lunt, Lindsay mimicked Margaret Anglin's performance and wore the apron she wore when playing the role. Lunt felt that Lindsay was being entirely too fussy, making the audition more stressful than was necessary.

Lindsay's impression of Lunt was even more negative. "He was, in my opinion, the most hopeless aspirant I had ever seen or heard," said Lindsay. Watching Lunt out of the corner of his eye while he read Anglin's lines, Lindsay saw a terrified youngster who seemed to be ashamed of his height. Rather than standing, Lindsay said, Lunt crouched over in an unsuccessful attempt to seem smaller than his six feet three inches. And he made himself look utterly ludicrous, according to Lindsay, by taking very small steps across the stage, again with the intention of diminishing his height. Reinforcing this impression of awkwardness was Lunt's voice, which Lindsay thought to be squeaky and unpleasant.

The reading continued for fifteen minutes, an unusually long audition. Lindsay could not understand why Anglin allowed it to go on, as Lunt was so obviously out of his depth. Finally, she called a halt and told Lunt, in the time-honored tradition of the theatre, not to call her; she would let him know by telephone whether or not he was to be hired.

As Anglin and Lindsay left the theatre, she asked him what he thought of Lunt's audition. "I told her I thought he was terrible," Lindsay said; "dreadfully inexperienced, no control of his body or his voice, quite impossible." Anglin remained silent for several moments. She then astounded her stage manager by telling him, "Make no mistake, Lindsay—that boy has quality. I like him."

As stage manager, it was Lindsay's job to telephone Lunt, informing him that he was hired. Certain that Miss Anglin had made a woeful error, Lindsay offered Lunt the job at a salary of $50 per week. The salary was more than Lunt had been earning at the Castle Square Theatre, his role was longer and more important than any he had played in Boston, and he would finally be given a chance to play a character who was close to his own age, but the real coup was simply in being allowed to work in Margaret Anglin's company. She was, in Lindsay's words, "one of the greatest stage directors and teachers of acting that . . . I have ever known." Lunt was still far from a polished actor in 1915, and Anglin sharpened his skills significantly during the several productions of hers in which he appeared.

Lunt had little more than a week to prepare for *Beverly's Balance*. He first appeared in the role of J. Courtland Redlaw in Chicago in early July, and then headed west with the company on the 11th, playing one-night stands in Cheyenne, Wyoming, Winnemucca, Nevada, and other cities on the way to Berkeley, where Margaret Anglin had agreed to perform a series of ancient Greek plays in the Greek Theatre at the University of California as part of a festival in conjunction with the Panama-Pacific Exposition. Meanwhile, the tour of *Beverly's Balance* was suspended, to be picked up again in September.

Anglin hired Lunt to perform in the Greek plays, but, because of his inexperience and lack of classical training, he was originally scheduled to appear only in the smallest of roles.

The plays—*Iphigenia in Aulis, Medea* and Sophocles' *Electra*—were each to be given for one performance only, on Saturday, August 14, and the two Saturdays following. Each would be given a magnificent production. Lunt's benefactor, Livingston Platt, was hired to design the properties, costumes and stage machinery; Walter Damrosch was to arrange the musical settings and conduct the orchestra of sixty pieces; and Gustav von Seyffertitz would direct *Iphigenia* and *Medea*. But most of the work fell to

Margaret Anglin, who directed *Electra* (and had a significant hand in directing the other two plays), played leading roles in all of them, selected each member of the cast and chorus (in addition to those who played speaking roles, two hundred chorus members and supernumeraries participated in the productions), helped to choose the costumes and, in short, took a hand in every aspect of production. So busy was she with her supervisory concerns that on the night of *Electra* she barely had time to get into costume and makeup before the performance began. Lunt was overwhelmed by the amount of work she did and how brilliantly she did it. "Certainly no other actress in the year 1915" could have accomplished as much, he said in 1971.

Platt used the permanent stage of the Greek Theatre somewhat differently for each of the three productions; his arrangements were simple but extremely effective. Damrosch's music was equally outstanding. But the focus of the performances was—as it should have been—on the acting of the major roles, and Anglin did not disappoint in any of them.

In *Iphigenia*, the first play to be given, Lunt played the small role of the Second Messenger. Anglin felt that he was too thin, so he was liberally padded around the waist and chest. He played his role quite effectively, speaking with sufficient projection and clarity so that he could be heard clearly by everyone seated in the vast amphitheatre.

Lunt was to have been a supernumerary in *Electra*, but Anglin gave him a special role to play. She inserted a procession before the entrance of Clytemnestra and asked Lunt to lead it; she wanted something suggestive of decadence, she told him, bordering on the obscene. In rehearsal Lunt gave his finest rendition of decadence, but, in his words, Anglin "said it was about the most wholesome entrance she had ever seen in her life. It was just a nice boy leading a few members of the family to church, and it wasn't the idea she wanted at all." Lunt asked if he could work on the scene by himself, and she agreed. At the next rehearsal he made his entrance looking thoroughly dissolute, and "what I did not only shocked but delighted her. She said we might be arrested, but to keep it in." According to one account, Lunt entered with his arms draped suggestively around two young boys, all of them drunk and all of them made up with painted fingernails and toenails.

As the performance of *Electra* came to an end, the great audience sat in utter silence for more than a minute. Anglin feared that the performance had been disastrous. Then, as if they had all been given a cue, the audience broke into cheers and shouts of "Bravo!" Those seated near the stage could not contain their enthusiasm; they ran onto the stage and mobbed the actors with their congratulations.

The production of *Medea* was a thorough triumph for Anglin, and a milestone for Lunt as well. The actor who was scheduled to play the Messenger broke his ankle just prior to the performance, and Lunt was asked to fill in. He did so with much apprehension, but he gave an electrifying performance, speaking with power and authority.

Lunt recalled later that Anglin had stunned the actors as well as the audience during the performance of *Medea*. She had conserved her energy during the rehearsals, giving no hint of the dynamism she would bring to the performance. "So," Lunt said, "when she came to the scene in which she dragged her two children off to be killed, using a great full and terrifying voice, the two children were literally so frightened she had difficulty dragging them offstage. This I doubt could ever be repeated. It was real. It was actual."

The reaction to the Greek plays was so positive that Anglin was asked to give a repeat performance of *Iphigenia in Aulis* on September 4. She agreed to do so, but Lawson Butt, who had played the important role of Achilles, had a commitment elsewhere. Remembering how well Lunt had done on short notice in *Medea*, Anglin cast him as Achilles. Howard Lindsay was given the task of preparing him for the role, as there would be only one rehearsal with the entire cast before the performance. Lindsay still had little faith in Lunt's abilities and believed that he would never be able to convey the warrior's physical and emotional power. In order to make Lunt more physically impressive, Lindsay saw to it that he would wear a heavy coat of armor, supplemented with a helmet, a sword, a shield and a dagger, during the performance. But he failed to realize that the heavy armor, combined with the tension of the performance itself, would sap Lunt's strength as thoroughly as it did. After Lunt made his first striking appearance as Achilles—looking eight feet tall in his great helmet—he began crossing toward the center of the enormous stage. As he walked, he grew shorter and shorter until, Lunt later said, "I don't think I was four feet tall." But although he was physically worn down by the weight of his costume, he did not allow it to interfere with the intensity of his performance, and Anglin was pleased with his work.

The *Californian* took note of Lunt's performance as Achilles, describing him as "manly, quick to anger, and incarnate with youth." And the *Argonaut* said, "Mr. Lunt took the stage centre with a splendid effort of self-forgetful exaltation, as he poured out a eulogy to the sacrificial daughter of Agamemnon."

Anglin told her husband and manager, Howard Hull, that Lunt deserved a reward for taking over the role at the last minute and playing it so well. Hull later took Lunt aside, expressed his gratitude and—unbeknownst to his wife, who would have been shocked by the cheapness of the gesture—handed him a five-dollar bill.

Margaret Anglin alternated appearances in the most ephemeral of modern plays with revivals of the classics on a grand scale. Already in the works was a production of Shakespeare's *As You Like It*, scheduled to be given outdoors in Forest Park in St. Louis in the summer of 1916. Meanwhile, however, she resumed her production of *Beverly's Balance*, with

Lunt again playing Redlaw. His performance at the Columbia Theatre in San Francisco in mid-September was praised by the critic for the *Argonaut,* who spoke of "the decidedly attractive person and personality of Alfred Lunt. . . . As played by Mr. Lunt, Jack Redlaw was a dear, loveable lad."

In October, *Beverly's Balance* began an international tour that took the company to Calgary, Edmonton, Saskatoon, Regina and Winnipeg in Canada, then returned to the American Midwest to play Sioux City, Fort Dodge and other locations in Iowa; Peoria and Springfield in Illinois; Battle Creek, Ann Arbor and other Michigan cities; and finally Boston's Plymouth Theatre.

For Lunt, this must have been a momentous occasion. *The Christian Science Monitor,* in its review of the production, took note of the fact that Lunt had spent several seasons in Boston and commented, "Alfred Lunt brings the same restraint and careful study to his part that he did in . . . 'Common Clay' [at the Castle Square Theatre], and is even more successful in the younger role of Redlaw."

The tour continued for three more months. When it neared New York, Lunt wrote letters to Broadway producers, requesting that they travel to Atlantic City to see him in one of the three performances of *Beverly's Balance* to be given there in February 1916, and offering to pay expenses if necessary. The tour was about to conclude and a new play, *The Vein of Gold,* was scheduled to open later that month. Lunt told the producers that "the bit I have in the new play is quite impossible & I want to get out as quickly as I can," but he remained with *The Vein of Gold*—which was subsequently retitled *The Lioness*—throughout its tour.

A brief period of unemployment followed, but only until preparations for *As You Like It* began. Lunt was to play two minor roles in the production, whose cast would include Margaret Anglin, Robert B. Mantell, a Shakespearean performer who had acted in Milwaukee during Lunt's boyhood and was still going strong, Sydney Greenstreet, who had played Waukesha with a British company during Lunt's Carroll College days, Howard Lindsay and Henry Hull, who had played with Lunt at the Castle Square Theatre.

Anglin's production of *As You Like It* was designed by Lunt's friend from Boston, Livingston Platt, who went to St. Louis in mid-May to supervise the construction of an amphitheatre in Forest Park which was to utilize the natural environment. First rehearsals were held in New York, where Anglin was completing an engagement in *A Woman of No Importance.* The actors spent only a week in St. Louis before the opening, but a great deal of work was accomplished in that time, for more than a thousand supernumeraries were used in an Elizabethan prologue, which included songs, dances and processions in four episodes and a recessional.

The performance, to be given for an audience of ten thousand, was scheduled for June 5, 1916, but bad weather forced a postponement to the following night, when again a heavy rainstorm made the outdoor performance impossible. On the night of the 7th, the grass stage was a soggy mess, a cold wind was blowing and a hard rain began to fall fifteen minutes before the scheduled starting time. Those in charge were about to cancel the performance when Margaret Anglin predicted that the rain would end soon and suggested that the audience be asked to wait. She put the question directly to the thousands who had assembled, and they shouted to her that they were eager to see the play and didn't mind getting a little wetter than they already were. Within a half-hour the rain had stopped and the skies cleared. The performance was given at last to a wildly enthusiastic crowd.

The year Lunt spent in Margaret Anglin's various companies provided him with far more than secure employment. In her presence he was able to renew the idealism he had felt when he had worked with May Rankin at Carroll College. Anglin was a woman of great integrity whose devotion to theatrical art was as thorough as his. She may have had to perform in plays of little merit a good deal of the time in order to maintain her appeal to commercial audiences, but she returned to dramatic literature of the highest quality whenever possible. Furthermore, her standards of performance were extremely high, and she held every member of her companies to that standard. She was exactly the role model Lunt needed in 1915 and 1916, and he always acknowledged the debt he owed her. Although he appeared in her company on only one other occasion, he never lost touch with her, consulting her about the Lunts' production of *The Taming of the Shrew* in the 1930s, and, as late as the 1950s, seeing to it that she was sent complimentary tickets to all the plays he appeared in or directed.

1916–19

In August 1916, Lunt was in New York looking for work when his agent told him that Laura Hope Crews, a well-known actress of the day, was desperately in need of an actor to play opposite her in a one-act play named *Her Husband's Wife* on a vaudeville bill in Philadelphia. The only catch was that the role would have to be learned overnight; the play was scheduled to open the following day.

Lunt assured the agent that he would have no difficulty learning a role in a one-act play overnight. There were nineteen "sides"—not an inconsiderable feat of memorization—but Lunt learned the lines and performed the next day. He later discovered that he had gotten the job on Margaret Anglin's recommendation. She had told Crews that he was a quick study and a hard-working actor of considerable promise.

Lunt had just passed his twenty-fourth birthday when he joined Crews's production. The actress, who was twelve years older, found herself powerfully attracted to her young leading man, and she and Lunt had a brief affair.

Lunt continued in *Her Husband's Wife* for two weeks, one in Philadelphia and the other in Washington, before he was approached by a renowned star whose best days were behind her, the legendary Lillie Langtry. In one of her many "farewell appearances," Langtry was appearing for the last time in vaudeville, performing in one-act plays, and she needed an immediate replacement for the leading man in a melodrama called *Ashes,* which would open in San Francisco in two weeks' time. Langtry asked her friend Laura Hope Crews if she could recommend an actor, and Crews took Lunt to Langtry's suite at the Savoy Hotel in New York.

Lunt described his meeting with the famous Jersey Lily. "It was late afternoon and I shall never forget her silhouette against the sky, exactly as she looked in her early photographs. It was a beautiful profile. I must admit that in the full light some of the aura was dissipated, but she was still a handsome woman, rather big, with the bluest eyes I have ever seen. She used to bead them with blue wax for the stage. Her hair was browny gold, but the color, she said, varied with her mood."

Langtry was taken with the young actor and offered him the job. Lunt learned the role on the train to the west coast, and the play opened after a single rehearsal.

Ashes was essentially a two-character play about a woman who is being blackmailed by her lover, who threatens to reveal letters she had written to him years before. The notion that Lunt and Langtry could have been lovers would seem to be ridiculous: the Jersey Lily was sixty-four years old in 1916. But the source of her attraction for audiences was her reputation as a *femme fatale* (the newspapers billed her as the woman "to whom two continents paid ardent court when her beauty reigned supreme"), and it is clear that Langtry still saw herself in those terms. Not for a moment did she betray any concern that Lunt might be too young to play opposite her, although many who saw the play found the relationship ludicrous. The gist of the critical response was: "When did she give him the letters, when he was in the cradle?" Langtry was furious, both at the critics and, for some reason, at Lunt. She refused to speak to him for several days.

Despite their acerbic comments on the disparity in the ages of Lunt and Langtry, a number of critics commented favorably upon Lunt's performance. "Mr. Alfred Lunt is a good aid to the star," said the *Argonaut;* "he has ease and deftness of method, and an ability to sink his own individuality into that of the character personated." Another review spoke of his "remarkably clever work in the role of a gentlemanly blackmailer."

Langtry's irritation with Lunt soon turned to flirtation. And, as in the case of Laura Hope Crews, the flirtation ended in seduction. Perhaps Langtry believed that it was her duty to give herself to her leading man— that she owed it both to him and to her public. Perhaps she needed to prove to herself that she was still capable of attracting young men. One can only guess at Lunt's reaction: astonishment, probably, but spiced with a bit of careerism as well. At this time in his life, he was certainly not above using every opportunity to advance his career. Making love to Laura Hope Crews and Lillie Langtry may have seemed no more than another way to establish himself in the theatre.

Lunt continued to tour with Langtry in *Ashes* and in another one-act play, *The Eleventh Hour,* for about twenty-six weeks, which he later described as "probably the most exciting weeks of my life." Lunt had been a fan of vaudeville since childhood, and he reveled in his proximity to the great acts of the time.

Lillie Langtry, on the other hand, felt that appearing among such performers diminished her dignity, and she regularly told the booking office of her attitude.

The quality of Langtry's performances varied greatly, depending upon the audience reaction to the other acts in the show. If she felt that the members of the audience were responding only moderately to the acts that preceded her one-act play—that they had come to the theatre primarily to see her—she acted with all the skill she could muster (which, it must be said, was never very great even on her best days). But if the audience laughed and applauded enthusiastically as they watched the acts she felt were beneath her dignity, she punished them by simply walking disinterestedly through her performance. Lunt, who was puzzled and disturbed by her behavior, composed a brief poem on the subject: "Mrs. Langtry, in the best of sashes / Every evening turns to 'Ashes.' / Many times the house grows chilly. / But no one dares to poke the Lillie."

Lunt's tour with Langtry not only allowed him to see and become acquainted with some of the vaudeville performers he had long admired, it helped to establish his reputation as an actor who could be relied upon to give a solid performance in any circumstance. But it was clearly not the sort of work he wanted most to do, and he left the tour as soon as his six-month contract was up to accept a job in the legitimate theatre. He never forgot Lillie Langtry, however, and years later, when the Lunts kept several Jersey cows on their farm, one of them was appropriately named Jersey Lily.

The new job offer Lunt received came from Margaret Anglin, who was to present a revival of one of her previous successes, *Green Stockings,* on an Eastern tour that would include a week in New York. Anglin sent Lunt a wire asking him to play opposite her, to which Lunt responded by telegram, "GLADLY, BUT NOT FOR LESS THAN ONE HUNDRED DOLLARS A WEEK." Howard Lindsay, who was still serving as Anglin's stage manager, recalled that the actress was not terribly pleased with Lunt's reply, which she regarded as ungrateful. Nevertheless, she met his demands and he joined her company once again.

Lunt played the role of Colonel J. N. Smith, D.S.O., and played it extremely well. The play opened in Albany, where Lunt gave a particularly

outstanding performance. Anglin surprised him by insisting that he take a
solo curtain call—a most generous gesture for the star to make, and one
that Lunt recalled with gratitude more than fifty years later. He was
stunned, and Howard Lindsay remembered the extent of his shock: "His
performance had had weight and maturity and dash. But in his solo curtain
call there crouched the same shaking, frightened boy of that night in Chicago" when he had first auditioned for Margaret Anglin.

By the time the tour of *Green Stockings* concluded, Lunt was in much
the same position Lynn Fontanne had been in at a comparable stage in her
career. He was making steady progress in his profession, but the big breakthrough—the occasion that could transform him from a competent supporting actor in vaudeville and in touring productions to an established
and respected performer on Broadway—had eluded him. He needed a
stroke of luck to bring about that transformation, and, like Lynn Fontanne's good fortune when she met Laurette Taylor, it occurred in an unexpected way.

There were no further offers to perform on the east coast in the late
summer of 1917, so Lunt accepted an invitation to play Ludwig Fulda's
The Pirate for a week's run with the Pabst Stock Company in his home-
town, Milwaukee. If nothing else, the engagement would allow him to see
his family once again and to play a leading role of a sort he had not played
before: a dashing, swaggering, swashbuckling pirate in a play set in eighteenth-century Spain.

A young British actress, Cathleen Nesbitt, was playing the girl who
falls in love with Lunt's character in the play, and she told a revealing story
about the "tall gangly young man" who "would eat an enormous Spanish
onion during one of our scenes. 'Oh! Alfred, couldn't it be a large apple?'
I moaned, as I was allergic to onions. 'The script says an onion,' said Alfred
firmly, and an onion it was every night."

Lunt's insistence that an actor must not tamper with the circumstances—some might say the minutiae—provided by the playwright may
seem finicky and unnecessary, but to a great extent it formed the basis of
his acting technique. The job of the actor is to create reality for the audience, and Lunt believed that he could do so only if he could first create it
for himself. Hence, no detail was too small to overlook and no deviation
from reality could be permitted: an onion was an onion.

Hundreds of instances could be cited of Lunt's attention to detail and
the way in which he used one detail or another as the basis of his characterizations. Here are only two examples:

When Lunt was rehearsing the role of Henry Higgins for *Pygmalion*
in 1927, he was convinced that Higgins would carry a green umbrella. The
umbrella could not be brown or black or any other color—it must be
green. Somehow the conviction that a green umbrella was an essential
prop for Higgins crystallized much of Lunt's thinking about the character;
he found that everything else in his characterization fell into place once he

had come to see the necessity of the green umbrella. Lunt and Fontanne later used the phrase "green umbrella" as a kind of code. When he said, "I'm looking for my green umbrella," she knew he meant he was searching for just the right prop, or costume piece, or any meaningful detail that would define the entire character for him.

And in 1958, when he was working on *The Visit* with director Peter Brook, Lunt, who played a poor and desperate man, asked Brook if it would be all right for him to take off his shoe at one point and shake some pebbles out of it. This gesture would be his "green umbrella"; it would convey to the audience the character's circumstances, and it would give Lunt just the feeling he needed in order to play the role convincingly. Brook agreed that the business would work well. After a few moments of thought, Lunt returned to Brook to ask: "But how many pebbles should there be? Three? Four?" The number of pebbles in his shoe would obviously be insignificant to the audience—or for most other actors—but it was crucial to Lunt.

His performance of Serafina in *The Pirate* in Milwaukee in 1917 showed "much ability," according to the Milwaukee *Free Press*. "He plays the role of the gay young stroller with airy insouciance," it said, and added that he was "sure of his lines even on a first night"—a comment that indicates just how difficult it was for actors to prepare fully for a production in a stock company that presented a different play every week. H. H. Ryan's review of the play said that Lunt "walked away with first honors" and that his portrayal "stands out as one of the most perfect characterizations of the entire season." The play offered the opportunity for Lunt to indulge his talent for romantic comedy, and he made the most of it. All in all, Lunt had such a good time in *The Pirate* that he persuaded S. N. Behrman to modernize it for a Broadway production in 1942, when Lunt once again played the leading character (renamed Serafin) and was rewarded with an Antoinette Perry Award for the best performance by an actor that season.

But in 1917 he was simply playing a single week in Milwaukee, which must have seemed to be a step down from the work he had been doing with Margaret Anglin, Lillie Langtry and Laura Hope Crews. It turned out, however, to be a step upward to theatrical prominence. The director of *The Pirate*, George Foster Platt, was scheduled to direct a Broadway production of *Romance and Arabella* in the fall. Impressed by Lunt's work in *The Pirate*, Platt decided to offer him a role in *Romance and Arabella* if the leading lady approved. The leading lady, as it happened, was Laura Hope Crews, and she had no objection whatever to Lunt's inclusion in the cast.

Romance and Arabella, which opened on October 17, was an inconsequential play that failed to strike a responsive chord with Broadway audiences, and it closed after only 29 performances. In terms of Lunt's progress, however, it represented a significant step—his Broadway debut. He played the relatively small role of a Greenwich Village artist, but a number of people took note of his performance. The New York *Sun* said, "Mr. Lunt has given us the most amusing character acting of the new season." Another who became aware of Lunt's skills for the first time was Lynn Fontanne, who was then rehearsing for the New York production of *The Wooing of Eve*. She did not see Lunt's performance, but she recalled that "everyone was talking about an extraordinary new actor and all the leading actresses wanted him to play opposite them."

One actress who did see Lunt's performance and was impressed by it was Alexandra Carlisle, who was playing the lead on Broadway in *The Country Cousin* by Booth Tarkington and Julian Street. The play's producer was George C. Tyler. Carlisle and Tyler were on the lookout for actors to tour with the play, and separately they had made the rounds of the New York theatres, looking for actors with the right comic touch. Several weeks of theatregoing had failed to yield any positive result until Carlisle attended a matinee performance of *Romance and Arabella*. Soon after Lunt made his first appearance, Carlisle knew that she had found the right actor to play the featured role of George Tewksbury Reynolds III. She told Tyler so, and he responded, "Oh, no, no, no, not the type." Carlisle said, "It hasn't anything to do with the type; I think he's a good actor." She was convinced that Lunt's comic flair, his surehanded grasp of character and his accomplished technique were precisely what was needed, and eventually she managed to persuade Tyler to offer him a contract.

The tour began in the spring of 1918 and continued for more than a year, playing large cities and the smallest of small towns. Lunt had only three days of rehearsal with the company, and his role was a large one. It was, in fact, second in importance to Alexandra Carlisle's, and the billing he received reflected that importance. For the first time, his name appeared in newspaper advertisements and on posters.

Since the tour was a long one and the actors did not want to become stale, they prepared a production of John Masefield's *The Tragedy of Nan* while they were in Boston, and they offered one matinee performance of it at the Hollis Street Theatre. The play—as complete a departure from the comedy of *The Country Cousin* as could be imagined—was throughly rehearsed and acted with devotion even though only a single performance was given.

Lunt's performance in *The Country Cousin* was acclaimed by reviewers throughout the country. The St. Paul *Daily News*, for example, spoke of his "skill and charm that make his appearance a keen delight." A Milwaukee newspaper said, "He stands in a class by himself among the American leading men by his work in his present role, which is a most artful combining of 'straight' leading business and slightly eccentric comedy methods." Another said of Lunt: "He is an artist; there is no other word for it."

Booth Tarkington, who spent his summers in Kennebunkport, Maine, was invited by Tyler to journey to Boston to see the opening-night performance of his play. Tarkington was apprehensive about the new actor who had been hired for the role that Eugene O'Brien had played so successfully on Broadway, but he was captivated by the freshness and invention of Lunt's approach. Tarkington visited Lunt backstage and invited him to lunch at his home in Indianapolis when *The Country Cousin* visited that city the following winter.

Tarkington was so impressed that he intended to write a play tailored especially to Lunt's abilities, and he spent much of the summer of 1918 trying to decide what sort of role would most effectively showcase Lunt's talents. He wrote to Tyler in October of that year: "Let me write a play for Lunt of my own kind. . . . You don't have to take it, but you got to let it go on my way if you do take it—only keep a holt on Lunt so we can get him. He's *it*."

When the tour reached Indianapolis in November, Lunt went to Tarkington's house for the long-planned lunch. Only later, as they sat upstairs in the study, did Tarkington inform Lunt that he was working on a play for him. He described the idea for the play in detail, and the meeting lasted for several hours. When the discussion ended, Lunt was unable to contain his enthusiasm. He slid down the banister and shouted to a surprised Mrs. Tarkington, "He's going to write a play for me! I'm made! I'm made!"

Following Tarkington's instruction to "keep a holt on Lunt," Tyler hired him to appear with the George C. Tyler Stock Company at the National Theatre in Washington during the summer of 1919. As far as Lunt was concerned, he would be marking time until Tarkington's new play was ready to go into rehearsal. He looked forward to the start of those rehearsals with a greater excitement than he had ever felt before. They would mark the most important occasion in his life, he thought. But, as it turned out, they marked only the second most important occasion. While he was rehearsing for the first production of the George C. Tyler Stock Company, he was introduced to a British actress who had been in America only three years and who had been making a name for herself by appearing in several plays with Laurette Taylor.

Chapter Four

TRIUMPH AND FRUSTRATION

"From these shabby, congenial rooms [at
Dr. Rounds's boardinghouse], we projected ourselves into future eminence.
We discussed, the three of us, over deli-
catessen potato salad and dill pickles, our
most secret dreams of success. Lynn and
Alfred were to be married. That was the
first plan. Then they were to become def-
initely idols of the public. That was the
second plan. Then, all this being successfully accomplished, they were to act exclusively together. This was the third
plan. It remained for me to supply the
fourth, which was that when all three of
us had become stars of sufficient magni-
tude to be able to count upon an individual following irrespective of each other,
then, poised serenely upon that enviable
plane of achievement, we would meet
and act triumphantly together."

Noël Coward

1919–21

Accouding to Alfred Lunt and Lynn Fontanne, their first meeting occurred in the late spring of 1919 at the New Amsterdam Theatre
in New York, where both were called to begin rehearsals for the leading
roles in the Tyler Stock Company production of *Made of Money,* which was
scheduled to open in Washington on June 9. Fontanne's call was later than
Lunt's, and when she arrived he was already on stage. Fontanne took a
chair in the wings and sat down next to Sidney Toler, another actor in the
company—later to become famous as the movies' Charlie Chan.* Already

* Many of the performers in Tyler's company were to become illustrious. The group
included Glenn Hunter, Cornelia Otis Skinner, Josephine Hull and an eighteen-year-old
ingenue named Helen Hayes.

aware of Lunt's reputation as an actor of great promise, Fontanne watched and listened to him carefully. She was immediately impressed by his voice and manner, as was Toler, who remarked to her, "That young man's voice is literally a gift from heaven. A voice like that can't be acquired. You have to be born with it."

Lunt had seen Fontanne once before, in *The Wooing of Eve* a year and a half earlier. He had thought her a fine actress, but he had not thought of her in a romantic way. As he came rushing offstage at the New Amsterdam Theatre to meet his new leading lady, however, he was instantly taken by her. In the manner of millions of young men throughout the centuries who have been introduced to women who powerfully attracted them, Lunt suddenly became awkward and tongue-tied. Wishing to impress Fontanne with his suave demeanor, he took her hand to kiss, accompanying the gesture with a sweeping bow. He had forgotten, however, that he was standing at the head of a short flight of stairs. His gallant gesture turned to instant farce as he fell backward down the stairway. Someone—various accounts attribute it to a stagehand at the theatre that day or to George S. Kaufman later on—commented wryly, "Well, he certainly fell for her."

Lunt later said that he felt no pain from his fall. "I was so exhilarated and happy," he said, "as though I had been drinking champagne." Fontanne commented that Lunt's pratfall was "prophetic," both in the sense of their having fallen for one another and because his assured and confident manner would always conceal a shy and uncertain attitude.

Neither of them was in any doubt about their feelings for one another. Fontanne confided to Laurette Taylor that she was in love with Lunt, and Lunt told Robert E. Sherwood that he had fallen desperately for Fontanne. When Tyler's company proceeded to Washington, Lunt and Fontanne began spending every moment together. They went for rides in a hansom cab through Rock Creek Park, ostensibly studying their lines. But since she spent most of the time sitting on his lap, it is perhaps not unreasonable to suppose that memorization was not uppermost in their minds.

Made of Money, a variation of the Pygmalion story, opened on June 9 at the National Theatre for a one-week run, marking the first appearance of Lunt and Fontanne in the same play. Fontanne's performance, as the shy and unfashionable Galatea who reforms the philandering man-about-town played by Lunt, was particularly fine. The Washington *Post* noted, "This is the first opportunity Miss Fontanne has had to give full rein to her talents. She proves that Mr. Tyler's judgment was sound. The success of the comedy will be closely associated with the personal triumph of a new theatrical luminary."

Lunt was less prominently mentioned and his notices were somewhat less enthusiastic, a not unusual response to the early performances of Lunt and Fontanne. She was more experienced than he, older than he, and had achieved a greater degree of vocal and physical control. This is not to say that Lunt was an unimpressive performer in any sense, only that she had already become a truly superior one while he was still in the process of perfecting his craft.

A Young Man's Fancy opened immediately after the brief run of *Made of Money*. Once again Lunt was appearing in a different play every week, but the productions were far more polished than any he had known in earlier stock situations.

Not only were Lunt and Fontanne playing the leading roles in *A Young Man's Fancy*, they were given something resembling star billing for the first time. The newspaper advertisement for the play read:

GEO. C. TYLER'S COMPANY

INCLUDING

LYNN FONTANNE   ALFRED LUNT

AND AN ALL-STAR CAST IN

A YOUNG MAN'S FANCY

The critical response to the play and the production was rhapsodic. Both Lunt and Fontanne were showered with superlatives. She was praised for her "wealth of delicacy and feeling," he for "one of the most effective impersonations . . . that a Washington audience has ever enjoyed." Such an enthusiastic response might well have led Tyler to cast Lunt and Fontanne in the same roles when he presented the play on Broadway. But Tyler was not about to allow anyone or anything to alter his plans, and after the summer he proceeded to recast the play for its Broadway production as he had always intended to do.

Later on, when *A Young Man's Fancy* opened on Broadway with Philip Merivale and Jeanne Eagels playing the roles Lunt and Fontanne had played in Washington, Tyler acknowledged that the original cast had given a better performance. He turned to Fontanne as the curtain descended and said, "I owe you and Alfred an apology." He must have been even more upset with himself when the play was given indifferent notices and forced to close.

Tyler's actors were originally scheduled for a five-week season in Washington, but the heat was so oppressive that attendance at the theatre was poor, and after the third week he disbanded the company. But he still had most of its members under contract, and while Fontanne prepared to go on a tour of New England with *Made of Money* he began rehearsals for Booth Tarkington's *Clarence* with Lunt in the title role.

Fontanne believed, no doubt with justice, that Tyler was underpaying her. Because of his contractual arrangements with his actors, he was often able to economize greatly on their salaries. He would sign an unknown and unheralded actor at the lowest figure he could persuade the actor to accept. Since the actor had no other options he would gratefully accept Tyler's offer. A year or two later, however, when the actor had gained in importance, he believed he was entitled to a raise in pay; but the long-term contract he had signed obliged him to work at the same figure for years to come. Many of the actors resented the hold Tyler had over them, but most were too frightened of him to say so. Lunt, for one, believed that his salary should be higher, but he held his tongue. Fontanne was more assertive.

She marched into Tyler's office, ignoring the astonished look on the face of his secretary. Full of righteous fervor, she looked down imperiously at the great man, who was seated at his desk smoking a cigar. "Mr. Tyler," she intoned, and, when he didn't respond, repeated "Mr. Tyler!" Tyler slowly looked up at her and growled ominously, "What do you want?" As she looked him full in the face, Fontanne's courage vanished. As Helen Hayes described the incident, "She backed out, thanking him for his many kindnesses in employing her, for paying her anything at all, and for allowing her to stay in the country."

Tyler may have paid his actors poorly, but he was a powerful producer and they knew that his interest in them could pay significant dividends in the future. Not only did he have many of the finest young actors of the day under contract, he also presented the great stars of the theatre in New York engagements. Mrs. Fiske, Sarah Bernhardt, Eleonora Duse, Arnold Daly and the Abbey Players from Ireland all had played under his banner. He presented Bernard Shaw's unconventional and iconoclastic plays to American audiences before most other producers dared to do so.

But it must have been difficult for young performers to tolerate Tyler's arrogance. He treated his actors with the contempt he thought they deserved, and he also believed it was his mission to educate the poor wretches. He would hand them inspirational books from time to time, encouraging them to raise their level of spirituality. However, he was more paternal in his relationship with some actors than with others. Neither Lunt nor Fontanne was among his favorites, perhaps because he had not been the first to recognize their talents. Lunt later said that Tyler "never wanted either of us—Laurette forced Lynn on him and Alexandra Carlisle did the same with me, and although we acted in his last two great hits, *Clarence* and then *Dulcy,* we were never his 'finds.'"

When Booth Tarkington notified Tyler that his script for *Clarence* was ready, a distinguished cast was assembled to play it. Tarkington was responsible for casting not only the leading role, but for at least one of the supporting roles as well. He had written to Tyler, "*Got* to have Helen Hays [*sic*] for the 16 to 18 year-old sister of the 16 to 18 boy: *Got* to! This is the best girl or woman part I ever managed to write . . . and needs just that one young genius-person H.H. to play it." He also cautioned Tyler against a practice indulged in by many managers of the time, warning him that the play "can't be altered substantially, because its whole substance is character and detail."

Tyler complied with Tarkington's instructions. The only liberties he took were to rewrite a brief speech at the end of the first act and, with the author's permission, to transpose two speeches in the third.

In another letter to Tyler, Tarkington said, "You'll see I've made use of Lunt's extraordinary good looks, by leading up to them; disguising them for a time—partly at least. I believe he has the full limit of 'manly beauty'; my idea was to take full comedy value of this endowment and not sell it for a nickel at first sight."

Lunt was to play an eccentric curator of entomology—one of the world's foremost experts on beetles. The character, just returned from the war, applies to Mr. Wheeler, a banker, for a job. Mr. Wheeler has nothing for Clarence at the bank, but takes him into his house as an all-purpose handyman. Much of the comedy is based upon Clarence's appearance and personality; at first he is presented as an awkward, painfully shy and foolish-looking object of derision, one who could never possibly appeal to women. He is described in stage directions as being sallow, with his hair in disarray, stooping "not only at the shoulders, but from the waist, sagging forward, and, for a time, to the left side; then, for a time, to the right; his legs 'give' slightly at the knees, and he limps somewhat vaguely." Moreover, he wears an army uniform that "was a bad misfit for him when it was new."

Clarence's physical appearance changes during the course of the play, however, and so do the perceptions of the women in the Wheeler household. In Act II he changes into civilian clothes and becomes "a more dashing figure." In Act III he wears dinner clothes, combs his hair and stands without stooping. By this time the Wheelers' maid, Della, has fallen in love with him; so has Wheeler's daughter, Cora; and Cora's young stepmother has developed a crush on Clarence. In the fourth and final act, Mrs. Wheeler is reconciled with her husband and a letter arrives offering Clarence his old position at the entomological laboratory. Clarence proposes marriage to Cora's governess, Miss Pinney, and they go off together, leaving Cora and Della heartbroken.

Clarence called upon Lunt to make full use of his talents, and to acquire some abilities he did not possess. The script required Clarence to play the piano, although both Tarkington and the director, Frederick Stanhope, made it clear that Lunt could perform in pantomime and the actual sounds could be produced in the wings. Clarence was also to play the saxophone, but all the playing was to be done offstage so that a hired musician would be able to perform on the instrument. Lunt was aghast. His insistence on realistic detail in his own performance would not permit such fakery.

Fortunately for him, Tarkington had told him long before rehearsals began that Clarence would play the saxophone and that Clarence's skill on the instrument would be one of the reasons why the women of the play fell in love with him. So Lunt began to learn the saxophone while he was still touring with *The Country Cousin*. His only opportunity to practice came after each performance, when the company returned to its hotel. Howls of anguish could be heard from the other actors as Lunt laboriously bleated away at his instrument in the early hours of the morning, but he had no intention of stopping until he had accomplished his goal.

His work on the piano did not begin until the *Clarence* rehearsals were under way. He had never had any musical education, but he was helped by the presence of Lillian Russell's sister in the cast. "She played the piano," Lunt said. "She put numbers in ink on paper and said, 'Now hit "one," now hit "six," ' and I learned to play the piano."

One of Lunt's objectives in *Clarence* was to play his comic role in a more natural and subtle manner than was usual in Broadway comedies of the time. "It is unnecessary to fill a play with 'hokum' to insure its popularity," he would say after *Clarence* opened. "This 'hokum' theory is wrong, I believe. You have only to overdo the catering to a notion of what the public wants to discover that what the public emphatically doesn't want is trite stage entertainment. . . . Nothing is too subtle for a theatre audience if it is lifelike. It is the business of the actor to take the author's truthful conceptions and put them over the footlights, and put them over truthfully, without resort on his own part to the 'hokum' of obvious acting tricks."

Ever since he had been a student at Carroll College, Lunt had experimented with new approaches to acting. In *Clarence* he was able to put some of them to use for the first time in his professional career. For example, there was his theory about the effectiveness of turning his back to the audience during an important moment in the play. In both the first and the last acts, Lunt played scenes of dejection with his back to the audience, and his slowly drooping shoulders spoke at least as eloquently as any gesture or facial expression would have. In Act IV, when dejection turned to elation as the letter Clarence had thought would never arrive finally reached him, the audience saw Lunt's back straighten with hope before they saw the expression on his face.

Lunt's preparation for playing Clarence was long and arduous. Through observation, imagination and close study of the play and the role, Lunt worked his way "inside" Clarence. Nothing whatever was left to chance. As an approach suggested itself, he would meticulously work out its representation in his room, then show the result to the director. And each approach was based upon the truth of the character in the circumstances provided by the playwright. Comedy was to spring from the character, not from irrelevant or incongruous jokes that might win momentary laughter but would detract from the character and his situation within the play.

One method Lunt evolved in playing the role, a method that would serve him well throughout his career, was to play the character with intense seriousness during the most comic moments and to find and portray whatever humor might exist in the role during more serious scenes.

Clarence, whose cast was composed of relative newcomers like Lunt and Helen Hayes and Broadway veterans such as John Flood and Mary Boland, opened in Atlantic City in July and remained "out of town" for a month. Even from the beginning, it was clear that something extraordinary was taking place. *Variety* wrote about the Atlantic City opening, "One of the warmest welcomes ever given a premiere at the Apollo Theatre was accorded Monday to 'Clarence' [which was] presented by George C. Tyler for the first time. Every act called forth applause so consistent the curtain had to be raised many times." About Lunt, the critic said he "rose to stardom in one bound. His personality is unique and thoroughly captivating . . . [his] methods are quite indescribable. In effect he is thoroughly charming, deft in comedy, and so genuinely convincing that one's admiration goes out to him." The following week in Philadelphia, the reaction was equally enthusiastic.

Everything was progressing smoothly toward the planned opening of the play in New York. But in early August, Actors' Equity Association, which had been formed several years before but still had not won anything resembling decent treatment for its membership, called a strike, immediately putting a halt to almost all theatrical activity in New York.* Equity demanded that certain reforms be agreed to by the managers. Among them were the understanding that actors should not be required to perform in more than eight performances in any given week, and that any performances given beyond that maximum should be compensated by extra pay; that actors should be paid a reasonable wage during rehearsals; that actors on tour should not be forced to pay for their own transportation; that actors could not be fired without reasonable notice and reasonable compensation; and a series of lesser demands. Equity initially proposed that these issues be submitted to arbitration, but the managers refused to accept that offer. Thus, Equity had no alternative but to call a strike.

The managers formed an organization called the Producing Managers' Association and vowed never to capitulate to what they regarded as excessive and arrogant demands. They agreed among themselves to assess a heavy fine against any producer who hired an Equity member or "compromised with the enemy" in any way. In return, the actors picketed theatres run by managers who were regarded as especially hostile to the union movement. They also adopted a tactic that made the majority of the public sympathetic to their cause: the actors gave free street performances and benefits on behalf of veterans returning from the World War.

Some performers disagreed with Equity's stand and formed what they called the Actors' Fidelity League. They contended that Equity, by joining the American Federation of Labor, had forfeited its right to speak for artists since, in their opinion, art and labor were antithetical. The member-

*One of the few exceptions was the Theatre Guild's production of *John Ferguson* (see Chapter 5).

ship of the "Fidos" was made up largely of actor-managers like George M. Cohan who had more to lose than to gain from an actors' strike, and actors of sufficient prominence—such as Mrs. Fiske, Lenore Ulric and David Warfield—who were already receiving substantial salaries and saw no reason to ask for more.

George C. Tyler was especially vehement in his opposition to the Equity movement and tried to persuade all the actors under his management to join the Actors' Fidelity League rather than Equity. Lunt and Fontanne sided with Equity, as did most of Tyler's performers, but Helen Hayes was persuaded to ally herself with the Fidos—a decision she later regretted, as many of her fellow actors accused her of betraying their cause.

The public, for the most part, sympathized with the actors' position. Other American workers had won basic rights, and most theatregoers believed that actors were entitled to protection from exploitation as well.

Because of the strike, the opening of *Clarence* was postponed, and Lunt returned to Wisconsin to wait until the dispute was resolved. While he was waiting, he invited Lynn Fontanne to join him in Genesee Depot and meet his family. She accepted the invitation and wired her time of arrival. But the telegraph operator made a mistake in the date, and she arrived at the Milwaukee railroad station to find no sign of Alfred Lunt. She then telephoned the Lunt home and took the suburban train to Genesee Depot. When Alfred greeted her, she barely recognized him. The sophisticated, well-dressed young actor she knew in New York had been transformed into a farmer in overalls, muddy boots and a battered, ancient hat. This was normal apparel for Genesee Depot, but Fontanne was astonished at the change in him.

Lunt introduced Fontanne to his mother, and there was an immediate coldness between them. Perhaps it is more accurate to say that Hattie greeted Fontanne without any enthusiasm whatever, and that Fontanne, puzzled by her antipathy, responded with a haughtiness born of self-defense. Hattie was not overtly rude to Lynn, but her attitude made it clear that she did not look with favor upon any relationship that might lead to her son's marriage.

Hattie had always been the most important woman in Alfred's life, and she jealously guarded that importance. To yield her position might result in several changes, all of them unfortunate in her eyes. Alfred's marriage would mean less money for her "three Finns," as she called her children by Dr. Sederholm; it would mean that Alfred would be less emotionally dependent on her, a dependence she had carefully cultivated ever since he had been a child; and it would probably mean the end of the European journeys she and her son had taken together.

Hattie also believed that Fontanne was not pretty enough for Alfred. Pauline Alexander, Alfred's childhood sweetheart, had been a beautiful girl, and Lynn did not measure up in Hattie's eyes. Of course, Hattie was hardly an objective observer, and Lynn was hardly plain. She was very thin in 1919 and had not yet achieved the beauty and grace that became her hallmark in later years, but only a prejudiced observer would have found her unattractive.

Hattie's resolution to dislike Fontanne and to make things difficult for her was not easily altered. Even after Alfred and Lynn became engaged, Hattie remained adamant, her opposition so strong that Lunt feared it could never be overcome. If he and Fontanne had not been so deeply in love and so determined, they would not have continued their relationship.

It is perhaps unnecessary to add that Fontanne's visit to Genesee Depot was less than happy. But while she was there, she and Lunt became engaged. They decided not to announce their engagement for a while, giving Hattie time to get used to the relationship, but their commitment to one another grew stronger than ever.

In the first week of September, the Equity strike came to an end, the actors and producers having reached a compromise. Immediately, Broadway relit its marquees. *Clarence* was scheduled to open in two weeks, and the cast reassembled for final rehearsals.

Clearly, the layoff did not harm the production. The New York opening of *Clarence* on September 20, 1919, was phenomenally successful. The audience called the actors back on stage for more than twenty curtain calls. They broke into a spontaneous shout of "Lunt, Lunt, Lunt!" and made the performance "as wildly exciting as Armistice Day," as Helen Hayes remarked.

In his New York *Times* review, critic Alexander Woollcott waxed enthusiastic in the lyrical style for which he later became famous: "Write it on the walls of the city, let the town crier proclaim it in the commons, shout it from the housetops that *Clarence,* the new and capitally acted play which so vastly amused its first New York audience at the Hudson Theatre Saturday night, is a thoroughly delightful American comedy, which the world and his wife and their children will enjoy.

"It is as American as *Huckleberry Finn* or pumpkin pie," he continued. "It is as delightful as any native comedy which has tried to lure the laughs of this community in the last ten seasons."

The New York *World* found Lunt's performance to be so natural and believable that it praised him for acting "with an unflagging sense of unconscious humor." Of course, the humorous touches he brought to his character were anything but unconscious; they were carefully planned, down to the smallest detail. But the comment in the newspaper reveals one of the secrets of Lunt's greatness: he was practicing the art that conceals art. Alan Dale in the *American* also mistook Lunt's characterization as being identical to his own personality. After saying, "Young Mr. Lunt is extraordinary," Dale continued: "It may be that his measure was taken in the play, and that he couldn't play Hamlet, but as far as *Clarence* went, he was perfectly flawless."

Tarkington was too nervous to attend either the rehearsals of the play or the early performances. This was not unusual for him; he generally spent his opening nights as far from the theatre as possible. But five days after *Clarence* opened, he sent a letter to Tyler, which the producer posted on the call board at the Hudson Theatre. The letter said,

> Please express my gratitude to all of the "Clarence" company, and tell them to note how nicely a play goes when the author keeps away from it.
>
> I'd like you to note a certain important thing—even more important than the author's staying away, viz., a cast as well fitted, well acting and personally attractive as this one could play the Telephone Directory and make a hit with it.
>
> If you had got one of those people wrong you would have lost. They have made New York dramatic critics face about—the play didn't do that, not for a minute—the cast did it.
>
> When I wrote "Clarence" I had a pretty accurate guess that Cora was what Helen Hayes needed as proof of her big range, just now—also, there was no Cora without Helen Hayes, of course. . . .
>
> Please shake Lunt's hand for us.

During the run of *Clarence,* Lynn Fontanne visited the theatre each night. She would generally come backstage during the third act and wait in Lunt's dressing room until the performance was over, and then they would go out together. But she dreaded those nightly visits because she had to run a gauntlet of hostility from the actresses in the play. Helen Hayes, Mary Boland and the other women in the cast had developed furious crushes on Lunt. Hayes even thought that "the company got on so well because all hostility was reserved for the beauteous Miss Fontanne."

Lynn was well aware of the unfriendly stares she received. "I could feel it, you know," she said later, "I could feel the daggers right between my shoulder blades."

Clarence ran for 300 performances in New York before going on a national tour. Having established his name so spectacularly on Broadway, it might be thought that Lunt would have wanted to take advantage of his newfound prominence by appearing immediately in another New York production. To Lunt, however, the play and the role were always more important than anything else. He loved *Clarence,* he loved playing the role and he thoroughly enjoyed the camaraderie that prevailed in the company. Only the necessity of leaving Lynn Fontanne dimmed his enthusiasm for the tour. But he must have found some solace in his new prominence as an actor. He had not received billing in the New York advertisements for the play, but he did on the road. At first the name was below the title: "CLARENCE with Alfred Lunt." Before long, however, the order was reversed: "ALFRED LUNT in CLARENCE."

When the tour reached Boston in early February 1921, Lunt wrote to Tyler, telling the producer that he intended, now that their contract had expired, to accept the offers of other managers, who were eager to pay twice the salary Tyler had been giving him. Tyler answered with a masterpiece of wounded indignation. The letter said, in part, "You need not have the slightest hesitation in doing whatever you feel will make you most happy. Happiness is all there is in life—and to most people quick money is the specific. Of course, I knew that there were managers who would be willing to take advantage of your growing importance and pay you more money than you are receiving from me at the present time—but if it had ever occurred to me that you would think of considering their offers, I should have been willing to bet that you would have written to them suggesting that they talk to me first." Tyler reminded Lunt that Tarkington had not written *Clarence* for him "until he had received my [i.e., Tyler's] sanction and approval of the idea." He told Lunt that, had he remained in the Tyler stable, "next season I suppose you would have been a [Broadway] 'star,'" and that the only reason he had not already promoted Lunt to that category was because "I don't believe in rushing where the developing of 'stars' is concerned." Alas, Tyler said, "What a fool I was! But . . . I wish you all the luck in the world. My thoughts and memories of you shall never be anything but pleasant. I beg of you not to blame yourself for an instant. In the line of reassuring you I want to say that in leaving me as you do you are not proceeding even in the slightest manner differently from all the others—many of whom are now making vast sums of money."

Tyler's letter was so cleverly calculated to appeal to Lunt's conscience that it achieved at least part of the intended result: Lunt agreed to appear again under Tyler's banner, although he would no longer act exclusively in Tyler's productions.

The *Clarence* tour came to an end in the spring of 1921 and Lunt returned to Genesee Depot. Shortly after that, an offer arrived from Robert McLaughlin, the manager of a theatre in Cleveland, asking Lunt to play *Clarence* for a week with a newly assembled cast. Although he had already played in *Clarence* for nearly two years, Lunt felt there was still more he could give to the role, and he told his mother he would be satisfied if he could play *Clarence* for one more week.

McLaughlin sent a wire to Genesee Depot, asking Lunt what his salary demand would be. Lunt gave the telegraph operator the figure and told him to wire the answer to McLaughlin. Soon afterward McLaughlin's reply arrived, stating that he would be glad to pay the requested salary— naming an amount precisely $100 less than Lunt had asked for. Lunt inquired of the telegraph operator if he had perhaps sent an incorrect figure. "Now, Alfred," said the operator, who had known Lunt since he was a child, "you know that that was too much for one week's work, so I just cut it down to size." Lunt swallowed hard, but he decided to honor the arrangement and play the week in Cleveland for $100 less than he would otherwise have gotten.

* * *

While Lunt was playing in *Clarence* on Broadway, Fontanne toured in *Made of Money* in late 1919. Perhaps intending to take advantage of Lynn's absence from New York, Hattie Sederholm visited her son. Indeed, Hattie seems to have used the opportunity to repeat her reservations about the relationship Lunt and Fontanne had developed. When Lynn returned she found a bewildered young man, torn between his love for her and loyalty to his mother.

Fontanne feared that Mrs. Sederholm's influence over Lunt might prove decisive. Arguments between the couple ensued, culminating at one point in Lunt's taking a train to Philadelphia in order to think the situation over away from the entreaties of his mother or his fiancée.

"A more miserable pup you never saw" is the way Laurette Taylor described Fontanne. "Many times she used to stay the night at our house. We would talk until two or three in the morning." Fontanne begged Taylor, who'd had plenty of experience with romantic entanglements, to advise her. Taylor said that the situation was indeed serious and that Lynn should take the train to Philadelphia and find out for herself exactly how things stood.

Fontanne was not at all certain this was a good idea. She didn't want to put Lunt in the position of having to choose between her and his mother. But Taylor argued that Fontanne's anguish was too great for her to allow it to continue. "Lynn," she said, "I wouldn't suffer in my soul the way you do—for any reason—without trying to end it. The longer you let this . . . stand between you and Alfred the more powerful it will become."

Fontanne took Taylor's advice and went to Philadelphia, where Lunt greeted her with open arms. He was more determined than ever not to lose her, he said, and there was no possibility that his mother could persuade him otherwise. Relieved, Fontanne returned to New York along with Lunt, who resumed his performances in *Clarence*.

But then something happened—an ultimatum from Hattie? another argument between Lunt and Fontanne? a telephone call?—that chilled the relationship once again. Taylor said later that she had no idea what had occurred, but that Lynn "seemed doubly hurt. One difference was that she no longer wanted to talk about Alfred. In fact you could imagine that no such person as Mr. Lunt had ever *met* Miss Fontanne."

Then, after an interval of several weeks, according to Maurice Zolotow, Hattie left New York; Lunt immediately telephoned Fontanne, asking forgiveness. The couple met, reconciled and shared a joyous dinner. Laurette Taylor's account is different, however: she claimed that the estrangement lasted for a considerably longer time.*

---

* Zolotow's version of the events, in his biography, *Stagestruck: The Romance of Alfred Lunt and Lynn Fontanne*, has Taylor playing a somewhat sinister role. Zolotow believed that Taylor intended to end the love affair between Lunt and Fontanne because she was determined to have no rivals. As Fontanne's mentor, she had no intention of allowing Lynn to escape her dependency, Zolotow claimed. Therefore, she tried to destroy the relationship by

In any case, in March 1920 Fontanne appeared in *Chris,* an early play by Eugene O'Neill, which later became *Anna Christie.* George C. Tyler wanted to capitalize on the success of O'Neill's *Beyond the Horizon,* which had opened to enthusiastic notices on February 2, by rushing *Chris* into production as quickly as possible. Tyler cast Fontanne as Anna and Emmett Corrigan as her father, Chris Christopherson.

Chris was intended to do for Fontanne what *Clarence* had already done for Lunt: make her a prominent name on Broadway. There was a problem, however. Whereas the role of Clarence was specifically tailored to Lunt's talents and a cleverly written part for a gifted actor, the role of Anna—a bland and vacuous girl (only in the later version did she become a prostitute)—was poorly developed; the play's focus was almost entirely on the father, and Anna had little life of her own. Fontanne expressed serious reservations about the play to Lunt, saying that she found it weak in several respects, only one of which was the development of her character. For his part, O'Neill was uncertain about the suitability of Fontanne for the role, thinking that only an American actress could play Anna believably.

Tyler scheduled an opening in Atlantic City for March 8, 1920. He also planned to tour *Chris* in other eastern cities before bringing it to New York, where it would join the successful *Beyond the Horizon* and, Tyler hoped, cement O'Neill's growing reputation as America's leading young playwright.

But rehearsals revealed *Chris* to be as weak as Fontanne had thought. Tyler asked O'Neill to join him in Atlantic City to work on revising the drama, but the playwright was reluctant—his father had just suffered a stroke and his wife had become seriously ill. He sent his regrets and returned to his home in Provincetown, Massachusetts.

The opening of *Chris* in Atlantic City confirmed Tyler's belief that the play was in urgent need of rewriting, despite the fact that the reviews were not entirely unfavorable. One critic said that "the play is full of red-blooded life," and praised Emmett Corrigan's performance in the title role. But the same critic found fault with Fontanne, who, he said, "missed in many ways the heights of emotion and soulful spirit that could have been hers." Tyler realized, however, that the main problem lay not with Fontanne's performance but in the way the role of Anna was written.

Atlantic City audiences avoided the Apollo Theatre, and those few who did attend found *Chris* slow-moving and lacking in dramatic impact. Tyler castigated the people of that city as "tango lovers and chewing-gum sweethearts," but he knew that the play stood no chance anywhere unless it was thoroughly overhauled. Another desperate appeal to O'Neill had

poisoning Fontanne's mind against Lunt. According to Zolotow, Taylor introduced Fontanne to several eligible bachelors, hoping that one of them would be so fascinating that she would lose her interest in Alfred Lunt.

little effect. The playwright responded that his wife was still too ill to manage without him, but he did recommend some revisions for *Chris,* and agreed that it would have to "be radically rewritten before the play has a New York showing."

Tyler made several drastic cuts while *Chris* was still running in Atlantic City, but they did not seem to improve it appreciably. A week later the play opened in Philadelphia and once again its flaws were all too apparent. Tyler decided that a New York engagement would meet with certain failure and informed the cast that the production would close in Philadelphia. O'Neill was not too upset because, he told Tyler, "In the back of my mind there are already inklings as to how" to take elements of *Chris* and use them to create a sturdier drama. "Suffice it to say that of the present play I would keep without change only the character of Chris," O'Neill went on. "I'd give you a real daughter and lover, flesh-and-blood people," he added, tacitly acknowledging that the role of Anna was unplayable as he had written it.

After the closing of *Chris,* Laurette Taylor and J. Hartley Manners asked Fontanne if she would like to act in the London production of Manners's new play *One Night in Rome,* which they planned to open late in April. Lynn was torn between the desire to see her family and friends in England and her wish to stay in the United States, close to the man she had secretly agreed to marry. But Laurette Taylor urged her to put some distance between herself and Lunt, since—according to Taylor's version of events—she wasn't seeing a great deal of him in any case. Give him time to think, Taylor recommended. "You love England," she said, "and if it proves unbearable there are always boats to bring you back." Fontanne agreed to Taylor's proposition.

She sailed for England with Taylor's company in mid-April. *One Night in Rome* opened at London's Garrick Theatre on Thursday, April 29, 1920—an opening unlike any other in the history of the theatre.

A distinguished audience, including the American ambassador, John W. Davis, and his wife, was in attendance to welcome Laurette Taylor, who had been such a favorite in *Peg o' My Heart,* back to England.

The scenery for the production had been used in the New York theatre where *One Night in Rome* had originally played, and was not properly designed for the Garrick. Patrons seated at the back of the gallery (i.e., the balcony) could not properly see the stage because the low ceiling of the set cut off their view of the actors. It is not surprising that some patrons shouted, "We can't see" as the first scene was being played. Order was restored only when the stage manager told the actors to move the furniture downstage and play the remainder of the first act near the footlights.

After Act I, Taylor went before the curtain to apologize to the audience—she charmingly said that the scenery had been built in America, "where we are accustomed to do things on a small scale"—and to promise that the difficulty would be remedied before the second act began. But whatever modifications were made did not solve the problem. The curtain could not be raised sufficiently to afford complete visibility, and the "gallery gods," as they were called, soon began howling indignantly and throwing candies and coins on the stage. Now they aimed their comments directly at Laurette Taylor, shouting "Go back to America!" and "We don't want you here!" Only a handful of men called out, but they prevented the actors from being heard.

Again Taylor spoke to the audience, offering to refund the money of the galleryites or to permit them to exchange their tickets for orchestra seats for another performance. This time, however, she was clearly shaken and on the verge of tears. The play's producer, Charles Cochran, rushed on stage, linked arms with Taylor and said he would not permit her to be insulted. If the gallery gods continued to behave inappropriately, he would ring the curtain down and postpone the opening to another night. He was cheered by the majority of the audience, the cheers momentarily drowning out the catcalls. But as soon as the actors attempted to continue, the din from the gallery began once more.

Someone in the front row of the gallery shouted that the pandemonium was not spontaneous, but the product of an "organized gang." By this time, members of the audience were howling at one another, pennies were still being thrown by protesters, and the actors had no chance whatever of being heard. They were also at risk of being injured by the objects being thrown upon the stage, although Fontanne later insisted that she was more angry than frightened.

Cochran ordered the stage manager to bring the curtain down and the conductor to lead the orchestra in "God Save the King." When the actors left the stage, many of them were visited in their dressing rooms by theatrical luminaries who had been in the audience and who had come backstage to express their dismay. Others remained in the auditorium to discuss the incident, trying to discover what could have prompted an organized demonstration, if indeed that was what it had been.

Among the hypotheses offered were these: it might have been an outbreak of anti-Americanism directed at a convenient target, an American actress. It might have been an expression of disdain specifically directed at Laurette Taylor, who had left England in the midst of the war only to return when she would be in no physical danger. It might have been an attack on Charles Cochran for casting an American actress in a role a British actress could have played. An American producer later claimed to know that another American actress in London—Peggy O'Neill—had arranged to destroy Taylor's opening night by organizing a gang of hooligans.

Whatever the reason for the demonstration, most of the audience was ashamed of the behavior of the gallery gods. London newspapers editorialized about the disturbance. And a group of leading figures in the British theatre, including Dennis Eadie, Gerald du Maurier and Sir Johnston

Forbes-Robertson, voiced their sympathy for the cast of *One Night in Rome* in a letter to the *Times*.

The riot was the talk of London for days, and when word filtered to America, it was discussed there with nearly equal fervor. The staid New York *Times* tried to put the incident in perspective by assuring its readers that "Anglo-American relations will not be strained" by the furor.

Cochran announced that *One Night in Rome* would reopen on Saturday night, May 1, "provided that Miss Taylor is well enough to appear." But he then postponed the opening until the following Monday, having heard a rumor that many of the troublemakers planned to reappear and to bring with them stink bombs and "electric snuff," a powder that caused uncontrollable sneezing.

The "second opening night" was performed to a sold-out house that again included the American ambassador. The audience responded with an enthusiasm that could not have been accounted for by the play, which had earlier been dismissed by the New York critics as a lamentably weak comedy. Clearly, the spectators were showing their support for Laurette Taylor and her company. The performance was not marred by any interruptions from the gallery, and each of the actors was cheered wildly at the curtain calls.

Given the remarkable nature of the evening, it hardly seems important to note what the critics thought about the play and the performance, but there was general agreement that the play was monotonous, that Laurette Taylor was as adorable as ever, and that Lynn Fontanne had given an excellent performance. Word of the play's deficiencies spread quickly, and it played to increasingly smaller houses for a total of 104 performances.

When Fontanne returned to New York, she took a third-floor room in a theatrical boardinghouse at 130 West 70th Street. The house was run by Dr. Rounds, a woman whose career was in medicine but whose great interest was in the theatre and theatre people. Somehow Lynn and Alfred must have patched up their differences, for Lunt was living in the basement of the same boardinghouse, waiting for the tour of *Clarence* to begin. One might have thought he would be living in a somewhat more comfortable fashion now, but although Tyler had raised his salary, it was considerably less than Lunt could have earned under another management. And most of his money—ninety percent of it, he later estimated—was being sent home to support his mother and her children. Perhaps this was the source of the argument that preceded Fontanne's departure for London in *One Night in Rome:* Lunt had made it clear that he couldn't marry until he was earning enough to support his Wisconsin family as well as his wife and himself.

Whether or not Alfred and Lynn sometimes spent the night in the same room at Dr. Rounds's boardinghouse is an open question. Both of them adamantly insisted they did not. "Dr. Rounds's house was run with

a rod of iron—no hanky panky there," Lunt said. And Fontanne maintained that Dr. Rounds, whose room was next door to Alfred's, "was eagle-
eyed and there was no question of an affair going on between us." On the
other hand, Noël Coward, in his autobiography *Present Indicative,* said
that Lunt and Fontanne "were, to put it mildly, 'courting' at . . . Dr.
Rounds," which would seem to imply something resembling the sort of
hanky-panky of which the doctor disapproved.

Fontanne's career was not progressing as rapidly as she had hoped.
Nearly five years after coming to America to play supporting roles in Laurette Taylor's company, she had just ended a run in still another play by
J. Hartley Manners in support of Laurette Taylor. It seemed as if her career
had been all but standing still.

George C. Tyler, however, was still intent on finding a play in which
she could play the leading role, and the right one finally appeared in late
1920. It was a comedy by George S. Kaufman and Marc Connelly. Kaufman and Connelly had tried their hands at collaboration once before, with
a musical called *Miss Moonshine* that later, under the title *Be Yourself,* had an
unsuccessful Broadway run. But Kaufman thought they had worked well
together, and he suggested to Connelly that they now try to create an entire play around the character of Franklin P. Adams's Dulcinea, the prototype for Mrs. Glendenning, the role Fontanne had played in *Someone in
the House.*

Kaufman and Connelly approached Tyler. Would he be interested in
producing such a play? He would, if the play was sufficiently amusing. The
authors, taking no chances this time that Adams might disapprove of the
use of his character after the fact, asked him for permission to use Dulcinea's name as well as her personality. Adams was pleased to give his approval—for ten percent of the box-office. The authors willingly agreed and
decided to call their play *Dulcy.*

Dulcinea, both in Adams's columns and in the play, was a dizzy young
woman who thought she was terribly original, but who spoke exclusively
in clichés. "It's just good to be alive," Dulcinea was fond of saying. Or,
"The moving pictures are still in their infancy." And, at various times, "My
books are my best friends," "All men are children" and "If a woman is
good-looking, no jury on earth will convict her."

The Dulcinea of Adams's invention became, in the play, Mrs. Dulcy
Smith, an inveterate meddler. The well-to-do wife of a manufacturer of
costume jewelry whose business is in danger, she arranges a party that is
intended to help him but instead creates comic chaos. Eventually, however,
the chaos is resolved by her scatterbrained ingenuity. Kaufman and Connelly wrote the play swiftly, delivering a final copy to Tyler about a month
after they had first approached him with the idea. Tyler expressed enthusiasm and immediately began to plan its production. Howard Lindsay, in
his first significant Broadway assignment, was hired to both direct and act
in the play, Elliott Nugent and Gregory Kelly were given important sup-

porting roles, and, of course, only one actress could be considered to play Dulcy: Lynn Fontanne, who had so brilliantly played the similar role of Mrs. Glendenning.

Fontanne was nearly overwhelmed. At last, at the age of thirty-three, she was being given the opportunity to achieve pre-eminence in the theatre. But, conversely, to fail in *Dulcy* would probably mean that she would never again be given such a chance. As soon as Tyler told her the role was hers she became ill and remained sick to her stomach throughout rehearsals. She had never before been called upon to carry an entire production. Although Lunt announced that her success was assured, she doubted her own capabilities.

As rehearsals progressed, however, Fontanne's fears were eased. Howard Lindsay was a compassionate director whose calm, professional demeanor helped her regain her confidence. But he had his own problems. Tyler insisted that Lindsay use some Italian furniture bought at a bargain rate. This was a favorite trick of Tyler's: saving money by economizing on sets and costumes. But Lindsay could not figure out how to incorporate the furniture into the set without destroying either the picture he wanted to present to the audience or his patterns of movement. One evening after rehearsal he was taking a walk when he ran into Lunt and Fontanne. He told them about the difficulty he was having with the Italian furniture and confessed that the only reason he had agreed to use it was to please Tyler. Fontanne said, "If you don't start out to please yourself, you'll never end by pleasing Mr. Tyler." Her comment gave him the courage he needed, and he eliminated the Italian furniture at the next rehearsal.

Where the costumes were concerned, Fontanne was adamant: Tyler's penny-pinching would not dictate the choice of her clothes. She knew exactly how Dulcy should be dressed, and when she was less than pleased with the costumes designed for her, she headed to the most expensive dress shop in New York and bought several dresses for the production. The bill, she told the clerk, should be sent to George C. Tyler. Tyler was furious, as she knew he would be, but he later admitted that the dresses she selected had contributed to the success of *Dulcy*.

Tyler chose to open the play in Indianapolis, the home of Booth Tarkington. His idea was that Tarkington would be able to offer the authors advice if revisions proved necessary. But, as it turned out, Tarkington's presence was superfluous. The play opened on February 13, 1921, at English's Opera House. Many of the audience were especially invited to attend, and they were wary of any play that had to invite its audience. As *Dulcy* progressed, however, they realized it was a sparkling comedy that could stand perfectly well on its own merits. The reviews were uniformly good. Critics spoke of the play's "good humoredly sophisticated, civilized viewpoint," of the "human, natural, and sly" humor which "comes out of character, not out of vaudeville," and mentioned that the opening night audience had given the actors more than twenty curtain calls. When Tyler called upon Tarkington for his advice, the writer responded, "There's no advice to give."

On February 20, *Dulcy* moved on to the Cort Theatre in Chicago, where it was even more successful. Not only did the audience laugh from beginning to end, they laughed louder and longer than the Indianapolis audiences had. And Percy Hammond's review in the Chicago *Tribune,* which was headlined "Lynn Fontanne Scores Triumph; Fine Play Admirably Presented," summed up the critical opinion. *Dulcy* ran in Chicago for months.

When Fontanne returned to New York and Dr. Rounds's boarding-house, Noël Coward, whom she had first met years before at a dance hall in London, was her most frequent visitor. Coward had managed to save enough money to come to the United States, but he arrived with only $75 in his pocket, and he remained by borrowing money from Fontanne and by dining with her and Lunt—usually eating delicatessen food in Fontanne's room—almost every night. Although, as Fontanne later said, "We weren't so damn rich either."

Coward was determined to make his mark as an actor and a playwright in the United States. In 1921, however, he had yet to encounter success in either capacity. While they shared the evening's repast, Coward, Fontanne and Lunt also shared their dreams for the future. The first step would be Alfred's and Lynn's marriage, after which they would both become Broadway luminaries. Then, when the theatrical world was at their feet, they would announce that they intended to act together in every production. And Coward added his own dream: after he, too, had become a star, he would write a play for the three of them to appear in, which would conclusively establish them all as the finest comic actors in the western world.*

Dulcy was scheduled to open on Broadway on August 13, by which time it had earned a well-deserved reputation as an ingenious comic success, and New Yorkers were eager to see it. Most eager of all the spectators, though, were Alfred Lunt and Noël Coward. They visited Fontanne in her dressing room before the opening performance, but left when it became apparent she was going to be sick, and spent the hour before the curtain pacing the streets around the Frazee Theatre. "We drifted in and out of soda fountains," Coward said, "consuming endless Coca-Colas and frosted chocolates, and behaving generally like anxious fathers expecting twins." At the last possible moment, they entered the theatre and stood at the back of the orchestra, nervously awaiting the rise of the curtain.

---

*Fontanne helped Coward achieve his first success in America. He showed some of the material he had written to Fontanne; in her words, "He'd hand me sheets and sheets of his writing and I knew he had something very special. Arrogant, but very special." Fontanne called her friend, the editor Frank Crowninshield, and sent him one of Coward's pieces. Crowninshield published it in *Vanity Fair* and paid Coward $400. That publication began Coward's immensely successful American career, permitted him to repay Fontanne for some of the dinners she had shared with him, and cemented their friendship for life.

They expected to see a frightened, insecure Lynn Fontanne, but were pleasantly surprised to find that she was completely in control when she made her first entrance, apparently brimming with confidence. The audience greeted line after line with appreciative laughter and frequently broke into applause. By the end of the second act, Coward said, he and Lunt "discovered that not only were we no longer pinching each other black and blue, but that we were quite relaxed and actually enjoying ourselves."

The critics were equally pleased with *Dulcy*. Leo A. Marsh, writing in the *Telegraph*, said, "If there are more entertaining, scintillating plays extant than *Dulcy*, we have yet to hear about them." Alexander Woollcott in the *Times* had favorable things to say about the play and said of Fontanne, "She is brilliant—no less. This English player has been with us for several seasons. . . . It was apparent from the first that she was an actress of uncommon quality, and not even the rich role of Dulcy, which offers her her first full-sized opportunity, measures up to her suspected stature. She can do great things and perhaps she will." In his Sunday article on the play, Woollcott added that "Lynn Fontanne is an actress of extraordinary gifts."

Howard Lindsay has said that Fontanne behaved like Dulcy offstage as well as on during the run of the play. Since he was serving as stage manager as well as actor and director, it was his job to see that she was in place for each entrance. "Many a time I made sure that Lynn was in the entrance ready to go on at the proper cue," he said. "Her hand would be on the doorknob. I would turn away to attend to something else, and soon would hear the actors on stage ad-libbing to fill in a stage wait. I would rush back to the entrance and find Lynn still standing there, her hand on the doorknob, her mind miles away."

Another instance of Fontanne's scatterbrained behavior occurred at the end of the pre-Broadway run of *Dulcy* in Chicago. The company returned to New York when the play closed on May 7, but Fontanne remained and spent most of her money on clothes, gifts and good food. Fortunately, Laurette Taylor's company was soon to play *Peg o' My Heart* in Chicago, opening on May 30. George C. Tyler wired the company manager to find Fontanne and bring her safely back to New York before all her money was gone. The manager located Fontanne, and reported to Tyler that she was "dead broke and totally unconcerned about it. She laughed when we kidded her about spending her money so fast." When Taylor's company arrived in New York with Fontanne in tow, soon after *Peg o' My Heart* closed in Chicago on June 25, Lynn asked the company manager if he would lend her ten dollars so that she could get home.

But Howard Lindsay was soon exposed to another, deeper side of Fontanne's character. "One night after *Dulcy* had closed, Lynn and I went together to see and examine a new play that was enjoying a successful reception," he wrote. "Over an after-the-theatre supper table, the two of us dissected the play and the performance. I had something of a surprise. When this scatterbrained girl pulled her brains together, she was an intel-

ligence to be reckoned with. . . . I simply did not know her capacity, and
I had underestimated both her brains and her strength of character."

Lindsay thought of Fontanne as an enormously talented actress, but
he believed that because of her appearance she would always be limited to
eccentric comic roles. She was still painfully thin (her "legs were as thin as
toothpicks," he said) and, despite the dancing lessons she had taken to
eliminate her pigeon-toed walk, he still found her ungainly.

On the other hand, Lindsay's opinion of Fontanne as an ugly duck-
ling in 1921 was certainly not shared by everyone. When she had played
Dulcy in Chicago that year, one critic had described her this way: "Much
of a beauty is Miss Fontanne, starry-eyed, dark-haired, her features well
defined, all luminous with a smile that plays over them like sheet lightning
across a summer sky."

Dulcy's success in New York was repeated on tour, with Fontanne continuing to play the role that had by then become associated with her. One
of her supporting players in the touring company was James Gleason, an
Irish actor of great skill whose personality often got on Fontanne's nerves.
He had "very little sense of humor," according to George Abbott, who was
also in the cast, whereas Fontanne was playful, "a hoyden, a fey girl who
exaggerated her eccentricities because they were charming." Fontanne
would drive Gleason to distraction by making Dulcy-like comments to
him in all apparent seriousness. "All policeman wear red underwear," she
once told him.

Gleason, whose family included a number of policemen, took um-
brage at her remark, as she had known he would. He irately told her so.
But once he had taken the bait, she was not about to let Gleason get away
until her teasing had thoroughly infuriated him, so she repeated the bro-
mide.

When Gleason sputtered with rage, insisting that his own relatives on
the force were living proof to the contrary, she sighed and said, "No
Jimmy, you just haven't observed. They all wear red underwear." With that,
she sauntered away from Gleason, who was ready to throw the nearest
heavy object through the nearest brick wall.

But Gleason didn't stay angry for long. Abbott concluded his story:
"A few hours later they were friends again."

Robert E. Sherwood eventually became one of America's foremost
playwrights, and wrote several plays in which the Lunts appeared. But he
was a struggling young writer in 1920 when he first met Alfred Lunt and
Lynn Fontanne. He liked both of them at once and admired their abilities
as actors, but, like Howard Lindsay, he thought their talents far too limited
to carry them to a higher plateau of success. They were "gifted grotesques,"
he wrote, "sure to shine in the sideshow but doomed never to achieve
prominence in the Main Tent."

Sherwood and Lindsay were not alone in this conviction. Everyone agreed that Lunt played Clarence to perfection and that Fontanne was the perfect Dulcy, but how could their talents possibly be used in different kinds of roles in other plays? How often would audiences enjoy seeing them repeat the same characterizations? Sherwood and others believed that their careers would inevitably be limited, like those of other actors who created specific stage personalities and then gave the same performance, however cleverly contrived, in each new play. They would never be out of work for long and their performances could always be counted on to elicit appreciative laughter, but they would never reach the top of their profession.

Sherwood characterized Lunt in 1921 as having the stage personality of "a shy, repressed, neurotic young man with some kind of physical deformity, as though he had been wounded in the liver. Lynn," he said, "was a funny, gawky English girl who didn't care how ridiculous she looked as long as the laughs came quickly."

Fontanne reinforced her reputation with occasionally eccentric off-stage behavior. One wonders now if that behavior was calculated in some way—if she was either trying to create a public image that would help her get roles of the only sort anyone was considering her for, or if perhaps she was trying to live up to the expectations of her audience. On the other hand, her peculiarities could have been a public mask to hide the shy woman underneath. Whatever the answer, her eccentric behavior during that time contrasted so remarkably with her behavior in later years that it is difficult to reconcile the two. Indeed, soon after she and Lunt were married, she seemed to discover her true personality, for she changed both outwardly and—apparently—within. From "a rather awkward English girl who showed her gums when she smiled," as Theresa Helburn described her, she became "one of the most beautiful women in the theatre," again in Helburn's words. Gawkiness somehow turned into elegance and grace, clumsiness into poise, silliness into shrewdness. And far from being regarded as a bizarre personality, she was looked upon as the more stable element in the Lunts' relationship, much less volatile than her husband.

1921–24

Lunt's first role after his great success in *Clarence* was in yet another play by Booth Tarkington, *The Intimate Strangers*. He might well have preferred to appear in another play, for the role he was asked to portray was not unlike the role of Clarence, and, even though it was the romantic lead, the director and producers encouraged him to repeat many of the mannerisms and bits of business that had served him so well in his first great success. All prominent actors have suffered from this problem; once they establish themselves in the public mind in one sort of characterization, they are offered similar roles. The serious actor's first impulse is generally to ask himself how he can perform each new role differently from others he has played, but he often discovers that those who have hired him have no intention of allowing him to experiment with a different approach. Instead, they are looking for a duplication of the performance that succeeded for him the last time, on the theory that the audience will be disappointed if the actor gives them anything unexpected.

It would probably have been best for Lunt to turn down all offers to re-create Clarence under another name. But that is a luxury only wealthy actors can afford. Lunt was not in that position. He needed to keep working in order to support himself, his mother, his brother and his sisters (one of whom was being put through college), and he also wished to put money aside so that he could get married.

For the first time in several years, Lunt was not appearing under George C. Tyler's management. *The Intimate Strangers* was produced by Florenz Ziegfeld, A. L. Erlanger and Charles Dillingham. Lunt's leading lady was Ziegfeld's wife, Billie Burke, who was the star of the production. All the other actors were omitted from the advertisements, which all but ignored the title and author of the play. And, just in case anyone was still uncertain who the leading attraction of *The Intimate Strangers* was, he had only to look at Miss Burke's touring retinue, which included two maids, a nurse for her little daughter, three dogs, a cook and, as Miss Burke noted in her autobiography, "a car with my faithful chauffeur Ernest."

Clarence had been Booth Tarkington's first substantial success in the theatre after many attempts. Now that he had finally achieved recognition as an accomplished playwright, it was inevitable that *The Intimate Strangers* would be compared to *Clarence,* and the comparison was thoroughly unfavorable; critics found the new play unsatisfactory by any standards, but especially so when compared to its predecessor. For Lunt, the Broadway engagement, which lasted for only 91 performances, and the tour that followed must have been anticlimactic. But perhaps he was preoccupied with his personal life at that time, for he and Fontanne announced their engagement on December 10, a month after *The Intimate Strangers* opened.

Those who maintained that Lunt was an actor with but a single string to his bow were confirmed in that opinion by his performance in *The Intimate Strangers*. Indeed, the performance *was* reminiscent of his portrayal of Clarence, but the skeptics were wrong about him. He was not limited to playing eccentric comic roles. Producers were limited in offering him only eccentric comic roles to play. Within a few years Lunt would be acting in a dazzling array of roles for the Theatre Guild.

When Fontanne came to see an early performance of *The Intimate Strangers,* Lunt asked her how she had liked his portrayal. Fontanne, who never was one to conceal her honest opinion, told him, "You worked too hard. Act being relaxed." On this occasion Lunt was overly sensitive to the criticism. "He didn't like that at all," Fontanne said. In later years, however, one of the sources of strength in the Lunt-Fontanne relationship was their ability each to point out the flaws in the other's performance and to do so directly and honestly. Each one genuinely admired the critical acuity of the other, each was hungry for criticism, and each was able to accept criticism without taking it personally.

In 1961, Fontanne told an interviewer, "We were two actors being perfectly honest with each other. To an outsider it might have sounded cruel. We didn't sound cruel to each other. It's just that we didn't have to bother with the 'now-darling-of-course-you're-the-most-marvelous-actor-in-the-world-but-there's-just-one-little-thing' beginning. We've always been pretty straight with each other."

When the engagement of Lunt and Fontanne was announced in the newspapers, for some reason he gave out the information that his real name was not Lunt but Ecklunt, a "fact" that appeared in most reporters' stories. The name had been changed only when he began his career in the theatre, he told them. Some reporters took this to mean that Lunt was not a native American, and stories began to circulate in and out of print that he had been born in Scandinavia—in Sweden, according to some, or in Finland. Why Lunt offered this fiction remains a mystery. Perhaps it was simply intended as a joke and never meant for publication. But he didn't repudiate the fiction for many years. Rather, he continued to tell interviewers throughout the 1920s and '30s that his original name was Ecklunt, Ecklund, Erklund or Egland.

The tour of *The Intimate Strangers* was torment for Lunt. He could think only of Lynn Fontanne. Billie Burke said that Lunt was so preoccupied he often forgot to eat, so she instructed her cook to concoct "special delicacies" that even a man whose mind was elsewhere could not refuse. But not even the cook's most elegantly prepared meals could turn Lunt's attention from his impending marriage.

Burke said that Lunt was especially concerned about his trousseau. He spent the afternoons when no matinee was scheduled shopping for clothes and then showing his purchases to her for approval, presumably on the theory that one woman would know instinctively what another woman would appreciate.

The wedding ceremony was planned for May 27, 1922, a week after Fontanne's tour in *Dulcy* had ended and during a week when the *Intimate Strangers* tour was taking a brief vacation. But on the morning of the 26th, Lunt was nervous and impatient. He and Fontanne were sitting on a bench in Central Park when he turned to her and said, "Let's get married! Now! Immediately!" The wedding was to be a civil one without pomp in any case, he argued. Why wait until tomorrow? She agreed that there was no special point in waiting, so, without telling a soul, they took a local subway train to City Hall and sought out someone who would perform the ceremony.

They found Deputy City Clerk James J. McCormick, who agreed to preside. But, McCormick asked them, where are the witnesses? Not having thought about that technicality, Lunt had to ask two employees of the City Clerk's office to serve as witnesses. After the ceremony had been performed in the chapel of the Municipal Building, one more formality remained: payment of the fee. An embarrassed Alfred Lunt had to admit he had forgotten to bring any money; an absent-minded Lynn Fontanne confessed she had forgotten her purse. So Lunt asked the hapless witnesses if they would mind lending him the two dollars to pay for the wedding. Each witness contributed a dollar, and Alfred and Lynn became the Lunts at last. Lunt jokingly telegraphed to his mother, "HAVE MADE AN HONEST WOMAN OF LYNN."

The New York newspapers were interested in this union of two Broadway players, and articles were written both before the wedding (announcing that it would take place on the 27th) and afterward. The stories focused their attention primarily on Fontanne, who was still generally considered to be the more prominent performer. On May 26, the *Times* headlined its piece, "LYNN FONTANNE TO MARRY; *Dulcy to Wed Alfred Lunt, Actor, at City Hall Tomorrow.*" And after the marriage had taken place, the newspaper headlined: "LYNN FONTANNE MARRIES." The story was inaccurate in many respects, but all of the inaccuracies had been furnished by the bride and groom; it gave Lunt's real name as Erklund, his age as twenty-eight (he was twenty-nine) and Fontanne's age as twenty-eight as well (she was thirty-four).

There was a brief honeymoon in Atlantic City, where Lunt rejoined the tour of *The Intimate Strangers*. When Billie Burke learned that the ceremony had taken place in City Hall, she was so upset that she insisted on being allowed to arrange for a church wedding. According to her story, the Lunts agreed to go through with it in order to please her. Their second wedding was held in the morning before a matinee performance of *The Intimate Strangers*. Lunt was nearly overcome with fright, and when the minister asked him whether or not he would take this woman, he was unable to produce a sound. A second attempt was no more successful. At last he managed to croak "Yes," and the minister was able to complete the ceremony.

Gamely, Lunt agreed to go through with the matinee, sure that his voice would return as soon as the play began. Although he was able to remember the blocking and the business, and although he moved his lips when he was supposed to be speaking, no sound came from his mouth. Lunt had no understudy, so the only option seemed to be to cancel the performance. But a full house was in attendance, and the manager of the theatre was loath to refund the audience's money, so, Billie Burke tells us, he came up with a novel solution. The stage manager was told to read Lunt's lines while seated behind a screen—or, when he could be hidden on the set, from behind the sofa or the stove.

Lunt's voice did not return for the evening performance either, and he may have wondered if his theatrical career had come to a premature end. Certainly the producers must have feared the worst, for they dispatched an actor named McKay Morris to Atlantic City with instructions to be ready to go on at the next performance. Fortunately for the groom and for two generations of theatregoers, Lunt's voice returned on the following day and he went back into the production.*

The first step in the plans that Lunt and Fontanne had made with Noël Coward was now complete: they had gotten married. The second step—to act together in all their plays—was less easily accomplished. They presented their plan to George C. Tyler, but the producer thought it a poor idea. Step two would have to wait.

The couple returned to Genesee Depot for the summer, where plans were made to build a second house, the original being too small to accommodate the Lunts, Hattie, Carl and Karin comfortably. (Louise, having married Jack Greene, was no longer living at home.) Hattie never fully reconciled herself to Lynn and Alfred's marriage. Although Hattie and Lynn were rarely openly antagonistic to one another, their relationship never became close, a relative characterizing it as an "armed truce."

The difficulties stemmed both from Hattie's refusal to treat her daughter-in-law with affection and from Fontanne's conviction that Hattie and Alfred should be left alone together as little as possible. Throughout her fifty-five-year marriage to Lunt, Fontanne made it a point to be present whenever Lunt was with *any* other woman, including his mother and his sisters. Fontanne apparently had little reason to be jealous—Lunt preferred her company to anyone else's, and there was never a suggestion that he had become significantly attracted (sexually or emotionally) to another woman—but she always maintained a close watch over him. Women were no less strongly drawn to him after 1922 than before, but Lunt seems to have been oblivious (or indifferent) to their feelings for him. The fact that Fontanne's obsessive watchfulness extended even to his mother and sisters betrayed an insecurity she never managed to conquer. Women—all women—were perceived as potentially threatening to her marriage, and on no account would she allow the threat to become a reality.

Fontanne's brilliance as an actress served her well in her relationship with her mother-in-law. If she felt little warmth for Hattie, she could mask her feelings effectively. For many years she made a genuine effort to win Hattie's friendship, writing to her regularly when the Lunts were in New York or on tour and often sending gifts to her. Hattie, too, was an accom-

---

* The story of the second wedding ceremony and Lunt's resultant problems was told by Billie Burke in her autobiography, and newspaper versions of it appeared in 1922. Much later, however, Lunt maintained that the entire story was "utter invention."

plished performer, although acting was not her profession. Thus, her unwillingness to accept Lynn was not overtly expressed after Lunt and Fontanne were married. On the surface Hattie and Lynn had a cordial, even friendly relationship. Only the members of their family detected the coolness that separated them.

Life at Genesee Depot was everything Lunt could wish for: informal, relaxing—and productive, too, as he began the process of turning the acreage into a working farm. George C. Tyler wanted Lunt to appear in William Harris, Jr.'s presentation of a play called *Banco,* but Lunt delayed his return to New York for as long as possible. The money was running out, however, and the new play was scheduled to open on September 11. By August, Tyler was becoming nervous. "I can quite understand how a man with a new wife and a new Ford is kept constantly occupied," he wrote to Lunt, but he reminded him that his presence at rehearsals was needed immediately.

The Lunts returned to New York and set up housekeeping in a small apartment equipped with a bare minimum of furniture: a bed, a bath mat, a complete set of kitchen equipment and an elegant Spanish cupboard Lunt had picked up in Cleveland during a tour. A friend asked them to look after his phonograph while he was out of the city, and the Lunts were glad to do so. Not only did it provide the music of which Alfred was so fond, it also served the couple as a chair—the only one in the apartment. Gradually, additional furniture found its way into the flat, most of it coming from nearby antique stores, where occasional bargains could be found.

Banco offered Lunt a role entirely different from the comic eccentrics he had been playing. The play, adapted by Clare Kummer from a French comedy by Alfred Savoir, was considered quite risqué for 1922, and it failed to find an appreciative audience. However, in terms of Lunt's career, it represented a significant opportunity. His role, the Count Alexandre de Lussac—a charming but dissolute gambler who unsuccessfully attempts to keep from falling in love with his own wife—gave him a chance to demonstrate the versatility so many observers thought he lacked.

Banco opened in Washington on the 11th, as scheduled, and came to the Ritz Theatre in New York on September 20. The reviews were so mixed on the subject of Lunt's performance that one finds it difficult to imagine that all the critics were watching the same actor in the same play. Kenneth Macgowan found Lunt as mannered as in his earlier Broadway performances. "All through the first act he is some sort of boyish Punch with knotted face and tense body," said Macgowan, although later conceding, "He improves steadily toward the close, when he is really very good." Heywood Broun found Lunt to be "enormously clever and able," but said that "by and by it [his performance] got on our nerves a little. . . . Our eyes grew weary of chasing gestures."

Other critics saw things differently. *Variety* said that Lunt "portrayed the role in such a whimsical manner and with such delightful light and shade that when the final curtain dropped you wished you could have even more of the man." The *Telegram* noted Lunt's "sure lightness of touch and never failing variety," and Alexander Woollcott, who had voiced his objection to Lunt's mannered performance in *The Intimate Strangers,* remarked that he played "without the visible effort and the fiddle-dee-dee mannerisms with which he has been hobbling himself."

The most vivid description of Lunt's performance was given years later by S. N. Behrman in his memoirs. Behrman had never seen Lunt before he saw *Banco*. "I was fascinated by Alfred's style and personality," he said.

> He captivated me. He had total command, not merely physically but mentally. You saw his brain digesting the lines and the situations and finding them funny. There was glee in his voice, in his expression, in his gestures. I went to see *Banco* time after time. I saw that Alfred changed his readings, changed his performance all the time, but he never changed his point of view, which was comedic. It was the comedy of intelligence. He was not always amused by the same things so that you got different facets almost at each performance.

Behrman was so impressed by Lunt's portrayal that he later wrote his first play, *The Second Man,* specifically with Lunt and Fontanne in mind. They did act in Behrman's play and in several others that he wrote or adapted for them afterward, and Behrman never wavered in his assessment of the Lunts as geniuses who could make a dull play seem exciting and a competent play seem brilliant.

The subtle alterations in Lunt's performances from night to night that Behrman observed were a hallmark of his approach to acting, and Behrman's statement could have been applied to Fontanne as well. She demonstrated the same ability to improvise within a prearranged framework in most of her performances. It was not sufficient for the Lunts to repeat what had worked for them yesterday, as it was for most actors; it was necessary that they *rediscover* the meaning of every scene, every line of dialogue and every reaction at each performance, so that every moment would be vivid, spontaneous and real.

Lunt was just beginning to confound Broadway's view of him as a limited actor. And perhaps that is the chief reason he accepted an offer to appear in a silent film called *Backbone*. The film would give him the opportunity to play a conventional romantic hero. It would also be financially rewarding. He was then earning $600 per week on Broadway, and the film offer was for substantially more money than that.

Before *Backbone* was released, a film writer named James Dean saw the unedited footage and predicted a great future for Lunt on the screen. "He is the most personable actor I have seen since Wallie Reid's heyday," said Dean. "All he needs now is a little pomade for his hair and a scene with a little passion in it—sheik stuff—and he will be well on his way to mount the idol's altar."

The altar remained vacant, however. Lunt's interest in filmmaking reflected his curiosity about a medium he had not yet tried rather than a burning desire to become an idol. But the picture, in any case, reflected no credit on anyone connected with it. Although the review in the New York *Times* of April 30, 1923, reported that Lunt was "quite good" as the handsome young man, it said that *Backbone* as a whole resembled a chocolate eclair more than it did "anything with real vertebrae."

Lunt himself was upset by his performance, and after sitting through *Backbone* once, he never wanted to see it again. "I know so little about the screen that I feel I made a mess of things," he said. "I was so conscious of the camera. . . . I was a novice and I was afraid to venture forth without the director's instructions."

He was glad to return to the stage, and particularly happy that he and Fontanne would be performing together for the first time on Broadway. The play was to be a revival of an old chestnut called *Sweet Nell of Old Drury*, produced by the Equity Players in order to raise money for that beleaguered organization. All the actors were asked to work for minimum salaries and all agreed to do so. The production would feature Laurette Taylor as Nell, with Lunt (whose credit on the program listed him as appearing "By Courtesy of Distinctive Pictures Corporation") as Charles II and Fontanne in the relatively minor role of Lady Castlemaine.

The play was chosen by Laurette Taylor, who had been given her choice by the Equity Council. *Sweet Nell of Old Drury*, the prototype of early twentieth-century comic melodrama, was hardly an adventurous selection. It was full of ridiculous situations and improbable dialogue, but Taylor selected it because of its history of success and its old-fashioned hokum, frankly acknowledging that the play had been chosen for its appeal to the tired businessman. The purpose of the benefit was to make money, and in that aim the production was successful.*

Sweet Nell represented Fontanne's chance to break out of her stereotypical casting. Lady Castlemaine was a calculating beauty, a character far removed from Dulcy or Mrs. Glendenning or any of the scatterbrained roles with which she had become associated.

Fontanne and Lunt were always conscious of the importance of the visual image presented to the audience—the costumes, accessories and makeup—in reinforcing the personality of the character, so for the role of Lady Castlemaine they spent a considerable amount of their own money on costume jewelry to enhance the character's physical beauty.

Fontanne's own opinion of her appearance was given to an interviewer in 1923. She said, "It's not that I'm homely. I am rather pictur-

---

* Perhaps Taylor also chose *Sweet Nell* because her husband had had so much to do with its creation. Two of the actresses in the original production (in London in 1900) stated that J. Hartley Manners had, without credit, contributed an act and a half to the play.

esque, in a gauche and angular way. With lots of trouble, with infinite care in the choice of clothes, I contrive to look smart." Lunt had helped his wife to achieve that image. Soon after their marriage he had determined that her skinniness was unhealthy; consequently, he taught himself to cook and he tempted her every morning with elaborately prepared breakfasts, a different kind for each day. The only thing the breakfasts had in common was that they were all large and filled with calories. This ruse of Lunt's led to his lifelong passion for gourmet cooking, and it was responsible for his wife's transformation into a stunningly attractive woman with a voluptuous figure and a lovely face. "She is the only woman I know whom twenty pounds of flesh turned into a beauty," said Laurette Taylor.* Now Fontanne's task was to apply that beauty to the role of Lady Castlemaine.

Long hours were spent in rehearsal, at the request of the Lunts. Their quest for perfection drove them to spend every waking moment discussing, then trying out new approaches. "Lynn and Alfred were untiring," said Laurette Taylor; "after rehearsing all day we would start again on individual scenes after dinner."

Fontanne's performance—helped, no doubt, by the costume jewelry—accomplished exactly what the Lunts hoped it would. John Corbin's review said that she was "superb" as Lady Castlemaine, "a part whole worlds removed from her delectable moron, Dulcy, yet as perfect in every accent, lineament and gesture." Woollcott, writing now in the New York *Herald,* said, "In a generally sumptuous cast, one performance stood out last evening as something of fine mettle, something true and shining. That was the performance of Lynn Fontanne as the frustrated and embittered Lady Castlemaine. . . . It might be noted in passing that she is growing beautiful."

Lunt's contribution to the production was less universally praised, although he was by no means ignored. The *World* commented, "Alfred Lunt we found particularly happy as Charles the Second," and Kenneth Macgowan in the *Globe* reported that "the real news about *Sweet Nell* is of course the fact that Alfred Lunt is having a fine time of it playing Charles II of England," but others were less impressed; Corbin said that he had been "well nigh submerged in the costume and the dummy personality of this Charles Rex." It seems likely, however, that Lunt would have been undisturbed by criticism of himself in his pleasure at the critics' enthusiasm for Fontanne's performance, which was even more highly praised than that of the play's star. Corbin noted that Fontanne "had even a bit of the 'authority' which Miss Taylor sometime lacked, carrying off the crude lines of her part with the distinction of an old master."

The theatrical world had finally been given a convincing demonstra-

---

*When looking at photographs of Lynn Fontanne taken before 1922 (especially in the role of Dulcy), one is surprised to find a lovely woman, thin by the standards of the time, perhaps, but by no means gaunt.

tion of Fontanne's versatility. She would not thereafter be regarded as simply an eccentric comedienne. She fully realized, however, that she would once again be relegated to character roles unless she cultivated her appearance, and from 1923 onward she spared no effort to make herself beautiful. If this involved daily naps, giving up late parties, taking special care of her hands, face and hair, and spending an hour or so each day on the application of makeup and the selection of her personal wardrobe, so be it. She would not allow her career to be limited by the insistence of producers, directors and the public that leading actresses must be beautiful, any more than she would let the fact that she was several years older than the public's perception of a leading woman stand in her way. If beauty was demanded, she would develop and maintain it. In the years that followed, one person after another was dumbfounded by the appearance of Lynn Fontanne. Could that ravishing woman possibly be the same person as the scraggly girl everyone was accustomed to seeing? It was. Moreover, Fontanne's appearance became a standard of beauty. In interviews she was continually asked for her secrets, and she occasionally responded by writing articles giving advice.

In 1927, for example, she wrote "Making the Most of Your Looks" for the *Ladies' Home Journal* and said she believed that all women should study "the many ways of becoming beautiful"—the artful use of makeup, the advantages of a beautiful carriage, careful attention to the selection of clothes and hairstyles. "I wash my face beautifully every night with cold cream," she wrote, "and very thoroughly. And then I wipe the cream off with a nice, soft cheesecloth. In my bath I shake a few drops of a bath essence which costs a good deal of money. . . . After my bath I dust with talcum. And then—I put on a nice, light, clean makeup."

Convinced that taking proper care of her teeth was paramount, she developed a fascinating—and obsessive—ritual which she practiced every day, regardless of her surroundings. She brushed her teeth in the morning for half an hour with exactly thirteen toothbrushes. She would then dry the brushes by laying them out in the sun. And that night each of the toothbrushes would be put to work once again for another half-hour of brushing.

What began as the desire to manufacture beauty ultimately became reality. Somehow Fontanne did not simply appear to be a beautiful woman; she *became* a beautiful woman. When a woman feels beautiful, she once said, she "is halfway to *being* beautiful." On another occasion she put it this way: "If a woman is determined she shall stay young and pretty, in some way just the determination affects her appearance." Howard Lindsay, who had thought her plain in 1921, was astonished when he saw her several years later and discovered she had become beautiful. "This," he said, "was no accident. It was a deliberate act and a personal achievement."

Many who saw her on stage and assumed that her appearance was simply a matter of makeup were amazed when they saw her at close range.

Her skin was described as "flawless" by one writer, as having the "strange whiteness of Wedgwood china" by another.

But Fontanne's attractiveness was not simply a matter of facial appearance. Her voice was low and sultry, her movement undulating and graceful, onstage and off. Whether she was appearing in a play or in someone's living room it was impossible for others not to look at her. She radiated a glow of such intensity that it transfixed every eye.

In time Fontanne's stunning, youthful appearance became legendary. While everyone around her grew older, she seemed somehow to remain the same age. Lawrence Lader wrote about her in 1948, when she was sixty-one, "The real source of her beauty comes from inside. It seems to bubble out inexhaustibly, expressing itself in a dozen ways, such as the saucy tilt of her chin or the way she shows off a new gown like a schoolgirl."

Fontanne's sister Antoinette said the decisive element in transforming Lynn from a plain to a beautiful woman was "the appreciation of Alfred." Antoinette believed that Lunt's perception of Fontanne's inherent beauty occurred long before others saw it and that her view of herself was completely altered when she looked at herself through his eyes.

The press agent for the Theatre Guild's road tours in the 1930s and '40s was Thoda Cocroft. Before Cocroft met Lynn, she had been told by another actress that Fontanne pasted "a transparent skinlike substance over her face when she made up for the stage to eliminate lines and wrinkles." When they did meet for the first time, it was backstage after a performance and Fontanne was still wearing heavy makeup. Cocroft decided that the actress's account had probably been true, that Fontanne's "youth was in her slim figure, flowing walk, ankles like a racing pony's, aromatic voice, and that her face, after all, required the disguise of grease paint for the complete illusion of youth." Later, however, Cocroft made a morning appointment with Fontanne and, as they were riding together in a taxi, she "inspected her at intimate range," and found that "her face was smooth and unlined. There was not the faintest indication of the betraying droop of middle age."

Fontanne continued to look so much younger than she really was for such a remarkably long time that other women took to peering at her intently whenever they saw her on the street, in an elevator, in a department store. This became a source of considerable embarrassment for her and for Lunt.

Rumors persisted for years that Fontanne dyed her hair, had regular facial treatments and periodically had her face lifted. She denied all such rumors, saying that she was "too lazy" for such procedures. Still, few could believe that her appearance was entirely natural. Undoubtedly the most skeptical of all was a woman who saw her perform in a small town in Texas in the 1940s. The house manager overheard the woman's companion ask her, "Hasn't Lynn Fontanne the most beautiful hands and arms you've ever seen?" "Yes," replied the woman, "but are they her own?"

Fontanne worked hard to maintain her image as a beautiful woman who looked far younger than her chronological age. She insisted that photographs of her be taken from the proper angle, and with the proper lighting. The Lunts' secretary in the 1940s and 1950s, Renée Orsell, recalled that whenever light rehearsals were held for one of the Lunts' plays, Fontanne would sit or stand on stage while "Mr. Lunt would go out front to check. Suddenly Miss Fontanne's voice would be heard asking, 'Alfred, do I look lovely?' His answer was always in the affirmative."

During the tour of *The Great Sebastians* in 1956, she and Lunt would spend many hours in each theatre, checking the lighting for each of her stage moves. With Lunt in the audience, she would take her position for her first entrance and ask him how the lights affected her appearance. Then she would move into her next position, then on to the next and the next, each time being assured that the lights were flattering. "How is this? Is it lovely?" she would ask. "Yes, Lynnie," came the answer. "And now I sit. Is this lovely?" "Yes, it's fine." "No, no, no, Alfred," she would say, "don't tell me it's fine. Is it *lovely?*"

Fontanne shared her knowledge of attaining and maintaining an attractive face and figure with her colleagues. Peg Murray, who was in the cast of *The Great Sebastians*, told me that Fontanne gave tips to the other actresses. One of her hints was to lie on a bed each day with one's head hanging over the edge. She helped a number of the actresses in that production with their stage makeups and all of them agreed that she had improved their appearances significantly.

In 1960, when Fontanne was seventy-two, Noël Coward, her friend of more than forty years, dined with the Lunts and recorded in his diary, "Lynnie looked so incredibly young and beautiful that I could hardly believe it."

Fontanne's growing reputation as a beautiful woman caused a rift between her and Laurette Taylor, who was envious of Fontanne's appearance. When Lynn first arrived in America, she had been regarded as terribly skinny, awkward and generally unattractive, and she certainly posed no threat to Taylor, who demanded constant attention from men. By 1923, however, Lynn had been transformed. Suddenly, Laurette discovered, everyone was looking at Fontanne as an attractive woman, and that meant that Lynn was providing unconscious competition for the attention Taylor craved and demanded.

Furthermore, Taylor was unhappy with Fontanne's growing reputation as a brilliant actress. As Lynn became more independent and self-confident and less in awe of Taylor, she found herself under frequent attack. Laurette accused her of being unintelligent, a verdict Fontanne accepted for many years, only to come to the realization much later in her life that Taylor's accusation had been based on jealousy.

Another issue that caused resentment between Taylor and Fontanne was Taylor's insistence that her guests perform when invited to her parties. Lynn was still shy and disliked being called upon to perform; she believed that an actress had ample opportunity for displaying her talents on the stage. On social occasions she wished only to relax. Her ego did not need the constant approval that some actors derive from being "on" in every conceivable situation.*

Finally Lynn also grew tired of Taylor's frenetic behavior. She longed to sit quietly and talk with her, but Taylor was incapable of repose, needing either to entertain or to be entertained. Lynn found herself unable to respond to Taylor's emotional demands. The jokes, the gossip and the giggling they had shared years before had been amusing and stimulating, but Lynn now yearned for a more mature relationship, which Taylor refused to permit.

Perhaps in an effort to retain her position of superiority in the mentor-pupil relationship she had established with Fontanne, Taylor began to treat Lynn with the malice she had previously reserved for others. As Lynn was engaged in conversation, Taylor would suddenly shout at her, "Oh, shut up! What do you know about it, anyway?" Or: "Sit down. What makes you think you're so smart?" Taylor was always caustic when she drank, though she had treated Lynn with friendliness in the past. Under the influence of alcohol, however, she could be vicious, and especially cruel to Fontanne—and beginning in 1923, she began to drink much more heavily than before. Marguerite Courtney has described an all-too-typical display of Taylor's crudeness:

> If Lynn attempted to take the center of the stage at a party or
> offer an opinion different from Laurette's, there would be a
> sharp, "See 'ere my girl, come off it!" or maybe just a plain, "Shut
> up!" To Laurette, Lynn remained the skinny girl in the hat with
> the velvet streamers whom she had taken under her wing. If re-
> minded that Lynn was very much a star in her own right, she
> was likely to answer, "I can't help that—she's not as good an
> actress as she used to be." When drinking, this "self-indulgent"
> honesty became downright abuse. Lynn left many of Laurette's
> parties in tears with Alfred glowering Teutonically at her side

*In 1924, Lunt and Fontanne invited Noel Coward to accompany them to several parties at the Taylor-Manners house on Riverside Drive. Coward participated in the elaborate charadelike games that Taylor loved to play, but he spent much of his time observing Taylor and her guests. The vehemence with which Taylor played the games (she insisted that there always be a game in progress and that everyone should play, and then she loudly criticized everyone else's ability; some of her guests became so offended that they left the party and refused all further invitations) and the dazzling displays of temperament and theatricality he witnessed at her parties became the subject of *Hay Fever*, one of Coward's first successful plays.

and muttering, "There is no reason for you to put up with such abuse, Lynn! We will not go there again." Finally Lynn could take no more, and left one evening, vowing never to return.

Lunt said later that Taylor had always been extremely kind to him, "but . . . I could not bear her behavior to Lynn and so could not continue to see her. . . . I was stunned and bewildered by her behavior—we both were."

Neither of the Lunts realized that Taylor's abusive behavior was caused to a considerable degree by alcoholism. When Fontanne came to understand that fact many years later, it helped to explain, if not to justify, Taylor's vindictiveness toward her.

Lunt's contract with Distinctive Pictures Corporation called for him to make another film in 1923, and he fulfilled that obligation with *The Ragged Edge,* a melodramatic adventure story set in China and the South Sea islands. The film was unremarkable in every way, but the publicity campaign caused a stir. A large advertising poster displayed outside theatres was somehow found "indecent" and "tending to corrupt the morals" by the Motion Picture Commission of the State of New York. The poster showed Mimi Palmeri, the film's leading lady, on a beach in a one-piece bathing suit with Lunt beside her, dressed in shirt and trousers and standing half-immersed in the water. Nothing in the picture appears to be remotely salacious to a viewer in the 1980s, and it is difficult to imagine what could have offended the Motion Picture Commission in 1923, but offended it was.

The publicity gave *The Ragged Edge* a notoriety it didn't deserve. Every indication is that the picture represented the height of absurdity. Even "trying to keep track of the tale hidden in *The Ragged Edge* brings out beads of perspiration on one's brow," said the *Times*'s reviewer, who added that Lunt was "fair in his part, but suffers from too much obedience to the director." As Lunt had observed the same failing about his performance in *Backbone,* it seems clear that he was uncomfortable in the film medium. Perhaps that helps to explain why he and Fontanne turned down so many film offers when they were at the height of their careers.

But they did not turn down the opportunity to appear together in a silent for Distinctive Pictures called *Second Youth*. Once again Lunt played the leading man to Mimi Palmeri, while Fontanne undertook a minor role for her first venture into film. *Second Youth* was a farce, although, according to the critical response, it was hardly filled with uproarious humor. Still, it seems to have been a pleasant enough diversion and a considerable improvement over Lunt's earlier movies.

After the film was shot, Lunt told an interviewer for *Motion Picture Classic* that he and Fontanne had enjoyed acting in the picture and that he was pleased with the result. Evidently he had reason to be. When *Second Youth* was released in 1924, the film critic for the New York *Times* said that he was "much better in this film than in either of the photodramas in which he appeared," and that "with a stronger story and a more whimsical theme, Mr. Lunt would do very well as a comedian." But one has the feeling that the Lunts did not regard their silent-film appearances seriously. They were simply diversions—albeit profitable ones—from the serious business of the theatre.

Capitalizing on her new freedom from Dulcy-like characterizations, Fontanne was cast in the summer of 1923 in a sophisticated romantic comedy called *In Love with Love,* which opened at the Ritz Theatre in New York on August 6. Robert Milton, who had directed Lunt in *The Country Cousin* and in *Banco,* directed Fontanne for the first time.

Ann Jordon, the character played by Fontanne, was a beautiful and charming woman who indulges in many flirtations. The comedy begins with her seemingly devoted to one man, follows her progress as she becomes engaged to another, and ends as she prepares to marry a third. She explains to him that during her previous romances she was merely "in love with love." The play was—except for its comic foundation—unlike anything she had played before, and called upon her to project a sensuality that none of her earlier characters possessed.

Noël Coward found her "gay and attractive" in the role, and added: "In *In Love with Love* she also began to be beautiful. There was a new fullness in her figure and her movements were smoother." But when he wrote in 1937 that he "suspected Alfred of rehearsing her in sex appeal" for the role, Fontanne was more than mildly irritated. She told him in a letter that "Actually Alfred has never rehearsed me in anything. . . . I imagine the sexy part you saw me in just called for it, that's all. And there the matter is closed."

The New York critics seemed still to be astounded by Fontanne's range; they must have suspected that her performance in *Sweet Nell of Old Drury* was an anomaly and that she would inevitably return to her more familiar style of acting. John Corbin said in the *Times,* "This is a new note in Miss Fontanne's scale, and one that is destined to delight many hearts." He spoke of her remarkable "blending of surface humor and latent passion," and, he said, although her role was "less original and less whimsically diverting than Dulcy" it was "no less true and, needless to say, as flawlessly, as delightfully acted."

The *Morning World* commented that "here already we have a performance with which to judge and measure whatever else may come after throughout the year in the playhouses." Fontanne, the writer said, "is deft and admirable throughout. . . . After the final scene we went away convinced that . . . Lynn Fontanne is one of the finest actresses of our day."

In Love with Love settled in for a successful New York run during the fall and winter of 1923, then took to the road for an equally successful tour in the spring. Everywhere the play was performed, Fontanne won new converts. A Philadelphia columnist spoke of the "glowing comedienne with the delectable lazy drawl." A Boston writer said that the play, which he found mediocre, "was saved by the acting of Miss Fontanne [who] is fair to look upon, a constant delight to the eye."

The critic for the Boston *Transcript* gave an especially vivid description of her performance. "To watch her," he said, "was to wish to paint her, so pictorial, so spontaneous seemed her poses and movements. She is mistress of quiet watching, listening, musing. In a part that she has played since last August, she still seems to speak and stir by the impulse of her personage and by the moment." Here was an acknowledgment of Fontanne's ability to keep her role spontaneous. The critic also spoke approvingly of "the brightness and suavity of her tones . . . the grace, economy, alertness and meaning of her gesture—the will or the anticipation of the instant become bodily motion; the light and shade of her face; the sensibility and the unbroken current, variously flecked and measured, of her acting."

Lunt had not yet given quite so convincing a demonstration of his versatility. He had shown his brilliance in comedy; it was time now to play a wholly dramatic role. He was offered a secondary part in an epic drama by John Drinkwater entitled *Robert E. Lee,* which, like Fontanne's play, was directed by Robert Milton. An actor who cared more for his image than for his art would have turned down a secondary role if, like Lunt, he had already established himself as a leading player. But image meant little to Lunt. Proving to the theatrical world—and to himself—that he was capable of portraying characters for which he was thought to be unsuited was his motivation, so he accepted the supporting role at once.

Robert E. Lee was to open in Virginia. Since *In Love with Love* was still running in New York, this necessitated the first extended separation for Lunt and Fontanne since their wedding. The remarkably close tie that bound the Lunts fiercely to one another throughout fifty-five years of marriage had already begun to take effect, and the separation was not easy for either of them. Both were too busy to write letters while Lunt was in Virginia and Fontanne in New York—and later when Lunt was in New York and Fontanne on tour—but they sent wires to one another several times each week and telephoned frequently.

When *Robert E. Lee* opened in Richmond, on November 5, 1923, with Berton Churchill as Lee, the presentation caused quite a stir. A group of Confederate organizations came together to protest the "many historical misstatements" allegedly made by the play, which, in the words of the group's resolution, "gives to the world a false idea of the principles for which Southern people fought and died." Especially upset was the president of the Sons of Confederate Veterans, who called the play "a hopeless failure as a portrayal of Southern life."

The New York engagement was far less controversial. Most critics agreed that Drinkwater's play, although sometimes poetic, was insufficiently dramatic. That the drama took considerably more than three hours to perform did not help its chances for success. It closed after a mere 15 performances.

But Lunt, playing the role of a young pacifist and poet, scored heavily. One critic after another noted how moving his performance had been in a leaden play. Alexander Woollcott told his readers that a trip to the Ritz Theatre would be worth their while despite the deficiencies of the play because "You will . . . see in one role a performance of distinguished beauty. That is the playing of Private David Peel by an actor whom chance had hitherto made known to this city only as a gay but highly mannered comedian. His name is Alfred Lunt and he is aflame in the new play."

Percy Hammond of the New York *Tribune* concurred. "Mr. Lunt, when he talks of the death of Jeb Stuart . . . with breaking voice and breaking heart, is as perfect an actor as any Russian of the Moscow Art Theatre," said Hammond, offering the highest possible praise. And the *World*'s review stated that "Mr. Lunt apparently can do anything he chooses, whether he decides to bring a Tarkington character into perfection or breathe force into Mr. Drinkwater's still-life."

As soon as *Robert E. Lee* closed, Robert Milton began directing the Broadway premiere of an English drama, *Outward Bound,* and he brought Lunt into the cast. The company was a brilliant one, including Leslie Howard, Margalo Gillmore, Dudley Digges and Eugene Powers. Lunt had never appeared with such an outstanding ensemble as this one.

Outward Bound is an imaginative allegory in which the passengers on a ship discover that they have died and are traveling to an afterlife. Lunt played Tom Prior, the first of the passengers to discover the real nature of the voyage. The play is intensely serious and highly demanding of an audience's willingness to suspend its disbelief. It is anything but escapist Broadway fare. But New York has always had its share of adventurous theatregoers who are willing to give a provocative drama a fair hearing, and this was especially true in the 1920s, when the American theatre was at last beginning to welcome the kinds of serious experiments in drama that had been widely accepted in much of Europe for the previous thirty years.

On the other hand, Atlantic City was not a community to eagerly accept dramatic innovation. Many who patronized the theatre in that resort city were there on vacation, and when they went to see a play, they expected to see something light and easily digested. Given that fact, it is difficult to imagine why William Harris, Jr., the producer of *Outward Bound,* chose to present the play there before bringing it to Broadway. But that is what he did, with results that seem in hindsight to have been almost predictable.

When the play was first presented, on Christmas Eve, 1923, the audience at the Apollo Theatre in Atlantic City divided into two camps. One was decidedly hostile, the other supportive. The hostile element, which was dominant, hissed loudly as the final curtain descended. The supporters were few in number and their applause was barely audible. The booing of the majority made it inadvisable for the actors to take a curtain call, and the stage manager wisely decided to leave the curtain down.

Subsequent performances in Atlantic City did not call forth such extreme responses, but there was a conspicuous lack of audience enthusiasm, and a decision was made by the play's management not to risk the taking of curtain calls after any performance. If the performance was unsuccessful, curtain calls would obviously be inappropriate; if, on the other hand, the audience had been moved, curtain calls would intrude upon the mood the play had created.

After two weeks *Outward Bound* moved to New York, where it received a highly mixed set of reviews. As in Atlantic City, observers tended either to be highly supportive or extremely negative. But in New York the percentages were reversed and the supporters outnumbered the nay-sayers. John Corbin wrote in the *Times* that "most of the first night's audience . . . sat breathless—thrilled and fascinated to the final curtain." *Outward Bound* played successfully for 144 performances. Never once, however, did the actors take a curtain call.

One evening the audience included a woman who arrived at the theatre just after the play had begun so that she had no time to look at her program. At the end of the first act, she turned to her companion and remarked on the performance of the young man who was playing the drunken passenger so brilliantly. She had a peculiar feeling about him, she said. "I know every motion that man is going to make. I know all the tones of his voice. But," she said, "I've never seen him before." The mystery was explained when she consulted the program and discovered that the actor was Alfred Lunt. The woman was May Massee, who had been Lunt's teacher in the second grade in Milwaukee and who had often encouraged him to read aloud to her class.

After *Outward Bound,* there could be no more doubt of Lunt's brilliance and versatility than of Fontanne's. He had conclusively demonstrated his range in the varied roles he had played since *Clarence,* and he had shown in *Outward Bound* and in *Robert E. Lee* that he was as accomplished in serious drama as in the comedies with which he had previously been associated. But versatility in itself does not guarantee success in the theatre. It can, in fact, be a sort of curse. It can prevent the performer from developing a stage personality with which the public can identify, thus inhibiting rather than furthering his career.

To a considerable degree, that was the problem both Alfred Lunt and Lynn Fontanne faced when he closed in *Outward Bound* and her tour in *In Love with Love* came to an end. That the versatility they had striven to demonstrate should have come to be a problem is an irony, but that was the case. As the 1923–24 theatrical season ended, both had reached critical points in their careers. Lunt was no longer considered to be a limited performer. On the other hand, he had exchanged his position as a leading player with a recognizable stage personality for that of a distinguished supporting actor whose theatrical persona was unclear.

Another factor that added to the public's confusion about Lunt was his appearance. A tall, imposing figure, he was described by Thoda Cocroft as "a remarkably handsome man" and as an "irresistibly sexy actor" who "radiates maleness" on the stage. That would certainly have been advantageous had Lunt aspired to be a matinee idol, but his ambitions did not lead him in that direction. He was determined to be an accomplished *actor*, in the best sense of the word: one whose personality is merged with, and often subordinated to, the personality of the character he is playing. Thus, the public didn't know quite what to make of this dashing, good-looking figure who enjoyed playing roles (such as Clarence) that called for him to be clumsy and unkempt. And how should they regard an accomplished comedian who confounded their expectations by playing in serious dramas? And why did this established star consent to play supporting roles?

At the age of thirty-one, Lunt was in no danger of being unemployed for more than a few weeks at a time, but the public recognition that was due him as one of the ablest actors in America had not yet come his way.

Fontanne's situation was not unlike her husband's. She had refused to become type-cast, expanding her range in a series of roles that demonstrated her ability to play comedy and drama, leading women and character parts. Her display of versatility was most satisfying to those who appreciated good acting, but puzzling to the public at large.

Fontanne's newly gained reputation as a beauty was certainly in her favor, but it was still another element in her blurred public image. Here was a beautiful, provocative woman with a haunting voice who was most closely associated with roles that called for gawkiness and eccentricity.

Fontanne was thirty-six years old in 1924 and an actress whose career had spanned almost twenty years, although she looked at least ten years younger. It was important that her next role should give her an opportunity to display her ample talents to full advantage.

Although they had appeared together in *Sweet Nell of Old Drury* in 1923, the Lunts had not yet become "The Lunts." They had received several offers to act together in the theatrical season just past, but—although the idea had great appeal to them—they had turned down the proposals of Lee Shubert, William Harris, Jr., Gilbert Miller and David Belasco because they disliked the plays those producers offered. Thus, neither they nor the public thought of them as an acting team. They had told Noël Coward that it was their ambition to act always with one another, but they had subsequently dismissed that goal as unrealistic. They regarded their careers as essentially separate and were looking for separate plays in which to appear. The fact that their great breakthrough, in which they emerged as two of the leading figures of the American theatre, was achieved by appearing together in the same play was thus a complete accident. It came about because the Theatre Guild had been rebuffed in its attempt to hire other actors and actresses to play the leading roles in its forthcoming production of *The Guardsman*. The Guild happened to settle on Alfred Lunt and Lynn Fontanne not because they were married to one another, but because each of them had by 1924 conclusively established an individual reputation as an outstanding performer.

Chapter Five

THE GUARDSMAN

"Those who saw them last night bowing
hand in hand, for the first time, may well
have been witnessing a moment in theatrical history. It is among the possibilities that we were seeing the first chapter
in a partnership destined to be as distinguished as that of Henry Irving and Ellen Terry."

Alexander Woollcott, 1924

1924–25

Dissatisfied with the conventional Broadway fare of melodramas and
escapist comedies, unhappy with the stagnant methods of production and acting generally given to these plays, and inspired by the examples
of such foreign organizations as the Moscow Art Theatre, a group of aspiring playwrights, actors, producers and directors in New York City
joined forces in 1915 and decided to call their organization the Washington Square Players, Inc. Their program called for the production of plays
of artistic merit—American plays, preferably—without regard to their
commercial possibilities. Furthermore, the Washington Square Players
wished to appeal to the widest possible audience by pricing their tickets at
a strikingly low level: fifty cents. They could afford to do so because their
members were, almost without exception, young, passionate in their idealism and content to devote time and energy to the group for little or no
remuneration.

But if amateurism brought the Washington Square Players into being,
it almost destroyed the organization as well. The first productions were
marred by painfully awkward acting and directing, and it must quickly
have become evident that good intentions alone would not bring about
the desired reforms in the American theatrical system. Consequently, the

Players began to pay salaries, hoping to attract more competent recruits. The salaries were low, but the $25 per week the Players offered did have the intended effect: by the middle of 1916, the performances were significantly improved, with the result that considerably more tickets—even at the new price of one dollar—were sold. The company was well on its way to establishing itself as a potent artistic force. The critics and the public were taking notice, playwrights were eager to have their work produced by the Players, and talented young performers, directors and designers were eager to join.

America's entry into World War I forced the Washington Square Players to disband in 1918, as many of their leading lights had joined the armed forces. But their accomplishments had been staggering: sixty-eight plays (most of them one-act) produced in three and a half years, and thirty-eight of them new works by American playwrights. The Washington Square Players had also given a start to many young theatre artists who would soon take their places among the finest in the country: actors such as Katharine Cornell, Glenn Hunter, Roland Young; scene designers Lee Simonson and Robert Edmond Jones; and director Philip Moeller.

When the war came to a close, Lawrence Langner, a patent attorney who had been instrumental in the founding of the Washington Square Players, approached several members of the original organization and suggested that the group be reconstituted. The others agreed, but this time the company would be different in one significant respect: the time for amateurism, they felt, was over; the new organization would be run along strictly professional lines. Enough money was raised to begin operations, the Garrick Theatre on West 35th Street was rented, and in 1919 the Theatre Guild presented its first production. The play, Jacinto Benavente's *The Bonds of Interest,* was a critical success but a popular failure, despite the presence in the cast of Helen Westley, Dudley Digges, Edna St. Vincent Millay and Rollo Peters, and the direction of Philip Moeller. Salaries, as before, were held to $25 per week, but nonetheless far more money was being paid out than was taken in at the box office. Only the financial contributions of Lawrence Langner and the banker Maurice Wertheim kept the Guild afloat and allowed it to begin preparations for a second production, St. John Ervine's *John Ferguson.*

Rarely in the history of the theatre could an opening night have been so critical to an organization's continued existence, for the treasury of the Theatre Guild amounted to all of $19.50 when *John Ferguson* was given its premiere. Fortunately, the public responded enthusiastically to Ervine's play, and it displayed its enthusiasm quickly enough so that the Guild was able to survive and prosper. One reason for its success could not have been anticipated: in August 1919, when the Actors' Equity strike occurred, *John Ferguson* was allowed to remain open because Equity regarded the Theatre Guild as an enlightened organization which did not exploit its performers. Indeed, the Theatre Guild had earlier agreed to share all profits with the casts of its productions, an arrangement that Equity looked upon with favor. So the Theatre Guild found itself in the enviable position of being almost the only game in town from the time the strike was called until it was settled on September 3. New Yorkers with a taste for theatrical entertainment had little choice but to patronize the Garrick Theatre, and they did so in sufficient numbers to permit the Theatre Guild to turn a significant profit on the production.

During the next several years, the Guild became firmly established as the leading purveyor of quality, noncommercial theatre in America. And the public, once exposed to the rapidly improving productions of fine plays that the Guild was offering, responded favorably. The Guild was succeeding as perhaps not even its founders had expected, turning "noncommercial" theatre into a modest commercial success. The clearest indication of this success can be seen in the Guild's growing list of season subscribers. From a total of 800 in 1919, the Guild saw an increase to 1,300 in its second season; by 1922–23 there were 6,000 subscribers, and that number doubled in 1923–24.

Still, as the 1924–25 season approached, the Theatre Guild found itself once again in a precarious financial position because it had undertaken to build its own theatre. The Guild raised enough money to cover the anticipated cost of $500,000, but prices escalated as the theatre was being erected on West 52nd Street, with the eventual total considerably in excess of a million dollars, forcing the organization to take out a large mortgage. The resulting annual repayments approached $100,000, creating a terrible financial burden on the Guild for many years afterward. And the treasury, at the start of the 1924–25 season, was very nearly as depleted as it had been in 1919 when *John Ferguson* opened. Only $1,000 was available to cover operating expenses. Once again the Theatre Guild was sorely in need of a successful production, one that would attract new subscribers as well as keep the old ones in the fold.

It was Theresa Helburn, the Guild's executive director, who decided that Ferenc Molnár's *The Guardsman* could provide the necessary success and that Alfred Lunt and Lynn Fontanne would be ideal for the leading roles. Both decisions were fraught with peril. Only thirteen years before, in 1911, the play had been given in New York under the title *Where Ignorance Is Bliss,* and it had been regarded as an utter failure, having run for only a week. This lightest of comedies required deft acting of the most subtle and brilliant kind, and evidently nothing of the sort had been achieved. The play was stigmatized in America as an elephantine bore— and, indeed, the original text of the play contained archaic devices that had contributed to that impression. A new translation, eliminating some of the awkwardness, was prepared by the agent who held the American rights and submitted to the Theatre Guild in 1922. The Guild was enthusiastic about this new version, yet unwilling to accept the agent's unyielding demand that the play be cast with two established stars, Lionel Atwill and Violet

Heming. The Guild had a firm policy against giving any actor star billing, believing that the star system was antithetical to the principles of an organization that prized art above commerce. The Guild thus made it clear that it was interested in producing the play, but only if given the authority to cast it as the managers saw fit. The agent was adamant, however, and for a time the project had to be shelved.

When at last the agent recognized that the Guild was not about to compromise its principles, he recommended another actor and actress. Then, however, a new problem presented itself. The actress to whom the play was submitted rejected it because she felt that the actor's role was superior to hers; and the actor who was approached to play the male lead turned down the opportunity because he believed he would be outshone by the leading actress, whose role, he felt, was the more appealing. The play was offered to other actors and actresses, but the response was always the same: each performer was convinced that the other role was the better one. At last Theresa Helburn suggested to the Theatre Guild's managers an idea that had appealed to her for some time: that Alfred Lunt and Lynn Fontanne be offered the roles. The Lunts seemed to her the ideal performers for Molnár's play. Both were already established as brilliant comedians; they were known to be more interested in the theatre as an art form than as a business, and they were, therefore, unlikely to insist on star billing; and, perhaps most importantly, the Lunts were known to be almost entirely lacking in temperament and jealousy. Surely, Helburn believed, Lunt would not be jealous of Fontanne's role or Fontanne envious of Lunt's.

When Helburn extended her offer, the Lunts eagerly accepted the chance to join the Theatre Guild and to play *The Guardsman*. As Lunt said years later, he and Fontanne admired the Guild's vision and its "sense of mission." In particular, they had great regard for Lawrence Langner's "vision" and "foresight," Theresa Helburn's acuity and the "great artistry" that Lee Simonson, another member of the Guild's Board of Directors, brought to his work as scenic designer. "The extraordinary thing about them," Fontanne said, "is that with their separate talents they made one good showman."

The Lunts' response to the Guild's offer was interesting in relation to the reactions of other actors and actresses. Lunt urged Fontanne to play the role of the Actress in *The Guardsman* because it was a wonderful role that would surely further her career; he didn't at all mind playing a role that was somewhat subordinate, he said. On the other hand, Fontanne felt strongly that Lunt must not pass up the opportunity to play the rewarding role of the Actor; she would be perfectly content to play a role that she believed would give her abilities somewhat less scope.

Financial arrangements, however, proved to be a considerable problem. For one thing, the agent who had held the rights to the play insisted that his percentage be increased by ten percent in exchange for allowing the Guild to cast Lunt and Fontanne. To that demand the Guild was forced to accede. In addition, the salaries offered the Lunts represented a considerable cut in pay for both of them. The Guild, as an art theatre, could not and did not try to compete with commercial managements in the salaries it offered to performers. This sensible policy permitted the Guild to produce worthwhile plays that were unlikely to pay substantial financial dividends, but it did present a problem to its actors. The Lunts had each been earning $600 to $700 per week in productions for commercial managements. Theresa Helburn offered them only $500, and made it clear that this was the most the Guild could possibly afford. Lunt said that he and Fontanne would be willing to make a small financial sacrifice in order to work for the Theatre Guild. Helburn hastily added, however, "Oh, I didn't mean $500 *each*. I meant $500 for the both of you." Certainly there can be no greater testimony to the Lunts' idealism than their acceptance of the Guild's offer.

While Lynn Fontanne had no reservations about accepting the salaries offered, she felt strongly about one area of financial concern. The play, originally set in Budapest in 1910, portrayed a world of elegance and glamour; the character Fontanne was to play represented the epitome of that world, a wealthy and sophisticated actress. It was important, she felt, that the costumes she wore suggest those qualities at once. Fontanne wanted to select her own costumes, which she proposed to do in Paris. Helburn agreed, but insisted that the Theatre Guild would pay no more than $50 for each dress. Fontanne argued that it would be impossible to outfit the Actress satisfactorily for that amount, and that the play would suffer as a result. But Theresa Helburn was unshakable, and the Lunts were forced to agree to what they perceived as a clearly inadequate sum of money—money that would be spent not on themselves, but on the production. This incident and the resentment it caused would fester to such an extent that it would, as much as any other issue, lead eventually to the break between the Lunts and the Theatre Guild.

It is important to remember that Fontanne's concern focused on the clothing the character would wear. As a performer who—like her husband—depended greatly upon the external circumstances of props and costumes to help her form her approach to each role, it was essential to her that the clothing worn by the character be appropriate in every detail. This was not a case of a temperamental actress who insisted on being beautifully gowned in order to satisfy her vanity. No doubt Fontanne wished to make a favorable appearance—what public figure would wish to do otherwise?—but her primary concern was the suitability of her costume to the character she was playing.

While the Lunts sailed for Paris in search of costumes and to Hungary to seek out Ferenc Molnár, Philip Moeller, who had been assigned to direct the play, set to work on a revision of the translation the Guild had purchased. Moeller cut and rearranged the text, and, when he felt it necessary, wrote additional material.

In Paris, Lunt found the costume he wanted for the role of the Guardsman. From a tailor he borrowed a Cossack's uniform (Moeller's new version had changed the Guardsman from Hungarian to Russian and the play's locale from Hungary to Vienna), sketched it carefully and later had it copied and tailored to his own specifications. The money he spent exceeded $50, but Fontanne's purchases went so far beyond the budget that the Guild, had they known how much money she was spending, would have been horrified.

Fontanne was not spending the Guild's money, however, but her own. Certain that the success of the production would depend, in large measure, on the magnificence of the Actress's wardrobe, she was confident that the Guild's Board of Directors would eventually see reason and reimburse her for her expenses.

The Lunts were advised by Noël Coward that a couturier named Captain Edward Molyneux, who maintained a studio in Paris, would be an ideal designer for the Actress's costumes. Coward told them about a cape of ermine and white feathers that would be perfect for *The Guardsman* with some slight modifications. Armed with letters of introduction from Coward and from other friends, the Lunts went to Molyneux's studio without an appointment. Molyneux at first refused to see them, but eventually relented when they sent in their letters of introduction. After they explained the reason for their visit, however, Molyneux made it clear that he had little interest in the project, although he agreed to draw a few sketches for their consideration.

The Lunts returned to the studio several days later and Molyneux's assistant showed them the sketches. They were disappointed and asked to see Molyneux again. No, they were told, "Captain Molyneux is an artist. He is very busy."

Fontanne stared coldly at the assistant. "Tell him," she said, "that Mr. Lunt and I are artists too and that we have changed our minds. . . . We will go elsewhere."*

Their next visit was to Poiret where they saw exactly what they wanted: a dress in purple velvet, banded with white crystal beads and pearls. Lunt suggested that the gown be remade in white velvet; otherwise it was perfect.

The dress and a heavily embroidered cloak cost $1,000. More money was spent on expensive imitation jewelry, and still more for five other dresses, although none of them was as expensive or as magnificent as the velvet gown.

Then the Lunts went on to Budapest in search of Molnár—a fruitless trip, for they were never able to locate him. Ironically, he had been in Paris

*They did not see Molyneux again until years later in London, when they attended a party of Noël Coward's. By that time all the world knew of the Lunts' artistry. Molyneux literally got down on his hands and knees and crawled to Fontanne, asking her forgiveness for his stupidity. She gave it and subsequently ordered many of her own clothes from him.

when they were in Budapest, and he was returning to Hungary when they were sailing home.

At last, on August 25, 1924, the Lunts returned to New York on the Hamburg-American liner *Albert Ballin*. The cost of their trip had amounted to $6,000, which constituted their entire savings. Two-thirds of that amount had been spent for costumes. So thoroughly had their capital been depleted that the Lunts were unable to pay their rent, and they were forced to borrow money from a friend—one of the few times in their lives that they ever borrowed money, for Lunt preached and practiced frugality, even if his wife did not always do so.

In desperation, the Lunts pleaded their case to Theresa Helburn once again. They understood that the Guild would not be willing to reimburse them for their entire outlay, but surely some compromise could be reached. No, said Helburn, a bargain was a bargain and the Guild fully intended to pay only $50 per costume. Still, neither Helburn nor the other members of the Board could conceal their pleasure with the Lunts' purchases. All of them agreed that the costumes were perfect and the white velvet dress was magnificent. Nevertheless, the Board refused to make any significant reimbursement, although they did begin to hedge on their original $50-per-costume budget.

Sensing an opportunity, Fontanne offered the Board a tantalizing proposition. The Theatre Guild, she quite rightly pointed out, was in need of a solid commercial success. Despite its many fine achievements of the past, it had managed to survive by paying minuscule salaries, cutting production costs to the bone and asking the managers—Langner, Helburn, Simonson, Wertheim, Moeller, and the actress Helen Westley—to work to the point of exhaustion for virtually no compensation. If *The Guardsman* were to become a genuine commercial success, Fontanne asked, would they be willing to reimburse the Lunts for the costume expenses? Intrigued, the Board asked just how Fontanne would define success. She answered—incorrectly, but with no less fervor—that the Guild had never been able to keep any of its plays running for ten weeks;* so ten weeks would serve as a good barometer of a successful production. If the play ran for ten weeks, would the Board pay the full price of the costumes? Perhaps because the Board members were in particular need of a money-making production at that moment, they agreed to the proposal.

Fontanne later said that it never occurred to her the play would not succeed. Since her arrival in the United States, her career had been marked primarily by success, and, as she said, conveniently forgetting such failed productions as *The Wooing of Eve, Someone in the House* and *Chris,* "I've never been in a failure, and I never thought of myself at all in terms of failure. . . . I got used to success quite early, and it wasn't conceit, it was just sheer habit. I had been very lucky, indeed, and didn't know it."

---

*In fact, twelve of the plays presented by the Theatre Guild between 1919 and 1924 had achieved runs of ten weeks or longer.

The plot of *The Guardsman* has to do with a worldly and successful Actor who suspects that his wife, a beautiful and equally successful Actress, is tempted to have an affair with a Guardsman—who is, in fact, an invention of the Actor (who has been sending his wife flowers, accompanying them with cards signed by the fictitious Guardsman). The Actor becomes obsessed with the notion that his wife is yearning to having an affair with the Guardsman. In order to test her fidelity, he appears to her one day as the Guardsman, dressed and made up for the occasion. He plays the role so convincingly that the Actress has no suspicion it is her own husband who is proposing to have an affair with her. Or does she? Is the Actor deceiving the Actress, or is it the Actress who is deceiving the Actor? Which of the two is the more skillful performer?

In a series of delightfully comic scenes, Molnár's play never resolves that issue. On the day after the Actress has arranged to meet the "Guardsman" in her home (believing—or apparently believing—her husband's story that he is away on a theatrical engagement), the Actor unexpectedly shows up and accuses her of infidelity. With perfect aplomb, the Actress reclines upon a sofa and denies the charges. The Actor, hidden from his wife's view, then dons his Guardsman makeup and triumphantly presents himself to her. Again, however, the Actress is equal to the challenge. She recognized him from the beginning, she assures him calmly, but decided to play along with the charade. When she tells him that she never had the slightest intention of being unfaithful to him, the Actor is understandably confused. He believed he had played the role of the Guardsman to perfection, thus bringing off a brilliant *coup de théâtre;* but the Actress now claims that it was *she* who was fooling *him*. Who has won this marital duel? Has the Actress genuinely been aware of her husband's disguise all the while, as she claimed? Was she skillfully exploiting his vanity? Or was she, in fact, taken in and ready to consummate an affair with the "Guardsman"? The question is unanswered.

In preparing for his role as the Guardsman, Lunt was troubled by the improbability of any man's being able to make his wife believe that he was someone else, regardless of the brilliance of his disguise. For that matter, it seemed unlikely that even a reasonably close acquaintance could be taken in by the use of makeup and a foreign accent. It was important to Lunt that *he* believe in the reality of the situation; otherwise, he was certain he would not be able to transmit that reality to his audience. So he determined to put the situation in the play to the test. After perfecting his accent and his makeup, Lunt dressed in a reasonable facsimile of the costume he would wear in the play and set forth to visit the grocer whose shop he patronized almost daily. Because of Lunt's avid interest in cooking, he and the grocer had had many discussions about food. Now he entered the grocery in his disguise and, speaking with the accent and the attitude of the Guardsman, carried on a lengthy conversation with the grocer, looking all the while for any sign of recognition on the man's face. But there was none.

Confident now that his disguise was indeed convincing, Lunt left the shop, ready to begin work on the production.

Rehearsals for *The Guardsman* did not run smoothly. The Theatre Guild had a well-deserved reputation for strained and tense rehearsal periods, largely due to its unique method of collaborative creation. All the members of the Board were welcome to attend rehearsals and to pass along criticism and advice to the actors and the director. This was intended to be constructive, of course, but it frequently resulted in a bewildered group of artists. And there were special runthroughs of each play, the first usually given two weeks before opening night, the second a week later, and often a third at the final dress rehearsal, that were known as "managers' rehearsals." The members of the Board attended these rehearsals equipped with pads and pencils. As the rehearsals progressed, they took copious notes. Afterward they climbed the stairs to the stage and sat around a table to discuss their criticisms with the play's director. Normally, the actors would be dismissed. In most circumstances the author of the play would be present, although in the case of *The Guardsman,* Molnár escaped this ordeal. Each Board member spoke frankly—often brutally—about his or her reactions. One might suggest replacing a performer; another might emphasize the weakness of the direction; a third might maintain that the comedy was being overplayed, while a fourth would be equally insistent that the comic values of the play were not being sufficiently projected.

With six individuals of diverse tastes and backgrounds freely expressing their opinions, it is no wonder that there were frequent disagreements, many of which ended in shouting matches. And it should be remembered that a number of the Board members were less than fully qualified to offer advice to actors, directors or playwrights. Maurice Wertheim was a banker, Lawrence Langner a patent lawyer, Lee Simonson a scenic designer—all of them vitally important to the success of the Theatre Guild, but perhaps not well versed in the matters under discussion. The impact of these sessions, which were known by the Guild's actors and directors as "the death watch," often resulted in confusing the director, who then tried to pass on the conflicting advice he had received to his apprehensive actors, which only contributed further to the tension inherent in any rehearsal process.

Furthermore, the Guild's actors were under an additional strain. They were only halfway through rehearsals when they were first asked to give "a performance" for the Board. Frequently, their lines were imperfectly learned, their characterizations only half formed, but they were being judged as if they were giving polished performances. Moreover, a negative judgment of an actor's work might result in his not being employed again by the Guild.

Sometimes an actor would eavesdrop on the Board's heated conversations. Invariably he would hear the most critical opinions expressed in the most vehement and tactless ways. One can easily understand why Theatre Guild actors dreaded these rehearsals and considered them personally and professionally demeaning.

Nor were actors the only artists who found the managers' rehearsals upsetting. Robert E. Sherwood, S. N. Behrman and Maxwell Anderson, all of whom wrote successful plays for the Theatre Guild, ultimately left the Guild for the Playwrights' Company specifically because they were exasperated by what they believed to be the unwarranted interference of the Guild's managers. Sherwood found Lee Simonson particularly objectionable. No one could fault Simonson as a scenic designer, but his personality was exceedingly abrasive. When Simonson believed he was in the right about any issue, he would argue the point vehemently and incessantly until he had driven everyone else to exhaustion. His arguments often involved personal attacks on those who held an opposing view, and he tended to shout his opinions at foghorn level.

It was especially difficult to rehearse a comedy before the Board. Its members were thoroughly familiar with the play, so they were unable to respond spontaneously to the humor, as a typical audience would. Instead, the Board members, in Theresa Helburn's words, sat "silent and apparently unresponsive, pencil in hand, flashing electric torches or cigar lighters every now and then in the darkened auditorium in order to indulge in the menace of a critical note." Laugh lines fell flat; elaborate comic bits of business were greeted with utter silence. It is no wonder that Alfred Lunt, on one occasion, stepped to the edge of the stage and shouted angrily to the six people seated in the house, "Playing light comedy for you is like feeding a soufflé to a horse!"

The director of *The Guardsman* was Philip Moeller, who cultivated a striking appearance. He affected an opera cape and was rarely seen without a long cigarette holder. Despite—or perhaps because of—his eccentricities, Moeller was well liked by most of the actors who worked for the Theatre Guild. There was an exuberance and an innocence about him that many found charming.

Actors also enjoyed Moeller's treatment of them as collaborators in the creative process. Rather than preparing meticulously in advance for each rehearsal, Moeller made it a habit to attend each session without preconceived ideas about characterization, timing, blocking or any other aspect of the process. Theresa Helburn even went so far as to say, "It would be nice if Phil would read a play before he [directed] it." But Moeller wanted to leave himself open to inspiration, and he feared that preparation of any sort might hinder the process. Rather than tell his actors what to do, Moeller solicited their opinions; he could hardly have done otherwise. His function was primarily to respond to the stimuli the actors provided, and he was confident that his responses, augmented by inspiration, would be sufficient to guide the actors to exciting and unified performances. Conscious of his own limitations, he said that he could not tell an actor what to do or to refrain from doing; however, when the actor, through trial and error, happened to hit upon a satisfactory line reading or bit of business, Moeller maintained that he would be able to recognize it. "I am like a conductor who cannot play the oboe, nor teach it," he said, "but who knows when it is played ill or well, and what its uses are."

Alfred Lunt enjoyed the freedom of the trial-and-error method and he also enjoyed working with Moeller in another respect, finding that the director "had—in doing comedy—a great and valuable quality. He could sit out front and he would laugh a great deal. Well, if you are playing a comedy, and the director sits out front and goes into fits, you immediately respond in your playing. It wasn't a trick. He meant it." On the other hand, Lunt and Fontanne went through some trying times with Moeller while working on *The Guardsman,* and there were many "terrible hours." For example, Lunt had decided to make the character of the Guardsman as ugly as possible, to contrast him with the debonair Actor. He wanted the Guardsman to have a "mysteriously ugly sex quality," he said. One aspect of this quality would be projected, Lunt felt, by the black Cossack uniform he had selected in Paris. But Moeller objected. "You can't play comedy in black," he insisted. This remark struck Lynn Fontanne as both pompous and ignorant, and she countered angrily, "Listen, Mr. Moeller, you can play comedy in a burlap bag inside a piano with the cover down, if the lines are funny and the audience can hear them!" Moeller backed down and Lunt wore his black uniform.

Rehearsals were further complicated by the director's limited view of his function. Moeller's greatest artistic passion was for music rather than theatre. Consequently, he tended to think of directing a play in terms of counterpoint and harmony. This approach was often useful, but a director also needs to maintain a good rapport with his actors and take care not to damage their self-confidence. At these tasks Moeller was frequently unsuccessful. He tended to be tactless and temperamental, and, in S. N. Behrman's words, he often "blurted out what was on his mind without thinking." Thus, Behrman noted, rehearsals occasionally degenerated into pitched battles between actor and director. Since Moeller seldom saw plays that he did not direct, he was also deficient in his knowledge of theatrical technique. Beyond that, he kept largely to himself and had little interchange with others.

One of the most difficult challenges the Lunts faced during rehearsals was to define the most appropriate acting style for the play. In the original production in Hungary, the actor playing the Actor/Guardsman had shifted instantaneously from one character to the other, playing the Guardsman for the benefit of the Actress, then turning to wink at the audience in the role of the Actor, then swiftly reassuming the Actor's role as he turned back to the Actress. Lunt determined early on that this method would not do, for the believability of the play depended upon the Actor's ability to convince his wife that he was not the Actor but the Guardsman.

As an actress, his wife would be the first to discover any false note in his portrayal, and the game would be up. In addition, no actor—and certainly not the Actor—would slip in and out of the role he was playing; an actor is trained to submerge his personality in the personality of the character he is assuming, and only a rank amateur would break character at one moment and return to it the next. Such a convention might be appropriate for farce, Lunt believed, but hardly for the urbane comedy of *The Guardsman*.

Still, the audience must never lose sight of the fact that the Guardsman is a fictional character behind whom stands the Actor. When the Actress responds, either flirtatiously or with reserve, to the Guardsman's advances, the audience must know that her husband, the Actor, disapproves of the flirtation and triumphs at her protestations of virtue—even while the Guardsman is conveying the opposite responses. How much more difficult a task this is for any actor than the farcical method by which the Actor overtly takes the audience into his confidence. Lunt's solution to this acting problem bespoke his thorough mastery of the comic form.

Fontanne met the equally difficult challenge of convincing the Actor/Guardsman that she believes unequivocally in whatever character he is assuming at the moment, while simultaneously conveying to the audience an ambiguous attitude. Is she skeptical? Is she genuinely taken in? Is she merely playing the Actor's game? It is important to the comedy that the audience *not* be able to answer these questions.

At last, as the play is about to end, the Actor reveals that he and the Guardsman are one. Theresa Helburn described how Fontanne played that moment:

> . . . the Actress is lying prone on the couch reading a book. There is no sudden gesture. Very slowly the book is lowered. The actress looks back and up at the figure towering above her, and her lips gradually curve in a smile. It may be the moment of recognition for her, it may be she has recognized him a few minutes before, it may be she has known him all along. Every member of the audience is free to answer the question. The sophisticated will take it one way, the romantic another and this, I believe, is Molnár's intention. No matter what he himself thinks on this subject—and he doubtless has a definite if unadmitted point of view—he wants his audience to form their own opinion.

It was during the rehearsals of *The Guardsman* that the Lunts first began to experiment with a technique for which they would later become famous: overlapping one another's lines. In 1961, Lunt recalled how he and Fontanne went about it:

> We would speak to each other as people do in real life. I would, for instance, start a speech, and in the middle, on our own cue,

which we would agree on in advance, Lynn would cut in and start talking. I would continue on a bit, you see. You can't do it in Shakespeare, of course. But in drawing-room comedies, in realistic plays, it is most effective. . . . [We] overlapped . . . in the middle of a sentence. . . . To do that on the stage, you see, you have to work it very, very carefully, because you overlap lines. So that once I say the line, "Come into the next room and I will get ready," your cue really is "the next room," and you say, "All right," and I continue and say, "and I will get ready," underneath, as it were. Of course, I must lower my voice so that she is still heard.

On another occasion Fontanne explained the technique more fully. "Very often," she said, "Alfred has come at me with a certain tone, and I've gone on half a tone higher, unconsciously. Nobody told me to, and I don't know why I did, but instinctively, like boxing, I avoided his tone and I knew I could be heard." The success of the method depended on both actors having a dependable musical ear, on their willingness to rehearse the effect endlessly, and upon mutual trust. The effect, once it was perfected, was stunning. "We could talk at the same time," Fontanne said, "and you would [still] be able to hear our words. We wouldn't jam each other." Moreover, the technique helped to illuminate the characters of the Actor and the Actress in *The Guardsman,* demonstrating to the audience that each knew so clearly what the other was about to say that there was no need to wait for the other to say it.

Philip Moeller and the other members of the Theatre Guild were skeptical. "They thought it couldn't be done," Lunt said. "They said you will never do it. And when we first played *Caprice* in London [in 1929], they were outraged because we talked together. Really outraged, the press was. But it was a great success. . . . It just happened because we knew each other so well and trusted each other."

Other actors have tried to adopt the overlapping technique, but few have been successful. "It's very difficult to do," Fontanne noted. "Very few have been able to do it. Sydney Greenstreet could, [Richard] Whorf couldn't. It drove him nuts. He couldn't shoot the words in quick, or use a lower tone."

Mastery of the technique did not come easily to the Lunts. When rehearsal was over, they continued to work on it at home for hours on end. Had they not been married to one another and able to rehearse at all hours of the day and night, perhaps the technique would never have been perfected. But the Lunts were never daunted by the necessity to work intensely and continually at their craft. Indeed, if there was one quality that separated them from other performers, it was their willingness to spend hour after hour upon what might seem to an outsider a minor detail. But when each detail had been polished to perfection and combined with every other detail, the mosaic that was formed represented acting at its most brilliant.

Having developed the overlapping technique for *The Guardsman,* the Lunts continued to refine it and use it again and again. Audiences came to anticipate the dovetailing of speeches that was the Lunts' specialty. But in 1924 the possibility that overlapping could be made to work seemed most unlikely to everyone except Lunt and Fontanne.

When the members of the Board attended the final "managers' rehearsal," only a few days before *The Guardsman* was to open, they were appalled at Lunt's characterization. There was no question that the Guardsman was ugly, they said, but the sexual quality for which Lunt had been striving was entirely missing; the character was simply too repellent to attract any woman. Moreover, they felt that the entire production was lamentable: it lacked wit, invention, comic flair—it was, in short, a disaster. Lunt, who was present to hear these comments, was devastated. The Board members had, in the most brutal terms, destroyed his confidence.

Any actor's ego is fragile at the best of times. Unlike a painter, for example, who can accept criticism of his painting with some objectivity because it clearly differs from criticism of the painter himself, the actor cannot easily separate his work—his characterization—from himself. The actor is told that he has an imperfect understanding of the character, that his performance is dull or overblown, that his articulation is muddy or that his personality is unappealing. The criticism may be aimed at the actor's work, but he is likely to take criticism personally unless it is offered in the most tactful and sensitive ways. To attack an actor's work tactlessly and insensitively is cruel; to attack his work in those terms shortly before the opening of his play is not only doubly cruel, it is also stupid. An actor cannot function without self-confidence. To have to appear before hundreds of people without that confidence can only be a humiliating ordeal.

For Alfred Lunt, lack of self-confidence was a lifelong problem. It may seem unlikely that a man often described as the world's greatest actor would be woefully uncertain of his own abilities, but that was unquestionably the case. Hardly a production was mounted without Lunt's begging the director, at some point in the rehearsal process, to replace him with another actor because he was, in his own view, unable to fulfill the demands of the role. Lunt was constantly tormented by the thought that he was letting down the other members of the cast. He said in 1932, "Tell me I'm rotten and I'll always believe you. Maybe I shouldn't have been an actor. Maybe that is why I'm always scared."

And scared he always was. No novice in his senior-class play has suffered from stage fright more acutely than did Alfred Lunt. Other actors became used to seeing him pace back and forth in anguish behind the scenes while he was waiting for his entrance. Some of them were convinced that the act of appearing before an audience was a kind of agony for him that made him unable to enjoy his own abilities. When in the middle of a scene he became aware of any noise in the audience—a cough, a whisper, the rustle of a dress—he would be convinced that the noise had been caused by the audience's dissatisfaction with his performance, and that belief led to many a sleepless night. Lunt's friends sometimes hesitated to congratulate him after a particularly brilliant performance because they knew what his reaction would be: "I was awful, and I can't think what to do about it. I wish you'd been here last night or the night before, but tonight I'm afraid I let everyone down." And this was no pose, no coy attempt to extract further praise. It was, perhaps, an inevitable consequence of his unrelenting perfectionism. Even in 1968, when he had been retired from the stage for several years, he told an interviewer, "When I see myself on television, I am revolted! I wonder how on earth I ever made a success in the theatre."

So lacking was Lunt in self-confidence that he managed to misinterpret words of praise and turn them, in his mind, to derisive criticism. Lynn Fontanne wrote a letter to her friend Alexander Woollcott in 1938, shortly after the Lunts opened one of their greatest successes, *Amphitryon 38,* in London. She told Woollcott that the audience had been wild with enthusiasm: "They tore up their seats and shouted from all sides of the house, 'Bravo.' . . . Alfred stepped down to make a speech, and you remember the last time when they called out 'Louder' and he thought they said 'Lousy'? Well, true to form, this time he made a speech. There were cries from all over the house, 'Welcome, welcome.' The curtain descended. Alfred turned a haggard face to me and said, 'What was that they were calling out? 'Rotten, rotten?'"

Fortunately for both of them, Fontanne maintained a much-needed sense of humor in the face of Lunt's moments of self-doubt. If she couldn't always cheer him out of his anguish, she could at least prevent herself from yielding to it. She, too, had moments of professional insecurity, of course, but they rarely approached crisis proportions, as Lunt's did. And at times her wit and common sense did help him to put his own agony in perspective. Noël Coward, in his autobiography *Present Indicative,* told of the time he saw Lunt play in *Outward Bound:*

> It was the first time I had ever seen him on the stage, and when I visited him in his dressing-room afterwards he went through all his hoops. I know those hoops so well now, that I can hear the paper crackling in anticipation before he dives through the first one; but then it was a surprise to me, rather a painful surprise. I had been deeply moved by his performance and was still feeling wrought up. I explained this to him from my heart, but no gleam of pleasure came into his rolling tragic eyes. He mowed down my praise with bitter self-recrimination. I had, he said, been privileged to see him give far and away the worst performance of his career. He had over-played, over-emotionalised, and used every ham trick that had ever been invented. Nothing I said

could convince him to the contrary. At supper afterwards I observed that Lynn was unmoved by his despair. She said: "Never mind, darling, you gave a lovely performance last Thursday matinee," and went on with her scrambled eggs.

Even Fontanne, however, was unable to apply a humorous touch when the Theatre Guild's Board savaged the Lunts' performances in the managers' rehearsal of *The Guardsman*. Perhaps the Board members were not aware of the fragile nature of Lunt's ego. But their assessment of the rehearsal they had witnessed was so brutal that it thoroughly humiliated Alfred Lunt, who got no sleep that night. He cried—"for the first and only time in my life," he said—and Fontanne did her best to comfort him. They talked together all night long, but he felt no better in the morning.

In desperation, the Lunts called their friend Howard Lindsay and asked him to attend the final dress rehearsal. They were deeply unhappy about their performances, they told him, and could not rely upon anyone in the Guild to help them. Lindsay went to the Garrick Theatre the next afternoon and was surprised to see that the Lunts' performances were flawless. It was clear to him, however, that the element of fun—so obviously necessary in comedy—was missing. The apprehension that the Lunts felt as a result of the Board's assessment of the production was evident. Despite the technical perfection of their performances, the Lunts were unwittingly transmitting their insecurity across the footlights. Lindsay went backstage to find his friends resembling nothing so much as beaten dogs pathetically eager to be patted on the head. Choosing his words carefully, Lindsay congratulated them on their polished technique, their expert timing, their superb characterizations. But, he said, the element of enjoyment was missing, and that was crucial to the play's success. Somehow, he said, it was necessary for the Lunts to enjoy themselves more, to feel and communicate a sense of having fun.

Fontanne could hardly contain herself. Lindsay later quoted her as saying: "Having fun! Do you think we could have fun under these conditions? Do you know what goes on around here? Do you know what they're doing to us? Do you know how they treat—" Suddenly she stopped, turned to her forlorn husband and said, "Alfred, he's right." It became clear to them that the only way to proceed was to ignore the comments of the Board members and to put their faith in their own instincts—which is precisely what they did.

But their ordeal was not over yet. Never having performed in a Theatre Guild production, the Lunts were unprepared for the boorishness of the opening-night audience. Somehow, the Theatre Guild's opening nights always seemed to attract an audience that was less interested in seeing a play than in being seen themselves. It was not unusual for a steady hum of conversation to be heard from the audience during those dreaded first nights. Moreover, the patrons could not be bothered to stay in their seats during curtain calls. As soon as the curtain came down, the Guild's subscribers began scurrying to the nearest exits. For Lunt and Fontanne, as well as for the rest of the cast, this was the final indignity.

At least the wretched evening was over. The Lunts returned to their apartment, thoroughly disheartened but happy in the belief *The Guardsman* would close within a week and they would be able to leave the Theatre Guild. They resolved not even to wait up for the reviews. Several hours later the telephone rang. The caller was Alexander Woollcott, then the drama critic for the New York *Sun*. Woollcott was later to become one of the Lunts' closest friends, but at this time they were barely acquainted. He told them how much he had enjoyed their performances and asked if they had read the reviews in the morning newspapers, which were just then hitting the streets. No, the Lunts replied, they had decided to spare themselves that ordeal. Woollcott wondered what they could be talking about. The critics, he told them, were almost uniformly enthusiastic about the play, the production and their performances.

Astonished, the Lunts ventured forth to confirm the accuracy of Woollcott's report. Percy Hammond of the *Tribune* said the "performance is perfect, and I think the acting of Miss Fontanne and Mr. Lunt and the stage direction of Mr. Moeller is perhaps superior to the play itself." Heywood Broun, in the *World*, said that the Lunts "both give brilliant performances," and the New York *Post*'s John Anderson rhapsodized: "Few performances within recent memory have had the easy flow of this one. It is timed with precision and executed with unfailing adroitness. Mr. Lunt played the desperate actor with comprehension and an elaborate shading of mood, which was as sure in its comedy as it was in its deeper significance. Miss Fontanne managed the quiet devilishness of the actress-wife with finely effective economy, giving to the merest sketch the color and reality of a full portrait." Other than Stark Young's lukewarm notice in the *Times,* the critics were captivated by the production.

It was left to Alexander Woollcott, however, to offer not only an enthusiastic review, but a remarkable prophecy. His column in the New York *Sun* reported that "Miss Fontanne played last evening with deep humor, now and again achieving a fleeting instant of such delicacy and shining rightness that the lover of good acting glowed to the point of incandescence. . . . Mr. Lunt was admirable, playing with infinite zest. . . .

". . . those who saw them last night bowing hand in hand, for the first time, may well have been witnessing a moment in theatrical history. It is among the possibilities that we were seeing the first chapter in a partnership destined to be as distinguished as that of Henry Irving and Ellen Terry."

Woollcott's statement is extraordinary not only for its insight but because it harks back to the relationship between Lynn Fontanne and her great teacher, Ellen Terry. Moreover, it may, in some subtle way of which Fontanne herself was not fully aware, have reconfirmed for her the impor-

tance of continuing to perform with her husband on a regular basis. Ellen
Terry had reached the pinnacle of her success by combining her talents
with those of Sir Henry Irving. Together they had won the admiration of
millions, and had ultimately been regarded as the most brilliant acting
team in theatrical history. The lessons in acting that Terry had given Fontanne had proved to be invaluable, and it is just possible that Woollcott's
review triggered in Fontanne's mind the notion that her on-stage partnership with Lunt might be as advantageous to the two of them as the Irving-
Terry partnership had been to the earlier pair.

The critics had responded favorably to Lunt's and Fontanne's inter-
playing. In many ways, their joint reviews were more uniformly enthusiastic than those either had received as an individual in earlier productions. Perhaps the talent of each brought out the best in the other.

After *The Guardsman* opened on October 13, 1924, there were seldom any empty seats at the Garrick Theatre. To the astonishment and delight of the Guild's Board of Directors, the production was an unqualified
hit. The Lunts' triumph was shared by Helen Westley, who played
"Mama," and Dudley Digges, the fine Irish performer who was one of the
Theatre Guild's leading lights, as the Actor's friend. To all of them, and to
Philip Moeller's direction and Jo Mielziner's brilliant settings, goes the
credit for turning *The Guardsman* into one of the most popular productions the Theatre Guild ever presented.

The Lunts were characteristically determined not to hog the spotlight,
and—in a decision that was to become a lifelong practice—they elected not
to take any curtain calls by themselves, but to share their calls with the rest
of the cast. In its own small way, this was a revolutionary act. The Lunts
also defied convention in another matter regarding curtain calls taken for
The Guardsman. At that time, it was traditional for actors to come before
the curtain and take calls at the end of each act. But the Lunts believed the
practice disrupted the illusion and the continuity of the play, and they refused to take any calls until the final curtain descended.

On November 22, *The Guardsman* was moved uptown to the Booth
Theatre so that *They Knew What They Wanted,* the Guild's next subscription production, could play at the Garrick. In all, *The Guardsman* ran for
248 performances in New York—and the Guild was compelled to repay
the Lunts the money they had spent on costumes and jewelry. It must have
been happy to do so, for the run far exceeded Lynn Fontanne's prediction,
which had once seemed so extravagant.

In late 1927 the Theatre Guild made still more money from *The
Guardsman*—and helped to spread the Lunts' fame in the process—when
it sent a company on tour with a repertory of four plays, each of them
featuring Lunt and Fontanne. At the Studebaker Theatre in Chicago, *Pygmalion* ran for two weeks, followed by *The Guardsman* for two. *The Second*

Man then played for two, and the engagement concluded with ten days of *The Doctor's Dilemma*. Again in 1928, the Lunts toured in *The Guardsman* for the Theatre Guild.*

Thanks to *The Guardsman,* the Lunts attained stardom in the eyes of the public. From that time on, a large and eager audience awaited their appearance in any play they chose to perform. The benefit to the Theatre Guild was incalculable because the Lunts gave the organization its only surefire box-office attractions. Still, the Guild maintained its policy against giving actors star billing, and the Lunts were perfectly happy with that arrangement. To the end of their careers, they believed that the written play was the most important element in the success of any production and that the playwright deserved to be the focal point of public attention. At no time did the Lunts insist on receiving the deferential treatment often accorded to stars, nor did they ever display "star temperament." When either of them did indulge in a fit of temper—and there were many occasions on which they did—it was caused by their own failure or the failure of others with whom they were working to measure up to the standards of perfection they had set for themselves and their companies. But the notion that they were "stars," and that this designation somehow separated them from the rest of the human race, would never have occurred to either one.

---

*Throughout the Lunts' long and illustrious careers, their names became associated with many fine plays, but none more so than *The Guardsman*. Clearly, this association was relished as much by the Lunts as it was by the public. On numerous occasions they flirted with the possibility of reviving the play. In 1938 the Theatre Guild went so far as to hire Richard Whorf to design sets for the production. In 1943, when they were in London appearing in *There Shall Be No Night,* they intended to add *The Guardsman* to their repertory. A year after that, they wrote to Richard Whorf, "We shall do *The Guardsman* after the tour [of *There Shall Be No Night*] if all goes well." And in 1946, Lunt and Fontanne told the New York *Times* that they were intending to stage a revival of *The Guardsman* early in the next Broadway season, to be played in repertory with *A Month in the Country* and *Reunion in Vienna*. But none of these productions ever came about, and except for their film in 1931 (see Chapter 7) and a radio broadcast on September 30, 1945, the Lunts never revived *The Guardsman*.

Chapter Six

ART THEATRE—OR
SWEATSHOP?

To have acted for the Theatre Guild "was the cruelest, most insulting procedure. [Actors], all of them, came away with inferiority complexes for the rest of their lives. And we played for them practically for nothing. Why did we play? I'll tell you why. Because for one thing the Guild changed the sound and the shape of the whole English-speaking theatre."
Alfred Lunt

1925–26

The Lunts' triumph in *The Guardsman* made it a foregone conclusion that the Theatre Guild would make every attempt to retain their exclusive services for future seasons. The Guild offered to raise each of their salaries in 1925–26 to $300 per week when the Lunts were playing in the Guild Theatre and $350 a week if they were performing in a Guild production in any other theatre. In addition, the contract called for the Lunts to receive five percent of the gross receipts if the weekly box-office take exceeded a certain amount. The offer was still far less than the Lunts could have received if they had chosen to work for commercial managements, but it was considerably more than many other Guild actors were being paid. Some who had already achieved prominence received as little as $75 per week.

Actors under contract to the Guild understood that they would play sizable roles in some productions and minor roles in others. The arrangement served as both a protection for the Guild, guaranteeing that even small roles would be well performed, and for the actors, assuring that they would not become physically and emotionally exhausted by being assigned leading roles in every production. But the managers of the Guild regarded the Lunts differently. Here were two performers who created theatrical magic together. It would have been pointless, the Guild's directors felt, to waste such talent in insignificant roles. Among the productions chosen for the 1925–26 season were *Arms and the Man, Goat Song* and *At Mrs. Beam's,* all of them designed to exhibit Lunt and Fontanne in significant roles. And in the seasons that followed, the Lunts were called upon to perform leading roles in even more productions. In 1927–28, for example, Lunt played leads in three plays that opened in New York and in three touring productions for the Guild. In that same year Fontanne played opposite her husband in all the touring productions and acted leading roles in two plays in New York, one of which was the excruciatingly long *Strange Interlude,* a psychological drama in nine acts by Eugene O'Neill.

But if the Lunts' energies were severely tested by their demanding schedules, it was not entirely the fault of the Theatre Guild. The Lunts added to their own workload when Alfred agreed to make two more films in 1925 and Lynn accepted a role in another. Most of the filming could be done during the summer, they reasoned, before *Arms and the Man* rehearsals were scheduled to begin.

Thus, both of them were involved in motion-picture projects that summer. While *The Guardsman* was concluding its New York run, Lunt played the leading man in D. W. Griffith's *Sally of the Sawdust.* Griffith was "not at his best" during the filming, Lunt said. "He seemed sometimes bewildered and sometimes indifferent." One of Lunt's costars was W. C. Fields, who improvised inane and "excruciatingly funny" dialogue (according to Lunt) while the silent film was being shot. Fields's performance was far and away the most interesting aspect of an otherwise pedestrian film, although Mordaunt Hall, reviewing it for the New York *Times,* had words of praise for Lunt.

While *Sally of the Sawdust* was being filmed, Fontanne began work on *The Man Who Found Himself.* And Lunt wasted no time in signing a contract to play opposite Bebe Daniels in *Lovers in Quarantine.* Fontanne's film proved to be a complete dud. Hall's review dismissed the screenplay, the direction and—with two exceptions—the acting as equally incompetent. The two singled out as giving "acceptable" performances were Frank Morgan and Lynn Fontanne.

Lovers in Quarantine received a significantly better notice from the *Times*'s critic, who found it an "amusing feature . . . with a thoroughly capable cast," including Lunt, who was "quite at home" in his role as a spurned lover. But Hall's highest praise went to Bebe Daniels and Ivan Simpson. *Lovers in Quarantine,* the last silent film either of the Lunts ever made, was probably also the best.

At the Theatre Guild, meanwhile, the managers had opened their new theatre, on which so much money had been spent, in April 1925. The

Guild Theatre was an impressive structure equipped with an enormous stage, ample seating capacity, and magnificent tapestries in the auditorium. Alexander Woollcott, present at the opening of the theatre, was concerned that *too* much money and effort might have been invested in matters unconnected with theatrical production. Looking skeptically at the tapestries, he admonished the Guild's manager: "The Gobelins'll get you if you don't watch out."

Indeed, the premiere production, *Caesar and Cleopatra,* was not a success, and once again the Guild faced the necessity of mounting a commercial success in order to salvage its losses and pay the mortgage on the new theatre. Where better to turn than to the Lunts, who had proved their appeal in *The Guardsman* and upon whom the Guild was counting in *Arms and the Man?*

Philip Moeller again served as the Lunts' director and the production was again subject to the blunt criticisms of the Board members, though with much less friction during these rehearsals than during *The Guardsman.*

Lunt's primary concerns in developing his characterization were to convey a sense of utter weariness on his first entrance (as Bernard Shaw's script requires him to do) while simultaneously winning the audience's sympathy for his character, Captain Bluntschli, and interesting them in Bluntschli's predicament. Bluntschli, an unromantic Swiss mercenary fighting in Bulgaria, has run away from his regiment in the Serbian army in order to save his life. He climbs the balcony of the first house he sees and enters the bedchamber of a shocked Bulgarian lady, Raina Petkoff. Thoroughly exhausted and desperately hungry, Bluntschli avoids capture by threatening Raina with a fate she believes is literally worse than death: he will allow his captors to infer that she invited him into her room, a most unladylike act for a proper Bulgarian in 1885.

To win the audience's sympathy for this antihero was by no means a simple problem. The character was shockingly unromantic in his attitudes toward war and thoroughly lacking in chivalry. Lunt believed the audience would sympathize with his plight, however, if he could convincingly convey Bluntschli's fatigue. But that in itself was a difficult task. He found it "very difficult, really, to be so exhausted . . . night after night. I mean to play it really true. It's awfully hard to summon things to make them true so many times a week." He felt, as he so often did, that to counterfeit exhaustion would have been unconvincing; that he had somehow to find a method of *becoming* exhausted (without wearing himself out for the rest of the performance) in order to play the scene genuinely and believably. He solved that problem by inserting thin slices of lead into the soles of his light leather boots. "Well, when these were laced up, I want to tell you you can't be anything but tired if you're walking with lead in these boots," said Lunt. "And when I fell on the bed I always managed to have my feet hanging over [the edge], and you know they were dead; they were really dead."

He took special pride in the fact that no one but he knew his boots were weighted. Still, everyone in the theatre received an overwhelming impression of utter fatigue, which, as Lunt had hoped, won the audience's sympathy for Bluntschli, a sympathy that was maintained throughout the play.

Lunt also took special care in the preparation of his costume, hanging it on a clothesline outside his apartment for several weeks, then spattering it with mud until it had just the disreputable look he wanted.

Fontanne was just a bit jealous of Lunt's role. The clever and supremely rational Bluntschli could not be anything but a sympathetic character, she felt, while her role—the giddily romantic Raina—was much more hazardous because the audience could easily dismiss her as a simpleton unworthy of Bluntschli's interest. This was the first of several occasions in the 1920s when Fontanne believed Alfred's role superior to hers. A year and a half later, she played a minor role in *The Second Man* while Lunt was acting the lead, and again thought he had been given the more gratifying opportunity. Eventually she told him so, and they were careful thereafter to appear only in plays that gave them roles of equal size and strength.

Opening night of *Arms and the Man* was an ordeal, especially for Fontanne. Unlike most New York openings, the Guild's first nights were precisely that: the very first performance to be seen by an audience. Other managements generally opened their plays out of town, giving performers the benefit of facing less demanding audiences and critics before opening on Broadway. But the Guild could not afford this luxury, with the result that their opening nights were particularly nerve-racking experiences. Fontanne's nerves, normally as steady as one could hope, gave way under the strain, and, as she said, she "dried up flat." It was the first—and almost the last—occasion on which she totally forgot her lines and was unable to think of a thing to say or do. Utterly helpless before an audience of more than a thousand people, she could only wait on stage for help from the prompter in the wings. Seconds later, however, she heard the prompter's voice, recovered her composure and continued the performance. Unfortunately, everyone in the audience heard the prompter's voice as well, and many of the critics commented upon it in their reviews.

Woollcott's notice was especially critical of Fontanne's lapse. Early in the performance, he said, "she seemed to be suffering a kind of nervous paralysis that made her inarticulate and a little laborious and which left the whole first act curiously deadened." However, "In the final act it was a beautiful performance," he added, "glowing with vitality, immensely skillful and at times richly comic."

Gilbert W. Gabriel, writing in the *Sun,* also referred to the lapse of memory, but other reviewers were less distracted by it. Percy Hammond in the *Tribune* called her portrayal "lovely and shrewd," and mentioned that she had endowed her role "with all of her dependable fascinations."

Lunt's performance, unmarked by apparent nervousness, was uniformly praised. Woollcott's comments are of particular interest:

Lynn Fontanne (standing, left) and her family

Lynn at the age of twelve

Alfred Lunt, age four

...and age ten

Alfred as he appeared in a school play

An advertisement for one of Alfred's early successes

Young Lunt "playing older"
at the Castle Square Theatre

Lynn Fontanne at about twenty-five

Lynn and Alfred
mugging for their
wedding photo,
taken at Coney Island

Lunt practicing the saxophone for his role in *Clarence*
and as he appeared in *Ned McCobb's Daughter*

Lunt and Fontanne in a pensive pose at Genesee Depot with two of their dogs

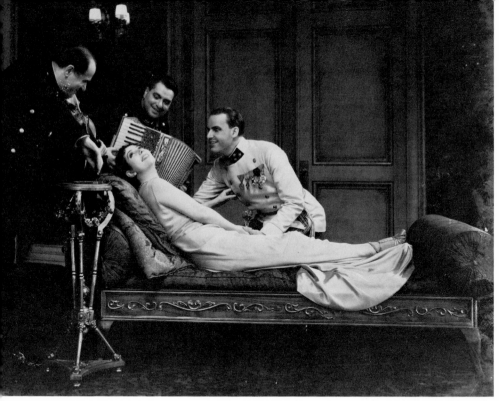

Reunion in Vienna, 1931

The Lunts on film in *The Guardsman,* 1931

The Lunts with their friend Noël Coward at Genesee Depot

in *Design for Living*, 1933

after the Tony Award presentations in 1970

Lunt in *Idiot's Delight* with Les Blondes

Flawless is surely no more than the just adjectival due to the performance given by Alfred Lunt. . . .

Nothing could be much more suave and engaging than Lunt's adroit handling of the light comedy which is the Captain's portion after the first act; nothing much more vivid and believable and fine than the scene of exhaustion which marks the Captain's advent into the play.

It is the kind of fatigue that possesses a man utterly, when the muscles of his face and eyelids give up their functions like an old and discouraged elastic, when his skull somehow becomes detached from his spinal column and finally seems to be someone else's skull. I never saw any player so completely express exhaustion. Come to think of it, I never saw any player express anything more completely.

The production of *Arms and the Man* improved as the run progressed. Indeed, the *Times* critic returned to see a performance two weeks later and said how much better it was than the one he had seen on opening night. *The Guardsman,* too, had become a more polished, more brilliant production the longer it ran. A clear pattern was emerging: often the Lunts would not be at their best on opening nights, when nerves and a hurried rehearsal period took their toll, but each succeeding performance would exhibit an improvement over the previous one. A theatregoer need have no fear that he would see a stale, mechanical performance in the sixth month of the run. In fact, he would be likely to see a performance whose quality far exceeded any given during the play's first week.

Arms and the Man, which was eventually moved to the Garrick so that the next subscription play could open at the Guild Theatre, ran for 180 performances in all, and confirmed the Lunts' position as outstanding comic performers.

For their next venture, however, the Guild chose Franz Werfel's enigmatic and symbolic folk-tragedy *Goat Song,* which opened at the Guild Theatre on January 25, 1926, while the run of *Arms and the Man* continued at the Garrick. *Goat Song*'s strength was its emotional power and sweep; its weakness was its obscurity. The play wove together political and sexual themes in an intriguing but (many felt) a bewildering way. So concerned was the Guild that its audiences would be hopelessly confused by the nature of the play that it printed an explanation of its intentions in the program: ". . . there are mystical undercurrents, hidden profundities, vague and devastating associations implied in *Goat Song* which will elude the spectator as they are unfolded upon the stage, but which, if his heart is open to the author's message, will return to trouble his memories and prick his thought."

Of the six members of the Guild's Board of Directors, only Theresa Helburn believed that Lunt and Fontanne were capable of undertaking roles that represented such radical departures from the sophisticated characters they had played in *The Guardsman* and *Arms and the Man*. Indeed, *Goat Song* had gone unproduced for several years because the Board members believed that many of the roles were virtually unplayable. Helburn proposed the Lunts for two of the most difficult, arguing that it would be wasteful to limit them to high comedy when she believed that their range was considerably greater. Somewhat grudgingly, the other Board members went along.

Lunt was assigned the role of Juvan, a revolutionary student, and Fontanne played Stanja, a young woman engaged to be married to the brother of a peculiar and terrifying creature who is half-man, half-goat. In the course of the play, Stanja's fiancé kills himself, Juvan is executed after leading an unsuccessful uprising and Stanja is made pregnant by the creature before he dies.

Goat Song was so different from any play in which the Lunts had appeared that, had they been less adventurous, they might have wished to turn it down. But the work they were doing with the Guild—acting in plays by the finest dramatists of the twentieth century, stretching their abilities by meeting the challenges of plays as diverse as *Arms and the Man* and *Goat Song*—conformed exactly to their ambitions. Both tended to view the theatre in idealistic terms, valuing its ability to uplift and inspire as well as to amuse. To the Lunts, as to the Theatre Guild, the significance of the theatrical event was cultural, social and esthetic. If a play that met the highest standards also attracted large audiences, so much the better, but the greatest importance lay in the work itself.

On the other hand, the Lunts would have had little sympathy for a theatre which was so obscure that it alienated its audience. But the Theatre Guild did not produce plays like *Goat Song* in order to antagonize its patrons. Instead, it was motivated by a desire to win the public over to an appreciation of drama that was vivid, striking and original. And the Lunts believed profoundly in that desire.

The production of *Goat Song* was expensive, requiring a massive cast, numerous settings and costumes. The Theatre Guild was following its credo to the letter, lovingly producing a determinedly noncommercial play. An impressive production team, including director Jacob Ben-Ami, designer Lee Simonson and a corps of actors which included Blanche Yurka, Albert Bruning, Helen Westley and Edward G. Robinson in addition to Lunt and Fontanne, attempted to infuse the play with pulsating vitality.

Blanche Yurka found the Lunts, who approached the rehearsals of the play with vigor and passion, "wonderful to work with. . . . Their fresh enthusiasm about their work is infectious," Yurka said, "their standards inspiring."

In commercial terms, *Goat Song* was not successful. The production ran fewer than 60 performances and the Guild took a considerable financial loss. Audiences were sharply divided on the merits of the play. Some found it moving and beautiful, others rejected it as bewildering, even disgusting. Laurette Taylor was so baffled by it that she asked the Lunts, "Do you have to do plays like this? Is it in your contract?" Some of the patrons were so upset, either by the play's social content (some audience members misinterpreted it as Communist propaganda) or by its frank sexual nature, that they canceled their Theatre Guild subscriptions. Most of the critics tended to praise the production but dismiss the play as confusing. Brooks Atkinson called *Goat Song* "ponderous and unwieldy" in the *Times,* although he conceded that there were "moments of great power" and that the ensemble had given an "excellent exhibition of acting." The *Tribune*'s critic said, "a more thoroughly dazed audience we have seldom seen. The paramount question between the acts was 'What is it all about?'"

Since the Lunts went directly from *Arms and the Man* into *Goat Song,* and played leading roles in both productions, they were becoming understandably tired. Nor were they given an opportunity to catch their breath in *At Mrs. Beam's,* in which they played leading parts opposite the British actress Jean Cadell, who was imported specifically to repeat the role she had originated in London where C. K. Munro's comedy had been given successfully three years before. Fontanne was cast as a voluptuous Brazilian temptress, Lunt as her lover, a glib British thief. In one scene the play called for the Lunts to engage in a battle of the sexes. But, unlike *The Guardsman* and *Arms and the Man,* in which the battles were fought with wit and innuendo, *At Mrs. Beam's* required a convincing physical encounter. Fontanne's character was to throw things at Lunt, to slap and maul him. "But," he said in a 1928 interview, "I couldn't get her to scrap as if she really meant it. Consequently, the scene lacked realism. Lynn would deliberately miss me when she aimed, and as for slapping my face, all I got was a gentle pat."

Irritated, Lunt told his wife not to hold back. But she was afraid that she would hurt him. In order to goad her on, Lunt shouted insults at Fontanne until she lashed out at him in frustration. "After that," said Lunt, rehearsals for the scene proceeded with no holds barred: "everything she threw at me *hit* me, my face got slapped good and hard, and she finished by pushing me over a chair backward. In fact, she put so much vigor into her performance that even some of the Theatre Guild people used to wonder how we could go home happily after such a scrap."

Audiences certainly wondered when the play opened in April 1926. The Lunts appeared to be pounding one another with terrifying abandon. But the fight was not as dangerous as it appeared. Every moment of the twenty-minute battle was carefully choreographed by the Lunts with the help of the director, Philip Moeller. For many who watched it, the scene was the highlight of the production, although both the critics and the Guild's subscribers were much impressed by Jean Cadell's performance as well. The scene also had a long-range effect, for the Lunts were able to use many of the same techniques during their battles in *The Taming of the Shrew* nine years later.

1926–27

Exhausted by the work they had done during the 1925–26 season (which also included Lunt's teaching in the Guild's newly formed acting school), the Lunts were given two months' vacation. They promptly sailed for Europe. In Paris, Lunt introduced his wife to Lillie Langtry. Although Langtry was now seventy-three, Fontanne graciously told interviewers that she was still very beautiful.

The European trip was intended to be a vacation, but the Lunts devoted much time to preparations for the next season. Most of their two-week stay in London was spent searching for costumes. Fontanne was particularly determined to find exactly the right accessories—a dilapidated hat, a wilted boa and a pair of disreputable shoes—to decorate her costume for Eliza Doolittle in *Pygmalion*.

The Lunts returned to the United States on August 31, refreshed and eager to begin work on the next season, during which the Theatre Guild scheduled Lunt to appear in four plays, Fontanne in three.

In September, Fontanne resumed performing in *At Mrs. Beam's,* while Lunt began rehearsals for another play by Franz Werfel, the historical epic *Juarez and Maximilian*. Soon afterward Fontanne started work on *Pygmalion*. This would be the first time they appeared separately in Theatre Guild productions.

Juarez and Maximilian had been brought to the Guild's attention by the author, who sent the managers a copy of the play after the opening of *Goat Song*. It required an enormous cast and many settings, which were provided by Lee Simonson. The rehearsals went splendidly. According to Lawrence Langner, "the final run-through of the play without scenery and costumes [was] so moving that all of us who witnessed the rehearsal were dissolved in tears"—a remarkable and unprecedented achievement for a managers' rehearsal. Then, however, the sets and costumes were added, and, perhaps because the scale of the sets was so vast, the performance suddenly lost much of its impact. In addition, the long and complex scene changes effectively destroyed the play's continuity, dissipating whatever excitement the performers were able to generate.

Brooks Atkinson, however, seemed not to perceive the problem. He praised the settings and costumes, but found the performance "sluggish," the movement "unwieldy" and the speech "droning." Alfred Lunt's articulation was singled out for criticism. "This Emperor of Mexico does not speak intelligibly beneath his bushy whiskers," Atkinson said. "Indeed, Mr. Lunt does not seem well cast in this sombre part of a weak monarch. . . . Mr. Lunt seldom penetrates the obvious surfaces."

John Anderson, writing in the *Post,* also expressed dissatisfaction with Lunt's performance. Although he had "portrayed perfectly the indecision and meekness of the part," Lunt "seemed to leave much else undone and unshown," Anderson wrote.

Juarez and Maximilian was scheduled to be the first play in the Guild's new "Alternating Repertory Company."* The idea was to produce one play for a week at the Guild Theatre, then substitute a second play using the same cast of actors. After a week, the first play would resume perform- ances and the two would alternate thereafter. Meanwhile, at a second the- atre, two other plays would be offered in repertory. The leading actors would be chosen from a permanent ensemble of performers which, begin- ning that season, was known as the Acting Company and whose nucleus consisted of the Lunts, Helen Westley, Dudley Digges, Henry Travers and Ernest Cossart. Within a year or two, the Acting Company grew to include Clare Eames, Glenn Anders, Edward G. Robinson, Margalo Gillmore, Claude Rains, Tom Powers, Philip Loeb and other fine performers. The notion of establishing a permanent repertory company, in the tradition of Shakespeare's Lord Chamberlain's Men and Stanislavski's Moscow Art Theatre, seemed to the Theatre Guild a logical extension of its program.

The advantages to the actors were considerable. Because no play ran for more than a week at a time, actors were less likely to grow stale in their roles. In addition, the opportunity to appear in two plays in alternation offered each actor the opportunity to work on different kinds of roles in contrasting styles of plays. The Guild's audiences benefited from the ar- rangement as well, because all the major roles were played by established performers who were familiar with and devoted to both the repertory sys- tem and the Guild's idealistic view of the theatre.

In *Pygmalion,* which opened in mid-November, with Reginald Mason playing Higgins to Fontanne's Eliza,† Lynn created one of her finest char- acterizations, playing both aspects of Eliza—the Cockney guttersnipe and the counterfeit lady—to perfection. The standard of excellence in the role had been Mrs. Patrick Campbell, who had been the first to play Eliza both in England and in New York in 1914. But many who saw the Theatre Guild's production thought that Fontanne's portrayal outshone that of her illustrious predecessor. Woollcott called the performance "resourceful, im- mensely competent and richly satisfying"; Gilbert W. Gabriel in the *Sun* said it was "a lovely piece of acting, keen, cleverly turned, completely win- ning." And when Brooks Atkinson looked back upon the production

*The production, however, was so immense and the notices so discouraging that the Board members decided not to inaugurate the system until *Pygmalion* opened.

† Alfred Lunt did not join the cast of *Pygmalion* until it went on tour in September 1927; the Lunts never played it together before a New York audience.

forty-four years later, he said that Fontanne was "the finest of all Elizas, realistic and unromantic."

Mrs. Patrick Campbell attended a performance at the Guild Theatre and went backstage afterward to see Fontanne, who was apprehensive at the prospect. "I mean, she was supposed to be the bitch of all time, you know," Fontanne said later, "but she wasn't at all. She helped me. She said, 'Now there's one thing you do that Mr. Shaw told me that I must do *this* way,' and . . . I said, 'I'm going to do it tonight, come and see it.' So I did, I put it in."

Fontanne and Cheryl Crawford, who served as assistant stage manager for the production, developed a playful relationship. One of Crawford's duties after each performance was to find the ring that Eliza angrily throws at Higgins and retrieve it so that it would be ready for use in the next performance. Fontanne intentionally tossed the ring into inaccessible places—the fireplace, underneath the furniture—so that Crawford would have to hunt for it. "After a few such experiences," Crawford said, "I bought a number of rings at the five-and-ten, keeping them in my smock, so it got to be no more fun for her."

Once *Pygmalion* opened, the Guild was able to put the Alternating Repertory system into practice. Lunt was assigned to play the lead in Sidney Howard's new comedy, *Ned McCobb's Daughter*, which opened on November 29 at the John Golden Theatre, having been postponed because Clare Eames, who played opposite him, became ill. The wonder is that the Lunts were able to maintain their health so well during this whirlwind of activity. Lunt's physical condition was always somewhat fragile after the removal of his kidney during childhood; if he did not retard his rehearsal or performance schedule, it was only because every possible moment away from the theatre was spent sleeping or relaxing.

The commitment the Lunts made to their careers in the theatre was so complete that, by design, it eliminated a full social life. When they were appearing in a play, they seldom attended parties. Occasionally (but rarely) they might invite a friend or two to their apartment for an after-theatre meal. Alexander Woollcott, Robert E. Sherwood, Noël Coward, Douglas Fairbanks, Jr., Marc Connelly, Gilbert Miller and Carl Van Vechten were among those who received such invitations. More often, however, Lunt would cook a simple meal for the two of them and they would discuss the quality of that evening's performance and how it might be improved, before going to bed.

During their first years with the Theatre Guild, they were constantly overworking. Asked by an interviewer in 1928 what they did in their spare time, Fontanne gasped in amazement. "Spare time!" she said. "Why, we haven't any. We are seldom outside the theatre except during the hours from midnight to eleven the next morning. And that often includes Sundays as well. Usually, we are acting in two plays that alternate every week and rehearsing a third one at the same time. And when we go on the road for a short tour, we have to brush up on the whole season's repertory."

Later, when the Lunts were no longer performing for the Theatre Guild, they did occasionally have an afternoon free, giving them a chance to see a play. But they rarely took advantage of the opportunity. "If you go to the matinee in the afternoon," Lunt said, "and it's good and it's thrilling, you're exhausted by the time you get to the theatre that night and you have to play a long part. We can't do that." Only after they retired did they attend the theatre on a regular basis. Night clubs never interested them. They probably saw the inside of a night club fewer than half a dozen times in their lives.* They never went to the Stork Club or El Morocco. Only once did they go to "21," and then only for a few minutes.

"They weren't members of the jet set, you know," Edward Bigg, their physician in later years, told me. "They could have had a Hollywood kind of life, but they didn't want it. They had a few chosen friends. But they never accepted very much in the way of invitations or socializing. It was all very quiet."

Lunt, who was marginally less fanatical about conserving his strength for the theatre than was Fontanne, did enjoy vaudeville and burlesque shows as well as opera. But he attended such events only when he felt they would not interfere with the energies he needed to devote to a rehearsal or performance. Still, neither Lunt nor Fontanne saw themselves as martyrs to the theatre. Giving up these activities was not regarded as a sacrifice; it was simply the prudent and professional thing to do.

Others saw the Lunts' self-discipline quite differently, however. Lunt and Fontanne were valued party guests. Both were lively and witty, and their friends regretted that they did not attend social gatherings more often. But the Lunts enjoyed parties only if they were intimate gatherings of those they knew well. Others often gawked at them, treated them as celebrities or requested them to put on a show, all of which made the Lunts uncomfortable—so much so that they worked out a series of ruses to get them out of parties they weren't enjoying. Even at their own apartment they occasionally found that a guest had brought uninvited friends and that awkward situations resulted. At such times Lunt would ask a relative or a close friend to announce loudly that everyone had better be going so that the Lunts could get some rest.

On days when they were performing, every detail of their lives was subordinated to the demands of the performance. They habitually arrived at the theatre at least an hour before the other actors checked in. They dressed and made up in separate dressing rooms so that each would be able to concentrate fully on the character he or she was playing. To relax before a performance, Fontanne would play several games of solitaire and Lunt might visit with the other actors as they arrived, but the purpose of

*In 1935, preparing to play a night club comedian in *Idiot's Delight,* Lunt attended night clubs frequently in order to study the behavior and attitudes of the comics. But those visits were made for business, not pleasure.

these activities—to relax so that the performance might be improved—was never forgotten. "Their whole life was dedicated to those three hours—from eight o'clock to eleven o'clock on the stage," Dick Van Patten, who played with them for two and a half years in *O Mistress Mine,* told me in 1983.

When the Lunts were scheduled to give a matinee and an evening performance on the same day, they were often reluctant to expend the energy needed to take a taxi to their apartment for dinner and return to the theatre. They were not particularly fond of restaurants (although they did occasionally dine at Voisin and at Ruby Foo's), so they were left with only one alternative: to bring food to the theatre and eat it in their dressing rooms between performances.

After the evening shows, they left the theatre as quickly as possible. This general rule of the 1920s became inviolable in the '40s. According to Dick Van Patten, the Lunts routinely turned down requests to visit them in their dressing rooms after performances of *O Mistress Mine.* "They wouldn't see them," Van Patten said. "They turned down the biggest people. Their stage manager would stand there and say, 'Sorry, Mr. Lunt and Miss Fontanne have to get home immediately. They cannot see you.' They didn't want to waste any energy."

Conservation of energy was always uppermost in their minds. Both Lynn and Alfred were determined to get at least eight hours' sleep unless circumstances made that impossible. By "circumstances," they had in mind such uncontrollable situations as a train that arrived late at a stop on a tour, *not* the fact that a party had lasted longer than anticipated. "They rest and they rest and they rest," said Noël Coward. "They wouldn't dream of going to a party if they have a matinee the next day."

The Lunts were so determined to get the rest they believed they needed that there was a standard joke, Helen Hayes said, that they were wrapped in cellophane and hung up with the costumes between performances.

Fontanne was always astonished to find that other performers led less ascetic lives than she. "I remember a party, it happened to be the night before *Victoria Regina* opened, and Helen Hayes was there," she once recalled. "I said, 'How can you go to a party the night before you open?' And she said, 'Oh, it takes my mind off it.' But we could never do that."

On another occasion the Lunts were invited to a party at Tallulah Bankhead's New York apartment. Bankhead said to the assembled guests, "Let's all have a little marijuana," and most accepted the invitation. Fontanne demurred, saying that she had a matinee the next day. On her way out the door, Fontanne said, "I rather rapped her knuckles. I said, 'Well, you may not know it, but I own a third of this play you're in and Alfred owns another third, and I'm very concerned that you're having a party on a Friday night before a matinee. I don't like it at all.'" Bankhead smiled condescendingly and returned to the party. The next day, as Fontanne was putting on her makeup at the theatre, she heard Tallulah's distinctive low voice outside the dressing room calling, "Where's Miss Fontanne's room?" Bankhead "stormed into my room," according to Fontanne, "and she said, 'There now. I had a party last night and I'm as good as new this morning and it hasn't made the faintest bit of difference.' I said, 'Look in the glass.' I had a glass with lights all around it. I said, 'Look in that glass.' She looked in it. She was absolutely drawn. And she said, 'Oh, my God,' and left."

The Lunts tried to maintain the same schedule each day. They would have breakfast at eleven o'clock or noon—a light breakfast for Lunt, comprised only of coffee and rye bread, an enormous breakfast for Fontanne, consisting of toast, Canadian bacon, coffee and either fish or eggs or kidneys. If there was no afternoon rehearsal or performance, they might visit friends, walk, attend to correspondence or shop, but these activities would immediately be curtailed if they threatened to tire the couple or to interfere in any way with the evening's performance. "We learned not to have any social life in the daytime," Fontanne said in 1972. "The [energy you use in social situations] is what you use in acting. If you use it during the day, there's not so much of it to use at night. We found that lunch with someone always meant a tired performance."

Except for the rare occasion when the Lunts had lunch with friends, they invariably skipped that meal, having a small dinner at five o'clock. Fontanne always made it a point to take an hour's nap before departing for the theatre. After matinees the Lunts took naps in their dressing rooms before the evening performance. Other actors were cautioned not to make a racket if they arrived at the theatre early. Fontanne became quite unhappy if her sleep was disturbed, and Lunt would become even more upset. William Le Massena, who often appeared with the Lunts in New York and on tour, told me, "I've been in on interrupting his naps. And he'd come forth from the dressing room where he was resting in a boiling rage that he'd been disturbed by people making noise. Or they'd have a couple of drawing rooms down at one end of the train when we were on tour and the rest of us would be making some wild kind of noise late at night, and he'd come forth and deliver a furious speech, and everyone would subside and quiet down."

After an opening night Fontanne, whenever possible, spent the entire day in bed. On more than one occasion, her husband testified that she had given so much of herself during a first-night performance that she slept for fifteen hours the following day.

Those who did not take the theatre as seriously as the Lunts were often at a loss to understand how acting in a play could be so tiring. "You work only a few hours eight times a week," they would say. The Lunts were energetic individuals who seemingly would not be fazed by such a schedule. But acting exacts a terrific toll, the Lunts would answer. The physical energy that is compressed into three hours of performance is comparable to the energy needed to run a marathon, and that does not take into account the emotional intensity required to represent a character in the throes of one sort of crisis or another. In addition, Fontanne said, "Being the focus of thousands of eyes produces an hypnotic magnetism which makes the actor physically stronger than he is himself, [but] when the eyes are withdrawn and the current is switched off he feels like a pricked balloon."

If the Lunts willingly sacrificed a full social life in favor of their careers, it is less clear whether they decided not to have children for the same reason. Every one of their friends and relatives to whom I've spoken found the very idea that they might have wanted children impossible to believe. The consensus is that they were far too determined to concentrate their energies on their careers to have seriously considered the possibility of parenthood. If the idea ever did occur to them, however (and it is difficult to imagine that the subject would *never* have arisen), and if they ever gave the matter serious thought, it would have been during their years at the Theatre Guild. Fontanne was thirty-nine years old in 1926; if children were in their plans, the plans would have to be made swiftly.

It may have been that they never had children because it was impossible for them to do so. If that was the case, they seem not to have mentioned it to anyone. Perhaps they simply regarded children as inconvenient. Peg Murray, who appeared with Fontanne in *The Great Sebastians* in 1955, said, "I think she would rather have died than gone through the business of having a child—and certainly changing a diaper, I couldn't in my wildest . . . I can't believe she was ever interested in that." Perhaps the conviction that having a child would temporarily distort the figure that Fontanne strove so mightily to achieve and maintain was enough to dissuade her from giving the possibility serious consideration.

Armina Marshall, who knew them well when they acted with the Theatre Guild, offered a typical reaction when asked about the possibility that the Lunts might have wanted children. "Well, I would just say that would be totally unacceptable," Marshall said. "They never discussed it. Acting was the thing they did. They lived and breathed acting all the time, and it was the play that we talked about whenever I visited them. Always, it was the theatre."

In 1978, five years before Fontanne died, a New York *Times* interviewer asked her whether she regretted not having had children. "No regrets," Fontanne answered. "I was too busy. My life was filled with hard work, so it was very difficult to have children."

Dick Van Patten once said to the Lunts' stage manager, Charva Chester, "Wouldn't they be wonderful parents?" And he remembers Chester's reply: "Are you crazy? They'd be the worst parents in the world. They would absolutely ignore the child. Their whole life is in each other. They're completely involved in each other. They would be terrible parents."

Dr. Edward Bigg said the Lunts were not very fond of children. "They were pleasant and nice around them, but children annoyed them. Once [children] were sixteen or eighteen or twenty, they were all right. But up until that point they were a nuisance. They didn't have much use for them."

Many of the actors I interviewed told me that the Lunts seemed to regard the members of their acting companies as their children. A deep family feeling existed among them, an affection that in every case lasted far beyond the professional association.

In the 1940s, however, the Lunts may have had momentary second thoughts about not having had children. One summer day in Genesee Depot, they were seated beside the pool with their young friend and lawyer Donald Seawell, who told me: "Lynnie said to me that Alfred and she wanted to talk to me about something. She said that it was very serious and very wonderful for us. And I said, 'What's that?' She and Alfred said almost simultaneously, 'We want you to be the son we never had.' Well, of course I was thrilled and honored. Alfred said, 'You know, I guess we were just too busy to ever think much about having children,' and Lynnie said, 'Well, Donny, we don't have to be sorry about that now.'" Years afterward, when Seawell and his wife, the actress Eugenia Rawls, had children of their own, the Lunts became very close to them, planning Christmas parties for them, shopping with them and taking them to museums and to the theatre. "They wrote [to the children] quite often," Seawell said, "and they couldn't have been more attentive or helpful or concerned about what they were doing."

The first contemporary American play in which Lunt appeared for the Theatre Guild was *Ned McCobb's Daughter* in 1926. The character he played, Babe Callahan, was a cheap hoodlum, a role unlike any he had ever acted before. Again he faced skeptics, but Theresa Helburn, who was responsible for casting decisions, felt that Lunt gave a "splendid" performance and that "the very change of type had a stimulating effect." Lunt used all his formidable powers of observation and fanatical attention to detail in creating a wholly convincing gangster. He observed the mannerisms of a New York bootlegger named Larry Fay, incorporating Fay's manner of speaking and movement into his characterization. And he found his "green umbrella" for the play in the notion that Babe Callahan would proudly exhibit a gold tooth; Lunt had one of his front teeth capped in gold for the role. Later on, when he was needed for a new play and was removed from the cast of *Ned McCobb's Daughter,* he told Philip Moeller, who was directing, that the actor who replaced him should not be restricted in any way but one: "Please don't let him have a gold tooth," he said. "I couldn't bear it. That's mine."

Critical reactions to the play were largely negative; one critic called it "unconvincing, lacking in beauty and . . . integrity." But Lunt's performance was uniformly and rapturously praised. George Goldsmith's review in the *Tribune* was typical: "Strangely metamorphosed since the close of *Juarez and Maximilian,* Alfred Lunt represented a wholesale bootlegger with unction, gusto and immense vitality. His was easily the finest performance of the evening."

In the *Times,* Brooks Atkinson said, "Mr. Lunt plays more buoyantly than ever before, with sure control of all the means of stage expression." Atkinson believed that the character had been especially well written and had been given most of the funniest lines of the play. But the critic read *Ned McCobb's Daughter* soon after he saw it and discovered that the humor he had seen in the role had been provided primarily by the actor rather than the playwright. "To read [the lines] in the printed text . . . is to realize just how much flavor Mr. Lunt brings to his part. Far from being an instrument of expression, he is a living character. . . ."

Only one comment could have prevented Lunt from being entirely happy with his critical reception. Alan Dale, writing in the *American,* referred once again to the problem that plagued Lunt on so many occasions. Dale said that "even though he spoke loudly, [he] often blurred his words so that they were quite unintelligible." Comments of this sort appeared so often during Lunt's early years with the Theatre Guild that they cannot be dismissed as critical nit-picking. Clearly, Lunt needed to refine his articulation, and it must have been at about this point in his career that he began attending to the problem in earnest. After *Ned McCobb's Daughter,* Lunt was seldom criticized for poor articulation; indeed, in time his delivery became so crisp and clear that it was held up as a standard for all American actors. Perhaps it was Fontanne who helped to rid him of the problem. From the beginning of her career, she was noted for the clarity of her speech, and in 1935 she was awarded a gold medal by the American Academy of Arts and Letters for the perfection of her stage diction.

The critical reception for Sidney Howard's play may not have been enthusiastic, but the performances of Alfred Lunt and Clare Eames were so highly praised that the production had a long and successful run. After *Ned McCobb's Daughter* established its place in the repertory with *Pygmalion,* the Guild sought two plays that could be alternated with them. They chose *The Brothers Karamazov,* with Lunt and Fontanne in the pivotal roles of the tormented sensualist Dmitri and the earthy Grouchenka, and *The Silver Cord,* in which the Lunts were not cast.

Jacques Copeau, the noted French director whose company, the Théâtre du Vieux-Colombier, had presented his (and Jean Croué's) adaptation of *The Brothers Karamazov* in French at the Garrick Theatre in 1919, was invited to direct an English translation of the same play for the Theatre Guild. Harold Clurman, then a young actor and playreader for the Guild, was chosen to be Copeau's assistant director, primarily because he was conversant in French and could translate Copeau's comments to the actors.

Clurman had great respect both for Copeau and for the Guild's performers, but he learned that even "a first-rate foreign director, who is also the
author of the play, working with such incomparable actors as Lunt and
Fontanne, does not inevitably produce a satisfying theatre event." The theatrical traditions of Europe and America "differ, often hopelessly," Clurman found, and although both the cast and the director went about their
work with goodwill and mutual respect, the clash of approaches produced
more confusion than light.

Most of the plays in which the Lunts appeared for the Guild had been
directed by Philip Moeller, who gave them near-total freedom to develop
their characterizations in their own ways. Both Lunt and Fontanne responded to this freedom eagerly. But Copeau's method was different. He
began the rehearsal process with a clearly formed idea of his characters and
expected the actors to adapt themselves to his preconceptions. Many of the
performers, including the Lunts, found such an approach stifling.

At one rehearsal Copeau whispered to Clurman that Lunt was *un
gosse:* a little boy. As Clurman noted, "He did not mean this at all unkindly;
there is in fact something tender, vulnerable, and invincibly boyish in
Lunt, which is the source of his acting. . . . Copeau could not altogether
understand the fluidity of Lunt's inspiration, the spontaneous emotional-
ism that makes him so poignant an actor, even in comedy."

Copeau and Lunt were not openly hostile to one another, but most
rehearsals found them at odds, engaging in a battle of wills. Copeau might
insist upon a specific approach to a scene or to a line of dialogue. Lunt
would respectfully object. Copeau, beginning to lose patience, would
shout, *"But I know the play; I've seen it performed for hundreds of audiences."*
Lunt would quietly demur, saying, "But not *American* audiences."

Clurman believed that Copeau would have benefited from listening
more carefully to Lunt's objections. Lunt was a finer actor, Clurman said,
than any with whom Copeau had worked previously, and the director
should have given him greater latitude in developing his characterization.

Ultimately, Copeau was unable to shape *The Brothers Karamazov* in
the way he had intended. After a time he became so frustrated that he
would retreat with Clurman to the rear of the darkened auditorium and
refuse to deal with the actors' problems. On one occasion, during a dress
rehearsal, Fontanne, who occasionally displayed her temperament when
she was feeling insecure, became so irritated by the arrangement of the
bedsheets on which she was lying that she called out into the darkness,
"Aren't you going to do something about this?" But Copeau remained
silent. She continued, "Monsieur Copeau, Monsieur Copeau, have someone fix this; I can't play the scene on this bed." Still Copeau did not respond; in effect, he had withdrawn from the rehearsal process.

At another dress rehearsal Copeau came out of hiding long enough
to tell Lunt that he needed to re-do his makeup, adding a scar on his cheek.

"But I have one," Lunt replied, indicating a scratch mark. Tired and irritated, the director shouted, "I want a big large wound right across your cheek, at once!"

"Very well, you shall have it," Lunt responded cheerfully. He retreated to his dressing room, reemerging in twenty minutes with "an enormous gaping wound painted in bright green right across his cheek, which gave the effect of a gangrenous protuberance," as Lawrence Langner described it. Copeau sighed and said, "We will have no wound at all." Lunt again retired to the dressing room. When he reappeared, his cheek showed a scratch mark nearly identical to the one with which he had begun the scene. "I've made a compromise," he said genially. Copeau smiled in a concession of defeat, and the rehearsal continued.

Although most critics responded enthusiastically to the Lunts' performances, *The Brothers Karamazov* was not entirely successful. It ran for only 56 performances before being withdrawn from the repertory. In its place the Guild decided to offer the Lunts in *The Second Man,* a new play by S. N. Behrman, rehearsals for which were a particularly severe test of Fontanne's energy and endurance. The Theatre Guild also decided to send *Pygmalion* to Philadelphia for one week. Thus, after the evening's performance in Philadelphia, Fontanne hastily removed her makeup and costume so that she could take the midnight train to New York. On the following day she rehearsed *The Second Man,* then rushed to the railroad station to catch a train back to Philadelphia, arriving just in time to make up and go on stage. She looked forward longingly to Wednesday and Saturday, when matinees of *Pygmalion* made it impossible for her to leave Philadelphia.

The Lunts were eager to appear in *The Second Man,* but the burden of preparing one play after another was beginning to tell. Each day was a struggle against fatigue. It is little wonder that a year later, after both the Lunts had played several more exhausting roles, Fontanne shouted angrily to the Board members, during a long and frustrating production meeting, "This isn't an art theatre, it's a sweatshop!"

The Second Man was S. N. Behrman's first play, a sophisticated comedy about a successful young writer, played by Lunt, who projected an air of urbanity and charm but was really guided by cynicism and malice. Behrman, who had been so impressed years earlier by Alfred's performance in *Banco,* had written the play with the Lunts in mind, but he had held out little hope that they would ever play the roles. The Guild rejected the play when it was first submitted, as did several other managements in New York. Later, however, Behrman's agent took the script back to the Theatre Guild; Lunt and Fontanne read it, liked it and persuaded the managers to put it into their schedule.

Behrman, a short, pudgy, endearing man, attended a number of early rehearsals of his play and was totally confused by the process. "Half the time I didn't know what [the actors] were doing or why," he said. The words he had written seemed to have no vitality, even to make no sense.

Seeing his confusion, Fontanne approached him on one occasion and said, "I suppose it all sounds like nothing to you." Behrman confessed that that was true. "You see," she said with a smile and a squeeze of Behrman's hand, "we're not thinking of the words now, just the movements, but I promise you it'll be all right."

Still, the playwright wondered. He found Lunt's readings especially perplexing: "very casual, only sporadically vital, and in the main, disinterested," he said. Behrman tried unsuccessfully to conceal his concern from the actors, and when Fontanne eventually advised him that he might be better off not attending rehearsals at all, he took her suggestion. Thus, when Behrman saw the play on opening night, he had no idea what to expect. The performance took him utterly by surprise, as he wrote in his autobiography, *People in a Diary*.

> I realized as I watched that first performance that I'd had not the remotest idea of what Lynn and Alfred could or would do. The illuminations of the script provided by the actors dazzled me because I had not perceived them during the rehearsals. Lynn's part was a small one but now in the performance I heard overtones that I didn't know were there. For example, I had written a line for her about another character who bored her: "He never has anything interesting to say." What I heard was: "He never has anything interesting to say—never—never—never—never—never," a perfectly graduated diminuendo of "nevers," conveying an endless vista of boredom, the last "never" faint—but audible!—faint with the claustrophobia of boredom.

Behrman was equally impressed by the way Lunt was able to give dimension to his character with a brilliant mimetic brushstroke.

> The nonhero has been abandoned by the older woman who loves him and by the young woman whom he, had he been less practical, might have loved. He has just seen the younger woman out the door. My stage direction reads: "He leaves the door, goes to the telephone." That walk, that walk from the door to the telephone, shafted a light on the play and the character which I had not foreseen. It was a moment of self-confrontation, of complete awareness. Why hadn't he taken a chance? Why hadn't he tested himself? Perhaps he was better than the louse he knew himself to be? Alfred's eyes, when he picked up the telephone to get back what he didn't want, went insane.

Another method Lunt used to reveal his character more fully was to reverse the inner and outer traits provided by the playwright. Instead of showing the audience a cynic who plays the role of an affable charmer, Lunt showed them a vulnerable, decent man who adopts a veneer of cynicism.

If Behrman, then a novice playwright, did not realize how effectively the Lunts were bringing his play to vibrant life during rehearsals, he could be excused. Less forgivable, perhaps, was the reaction of the Guild's Board members when they attended a managers' rehearsal and vehemently insisted that a scene should be cut. The Lunts countered that there was nothing wrong with the scene, that it just needed more rehearsal. A battle ensued—this one resulting in a victory for the Lunts—that confirmed their belief that the managers' judgments vis-à-vis light comedy were not to be trusted.

Behrman later said that the Lunts' playing of the roles he had created in *The Second Man* was "the luckiest thing that ever happened to me." Eventually he wrote or adapted a total of five plays in which the Lunts appeared.

Until *The Second Man* opened on Broadway, some holdouts still regarded Lunt as overrated. But the premiere at the Guild Theatre, on April 11, 1927, put all such thoughts to rest. Percy Hammond in the *Tribune* wrote that Lunt was "the First Actor" in America; the *Telegram*'s Frank Vreeland said that he had given "the best individual performance this season"; Kelcey Allen said in *Women's Wear Daily* that his performance "strengthens the ripening feeling among many that he is today one of America's greatest and most protean of the legitimate actors"; and Charles Brackett in the *New Yorker* called Lunt's portrayal "the best high comedy performance I have ever seen given by a man."

Fontanne was always concerned about the harm that overwork could do to her husband's health. Her own constitution was so strong that she rarely suffered from any kind of illness, but it was she who fell ill in April 1927 and required hospitalization for an attack of appendicitis. She missed several performances of *The Second Man,* during which her role was played by another actress. But she had become so closely identified with the role of Eliza that the Guild canceled performances of *Pygmalion* until she was ready to return.

Fontanne's determination to perform as soon as possible impelled her to leave the hospital and rejoin the *Pygmalion* cast after an absence of less than a week. But her system was not equal to her determination and she returned to the Park West Hospital early in May, when her appendix was removed without complication. This time she remained in the hospital for three weeks, returning to the Guild Theatre to play in *The Second Man* on May 29. But she was not yet up to the strenuous role of Eliza, and the Guild, thinking it unwise to postpone *Pygmalion* indefinitely, was forced to send an understudy on in her place.

In a poll of New York theatre critics, Lunt was voted the best stage actor of the 1926–27 season. The award, presented to him on the stage of the Guild Theatre after the first act of *The Second Man,* was based upon his work in that play as well as in *Ned McCobb's Daughter* and *Juarez and Maximilian*. Fontanne received honorable mention among the actresses, along with Ethel Barrymore, Jane Cowl, Alice Brady, Ruth Gordon, Helen Menken and Blanche Yurka. The winner was Pauline Lord, who was recognized for her performances in *Sandalwood* and *Mariners*.

In July the Lunts were at long last given a sorely needed rest. They literally wasted no time beginning their vacation, performing *The Second Man* on Friday evening, July 8, then rushing to catch the midnight sailing of the *Olympic* for Europe.

During their stay in England, the Lunts visited their old friend Noël Coward at his farmhouse, Goldenhurst. They brought with them the script of *The Second Man*, which, they suggested to their host, should be produced in England with Coward in the title role. Coward took their recommendation, and opened in *The Second Man* in London during January of 1928.

When the Lunts returned from their vacation in early September, the New York *Times* ran a brief story announcing their arrival in New York. The story reflected Lunt's new eminence. Previously, when the *Times* had run such items, they had invariably begun, "Lynn Fontanne, accompanied by her husband, the actor Alfred Lunt . . ." On this occasion, however, the story began, "Alfred Lunt, actor and his wife, Lynn Fontanne, returned yesterday on the Holland-American liner *Rotterdam* from their vacation in Europe."

1927–28

The Lunts received their customary raise of $50 each for the 1927–28 season. They would be paid $400 per week when they were playing at the Guild Theatre and $450 per week when playing elsewhere, in addition to their usual five percent of the weekly box office receipts over a specified minimum. By this time, firmly established as the finest acting couple of the American theatre, the Lunts might have been commanding salaries of five to ten times as much. Ed Wynn, for example, was earning $7,500 a week in *Manhattan Mary* in 1927, while Marilyn Miller's weekly salary in *Rosalie* amounted to $3,000. And there was no shortage of commercial plays in which they might have appeared. Robert E. Sherwood's *The Road to Rome*, one of the greatest hits of the previous season, had been written for the Lunts, but they had turned it down. They gave no thought to leaving the Theatre Guild because they were grateful to the Guild for providing them with magnificent roles in outstanding plays.

In addition, the Lunts were in fundamental agreement with the Guild's notion that the playwright's work should always take precedence over the work of the actor. As Helen Westley, one of the Guild's managers, said, "The popular theatre is sustained by the mass worship of a certain actor or actress. This public does not swarm to see So-and-So's play. They swarm to see So-and-So act. . . . The audience of the art theatre is interested in [the play]. . . . Therefore, the actor's relation to the art theatre is one of respect and service. This tends to dim the ego. In adhering truthfully to a great script there is something of religion. The play is the star."

Lunt and Fontanne often expressed their agreement with this concept. "The actor is not a creative, but an interpretive artist," Lunt said. "His one and *only* job is to work *within the play*, to translate the ideas of the author." Fontanne put the idea more colloquially, but just as succinctly: "The thing is to appear with the goods, and if you haven't got the goods, then you're dead. . . . You can't make a success unless you have the material."

The Lunts did not waver in their loyalty to the Theatre Guild even though they found the attitudes and policies of the managers toward the actors demeaning. "They were bitches and bastards and all this, that and the other," Lunt said, "but they had a vision." And the vision was so powerful that it overrode all other concerns. "The Guild raised the tone of the theatre," Fontanne agreed. "They did plays that were literature, plays written by good writers, plays that had a mind back of them, not just silly entertainment."

"And actors knew the Guild was doing the most distinguished plays in town. So of course you wanted to go with the Guild," Lunt added.

The 1927–28 season began with a tour, opening in Cleveland on September 12, with *The Guardsman* and *The Second Man* performed in repertory while Lunt rehearsed the role of Henry Higgins with the cast of *Pygmalion* during the mornings and free afternoons. By September 26, when the tour arrived in Chicago, *Pygmalion* was added to the repertory. Immediately thereafter, the company began rehearsals for *The Doctor's Dilemma,* with the Lunts once again in leading roles. When that play was inserted into the performance schedule, on October 31 in Chicago, it meant that Lunt was playing leading roles in four plays and Fontanne was playing leading roles in three, plus her supporting role in *The Second Man.* The season had barely begun and the couple's energies were, once again, overtaxed.

While the tour was in progress, the Lunts got a nasty surprise. From the beginning of their association with the Theatre Guild, they had willingly agreed to forgo star billing, but they had made it clear that they expected the same policy to apply to all its other actors as well.

A second Theatre Guild company, headed by George Gaul and Florence Eldridge, was touring other cities when the Lunts and their company reached Cleveland. By mistake, the posters for the two tours were mixed up, and the Lunts arrived at their hotel to find the wrong posters awaiting them. To their consternation, the posters announced that George Gaul and Florence Eldridge would star in a repertory of productions for the Theatre Guild. Lunt was in the midst of signing the hotel register when the poster was called to his attention. He put down the pen, turned to Fontanne and said, "We're going back to New York." Eventually they were persuaded to call the Guild offices in New York before making a final decision. Lunt called and, as he described it, "Well, they came out right away. And boy, they were right there. They were there right away and burned up all the wrong posters." But the incident further drove a wedge between the Lunts and the Guild, which, they were convinced, had taken advantage of their naïveté in not specifying that all such agreements be included in a written contract. From then on, they never fully trusted the word of the Guild's managers.

The Doctor's Dilemma, which opened in Baltimore on November 14 before moving to New York on November 21, was the third play by Shaw in which the Lunts had appeared, the playwright having given the Guild exclusive American rights to his work.

The Doctor's Dilemma had been seen once before in New York. In 1915 a troupe headed by Harley Granville-Barker and his wife, Lillah McCarthy, had performed the play in what many had regarded as a defin-itive production. But most observers revised their opinion when they saw the production that Dudley Digges directed for the Theatre Guild.

The role of Louis Dubedat was a favorite of Lunt's. He called it "the easiest and most satisfactory part ever." After the long and difficult roles he had been playing, Dubedat seemed almost a vacation. "Oh boy," said Lunt, "he doesn't get in until the end of the second act—and then he has that marvelous death. Well, that's all he has. Boy, that's the dream."

Still, the part presented problems, as did any role of Shaw's. Lunt believed that Shaw's characters often behaved inconsistently because the author was willing to sacrifice consistency in order to make his social point.

> With Shaw, you can't ask why do I have to say this? You signed a contract to play Shaw, and you have to do what you can. Now, Shaw is a very tricky man. He's always betraying his actors. Du-bedat, for instance, is supposed to be the cleverest, shrewdest little bastard who ever walked the earth. He has one scene in which he's supposed to be clever and he isn't that at all, and it's quite apparent to the audience, and you have to play it with your head under the pillow, practically. So often, Shaw will leave your character here so he can preach one of his sermons at you, and you have to do it, because Shaw jolly well wants you to.

Fontanne's performance as Jennifer Dubedat was one of her finest. S. N. Behrman recalled it years later, saying, "I'll never forget Lynn's voice in *Doctor's Dilemma* when Dubedat is dying and she says, 'Is that death?' But the voice in which she said that line was a voice she'd never used be-fore, in that play or any other play. It came out of a cavern—a dark cavern."

The New York critics were equally impressed. "Miss Fontanne's per-formance is a clear-browed delight, understanding, warm, as alive as poised," said Gilbert Gabriel. "Hers is infinitely better than Lila [*sic*] McCarthy's playing of the part here in the Barker troupe." John Anderson concurred, "Miss Fontanne, for all the fine things that she has done, seemed better and truer and deeper than ever."

Lunt's notices were equally good. Anderson called his portrayal "delicately imagined, brilliantly played," and Gabriel proclaimed it "vividly clever." Woollcott's review summarized the critical opinion: "It may be doubted if ever anywhere the crucial roles of the dying blackguard of an artist and his exalted, exalting wife have ever been so illuminatingly acted as they were last night by Alfred Lunt and Lynn Fontanne. It may be doubted if ever anywhere in our time they will be so well acted again."*

The Lunts always felt that *The Doctor's Dilemma* had been one of their most satisfying experiences. Fourteen years later, in 1941, Fontanne heard that Katharine Cornell was planning to appear in a new production of the play. "I have always thought that she would make a lovely Jennifer," she wrote to a friend, "but I am afraid she will never be able to, in this day and age, get a cast like we had with Henry Travers, Dudley Digges, Phyllis Connard, Earle Larimore, Baliol Holloway, Philip Leigh and Alfred and me."

The Lunts met Bernard Shaw once. Along with Lawrence Langner and Armina Marshall, they were invited to lunch at Shaw's apartment on the bank of the Thames. As the guests arrived, they were greeted by Mrs. Shaw. The playwright himself was still conspicuously absent when they all sat down to lunch. Mrs. Shaw explained to her puzzled guests, "Mr. Shaw is always a little late because he likes to make an entrance." At last the great man entered the dining room. Despite his reputation for irascibility, the Lunts found him "charm itself," as Fontanne said; "he was simply marvelous. I could have fallen in love with him at once." Lunt was equally taken with Shaw's wit and charm, and the playwright remained one of their idols ever afterward.

The Doctor's Dilemma ran for more than 100 performances, during which time the Lunts went into separate productions of two Eugene O'Neill plays: Lunt spent his "free time" rehearsing for *Marco Millions* and Fontanne prepared for *Strange Interlude,* both of which were scheduled to open in January 1928. The Guild was enthusiastic about presenting two works by America's foremost playwright, but apprehensive about the cost of the former (it called for many sets and costumes and an exceptionally large cast) and the extraordinary length of the latter. O'Neill, who gener-

---

*Woollcott's enthusiasm for the Lunts is evident from this and other notices he gave them. That, and the fact that they were close friends, may lead one to question his objectivity. But it should also be noted that Woollcott did not hesitate to pan Lunt's performances in *The Intimate Strangers, Goat Song* and—later—in *Marco Millions,* or to point out Fontanne's lapse of memory in *Arms and the Man.* Moreover, Woollcott tended to characterize art and artists either as brilliant or as mediocre; rarely did he recognize a middle ground. The Lunts were among those he ranked as brilliant, but he was no less enthusiastic about several other performers.

ally permitted no tampering with his plays, agreed to eliminate some characters and settings from *Marco Millions* and to shorten *Strange Interlude* to conform to the wishes of the Theatre Guild.

Despite his great reputation, O'Neill had difficulty finding a producer for *Marco Millions,* a play about Marco Polo which the playwright intended as a satire on American big business. Both Gilbert Miller and David Belasco had turned it down as too expensive, and O'Neill, who wanted a lavish, expensive production, was not enthusiastic about the Guild's intention to produce the play. He wrote to the critic George Jean Nathan, his friend and supporter, "I am getting a bit sick of these groups that never have the dough to do right by me." But in fact he did not have much choice.

Lunt was chosen to play Marco Polo, and young Rouben Mamoulian, who had recently directed *Porgy* for the Guild to great acclaim, was assigned to direct. At first O'Neill rebelled against Mamoulian's selection, but he was persuaded by the Guild's managers to see *Porgy* before rendering a final judgment. After watching the first act, O'Neill gave his approval.

The Guild appealed to Actors' Equity Association and received permission to rehearse the play for five weeks instead of the customary four because of the size and scope of the production.

Lunt liked the play, but he had reservations about his own role and hoped to be able to speak to O'Neill about them. But, he said, although "O'Neill was there during rehearsals, seated at the back of the theatre . . . I did not get to know him; he was not an easy man to know."

Mamoulian planned to end each performance with a surprise. Lunt, dressed as Marco, would step off the stage and stride down the aisle of the auditorium. Outside, he would step into a waiting limousine, which would carry him away. The effect was intended to suggest that Marco Polo was just another "tired businessman." But Mamoulian's idea was not popular with the Guild's managers, and it was eliminated before opening night.

When *Marco Millions* opened on January 9, 1928, it was still unwieldy. Twenty-one actors were required to play thirty-two characters in a long play of eleven scenes. As in *Juarez and Maximilian,* Lee Simonson's sets tended to dwarf the actors, dominating the production to the detriment of the play.

Some critics found the play to be "original, powerful, searching . . . a splendid and thoughtful burlesque." Others were far more critical. Robert Littell, in the *Post,* called *Marco Millions* "surprisingly simple-minded, obvious, and at times actually foolish. . . . The eleven scenes show us, in ABCs which can be read a mile away, the contrast between Western money-grubbing and Eastern wisdom, between materialism and idealism, between the dollar and the dream."

Lunt's performance as Marco was praised by many observers. Brooks Atkinson, who had in the past been more critical of Lunt's performances than any other New York reviewer, applauded his work in *Marco Millions,* saying, "Alfred Lunt plays the most conspicuous role expertly. Without ever betraying the character, he catches the selfishness and the vigor of a cheapjack merchant." E. W. Osborn said that Lunt's portrayal was "a marvel . . . the perfect characterization," and Leonard Hall in the *Telegram* called his playing "delightful . . . his finest chore in years."

But it seems probable that Lunt's performance was less effective than many he had given in the past. The weariness caused by performing leading roles in so many plays in such rapid succession was taking its toll. If no one else noticed that weariness, Alexander Woollcott did. Woollcott, who found the play "an almost grotesquely elaborate and solemnly pretentious way of saying a very little," commented in his notice in the *World* that Lunt's "performance [had] the effect of lapsing between each speech. It was, of course, a perfectly conceived and supremely competent performance, but . . . it was marked by an almost hypnotic weariness, each line of the long role parting from him as if, although he was quite certain what the next might be, he had not quite decided whether to buck up and say it or just to curl up there on the Guild stage and take a good, long nap."

The production was, nevertheless, modestly successful, playing for 92 performances. It was placed in the repertory, alternating with *The Doctor's Dilemma* and, after that play closed, with *Volpone*.

Marco Millions was simplicity itself compared to the difficulties presented by *Strange Interlude*. That play, in which O'Neill attempted to reproduce the rich texture of a psychological novel, featured characters who spoke their lines of dialogue to one another, then described their real thoughts—which were often at odds with the words they had spoken—to the audience.* The technique had never been attempted in American drama before, and the Guild was challenged to find a way to make the convention understandable to its audiences. Furthermore, the play was immensely long, written in nine acts requiring more than five hours to perform.

Because of its length, its innovations and its reliance upon Freudian psychology, *Strange Interlude* was thought by the managers of the Theatre Guild to have little chance of success with the public. They expected critical approval, to be sure, but they were so certain that most theatregoers would have no interest in the play that they considered offering it to subscribers only, as a special matinee attraction.

Eventually it was decided to incorporate *Strange Interlude* into the Guild's regular program, but that decision in itself created problems. Because the play was so long, it was first scheduled to be presented on two consecutive nights. O'Neill then shortened the play somewhat, and the managers decided to give it on a single day, beginning it at 5:15, breaking for dinner at 7:30 and resuming at 9:00; the final curtain would descend

---

*The process was also reversed. Often, the characters first articulated their thoughts, then delivered their lines to the characters on stage.

shortly after 11:00. That schedule, however, necessitated even further cuts in O'Neill's script. The playwright obliged by eliminating all the humorous moments, a tactic that disturbed the director, Philip Moeller, who believed the humor was necessary to provide relief from the prevailing tone of stark drama.

With one exception, the Guild was able to cast the play without difficulty. The role of Nina Leeds—the principal character, who begins as an innocent but gradually becomes a cynic who employs her sexual attractiveness and her possessiveness to exploit the men with whom she comes in contact—had first been offered to Katharine Cornell, who rejected it. O'Neill recommended Ann Harding, but agreed to the managers' suggestion that it be offered to Alice Brady. Brady turned it down because of her concern that the role was an unsympathetic one. Other actresses were then approached, but all of them expressed the fear that the Freudian implications of the play would be misunderstood and that the character of Nina would be disliked by the audience. Finally, Lynn Fontanne was offered the part. She took the script of the play on the road with her, and she and Lunt both read it carefully.

Neither Lunt nor Fontanne was impressed by *Strange Interlude*. Fontanne thought the role of Nina was "impossible," but Lunt believed she should accept it because, he said, the play was sure to be "the event of the season." "Everyone will be writing about it and talking about it," he told her. "Even if it is a flop, it will be important and you will gain something by having played in it."

Lawrence Langner and Theresa Helburn were deputed by the Guild's managers to use their powers of persuasion on Fontanne. They caught up with the tour in Baltimore, having rehearsed their arguments on the train from New York. But when they sat down to dinner in the Lunts' suite at the Belvedere Hotel, they found, to their surprise, that she had already decided to accept the part.

O'Neill had the right of approval concerning the actors to be cast in his play. He expressed enthusiasm about Earle Larimore, Tom Powers and Glenn Anders, but he was reluctant to approve the casting of Fontanne. His only previous experience with her had been when she played Anna in his play *Chris* in 1920, and he had not been impressed with her. As he rarely attended the theatre, he had not seen her perform since then. He was persuaded to attend a performance of *The Doctor's Dilemma* in Baltimore, but the experience did little to change his opinion. He was much impressed by Lunt, but predicted that Fontanne "will give a very adequate performance but she will be far from . . . my 'Nina.' However, who would be?"

Fontanne was given the role. Soon afterward O'Neill approached her and, in her words, "asked me if I remembered a conversation we'd once had during the production of *Chris,* when I told him that I wished someone would write a play exposing possessive mothers, showing how some of them ruin their children's lives. 'This is it!' O'Neill said, pointing to a script of *Interlude*." Since Fontanne was vying with Hattie Sederholm for Lunt's affections at the time she was playing in *Chris* (and appeared to be losing the battle), one wonders if she had Hattie in mind as the prototype of the possessive mother.

Rehearsals for *Strange Interlude* began early in December 1927. As it had with *Marco Millions*, the Theatre Guild appealed to Actors' Equity to allow them a rehearsal period longer than normal. Essentially, the Guild argued, they would be presenting two plays when they were offering *Strange Interlude*. Equity agreed and allotted the Guild seven weeks of rehearsal time.

O'Neill, whose father had been a prominent actor in America but had sacrificed his idealism in favor of making a fortune by appearing in mediocre melodrama, was generally contemptuous of actors. He found them intellectually inferior and insufficiently creative. It may be said that the very form of *Strange Interlude* reveals his distrust of actors. By forcing the performers to speak their thoughts aloud, he was not permitting them to communicate those thoughts by unspoken means, which is the actor's constant task. He was, in effect, eliminating much of the impact that an actor can have upon a production. He admitted as much in a conversation with Lawrence Langner, saying that he believed most actors were not competent to communicate unspoken thoughts and that he had therefore articulated those thoughts for them.

But how should the lengthy asides be treated in production? That was the most serious problem faced by the director, Philip Moeller. As Moeller put it, "In the midst of the action and the usual sort of dialogue the play had to seem suddenly to stop and, at the same time, not to stop so that the characters involved in the various scenes might speak out their supposedly silent thoughts in a new kind of audibility. The audience was to accept the peculiar psychological problem of hearing what the characters in the play were thinking while they were saying one thing and simultaneously, in their minds, commenting on it."

Several ideas were discarded. One of them was to set aside a special area of the stage that the audience would be given to understand was an area in which spoken words represented a character's thoughts; but that seemed overly cumbersome, as actors would have to move back and forth continually between the acting area proper and the "special area." Another possibility was to alter the lighting each time a character expressed his thoughts, perhaps by focusing on that character alone; again, however, the method seemed to have as much potential for distraction as for clarification. Perhaps the actors could deliver the lines of dialogue in one tone of voice and alter their voices during the moments of mental commentary. At least five different possibilities were considered, but the director eventually rejected all of them.

Finally, as Moeller was on the train returning from Baltimore, where he had gone with O'Neill to see *The Doctor's Dilemma,* the answer came to him. As he described the moment, "Suddenly the train stopped. Unconsciously, this may have been the hint; this may or may not have been the way my mind got it. 'Why not, for a moment,' I thought, 'stop the physical action of the play and allow the mental commentary to tell us its hidden secret simply, directly and without any obviously elaborate and intimate preparations?' I decided to do it this way."

The rehearsal process was long and tedious, especially for Fontanne, whose dislike of the play became stronger as time went on. She objected to the excessive length, which she thought unnecessary, to the facile psychologizing and, most of all, to the wooden dialogue. "I respect authors, I really do," she said, "but I have a great sense of what will 'go,' and I didn't care much for the writing in *Strange Interlude.* There was a woodenness at times, and so much of it was repetitious. There were a good many lines intended by O'Neill to be taken seriously, that I thought would get belly laughs from the audience. It would have hurt the play. For instance, I would have to say in an aside something like, 'Ned has the bluest eyes I ever saw; I must tell him so.' Then I would go to Ned and tell him he had the bluest eyes I ever saw. I felt it was unnecessary to say this twice. I told O'Neill I thought it would be better if I looked at Ned's eyes with admiration the first time, silently, instead of saying the line as an aside. I asked him if I could cut the line. He said, 'No, you can't. Play it as I wrote it.' I asked O'Neill to cut [other] lines and he wouldn't do it, so, without telling anyone—Moeller, Helburn, Langner, anyone—I cut, cut, cut, and nobody ever realized it."

Lunt's opinion of the play was similar to his wife's. He described it to his friends as "a six-day bisexual race." Time did not soften his negative opinion. Years later he described the play as "utterly dated, quite unreadable." He also said, more genially, when Fontanne was no longer in the production, "If *Strange Interlude* had had two more acts, I could have sued Lynn for desertion."

Still, O'Neill and Moeller were pleased with the progress the actors were making during rehearsals. Shortly before the play was scheduled to open, O'Neill told Fontanne, "You are so exactly right for the part that it might have been written for you."

Fontanne may have given her script to Alexander Woollcott to read, for an article containing a scathing review appeared in *Vanity Fair* days before *Strange Interlude* opened. The general belief was that no one else would have given Woollcott a copy of the play, but that Fontanne might have done so because she and Woollcott had become such close friends. Woollcott had never been fond of O'Neill's dramas, but his attack on *Strange Interlude* was particularly strong. (He saved his most biting phrase until after it had opened, calling it "the *Abie's Irish Rose* of the pseudo-intelligentsia.") Outraged at this pre-opening assessment, the Guild contacted Woollcott's editor at the *World* to ask that Woollcott not be permitted to review the play for the newspaper. The editor agreed, promising to send another critic in his place.

A preview performance of *Strange Interlude* was given on January 29, the day before the official opening. The reaction of the audience was far more intense and appreciative than the Guild's managers had anticipated, and for the first time they realized that the long psychological drama, which they had produced only because they thought it would bring prestige to the organization, might turn out to be a commercial success.

The audience at the opening performance was similarly impressed, as were most of the critics. "The most significant contribution any American has made to the stage" was Gilbert Gabriel's verdict. Dudley Nichols, who replaced Woollcott as the reviewer for the *World*, called *Strange Interlude* "the top of O'Neill's career. . . . It would seem that [O'Neill] has not only written a great American play but the great American novel as well . . . a psychological novel of tremendous power and depth." But not everyone was so enthusiastic. Brooks Atkinson said the play "commands the respectful interest of the enthusiastic playgoer to whom experiment is never dull. [But this can be reported] without believing that *Strange Interlude* is distinguished as a play."

Fontanne's skeptical attitude obviously had no ill effect on her performance, which was universally admired. Atkinson singled her out, along with Earle Larimore, for special praise. They "play with admirable distinction and resourcefulness," he said. "More than any of the others they have mastered the technique of this strange play; and without upsetting the flow of drama they contrive to give their 'asides' a true value. Meanwhile they describe two characters completely. One cannot speak too highly of their skill."

To everyone's surprise, *Strange Interlude* became a runaway box-office success, playing in New York for 441 performances, always to packed houses. It was not part of the alternating repertory—its length made it unsuitable for that system—so it ran continuously at the John Golden Theatre. The fear that audiences would object to the long intermission did not prove to be the case. If anything, people seemed to enjoy it, and a number of restaurants in the neighborhood of the Golden Theatre reaped the benefits.

Noël Coward saw a performance of *Strange Interlude* and was asked by Fontanne what he had thought of her performance. After offering his compliments in general, he added, "In the seventh act you overacted, you groaned a bit too much." As soon as he made the comment, Coward said, "I could have bitten off my tongue." He knew he had let himself in for hours of questioning, and the probability that he would be asked to attend another performance in order to see if she had tempered her overacting.

Coward said about both the Lunts, "They cross-examine you like the Gestapo, you know, on every detail." As he had expected, Fontanne grilled him endlessly about her performance. Then, "Ten nights later she called me and said, 'You can come see it,' and I couldn't just see the seventh act, I had to sit through the whole boring thing from the beginning. And of course she had the seventh act down perfectly."

While Fontanne played *Strange Interlude* at the Golden Theatre and *Marco Millions* was still running at the Guild, there was a meeting of the Guild's Board and its leading actors at which Lunt was asked to play the role of Mosca in Stefan Zweig's adaptation of Ben Jonson's *Volpone,* to run in repertory with *Marco Millions.* The role was a fiercely energetic one for a man who was already as tired as Lunt's performance in *Marco Millions* had shown him to be, and Fontanne lashed out at the Guild's managers for suggesting that her husband play yet another demanding role. She produced a letter from a physician saying that Lunt's health was in danger, that he must be given a long rest. She insisted that Lunt's voice was overstrained—that he could barely whisper, much less project to a crowded theatre.

The managers were about to relent and cast someone else in the role. Before they could announce their decision, however, a small voice was heard from the back of the room. It was Alfred Lunt, speaking with what little voice remained to him, saying that he would enjoy playing Mosca, actually.

One can imagine Fontanne throwing up her hands in irritation at Lunt's response. However, his instinct never to turn down a challenging role was too strong for him to resist. The opportunity to play Mosca might never be offered him again; thus, it *had* to be accepted, regardless of his weariness.

Lunt, as Volpone's wily servant, was always on the move, often performing feats of near-acrobatic skill. "I had to crawl on my knees so much that I developed painful calluses," he said, "and I was plentifully covered with black-and-blue spots through falling over chairs, beds and other stage furnishings."

But Lunt always enjoyed playing low comedy, and he reveled in the role of Mosca. On one occasion the revelry got a bit out of hand. Noël Coward was in the audience and Lunt was keyed up, wanting to please his friend with an especially rollicking performance. In his enthusiasm, he inserted some unrehearsed business that proved distracting to the other actors. During one scene he suggestively toyed with a basket of oranges and bananas. At the end of another, when the curtain was supposed to come down with Mosca standing at one side of the stage while Volpone lay in bed at the other, Lunt suddenly leaped across the stage to the bed, hurled the covers back and jumped into bed beside Volpone. The curtain fell on an astonished Dudley Digges (Volpone), who must have thought that

Lunt had lost his mind. Digges refused to speak to Lunt for days afterward.

Lunt may also have been a bit ashamed of his uncontrolled enthusiasm, because in later years he rarely gave in to the temptation to indulge in unrehearsed business. And when he began directing, in 1934, he certainly would not have tolerated such improvisation from anyone else.

Even when he stayed within the confines of the Jonson-Zweig script, Lunt's performance was apparently a devilish one. "He is agile and artful, but he is also mocking and crafty," Brooks Atkinson said in his review; "his acting is shot through with the Jonsonian spirit. . . . As Volpone's rascally parasite, Mr. Lunt infuses his acting with the buoyant, knavish irony of the play." And Woollcott said, "Quite obviously he has the time of his life as the wind-blown, scheming, lick-spittle Mosca. . . . Swift, sure, gleaming—he darts and buzzes and stings his way through the play. . . . I know only one other actor of our stage who would so enjoy playing Mosca, or who would play it so well. That is the truant [John] Barrymore [who was in Hollywood making films]. More than their fellows, it seems to me, these two bring a great and leaping thing to the theatre. It is called imagination."

If *Strange Interlude* and *Volpone* were successful, both were also highly controversial. Some viewers were outraged at *Strange Interlude*'s sexual frankness; some found the risqué business in *Volpone* offensive. And some went further, suggesting that the plays should not be permitted to continue. They were symptomatic, it was said, of the too casual approach the New York theatre took to the presentation of "immoral" plays. The plays thus became a target for those who wanted to impose censorship on the American theatre.

More than a year earlier, on February 4, 1927, a symposium on censorship had been sponsored by the New York *Times*. Many prominent actors and actresses attended and some of them offered their opinions. John Drew, a star for fifty years, said he thought the actors themselves should lend a hand in cleaning up the New York stage. He was supported by Fred Stone, Bobby Watson and Estelle Winwood (who said, "I favor a censor. . . . It is a means by which the theatre may keep its decency and self-respect. Anyone with good taste and good judgment—in other words, with the right moral and intellectual background—would be suitable as a censor"). Most emphatic in his support of censorship was the British actor Clarence Derwent, who said, "I am not one of those who fear the coming of dramatic censorship as the end of all things. We have had it for many years in England and it has worked very well. In fact, some fifteen years ago when there was a question of the censor being abolished I appeared in the House of Lords as official representative of retaining in the censor. The movie industry in America has flourished as never before under the strict supervision of a czar, and the theatre, under similar benevolent autocracy, would quickly regain the confidence of the public."

Other actors were less certain that censorship would work, although they agreed that it was desirable. Such performers as Sidney Toler, E. H. Sothern and Frederick Perry said they would support censorship if a board were appointed that would include people within the theatrical profession.

But most of the assembled actors firmly opposed the idea. Among them were Blanche Yurka, Jane Cowl, Walter Huston, Ethel Barrymore, Eva Le Gallienne, Leon Errol, Vivienne Segal, Genevieve Tobin, Helen Gahagan, Wilton Lackaye and a contingent from the Theatre Guild thatj included Helen Westley, Dudley Digges and Alfred Lunt. Lunt's views were expressed simply but eloquently. "As an actor," he said, "I would find it distasteful to appear in any play which offended my own sense of decency or which offended the sense of decency of any intelligent audience. As to censorship as it might be practiced, I believe it brings far more dangers into the theatrical world than it removes."

Lunt and the other members of the Theatre Guild were clearly concerned because the plays the Guild produced often contained just the sort of frank treatment of adult material that was grist for the censor's mill. Indeed, in 1928, District Attorney Joab H. Banton announced that the Theatre Guild's productions of *Strange Interlude* and *Volpone* would be investigated and, if found to be immoral, prosecuted under the law. Banton had received written complaints from the counsel for the Shubert brothers and the editor of the Shubert publication, the *Review,* asking him to investigate the morality of *Strange Interlude* and *Volpone*. It is not difficult to discover why these theatrical producers would have filed such a complaint. Until earlier in 1928, the Shubert brothers had been the booking agents for the Guild's road companies, but the Guild had arranged to turn its road bookings over to A. L. Erlanger for the 1928–29 season. Immediately following that action, editorials in the *Review* began to attack the Theatre Guild, focusing primarily upon *Strange Interlude* and *Volpone*. The Shuberts' counsel complained to the District Attorney that plays like *Strange Interlude* present "a sex appeal which does not help to mold the mind of the young girl." The counsel admitted, however, that neither he nor his clients had seen a performance of the play.

Banton revealed that he regarded the Shuberts' complaint with some suspicion, and he might have dismissed it as a matter of internecine theatrical warfare if, shortly afterward, he had not received a second complaint, this one from an unidentified Theatre Guild subscriber.

Banton agreed to investigate. He or his men would personally view the productions and decide their fate, he said. There was only one catch. *Strange Interlude* was sold out until May 28 and seats were not available even to a crusading District Attorney. So his investigation of that play would have to wait for a month.

If Banton could not get tickets, however, he could read the play, and he did so on April 25. Also on that date the Theatre Guild sent him two complimentary tickets. He then announced that his deputy, Assistant District Attorney Wallace, would attend a performance of *Strange Interlude* on Saturday, accompanied by a representative of the Police Commissioner's office. They would determine whether the Theatre Guild was in violation of the Wales Padlock Law "against objectionable performances."

Assistant District Attorney Wallace and the Police Commissioner's representative, James P. Sinott, attended *Strange Interlude* on April 27. As they watched the performance from fourth row center, they also followed the written text of the play, which they had carried into the theatre with them. A day later the same two public servants ventured to the Guild Theatre to see *Volpone*.

On May 1, having received the report of his assistant, District Attorney Banton made the surprise announcement that neither *Strange Interlude* nor *Volpone* would "tend to corrupt the morals of youth or others." Banton revealed that Wallace and Sinott had discovered that many of the most objectionable features of both plays in written form had been eliminated in production. "Many of the lines in the manuscript [of] the plays, which might offend good taste, are not read by the actors," Banton said. His assistants did report that the performances contained some coarse language, offensive to good taste, but that this was insufficient for them to recommend that the full weight of the law be brought to bear against the Theatre Guild.

Did the Guild instruct its actors to launder the productions seen by the lawmen? Was Eugene O'Neill, who was quite fanatical on the subject, angry when he heard that the actors were omitting some of his dialogue? Is it possible that the cuts that Lynn Fontanne had made in her dialogue during rehearsals helped save the Theatre Guild from prosecution? Unfortunately, history is silent on all of these subjects.

Reactions to Banton's announcement ranged from the Shuberts' grudging admission that "Mr. Banton's ruling is the last word, and we have to abide by it," to Theresa Helburn's statement on behalf of the Theatre Guild, "Of course, the District Attorney's ruling makes the Guild very happy."

Neither of the Lunts remained in their productions until the runs were concluded. Fontanne appeared in *Strange Interlude* only for six months and, at the end of June, was replaced by Judith Anderson. At the same time Lunt turned over his role in *Volpone* to Douglass Montgomery so that he and Fontanne could take a two-month vacation before setting out on tour with *The Guardsman* and *Arms and the Man* at the beginning of the 1928–29 season.

Within a few years the unrelenting pace of the Lunts' activities, combined with their distaste for the methods of the Theatre Guild's managers, would prompt them to sever their connection with the Guild. In 1928, however, their workloads were so staggering—and the rewards so gratifying—that they had neither the time nor the inclination to think purposefully about anything beyond that night's performance or the next day's rehearsal.

Chapter Seven

TEAMWORK

"Isn't it nice, my dear, to know that they
really are married?"
A member of the audience, 1929

1928–29

O n August 30, 1928, the Lunts returned to New York from a vacation
trip to Spain and plunged immediately into work for the 1928–29
season, which began for them with a tour of Baltimore, Cleveland, Pittsburgh, Philadelphia, Chicago and Boston, where on December 17 they
opened in *Caprice,* which had been in rehearsal throughout the tour. The
play marked a historic occasion: it was the beginning of the indivisible
acting partnership of Lunt and Fontanne. From the time it opened until
the Lunts retired from the stage after the run of *The Visit* in 1960, they
never again appeared separately.

The Lunts had arranged the year before that the Theatre Guild would
not require either of them to perform in one city while the other was acting
elsewhere. But in 1928–29 they went further, informing the Guild that
they wished always to appear together in the same plays. Several elements
contributed to this decision: the Lunts were convinced they did their best
work together, they hated to spend time apart, and they believed the Guild
was putting commercial concerns before artistic ones by casting them in
separate plays. Not content with paying them salaries far below what they
could have commanded elsewhere, the Guild wanted to keep them acting
separately, the Lunts believed, so that they would provide drawing power
for two plays rather than one. But the Lunts felt their contributions to the
box office were quite sufficient when they were cast together.

Caprice, under the title *Playing at Love,* had been scheduled to open
at the end of the previous season with a different cast, including Richard
Bennett and Cathleen Nesbitt. Rehearsals had gone poorly, however,

largely because Bennett was drinking heavily, so before the play could open, the Theatre Guild decided the cast should be disbanded and the production postponed until the Lunts were available. *Caprice,* written by the Viennese playwright, novelist and essayist Sil-Vara, was the sort of sophisticated comedy in which Theatre Guild audiences most enjoyed seeing them perform.

Caprice was adapted and directed by Philip Moeller, who had also staged *Volpone, The Second Man, At Mrs. Beam's, Arms and the Man* and *The Guardsman,* the other light comedies in which the Lunts had scored such success. Clearly, Moeller must have had a deft comic touch, even though Fontanne in 1978 said that "he really wasn't a very good director." She also told George Schaefer that Moeller believed the old-fashioned elocutionary style of acting, in which the actor slowly and ponderously intoned his words, was superior to the more natural and realistic kind of performing the Lunts exemplified at the Theatre Guild.

Lunt played Albert von Echardt in *Caprice,* a middle-aged bachelor with an unquenchable thirst for attractive young women. Fontanne appeared as the beautiful and sophisticated Ilse von Ilsen, whose appetite for amorous adventure is equal to that of von Echardt.

While the Lunts were on vacation the previous summer, Fontanne had selected Ilse's costumes for *Caprice.* The Theatre Guild thought it was showing remarkable generosity when it allocated $2,500 for her outfits. But that "was nothing, not even a drop in the bucket," as Lunt said after the purchases were made. As they did so often, the Lunts wound up spending a good deal of their own money on their costumes.

The Doctor's Dilemma had been the first production of the Theatre Guild ever to open outside New York. *Caprice* was the second, beginning a trend for the Guild, which thereafter opened most of its plays "on the road." *Caprice* was greeted enthusiastically by the Boston press and theatregoers. After two weeks, the production moved to New York, opening at the Guild Theatre on December 31, 1928. If ever a play opened on an appropriate day, this was it. Charmingly risqué, as light as air, inconsequential, full of good spirits, *Caprice* was the perfect play for New Year's Eve.

Brooks Atkinson expressed the general critical opinion when he wrote that *Caprice* "is a dextrous comedy edged with alluring insight . . . piquant, sly, insinuating and frolicsome," but "the supreme pleasure is having Lynn Fontanne and Alfred Lunt back again, playing with original charm and skill, picking up every hint in the script and tossing it brilliantly into the air." Atkinson went on to say, "Miss Fontanne and Mr. Lunt are a matchless pair of volatile comedians. *Caprice* lives in their style of walking, their toying with boutonnieres, and in their spontaneity with the lines and colloquies. . . . They have played similar parts before, but with no such effervescence and versatility as they summon in *Caprice*. Now they play with infinite subtlety, resource and drollery. . . ."

On June 4, 1929, the Theatre Guild's production of *Caprice* opened at the St. James's Theatre in London with the New York cast nearly intact. New York audiences had by no means tired of the play, but the Guild sent *Caprice* to London both in order to expand its influence and as a sort of reward to the Lunts for their contributions to the organization and their willingness to forgo the offers of commercial managers and motion-picture producers. The London engagement was of special importance to both the Lunts, as it represented Fontanne's first appearance in her home country as an internationally renowned performer and Lunt's British debut.

If the opportunity to play in Britain was welcomed by the Lunts, it also created a degree of tension for both of them. The awful memory of her last London opening, with Laurette Taylor in the ill-fated *One Night in Rome,* combined with the personal significance of her return to the British stage, made Fontanne far more nervous than she customarily became on an opening night.

Lunt was always apprehensive on first nights, but the stories Fontanne had told him about the rowdiness of English audiences had him especially worried. He had the misfortune to ask the Cockney wardrobe mistress if it was true that British audiences were given to booing when they disliked the production. According to British writer Wilson McCarty's 1929 account, the woman responded, "Oh, sir, they boos something terrible in this theatre, but don't you worry. Don't you pay any attention. You just go right on talking, like as if you didn't 'ear it, sir. That's wot they all does, sir."

Lunt shivered and asked if the last play produced at the St. James's Theatre had been booed. Yes, replied the wardrobe mistress, it had been given a thorough booing. Did the audience throw anything at the actors, Lunt asked. Eggs, for instance?

"Yes, sir, eggs, too; but don't you mind an egg or two, sir. I'll get it off your clothes, sir. Don't you worry."

Not feeling very reassured, Lunt went on stage to begin the play. He said afterward that he felt like an uncertain boxer, "tossing out a line, then jumping back and watching the effect."

Fontanne stood in the wings, waiting for her entrance. "I was frightfully upset," she said. "All of a sudden my knees began to tremble, then to wobble and finally to rattle against each other. . . . It was exactly like my first performances in England as a girl." But when she heard her cue and walked on stage to deliver her first line, her nervousness disappeared. The Lunts gained confidence as the evening progressed and the audience's enjoyment of the play became evident.

Another reason for the Lunts' apprehension on this occasion was their fear of critical reaction to the overlapping technique they had developed. But the response of most of the English critics could hardly have been more favorable. Charles Morgan called the company's performance "immeasurably more highly finished than our own. . . . The Theatre Guild's

Acting Company is more professional than any I have ever seen." *Punch* called it "the best presentation of a comedy in English on the English stage since the Barker-Vedrenne association at the Court Theatre" more than twenty years before. And another critic declared that the response of the audience "was the greatest ovation I have ever seen accorded to an American company."

J. B. Priestley was taken against his will to a performance at the St. James's Theatre. He expected to be bored beyond words by a trivial comedy of manners. But by the end of the first act, he said, "I was sitting in an enchantment . . . because I had fallen under the spell of its leading players . . . the fabulous Lunts." Priestley went on to describe in more detail the sensations he experienced:

> . . . there is both an aesthetic and intellectual delight, and one very rarely discovered, in being offered direction and acting raised to an unusual high pitch, brought close to perfection. In an ordinary way, with a run-of-the-mill director slogging away during his three-week rehearsals, what we get is little more than a rough sketch of a play. . . . We need something much more, both from the director and his leading players. Now . . . the Lunts gave us that *something much more*. Over and above their exceptional individual talent or his reserve of strength or her bewitching femininity, their secret was that they took over where the director left off. They were capable of rehearsing and rehearsing, making another tiny cut or adding a nuance, when they were already playing to crowded houses bursting with applause. . . . The result to an intelligent member of the audience would reach beyond mere satisfaction to sheer exhilaration.

The capacity for endless rehearsal noted by Priestley was in part a reflection of the Lunts' fascination with the technical aspects of acting. On occasion it was impossible to test a particular technique unless it was tried in front of an audience. Consequently, while he was appearing in *Caprice,* Lunt conducted an experiment based upon a supposedly surefire theatrical technique. "I'd always heard about the handkerchief trick, that if you pulled out a handkerchief, a white handkerchief, in a speech, it spoiled someone else's laugh," he told Maurice Zolotow. "The theory is, the audience's eye is attracted to the white handkerchief and the lines are not heard." During the London run of *Caprice,* Lunt and Douglass Montgomery determined to test the White Handkerchief Theory. "I had a line with a tiny laugh and he had a tiny laugh and I thought if I could kill his laugh with the handkerchief trick I'll get myself a bigger laugh on my line. He said his line and got the biggest laugh he ever got. I said my line and got nothing. I put the handkerchief away and never used it again."

Years later, when the Lunts were acting in *O Mistress Mine,* Lunt decided once again to experiment with technique. He and the other members of the cast made slight alterations in their playing to see if they could discover precisely which techniques would elicit laughter and which would inhibit or destroy audience response. "We spent several nights doing one scene in every way possible," Lunt said. "We tried reading lines with our faces down . . . it didn't make any difference at all [as long as] they could hear it—they laughed. We read it with our backs to the audience, behind furniture, etc., and you know, we got every single laugh we got before! I said to the young man in the play [Dick Van Patten], 'Play the whole last act upstage and see what happens.' It didn't make any difference. It happens that the lines were good. That's the author, you understand? Not the actors. So it doesn't matter what you do if you can be heard. You know, they tell you the audience has to see your face in order for you to get certain laughs. Well, Lynn had a line she was positive was a laugh in *Mistress Mine* and no matter what she did she couldn't get it. Then one night she decided to say the line *offstage*—and she got the laugh."

When Lunt was asked to define and explain acting technique, he would candidly admit that he hadn't the least idea. He had come to the conclusion that rules simply do not apply to acting. He told Morton Eustis, "No good actor is bound by any rules. It's absurd to say there are any set formulae for acting comedy or tragedy—one set of gestures the actor pulls out of the hat when he is a clown, another when he is a tragic figure. What you do and how you do it depends entirely on the play and the part you portray. . . . You play serious and comic scenes differently. Of course. The timing is quite different, the whole interpretation—just as it is in life. But that depends on character more than on technique. Often you do the best you can and then something happens you hadn't expected at all. You plan one piece of business to get a laugh. It falls absolutely flat. Something you hadn't thought out at all brings down the house. You can't be sure of anything."

Shortly after the end of World War II, Lunt was asked by the American Theatre Wing to teach a class in acting to American servicemen. One of the GIs brought up the question of technique, and, knowing that the Lunts were regarded as consummate technicians, asked him to define the word. Lunt pondered for a moment and said, "I haven't the slightest idea. I have to go home and ask my wife." When he returned for the next session, the soldiers asked him what Fontanne had said. Lunt answered, "Well, she said to read the lines with as much reality as possible, as if you were in a room, but a little louder than in a room, so the back row and the gallery can hear. And be careful not to bump into each other."

Despite their claim of ignorance regarding technical know-how, the Lunts' reputations as actors who had achieved near-total command of theatrical technique was well deserved. The technique they had mastered, however, grew not out of a predigested set of conventions but out of trial and error, a laborious working out of alternatives calculated to produce the most effective ways of communicating every nuance of attitude and behavior. If they could not (or would not) articulate their understanding of technique, they were no less masters of the skill.

During a matinee performance of *Caprice* early in the play's New York run, Cheryl Crawford witnessed one of the rare occasions on which the Lunts were guilty of a serious breach of stage discipline when Fontanne, in her character of Ilse, slapped Lunt as Von Echardt in the face with her gloves. Lunt glowered angrily at his wife for delivering a harder slap than he was used to receiving. He muttered something to her under his breath, and she angrily responded with a muttered oath of her own. The play called for her to exit a moment later and then to return immediately. In the character of Von Echardt, Lunt poured himself a bicarbonate of soda while waiting for Fontanne's entrance so that the scene could continue. But he waited in vain. A horrified Crawford watched from the mezzanine as Lunt slowly drank the headache remedy. He turned pale and began to shake with fury, but Fontanne did not reenter. At last the stage manager called for the curtain to be brought down. Thinking that she might be able to help, Crawford ran backstage, but was intercepted by the stage manager, who said, "Stay out of it, for God's sake! They're furious. Give them time to get over it."

Such outbursts of temper aimed at one another were rare, and the way they had, on this occasion, allowed their private anger to spill over into the performance was unprecedented for either of the Lunts; nor was it repeated during the remainder of their careers. The public regarded them—accurately—as individuals who had the greatest love and respect for one another. This perception of the Lunts' offstage lives also had an effect on the public's attitude regarding their performances. With each new play, audiences anticipated what sort of relationship Lunt and Fontanne would share. Would it be erotic? violent? both? Such plays as *Caprice, At Mrs. Beam's, The Guardsman* and *Arms and the Man,* in which they played married or unmarried lovers who often feuded with one another, physically or otherwise, stimulated the public's taste for the sophisticated and slightly risqué humor at which the Lunts were so adept.

Audiences in the 1920s were often unwilling to accept the overtly sexual on-stage language and behavior that became commonplace in the 1960s and thereafter, but the Lunts were permitted liberties that other actors were denied. Perhaps it was partly because they were known to be happily married to one another. Perhaps it was because their most erotic love scenes were always stylish and good-natured rather than salacious. But the scenes reeked frankly and wholeheartedly of sex.

On one occasion during the run of *Caprice,* one of the Lunts' love scenes became so steamy that an elderly matron in the audience began to squirm uncomfortably in her seat. Her companion, also a respectable old woman, whispered comfortingly, "Isn't it nice, my dear, to know that they really are married?"

A scene in *Reunion in Vienna,* produced in 1931, was described in detail by Alexander Woollcott. As Fontanne entered, Lunt was seated with his back to the audience. "The meeting is electric," Woollcott wrote. "He sees her in a mirror, turns slowly around, scorches her from head to foot with his eyes, circles silently around her, comes close, lets his hand play over her bosom and buttocks, then slaps her in the face and gives her one long, exhausting kiss. All that time she never speaks, never moves a muscle, but when he straightens up again, you can see that . . . everything about her has wilted in the heat."

During the Second World War, the Lunts gave a performance of *Love in Idleness* in an unheated London theatre with an audience composed largely of soldiers on leave. At the beginning of the performance, the soldiers all wore their overcoats, but each love scene on stage seemed to raise the temperature in the auditorium. By the end of the performance, according to George Freedley, most of the assembled military personnel had removed not only their overcoats but their sweaters as well.

A few months later *Love in Idleness* was retitled *O Mistress Mine* and brought to America. During one performance Lunt lay exhausted on a couch, his legs across Fontanne's lap. "And suddenly," as he described the business when he and Fontanne appeared on Dick Cavett's television show in 1970, "she ran her hand up inside my trouser leg. The audience was delighted with the business and so was I. And we just kept it in for a couple of years."

After the Lunts' stage careers were over, Lunt looked back on this aspect of their performances and offered the opinion that audiences in the 1960s were no longer able to enjoy sexual byplay because "some awfully talented writers have come along who think sex is terrible and ugly, and they write those kinds of plays. . . . They're so worried about it, so tormented, tortured. Sex really isn't a ghastly thing, you know." By contrast, he said, the plays in which he and Fontanne performed regarded sex as healthy and enjoyable. "Sex is fun," he said. "Honestly, it is. Lynn and I did the most outrageous things on a stage, and we enjoyed it and the audience enjoyed it. It was done graciously and with pleasure, rather than with a sense of doom and terror."

Now that the Lunts were performing together exclusively, their rehearsals at the Theatre Guild were extended by many hours after they returned to their apartment at 163 East 36th Street. It might, in fact, be more accurate to say that rehearsals at the theatre became extensions of the work they did at home, for that is where the bulk of their preparation was done.

They worked out a meticulous routine for their sessions at home. Memorization of lines came first. Since the apartment had three stories, with the dining room on the ground floor, the bedrooms on the second and a studio-living room on the third, Fontanne would take the top floor and Lunt the lowest. Each would thus be able to shout out the lines of the play without disturbing the other. Memorization came more easily to Lunt, but neither of them was a quick study. After both felt reasonably secure in their lines, they worked in the same room, sitting facing one another on two plain wooden chairs. With legs interlocked and eyes focused squarely on each other, they began to exchange dialogue. If one of them faltered or gave the wrong line, the other clapped his knees together and the scene began again. After several such sessions, their knees may have been bruised but they were letter-perfect in their lines.

Once the memorization was out of the way, the Lunts approached each scene with a sense of improvisation. A scene would be played first one way, then another, then still another. The lines would remain the same, but the attitudes and intentions of the characters would undergo a change each time. After trying numerous approaches, they would then come to an agreement on which had been the most interesting, the most useful in terms of suggesting character traits and relationships. The scene would then be played again and again, with the Lunts stopping frequently to discuss points of contention, to recommend the addition of a look here, a gesture there, the modification of an inflection or the deletion of an element that was not working as well as had been anticipated. None of this was performed halfheartedly. They would rehearse with as much energy, speed and vocal projection as if an audience were watching. ("We work like mad," Lunt said, "especially at home. We'll do scenes over and over again, throw out what we do not like, keep what's good, and then we polish, polish, polish.") In this way their characterizations, interaction and timing were well established before they began working with the other actors in the production, when they would try out the conceptions at which they had arrived during their "homework."

A remarkable aspect of the Lunts' method was that the many hours they worked on their characterizations before attending the first rehearsal did not prevent them from altering their conceptions at the suggestion of the director. Perhaps George Schaefer put it best after he directed them in a television production of *The Magnificent Yankee* in 1965.

> I think that any director who can come into rehearsal and find that his two stars have arrived after literally months of preparation, with all the words behind them, with the reading and the thought behind them, ready to get on their feet . . . and to help put the whole thing together, is in such clover to begin with that it's very easy for him to say, "You don't direct them." You don't stage-manage them. You don't scold them or boss them the way you have to certain actors in certain times. But the kind of exchange that real directing should be between people who know what they're doing and what we're all searching for and the ways

to get at it—I've never found two more receptive people to work with.

Schaefer told me that there was "a great deal of interchange" between himself and the Lunts concerning details of characterization and timing. "As soon as there would be some conceivable little value that either was missed or that I felt they could do a little more with, all I had to do was toss a clue in their direction and say, 'You know, that really is nice, but what would it be like if instead of letting him know you're glad to see him, you're a little grumpier?' They'd jump on something like that," Schaefer said. "'Wonderful,' they'd say. 'Yes! That's wonderful.' Then they'd work on that and try it. Then they'd make it their own, but they would sop up suggestions like a vacuum cleaner."

The Lunts' method of homework did not change with time. If anything, it became more intense. When they were no longer living in the triplex on 36th Street, each would retire to a separate room on the same floor to memorize their lines, with their company manager, Lawrence Farrell, seated in the room between them, holding the script of the play and rushing back and forth between rooms to offer assistance when needed. When the Lunts emerged to work together, they repeated each scene over and over again, discussing (and sometimes arguing over) every line reading, gesture and attitude.

Alexander Woollcott's comment about Lunt could have been applied with equal accuracy to Fontanne. "It is easy to tell Alfred Lunt from other American actors," Woollcott said. "He is the one who is always working."

When the Lunts went to the theatre or rehearsal hall to work with the other actors, they repeated the process, concentrating upon the refinement of each minute detail. If for any reason the rehearsal did not progress smoothly, Lunt was prone to nervous irritation, and it was up to Fontanne, who remained cool and unemotional under all but the most severe stress, to soothe him.

Noël Coward enjoyed watching them at work. "To see the Lunts building a scene as they rehearse, fighting over how they will play it, is something," he said. "They construct it out of bits and pieces, painstakingly, and they will take any criticisms, no matter how severe, from anybody, provided they accept his judgment." When they did ask for a viewer's reaction, they had no interest in "stupid flattery," as Coward put it, wanting instead a searching and detailed critical judgment.

Fontanne's approach to her roles was characterized by restraint. Even when playing a character or scene that might have lent itself to melodrama, she practiced the art of understatement. But her performances, whether in comedy or in serious drama, would be so arranged that at one point in every play she demonstrated a flash of great intensity. As one critic put it, "when she plays tragedy, she can blaze with transforming fires, all the more terrible because they can be seen smouldering long before they leap forth."

When an actor played a scene with Lunt for the first time, he often found himself unnerved by the experience. During rehearsal Lunt would stare with such force and concentration at the other performer that the unsettled actor might assume he was doing something wrong. But Lunt's intense stare was not the glare of a dissatisfied actor; it was the passionate involvement of the character, whose attention was thoroughly focused on the words, ideas and attitudes conveyed by his partner in the scene.

At the end of each rehearsal, the Lunts returned home to continue refining their characterizations. Over a period of weeks, each scene was repeated, with modifications, hundreds of times. "You stumble along until you know it," Lunt said, and "when you really know it—you begin playing it to each other, into the eyes, as it were, until it has some reality." What "some reality" meant to the Lunts was quite different from what it suggested to other actors. They were referring to a subtle interrelationship in which every nuance of character and timing was explored and perfected.

There was an element of mystery in the process. Lunt said he could not articulate how he went about creating a characterization; Fontanne, when asked her procedure, said, "I just slug at the words, and when I have learned them, I get the feel of the part, and allow the part to play itself." When asked what it felt like to create a role, she answered, "Falling off a hill. You don't know while you are falling whether you will land in a flower-garden or a gravel pit." When asked how she had mastered the ability to pitch her voice to the size of each theatre in which she played, she said, "How? How? I don't know. . . . All I can say is that it requires long and arduous training."

Lunt did say that he always began work on a role by attempting to differentiate the character from himself and bring to it some quality he had not used in any previous role. He disliked the approach of the personality actor who played every role in similar fashion, forcing the character to conform to his own personality. Lunt went to the opposite extreme, as the critic R. Dana Skinner attested. Skinner said that in each performance Lunt "transforms every fibre of his body. Those who saw him as the gangster brother in Sidney Howard's *Ned McCobb's Daughter* could not possibly imagine him in *Outward Bound,* nor as the Emperor Maximilian, nor . . . above all, as the fanatic revolutionist with a touch of diabolism in Franz Werfel's *Goat Song.* The number of his roles is legion—but in each of them he literally becomes the character, in carriage of his body, in manner and gesture and in smallness or greatness of spirit."

Fontanne offered infrequent clues to her work process, but the few observations she gave were cogent. She said, for example, "I have discovered for myself little things that help, such as—when you have been playing a part for a long time and you begin to feel stale and unnatural-sounding, in your imagination pull down that curtain and be in a room, not on the stage, and I found all my readings are entirely different and, I *think,* for the better."

Homework also involved a critique of one another's performances while a play was running. Asked in 1961 if Fontanne let him know about any flaws in his performances, Lunt answered with an emphatic affirmative. But, he said, "there is nothing personal about it at all. But if, for instance, I should jump in on a line, I hear about it, and vice versa. There is nothing personal about it, mind you. . . . It's strictly impersonal, it's business."

The Lunts' rehearsals continued regardless of their surroundings. If they weren't in the theatre or at home, anywhere else would do. S. N. Behrman described an occasion when, as the three of them were walking through the streets of Boston one December night, the Lunts began loudly speaking the lines from *Meteor,* which was then in rehearsal. Passersby stopped to eavesdrop on their conversation, not knowing it was from a play, but the Lunts were so thoroughly involved that they did not realize they were being overheard. "You couldn't *be* with the Lunts without rehearsing," Behrman said.

When Lawrence Langner suggested to an actor and an actress that they invest the scene they were rehearsing with the subtlety and care for which the Lunts were famous, the actress turned to Langner and exploded bitterly, "How can any other actors expect to play together as well as Alfred and Lynn? They rehearse in bed!"

While in England during World War II, the Lunts invited a friend, Arthur Marshall, to attend a rehearsal of *Love in Idleness.* Marshall reported that he saw "the elaborate jigsaw of their acting being assembled piece by piece. They repeated a dozen times, and then either rejected or adopted, a bit of stage business that might take only a second to do but which would add point to a line. You may say that this is what all actors do, but it can never have been done with more devotion and dedication and expertness."

Every instant in every performance represented one piece of a vast mosaic of details, each of them created for a specific purpose and each of them integral to the overall design. Renée Orsell, the Lunts' secretary during the 1940s, recalled a time when Fontanne came offstage during a performance and spoke to the stage manager, Charva Chester. "Charva, what was wrong?" she asked. "That scene went so badly." The stage manager answered, "You started off on your left foot." Fontanne nodded and said, "Ah, yes. Thank you, Charva." After that the scene went perfectly.

1929–30

The Theatre Guild's production of *Meteor,* which opened on December 2, 1929,* in Boston, reunited the Lunts with S. N. Behrman, who had writ-

*The American tour of *Caprice* had ended only two days earlier in Philadelphia. *Meteor* was rehearsed as the tour was in progress.

ten the play expressly for them. Three weeks later *Meteor* opened at the Guild Theatre in New York. The passage to Broadway was a rocky one. Behrman's skill at writing vibrant dialogue and creating intriguing characters* was not always matched by his skill at dramatic structure, and the play's structural failings proved to be its undoing.

The Lunts, the director, Philip Moeller, and the managers of the Theatre Guild all knew that the play needed a stronger underpinning, and said so from the outset. The previous September the Lunts had told a meeting of the Board that they were not enthusiastic about the play and would act in it only if Behrman could alter it drastically. Moeller, too, said he would accept the directorial assignment on condition that the play be substantially improved. No one, however, could figure out precisely how that should be achieved. Behrman did his best, condensing his play from four acts into three, writing additional material to give added dimension to the characters, and continually revising, but no amount of tampering seemed to help. After one rehearsal shortly before the Boston opening, the managers told Behrman that the play needed scenes with a greater sense of conflict and other scenes that displayed the characters' tenderness. The elfin playwright retreated to his room at the Ritz-Carlton Hotel, emerging the next morning with nine new pages of dialogue. He handed them to Lawrence Langner, saying, "Here, Lawrence, are six pages of conflict, and here are three pages of tenderness."

Langner said that Ina Claire, who often performed in Behrman's plays, was able to force the playwright's works into a structural unity better than anyone else. She would stand in the center of the rehearsal room, look Behrman in the eye and say, "Sam, this play is about me, isn't it, so what do I do next?" Thus Claire continually reminded Behrman that his plays needed to concentrate upon their central characters and that the digressions of which he was so fond, regardless of the elegance and wit with which they were composed, had to be excised. The Guild tried the same approach with *Meteor,* but every attempt to structure the play more tightly met with failure.

When the *Meteor* company went to Boston, everyone was on edge. Behrman had been unable to devise a satisfactory ending for the play, leaving the actors and the director in a state of monumental uncertainty about the direction in which the production should be guided.

Tensions continued to build. At one session everyone's nerves had become so frayed that an explosion of temper seemed imminent. Moeller suddenly burst into tears. He shouted, "I can't stand it any more! I can't stand it!" Dropping to the stage floor, Moeller sobbed uncontrollably

---

*Playing Raphael Lord, a vain, ambitious, selfish businessman, Lunt modeled his appearance as well as certain aspects of his characterization on his neighbor, Jed Harris. The clothes he wore as well as his makeup contrived to reproduce Harris's sinister look. Fontanne played Lord's wife, who ultimately leaves him when she realizes the depth of his egomania.

while the Guild's actors and managers carried him to a couch and attempted to console him. Lunt turned to Langner and said, "Get him home as soon as possible. It's been too much for him, and I don't wonder at it."

Langner escorted the weeping director out of the theatre, and Moeller stopped crying the moment the stage door closed behind them. Langner asked him how he felt. "Fine," said Moeller jauntily. He explained that so many of the actors were on the verge of hysterics that he had feared a free-for-all would ensue, so he had decided to anticipate them with his own outburst.

The tensions, however, did not dissipate as Moeller hoped they would. Instead, they grew sharper as Behrman wrestled with the problems of the play and the actors wrestled with the problem of not knowing what shape the play would take. Even at the final dress rehearsal, Behrman had not provided the actors with the last scene, although he promised it would be ready by the next morning. But Behrman and Moeller had a furious argument that night, both of them storming out of the theatre vowing never to work with one another again. The actors were left to face the opening-night audience without an ending for the play. Lunt turned to Theresa Helburn, saying, "What are we going to do, Terry? We can't open." Helburn could only reply, "But you'll have to. We're completely sold out."

Thus, the performers opened *Meteor* without having the slightest idea how they would bring the play to an end. The last scene Behrman had written was one in which Lunt was speaking on the telephone. Lunt hoped to be able to improvise a reasonably convincing ending, but in case no inspiration came to him, he arranged with the stage manager to bring the curtain down whenever he said the word "schlemiel." When the moment came, inspiration failed to strike, Lunt managed to insert "schlemiel" into his telephone speech and the curtain descended, separating a group of frustrated actors from a houseful of bewildered spectators.

As one might expect, critical opinion in Boston was hostile to the play. "Pretty doubtful entertainment" was the summation of one reviewer, Francis R. Bellamy, who went on to say that he found the work of the Theatre Guild rather pedestrian except for the contributions of Lunt and Fontanne. "We begin to wonder about the Theatre Guild, were it deprived of these two."

Fortunately, Behrman and Moeller were reconciled before the New York opening and Behrman supplied a final scene. But the other problems plaguing *Meteor* had not been solved. John Mason Brown wrote that "the Lunts play together as no other actors in our theatre do, with a fluency that is matchless, and an unselfish and precise sense of give and take which is a constant joy to watch." But the play steadfastly refused to come to life. Perhaps the crash of the stock market only weeks before the opening, combined with the play's layer of bitterness concerning the ethics of

American businessmen, also had something to do with *Meteor*'s failure.

Shortly after it opened, Lunt was forced out of the cast by an attack of acute neuritis. The Guild sensibly decided to suspend the production until he was well enough to play. When Lunt returned, he was forced to perform with his arm in a sling. After several weeks, during which Lunt was in considerable pain, the Guild withdrew him from the cast and gave him a six-month leave of absence. Fontanne continued to appear in *Meteor* until the end of its run in March, when the Lunts journeyed to Bermuda for two months and then returned to Genesee Depot.*

The summer was a restful one, during which Lunt spent most of his time gardening while Fontanne was designing and sewing clothes for herself and their friends and relatives. The vacation was so soothing that they determined to repeat it every year. Their trips to Europe had been highly enjoyable, but left little time for genuine relaxation, as life at Genesee Depot always did. From this time forward, the Lunts returned to their Wisconsin home as often as possible: invariably during the summers, and at Christmas and other holidays whenever it was feasible for them to do so.

That summer also brought Lunt his first honorary doctorate. Carroll College, where he had been an undergraduate eighteen years before, awarded him the Doctor of Letters on June 16, 1930.

Another result of that long summer was that it afforded Lunt an opportunity to give some serious thought to the state of his health. Despite the fact that he had been functioning on one kidney for nearly thirty years, Lunt was blessed with a strong constitution and, except for periods of exhaustion brought on by overwork, he was rarely ill. Moreover, never having experienced serious illness during his adult life, he had a difficult time understanding that illness could interfere with one's work. When Fontanne was in *Strange Interlude* and suffering one night with a high fever, she woke her husband and asked him to call the doctor. As Noël Coward told the story (perhaps with some exaggeration for the sake of a good anecdote), Lunt "looked at her with outraged resentment." He explained to her through clenched teeth that he had a matinee performance of *Volpone* scheduled the next day and that she had no right to deprive him of his sleep. He "picked himself up with his quilt and slept in the living room," Coward said.

The bout of neuritis that forced him out of *Meteor* gave him pause, however. When he was a young man, a doctor had told him he would be lucky to live until he was forty. In August 1930 he observed his thirty-eighth birthday, an occasion that may also have contributed to reflection on the state of his health. Perhaps it would be wise to consider the possi-

---

*Like many other Americans, the Lunts suffered disastrous financial reverses in 1929. Unlike most, however, their money was not lost in the stock-market crash. Rather, their broker embezzled all the money they had invested. They discovered the broker's theft only after he committed suicide. Still, they had sufficient funds to be able to afford a vacation that summer.

bility that the frantic pace he had maintained in the past would have to be curtailed even if it meant missing out on some choice roles. From this time on, if one can judge by his correspondence, Lunt became nearly obsessive on the subject of his physical condition. Rarely did he write a letter to anyone without noting the state of his health, which, according to him, was always considerably less than ideal. His conversations with some of his friends were also peppered with references to various maladies.

Fontanne also grew more concerned about Lunt's condition with each passing year. Her letters, too, nearly always mentioned how poorly Lunt was feeling at the time or how nicely he was recuperating from his most recent illness.

Was Lunt often genuinely ill or did he become something of a hypochondriac? One could perhaps make good cases for both theories. He certainly suffered from his share of diseases as he grew older: arthritis, prostate trouble, an abdominal aortic aneurysm, a bleeding ulcer, acute attacks of gout and, ultimately, cancer. On the other hand, Dr. Edward Bigg, his physician during the last twenty years or so of his life, said that Lunt "appeared to have a great deal of strength and vigor [although] he was always very careful about himself." Other than the difficulty produced by his ulcer, Dr. Bigg was unaware of any prolonged periods of pain. The physician thought the prediction that Lunt would not live beyond forty was probably based on faulty diagnosis. "As far as I was concerned, there was no reason to believe that that might have been true. He would fatigue rather easily, but other than that his general health was good. There was no evidence of heart problems or life-threatening disease."

I asked Dr. Bigg why Fontanne was always so solicitous about Lunt's health—why, for example, she often asked a prospective visitor to postpone a trip to Genesee Depot because her husband's health was not up to entertaining guests. He answered that the Lunts were remarkably devoted to one another, that she was overly apprehensive when he complained about feeling out of sorts, and perhaps she tended to overdramatize, as well. She may have picked up this attitude from his mother and sisters, Bigg suggested. "They were constantly concerned about him since as a young boy he'd been so sickly."

1930–31

The Theatre Guild intended to present the Lunts in only two productions in 1930–31, *Elizabeth the Queen* and *Much Ado About Nothing*. Although both Lunt and Fontanne had had some experience in verse plays in their early years in the theatre, these two plays would give them their first opportunities as mature performers to meet the problems presented by blank verse. Ultimately, however, only the first play was produced.

Maxwell Anderson, the author of *Elizabeth the Queen,* believed strongly that it was not coincidental that the great tragic plays of the past had been written in verse. The use of verse alone gave a play a lofty tone, he felt, and he called for its reintroduction into the modern theatre. When no playwrights leaped to follow his recommendation, he decided to set an example himself, even though he recognized that his abilities as a poet were limited. He determined to write a tragic play in verse and, to make the use of verse readily acceptable to the public, to set his play in Renaissance England, during the time when Shakespeare was active. *Elizabeth the Queen* was the result, a play about the possible romance between the "Virgin Queen" and Lord Essex, ending with Elizabeth's politically astute but personally heartbreaking decision to have Essex put to death for defying her orders.

Elizabeth was essentially Lynn Fontanne's play. Her role was the focal point of the drama, larger, flashier and with more potential for brilliance than the role of Essex, which was given to Lunt. If anyone had believed in the past that Fontanne was too concerned with her appearance, that she was unwilling to wear an unflattering costume or to be made up unattractively, her physical characterization of Elizabeth put such thoughts to rest. She shaved her eyebrows, donned an unflattering crimson wig, applied a putty nose and added a layer of "skin" to give the impression of sagging flesh. When she was assigned the roles of elegant and sophisticated women, her attention to expensive designer costumes and flattering makeup was perfectly justified. But the requirements of *Elizabeth the Queen* were quite different, and Fontanne's makeup in the role revealed her concern to express the character rather than to look beautiful.

Before rehearsals began, the managers expressed dissatisfaction with the pitch of Fontanne's voice, claiming that it was too high. For a time there was talk of using another actress in the role. Instead, Fontanne asked to be given three weeks in which to transform her voice. Each day she worked to lower its pitch, and each day she managed to drop it by a fraction. At the end of the three-week period, the managers agreed that Fontanne's voice had achieved precisely the pitch and quality they wanted.

The play opened in Philadelphia on September 29, 1930, and certain problems soon became apparent. Reviewers called it a "cold historical romance" in which "there is no dash, no sparkle, no lustiness whatever." The managers asked Maxwell Anderson for revisions, which he agreed to make. Each day, however, Anderson confessed that he had no new material ready. The New York opening was imminent and the managers grew more and more nervous. At least, Lawrence Langner noted, the weather in Philadelphia was beautiful.

When it became apparent the play would not be in shape to open at the Guild Theatre as scheduled, the Guild postponed the premiere and moved the production to Baltimore. Already unhappy, Langner was further depressed by the violent storm that raged during the evening of the first performance. The next morning Langner and Anderson met in the lobby of the Belvedere Hotel. Ready to be disappointed once again, Langner asked if Anderson had completed any work on the play. To his delight, the playwright produced pages and pages of revisions, strengthening every scene that had been judged weak. "When did all this happen?" the amazed Langner asked. "Well, Lawrence," Anderson answered, "I really only write well when it rains."

Time was needed to incorporate the new and revised scenes into the production, so the play was taken to Pittsburgh for a week and Cincinnati for another. Further additions and revisions were made at each stop, some of them by the Lunts, "with, of course, the help & consent of Max Anderson," Lunt said. Improvement was evident with each succeeding performance, and the Guild felt confident when *Elizabeth the Queen* finally opened in New York on November 3.

Opening night was an extraordinary event. The usually reserved Guild subscribers went wild with enthusiasm, giving the production a total of seventeen curtain calls. And Broadway's critics were overwhelmed by Fontanne's performance. "Miss Fontanne gives the most colorful characterization of her career," wrote John Mason Brown. "Her Elizabeth, with her amazing make-up, her booming chest tones, her imperiousness, her lusty oaths, her good nature and her pathetic craving for Essex, is a glorious, vigorous portrait. . . ." Burns Mantle added, "Lynn Fontanne is ever dynamic, interpretive, and magnificent. Miss Fontanne's performance . . . has taken the town. In every way it is her greatest personal triumph." "This is acting of the very highest order—selfless, thorough, vigorous, luminously intelligent," agreed Brooks Atkinson. "With Miss Fontanne it is a case of transmutation, not merely of make-up, which masks her true features completely, but of voice, gesture and bearing. She is no artfully bedizened Queen of the theatre. She is every inch Queen Elizabeth."

Lunt was clearly overshadowed in the role of Essex. Nevertheless, Brown noted that Lunt's "Essex is volatile, impulsive and touching, acted with a fine fervor and a pleasing freedom. And, as is always the case with Miss Fontanne and Mr. Lunt, the manner in which they play together is as sincere and deep a source of satisfaction as is the skill of their individual performances."

The critics were divided over the merits of Anderson's play. Some of them found certain scenes wanting in dramatic impact and considered the playwright's language flat and disappointing. Others felt, as Brooks Atkinson did, that the play was "a searching portrayal of character, freely imaginative in its use of history, clearly thought out and conveyed in dialogue of noble beauty."

A scene in the play called for Essex to bury his face in Elizabeth's bosom. During one performance Lunt dropped his head on Fontanne's chest a bit too violently, breaking her string of pearls. Most of them fell harmlessly to the stage floor, but one became lodged in Lunt's nostril, making it rather difficult for Elizabeth and Essex to concentrate on the remainder of the scene.

An accident of this sort is always discomfiting at the time it happens, but ordinarily it becomes more and more amusing to actors as they look back upon it. The Lunts, however, were generally unamused by the minor accidents that will occasionally plague a performance. They disliked any incident that threatened to interfere with their concentration. They were also appalled by the tendency of some actors to alter the words of the play-wright for the sake of an ad-libbed comment designed to amuse the other performers (although Lunt did spontaneously rearrange the dialogue of *Design for Living* on one occasion, to Fontanne's intense displeasure). In-deed, Lunt told Helen Ormsbee in the late 1930s, "I take my job during a performance seriously. I have no humor at all about things going wrong—somebody being late on a cue, or the curtain sticking. There are actors who think such things are funny. I don't. My idea is that people in the audience have paid for tickets, and they are entitled to the best we can do."

On December 8, only a month after *Elizabeth the Queen* had opened, rehearsals began for a production of *Much Ado About Nothing,* to be di-rected by America's foremost scenic designer, Robert Edmond Jones. The Lunts were enthusiastic about appearing together in their first Shake-spearean production.

When *Much Ado* had been announced the previous June, it was not scheduled to open until May 1931, after the New York run and a fifteen-week road tour of *Elizabeth* had concluded. But the Guild must have been excited about the director's concept, for it decided to move the opening date forward by six months and to alternate *Much Ado* with *Elizabeth.* Jones had seen a novel production of a Shakespearean play in Germany which he believed could be adapted for the Theatre Guild. The front cur-tain would be raised when the audience entered the theatre, with a dressing room on each side of the stage. Lunt, making up for his role of Benedick, would occupy one dressing room, while Fontanne, preparing to play Bea-trice, would use the other. The dressing rooms would remain visible throughout the production. When the Lunts were not taking part in the action of the play, they would retreat to their on-stage "dressing rooms" to change costumes, study their lines, chat inaudibly with other actors, read and wait for their next cues. The problem with this scheme was that the spectators at the dress rehearsal proved to be far more interested in the sideshows than in the play itself.

Ultimately, the managers convinced Jones that the play could never hope to succeed if his original idea was retained. He agreed to scrap it entirely and to begin anew, but other difficulties, unrelated to the produc-tion scheme, persisted. The Guild had lost several of its actors to Broadway and Hollywood in recent years, with the result that the company was seriously weakened, and some of the roles in *Much Ado* were not being given the sort of acting skill they required. In addition, the Guild's managers lost faith in Jones's ability to redirect the production and asked Moeller to take over the assignment, but Moeller refused. From a commercial point of view, the managers also began to wonder whether the enterprise was worth the losses in revenue the Guild would suffer if the sold-out *Elizabeth the Queen* was presented only in alternate weeks.

Thus, *Much Ado* was canceled before its scheduled opening in January 1931. The Guild initially announced only that the production was being postponed, but subsequently admitted that it would be dropped from the schedule. The official excuse was that "Alfred Lunt, Lynn Fontanne and others who were to have appeared in the play could not rehearse it properly while appearing at the same time in *Elizabeth the Queen*. Since the latter play is scheduled to go on tour early in March, it was also felt that insufficient time remained for a New York engagement of the Shakespearean production."

The cancellation was expensive. *Elizabeth the Queen* had already been moved to the Martin Beck Theatre so that the Guild would be available for the Shakespearean production, and the costumes and scenery for *Much Ado* had been completed. The Guild had to absorb a loss of something between $22,000 and $60,000 (depending upon whose account is accurate), which represented a considerable sum for the production of a non-musical play in 1931.

The Lunts, however, were pleased with the decision to cancel a production that had clearly been heading for disaster. Lunt wrote to Rouben Mamoulian, "We have been nearly dead from overwork—'Much Ado' was at last called off and strangely enough we are delighted—"

So *Elizabeth the Queen* continued its run uninterrupted. And after 147 performances in New York, it was taken on a tour of Washington, Boston and other Guild subscription cities, where Fontanne repeated her Broadway triumph.

It seems, in retrospect, most unfortunate that the Lunts never played Beatrice and Benedick. So perfectly suited were they for those roles that years later, when critics looked back upon the Lunts' careers, the greatest regret of many was that they had been unable to see them in *Much Ado* or in the roles of Mirabell and Millamant in Congreve's *The Way of the World*.

The Lunts appeared together in only one play of Shakespeare's—*The Taming of the Shrew* in 1935 and again in 1939–40—and the loss to theatregoers was regrettable. They did plan productions of *Twelfth Night* and *Macbeth*, but the plans were never realized.

Late in their careers the Lunts were often asked why they did not perform more frequently in Shakespeare's plays, as the great British performers of their generation had done. Lunt's answer was that American actors "should leave Shakespeare's tragedies to the British. Only they can do justice to him. We are good in the comedies, but not *yet* the tragedies." He believed that the cadences of British speech patterns were necessary to portray Shakespearean roles with distinction, and he distrusted his own ability to reproduce those rhythms. Consequently, Lunt never acted any role with a British accent, whether in a classical or modern play.

Fontanne, being English, had no such difficulty, and perhaps she would have liked to try her hand at other Shakespearean roles. A reporter asked the Lunts late in their lives whether they regretted not having played Romeo and Juliet. Lunt said that he had no regrets whatever. He saw Romeo as an asinine, bumbling fool, hardly worthy of a mature actor's attention. Fontanne listened carefully to her husband's reply, then said plaintively, "Juliet has some lovely lines."

When Lunt and Fontanne were interviewed in 1965, several years after their retirement from the stage but while they were still performing occasionally on television, the seventy-three-year-old Lunt surprised reporters by saying, "The only thing that we can do together now in a classic is *Romeo and Juliet*." After a well-calculated pause, he added, "Friar Laurence and the Nurse."

With the advent of sound movies in 1927, Hollywood became particularly eager to hire prominent actors with stage experience. The Lunts were high on the studios' lists of coveted performers, but they resisted all offers to appear in a "talkie" until the chance came in 1931 to repeat their success in *The Guardsman*. Irving Thalberg, who was running MGM, happened to be in Chicago for a sales convention when the Lunts were on tour with *Elizabeth the Queen*. They agreed to meet him at his hotel room at 7:00 a.m., the only time the busy mogul was able to see them, but his proposal that they film *The Guardsman* was initially met with skepticism. Fontanne must have feared that she and her husband would be asked to distort their stage performances grotesquely, for she told Thalberg, "Alfred and I will not do any swimming, high diving, fast horseback riding or any of those other things you do out there in movies." With that potential difficulty out of the way, Thalberg proceeded to persuade the Lunts to bring their talents to the west coast. It was agreed they would receive $75,000 for the film, they would have their choice of either Sidney Franklin or Robert Z. Leonard as director, they would have top billing, and they would not be required "to grant any interviews whatever to any party or parties, but it is understood that you will cooperate with our Publicity Department."

Sidney Franklin, who was chosen by the Lunts to direct the film, followed the tour to Minneapolis. His intention was solely to discuss the film with them, but when he saw *Elizabeth the Queen*, he suggested that a section of that play be used as the opening sequence in *The Guardsman*, to establish the characters of the Actor and the Actress. Franklin's suggestion was seized upon, and a scene from *Elizabeth the Queen* was incorporated into the film.

The arrival of the Lunts in Hollywood in June was not auspicious. The studio policeman guarding the gates of MGM turned them away when they were unable to produce passes confirming their identities. The incident convinced the Lunts they had made a terrible mistake in accepting Thalberg's offer, and they promptly turned their car around, heading for their rented apartment to begin packing. Only the intervention of Sidney Franklin and his willingness to escort them inside the studio gates himself prevented the project from coming to an early conclusion.

Lunt wrote to Maxwell Anderson on July 11, 1931, a month after their arrival, "Our stay so far has been extraordinarily pleasant. Everyone is amazingly pleasant and helpful. We've not yet run across a glimmer of 'Once in a Lifetime'* but of course there's always to-morrow."

During the filming of *The Guardsman,* the Lunts were warned that their technique of overlapping one another's speeches would not work for the film. The state of the sound equipment was such that it would not be able to pick up both voices distinctly, they were told. One voice would blot out the other. But their technique was so highly developed that even the primitive microphones of 1931 could not defeat it. The Lunts' speeches overlapped one another on film just as successfully as they had on the stage.

Donald Seawell, the Lunts' friend and lawyer, spoke to me in 1984 about one of the most remarkable achievements of the Lunts during the filming of *The Guardsman.* "I was told that the longest sequence that had been shot in Hollywood until that time was something over forty seconds," he said. "Their first shot went for fully nine minutes. And why did it end? Because the camera ran out of film."

Still, the process of making the film was irritating to the Lunts. Not every scene was shot in a single take, by any means. Accustomed to the continuity of the stage, they found that the constant interruptions of film work played havoc with their concentration and threatened to interfere with their consummate ability to modulate in intensity from one moment to the next. Because they were new to talking films and because both the Lunts were expected to have difficulty in an area that had confounded other theatre-trained actors before them—playing units of scenes out of sequence and yet finding the right pitch of emotion so that when the units were patched together the entire scene made emotional sense—Franklin closed the set to all visitors.

In one scene Fontanne was being filmed taking a bath and then had to answer the telephone. She was nude from the waist up, and the camera was set up behind her so that only her back could be seen. But the telephone was also placed behind her, and when it rang, Fontanne turned directly toward the camera. Franklin stopped the scene immediately and explained that it would never do to have her turn toward the camera and

---

* Once in a Lifetime, the brilliant farce by George S. Kaufman and Moss Hart portraying Hollywood as a haven for idiots and megalomaniacs, was then running successfully on Broadway.

expose her breasts. "But the telephone bell sounded from that direction," she replied. "Naturally I would turn in the direction from which it came." Such a story about another actress of that time might be difficult to believe, but Fontanne habitually became totally absorbed in the job at hand when she was acting, and on such occasions modesty was entirely forgotten.

Filming progressed swiftly. By 1931 the Lunts had performed the play *The Guardsman* hundreds of times, and the number of takes usually necessary to achieve the desired results simply weren't necessary for them. Often they required only one. The entire film, therefore, was shot in an astonishing twenty-one days.

Perhaps Irving Thalberg believed that no actors were capable of completing a first-class film that quickly. Although he expressed his general satisfaction when he saw the rough cut of *The Guardsman,* he insisted that one scene be reshot and its emphasis altered. Lunt demurred, claiming that the new scene Thalberg had in mind was inconsistent with the characters of the Actor and the Actress as Lunt and Fontanne were portraying them. But Thalberg was adamant, and the scene was retaken. Thalberg may have been pleased that he had asserted his authority over the famous acting couple, but his pleasure proved short-lived. When he watched the rushes, he noticed that one of Lunt's eyeballs kept rolling to the edge of his eye, which proved so distracting that one could not maintain one's interest in the scene. Thalberg accused Lunt of having purposely ruined the take. Lunt replied that he could not possibly control the rolling of his eyeball and that the condition had been caused by fatigue—fatigue that had probably been caused by Thalberg's maddening insistence on reshooting a scene that was already perfectly satisfactory. Thalberg was more determined than ever as the meeting came to an end. But Lunt was equally determined not to do another retake. The issue was settled at last when Lunt got a short haircut that made the retake impossible.

During the making of the picture, the Lunts decided to look at the rushes. At the last moment, Lunt said he would rather not see them, so Fontanne went in alone. Lunt met her eagerly when she emerged. She got into the car and they began to drive back to their apartment. Well, he asked, how does it look? Fontanne replied: "Oh, it seems to be going well. In fact, you're wonderful, Alfred. Your voice, your manner, your timing—they all register beautifully. Of course, you could use a little more makeup to define your mouth, you look as if you have no lips. But that's a trivial matter. You have such flair, such panache, it's just wonderful. But, oh, Alfred, I am *dreadful*. I look scared to death, very plain and haggard with awful lines under my eyes—no shine in my hair—I look as if I'd been buried and dug up again. It's terribly disappointing. No, if the film succeeds, it will be your doing, there's no doubt about it."

Lunt nodded thoughtfully and lapsed into silence. The car wound slowly through the streets. Lunt was deep in thought. At last, as the car pulled up in front of the apartment, he turned to Fontanne with a worried look and said: "No lips?"*

The completed film was previewed in San Bernardino. The members of the audience, as was customary, were asked to fill out brief questionnaires offering their opinions. Fontanne despaired of the results even before they had been tabulated. "The audience was composed of what we now call bobby-soxers—schoolchildren," she said when she recalled the incident years later.

The day after the preview, Thalberg and the Lunts met in Thalberg's office and he began reading the answers on the questionnaires aloud. According to Fontanne, the responses "were written in a most illiterate style—naïve—some were flattering and some were not." Growing angrier by the minute, Fontanne interrupted and said, "Don't read us any more if they're all like that. These people sound like children."

Thalberg agreed. "They *are* children, mostly," he said.

"Then why on earth are you reading them?" Fontanne exploded. "This film, in sophistication and maturity, is way outside their world. These children cannot possibly like it. It is a subtle, brilliant comedy, and you will find an audience for it, but it won't be made up of children."

"But this *is* our audience," Thalberg protested.

From that moment the Lunts knew the studio would not be acute enough to target the film for its appropriate audience. Indeed, from the beginning, the MGM publicity department had been uncertain how to promote the film. Most of the studio bosses were convinced that the Lunts could not possibly interest the moviegoing public. For one thing, they said, the Lunts were too old. (He was thirty-nine at the time, she forty-four.) Another problem was that Lunt and Fontanne had given interviews in the past saying that they were happily married to one another—a sure way to destroy the audience's dreams of mystery and romance. Furthermore, no breath of scandal touched either of them. They were, in short, a publicity man's nightmare.

Lunt gave an interview to the New York *Times* in 1931 in which he suggested that all stage actors should perform in films periodically, if only for the opportunity to explore new techniques and methods of expression. Lunt's primary recollection of his work on *The Guardsman,* however, was of how exhausting the whole experience had been. "Most persons who have not had any picture experience little know of the physical exertion and nerve-racking tension associated with film work," he told the interviewer. "It's a steady drain on one's energy, with no let-up." Lunt described how he and Fontanne had studied the film script on the train to Los Angeles and had been put to work the moment they arrived. "We both had

---

*Fontanne always claimed that the true story was not nearly so elaborate—that Alexander Woollcott, when he heard the anecdote, had thought it delightful, and every time he retold the story it became longer and more detailed.

put in some rather strenuous periods for the Theatre Guild, but they seemed rest periods, in retrospect, when we got out on that studio set," he said. And although many of their scenes were completed in a single take, Lunt said that having to repeat other scenes many times over "through some slight flaw or technical error" was "perhaps the most tiring thing." Still, he maintained, the experience had been more positive than negative, and he looked forward to making another film in California the following summer.

Fontanne was less enthusiastic about the possibility. She was still upset by the studio's reliance on the opinions of an audience she believed incapable of responding to the sort of work at which she and Lunt excelled. "I suppose when you run a business like that you must think of all kinds of audiences," she said, "but there is a [separate] audience for every kind of play, from the sheerly intellectual down to the most rabid farce. . . . They shouldn't try to drag an interest to a special group of people who wouldn't care for that kind of play anyway."

When the film was released, it proved to be a modest popular success. Lunt and Fontanne were both nominated for Academy Awards, and many were dazzled by the brilliance of their playing. The reaction was sufficiently favorable to indicate that subsequent films with the Lunts would have box-office appeal.

Critics with a belief in film as an art form were enthusiastic about *The Guardsman*. Mordaunt Hall, reviewing the picture for the New York *Times* in September 1931, said, "It is a pity that there are not more Fontannes, Lunts and Molnárs to help out the screen, for then this medium of entertainment would be on a far higher plane. It is a wonderful relief to sit through such a production. . . .

"When Mr. Lunt as the conceited Austrian actor decides to test his wife's fidelity, every change of his expression is visible. His agony is so well pictured that two or three times the audience applauded. . . .

"There are dozens of subtle, witty scenes in this film . . ."

Ten days later Hall expanded on his response to *The Guardsman,* writing:

> The work of Miss Fontanne and Mr. Lunt is deserving of the highest praise, for nothing quite like it has been seen on the screen. . . .
>
> Miss Fontanne's enunciation, the wealth of expression she puts into her lines, is the work of an artist. . . . Every line she utters and every change in her facial expression are most compelling.
>
> As for Mr. Lunt, his impersonation is, if anything, more difficult. . . . Here is acting that few, if any, of the Hollywood celebrities know much about, for Mr. Lunt skillfully resists all the many temptations to overact or to be repetitious. . . .

The critic for *Liberty* also noted the difference between the Lunts' performances and those of most film actors. "Here are two actors who pay no attention to the three P's of Hollywood," he said, "personality, pose, and profile. They are concerned merely with getting the most out of a playwright's work."

Such comments helped *The Guardsman* fill the Astor Theatre in New York. However, there were few packed houses in the rest of the country, a circumstance that can only be described as the public's loss. To many of those who did see it, it had the force of a revelation. One such viewer was Robert Downing, then a seventeen-year-old usher in a Cedar Rapids movie theatre, and much later to become the Lunts' stage manager. The very first film Downing saw in his Cedar Rapids job made him an admirer of the Lunts forever. "Nothing I had ever seen on film prepared me for *The Guardsman*," he said. "The electricity of the Lunts' playing was unlike any acting the cinema had had before. I was fascinated by the trick of overlapping dialogue, by their unique comedy pace, by the excerpt from *Elizabeth the Queen* that was part of a play-within-the-picture."

As a result of *The Guardsman,* the Lunts received many film offers. Carl Laemmle of Universal Pictures dangled $250,000 before them to make one film, *Tristan and Isolde*. Thalberg was more ambitious; he wanted to sign the Lunts to a three-year contract which called for them to film their stage success *Elizabeth the Queen,* among other projects. Thalberg would pay them the quite remarkable sum of $990,000, a great deal of money at any time but an unheard-of salary in 1931 for a couple who had made only a single film. The Lunts, however, had decided to reject all film offers unless they were given creative control of their pictures, including choice of vehicles. That was a demand that the studios could not accept, as it would lessen the absolute control they had achieved over creative artists. So the Lunts returned to the theatre, their attitude toward the movies summed up by the terse telegram they sent to Carl Laemmle after his *Tristan and Isolde* offer: "We can be bought, my dear Mr. Laemmle, but we can't be bored."

Although millions of filmgoers have seen and admired *The Guardsman*—it has become a "cult" picture, partly because of its inherent brilliance and partly because it is the only sound film in which the Lunts can be seen*—two people who did not see the film for more than forty-five years were Alfred Lunt and Lynn Fontanne. But in the mid-1970s, when they were in retirement and Lunt's health was failing, that situation was rectified. Fontanne, who was then nearly ninety, told the story this way: "We had the most extraordinary experience. We were on a cruise not long ago and they showed *The Guardsman*. I knew exactly what I'd look like: a

*Lunt and Fontanne appeared in *Stage Door Canteen* in 1943, but this hardly qualifies as an exception. They played themselves, as did many other stage performers, their roles were minuscule, and their motivation was to aid the war effort, not to bring their art to film.

plain creature, a schoolmarm. Well! I didn't at all. I was a lush piece! I had no idea I was anything like that. And Alfred was absolutely astounding. It was like seeing two other people. But I thought we were simply marvelous.

"When people came up to speak to us afterward, I said, 'Yes, weren't we wonderful.'"

1931–32

Many could not believe that the Lunts would not remain in Hollywood, with its twin lures of money and worldwide stardom. Rumors circulated that they would appear in various pictures. *Vanity Fair,* for example, announced in July 1931 that the Lunts had agreed to appear in the film version of Noël Coward's *Private Lives,* which had achieved considerable success on the stage in London and in New York. But the announcement was erroneous. Instead, the Lunts returned to New York to prepare for the Theatre Guild production of Robert E. Sherwood's *Reunion in Vienna.*

As he had done with *The Road to Rome,* Sherwood wrote his play with the Lunts in mind. "I suppose every playwright at the end of the second act or so thinks, 'Now this won't be so bad if I can get the Lunts to appear in it,'" he said later. For Lunt he created the role of the Grand Duke Rudolf Maximillian von Hapsburg, whose most recent employment has been as a taxi driver in Nice; for Fontanne he created Elena, Rudolf's former mistress and currently the wife of a psychoanalyst. The title refers to their reunion after a separation of ten years (and to a gathering of ex-courtiers to commemorate the 100th anniversary of the birth of Emperor Franz-Josef). *Reunion in Vienna* was submitted to the Lunts while they were on tour with *Elizabeth the Queen.* Fontanne read it first, liked it and passed it on to Lunt, who also approved. When they recommended to the Guild that the play should be incorporated into the 1931–32 production schedule, the Guild agreed to do so, but asked the Lunts if they wouldn't prefer to be in Eugene O'Neill's thirteen-act marathon, *Mourning Becomes Electra,* instead. Having already appeared in plays by O'Neill, and wishing to act again in a comedy after their long run in *Elizabeth the Queen,* the Lunts chose to perform *Reunion in Vienna.*

While the Lunts were in Los Angeles filming *The Guardsman,* Sherwood was in the same city working on several screenplays. The three of them met frequently, and Sherwood was surprised to discover that they had already memorized and worked upon several of their scenes. He realized that their understanding of his play and characters was complete and that they had begun the process of translating that understanding into theatrical reality.

The Lunts and the play's director, Worthington Miner, made a number of suggestions for revisions that would clarify the action and add dimension to the characters. Sherwood made the changes willingly, claiming that the suggestions were "tremendously helpful." His collaboration with the Lunts was a joyful one in every way. He said afterward that he was astounded by their genuine humility, their refusal to play the roles of "stars," and by the energetic way they approached his play as if it were to be their first Broadway production.

The playwright looked forward eagerly to rehearsals, which began in New York in September. But his enthusiasm for the project was severely tested by the Theatre Guild's system of managers' rehearsals and conferences. Lee Simonson, who had voted against the Guild's acceptance of the play, calling it "very superficial," confronted Sherwood immediately, telling him that he had little regard for *Reunion*. Simonson, who claimed that his knowledge of psychoanalysis was profound, continued to badger Sherwood throughout the production process, arguing over whether the analyst in the play was orthodox or not. In one particularly acrimonious session shortly before the play opened, Simonson's attack on Sherwood became so vituperative that the other members of the Board attempted vainly to stop him. Worthington Miner protested Simonson's behavior by walking out, and Sherwood himself finally joined the director, declaring bitterly that he would "never give a play of mine to the Guild again."* Even that did not end the dispute. After the play began its out-of-town performances, Simonson continued to deliver long harangues on psychoanalytic theory, insisting that Sherwood's ignorance of the subject destroyed the play.

The tryout performances got off to a bad start in Pittsburgh, but seemed to improve greatly in Buffalo. Each stop on the tour provoked an entirely different reaction from audiences, so that the Guild had no idea whether the production was heading for success or failure. The performances in Baltimore were so negatively received that the managers discussed closing the play before the scheduled New York opening. But the response in Washington was just the reverse: the production was greeted with cheers and critical acclaim.

Reunion in Vienna opened at the Martin Beck Theatre in New York (the Guild Theatre was reserved that season for *Mourning Becomes Electra*) on November 16, 1931.† Richard Lockridge wrote that the play was "light and frisky as one always believes Viennese comedy should be, and

---

* Sherwood did not follow through on that threat immediately, but his later plays were turned over to the Guild grudgingly and warily. Finally, in 1938, when he was joined by Anderson, Elmer Rice, Sidney Howard—and soon afterward by Behrman—in the formation of the Playwrights' Company, Sherwood left the Theatre Guild without regret, still furious over the treatment to which artists were subjected by the Board.

† The film of *The Guardsman* was playing at the same time at the Astor Theatre, where it had opened two months before.

as one so seldom finds Viennese comedy is." Gilbert W. Gabriel added, "Miss Fontanne and Mr. Lunt play it to the hilt. They play it swiftly, dashingly, humorously . . . and ornamentally. They revel in it, on tabletops and couches and canopied beds, to music, to cheers, with the gusto and brightness to which they seem to have captured the key for all time."

When Sherwood looked through the newspapers on the morning after the opening, he began with a discouraging notice in the *Herald Tribune*. He was halfway through his second review when the telephone rang. Lunt was on the phone, asking, "How is the press?" Before Sherwood could begin, Lunt added, "Don't tell me what they said specifically because Lynn and I never read them [and] we don't want to know really what they said, but what was the general overall opinion?"

Sherwood was impressed by the Lunts' remarkably detached attitude toward critics. "Well," he began, "I haven't read much yet myself, but the *Herald Tribune* is pretty bad. The *Times* seems to be a little better as far as I've—"

Lunt cut in at that point, shouting that the review in the *Herald Tribune* was hardly worth reading because they had sent a second-string critic to the production and it was clear that the critic had no idea what the play was about. But wasn't Gilbert Gabriel's notice a gratifying one, Lunt asked, and what about Richard Lockridge in the *Sun*? Lunt continued to describe each notice in detail, ending with his evaluation of the review in *Women's Wear Daily*.

Two months later, one critic was still particularly enthusiastic about the play and the production. Alexander Woollcott wrote to the Lunts in December, "When your grandchildren (on whom you have not yet made a really effective start) gather at your rheumatic knees and ask you what you did during the great depression, you can tell them that you played *Reunion in Vienna* to crowded houses, and enjoyed the whole depression enormously."

Woollcott also wrote to Paul Hyde Bonner, telling him of his enthusiasm for the Lunts' performances, "particularly, I think, by Lynn, who plays with a kind of exquisite delicacy that can't even be described."

The play featured Helen Westley as the proprietress of the hotel where the reunion took place. Lunt's dialogue in one scene, as Woollcott reported in his letter to Bonner, called for him to speculate "as to whether she still wears her old red flannel drawers, and at an opportune moment [he] lifts the skirt to see. The glimpse of Helen's behind incarnadined in flannel is a nightly joy to the Guild subscribers. The other evening, unfortunately, even Helen knew by the gasp of the minor actors on the stage that she had forgotten to put them on. . . . Alfred came out of his catalepsy at last unable *not* to speak the line which was then due. It was, 'Well, thank God there is one thing in Vienna that hasn't changed.'"

An article about the Lunts' performances in *Reunion in Vienna*, called "The High Art of Comedy Acting," was published in *Theatre Guild Mag-*

azine in March 1932. The author, Hiram Motherwell, described the artistry and technique the Lunts brought to individual moments in the production. For example, the moment when Lunt slapped Helen Westley's backside turned the play from low to high comedy, Motherwell said, by its revelation of character:

> Rudolph von Hapsburg, in this single moment, tells the audience all that needs to be known about himself, about the milieu in which he moves, about the theme of the play. He is of the old aristocracy. He has been accustomed to regard all other human beings as his inferiors and proper prey for his insults; he is himself an ordinary human being (except for his extraordinary vitality); he knows in his heart that he is ordinary and compensates by eternally pretending that he is superior; he demonstrates his superiority in the most vulgar ways; and he vainly flourishes the evidence of his mean superiority to all who will watch, or if nobody is watching, to an invisible audience. That is the meaning of the upraised hand (which is not dictated in the script). Triumph—a silly but soul-satisfying triumph. You know the man instantly.

Fontanne, too, was praised for her ability to convey a world of information in the subtlest manner:

> Observe Miss Fontanne as she stands at the doorway to her bedroom, deciding whether or not to join her lover. She has no line to speak. She has . . . two steps to take which are visible on the stage. By the way she strides those two steps she tells all that is in her mind and heart. . . . When Miss Fontanne hands Rudolph his officer's coat she says, "You will always wear it gallantly." To that last word she gives a slight upward inflection of the voice— an inflection so slight that a skillful violinist would have difficulty in fixing so fine a gradation. Yet in just that inflection is conveyed to the audience the fact that, after all, she loves this worthless scamp of an aristocrat.

Motherwell was particularly taken with a scene between the Lunts in the second act. "You will find in it a variety of light and shade, of tone and tempo and rhythm, which would delight a musician or an artist," he wrote. "But unless you are a seasoned actor you cannot know what art and calculation goes into this splendid impromptu of recklessness and hesitation and bravado and shrewdness and passion. To appreciate this one scene . . . is to know all that we now know about comedy acting."

Before the 1931–32 season had begun, the Guild had given serious thought to instituting a true repertory system (i.e., with the plays changing daily instead of weekly) built around the Lunts. However, the enormous success of *Reunion in Vienna,* which ran for 264 performances, put an end to the idea. The managers found the box-office returns for *Reunion* so alluring that they decided to allow it to run at the Martin Beck Theatre as long as the Lunts were willing to continue playing in it.

Alfred Lunt and Lynn Fontanne were clearly the leading acting team in America. Already, in 1932, some were beginning to suggest that they rivaled the most illustrious teams in American theatrical history: E. H. Sothern and Julia Marlowe; John Drew and Ada Rehan. Their interplay had become legendary, their success extraordinary. Only one aspect of their professional lives was less than satisfactory: the recurring battles with the Theatre Guild. Not only were they disturbed when they came in direct conflict with members of the Board over character interpretation and billing, they were equally upset by the Guild's treatment of playwrights like Robert E. Sherwood. They shared a deep respect for the Guild's objectives and for its influence in bringing the American theatre a new maturity and adventurousness; they felt satisfaction in having played a significant part in the Guild's success; but the daily frustrations they encountered in dealing with the prickly individuals on the Board often vitiated both the respect and the satisfaction. In consequence, the Lunts found it increasingly difficult each year to decide whether or not to commit themselves to the Guild for another season.

In October 1931, when *Reunion in Vienna* was in rehearsal, Maurice Wertheim and Theresa Helburn had approached the Lunts about signing a contract for the 1932–33 season and were told the couple was not ready to give a definite answer. As *Reunion in Vienna* continued its run, the Lunts remained uncertain. Philip Moeller and Helen Westley, on behalf of the managers, asked them again in November if they had reached a decision. The Lunts responded that they needed more time to think about it and intended to take a long vacation after the Broadway run and the road tour of *Reunion in Vienna*.

The more the Lunts thought about signing another contract with the Theatre Guild, the angrier they became. After eight years of working for the Guild, they had accumulated a number of grievances, some more significant than others. The low salaries they were paid did not rankle nearly as much as the cavalier attitude the Board members took toward the artists associated with their company. "Why are we putting up with this? We don't need it," George Schaefer quoted them as having said.

By the time the tour of *Reunion* began, the Lunts had firmly decided not to return to the Guild. They informed the organization, adding that they intended to sever their connection as soon as their contract ran out— which would occur before the tour was scheduled to end. The Guild made every attempt to keep them in the fold. A London production of *Reunion in Vienna* could be arranged, as could New York productions of *The Taming of the Shrew* and Bernard Shaw's *Captain Brassbound's Conversion*. If, as the Board members had heard, the Lunts wished to appear in Noël Coward's new play, the Guild would be pleased to produce it. But these appeals went unheeded. The Lunts had reached a firm decision to leave and no temptations the Guild could offer would lure them back.* They did hint that they might be willing to return after a year or two, but no firm commitment was made.

So their longtime collaboration with the Theatre Guild was temporarily severed. Early in 1932 they sent a cablegram to Noël Coward, who was vacationing in Argentina, saying, "CONTRACT WITH THEATRE GUILD UP IN JUNE WE SHALL BE FREE STOP WHAT ABOUT IT?" When Coward responded that he would get to work immediately writing a play in which they could appear, their course was set. On May 5, 1932, Lunt told his old friend Ray Weaver that he and Fontanne had been reading plays at a frenzied clip in order to find one they liked. "But now we've decided . . . to act with Noël Coward in a comedy of his next January." Two weeks later the news became public when the New York *Times* announced that the Lunts would appear in Coward's *Design for Living* early in 1933.

---

*According to Hobe Morrison, whose article appeared in *Variety* many years later, the incident that decided the Lunts to end their connection with the Guild occurred while *Reunion in Vienna* was playing in Omaha, after the Broadway run. Lunt sent word to the Guild's New York office that the uniform jacket he wore for the play was becoming tattered and he requested permission to buy a new one. The answer came back that Lunt should have the jacket mended, as a new one would cost $90, and the Guild did not want to spend that much money. Without replying to the managers, Lunt purchased a new jacket with his own funds. But he and Fontanne were furious.

At the end of the tour, according to Morrison, the Lunts did not return to New York, as they customarily did, to consult with the Guild's managers. Instead, they went directly home to Wisconsin. The managers began to realize that something might be wrong. They sent letters and telegrams to Genesee Depot, but the messages went unanswered. They telephoned and were told the Lunts were not at home. At last they decided to call on the Lunts in person.

When the managers arrived, intending to discuss the Lunts' new contract, Lunt said he wanted instead to discuss the matter of the jacket he had been forced to buy because of the Guild's miserliness. As a result, he said, he and Fontanne no longer wished to continue their association with the Theatre Guild.

These incidents may well have taken place, but they could not have occurred when Morrison says they did, since the *Reunion in Vienna* tour did not begin until after the Lunts had announced publicly that they would appear in *Design for Living*.

Chapter Eight

NOW APPEARING UNDER NEW MANAGEMENT...

"The actor is as much dependent upon his part as a table is upon its legs. No great actor ever made a poor play great, and no poor part ever produced a great actor."

Alfred Lunt

In Russia, if actors "forget 'the play is the thing' then it is their misfortune. It has been this trouble in America which is responsible for so many failures."

Lynn Fontanne

1932–33

When the Lunts cabled Noël Coward asking, "WHAT ABOUT IT?", they were referring to the plan made years before, which called for Coward to write a comedy in which the three of them would appear. Now as securely established as a performer-playwright as the Lunts were as actors, Coward was able to turn his mind to the fulfillment of those plans.

The most difficult challenge for Coward was to write a play with three roles which would be equally substantial. For the past eleven years the threesome had periodically discussed the possibility of such a play. According to Coward, "At one moment we were to be three foreigners. Lynn, Eurasian; Alfred, German; and I, Chinese. At another we were to be three acrobats, tapping out 'Allez Oops' and flipping handkerchiefs at one another. A further plan was that the entire play should be played in a gigantic bed, dealing with life and love in the Schnitzler manner. This, however, was hilariously discarded, after Alfred had suggested a few stage directions which, if followed faithfully, would undoubtedly have landed all three of us in gaol."

Coward wrote *Design for Living* while traveling on a small Norwegian freighter from Panama to Los Angeles, working only in the mornings and completing it in ten days. He created the characters of Gilda, Leo and Otto, "glib, over-articulate, and amoral creatures" (in Coward's words) who form a *ménage à trois* that proceeds from Paris to London to New York. Although each of them attempts to choose only one lover, no one can do so; they are utterly dependent on one another, and the play ends with the three of them having decided to continue their "design for living" as a threesome. *Design for Living* is something of a black comedy, more philosophical and less glib than most of Coward's comedies, though no less dependent upon verbal wit.

When it became known that the Lunts and Coward planned to appear in *Design for Living*, Coward was wined and dined, sent expensive gifts and courted by every important producer in New York. Eventually he decided to give the play to Max Gordon, who sent no presents but used a more dramatically effective tactic: he appeared one day at Coward's apartment threatening to cut his throat if Coward did not permit him to present the play.*

Gordon's tactic was as audacious as it was effective. Unbeknownst to Coward, Gordon was broke, unable even to pay the actors of the play he then had in production. However, when Coward agreed to let him produce *Design for Living*, Gordon was able to use that promise as collateral to raise enough money to meet his current payroll and present Coward's play as well.

The play was initially scheduled for a limited three-month run (Coward found it difficult to sustain his enthusiasm for acting in any play longer than three months), but its enormous success eventually persuaded Coward to extend it to four.

Max Gordon expected the rehearsals of *Design for Living* to be a lark, but they proved extremely demanding. The play had to be played by actors with perfect command of light comic technique in order to get full value from its wit and artificiality. The end result had to look effortless, but could be created only by prolonged, intense rehearsal. Gordon said the Lunts drove themselves to exhaustion during the rehearsal period; perhaps, after so many years of working for the Theatre Guild, they could not have functioned in any other way. Perhaps, too, the three-week rehearsal schedule was so brief that it galvanized them into more furious activity than might otherwise have been the case.

*This is the account given by Coward's friend Cole Lesley, at any rate. Max Gordon's story was a bit different. He insisted that Coward had contacted *him* and offered him the play, although on very stiff terms: ten percent of the gross for each of the three featured performers and another ten percent for Coward as the author. Coward and the Lunts would put up $20,000, Gordon was told, but he would have to raise the remainder of the $30,000 production cost.

Fontanne was confronted with a difficult acting problem. She faced the necessity of beginning the play in a high state of emotion. Most plays are written so that the characters build gradually to an emotional climax. In *Design for Living,* however, Fontanne as Gilda made her first entrance in an agitated state and had to sustain that pitch without allowing the audience to experience a letdown. Eventually, she was able to structure her performance so that the audience became increasingly interested in her predicament, but she called it one of her greatest challenges.

Coward was billed as the director of the play, but Lunt said, "Noël really [did not] try to direct either of us." Although the Lunts were perfectly willing to accept Coward's direction, the rapport among the three of them was so great and the way they envisioned the style of the production so similar that it was unnecessary to have one individual in charge of artistic matters. Questions of interpretation did not arise; decisions regarding blocking, line readings or selection of business were reached by consensus. Still, Fontanne said that *Design for Living* represented the first occasion in her career when a director was able to provide help when called upon. In her earlier experiences—especially with J. Hartley Manners and Philip Moeller—the director had been unable to suggest approaches to character, she said; normally, they even permitted the actors to determine their own patterns of movement.

Although Max Gordon was the nominal producer of the play and Noël Coward the nominal director, the Lunts contributed significantly in both areas. Perhaps because *Design for Living* marked the first time they were responsible for the welfare of others as well as for their own performances and because that responsibility created pressures they had not previously experienced, tempers occasionally flared. Lunt and Fontanne got into a battle royal during one rehearsal, and those who observed it were hard put to understand that the reasons were purely professional. "She went up on a line and she refused to admit she had forgotten it," Noël Coward said, "and she said that Alfred had thrown her off by changing his movements." Fontanne asked him, "Are you going to put down that glass there?" He replied testily, "I've always put down that glass there." "No, you haven't," she said. "You put it down here. You're doing it purposely."

The argument reached such an emotional pitch that, in Coward's words, it looked as if they were "going to tear each other into shreds." Discussions between actors about the proper placement or timing of a piece of business are as commonplace as they are essential, and, as we have seen, the Lunts concentrated upon such details with near-obsessiveness. Occasionally, their discussions became contentious. They often bickered with one another; once in a while the bickering turned to pouting; but only rarely did it end in an angry scene. Coward said that on this occasion the cast was certain the production would be closed on the spot. However, the Lunts suddenly realized they were behaving childishly and abruptly ended the argument. The same conclusion was repeated whenever such an incident occurred between them; a show of temperament would be followed by a sudden and unconditional peace. Fortunately, the Lunts confined these arguments to the rehearsals and forgot them the moment the stage door closed behind them. After the outburst during the *Design for Living* rehearsal, Coward said, "they [walked] out arm in arm as if nothing had happened."

The play was first presented in Cleveland on January 2, 1933,* moving on to Pittsburgh and Washington (where the Lunts were astonished to be invited to a gala ball by Franklin D. Roosevelt) before opening at the Ethel Barrymore Theatre in New York on January 24. As Fontanne stood waiting in the wings, she thought how inconsiderate it was of Coward to send her onto an empty stage with a coffee pot and a milk jug in her hands, all conspiring to increase her nervousness, as she had to worry about beginning the play alone and keeping her hands from shaking. She turned to the playwright and said, "I suppose if your house in Kent were invaded, you'd send your mother out to face the guns!"

Fontanne had little to worry about, as it turned out. Some critics expressed discomfort with the "immoral" content of the play, but there were no reservations whatever about the production. Everywhere it went, it was greeted with the same enthusiasm. "Theatrical history in the making," said the Cleveland *Plain Dealer.*

The New York opening confirmed the verdict of the Cleveland critic. Brooks Atkinson, who called the play an "audacious and hilarious . . . artificial comedy that bristles with wit," said of the actors: "They are an incomparable trio of high comedians. And they . . . transmute artificial comedy into delight." He described Lunt's performance as being characterized by exuberance and boyish enthusiasm, Fontanne's by "slow, languorous deliberation," Coward's by "nervous, biting clarity." The three diverse characterizations meshed perfectly, creating glorious comic chamber music. Gilbert Gabriel echoed Atkinson's description of the actors, calling them "a matchless trio at wit, audacity and polished glee," and the remaining critics concurred.

Alfred Lunt generally detested any actor who departed from the script, but he was guilty of doing just that during a matinee of *Design for Living*. During a drinking scene between Coward and Lunt at the end of the second act, Coward for some reason (he claimed it was by accident) said Lunt's line. Lunt countered with Coward's line. When Coward proceeded to speak Lunt's next line, the course of the scene was set. For nearly twenty minutes they performed the scene speaking one another's dialogue, until Coward recalled that one of his lines called for his character to burp and Lunt simply could not call forth a burp. So, with a nod to Lunt, Coward picked up his own line and the two of them completed the scene in their own characters. Lunt claimed that "the scene was just as funny as

---

*For the first time in their career as a team, the Lunts received star billing. "Alfred Lunt / Lynn Fontanne / Noël Coward in *Design for Living*," the advertisements proclaimed.

ever" and that he would never have been guilty of "ad libbing or changing business [except in] a very special type of comedy, and then one in which you happened to be playing with the author." Coward said "it didn't matter because it was a drunk scene, so it didn't matter psychologically."

But Fontanne was furious with both of them. When they came off stage, Coward and Lunt were hugging one another jubilantly, giggling at their triumph—until they saw the stern-faced Fontanne, who broke their mood by pointing toward the audience and saying, "You don't hear anyone out there laughing, do you? I don't think anything either of you did was even remotely funny. You ought to be ashamed of yourselves. It's disgraceful!"

Lunt was immediately cowed by his wife's disapproval. At the end of the matinee, he quickly removed his costume and makeup and walked miserably on the street outside the theatre until he found a movie house. Not caring what was playing, Lunt bought a ticket and entered the theatre, wanting only to sit quietly and repent his sins. After nearly an hour he became aware of another person seated beside him who also seemed preoccupied. As the lights came up at the end of the picture, Lunt stole a glance at his neighbor. It was Noël Coward, who, equally chastened by Fontanne's rebuke, had also slunk into the nearest movie theatre to find solitude. Only by the sheerest coincidence had they wound up sitting side by side.*

Lunt's shame was genuine. Never again did he permit himself to become so carried away by exuberance. As the years progressed, his attitude became more like Fontanne's: theatre was a serious business and comedy was the most serious aspect of that business. The Lunts' performances were governed by an iron discipline, one that they came to demand from every actor with whom they worked.

Coward, never so disciplined a performer as the Lunts, was less affected in the long run by Fontanne's disapproval. But the difference between Coward and the Lunts was essentially the difference between a writer who also performed and performers who also contributed to the creation of plays. As Carol Channing told me in 1983, "We all know that Noël Coward was one of the great creative forces of the world, but he could not *re-create*. Those are two different talents. The Lunts could also create—they could create the characters—but their great talent was the talent for re-creating. Coward said that after three weeks in *Design for Living* he was sick unto death of it. But when people said to the Lunts, 'You must be sick of doing this show after all these months,' they couldn't understand that. Neither can I. That's how we get ignited—re-creating—that's our joy in life."

---

*This is the story Lunt told Donald Seawell. In the less elaborate version he related to another friend, "Coward had a hamburger by himself at some joint [and] although [Lunt] did go home with Fontanne after the matinee . . . she wouldn't speak to him."

That basic difference was illustrated during the run of *Design for Living* when Coward developed a sore throat and a high fever. One Saturday morning he told Lunt he would be unable to give the two performances scheduled that day. Two days of rest would do him a world of good, he said, and his voice would be in good shape by Monday night. Lunt, who simply could not comprehend the idea that Coward would voluntarily miss two performances because of any illness that did not require hospitalization, insisted he would not hear of it. But, Coward said, his understudy was perfectly capable and ready to go on. Besides, the understudy had been recommended to him by the Lunts themselves and was being paid a handsome salary for just such an emergency. Nonsense, Lunt answered; Coward must go on. In fact, he said, he would be willing to speak as many of Coward's lines for him as he reasonably could, thus saving Coward's voice. At last Coward could do nothing but agree reluctantly, knowing that the Lunts would physically drag him to the theatre if all else failed.

That afternoon Coward waited for Lunt to deliver Leo's lines, as he had suggested. But the plan dissolved when Lunt dried up so thoroughly that he forgot not only Coward's dialogue but his own as well. In his irritation, Coward bellowed the lines at the top of his voice, entirely forgetting that his throat was sore. "He felt not a scintilla of guilt about his badgering me to go on stage with a fever of 103 and an inflamed throat," said Coward. "He felt my appearance was necessary for a good performance. He cared only about the theatre."

Lunt's focus on each performance as critical, a never-to-be-repeated opportunity to approach perfection, may have been responsible for his habitual dissatisfaction with the result. During *Design for Living* he regularly characterized each of his performances as less than satisfactory. Even Fontanne picked up the theme, often apologizing to Coward for having let down the side. Asked by Dick Cavett in 1970 if the trio criticized one another during the run of *Design for Living*, Coward answered, "Without ceasing. Every night. We never got out of the theatre until two in the morning—that was known as our coffee break. . . . It would always start with Alfred saying how awful he'd been. 'Oh, Nöelie, I was terrible tonight!' Then Lynn'd shout out, 'No, no, *I* was awful, worse than I've ever been.' And I used to get sick of this, and say, '*I* was wonderful.'"

Finally, Coward could stand it no longer. He wrote a comic sketch about three actors who are continually abasing themselves before one another although they are appearing in a greatly successful production. The Lunts, delighted with Coward's sketch, appeared in it with him for a charity benefit.

Fontanne's fierce determination to improve every performance she gave is perhaps best typified by her behavior on the last day of *Design for*

Living's run of four months in New York. During the afternoon performance, in a scene that involved placing two letters on a mantelpiece, Fontanne managed to get from the audience exactly the reaction she had been
striving for since the play began. She came offstage flushed with victory.
"At last I've got it right!" she said jubilantly. Coward was puzzled at her
enthusiasm, saying, "My dear, you're a little late, we're closing the show."
She gave him a puzzled look, followed by a cold stare. "There's still tonight, isn't there?" she said.

So great was the success of *Design for Living* that police had to be
summoned to control the crowds attempting to buy tickets during the final
week of the run. The play closed at the end of May 1933 only because
Coward had become utterly bored.

Not everyone who saw the play was impressed, however. Some observers felt it was too trivial an enterprise to merit the Lunts' participation.
One was Lunt's old school friend Ray Weaver, who had become a professor of speech at the University of Michigan. Weaver claimed that Coward
had corrupted Lunt's taste and altered his serious philosophy of the theatre. He said Lunt had once "believed [theatre] had a profound humanist
function in a democratic society and was to replace organized religion. It
was to uplift and purify man. A theatre is a church rather than a place to
be amused." Lunt's view of the theatre did indeed take into account its
civilizing and didactic capabilities, but he never overlooked its function as
a place of pure entertainment. To Weaver's accusation, he replied succinctly, "Oh, nothing of the kind. Ridiculous. Noël had no such influence
on me."

Weaver's contention and Lunt's rejoinder should be seen in terms of
the Lunts' mission in the theatre, as they saw it. Certainly there were more
significant plays in the dramatic repertoire than *Design for Living,* and it is
unfortunate that the Lunts were not able to appear in every one of them.
Given the impossibility of that task, however, they were forced to choose
the direction their careers would take. One choice they made was to appear
in new plays by living playwrights, plays they could help to shape not just
by the quality of their performances but by close collaboration with the
authors. Of the seventeen plays in which they appeared after deciding to
act exclusively as a team, all but two were written by living playwrights.
Their commitment was primarily to help ensure the vitality of the theatre
of the present and the future rather than devote their energies to the recreation of the plays of the past.

The Lunts were as skilled in playing serious drama as they were in
comedy. Without question, they could have applied themselves to the performance of tragedies, if they had wished to do so. Again, however, they
were required to make a choice. Without ignoring serious drama (such
plays as *There Shall Be No Night, Strange Interlude, The Sea Gull* and *The
Visit* hardly qualify as frivolous), the Lunts chose to concentrate their ener-

gies primarily upon the performance of comedy, and particularly to the comedy of manners. In doing so, they raised the level of performance of such plays to a higher plane than had been achieved before. Moreover, they created an appetite for witty, artificial modern comedy among millions of theatre- and film-goers. Even those who never saw the Lunts felt their influence. It can be argued that the public's acceptance of the wonderful comic films Katharine Hepburn made with Spencer Tracy and Cary Grant in the 1930s and '40s, for example, was an outgrowth of the work the Lunts were doing on the stages of New York, London and the scores of American cities to which they toured.

Finally, the Lunts chose to make the *play* the focus of their work. Unlike some actors who use the work of the playwright merely as a springboard for their own abilities and who are not averse to distorting a play for the sake of demonstrating their performing talents, the Lunts treated the authors' conceptions as sacred. Lunt made his attitude clear in an article he wrote for the New York *Times* in 1930, saying that acting is "merely a secondary medium through which the playwright reaches his audience. The actor is but an interpreter and must remain so. . . ." He reinforced those sentiments in a 1937 interview when he said, "The actor is not a creative, but an interpretive artist. His one and *only* job is to work *within the play,* to translate the ideas of the author. The play itself is what counts."

The Lunts were often credited with having made a poor play seem much better than it was, but they dismissed such notions. "The actor is as much dependent upon his part as a table is upon its legs," Lunt said. "No great actor ever made a poor play great, and no poor part ever produced a great actor."

Fontanne agreed. She claimed that she and her husband had never been directly responsible for creating a successful play. If they deserved credit, it was due primarily to their shrewdness in selecting good material, she felt. As evidence, she offered the experience of *Design for Living*. "Noël Coward wrote [the play] for us and we played it with him on Broadway," she said, "but it ran even longer in London, with Diana Wynyard, Rex Harrison and Anton Walbrook in the cast. Obviously, we are not indispensable."

Those were public comments, given to interviewers or written for publication. But the Lunts' private feelings were precisely the same. Shortly after the London production of *Reunion in Vienna* opened in January 1934, Lunt, who was upset about reviews claiming that the performance was superior to the play, wrote to Robert E. Sherwood, "My only reason for being in the theatre either as an actor or as a director of acting is to project the author—not obscure or use him for my own purpose but to clarify & heighten whatever *he* wishes to say—

"if I have failed you in this then sock me baby & let's call it a day."

1933–34

At Genesee Depot in the summer of 1933, Fontanne was beset by a series of misfortunes. On July 24, she was thrown from a horse and taken to a hospital, but X-rays showed no fractures or serious injuries. Shortly thereafter she cut her toe severely with a piece of glass and on the very next day was stung by a hornet. There was one great compensation, however. In August the Lunts finally saw the completion of their swimming pool, a project they had been planning for several years.

The money they had made from the film of *The Guardsman* and the Broadway production of *Design for Living* allowed them not only to expand and develop their property at Genesee Depot; it also gave them a freedom they had never had before. They planned a long vacation trip to Copenhagen, Stockholm, Helsingfors and Moscow for September 1933, after which they intended to spend a week in London helping to cast *Reunion in Vienna*, which they were to present in that city under Gilbert Miller's management. A trip to Egypt would come next, followed by a return to London. They would be gone from the United States for at least a year.

Few Americans were traveling so extensively during the Depression, but few Americans had the wherewithal. A year's absence involved more than spending a great deal of money, however: the Lunts were warned that it would be detrimental to their American careers to be out of the public eye for such a long period. But, Fontanne said, "In these days you either spend your money or lose it in a bank," and Lunt added, "We are going to spend it, and the devil with the bank and the future. If everyone has forgotten us when we return, we shall go right back to Genesee Depot."

There was little chance that the Lunts would be forgotten, of course. But if their new status as star performers brought the satisfactions of extended periods of leisure and heretofore undreamed-of amounts of money,* it also carried with it the pressures of responsibility, which the Lunts had not felt before. The necessity to achieve success in *Design for Living* in order to provide assured employment for everyone else associated with the project had led to unaccustomed tensions during the rehearsal process. And the freedom to select the plays in which they would appear was a great opportunity, but it was also a daunting responsibility that kept them busy reading scores of scripts. The Theatre Guild had for eight years made those decisions for them, and most of the decisions had turned out to be wise ones.

It may have been a subconscious desire to escape their new responsibilities that prompted Lunt to realize a childhood dream. On a Sunday

---

*The financial return for the Lunts from *Design for Living* was far greater than any they had previously received in the theatre.

night in April 1933, Lunt, whose love for the circus was as strong as ever, finally made his debut in that medium at the age of forty. Lunt, Fontanne and Noël Coward all rode elephants in the Ringling Brothers Circus at Madison Square Garden. Lunt was costumed as the Mahout of Bolivar. Since this appearance was not announced in advance, one must assume that it was not intended as a publicity stunt. Rather, it was the fulfillment of a lifelong fantasy. Readers can draw their own conclusions about any sub-conscious aspect of the circus appearance, but "running away to join the circus" has long been a metaphor for escape.

The Board members of the Theatre Guild may have been aware of the Lunts' ambivalence, for they continued to pursue the possibility of a rec-onciliation. In the fall of 1933 the Guild asked for and received a meeting with the Lunts. Although their anger with the Board members had cooled considerably, they declined to rejoin the Guild because of the scripts avail-able to them. The Board recommended that they appear in Ferdinand Bruckner's *Races,* an indictment of racism and Nazism, but the Lunts thought the play a poor one.* Lawrence Langner and Helen Westley sug-gested the Guild contact its stable of American playwrights—Behrman, Anderson, O'Neill, Howard, Sherwood—and ask for any plays they might have that would be suitable for the Lunts. In addition, they would ask those playwrights and others to consider writing new plays in which the Lunts could perform. The couple readily agreed to these suggestions and added that during their forthcoming trip to Europe they would look for plays in which they could appear under Guild auspices. Until such plays turned up, however, the Lunts would not sign a contract with the orga-nization.

The Lunts' trip abroad nearly had to be postponed when they mis-placed their passports. Their attempts to secure new ones met with the same red tape encountered by other Americans in their situation; for once, their celebrity seemed to have no effect. "I never knew such uninterested people as they have at the passport office," Lunt told the New York *Tribune* on September 14. "First they wouldn't believe we were born; then they didn't seem to care." At last, however, the Lunts convinced the govern-ment that they had indeed been born and they were awarded new pass-ports. Then, on the day they were scheduled to leave, a call from Genesee Depot informed them that the missing passports had been found under a stack of books. At last, on September 17, they boarded the *Bremen* for the trip abroad.

The vacation was gloriously successful. Its highlight, undoubtedly, was the three weeks they spent in Moscow, where, to their surprise, they discovered that their reputations had preceded them. Russia's leading ac-tors and directors entertained them on several occasions, treating them with the respect and admiration due to America's foremost actors. For

---

*Events seem to have proved them correct. When the Guild produced the play, it ran for two weeks in Philadelphia, received poor reviews and was closed.

their part, the Lunts went to the theatre or the opera every night of their stay and were thrilled by the taste and imagination lavished on every production. "You never saw anything like it," they told the New York *Herald Tribune* in December 1933. To Noël Coward they said, "As far as lighting, teamwork, underplaying, and psychological subtlety [are] concerned, the Russians [have] left us a long way behind."

The Lunts saw the Russian theatre at its height. The great actors Moskvin and Kachalov were appearing in such Russian classics as *Dead Souls* and *The Cherry Orchard,* the latter at the Moscow Art Theatre, where Stanislavski's and Gordon Craig's production of *Hamlet* was also playing. Lunt described it many years later as the finest production of that play he had ever seen. Two interpreters accompanied them to each play, whispering translations of the dialogue in their ears. But the interpreters became superfluous after a short time, Fontanne said. The actors communicated states of mind and attitudes with such clarity that understanding the spoken words became unnecessary.

Russian directors such as Stanislavski, Meyerhold, Tairov and Okhlopkov, each of whom had the ability to articulate his own theory of the function of theatrical art, still had the freedom to present their conceptions in radically experimental productions. The Soviet government subsidized many of the finest theatrical organizations and exerted little censorship. Within a year the regime would impose the standard of Socialist Realism upon all art in the U.S.S.R., and many of the great directors would be accused of the sin of Formalism. But in 1933 the Soviet theatre was undoubtedly the most dynamic and innovative in the world.

Lunt told a reporter for the New York *Times* that the Russians "do things on a grand scale. . . . They are unmistakably the most amazing people for observing, with respect to a play. It is never distorted. It is produced as the author felt it should be."

Fontanne added that one of the reasons for the impressiveness of the performances given by the Russians was their system of actor-training. An actor "must go through a kindergarten experience playing minor parts, and he never graduates into the leading role until he can feel it," she explained. "Their system is elastic. A man shows a faculty; a woman shows a talent. They are given a chance to go forward, but if they forget 'the play is the thing' then it is their misfortune. It has been this trouble in America which is responsible for so many failures."

During their visit to Egypt, the Lunts enjoyed the best of two worlds. Although they left Cairo to journey into the wilderness on a camel safari, they carried along iron beds with box springs that were assembled and placed inside their tents each night. Among their entourage was a French chef, who prepared their meals from the ample supply of food brought along. Somehow their method of travel seems peculiarly appropriate for them, for so much in their lives was contradictory: the worldly sophisticates who were most at home in rural Wisconsin, the urbane conversationalists who avoided social gatherings, the brilliant theatrical technicians who claimed little knowledge of technique.

After their sojourn in Egypt, the Lunts returned to London to begin rehearsals for *Reunion in Vienna*. The production promised to be a lucrative one, for each would receive ten percent of the gross receipts. It would also represent a significant challenge to Lunt, who would be given his first opportunity to direct. Lunt's insistence on taking pains as an actor to polish every aspect of his performance also characterized his approach as a director. He completely restaged the play for its London production, employing the services of an expert in old Viennese manners and court etiquette to ensure the accuracy of the stage business.

Reunion opened at the Lyric Theatre on January 3, 1934, to a tremendous ovation. The formally dressed audience, men in white tie and tails, bejeweled women in evening gowns, gave the actors a total of ten curtain calls.

"Everybody in this country to whom beautiful polished acting gives pleasure must contrive somehow at the earliest possible moment to go to the Lyric Theatre and see Alfred Lunt and Lynn Fontanne in *Reunion in Vienna*," said the London *Daily Telegraph*, adding, "You will probably have to fight your way to the box office." The review in the *London Stage* paid tribute to Lunt's direction, which "does full justice to the play," but concentrated upon the "exquisiteness" of Fontanne's acting and the "equally perfect performance" given by Lunt.

The evaluations of Sherwood's play were somewhat less ecstatic, and that destroyed whatever enjoyment the Lunts might have taken in the notices for their performances. Lunt wrote a long, apologetic letter to the playwright, which began, "I hope you will not be embittered or angered over the press here for *Reunion in Vienna*. The management and the friends we have seen since the opening appear to be delighted and consider the notices a triumph. But to you, and may I add humbly, to me, they seem for the most part pretty stupid and far from discerning or articulate."

Lunt's irritation extended to the performances he and Fontanne were giving ("G. B. Stern . . . could not understand why Lynn and I were so unhappy and suicidal for the two days following [the performance she saw]. We felt we had played badly, and that's the answer to that"), to the inability of English critics and audiences to recognize the skill of their native actors ("I am angered to desperation that the people here do not know what extraordinary actors they possess. Never have I seen small parts played so well. Never have I seen actors work so hard for their play, and not for personal acclaim") and particularly to the criticism of one observer that the Lunts' articulation had been poor ("Will you tell me why, if we were not heard, why then did the audience respond to every line, and why did the play come through so clearly? One [member of the audience] at the end of the play [during Lunt's curtain speech on opening night] shouted 'Louder,' and that voice was hushed by the entire gallery, and was followed by as pretty a scream as we have ever heard, 'We think you're both marvelous' ").

One can only attribute Lunt's frustration to his desire for unalloyed perfection. It is difficult for an objective observer to read the critics' notices and see them as anything but enthusiastic. But a review that was ninety-five percent favorable always left Lunt feeling unhappy, as he could not help focusing his attention on the few critical comments.

Fontanne, however, seemed undisturbed by the occasional caveat. "*Reunion* is a success, as you no doubt know, and the company is marvelous," she wrote to Alexander Woollcott a month after the opening.

By March 29, Lunt's anger seems to have abated and he was enjoying the performances. He told Woollcott of "the extraordinary goings-on in the audiences" during the play.

> It's sometimes hair-raising, and one hardly knows whether to speak your lines to the actors or across the footlights. For instance, one night in the last act I said to the husband, "Oh, I see I'm the only one seated," when an elderly woman's voice from the front row said, "Yes!" I continued with, "Won't you please sit down?" and the same voice said, "Well, that's better," and then relaxed for the rest of the performance.
>
> A week ago Saturday I said (again in the last act), "You don't mind my talking about myself, do you?" and a man's voice from the gallery said "No, not at all." Now I ask you. But the strangest was a couple of weeks ago. When I waltzed Lynn into the bedroom, a very old gentleman rose and yelled after us: "Lecherous mountebank!!" Oh, it's a very strange business, this acting in London.

Many London theatres were only minimally heated during the winter months in the 1930s. The stage of the Lyric was particularly frigid and Fontanne, who wore light summer clothing for the play, suffered more than anyone. "Poor Lynn," Lunt recalled years later. "I used to watch her grow bluer and bluer and bluer through the first act and at the end her arms looked like two alligators hanging from her shoulders." Fortunately, Gilbert Miller installed electric heaters in the dressing rooms, earning the everlasting gratitude of the Lunts.

During the run they moved from Claridge's Hotel to a rented five-room house in Chelsea, where they were able to warm up after each performance. The house, equipped with central heating, was described by Fontanne as "most comfortable, nay, luxurious." Four servants were hired, including a French cook, to maintain the luxury.

Just as Fontanne had worked until the final performance of *Design for Living* to perfect a piece of business, she exhibited the same relentless determination in *Reunion in Vienna*. One of her lines invariably received a small, appreciative laugh, but she was dissatisfied, believing that the line should get a much greater response. At last, at the final matinee in London, after having worked on the line for hundreds of performances, she got the big laugh she wanted.

John C. Wilson, Noël Coward's business manager and American representative, came to see the Lunts during the run of the play. Wilson proposed that Coward and the Lunts form a production company, with Wilson acting as business manager. The result was Transatlantic Productions, Inc. Fontanne wrote to Alexander Woollcott from the Lyric Theatre on March 31, 1934, "I suppose you know that Noel, Alfred and I have gone into management with Jack Wilson as business advisor, and the company will operate under his name. The arrangement is very nice because it leaves us all perfectly free, that is, if another management has a play that Noel or Alfred and I want to do, we can. It seems to us the best way of investing our money at the moment. We are reading all scripts like mad. . . ."

In addition to producing plays, the arrangement called for the profits made by any one of the participants to be shared with the others. The Lunts would profit from any plays written by Coward or produced by Wilson, while Wilson and Coward would share in the profits of any work the Lunts did for another management.

The Theatre Guild was unaware of the formation of Transatlantic Productions when the managers corresponded with the Lunts early in 1934. Still trying to woo them back to the fold, but unable to find any new plays worthy of their participation, the Board, at Lee Simonson's suggestion, offered them the opportunity to act in *Antony and Cleopatra*. The Lunts turned it down, however, asserting that they saw no point in doing Shakespeare simply for the sake of doing Shakespeare. When they were able to formulate a novel production scheme for a Shakespearean play, they implied, they would then be more enthusiastic.

The Guild refused to give up, perhaps because it could ill afford to. Despite the participation of Helen Hayes in *Mary of Scotland* and George M. Cohan in *Ah, Wilderness!* in the 1933–34 season, the subscribers let the Guild know they were unhappy about the absence of their favorite performers, the Lunts.

Then the news of Transatlantic Productions' formation was released to the press and its first production—S. N. Behrman's *Biography,* featuring Ina Claire and Laurence Olivier—opened in London in March. On April 10, 1934, Warren Munsell, the business manager of the Theatre Guild, wrote to the Lunts, "I saw an announcement in the papers the other day to the effect that you and Noel Coward were forming a producing corporation. . . . I don't want to pry into your private affairs but in view of the fact that you told Lawrence [Langner] and me that you would come back to the Guild next fall if we found a suitable play for you, I am wondering if this report is correct?" The Lunts presumably answered that their return to the Guild would have to be delayed for at least a season, for by this time they were already planning to appear in another play by Noël Coward under their joint management.

Reunion in Vienna closed only because the summer was approaching and the Lunts did not want to give up the Wisconsin vacation that had become so precious to them. They returned to New York on board the *Ile de France* on July 3, 1934. After a short stay, they went home to Genesee Depot, where Coward joined them in the fall so that they could all work on his new play. One of the requirements of Lunt's role was that he play the accordion, so, typically, he used the time in Wisconsin learning to give at least a passable performance. Then, early in December, Coward and the Lunts returned to New York to begin rehearsals for *Point Valaine*.

1934–35

From the first, the Lunts were reluctant to appear in Coward's play. It offered such a departure from the roles they had been playing in recent years that it was a challenging opportunity, but they doubted that the play could succeed, and tried to make their doubts known to Coward. Fontanne predicted that *Point Valaine* would be unlikely to run longer than six weeks. But Coward's belief in his play was unshaken. According to Fontanne, he responded by saying, "Nonsense! Absolute nonsense!" He had written the play especially for them, he said, and he was convinced that it would be successful. Fontanne told George Schaefer that she replied to Coward, "Of course you did *Design for Living* for us. That was a great success and we owe you something for that. We'll do it if you like."

An excellent cast, including Louis Hayward and Osgood Perkins, was assembled, but, as Coward later noted, "everything seemed to go wrong from the beginning. Alfred and Lynn and I were irritable with each other, which we had never been before." Again, the weight of responsibility for every aspect of the production seems to have been a heavy burden for the Lunts, creating unusual tensions.

The most serious problem with *Point Valaine*, as Coward ultimately acknowledged, was the play itself. Neither comedy nor tragedy, it was a lurid study of sexual obsession. Fontanne played Linda Valaine, the owner of a gloomy hotel on a semitropical island, who is having a passionate affair with Stefan, the hotel's animalistic Russian headwaiter, played by Lunt. None of the characters, Coward said, "was either interesting or kind." Given no one to sympathize with or admire, spectators refused to take more than a mild interest in the play.

The difficulties were compounded by audience expectations. When it was announced that Alfred Lunt and Lynn Fontanne would appear in a new play by Noël Coward, theatregoers anticipated another witty romp.

Point Valaine was under no obligation to comply with those expectations, of course, but its failure to do so left audiences confused if not downright hostile. Spectators were disappointed that Lunt had only about half a dozen speeches in Acts I and II; and they were shocked when, on two different occasions, he spat in Fontanne's face.

In other ways, too, the play seemed to be under a curse. During the first performance, at the Colonial Theatre in Boston on Christmas Day, 1934, the sets designed by Gladys Calthrop proved to be too heavy to be moved as quickly as the scene changes required, and a machine designed to produce rain did its job much too well, flooding the stage. Following the opening performance, the rain machine was scrapped, the sets were made less cumbersome and the lighting was entirely redesigned.

In Philadelphia another disaster occurred. The stage manager called too early for a scene change to be made. As most of the scenery was whisked away in full view of the audience, Lunt was revealed standing on a huge rock, the one remaining scenic element. He was supposed to leap from the rock to his death—but he was unable to jump because a stage-hand had removed the offstage mattress when the stage manager called the shift cue. Lunt could do nothing but wait in embarrassment until the curtain came down. The audience, puzzled, had no idea whether to laugh or applaud politely. Utterly humiliated, Lunt left the theatre alone immediately after the performance and walked disconsolately through the streets for several hours. When he finally returned to his hotel, he swore to Fontanne and Coward in all seriousness that they had just witnessed the end of his theatrical career.

He persevered, however, and *Point Valaine* moved on to New York, where the critics at the Ethel Barrymore Theatre on January 16 savaged the play and the production. Of all the performers, only Louis Hayward (who played the one role that might be considered remotely sympathetic) received consistently favorable reviews. Brooks Atkinson praised Fontanne for "that restlessness and reserve that throw [her] character up into high significance" and Lunt for the "energy and garish detail" with which he invested the "monster and fiend" he was called upon to play, but Atkinson was in the minority.

Although the Lunts had never been fond of *Point Valaine*, they became fiercely defensive once it was subjected to the scrutiny of the public. Worthington Miner, who had directed them in *Reunion in Vienna*, came backstage and, asked his opinion, confessed that he found *Point Valaine* to. be sordid and poorly written, unworthy of the Lunts' talents. Fontanne answered snidely, "You are the first intelligent person of the theatre to feel this way. Have you lined up with the critics?" Miner was stunned by her reaction and even more stunned when she turned to Lunt and referred to Miner in tones of mockery and disdain. The director, deeply unhappy at her attitude, fled the theatre.

Fontanne's defensiveness revealed her loyalty to Noël Coward, but it also demonstrated a less attractive side of her personality. When she took a position—any position—she defended it fiercely and often unreasonably against those who disagreed with her. She was not incapable of seeing her error after she had been given time to gain objectivity, but it must be said that she often needed an inordinate amount of time before she changed her attitude.

Fontanne herself had predicted that *Point Valaine* would run for only six weeks in New York. Instead, it ran for seven, but it was a decided failure in every respect, losing considerable money for Transatlantic Productions. Ultimately, *Point Valaine* proved to be the only flop of the Lunts' career after they reached the decision in 1928 to appear as a team in all future productions. Evidently it taught them a lesson, however, for they never again appeared in a play simply out of loyalty or friendship or for any reason other than their belief that the play was a good one. This required them to reject plays that had been written especially for them and occasionally led to hard feelings, but they had learned that personal relationships should not be allowed to interfere with their sound professional instincts.

When the Lunts rejected the Theatre Guild's offer to appear in *Antony and Cleopatra,* they had said they might be willing to appear in another Shakespearean production if they could evolve a new and imaginative concept. When *Point Valaine* closed early in 1935, the Guild asked the Lunts if they would be interested in acting in *The Taming of the Shrew,* a play that seemed perfectly suited to their comic talents. They were promised virtually free rein in conceiving and mounting the production.* In addition, the Guild offered to share the profits of the play with Transatlantic Productions. The offer was simply too good to reject, and the Lunts were reunited with the Theatre Guild in April 1935, after a separation of more than two years.

Thus, when the Lunts returned, it was as part of a corporation, an arrangement that made it possible for them to receive a considerably higher share of the profits than in the past. An example of how well the arrangement worked for the Lunts was the 1937–38 Theatre Guild production of *Amphitryon 38:* the Guild received half the profits brought in by the presentation, the other half going to the coproducer, Transatlantic Productions.

Moreover, when the Lunts agreed to rejoin the Theatre Guild, it was no longer necessary for them to appear wherever, whenever and in what-

---

*Lawrence Langner proposed to the other Board members that he be part of the production team for *Shrew.* But Lee Simonson felt it would be unwise for any Board member to attempt to impose his ideas upon the production, and this applied particularly to Langner, whose firm ideas about the correct way to produce Shakespeare might conflict with the Lunts' conception. The other members agreed that care must be taken not to alienate the Lunts. At Simonson's suggestion, Langner withdrew his request.

ever the Guild chose for them. Instead, they were able to select their plays and produce them in accordance with their own conceptions with a minimum of interference. The satisfaction they received from this artistic independence surely meant more to them than the additional money they received.

One other element may have played a part in the Lunts' decision. During their association the Theatre Guild had always attended to the drudgery of production work: finding acceptable scripts, raising money, dealing with theatrical unions and actors' agents, etc. It is not unreasonable to assume that the Lunts returned to the Guild partly in order to be relieved of these responsibilities. To rejoin the Theatre Guild as members of its acting company with the special privileges they were able to arrange as partners in Transatlantic Productions appeared to offer them the best of both worlds.

Chapter Nine

RETURN TO THE THEATRE
GUILD

"With these people it never stops until
they fall into their graves."

Uta Hagen

In many respects, the 1930s were the most exciting decade in the history of the American theatre. Although the Depression forced the closing of many theatres and caused mass unemployment in the theatrical community, it also stimulated the careers of young playwrights, directors, actors and producers, many of whom were motivated by their determination to protest a social system that they believed had failed, as well as by their eagerness to present their views in theatrical form. A new social consciousness thus pervaded the American drama of the period.

The movies had become the mass entertainment medium of America, drawing away millions of potential theatregoers. But those who remained were, in general, looking for something more vivid, more exciting and often more intellectually stimulating than the movies could provide. In many respects, the theatre in New York had finally caught up to the aspirations of the Theatre Guild, which had begun to present artistically challenging plays more than a decade before.

Many well-established theatrical personalities had difficulty adjusting to the "new" theatre of the 1930s. The Lunts had no such difficulty. They were well known for their devotion to the artistic principles of the Theatre Guild. At the same time, they were great box-office attractions. Thus, they were in a unique position, able to pursue their ideals without having to adjust to the new realities of the theatrical world.

1935–38

Confronted with the choice of appearing in Robert E. Sherwood's adaptation of Jacques Deval's scintillating—and, in all probability, highly profitable—comedy *Tovarich,* or acting in a Theatre Guild production of *The Taming of the Shrew,* the Lunts unhesitatingly chose to return to the Theatre Guild; but they returned to the organization firmly in control of the mechanisms of production—casting, selection of directors and designers, and so on. Transatlantic Productions (under John C. Wilson's name) would receive twenty-five percent of the profits on the production. Moreover, Lunt became a member of the Theatre Guild's Board of Directors, which assured that he would be fully informed of any discussions regarding the play.

Work on *The Taming of the Shrew* began in March 1935. Lunt and Fontanne, who had worked out a complete production concept, were given appropriate credit on the posters and programs. They were also given something approximating star billing for the first time in their association with the Theatre Guild. The program, which also acknowledged Transatlantic Productions' hand in the proceedings, was headed:

The Theatre Guild presents
(in association with John C. Wilson)
WILLIAM SHAKESPEARE'S COMEDY
THE TAMING OF THE SHREW

with
ALFRED LUNT AND LYNN FONTANNE
PRODUCTION DIRECTED BY
HARRY WAGSTAFF GRIBBLE
Scheme of production devised by Mr. Lunt and Miss Fontanne

The Lunt's production scheme began with a determination to investigate the play as if it were a new script never performed before. Ultimately, they became convinced that Shakespeare's purpose would best be served by emphasizing the farcical nature of the play and by providing constant diversion. The presentation came to resemble nothing quite so much as a three-ring circus.

Modern productions of *Shrew* often eliminate the Christopher Sly scene which, in Shakespeare's text, opens the play and provides a rationale for its action. But for the Lunts it was integral to their concept. They used the scene as written, so that *The Taming of the Shrew* became a play about a group of touring players who offer a performance at the request of a jovial nobleman in order to play a joke upon the drunken Christopher Sly, who, in their production, was seated in a box during the performance and periodically shouted at the actors. He also referred directly to the audience, particularly to anyone who had the misfortune to arrive at the theatre after the curtain had gone up. As the latecomers walked down the aisle, Christopher Sly made noises at them and pantomimed "Sit down" or "Be quiet." Furthermore, the actors stopped their performance and stared at the latecomers. If anyone in the audience coughed loudly, all the actors on stage also began coughing. In the Lunts' hands, *The Taming of the Shrew* focused not upon the reality of Petruchio and Katharine but upon the situation of the troupe of actors that was giving the performance. The Lunts built elements into the production—such as intentionally missed entrances followed by the on-stage actors repeating their cue lines more loudly; entrances made from the wrong side of the stage that forced all the actors to adjust hastily to the unexpected situation—that would constantly remind the audience that the actors on stage were playing actors who were, in turn, playing assorted characters. When Kate shrieked at and kicked Petruchio, the actors responded not as characters to Kate, but as actors to the actress who was playing Kate. Often the actors looked directly at the audience, inviting them to share in the fun of the play they were performing for Christopher Sly.

The Lunts chose Claggett Wilson to design costumes and, among the actors, Sydney Greenstreet as Baptista, Dorothy Mathews as Bianca, and Alan Hewitt, Bretaigne Windust and S. Thomas Gomez in smaller roles. A young actor named Richard Whorf, so eager to be cast in the production that he read everything from Tranio to the Widow during auditions, was cast as Christopher Sly, thus beginning his long association with the Lunts. These actors formed the nucleus of a new acting company that would perform in numerous Theatre Guild/Lunt-Fontanne productions during the next several seasons. In all, there were thirty-six performers in *The Taming of the Shrew*, including musicians, midgets (who, Lunt insisted, must always be referred to as "little people") and acrobats. When the production went on tour, it also included several personal servants of the Lunts: Fontanne's dresser, Lunt's valet and chauffeur.

The director, Harry Wagstaff Gribble, was responsible for cutting the text and selecting the songs, as well as staging the production. He also permitted the actors to invent comic business that seemed appropriate to the characters and the situation. Lunt skipped rope with a string of sausages during one scene; Fontanne as Kate, refused food by Petruchio, stuffed sausages and oranges into her bodice and pineapples into her bustle when Petruchio was not looking.

The Taming of the Shrew was first seen at the Nixon Theatre in Pittsburgh on April 22, 1935. The Theatre Guild wanted to bring the production to New York that spring, but Lunt decided against it. His plan was to tour the play briefly, pause for a summer vacation, resume the tour early in the fall and open in New York in late September. In that way, he hoped, any production problems discovered during the spring tour could be eliminated before the New York opening.

The Pittsburgh premiere was spectacularly successful. When the curtain dropped at the end of the first act, the audience cheered for five full minutes. Critics lavished praise upon the concept and the players, particularly the Lunts.

Lunt, whose previous professional experience in Shakespearean plays had been limited to the ill-fated *Much Ado About Nothing,* a few lines in Margaret Anglin's production of *As You Like It* and small roles in several productions at the Castle Square Theatre, found playing Petruchio a delight. He particularly enjoyed the richness of the character and the many different possibilities for interpreting individual lines and scenes. "You read a speech or do a scene, giving it a certain meaning," he said. "Then, all of a sudden, a wholly different implication dawns on you, and you say to yourself, 'Of course! *This* is what it really means. Why didn't I see it long ago?' And that keeps happening constantly. There is so much room to turn around in, in Shakespeare. No other dramatist old or new gives you so much."

The production was full of bruising physical encounters between Petruchio and Kate—and Lunt and Fontanne bore the scars to prove it. Even before the production reached Broadway, Fontanne tore a cartilage in her knee during one of the more active scenes. With the knee encased in a cast, she almost collapsed in her dressing room following one performance. Although the injury never forced her to withdraw from the production, it continued to cause her pain throughout the run.

Lunt's Petruchio was not at heart the insensitive male chauvinist he seemed to be. Although he treated Kate with the brutality required by Shakespeare's play, Lunt inserted a silent moment that revealed unsuspected depth of character. After one particularly fearsome brawl in which Petruchio established his dominance over Kate by thrashing her soundly, Kate left the stage in tears. At that point, G. B. Stern recalled, "Petruchio suddenly collapsed from sheer weariness and leaned exhausted against the door . . . by his complete surrender conveying how hatefully the masquerade had gone against the grain, and that he loved Kate, really loved her, but in carrying on in this abominable fashion until she capitulated lay their only hope of ultimate happiness."

From Pittsburgh, *Shrew* moved on to Cincinnati, Cleveland, Detroit, Toledo, Dayton, Louisville, Indianapolis, Rochester, Buffalo and Toronto. At each stop the production was further sharpened, and reports of the play's success created a sense of heightened anticipation among New York's theatregoers. Still, the Lunts resisted all temptations to hasten the Broadway opening. After the final Toronto performance, on May 25, the company was disbanded for a summer layoff.

That summer the Lunts dropped in at a movie studio on Astoria, Long Island, where Noël Coward was acting in a Ben Hecht–Charles

MacArthur film, *The Scoundrel*. Taking advantage of the Lunts' presence, along with that of Edna Ferber and George Jean Nathan, Coward prevailed upon them to act as extras in a crowd scene, thus making *The Scoundrel* a footnote to their cinematic history.

Also in the cast of that film was Alexander Woollcott, who called Coward "the czar of all the rushes." Woollcott, one of the few critics with whom the Lunts became friendly, was the most important tastemaker of his time, helping to shape the public's attitude toward hundreds of books and plays, even though he was accused by some of having no critical standards, only his own erratic likes and dislikes. His opinions were widely heard as well as read, for, despite his high, squeaky voice, he was one of the most popular radio commentators of the day.

Those who liked Woollcott were thoroughly devoted to him, whereas others detested him. Many feared his caustic wit. He could be either remarkably kind or a fearsome bully. Fontanne said, "Aleck was so witty and wonderful. I felt very honored by his liking me." When she spoke about him, she called him "my dear friend." Without question, the Lunts respected him greatly, often inviting him to Genesee Depot. When Woollcott visited, he and Lunt would have breakfast together, Woollcott's breakfast consisting primarily of thirteen cups of coffee. Then, while Lunt worked in the garden, Woollcott would return to his bedroom and, despite his enormous intake of caffeine, somehow manage to go back to sleep. Afterward, he would descend the staircase in bright orange pajamas and spend hours sitting on the front porch of the Cottage. The Lunts' cook described him as looking exactly "like a big Halloween pumpkin."

According to Carolyn Every, the Lunts' secretary in the 1930s, Fontanne respected Woollcott, but she was also terrified of his deriding her for lack of wit. Fontanne would spend hours perfecting metaphors and crafting epigrams for her letters to Woollcott, Every said. "Woollcott would make Miss Fontanne feel so silly all the time," she noted.

But others who knew the Lunts well felt differently about their relationship with Woollcott. William Le Massena said that they "adored him." Alan Hewitt believed that theirs was a deep and genuine friendship, and Lunt's brother-in-law said the Lunts idolized the critic. Evidence of Woollcott's closeness to the Lunts could be seen for years at Genesee Depot. He presented them with two dozen birch trees, which graced the estate thereafter; and they hung a painting of Woollcott in their library, above Lunt's desk.

His feeling for the Lunts is clearly revealed in a letter he wrote to them on June 7, 1934, when they were in England performing *Reunion in Vienna*. He told them that the year had been "the most generally satisfying" he had ever spent, with one exception: "The chief flaw in it was that you two who are both most dear to me were flourishing so far away."

Woollcott's love for the theatre went beyond critical enjoyment. He fancied himself an actor, and on several occasions tried his hand at it, but with scant success. In 1931 he acted in the Broadway production of S. N. Behrman's play *Brief Moment* and endeavored to reproduce the style of the Lunts. He had long been impressed by their ability to act without seeming to act. Their speech, so clear and audible, yet so easily projected that it appeared they were speaking in conversational tones; their gestures, so appropriate to character, yet so minimal; their use of emotion, so meaningful, yet so understated—all represented acting at its best for Woollcott. During the run of *Brief Moment,* Woollcott decided to emulate those qualities. On the night he first attempted this technique, the other actors were puzzled by his curious passivity on stage. His character seemed to have become invisible. Not only did he fail to communicate emotion, his voice could barely be heard. When they told him how ineffective his performance had been, he refused to believe them. After all, he had based his approach on the methods used by the finest of all American actors. Only after many hours did Behrman, Herman Shumlin, the director, and the other actors manage to convince him that what seemed in the Lunts to be conversational was really based upon superb vocal projection, that their technique of understatement was carefully calculated to produce the *appearance* of understatement, not the actuality.

The Lunts' closeness to Woollcott resulted in their becoming acquainted with many of his friends, and occasionally they dropped in at the Algonquin Hotel for one of the regular luncheon sessions of the Round Table—Lunt more frequently than his wife, who believed she was not quick-witted enough to keep up the group's level of repartee. Her brother-in-law disputed that verdict, however. "She could hold her own in a battle of wits," he said.

The Taming of the Shrew resumed its out-of-town performances on September 16, 1935, in Philadelphia. The audience, which seems to have been prepared for a long, dull evening, was reminded "of something that we are apt to forget," said a Philadelphia critic, "that the Bard of Avon wrote his comedies to be laughed at by audiences and not to provide required reading for sophomore courses . . . or to furnish a living for generations of academic commentators."

The New York opening, on September 30, was equally triumphant. "Most exceeding low," said Atkinson, "and most exceeding funny." The Lunts received accolades for their comic playing, and Richard Whorf was praised for his bulbous-nosed Christopher Sly, whose "befuddled, coarse, snoring, belching, thick-witted neighborhood drunk is a masterpiece of vulgarity." John Mason Brown, writing in the *Post,* devoted much of his review to Lunt's portrayal, which, he said, "takes its place among his most distinguished performances. It misses no chances, finds him reading Shakespeare with surprising ease, is richly humorous, has tremendous drive and variety, benefits by an unfailing invention, and is a memorable achievement in acting." John Anderson in the *Evening Journal* said that

Lynn Fontanne "sustains a portrait of magnificent comic proportions and (in spite of serious injury to her knee) she matches Mr. Lunt's Petruchio with a shrew that is a shrew, a yowling, kicking, biting hellion projected into the play like a bat out of hell."

With some notable exceptions, Shakespeare's plays had fared rather poorly on Broadway throughout the 1920s and '30s, but the Lunts' production of *The Taming of the Shrew* changed the attitude of thousands of playgoers, who eagerly paid premium prices for tickets.

After two months of full houses in New York, *The Taming of the Shrew* began to play before somewhat smaller audiences. Lunt informed the other Board members that he and Fontanne would be willing to take salary cuts in order to keep the production alive. Two months later the Board decided to send the production on another tour. Thus, in January 1936, *Shrew* played for two weeks in Boston and two in Chicago, where the engagement was a complete sellout.

At one of the last performances in Chicago, a couple drove two hundred miles, only to find that all the tickets were sold. They contacted local ticket agencies, but were told that nothing was available. At the theatre they found the stage doorman, known as Uncle Billy, and offered to give him $25 if he would allow them to stand in the wings. Tempted though he was, Uncle Billy knew that the couple's presence would be a distraction for the actors and stagehands, and he turned them down. After the performance, as the Lunts were leaving the theatre, Uncle Billy told them about the disappointed couple. Lunt answered, "Next time you get a chance like that, Billy, come and tell me and we'll slip them in and split the gate fee fifty-fifty."

One legacy of the Lunts' production of *The Taming of the Shrew* was the musical *Kiss Me, Kate*. A backstage observer, Arnold Saint Subber, once watched Lunt and Fontanne, dressed as Petruchio and Kate, engage in an argument while waiting for their entrances. Years later he produced *Kiss Me, Kate*, with songs by Cole Porter and a book by Sam and Bella Spewack. The musical shows the travails, on stage and off, of Fred and Lilli (Lillie Louise was Fontanne's real name), famous actors who are portraying Petruchio and Kate in *The Taming of the Shrew*.

Lunt's contributions to the Theatre Guild's Board meetings went beyond discussions of present and future Lunt-Fontanne productions. For example, he proposed a young British director named Tyrone Guthrie for the Guild production of *Call It a Day* in 1936. Primarily, however, his function on the Board was related to the productions in which he and his wife were planning to appear. In that connection, he had an announcement for the Board in December 1935. Transatlantic Productions had purchased Robert E. Sherwood's new play, *Idiot's Delight,* and, he said, the Theatre Guild was welcome to participate in the production. However, because of the play's topicality, it would have to be presented the following spring. The Guild assented enthusiastically.

Lunt had actually given Sherwood the original idea for *Idiot's Delight* in a letter congratulating him on the success of *Tovarich*. Lunt had mentioned that he and Fontanne were looking for a new play to appear in when the run of that "old flapdoodle farce" *The Taming of the Shrew* came to an end. "Seems to me, Mr. Sherwood, you'll really have to do something about *that!*" Lunt wrote. "You could put us in Budapest this time—say a Chicago punk on his way to Bucharest to put in those old slot machines or a former 'barker' now managing a troupe of midgets—who meets the elegant fakiress between a couple of hot violins and a zimbalum. Easy! Bobby, you could do it on your ear."

Sherwood, intrigued by Lunt's suggestion, sent word in November 1935 that he would begin working on such a play immediately. Coincidentally, he had long had a play in mind that was not unlike the notion Lunt presented to him, so the characters and plot did not take long to devise. By mid-December, Sherwood had completed the play and sent a copy to the Lunts.

Fontanne read it first and became absorbed immediately. As she was reading, Lunt asked her how far she had gotten in the script. "At the beginning of the second act," she replied, "and we must do it." Ten minutes later her resolve was even stronger. "We've got to do it, Alfred," she said, "we really must do this, it's most interesting and exciting."

"How is your part?" Lunt asked. She responded, "I haven't come to it yet."* Fontanne's enthusiasm for the play even before she knew the scope of her role represented a significant change in her attitude. Earlier in her career she had concentrated only upon her own part when deciding whether or not to appear in a production. By 1935, however, she had come to believe that the quality of the play was paramount.

Idiot's Delight was a comedy played against a backdrop of intense seriousness. The need for pacifism in a world about to be engulfed by war was the underlying theme, and events made the theme more topical each day. Ethiopia had been invaded by Mussolini when Sherwood began the play; when it opened in March 1936, Hitler had remilitarized the Rhineland and all Europe was contemplating the possibility of war.

The play concerns Harry Van, a moderately successful night-club comic and hoofer who is traveling throughout Europe with a troupe of chorus girls called Les Blondes. When they reach the Hotel Monte Gabriele in the Italian Alps, near the border of Switzerland and Austria, their tour is suspended because the onset of the war makes further travel impossible. Although international politics threaten the world's continued existence, Harry retains an incurable optimism. "I've known millions of

---

*Actually, the character of Irene enters during Act I, but she does not figure prominently in the play until later.

people, intimately," he says, "and I never found more than one out of a hundred that I didn't like, once you got to know them." His optimism is further expressed in his line: "No matter how much the meek may be bull-dozed or gypped, they *will* eventually inherit the earth."

Also stranded at the hotel is Irene, a woman of uncertain nationality who passes herself off as a Russian aristocrat. Irene is now the mistress of a ruthless munitions maker, but once, years before, when she was playing in vaudeville, she had a brief affair with Harry Van in Omaha, Nebraska. Harry recognizes her but Irene denies that she ever knew him.

Irene's disillusionment and bitterness at the state of the world are evident when she refers to God in the most hopeless terms: "Poor, lonely old soul. Sitting up in heaven, with nothing to do, but play solitaire. Poor, dear God. Playing Idiot's Delight. The game that never means anything, and never ends." Given characters of such contrasting attitudes and a play whose comic surface was only remotely suggestive of its content, the chief problem facing the playwright was to ensure that the comedy would hold the audience's attention without obscuring the serious theme.

Preparations for playing Harry Van were a joy for Alfred Lunt. He loved the idea of playing a vaudevillian whose "sincerity was greater than [his] artistry," as he put it; whose "eagerness to please was beyond [his] capacity to please." He asked for and received lessons in singing and stand-up comedy from Sophie Tucker and Milton Berle. After performances of *The Taming of the Shrew,* he went to different night clubs, studying "that forced bravado, that gay camaraderie," as he described the attitude of night-club comedians. "I pieced Harry together from these experiences and observations." He also used his own background. Harry's "accent, personality and appearance" were a composite of "three people I used to know in vaudeville. I took something from each one of them and added a general impression based on my own experiences. . . . Externally, I envisaged [Harry] with a pasty-faced expression—the look you see on men around Times Square who don't get out enough into the air—and black, shiny hair, slicked back around graying edges."

For Fontanne, going from the physical exertion of *Taming of the Shrew* to the relatively painless demands of the new play "was like going from something which is driving you to a nervous breakdown to lying in a feather bed." But she was frustrated by the sketchiness of her role. Its size did not bother her, but its lack of detail did. Irene "was not written," Fontanne said. "She was like a paper 'cut-out.'" She confided her feelings to Sherwood, who told her to include any details that would help her to present a complete characterization. It was Fontanne's idea to make the character a Cockney with a fake Russian accent. Even with the additions and changes, however, she felt that her role was underdeveloped. Still, she maintained her enthusiasm for the play and the production. "It is a lovely play and I am simply mad about it," she wrote to her British friend Graham Robertson in late January.

The Lunts chose Bretaigne Windust, who was acting in their production of *The Taming of the Shrew*, to serve as director for *Idiot's Delight*. From the beginning, it was conceived of as a play in which the actors' contributions would be predominant. Thus, at rehearsals, most of the creative ideas stemmed from the performers rather than from the director. And, by prearrangement with Windust, Lunt clearly took over many of the functions normally considered directorial. For example, when a scene did not seem to be making satisfactory progress in one rehearsal because the actors were not clearly communicating with one another, Lunt told the performers to repeat the scene, but to move about the stage only when motivated rather than when they had been instructed to do so, and to replace the playwright's language with gibberish. The purpose was to force each actor to affect the others not by the words he used but by physical proximity and by the urgency and tone of his voice.

So thoroughly did Lunt assume the reins that Lawrence Langner wrote in his autobiography, *The Magic Curtain*, that Lunt had been the director of the play. Windust himself cheerfully acknowledged that he had relatively little to do with the direction of *Idiot's Delight*. As Alan Hewitt noted, "When push came to shove, the nominal director simply got out of the way." The Theatre Guild's programs contained a note similar to the one that had appeared in the programs for *The Taming of the Shrew:* "Production Conceived and Supervised by Mr. Lunt and Miss Fontanne."*

Other actors who appeared in *Idiot's Delight* included Richard Whorf, Thomas Gomez, Barry Thomson, George Meader, Alan Hewitt and Sydney Greenstreet, all holdovers from *The Taming of the Shrew*. Whorf, Gomez and Greenstreet were to appear in five consecutive plays with the Lunts, spanning a period from 1935 to 1941.

Sherwood's stage directions called for the set design to suggest "a vague kind of horror," and Lee Simonson's setting provided just that feeling.† If Sherwood was grateful to the designer in one respect, he was frustrated in another, however, for Simonson's feud with Sherwood, begun during the production of *Reunion in Vienna*, broke out again. Simonson insisted that Sherwood's mixture of comedy and serious matter were incompatible, that the declaration of war in the play would destroy the

---

*Charles Bowden, who stage-managed the Lunts' production of *I Know My Love* in 1949, was asked to direct the scenes in which Lunt appeared. But, he told me, "Nobody can be said to direct the Lunts. Their first impulse was always so true and on the button. They had an unfailing instinct and a deep insight into the characters. When I say I directed them, I mean that I'd serve as their memory. They'd do something instinctively one day and then the next day try something else and then, the day after that, something else. I would just say to them, 'You know, if you didn't move there, I think it would be more effective.' And they'd say, 'Oh, my, yes, you're right. Oh, good.' As far as I'm concerned, nobody ever really directed the Lunts."

† Lunt requested an unusually high setting, made of flats twenty-four feet tall, believing that the sense of horror called for would be aided by a set that dwarfed the actors. But Simonson and the other Board members resisted, insisting, "You can't play comedy in a twenty-four-foot set." Lunt was adamant, however, and the set was built to his specifications.

comedy. Lawrence Langner, too, objected to the play's duality, saying that *Idiot's Delight* was "too light for its significant content."

Sherwood and Lunt believed that the Theatre Guild's managers were interfering with the progress of the production with their hypercritical attitudes and their penchant for calling a conference to discuss the smallest detail. At one such conference Sherwood was closeted in a hotel room with members of the Board, who loudly informed him where the problems lay and how they should be overcome. Sherwood, who normally accepted criticism with equanimity, argued back with equal vigor. According to Sherwood, Lunt's footsteps could be heard in the hallway as he approached the door of the room. But when Lunt heard the commotion within, he abruptly reversed direction. Shouting, "Oh, *shit!*" Lunt walked briskly away.

However, as rehearsals progressed, the Lunts and Sherwood firmly wrested control from the Theatre Guild. Little by little, the Board members found that their presence at rehearsals was unwanted, their criticism ignored. The minutes of one Board meeting stated, "Mr. Langner felt that the Guild's cooperation was not wanted in the sense that we had formerly cooperated in productions with the Lunts. . . ." Of course, the Guild would have been within its rights to insist upon full participation, but the managers were well aware that any attempt to impose their will too firmly might be met by the Lunts' withdrawal of their services from the Theatre Guild.

The Lunts provided considerable help to Sherwood in his attempt to balance the play's comic and serious sides. Fontanne recommended the inclusion of a scene between her character and the munitions manufacturer, Weber, which would serve to shift the emphasis from comedy to the impending war. Sherwood gratefully accepted the suggestion and wrote the scene. The Lunts also met frequently with an old friend, Irving Berlin, who wrote special lyrics for some of the songs performed by Harry Van, one of which was "Puttin' on the Ritz."

While *The Taming of the Shrew* was still playing in New York, a search for six chorus girls to play Harry Van's Blondes was begun. Those who had a hand in the casting process were divided on the most important attributes of the Blondes. Some felt that dancing ability was the prime requisite, but Sherwood said he "voted steadily for physical allure. They can learn all the dancing that's necessary."

Rehearsals, begun early in January 1936, were held in the afternoons (except on matinee days) while *The Taming of the Shrew* toured in Boston and Chicago. In the mornings Lunt could be found at the theatre working diligently to acquire a new skill required by the role: tap dancing. Harry was not supposed to be a particularly good dancer, but he had to carry off his routine with professional aplomb. Alan Hewitt recalled that one of the acrobats in the *Shrew* company tutored Lunt in the intricacies of the time step. Ultimately, however, Morgan (Buddy) Lewis, who was hired as dance director, decided that Lunt's barely adequate time step would have to be replaced by a soft-shoe routine.

Harry Van also played the piano in *Idiot's Delight*. For once, Lunt decided he need not actually acquire this skill. His other duties—acting in *The Taming of the Shrew*, rehearsing in and directing *Idiot's Delight*, learning to tap-dance—left him too little time. Besides, Lee Simonson came up with a seemingly foolproof arrangement. Simonson borrowed a mock-up of a baby-grand piano he had designed for the Hardman, Peck Co., which was placed against a stage flat representing a wall. Through a peephole in the "wall," an offstage pianist could watch Lunt's hands on the dummy keyboard while providing the actual sound. Lunt could see no possibility of anything going amiss.*

The prototype of Fontanne's role was the Russian couturière Valentina, who designed Fontanne's costumes for *Idiot's Delight*. Fontanne's preparation included mastering the Russian accent she had devised for the character, and to that end she took lessons from a Russian princess employed as a salesgirl at a New York department store. The princess and the actress met in Fontanne's dressing room before evening performances of *The Taming of the Shrew*.

Sherwood saw a rehearsal of his play in Boston which put him "in an absolute stew of excitement," he told Lunt in a letter. "The cast is perfect, the whole feel of the thing is perfect. When anyone asks Madeline [Mrs. Sherwood] or me how the show looks, we just come out with the statement, 'Absolutely magnificent!' Which may be terribly unwise, and flying in the face of destiny, and all that—but it can't be helped."

The play was scheduled to give its initial performance on March 9 in Washington, D.C., but after a long and abysmally unsatisfactory final dress rehearsal, Lunt very nearly postponed the opening. Although the rehearsal was scheduled to begin at 7:00 p.m., the next five hours were spent adding final touches to the sets and lighting. At midnight the rehearsal at last began, but was halted again and again for further technical adjustments. Not until nearly 4:00 in the morning did the final scene begin. The production ended with a series of intricately interwoven offstage sounds, including exploding bombs, air-raid sirens, machine guns and rifles fired into iron barrels while Harry and Irene sat at the piano playing and singing "Onward, Christian Soldiers" as they waited for certain death. The sound of the explosions, the playing of the piano and the on-stage dialogue and singing had to be perfectly synchronized; otherwise, the result would be meaningless chaos.

---

*He was wrong. One night the regular pianist was too ill to play for the performance. A substitute was hastily arranged for, and all went well until Lunt, seated at the piano, was supposed to break off his playing suddenly so that he could jump to his feet and stop a fistfight that had broken out. The substitute pianist forgot to watch Lunt's hands and continued playing. Lunt was therefore unable to leave his piano until the stage manager could get the attention of the offstage musician. From then on, a well-rehearsed understudy pianist was hired to attend every performance in case the first-string pianist was unable to perform.

"Everything imaginable went completely haywire," said Thoda Cocroft, who watched the rehearsal. "Bombs refused to explode, cues were late, stagehands bungled. A second time it was rehearsed and then a third time. Still it fell far short of perfection."

Lunt called everyone onto the stage. Exhausted actors and stagehands gathered, prepared for an angry outburst. Instead, quietly but firmly, keeping his temper in check, Lunt announced, "We will not give a performance tonight nor tomorrow night. We will not open this play until it is ready. We will stay here if it takes all day and all tomorrow night and we won't leave the theatre until we get it *right*."

The effect upon the stage crew was immediate. The actors were allowed to leave, but the stagehands, who moments before had seemed overwhelmed by fatigue, were galvanized into purposeful activity. From that moment on, they managed to bring renewed energy and concentration to their work. The rehearsal continued until 5:30 a.m., but when it was concluded, all the problems had been solved and *Idiot's Delight* opened that evening as scheduled.

It was a deceptively happy occasion. The audience laughed in the right spots and maintained a respectful silence during the play's serious moments, providing what the Lunts and Sherwood believed to be an encouraging response. The play had "opened fine," Sherwood noted in his diary, and added, "The Lunts terrifically happy." Fontanne's report to Graham Robertson was nothing short of ecstatic.

> Well, the first night audience was so friendly and so prepared to enjoy it, and so touchingly convinced that they were not going to be let down, the play and the company rose to them, and we gave a performance the like of which I, for one, have never been able to produce from the nerves of an opening night. And everybody tells me that they felt the same. The consequence was that Bob's beautiful play went over with a bang. We took 15 or 16 curtain calls, and the whole thing was a great triumph. Every seat is sold for the week we are here. We are giving an extra matinee on Friday, which was sold out completely the first day it was advertised. The play is passionately anti-war—marvelous theatre and a very exciting story. In fact, frankly I like it better than any play I have ever been in, and consider it by far Bob's best, no matter what happens to it.

But the reviews the following morning reported that the play's mixture of serious and comic matter was bewildering. On reflection, the Lunts and Sherwood agreed that considerable rewriting was necessary.

When Sherwood arrived at the theatre for rehearsal that day, he found the Lunts and the other actors depressed. But the new material he provided was immediately incorporated into the production, and the end of the first act was restaged. All those present were certain the changes had improved the play and production materially, and that night's audience seemed to agree. "All is now lovely," Sherwood wrote in his diary the following day. "The matinee was riotously successful—the few new lines in the play help considerably—and there doesn't seem to be any doubt now that we're in."

On March 16 the production began an eventful week in Pittsburgh. Torrential rains and heavy snows had plagued the area all fall and winter, and some sections of the city were flooded. Skies were clear when the company arrived, however, and there was reason to hope the flood waters would recede. But the rivers ominously continued to rise.

As the company rehearsed during the afternoon of the 17th, flood waters rose dramatically, swollen by a fearful snowstorm. There was concern that the flood would exceed the 1907 record of thirty-five feet.

By the next day that concern seemed trivial. The flood waters stood at forty-eight feet, filling the streets of downtown Pittsburgh and reaching almost to the theatre where *Idiot's Delight* was playing. The hotel where the musicians stayed was totally surrounded by water. Two members of the orchestra, stranded on the second story, waited for rowboats to take them to dry ground, about a block from the theatre.

It was clear to most observers that the remainder of the scheduled performances should be canceled and the company removed to New York. But the Lunts, whose belief in their obligation to perform if humanly possible was absolute, insisted on going through with the next performance, even if—as they were informed—few members of the audience would be able to reach the theatre. Those patrons who were willing to make the effort deserved to see the play, the Lunts insisted.

On the afternoon of March 19, with the streets around the theatre now inundated by the flood, the handful of people who could manage to do so arrived at the theatre in rowboats. The Lunts told the house manager to put everyone together in the best orchestra seats. The theatre's electricity failed, but an emergency generator was pressed into service for the first act. Then the flood waters poured into the cellar and the generator was rendered temporarily unusable. All lights went out during one of the musical numbers, but Lunt and the Blondes kept dancing. Still determined to continue the performance, Lunt lit his cigarette lighter and the other actors used candles and flashlights to illuminate the stage until the generator could be made to work again.

Sherwood, who had returned to New York two days before, heard a report on the 20th that typhoid had broken out in Pittsburgh. He called the Lunts and urged them to leave the city. The Pittsburgh police settled the matter by informing the Lunts that no additional performances of the play would be allowed. Convinced at last, they agreed to take a special "refugee" train to New York.

As the company was boarding the train, a young girl spotted Fontanne on the platform and spoke to her. She "said she'd come from Harrisburg by train just to see us [the night before] and thanked us for playing to so small an audience," Fontanne said, concluding, "so it was worth while."

The entire company—each member carrying his costumes, as Lunt ordered—was crammed into a single Pullman car. As the train pulled out of Pittsburgh, Lunt looked out the window and saw that the adjacent track was covered with water. He signaled to Alan Hewitt not to say anything to Fontanne, who was absorbed in a game of cribbage with Sydney Greenstreet.

Because of the flooding east of Pittsburgh, the train was rerouted north. The journey to New York took nearly twenty-four hours. Getting the set out of Pittsburgh was a thornier problem, one with which the stage manager, George Greenberg, had to deal. Somehow, Greenberg managed to persuade the governor of Pennsylvania to permit a special train, loaded with *Idiot's Delight* scenery, to leave Pittsburgh despite a statewide embargo on freight. Uncertain whether the scenery would arrive in time, Lunt told the cast that the play would open in New York as scheduled even if the only background was a set of black drapes. When he heard that the scenery would reach New York after all, he was disappointed; he had been looking forward to testing his theory that a play could be more fully enjoyed when the audience was called upon to use its imagination to fill in the details usually provided by the setting.

On March 24, *Idiot's Delight* opened at the Shubert Theatre in New York. The nervous Sherwood stayed away from the theatre as long as he could, but finally arrived at 9:30, in the middle of the second act. He was rewarded by a fine performance and a wholly appreciative audience which gave the play a tremendous ovation and the actors nineteen curtain calls.

The return of the Lunts to the Theatre Guild had made the Guild's 1935–36 season a great success, "after a year or two of indecision and mediocrity," in Brooks Atkinson's words. The Guild "has spread its canopy once more over Alfred Lunt and Lynn Fontanne, and that appears to be an excellent arrangement for both parties to the contract. The Theatre Guild and the Lunts have always been at their best together."

Idiot's Delight played before larger-than-capacity houses. "Had 81 standees last night," Fontanne wrote to Graham Robertson on April 4. "The fire laws only allow 40, so I'm sure I don't know how they got away with it."

Audiences and critics alike were delighted with Lunt's portrayal of the third-rate song-and-dance man. The mere fact that the actor, now widely acknowledged to be the finest in America, had gone from a Shakespearean play directly to the brassy buffoonery of *Idiot's Delight* astounded and thrilled the public.

Fontanne's notices were not as uniformly enthusiastic. Brooks Atkinson, for example, wondered if she was enjoying her Russian accent a bit too much; her timing "makes the character a little irritating and also delays the show," he said. Perhaps those critics who found fault with her performance in a relatively small role failed to recognize its importance to the production. Sherwood, as upset as Fontanne was, wrote to Alexander Woollcott in mid-April that her "performance, which carries the greatest part of the play's real purpose, fails to get anything like the recognition it deserves."

As indicated by Lunt's thorough knowledge of the critics' evaluations of Sherwood's *Reunion in Vienna,* the Lunts were well aware of critical opinion, even though they often pretended not to be.* And their opinions of critics were not generally flattering.

However, they did not reject all critical opinion. Donald Seawell recalled an occasion in Boston when Lunt, directing *First Love,* read a criticism he found particularly perceptive. The notice was not entirely favorable, but Lunt said to Seawell, "Donny, could you arrange a luncheon? I want to talk to that critic. It's as if he could read my mind. And some of the things that have concerned me concerned him. I'm just delighted with it." Lunt and the critic met and discussed the writer's evaluation at length.

The Lunts respected the opinions of several other critics. Richard Coe in Washington, Elliot Norton in Boston and William F. McDermott in Cleveland were all reviewers for whom the Lunts had genuine admiration.

A series of unexpected incidents enlivened the New York run of *Idiot's Delight.* One problem concerned *Victoria Regina,* which was playing at the Broadhurst Theatre next door to the Shubert. The explosive finale of *Idiot's Delight* disturbed the spectators in the Broadhurst, so the stage managers of the two productions arranged to minimize the problem. Each night before the performances, George Greenberg and Felix Jacoves synchronized their watches. The productions were then started according to a prearranged schedule so that the bombardment from the Shubert Theatre would occur during a scene-shift in *Victoria Regina.*

Even so, the problem was not resolved to everyone's satisfaction. Directly behind the Shubert Theatre stood the Booth, which housed a production of Kaufman and Hart's *You Can't Take It with You.* Normally, no sound made in one theatre would be heard in the other, but the cannon fire and air-raid sirens in Sherwood's play threatened to alarm the audience watching the Kaufman-Hart comedy. To prevent that, Kaufman arranged for his play to end just as the final scene of *Idiot's Delight* was beginning. The scheme worked perfectly until one night when *You Can't Take It with You* ran longer than usual. The explosions from the Shubert occurred just

---

*Charles Bowden maintained that they never read reviews and were annoyed when other actors in their companies paid attention to the critics' opinions. But they responded to critical verdicts far too often to allow one to believe they were ignorant of the notices.

at the quietest moment—when Grandpa was offering a prayer as the family sat down to dinner—and the bewildered audience in the Booth must have wondered why God was so loudly rejecting Grandpa's prayer.

Because MGM was interested in filming *Idiot's Delight* with Clark Gable in the leading role, Gable was brought by his manager to see the Lunts' performance and to go out with them afterward. The news that Gable was attending the theatre that night was circulated up and down Broadway, and thousands of the curious flooded the area, hoping to catch a glimpse of the famous star. Policemen cleared the streets of pedestrians so that Gable's limousine could pull up to the stage door, then held the crowd back while he, his manager and the Lunts got in. The following day Lunt told Alan Hewitt that Gable's manager had instructed the Lunts to "lean in toward the center of the car in case the windows were pushed inward. I've never been so terrified in my life, seeing all those shrieking, crazy people," Lunt said. "But Gable was very cool. He's used to it. Thank God, *we're* not movie stars."

On Broadway, in London and in the cities to which they had toured, the Lunts were recognized as "stars," but the designation meant little to them. Lunt said, "When I first saw my name up in lights, I was very embarrassed."

Carol Channing said the Lunts "were so busy working on the next project all the time they had no perspective on themselves. They didn't know other people thought of them as stars."

As was her habit, Fontanne continued looking for ways to improve her performance all during the long run of *Idiot's Delight*. But in this case, since she had contributed to the development of Irene's character during rehearsals, she felt free to contact Sherwood about possible script changes. On July 1, 1936, she wrote to him suggesting that certain lines be altered. Moreover, she confessed that she had already changed them in performance: "Knowing that you would not mind my experimenting, I changed the lines three times running," she said.

Again, in September, she wrote the author about additional dialogue between herself and Weber, the munitions manufacturer, which she and Lunt had devised. She told Sherwood that she felt "very guilty" about presuming to rewrite his play, but said, "Anything that will lend another dimension to Irene and make her less of a silhouette is all to the good of the play." Enclosing two pages of dialogue, Fontanne explained why she felt the additions would be desirable and asked that Sherwood cable her immediately "because I think I shall put this in to-night and take the chance as it seems to me to be so awfully good." She added, "I feel terrible risking your anger like this, but it does seem to be so right that I feel sure you will agree to this method of doing it. Alfred thinks my writing is tremendously in your own vein."

The day after Fontanne's letter was posted, Lunt followed with a message of his own. "Dear Bob," it began, "I do hope you approve the little scene Lynn added to the play last night. If you don't, you're crazy! . . . The lines that were inserted last night were not only amusing in themselves but cleaned up her whole character and the audience, therefore, were more relaxed. The play never went so well. . . . People who came back last night who were seeing the play for the second or third time, said they did not know why but the play seemed finer and clearer and more immediate than ever before, and didn't realize a new scene had been inserted. . . . I do hope you will let us keep it in as it makes the going for us so much easier." Whatever Sherwood's private thoughts may have been, he allowed Fontanne's alterations to remain in the production.

Despite the competition of such fine dramas as Maxwell Anderson's *Winterset* (which won the New York Drama Critics' Circle Award in 1935–36), *Idiot's Delight* was given the Pulitzer Prize as the best play of the season. When the play was published (minus Fontanne's additional dialogue), it was "lovingly dedicated to Lynn Fontanne and Alfred Lunt," who had brought the play to the Theatre Guild, helped the playwright to improve it in a hundred ways and brought to its performance the flair and *élan* necessary to its success.

Idiot's Delight became one of the Theatre Guild's most acclaimed productions, running for 300 performances at the Shubert Theatre. It was also one of the three biggest commercial hits on Broadway that season, the others being *Victoria Regina,* featuring Helen Hayes, and *Saint Joan,* with Katharine Cornell. The public took to *Idiot's Delight* so unreservedly that the Lunts even gave up most of their usual vacation. The play ran until July 4, then, after a break, reopened on July 31.

During the run of *Idiot's Delight,* the Lunts moved into an apartment at 130 East 75th Street. Lunt, Claggett Wilson and Richard Whorf decorated it in Swedish style, with different shades of gray for the bedroom, a rich blue-green for the dining room, and baroque floral designs on many of the walls. Fontanne proudly purchased a large bed, six feet six by five feet, which she described to her friend Graham Robertson as "the best in America and why not?"

Lunt and Fontanne, who were forty-five and fifty respectively in 1937, had begun, in the words of Bretaigne Windust, to "evince strong paternal and maternal feeling for all of us—their professional family. Indeed, we . . . adopted them 'in loco parentis.'" One of their favorites in the company was a young actor named Tommaso Tittoni, who played a small role as an Italian officer. The Lunts regarded Tittoni as a highly promising performer and intended to include him in the aggregation of actors that had by then become associated with Lunt-Fontanne productions. But Tittoni came down with pneumonia and died of its complications late in January. The effect on the Lunts was very much as if they had lost a son.

In February 1937 the production began a twenty-two-week cross-country tour, always playing to sold-out houses. It was the most successful road attraction in the history of the Theatre Guild, breaking box-office records in nearly every city. And, with Sherwood regularly providing new material, the dialogue continued to reflect the current political situation.

The most publicized stop turned out to be Omaha, Nebraska, where the mayor, Dan Butler, decided *Idiot's Delight* was not fit to be seen by the citizens of his community. Mayor Butler had already had some success as a censor, having banned the film *Ecstasy* from Omaha. His attempt to keep *Tobacco Road* from playing had failed, but those who favored censorship gave him credit for having fought the good fight. In the case of *Idiot's Delight,* the mayor insisted the play could not be shown unless its language was altered. The script mentioned that, years before, Harry Van and Irene had illicitly spent a night together in the Governor Bryan Hotel in Omaha. Mayor Butler objected on two grounds: Omaha was not the sort of town that would permit unmarried couples to spend a night together, and, even more shockingly, the use of the name "Governor Bryan" was a slur on the reputation of the great Nebraska politician Governor Charles Bryan. In all, the Lunts would have to make sixteen cuts in the text if the play was to be presented in Omaha.

The Bishop of the Methodist Episcopal Church in Nebraska, G. Bromley Oxnam, publicly regretted Mayor Butler's stand. "It is a thousand pities that our Mayor should make our city ridiculous," the Bishop said. "A gentleman astute enough to become a successful politician should be wise enough to know that censorship is more dangerous than an occasional realistic line." *Idiot's Delight* had been seen by thousands without inflicting moral damage, Bishop Oxnam claimed, and there was no reason to believe Omaha's citizens would be contaminated. To Butler's charge that "such garbage" should not be seen by a seventeen-year-old, Oxnam countered that he intended to take his fourteen-year-old daughter to see the play. Perhaps, he continued, the mayor should adopt as his theme song a ditty entitled "Every Little Damma Must Be Taken from Our Drama."

The Lunts were caught off guard by the controversy. Some people had objected to *Idiot's Delight* because of its pacifist theme, but no one had suggested it be banned because of "immoral" content. Uncertain whether to try to effect a compromise with the mayor, Lunt telephoned Alexander Woollcott in New York to ask his opinion. He was willing to make the suggested cuts, he said, but he planned to precede the play with a statement objecting to the entire procedure. Woollcott was furious. As he told a mutual friend of Woollcott's and the Lunts, "I denounced [the Lunts] as poltroons not fit to be trusted with a play by Sherwood or anybody else if they didn't have the gumption not to play at all."

Meanwhile, according to Fontanne's story, she put through a telephone call to the United States Supreme Court and asked to speak to Justice Felix Frankfurter, whom she had met at a dinner party. Fontanne, less willing to compromise than Lunt, was going to tell Frankfurter that she would refuse to accept Mayor Butler's terms and ask the judge's advice. When the call reached the Supreme Court, Frankfurter was in a meeting with the other justices. A page informed him that Lynn Fontanne wished to speak to him on the telephone. All the justices burst out in laughter as Frankfurter excused himself and answered the telephone, but by that time Fontanne, too agitated to hold on, had hung up.*

Bolstered by Woollcott's advice, the Lunts announced that the production would be canceled and the citizens of Omaha could blame their mayor for having deprived them of seeing the Pulitzer Prize–winning play. Mayor Butler, stunned by the Lunts' announcement, capitulated at once, saying he had had a change of heart and the play could proceed after all. "Since a Bishop and other public people are backing the show, I think it should go on, with the people to be the judges," said the mayor.

Idiot's Delight was performed on May 19, 1937, to a sold-out house without a single cut in its text. "It was a most strange performance," Fontanne said later. "Every time it came to that line [or any other reference to the Governor Bryan Hotel] the audience just stood up and roared. The audience was wonderful, and we were beyond ourselves."

During the tour's stopover in Chicago in May 1937, the Lunts received an award for distinguished achievement in drama from a conference of club presidents and program chairmen. "The award is not only for dramatic achievements," the president of the conference said, "but is high commendation for their effective service in the cause of peace as exemplified in their current play."

Fontanne was terrified of occasions on which she was asked to speak. For the Chicago ceremony, Lunt carefully rehearsed a speech which began, "I am inarticulate without an author to write some lines for me." Fontanne groaned when she heard him rehearsing. "Darling, don't say that," she said. "Oh, please don't! You know every actor always says that when he is called upon to make a speech." Lunt, realizing that she was correct, set to work to devise a new speech.

At the ceremony Fontanne was presented with a silver bowl and an illuminated parchment, and asked to say a few words. She stepped uncertainly to the microphone, nearly shaking with fright. "I don't know what to say," she mumbled. "I never made a speech before. I—I—er—I am bereft of speech without an author to write one for me." Those club presidents who were watching Lunt must have been puzzled to see a wicked grin cross his face.

When it was his turn to speak, Lunt charmed the assembled guests with his seemingly extemporaneous remarks. "I can't think of anything

* S. N. Behrman heard quite a different version of this story. According to him, Fontanne "called Felix up in Cambridge. He was at a university meeting and he broke out to answer the call. She didn't know he was the greatest authority on constitutional law, and she argued so vehemently that he didn't know where to turn."

appropriate to say," he began. "My mind is like one of those untidy sewing baskets, and strangely enough the only thing that keeps running through it is a recipe for roast lamb." The audience applauded, indicating that they would like to hear the recipe. Lunt complied. "Rub a leg of lamb with salt, pepper, and one-half teaspoon mustard, and roast. When it's half done, drain off the juices and add one cup of coffee and cream and sugar for basting, then finish roasting."

Between its New York run and its performances on tour, *Idiot's Delight* ran considerably longer than any play the Lunts had previously appeared in. Unlike so many actors of the time who simply tolerated touring as a necessary but unfortunate aspect of stage acting—if they agreed to tour at all—the Lunts were so invigorated by the experience that they determined to tour most of their plays thereafter.

Even their most devoted followers were surprised to see that the production of *Idiot's Delight* improved the longer it ran, but this was true of all their productions. Being in a long-running play can be something like working on an assembly line: the same circumstances are repeated again and again, calling forth the same responses. Generally, an actor's reaction to this—sometimes conscious but often unconscious—is to turn off the mind and allow the performance to continue on automatic pilot. Spectators who have seen a production soon after its opening and return to see the same production a year later are painfully familiar with this phenomenon. What was once crisp and exciting often becomes limp and stale through repetition.

Some actors guard against this by refusing to act in the same play for more than six months or a year, on the assumption that no one can be expected to keep a performance fresh for longer. But the Lunts continually offered proof to the contrary. Throughout their careers they were known for the remarkable enthusiasm they brought to every performance. They might act in the same production for a year, two years or more, but their performances would only grow richer with time. Rather than allow the production to deteriorate, the Lunts used the time afforded by a long run for experiment, rethinking and revising their performances.

It made no difference whether they were acting in New York or in Omaha, in Chicago or in Tacoma. They might be performing in a beautifully appointed theatre with perfect acoustics or in a high-school gymnasium that sounded like an echo chamber. The aim of every presentation was the same: to improve on the performance given the night before. And, beginning with the *Idiot's Delight* tour, when the Lunts were essentially managing their own company, they infected their casts with the same mania for perfection. As a result, a spectator in any part of the country could be certain the Lunts would offer him the best performance of which they were capable, and the Lunts at their best were incomparable.

As G. B. Stern observed of them, "Their attitude can most nearly be expressed by a child's copybook maxim about *duty;* doing their duty towards the play, towards the dramatist, towards the audience, according to their own standard; but a standard planted so high that it stays totally invisible to anyone except themselves."

During the tour the Lunts and the *Idiot's Delight* company began working on another play, S. N. Behrman's version of Jean Giraudoux's *Amphitryon 38*. Behrman adapted the play not just with the Lunts in mind, but with all the actors who had by then become "their company," just as Sherwood had written *Idiot's Delight* with the knowledge that many of the actors in *The Taming of the Shrew* would be cast in his play. The idea of forming a permanent company for which playwrights would be encouraged to write appealed more and more to the Lunts. As Fontanne pointed out, "That was the way Shakespeare worked. He had his own company and wrote his plays around it."

Giraudoux, the original author of *Amphitryon 38,* was a diplomat as well as a playwright. If diplomacy at its best includes the virtues of clear and logical thinking, wit and urbanity, Giraudoux would seem to have mastered those skills, for they characterize all his plays. *Amphitryon,* a retelling of an ancient myth from a modern point of view (the inclusion of the figure *38* in the title was Giraudoux's way of saying that his play was the thirty-eighth time the fable had been told in one fictional form or another), required just the qualities of sophistication, delicacy and precision that Giraudoux could bestow upon it. Behrman's skills as a playwright were very much the same as Giraudoux's, and he invested his adaptation with those qualities as well. The contrast between the high comedy of *Amphitryon* and the low-comic seriousness of *Idiot's Delight* was a tonic to the Lunts, who could hardly wait for rehearsals to begin. "Alfred and Lynn are very excited—like two kids in fact," Bretaigne Windust wrote to Behrman early in February 1937. "The whole company is straining at the leash and we all await your first page of manuscript with bated breath." Again the Theatre Guild would officially produce the play, but artistic control would be exerted primarily by the Lunts. Again, too, Windust was given the directorial assignment, but, as in *Idiot's Delight,* his function was essentially that of assistant to Lunt.

The play's premise is that the god Jupiter decides to have a fling with the very human wife of the Greek general, Amphitryon. Taking mortal shape, Jupiter descends to earth and, amid many complications, proceeds with his plan to seduce the beautiful Alkmena.

Originally, the Lunts hoped that Igor Stravinsky would compose a musical score, but in February 1937 Windust wrote Behrman that "after about a dozen conferences . . . it was mutually decided not to have him do the music [because] there was not enough music necessary . . . to allow for the amount of scope which he would need to employ his peculiar talent and to make his particular quality come to life. It was also apparent that the music under his hand might overshadow the play." Instead, Samuel

Barlow was asked to write the score. Lee Simonson and Valentina were once again engaged to design the sets and the costumes. As part of his costume, Lunt was outfitted with a long blond beard that, he said, made him look as if he had swallowed Shirley Temple.

When rehearsals began, Lunt was concerned that the opening scene, in which Jupiter and Mercury discuss Jupiter's lust for Amphitryon's wife, would seem unsavory. To Richard Whorf he said, "Wouldn't it be marvelous if we could be up on top of a cloud looking down?" Later, Lunt drew a sketch of Jupiter and Mercury, using his nephew John as a model. "I drew his picture and gave it to Dickie [Whorf, who was also a talented artist], and I said, 'This is what it should be: two people sitting on a cloud, looking down,' and Whorf drew it and gave it to Lee Simonson and he said, 'Well, how can we do it?' [I said,] 'Couldn't you make it out of papiermâché?' Lee said I was a fool, [but] he had it made."

As Simonson modified Lunt's original design, the faces of Lunt and Richard Whorf were seen attached to the naked, well-muscled papiermâché bodies of Jupiter and Mercury, who were lying on their stomachs on a cloud, peering over its edge to the world below. Lunt and Whorf simply stood on a platform and thrust their heads through a backdrop. "It was a wonderful opening," Lunt said. "As soon as you looked down from a cloud, you took all of the obscenity out of it. It made it very, very gay, and there was nothing offensive about it at all." Behrman concurred, saying in 1953, "In all my thirty years of stage experience, this is the most brilliant creative staging idea I have ever encountered. . . . The opening effect was so strong and it got such a gale of laughter it was hard to follow."

After the play opened, Jean Giraudoux saw Lunt's prologue (with dialogue by Behrman) for the first time and, far from being upset by the alterations to his play, said he was enchanted with it.

Rehearsals began early in April, with an opening in San Francisco scheduled for June 23. An early crisis was survived when, according to George Freedley, Lunt called the actors onto the stage during rehearsal and announced, "Ladies and gentlemen, it is impossible for me to play this role, so we can not go on with this play. Please consider the production canceled. . . . I can't go on. I can't find the green umbrella." With that, he strode up the aisle and out of the theatre.

Fontanne calmly took a seat and said to the distraught actors, "Don't worry, we'll go on, and he will find it."

Half an hour later Lunt returned. As the actors saw him approaching the stage, he waved to them and called out, "Don't worry, I've found it. We'll start again at the beginning of the act."

Fontanne wrote to the critic and playwright Stark Young from her dressing room in Milwaukee on May 12, between acts of *Idiot's Delight,* "Alfred is going to be truly remarkable as Jupiter." But, she said, "I feel as if I am going to make the most spectacular failure of my career. It all seems pretty bad, my part of it, but there are a few weeks left and perhaps I can do a little bit better later on." In earlier productions Lunt had always been the one to doubt his capabilities while Fontanne had maintained a quiet self-confidence. But as she grew older she became less and less certain that everything would turn out well. Most actors are plagued by self-doubt to one degree or another; Fontanne was just late in joining their ranks.

Initially, Behrman did not attend rehearsals. The Lunts and Windust noted which scenes played satisfactorily and which needed revision, then sent their notes to Behrman. Sometimes the letters simply asked for cuts; at other times they recommended revisions of a particular nature (Fontanne wrote on April 5, for example, "Put some remarks for me in [the scene], not too many . . . just one or two amusing things to say"); and on occasion they included portions of dialogue the Lunts had written in order to suggest precisely what they wanted.

Eventually, Behrman joined the company during rehearsals. As he watched the Lunts work on his play, he was impressed, as always, by "the amount of time that [the Lunts] spent in reorchestrating the harmonics of the dialogue scenes between the two of them. . . . They had played together so much that Alfred, who was very musical, knew exactly what he wanted, the tone and the lift of every second, the diminuendo of every suspension."

Behrman acknowledged the Lunts' contributions to the writing of *Amphitryon 38*. "The way they made me work on the scenes between Jupiter and Alkmena, the juxtaposition of sentences, the cuts and rearrangements of lines, so that they could do the things they did best—Alfred even contributed many scenes which were neither Giraudoux's nor mine."

But Behrman was not entirely happy with the Lunts' never-ending stream of suggestions. Theresa Helburn, in her autobiography, *A Wayward Quest*, referred to their insistence upon changes as "harassment." Behrman's "own ideas conflicted with the Lunts'," she said; "there was an endless struggle between Alfred's sound ideas for a vehicle and [Behrman's] sound ideas for a play."

After *Idiot's Delight* played for two weeks in Los Angeles, two more weeks were offered in San Francisco, where, on Saturday, June 18, 1937, the play closed. Five days later *Amphitryon 38* was given its first performance in the same city. It was an enormous success. Fontanne wrote to Woollcott, "The audience was so kind, so sure that it was going to enjoy itself, it was most heartwarming, and strangely enough, after we got over the first cold douche of nervousness, we actually enjoyed our first night!!! Every one of them seemed to have some kind of education, and to quite understand the meaning of the few words that have more than two syllables, and received the mythological allusions hilariously. They seemed like one mature and cultivated mind, but kindly withal. Where in the world could you find such another, I don't know. Certainly not in our experience, ever."

On the evening after the play opened, John Hobart, a writer for the

San Francisco *Chronicle,* waited to interview Fontanne in her dressing room after the final curtain. He was surprised to discover that she could give him only a few minutes because a rehearsal had been called for that night. The next day, too, a rehearsal was scheduled. As Hobart wrote, "Miss Fontanne is at the top because she believes she can always be better. Her goal is perfection, and to achieve that goal she realizes she must keep working, ceaselessly."

During one of the San Francisco performances, Fontanne displayed, more remarkably than ever, her thorough absorption in her craft. The Lunts were playing a scene while seated together at a table; suddenly, Lunt realized that Fontanne's silk-jersey costume must have stretched, for her left breast was exposed. He coughed, trying to attract her attention. He tried to indicate with his eyes the source of the problem. Fontanne continued with the scene, taking no notice of Lunt's peculiar behavior. When the curtain descended, he said, "Did you know your left breast was bare to the audience?" An irritated look crossed her face. "Don't bother me with things like that until I know my lines," she said.

After the San Francisco engagement, *Amphitryon 38* moved to Los Angeles for a two-week run before the Lunts' customary summer vacation. In October the company reassembled at the Shubert Theatre in New York for ten additional days of rehearsal before beginning another tour prior to the Broadway opening. An hour's worth of material had already been excised, but the Lunts believed that still more changes could profitably be made.

Thus, in the middle of a scene he was playing, Lunt stopped to remark, "I think that line's too long. Why not just cut it all out?" Fontanne, who was seated offstage but watching intently, commented, "Not all of it, Alfred, just the first half." Lunt agreed with her suggestion and Windust noted down the change. Later, during a speech of Fontanne's, she broke off, saying, "That's wrong, that speech. I must say something much simpler, something direct."

The play had been revised so often—nine different versions had already been played—that the actors, without realizing it, occasionally reintroduced material that had been eliminated. At one point in a rehearsal, Lunt spoke a line, then stopped and said, "What version *are* we playing?"

Morton Eustis, who watched the rehearsals and recorded his observations for an article in *Theatre Arts,* noted that the actors began the first rehearsal in a desultory manner. Then, he said, Fontanne made her first entrance. "Perhaps because she thinks the rehearsal has been a little casual so far, Miss Fontanne plays the scene in which she bids her husband farewell with an actor's full equipment. The effect on the other players is electric. They stop whispering, reading their lines, pacing up and down, and watch in silence." The rehearsal was suddenly transformed as the other actors picked up Fontanne's sense of spontaneity and commitment.

Fontanne also contributed materially to the direction of the play. At one point Lunt was having difficulty timing a particular movement with his lines in order to produce the best effect. After he repeated the business several times without any improvement, Fontanne offered, "Change the order of that speech, Alfred, so that you'll cross before you speak instead of after." Her recommended change solved the problem instantly. Later, when Lunt and Richard Whorf were rehearsing a scene, Fontanne, seated offstage, called out to Whorf, "Cut that line." "Thank God," said Whorf, "I've always hated it."

During a scene between Lunt and Fontanne, Lunt stopped to say, "This scene is too complicated. Let's try ad-libbing it, Lynn, and see what happens." Their improvised dialogue was far from polished, but it communicated the sense of the scene more clearly than before. Windust, who wrote down as much of the improvisation as he could, said he would send his notes on to Behrman "and let him work it out."

Another scene with which the Lunts were dissatisfied was not rewritten but was rehearsed with Fontanne offering an interpretation entirely different from the one she had been accustomed to playing. Lunt immediately altered his performance in response to hers. Windust's verdict was that the scene played as if it were "entirely new," and that the new interpretation made rewriting unnecessary.

Lunt directed one scene of relatively minor importance between Sydney Greenstreet and George Meader as if "the failure or success of the whole show hinged on it," Eustis said.

> First they run it through without interruption, while Lunt paces up and down in the wings, apparently not paying any attention to them. Then he takes hold. The intonation was wrong here, the gesture there. This speech must be cut, that transposed. That cross is bad. In high good humor, he plays both roles himself, exaggerating each effect he wants the actors to achieve. . . . "Now play the rest of the scene that way," Lunt exhorts them. . . . Then they act it again, . . . and, miraculously, a scene that was an hour ago dull and inconsequential becomes gay and spontaneous—an entirely new scene, in fact.

Lunt worked closely with Alan Hewitt on a speech with which the young actor was having difficulty. After listening to Hewitt's delivery, Lunt stopped him, saying, "You can't go on, Alan. You've got no place to go. You started on such a high key, you haven't anything left for 'War! War! This is war!' Start much lower. . . . You don't have to yell to create excitement. It's a question of tempo, not of volume." After working on this new approach, Hewitt repeated it in the manner Lunt had suggested. "His voice is keyed much lower but he is making twice the effect," Eustis commented. "The scene immediately becomes exciting, electric."

On another occasion the Lunts came to rehearsal with what was in effect an entirely new scene between Alkmena (Fontanne) and Leda (Edith

King). Lunt had constructed the scene from the remains of the nine different versions that had already been played, but with the dialogue completely rearranged. Fontanne and King rehearsed the scene all morning, until the actresses, Lunt and Windust agreed it had achieved far greater clarity and variety than in any of its previous incarnations.

Amphitryon 38 reopened in Baltimore, then moved on to Washington. Noël Coward and Neysa McMein attended a performance on October 14. "They all seemed pleased with the play and seemed to think we might have a success in New York," Fontanne told Woollcott. "The papers were superb about Berri's [Behrman's] adaptation, and the dear little thing was 'over the moon' today."

The impact of the work done in rehearsals can be seen in the Washington *Post* review of October 19. The Lunts "perform on even terms, with equal opportunities that are embraced with perfectly balanced skill," the critic commented. "Their reading of speeches that are sometimes abstruse is always lucid, illuminating and dramatically forceful. . . . The sum total of effect is that of a scholarly comedy interpreted by actors fully up to their formidable task."

After another stop in Cleveland, the presentation arrived at the Shubert Theatre in New York on November 1, 1937. Brooks Atkinson called it "the most distinguished piece of theatre the Guild has had the pleasure of presenting to the subscribers in some time. . . . [The Lunts] go the full distance in extravagance and stage perfection. They twist lines around their tongues until they have tasted the full savor of the humor; they wrap a play around them like a costume."

Overall, however, the critical reception *Amphitryon 38* received in New York was generally less enthusiastic than one might have expected, very probably because the production's reputation as a shimmering piece of theatrical sophistication had preceded it. "It is not the best thing for a play to be so publicized and praised so widely before it opens, for the reviewers are likely to be led to expect too much," Helen Deutsch, the Theatre Guild's publicist, said on the day before the opening. As she feared, many New York critics called the play less witty and inventive than they had been led to believe.

Stark Young was one critic who appreciated the play, however, and particularly admired the Lunts' performances. "With patience and taste Mr. Lunt and Miss Fontanne have slid over places that might have passed for wisecracks and even been guffawed upon as such," Young wrote. "To have been salacious, smarty and boffo would have been only too easy. They have preferred to seek instead dignity, a genuine inner rhythm, and distinction, and have accomplished a degree of profound meaning beyond any play I have seen them do."

Giraudoux saw the much revised version of his play in the company of S. N. Behrman. They watched the first act from the orchestra, the second from the balcony and the third from the second balcony. *"Quel vital-*

ité," he commented to Behrman about the Lunts' performances. According to the adaptor, Giraudoux "thought Lunt was 'majestic' and loved Miss Fontanne. He was so entranced with both of them that he became a friend of theirs, and, on one of his diplomatic tours, suddenly appeared at their home in Genesee Depot and spent several days." Although Giraudoux spoke almost no English and the Lunts were not fluent in French (Fontanne studied the language for years, but never made much headway), they got along superbly. Giraudoux mused that Lunt must have been out of his element in rural Wisconsin. "Oh, no," Lunt answered, "I am a man of the countryside."

Maxwell Anderson told Lunt he was certain the run of *Amphitryon 38* would be a long one. But on November 23, 1937, Lunt answered, "Being of a pessimistic nature I never believe a play has run until it actually has run!"

Anderson proved to be correct. Despite the lukewarm reviews, the public flocked to the Shubert Theatre, where *Amphitryon 38* ran for 153 performances, enough to qualify it as a commercial success. The production was still doing capacity business when it closed; it could have run considerably longer except that the Lunts had decided to present the play in London in May 1938. If they were going to add another play to their repertoire first, as they planned to do, *Amphitryon* had to be closed so that the new play could give enough performances to satisfy the demands of the Theatre Guild's subscription audiences.

The Lunts' longtime goal of managing their own repertory theatre with a permanent acting company was becoming a matter of established fact. Their company had now given successful performances of *The Taming of the Shrew, Idiot's Delight* and *Amphitryon 38,* all of which the Lunts planned to tour, beginning in the fall of 1938. The additional play needed to round out the repertory, they felt, should offer a marked contrast to the others. They chose one of the masterpieces of dramatic literature and one of the most difficult plays to perform satisfactorily, Anton Chekhov's *The Sea Gull.*

One evening, on the way to a party, Lunt mentioned to Alan Hewitt, a passenger in the car, that he had been impressed by a scene he had watched Alfred Ryder perform from *The Sea Gull.* He was fascinated by the play, Lunt said, and several people had recommended that it be added to the Lunt-Fontanne repertoire. Hewitt, who, like Ryder, was working on a production of Chekhov's play as an adjunct to Benno Schneider's acting classes, said, "Well, as a matter of fact, I have a copy of it right here in my coat pocket." Lunt borrowed the play and read it that night. The next evening, before the performance of *Amphitryon,* Lunt returned Hewitt's book, remarking, "My God, that's good. We really ought to do that." Shortly afterward he decided to hold read-throughs of *The Sea Gull,* without yet having made a definite decision whether to proceed with a production.

On December 20, 1937, a group of actors read the play aloud on the stage of the Guild Theatre. Fontanne portrayed the provincial actress Madame Arkadina, and Lunt played Arkadina's lover, Trigorin. Many of the other roles were taken by members of the Lunt-Fontanne company, but at least two of the characters were read by outsiders: Margalo Gillmore as Masha and Leo G. Carroll as Dr. Dorn.

When the second reading was held a week later, several of the roles were reassigned. Ernestine de Becker now read Masha and Dr. Dorn was taken over by Barry Thomson, both of the Lunts' company. Edith King, who had replaced Hope Williams in *Amphitryon 38* during that play's pre-Broadway tour on the west coast, read Paulina. As before, Richard Whorf played Constantine, Sydney Greenstreet read Sorin and George Meader was assigned the role of Medvedenko.

The company read from the old Constance Garnett translation of *The Sea Gull,* which none of the actors liked. Consequently, the Lunts asked Alan Hewitt, who was reading Shamrayeff, to work with Fontanne in preparing a new version. Hewitt knew no Russian, but attempted to assemble a collation from existing versions. "Preposterous though the idea was, I located two or three other translations of *The Sea Gull* and set to work," Hewitt said.

After conducting several more read-throughs and tentatively blocking the first act, Lunt began to think more concretely of offering a production of the play. Robert Edmond Jones, who had heard about the readings, asked to do the settings and costumes. The Lunts, eager to use the talents of one of America's foremost designers, readily agreed. Another significant addition to the group occurred when Lunt asked Robert Milton, with whom both the Lunts had worked as early as 1918, to take over the direction of the play. Milton, who was Russian by birth and whose father had acted and directed with considerable success in that country, was reputed to be an expert on Russian drama.

Originally, the Lunts intended to give performances of *The Sea Gull* on Mondays and Tuesdays only, exclusively for subscribers of the Theatre Guild. As rehearsals progressed, however, that idea was dropped. Instead, *The Sea Gull* would be offered to general audiences, but only for a limited run. Lunt suggested to the Guild's Board that he and Fontanne would be willing to accept a considerable reduction in their usual salaries.

The Theatre Guild agreed to sponsor the presentation, but it was billed as "The Alfred Lunt and Lynn Fontanne production of Chekhov's *The Sea Gull*." The Guild's influence on Lunt-Fontanne productions had diminished to such a degree that there was hardly any involvement beyond the financial.

Chekhov's plays, with their ambiguity, their seeming lack of structure, their peculiar mixture of comedy and pathos, have never been popular with Broadway audiences, and the Lunts did not expect *The Sea Gull* to achieve commercial success. Their primary motivation was to add a very different kind of play to their repertoire, one with which they could tour the country. Consequently, they announced that the Broadway production would be offered for a limited run of forty performances.

A transformation of historic proportions was taking place. And, because of it, the Lunts were becoming what only a handful of other twentieth-century American stage actors have become: not merely Broadway stars, but truly *national* performers. *The Sea Gull* was, in essence, being tried out in New York. Then, when the production had achieved a level of excellence, the Lunts would take it on the road. If the Lunts had earlier thought of Broadway as the pinnacle, the final arbiter of quality and taste, they had come to accord the same respect to audiences across the country.

Readings of *The Sea Gull* were conducted on an irregular basis, with the Lunts continuing to rotate different actors among the roles. Alan Hewitt, for example, who began by reading Shamrayeff, also read Sorin and Medvedenko, ending by playing the role of the servant, Yacov. Had the Theatre Guild been paying the actors for their participation, the Board members would surely have objected to such a leisurely process of casting and rehearsal. But the Guild was not yet parting with any money. As Alan Hewitt said, "The Lunts were . . . violating every conceivable Equity rule, even assuming that Equity then had such rules. Nobody had a contract. Nobody was being paid. But nobody complained. A great venture was a-borning. *That* was what mattered."

Even as late as mid-January 1938, the readings had not been entirely cast. But on the 17th several new actors were added, one of them Margaret Webster, who was already established as a director as well as an actress. A year before she had directed Maurice Evans in *Richard II* in New York. Webster was given the role of Masha.

Another part that had to be cast from outside the regular company was the pivotal role of Nina, the aspiring young actress who is driven to madness in the course of the play. No production of *The Sea Gull* can succeed without an inspired Nina, and the Lunts were determined to find exactly the right actress for the role. Several weeks after readings had begun, *The Sea Gull* was still without its Nina. But an actress was finally chosen after a lengthy search.

Earlier in January the Lunts had begun holding auditions for young actors, the purpose being not so much to find performers for their own company as to identify youngsters with talent whom they could recommend to other Broadway managements. A seventeen-year-old actress named Uta Hagen, who was preparing the role of Nina for another production of *The Sea Gull,* had been working on scenes from the play in her acting class. Her teacher, believing that the Lunts had not yet cast their Nina, arranged through the Theatre Guild for Hagen to audition for the Lunts. As far as they were concerned, however, Hagen's audition was not for any specific role.

Hagen was told to prepare a scene for Lunt, but, he cautioned her, it should *not* be a scene from *The Sea Gull*. Since it was common knowledge that the Lunts were currently rehearsing that play, most of the young actors auditioning for them had given scenes from Chekhov's drama, and the Lunts were sick unto death of seeing them. Consequently, Hagen prepared a monologue from *A Doll's House*.

On the day of the audition, the stage manager announced her name. As she moved onto the stage, Hagen was overcome by the conviction that her *Doll's House* monologue was not sufficiently well prepared. Thoroughly familiar with the role of Nina, she quickly reached the decision—totally unpremeditated—to perform a speech of Nina's despite Lunt's clear admonition.

Hagen played her scene and began to walk off the stage, but Lunt called to her from the auditorium, "Miss Fontanne says to wait." A moment later Fontanne rushed on stage, closely followed by Lunt. They both praised Hagen's scene and offered suggestions on how it could be improved. Fontanne and Hagen then did a scene from the play together, working on it for several hours. Finally, Lunt and Fontanne asked her to come to the company's next *Sea Gull* rehearsal.

The Lunts were in a quandary. They had already cast the role of Nina, but they had suddenly discovered a young actress who seemed even better suited to the role. They gently informed the actress who had been cast that Hagen would read Nina at the next rehearsal, although they had not yet decided which of the two would ultimately play the role. Thus, Hagen's reading with the cast on January 17 served as a final audition.

Naturally enough, there was considerable tension during the read-through. Perhaps Fontanne's nervousness was responsible for her outburst, but in the middle of the rehearsal she suddenly announced that the translation of the play was such a poor one that she refused to rehearse any longer. She became nearly hysterical, insisting that if an improved version could not be found, she would quit the production altogether. Lunt angrily told her to stop being temperamental and to continue the rehearsal. Fontanne sulked, reading the lines in a desultory, singsong manner for the rest of the afternoon. Hagen feared that the production would be canceled then and there. But Lunt calmed his wife by stroking her cheek softly at the end of the read-through and calling her "my sweet little girl." As always happened when one of the Lunts misbehaved, the incident was forgotten as quickly as it had arisen.*

As the actors began to leave, the Lunts told Hagen to return to the

---

*Among several visitors at this rehearsal was the critic Stark Young, who, excited by reports of the Lunts' work on *The Sea Gull*, had already volunteered to create a new adaptation of the play. Perhaps Fontanne would have been delighted with any alternative, but when she and Lunt read Young's completed version of Act I—only four days after Uta Hagen's first rehearsal—they found it superior to the one the company had been using, and it was adopted. Young's adaptation, like Alan Hewitt's, was compiled from several existing translations.

theatre that evening, by which time they would have reached a definite decision. On her arrival, Hagen was told the role was hers. Then Fontanne invited her to visit in her dressing room as she made up for *Amphitryon 38*. Together they discussed Nina for nearly two hours, Fontanne offering specific suggestions to the young actress.

The Lunts continued to work closely with Hagen throughout the read-throughs and the formal rehearsals, which began on February 15. On one occasion they invited her to their apartment for a three-hour discussion and rehearsal of the scenes between Nina and Trigorin. On another, Fontanne showed Hagen a more artful use of theatrical makeup than she had known before. As Fontanne was concluding her lesson, the company's business manager, one of the musicians and Robert Milton happened by the dressing room. All of them asked Hagen how she had suddenly managed to become so gorgeous.

Milton's contribution to the Lunts' performances was thought by some to have been significant, but others minimized its importance. Uta Hagen felt that Lunt was more dependent upon Milton's direction than he would have been had he not been so insecure about his ability to play Chekhov satisfactorily. She felt that the relationship between Milton and Lunt was a creative one. Lunt listened carefully and eagerly to Milton, she recalled, and relied heavily upon his suggestions. But Margaret Webster, a close observer of the directorial techniques employed in the production, concluded that the Lunts did a great deal of the actual direction and that their performances were based entirely on their own conceptions. Milton's directorial methods, Webster said, were entirely external, paying a great deal of attention to such matters as movement and gesture but almost none to characterization and motivation. Webster found it difficult to respond to Milton's approach, but was surprised to find that the Lunts did not seem to be bothered by it at all. They, too, developed their characters' external qualities first, allowing the mechanics to aid in the development of internal characterization.

Webster felt that the Lunts "took a curiously outside-to-inside path," but she was overwhelmed by their command of technical resources and their ability to create "extraordinary jets of emotional feeling" by technical means.

> Lynn came to me one day and talked of the scene at the end of the first act where Masha suddenly breaks down and pours out to Dr. Dorn all the bottled-up anguish of her heart. "I think," said Lynn, "it should start like this . . ." and she gave a cry of agony, like an animal in unbearable pain. I was taken entirely by surprise. It wasn't my cry or my pain; it wasn't anything I should ever have dreamed of for myself; it was grotesque, uninhibited, revealing, wholly right. I went home and worked very hard. I made it into my own pain and wrung from it my own cry—I

mean, of course, Masha's cry. Afterwards, I found it frighteningly difficult to bring myself, at every performance, to the pitch where the cry broke from me irrepressibly, inevitably, not forethought or manufactured. That, obviously, is where craft and discipline must come in—commodities which the Lunts had in abundance. . . .

Although they worked on many scenes from a technical point of view, the Lunts applied a quite different approach to the play's final episode. In that scene Trigorin and Arkadina go offstage with several other characters to have dinner before returning at the very end of the play. During rehearsals the Lunts complained on several occasions that they could never truly create the sense that they were either going to or coming from dinner. In order to create the reality for themselves, they had a full dinner set up at a table backstage, with glassware, china and silverware. Each night they and the other actors proceeded to eat the meal, talking to one another in character. The device added to the production in two ways: it provided the sense of reality the Lunts needed, and it also contributed to the on-stage reality, for the sounds of the characters dining and conversing could be heard in the background while the on-stage scene was being played. As Uta Hagen said, the Lunts were greater devotees of Stanislavski's "Method" approach to acting than any other actors she ever knew.

Webster watched the Lunts rehearsing Trigorin's and Arkadina's first entrance. They were dissatisfied with the progress of the scene and baffled as to how to play it for greatest effect. "Lynn and Alfred tried it sitting, standing, walking, crossing, lighting a cigarette, picking up a glass, sitting on a chair, with innumerable permutations and combinations of these things," Webster said. "Bob Milton suggested everything under the sun." But nothing seemed to work. In this and other scenes, the Lunts became increasingly frustrated by their inability to find the key to the material. They never doubted that the play was a great one or that it could be magnificently performed; but how to unlock its secrets?

Fontanne often became angry during rehearsals because she was dissatisfied with her own work. Uta Hagen recalled that she might repeat a line fifty or sixty times in order to get it right, and would grow increasingly irritated at her inability to find a reading that satisfied her. As during the production of *Amphitryon 38,* Fontanne's self-confidence failed her during rehearsals for *The Sea Gull.* Try as she might, she simply could not come to grips with her character. At one rehearsal Alan Hewitt overheard her say to Lunt, "Alfred, let me out of this. Get Judith Anderson. Judith is a personality. She will understand this woman better than I will. Postpone rehearsals, postpone the opening, persuade Judith to play it and let me out."

On one occasion, according to Harold Clurman, Lunt became so frustrated by his and the other actors' difficulties that he muttered, "Perhaps we're not good enough for this play." His insecurity was revealed on the closing night of *Amphitryon 38*. At the curtain calls, cries of "Speech, speech!" were heard throughout the auditorium. Lunt spoke a few words, concluding with, "We'll be back in two weeks in *The Sea Gull*. Heaven help us."

The Lunts' misgivings were often evident during rehearsals. They shouted at one another during some sessions; at others, they joined together to argue vehemently with Milton; Fontanne threatened to leave the production; Lunt threatened to cancel it altogether. But, with one exception, the temperamental outbursts of the day were always resolved by evening. The exception occurred after one rehearsal when Lunt sat down next to Uta Hagen and, believing that Fontanne was in her dressing room, said, "Don't mind Lynn, she's always like this at this stage of the game." Fontanne overheard the remark and was furious—not only with Lunt, but with Hagen as well. For several days she treated Hagen coldly. She seemed even to have become jealous of the young actress, apparently believing that Lunt had developed a crush on her. After a scene in which Trigorin kisses Nina had been rehearsed numerous times, Lunt said, "I guess it's all right," to which Fontanne answered sarcastically, "It should be good by now." Later, when Hagen and Fontanne played a scene together, Fontanne continually cut off Hagen's lines by jumping in with her own.

The day after that incident, Fontanne apologized to Hagen and gave her an expensive gold-and-pearl necklace. Later, Lunt told Hagen that his wife had been feeling ill and unhappy, and that the Lunts both hoped any hard feelings would be forgotten.

In a conversation with me in 1983, Hagen remembered the Lunts as "unbelievable disciplinarians" who insisted that all actors (including one who did not make his first entrance until the third act) must be in the theatre at 7:00 for an 8:30 curtain; moreover, they made it clear that they preferred all actors to check in by 6:30. Their attitude toward drinking was clearly communicated: any actor who allowed alcohol to interfere with his performance or with rehearsals would immediately be dismissed.

At one of the last rehearsals before the company traveled to Baltimore, where they would give the first performance of *The Sea Gull* on March 16, 1938, Alexander Woollcott watched a runthrough given on the bare stage of the Shubert Theatre.* Most of the actors felt the rehearsals had not been going particularly well and were afraid Woollcott's reaction would be negative. The Lunts, after a brief private conference with the critic, called the actors together in a dressing room so that Woollcott could address them. To the surprise of many, Woollcott, nattily attired in a long black cape, told the cast he had been moved beyond description by their performance. He

---

*The only other person in the audience was Helen Westley. The other members of the Board were firmly asked *not* to attend a rehearsal. They did not see the production until it opened in Baltimore.

said the production was like a beacon in the darkness, "a sanctuary for the spirit of man amid the bloody violence of a marching world." Many of the actors wept, and the morale of the company rose perceptibly.

Morale remained high in Baltimore. Woollcott wrote to Graham Robertson in England that the play had opened "with the audience demanding twenty-eight curtain calls and then going home only by request. I saw a single rehearsal of it," he added, "the first complete run-through of the play. I have never seen anything better anywhere. [The Lunts] have never done anything so good. It can never be so good again, I expect, as it was in that stripped, unadorned, hair-trigger performance."

The day after the Baltimore opening, the Lunts called a rehearsal which lasted almost until it was time for the actors to get into makeup and costume for the second performance. "With these people it never stops until they fall into their graves," Hagen wrote to her parents. And after the Friday-night performance, when Hagen's last scene went poorly, she and Lunt stayed to rehearse that scene yet again.

After a week in Baltimore, *The Sea Gull* played a week in Boston to equally enthusiastic audiences. Opening night was a triumphant occasion by almost any standard, but most of the actors were disappointed that they had received "only" ten curtain calls. A number of them, including the Lunts, went out to dinner afterward and cursed the unappreciative audience. They felt better in the morning, however, for critical response was overwhelmingly favorable. Elinor Hughes wrote in the Boston *Globe* that the play "requires and in this case has received the best possible acting and direction." Still, Lunt was not satisfied with his performance or that of the company. There were rehearsals each afternoon and, several times, after the evening performance as well. Alan Hewitt estimated that during the course of rehearsals, about fifteen to twenty hours were spent on a scene in the first act in which the characters enter in groups of twos and threes. Even though he had appeared in three other plays with the Lunts, Hewitt was astonished at "the incredible number of hours that was spent on bringing the people on stage and placing them."

But all the rehearsal in the world could not quell Lunt's fear that the company had just begun to penetrate the surface of Chekhov's play. In an interview published in the New York *Journal and American* the day before the New York opening, he said, "I don't see how actors can ever exhaust or reach the bottom of [the play's] subtleties, its complex meanings, its unspoken emotions. The longer we rehearse, the more amazing things we find in it. It is the most difficult and wonderful play I ever read; it is tender and human and profound, and ah, so difficult to play! The values are all there, but so elusively, so delicately expressed."

As Lunt feared, the premiere at the Shubert Theatre in New York on March 28 was not universally acclaimed. Usually, there was a clear critical consensus regarding the artistic success or failure of the productions with which the Lunts were associated—but about *The Sea Gull* there was no consensus at all. Some critics fell under the production's spell. Richard Watts, Jr., expressed the view of several when he wrote in the New York *Tribune,* "That fascinating cascade of melancholia and soul-probing that is Chekhov's *The Sea Gull* comes to bitter, brooding life in the splendid production . . . beautifully acted by Miss Fontanne, Mr. Lunt and an excellent company . . . and capably directed by Robert Milton." But others remained quite untouched. Brooks Atkinson complained that "Mr. Lunt and Miss Fontanne remain brightly on the surface of an introspective play." Fontanne overacted, Atkinson said, which "cheapens the part considerably."

One aspect of the production that received considerable criticism was the red wig Fontanne wore as Arkadina. A number of critics implied that she had worn it only to call attention to herself. Perhaps the wig was a distraction (it was discarded when the play was performed on the road), but it had nothing to do with projecting Fontanne's image. Instead, it had everything to do with projecting the image of the character, Irina Arkadina. Fontanne had considered the alternatives carefully, she said:

> Irina was a woman no longer young. . . . Her hair was dyed. In those days dyes were not what they are now, and she would have had little choice in the matter of color. The red hair which she chose was certainly to be preferred to the awful, dead-black, varnished-looking locks which were the most common result of hair dye in that era. Another color which she might have had for her money was a terrible peroxide blonde, but Irina would have chosen the nice bright orange, I think.

Although she was able to justify specific choices she had made in connection with the role, Fontanne was never pleased with her portrayal during the New York run of *The Sea Gull*. Not until later, when the Lunts toured it, did she begin to feel comfortable in the play.

Whatever the reason for the failure of *The Sea Gull* to achieve the near-universal accolades of most other Lunt-Fontanne productions, it was surely not because it was a "dull play," as Sidney B. Whipple said in the New York *World-Telegram*. Whipple was not alone, however. In Baltimore and Boston, several reviewers had betrayed their ignorance of the value of Chekhov's work, seemingly because they expected the Lunts to appear in the sort of comedy in which they had specialized in recent years. The Boston *Daily Record*'s E. F. Harkins said, "As diversion it is no dish of bonbons."

On a more serious level, Lawrence Langner of the Guild's board said that the individual cast members had been brilliant, but that no sense of ensemble playing had been developed. He concluded that "no one, including director Robert Milton, approached it as Chekhov must be approached—with the awareness that the subtext, rather than the text, is the heart of the drama." But Uta Hagen's attitude was precisely the reverse. "In terms of the ensemble, the attention to detail, and the understanding of the play," she said, "it was brilliant," achieving a perfect blend of the tragic and comic moods. Especially outstanding among the actors were the Lunts and Sydney Greenstreet, she felt. On the other hand, Margaret Webster said, "Some of the play's quality came through brilliantly; but there was a lack of rhythm, of wholeness, possibly of a kind of trust. We never let ourselves be carried along by the flowing current of the play." Harold Clurman placed most of the blame on Robert Milton, "whose only qualification" for directing the play, he said, "was that he happened to be the son of a famous Russian actor" and who had been "unable to bridge the gap" between talented American actors and a Russian playwright of genius.

George Jean Nathan's opinion of the Lunts' performances bordered on the contemptuous. "There were moments when one felt that the Lunts had unwittingly confused Chekhov with Molnar," he said, "by the apparent increasing inability on the part of the Lunts to suppress those acting idiosyncrasies which have so joyously in the past embellished the lighter plays that have been their greatest successes."

Nathan was one of a distinct minority who felt the Lunts' distinguishing characteristics tended to distort the roles they played. In the opinion of most other observers, however, the Lunts' most remarkable attribute was their ability to transform themselves in each successive role. In 1930 eight of New York's major drama critics received a questionnaire from *Theatre Guild Magazine* asking which American actors and actresses possess "a mature technique which enables them to act many dissimilar roles with equal sureness." Alfred Lunt was named on all eight lists, Lynn Fontanne on seven. No other actor or actress received more than five votes.

It is true, of course, that no actor can *completely* eradicate his own personality when playing a role. Even if that were possible, it would be undesirable, for it would result in superficial characterizations not grounded in reality. But some actors do go to greater lengths than others to mask themselves, and the Lunts were generally counted in that category.

If there is one aspect of the Lunts' personalities that was present in each role they played, it was the manner of speaking. Lunt developed a unique speech pattern which seemed to combine elements of standard American, British, and the hint of a Scandinavian intonation, and he used essentially the same quality of speech regardless of the character he portrayed. Fontanne, on the other hand, never attempted to conceal her native British accent, even when playing an American.

Few who saw the Lunts perform could deny the magic they created, whatever the method. But the argument continued for years: were they essentially actors who created a gallery of diverse characters, or were they performers who distorted the roles they played until the characters came to resemble themselves?

The Lunts and the Theatre Guild had realized in advance that *The Sea Gull* could not succeed commercially. The mixed reviews it received would have seemed only to make that outcome inevitable. Peculiarly, however, the public was not put off by either the tragic tone of the play or the caustic comments of the critics. During its limited run *The Sea Gull* was played before remarkably enthusiastic standing-room-only houses.

But Lunt remained unhappy. As he applied his makeup for the second performance of the play in New York, he said to an interviewer, "Well, we've got a flop on our hands." The reporter, Wilella Waldorf, pointed out that, on balance, the production had received "the best set of reviews that ever greeted the Chekhov play in this city." During the interview the box-office manager visited Lunt's dressing room to tell him that every seat for the performance had been sold out and all available standing-room tickets would probably be sold as well. Still, Lunt would not be consoled.

Perhaps, however, he took solace in the fact that the production improved after its opening. "We got better as we went along," Fontanne said.

Uta Hagen confirmed Fontanne's remark, and attributed the improvement primarily to the influence of the Lunts. "They got better and better," she said. "They never became mechanical in anything they did; never walked through any scene."

Hagen received a severe lesson in discipline while playing in *The Sea Gull*. One night, when she was to have made an entrance near the end of the third act, she was engaged in a discussion with another actor. When she heard her entrance cue, she was a considerable distance from the stage, and although she quickly ran onto the set, she caused Lunt to wait for several embarrassing seconds. Moments later Trigorin (Lunt) kissed Nina. On this occasion Lunt did more than kiss her—he bit her lip angrily. When the curtain came down at the conclusion of the scene, he shook her, nearly quivering with rage. Fontanne then came up to Hagen, kicked her lightly and said, "You're a rotten amateur!" Hagen was resentful, feeling that the Lunts had overreacted, but years later she came to understand their anger at her carelessness. As she told me the story, she ended by saying, "I never missed another entrance in my life."

The Lunts' influence on Hagen was profound. "They were fanatical about the theatre," she said, "as I wish others were." She regarded them both as great artists who were unjustly held by some to be capable only of playing light comedy.

At the conclusion of the 1937–38 season, *Stage* magazine gave special awards to four theatrical personalities who had dominated the Broadway scene: Orson Welles, Thornton Wilder, Alfred Lunt and Lynn Fontanne.

Their tribute to the Lunts saluted them as producers, directors and performers:

> To Alfred Lunt and Lynn Fontanne, actor-managers in the grand tradition, for holding that tradition high through another season. For two superb productions, made in association with the Theatre Guild, *Amphitryon 38* and *The Sea Gull*. For two acting performances in the Giraudoux-Behrman comedy . . . which demonstrated the art of high comedy at its most expert and electric. For two acting performances in *The Sea Gull* . . . which overrode the brooding, introverted Chekhov legend; set two human, lucid, and plausible people in the middle of a brilliantly played, brilliantly adapted revival of a moss-grown masterpiece. For the future promise of a joint career which remains one of the proudest ornaments of our stage.

As the Lunts prepared to leave for London on May 4, 1938, to offer their production of *Amphitryon 38,* they could look back upon the previous three years as a time of remarkable accomplishment. Within the Theatre Guild structure, they had managed to become a semi-autonomous unit, controlling nearly every aspect of the productions they appeared in. They had produced and acted in four very different kinds of plays in New York and on tours of varying lengths. They had assembled a company of actors who were talented, personable, attuned to their methods and willing to devote themselves to theatrical perfection. One step remained to be accomplished: to offer their productions in repertory on a nationwide tour. Following the London engagement of *Amphitryon,* that was precisely what they intended to do.

Chapter Ten

TOURING IN REPERTORY

"Why the word 'touring' conjures a picture of dismal weeks in dull cities is something Lynn and I have never been able to comprehend. To us it has been high adventure. . . . It has been a glorious experience and we have learned there are as appreciative and discriminating audiences in San Francisco and Edinburgh as in New York and London."

Alfred Lunt

"I hope to be like Mrs. Fiske in one way and spend my old age doing one-night stands."

Lynn Fontanne

1938–40

If there is any phrase calculated to set an actor's teeth on edge, it is "one-night stands." The very words conjure up images of long, uncomfortable rides between one smallish city and another (the cities are necessarily smallish, or performances would be given for more than a single night), bad food served in greasy restaurants, nights spent in hotels trying to sleep on too hard or too soft beds, and performances given in all sorts of environments, from massive auditoriums to high-school gymnasiums. Many actors have gotten their starts touring with companies playing one-night stands, but invariably their ambition is to escape that grind and find a more secure niche in the theatrical profession.

The Lunts could not be counted among their number. They were not oblivious to the hardships imposed by touring (and they managed to insulate themselves from some of them), but they loved it nonetheless. Recognized as the foremost stage actors in America, they could easily have insisted that they would tour only to the largest cities where their plays would perform for months at a time, but they did not do so. On their nationwide tours in 1938–39 and 1939–40, they played wherever people were eager to see them and theatres (or structures that could be outfitted as theatres) were available. One-night stands were liberally mixed with week-long engagements. In a way, the one-night stands were the most exciting aspect of the tours. As Fontanne said, "Every night is like opening night."

    Before embarking on their repertory tour of the United States, the Lunts took their company to London, where they played *Amphitryon 38* for a limited run beginning on May 17, 1938. The first performance was marred by Lunt's customary bout of nerves, but few members of the appreciative audience noticed it. W. A. Darlington, writing in the *Daily Telegraph*, lauded both the Lunts unreservedly, describing their joint playing as "the most fascinating thing of its kind that the theatre has had to show in my experience."

    The Lunts had already played *Amphitryon 38* about 200 times and were totally at home with its style of whimsical understatement. Early in its run, their performances had been marked by a good deal of movement from place to place, perhaps to ensure that audiences would be able to respond to physical comedy in case the verbal humor was not successful. By the time the production reached London, however, movement seemed more a distraction than an asset. "The longer we played it, the less we moved," said Lunt. "And by the end of the run, we hardly moved a muscle."

    Charles Morgan, the critic for the *Times* of London, found Lunt's performance as Jupiter more than a comic masterpiece. Lunt found deeper undertones in the character and his situation, Morgan said, demonstrating that Giraudoux's play was "something much more than a 'smart' or a 'sophisticated' or an 'amusing' enchantment of a classical legend." By contrast, he found Fontanne's performance limited. He acknowledged her "extraordinary charm of grace and lightness of touch . . . so rich in intelligence and high spirits," but he lamented that she had deliberately chosen not to explore the "ironic pathos" inherent in the role of Alkmena. Never attempting to overstep her limitations was characteristic of her, Morgan said; she had carefully assessed her histrionic abilities and knew their limits precisely.

    Morgan was not the only critic in England or America to express the opinion that Fontanne's range was narrower than her husband's. George Jean Nathan conceded that "as a comedienne she is uniformly delightful," but said that her performances in serious drama "have clearly betrayed her shortcomings." (It must be noted, however, that Nathan's acerbic comments about Fontanne's abilities were echoed by few others. For example, he accused her of "listening lovingly to the sound of her own voice" in

Pygmalion, a fault of which no one else seems to have written.) Several years later Kenneth Tynan concurred that her range was limited, either by conscious choice or by an inability to express the depth he perceived in those actresses who he felt were truly great.*

Most observers, however, agreed that the Lunts' performances in *Amphitryon 38* had been perfectly matched. Fontanne herself observed in a letter to Alexander Woollcott in June:

> . . . it is a great success, as you predicted. Giraudoux was here and it was a great opening night, with the best that London can do when they like it. They tore up their seats and shouted from all sides of the house, "Bravo," "Speech," and behaved very much like *Reunion in Vienna*. . . . Others, just like old friends, cried out, "Why have you stayed away so long?" It was all very touching, and a happy but highly emotional company rushed to their dressing rooms to dress for the various parties that were being given them all over town. Since then we have sold out. It is a real hit, and apparently we could stay here for another run like *Reunion in Vienna,* but we are finishing firmly on the 9th of July and going to Sweden.

The most exciting social event of the Lunts' London stay was a party given for them by Noël Coward. Among the guests were the Duke and Duchess of Kent and Anthony Eden, who was seated next to Fontanne at dinner. She reported to Woollcott, "You can get a rough idea of his charm when I tell you that he was asking *me* what he should do on his return to the House, and what his line of attack should be." Fontanne, whose naïveté about politics was matched only by her lack of interest in the subject, was flattered by his question. "And you can get a rougher idea of my gullibility," she said, "when, nothing daunted, I gave him my advice, which he received with the utmost respect."

A Scandinavian trip occupied the rest of the summer. But even in the midst of the most enjoyable vacation, the Lunts' thoughts were seldom far from the theatre. They communicated with the Theatre Guild in August, saying they wanted to revive *Idiot's Delight* for the road tour they were planning to make that fall, combining it with the productions of *Amphitryon 38* and *The Sea Gull*. They were not daunted by the imminent release of the motion picture of *Idiot's Delight* with Clark Gable and Norma Shearer. Nor was their determination lessened by the fact that another tour of that play, featuring Phil Baker, was about to begin.

When the Lunts returned to New York on September 13, 1938,

---

*Fontanne expressed dissatisfaction with her own work on at least one occasion. She told Morton Eustis in 1937 that her performances "vary so distressingly. Sometimes, you know, they are so bad I should like to advance to the footlights and urge the audience to get their money back."

aboard the *Normandie,* they reported that there seemed no way for war to be averted. "The atmosphere [in Europe] is so tense and ominous that one can scarcely breathe," they said. Still, they hoped to perform in England once again in the spring of the following year, unless, Lunt said, "events abroad change everything for all of us."

Rehearsals began immediately for the nationwide tour, which would open in Boston on October 3. The Lunts planned to start with a repertory of *Amphitryon 38* and *The Sea Gull,* to which they would add *Idiot's Delight* in early 1939. The actors in the company would be substantially the same as those who had appeared in the productions in New York, but there were a number of replacements who required every moment of the two weeks' rehearsal time.

The Lunts' aim in rehearsal was not simply to duplicate the productions given on Broadway, but to achieve tighter, richer performances. *The Sea Gull* in particular went through a process of significant revision.

The first week of *The Sea Gull* performances, given in Philadelphia, Fontanne described as "a kind of nightmare." During the dress rehearsal, she wrote to Woollcott, "Mike, the Guild's head electrician who has lighted every show that Alfred and I have been in since we started with the Guild, suddenly keeled over, and 20 minutes later was dead of a heart attack. During that 20 minutes we could get no help whatsoever, with a hospital only one-half block away. You can imagine the horror of watching a man die when there was a possibility that he might have been saved. A doctor arrived, but only in time to pronounce him dead."

Philadelphia was in the grip of an unusual November heat wave. The heat, combined with the fact that *The Sea Gull* was distinctly not a typical Lunt-Fontanne production, meant that audiences were smaller than those to which the Lunts were accustomed. They realized they were risking financial failure by presenting Chekhovian drama to a public that was not eager to see such a challenging play (despite excellent notices in the Philadelphia newspapers), but, Fontanne told Woollcott, "Well, to hell with them. We're doing *The Seagull* [*sic*] anyhow. Kit [Cornell] had to make *The Barretts* [*of Wimpole Street*] pay for Juliet, which they wouldn't come to see, so if they don't come to *The Sea Gull,* we'll have to make Amphitryon pay for it."

During their week in Philadelphia, the Lunts called upon Eva Le Gallienne, who was performing in a pre-Broadway tryout of a play called *Madame Capet.* They told her they were still unhappy over the performances they had given in New York and that they wished to rethink the production in its entirety. They asked Le Gallienne, who had had extensive experience in Chekhov's plays, if she would redirect the production for them.* Le Gallienne was flattered but unsure that she could bring any sub-

---

*Le Gallienne had seen *The Sea Gull* in New York. Although she was Uta Hagen's teacher and a good friend of the Lunts, she did not visit backstage after the presentation, primarily because she had not liked Lunt's performance. Fontanne, who always dreaded oc-

stantial improvements to the presentation. In any case, she told them, she was obligated to open *Madame Capet* in New York within two weeks. Typically blunt and typically engrossed in her own work, Fontanne blurted out, "But *Madame Capet* will close in a week!" (Fontanne's prediction was remarkably accurate; the production lasted only seven performances.) Le Gallienne could only repeat that she was bound by her contract. Next the Lunts consulted Margaret Webster, the production's original Masha, who was not a member of the touring company. Webster recommended, among other things, that Fontanne discard the red wig she had worn in New York. Fontanne did so, and the Lunts incorporated a number of Webster's other recommendations into the touring performances. In addition, they constantly re-rehearsed the production during the tour, adding elements here and removing others there.

Fontanne's spirits improved when *The Sea Gull* moved to Washington, D.C. "Chekhov seems to be Washington's dish," she reported to Woollcott. "The press this morning were beside themselves. The company are beside themselves. And most sensational of all, we have been asked to give an extra matinee, and we are so touched at this sudden appreciation for *The Sea Gull* that we are going to do it."

Uta Hagen played Nina in the touring production of *The Sea Gull* as she had on Broadway. She also played a minor role in *Amphitryon 38*. But she was deeply unhappy. Her mother died just as the tour began, leaving her with a great sense of emptiness. Moreover, she had fallen in love with José Ferrer and would have preferred to remain in New York where she could be close to him. In addition, George S. Kaufman had approached her about appearing in a play on Broadway in 1938–39. Still, she had signed a contract with the Lunts, so, after returning home for two weeks to attend her mother's funeral and to be with her family, she dutifully began the tour as scheduled.

When the company played Philadelphia, Marc Connelly approached Hagen to offer her the leading role in a new play he had written. Hagen told him she was under contract to the Lunts, but Connelly answered by saying, in effect, that he had given Fontanne her first big break in *Dulcy* and she was eternally grateful to him; a word from Connelly would be all that was needed to get Hagen out of her contract. Connelly learned differently when he broached the matter, however. The Lunts advised him that if he wanted Hagen badly enough, he should postpone his play until the conclusion of the tour.

As time went on, Hagen felt more and more miserable. At times she broke into tears during rehearsals or while making up for a performance.

casions when she knew that highly accomplished theatre artists were in the audience, called Hagen into her dressing room and asked why Le Gallienne had not come backstage. Then, before receiving an answer, she worked herself into a temper, saying, "You can tell her from me it serves her god damn right if she didn't like it. She shouldn't come after a matinee when we're tired. . . . It's her own god damn fault."

Fontanne, genuinely concerned and trying to be helpful, suggested that Hagen move in with her and Lunt. But Hagen was in such awe of the Lunts that she could not envision living with them. In despair, she returned to her hotel room and took an overdose of sleeping pills, not really wishing to kill herself, she later said, but simply because she could see no other way out of her dilemma. Fortunately, José Ferrer and Hagen's brother arrived in Philadelphia only hours after she had taken the pills. When they entered her hotel room, they found her lying unconscious on the bed. Together, they marched her back and forth until she was out of danger.

When the Lunts heard about the suicide attempt, they were horrified. Hagen believed they were primarily concerned because of the scandal that would be created if the word got out. Undoubtedly, they were also concerned that she might try to kill herself once again. As a result, they sent Hagen to a doctor, who reported to them that the young actress was so deeply depressed she could no longer function professionally. He recommended that she be excused from her contract. Still, the Lunts could not fully accept his verdict. They released her from her commitment in *Amphitryon 38,* but insisted that she continue to perform in *The Sea Gull*. Since *The Sea Gull* was performed less often than *Amphitryon* and sometimes was not given for a week or more, Hagen was able to return to New York periodically. She maintained that schedule until the tour reached Chicago in January 1939, at which point she told the Lunts she simply could not remain with the company any longer. The Lunts voided Hagen's contract, but were clearly bitter about what they regarded as her desertion. As Hagen bade them goodbye, Lunt assumed a curt manner; Fontanne refused even to speak to her. The role of Nina was taken over by Hagen's understudy, Thelma Schnee, who became one of the Lunts' protégés.

For the Lunts, an unswerving commitment to the theatre was invariably the best medicine. Regardless of how irritated they might become at one another or at a third party, everything became trivial in comparison to their work. They seemed unable to understand that this sort of absorption would not necessarily have the same effect on everyone else. As late as 1980, in a discussion with George Schaefer, Fontanne referred to Hagen's behavior on the tour as "naughty," and said she hoped Hagen had learned a greater sense of discipline in the meantime.

The traumatic events involving Uta Hagen coincided with the Lunts' conviction that the production had finally achieved the level of artistry they had been striving for. Fontanne wrote to Woollcott on January 18, "*The Seagull* [*sic*], we think and hope, has improved—at least we seem to give more good performances than we did. . . . The papers raved about the acting of the whole company after the opening [in Chicago], and the following night each scene was applauded. People must be coming to see it twice, as the members of the cast are now getting receptions as they come on. It is all very nice and encouraging and everyone is very happy." She also reported, "The audiences sometimes take the scene between Alfred and me very seriously and seem quite shocked when Alfred tells me he is in love with a young girl. They are all on my side about the whole thing—you'd think it was a private romance of their own that had been shattered, especially at the matinees, clicking their tongues in horrified 'Oh's [*sic*], isn't that sweet.' And then when I triumph at the end, the applause is terrific."

The *Idiot's Delight* company featuring Phil Baker had already embarked on its tour when the Lunts began to include that play in their repertory. Although Baker had been told in advance that the Lunts would appear in the larger cities of the East and Midwest and that his tour would therefore be limited to the west coast and the smaller cities east of the Mississippi, he was resentful that the Lunts' tour would interfere with his, and said so on frequent occasions, in public as well as in private.

In December, Lunt wrote to Sherwood, "Well now, really, but don't you think that Mr. Baker has behaved in an extremely odd fashion. I thought for a while that I must be the one who was mad, but I sent for a copy of the telegram that I had written to Baker from Philadelphia, and sure enough, I had said that he could play everywhere but New York, New Jersey and Delaware. I also spoke to him to that effect on the telephone, and there you are."

Still resentful, Baker decided to end his tour in mid-December in Toronto, where he said, "I began the tour on November 24 with the understanding that I would be able to take the play to the best centers. But it seems that Mr. Lunt wants to play it later in repertory and through the Theatre Guild has forbidden me to go to cities like Chicago. He will not even let me take the play where he has [already] been with it."

The day after Baker's statement, the Theatre Guild tried to clear the air, denying that Baker had ever been given the right to perform *Idiot's Delight* in the large cities of the East and Midwest. Besides, the Guild said, the Baker production had proved to have limited commercial appeal. Both companies had played in New Haven, which provided a basis for direct comparison. The Lunts had taken in $9,932 during three performances there, while Baker's company had grossed only $1,648 for four performances. The Guild suggested that Baker was using his feud with Lunt as a cover for the real reason he was ending his tour: his company was not doing satisfactory business.

Neither Baker's tour nor the film of *Idiot's Delight* diminished the audiences for the Lunt-Fontanne production. When they gave the play in St. Louis, the movie was playing concurrently, and still the Lunts sold out every performance. In Cleveland, they broke all records for a visiting production.

From October 1938 until April 29, 1939, the Lunts and their company toured almost continuously (with a break for Christmas), playing in the East (Philadelphia, Washington, Pittsburgh, etc.), the Midwest (Chicago, Milwaukee, St. Paul, Minneapolis, Madison, Kansas City, Wichita,

Des Moines, Davenport, Sioux City, Cedar Rapids, etc.) and the South (Oklahoma City, Dallas, Waco, San Antonio, Austin, Houston, Fort Worth, Little Rock, Memphis, Chattanooga, Atlanta, Birmingham, Montgomery, New Orleans, Nashville, etc.). Performances were given in theatres, municipal and high-school auditoriums, city centers and motion-picture houses. In a large city such as Philadelphia, they spent as many as three weeks, but other periods were far more hectic.

Lunt wrote to Sherwood from Chicago, with only slight exaggeration, "Did you know—and I want you to look at this sentence for a long, long time—did you know that after Chicago we start on *twelve weeks* of one-nighters with *Idiot's Delight?* . . . If you are not touched by this, you are not the man I think you are."

New actors were added to the ensemble to fill out the large cast of *Idiot's Delight*. Lunt was pleased with the casting, and after the first reading he told Sherwood, "I do believe the cast is better than the original."

The Lunts kept Sherwood busy revising the script so it would be current with world events. Lunt wrote to him, "You will be amazed how even more up-to-date [the play] is now than it was three years ago, and we are really thrilled at getting back into it again. When we rehearse next week, if you don't mind, I will make little notes where you can add a line here and there, although I would rather you do it. References to Ethiopia, for instance, which we changed to Spain [where the Civil War was drawing to a close], and later to Czechoslovakia."

The company traveled by train, filling up two sleepers and three baggage cars. The Lunts had their own compartment, where Fontanne spent most of her time reading and sewing. The more sociable Lunt was often found in the car with the other actors. Two complete road crews manned the productions, one of them setting up in one town while the second carried the scenery for the next play to the following location.

At each new theatre the Lunts would inspect the stage hours before the performance, testing the acoustics, checking the lights and walking from point to point on the stage simply to get the proper "feel" of the space. In order to ensure that the company could be clearly heard regardless of the size or acoustical properties of the theatres in which they played, they stationed several "listeners" in the audience at each stop. If the actors' voices were indistinctly heard, the listeners were instructed to rush backstage and signal from the wings for the actors to raise the level of their projection.

But some eventualities could not be foreseen. The performance of *Amphitryon 38* in Tulsa was given on a steeply raked stage, slanting downward toward the audience. Every stagehand in the company was required to hold the platform on which Lunt and Richard Whorf were standing, their faces attached to papier-mâché bodies, in order to prevent it from sliding into the auditorium.

Sometimes Lunt needed a release from the rigors of touring. Occasionally, he and Richard Whorf would vary the playing of a scene in order to stave off boredom. Invariably, however, they would come offstage to encounter a furiously disapproving Fontanne. At such times she would resolve not to speak to Lunt in order to punish him. But he knew how to break through her resolve: he spoke to her through their dachshund, Elsa, a tactic Fontanne could not resist.

The week of December 19 was free so that members of the company could go home for Christmas. The Lunts returned to Genesee Depot, where they enjoyed a family dinner on Christmas Day with Lunt's mother, his sisters, Karin and Louise, their husbands, George Bugbee and Jack Greene, and their children, and a few friends, including Claggett Wilson, who was decorating the house. The vacation allowed Lunt to enjoy his first family Christmas in twenty-seven years.

Fontanne reported to Woollcott afterward:

> Christmas was lovely with the family. The growing-up children are a delight—such good manners and so amusing. We sat down 20 to dinner, including the two little nieces and one little nephew, aged eleven, twelve and thirteen respectively, Johnny the youngest. They all had milk by their places but were allowed each a glass of champagne, and one of the little girls was heard to say, in one of those sudden lulls, "It tastes lousy after champagne, doesn't it?" They both wore long hostess gowns and were quite blissful imagining themselves grown up. Johnny finished his dinner quickly and accompanied the dessert course on his concertina with "Jingle Bells" and "Home Sweet Home." We played all the old favorites on the gramophone, too, and it was all very sentimental and lovely. Karin and Louise (Alfred's sisters) sang carols softly in high sweet sopranos with their heads together, looking like the children they were when I first knew them. We left with the whole family group at the top of the stairs, three generations from Hattie downwards in tears, because the Christmas that they had so long looked forward to was over.

After the Christmas layoff, the tour resumed, the schedule as hectic as ever. There were, however, performances scheduled in Milwaukee and Madison for March 1939, which the Lunts looked forward to with special enthusiasm because they would be able to spend more time in Genesee Depot.

During the 1939 stopover in Madison, the Lunts opened the University of Wisconsin's new theatre with their production of *The Taming of the Shrew.* They enjoyed the experience so much that several of their later plays also opened in that theatre. The University recognized their contributions in 1941 by awarding the Lunts honorary doctorates.

This was the first tour on which the Lunts had played in the South.

People who had never been to the theatre before drove hundreds of miles to see them perform, and Fontanne particularly found their enthusiasm refreshing. Although the Lunts usually insisted on resting before a performance, they often sacrificed their leisure time in order to reach out to their audiences. Fontanne estimated that during the tour she shook hands with 6,500 schoolgirls and signed at least as many autograph books. "When they travel so far to see a play, the least I can do is see them after the play," she said.

There were, of course, the inevitable surprises—but these were met with good humor by the members of the company. In Little Rock, Arkansas, for example, the auditorium was located on the fourth floor of the high school. All the members of the company, assisted by students, helped carry the scenery through the front door of the school, up three flights of stairs, through the hallway, down the aisles and onto the stage. It turned out that the "stage" was a gymnasium enclosed by a massive proscenium arch, and the gym was alive with young athletes playing basketball. When the stagehands attempted to move the scenery onto the floor, they were told they would have to wait until recess at 11:00. Then, when the basketball players left the floor and the set-up began, the stagehands discovered that the ceiling of the gym was barely high enough to accommodate the set.

The set-up was further delayed by a constant stream of students roaming freely throughout the stage and auditorium, questioning the stagehands about every detail. The Lunts arrived in the afternoon to see how things were going and were mobbed by students seeking autographs.

Because the proscenium opening was a gaping ninety feet, black curtains had to be drawn in from each side for a distance of nearly thirty feet. The set, occupying the thirty feet in the middle, resembled a toy theatre, so tiny did it seem in the vast space.

The auditorium was sold out, but that, too, created problems. Customers with side seats near the stage would barely be able to see the set, which stood in the middle of the gymnasium floor.

When the actors arrived to apply their makeup, they were shown to the only available dressing rooms: the locker rooms for the Home Team and the Visitors, one floor below the stage area. Because Fontanne and Edith King had fast changes to make, a temporary canvas dressing room was erected beneath a basketball net. But the rest of the cast had to descend a flight of stairs to reach their "dressing room."

The auditorium's acoustics were disastrous. The actors had to "scream at the top of [their] voices," Lunt said, in order to be heard and understood. The auditorium was also not equipped to handle all of the current required by the lighting instruments for *Idiot's Delight,* but even with fewer lights, fuses blew during the Lunts' big scene, causing them to play in semidarkness.

Remarkably, everyone—actors, stagehands and audience alike—accepted these difficulties with good spirits. The performers looked upon the

acoustical deficiencies of the auditorium and the primitive dressing arrangements as obstacles to be cheerfully overcome. The audience, even
those who could barely see the stage, seemed to enjoy the performance as
wholeheartedly as if they were seated in the center of the seventh row at
the Shubert Theatre in New York. And the stagehands calmly dismantled
the set after the performance, carried it down three flights of stairs and
loaded it onto the waiting trucks.

The long train ride to Memphis, where two performances were scheduled the following day, was so bumpy that no one was able to get much
sleep, and the company arrived in Tennessee depressed and weary, certain
that the performance would be uninspired, at best. But the audience's enthusiasm for *Amphitryon 38* lifted the actors' spirits, turning their exhaustion to elation. Afterward Lunt sat in his dressing room, exulting, "Wasn't
the audience *wonderful?* And *what* happened to us? . . . I've never given a
performance that satisfied me as much. I've never seen Lynnie better, but
never! And . . . the whole company—and we were all so tired we could
hardly stagger out of our dressing rooms."

Fontanne was equally thrilled. "We've never given a better performance, any one of us, that I can remember," she said. "I suppose we were *so*
tired that we just—you know, it's this kind of thing that makes trouping
worth while."

The difficulties the Lunts had encountered in Omaha in 1937 were
repeated in Memphis in 1939. After the two performances of *Idiot's Delight,* the chairman of the City Censor Board, Lloyd T. Binford, announced
that in future the Lunts must submit advance copies of any plays they
wished to produce in Memphis. He had not attended either of the performances, but he had been told that objectionable language had been used
in the production. Binford posted a sign backstage warning the actors of
legal consequences if any profanity was uttered during the performance.

Another bout with censorship threatened to disrupt the performance
of *Amphitryon 38* in Philadelphia. George Woodward, a Republican state
senator and a member of the Philadelphia Forum ("the learned and genteel
Philadelphia Forum," as it was sarcastically referred to in the Philadelphia
Record), which presented the play in that city, attacked the sponsoring organization for "subjecting us to the demoralizing influence" of a play
about seduction and infidelity. Lunt responded directly to Woodward's
charges. "Queen Mary came to the play in London, and," he said, "Queen
Mary doesn't go to plays that are immoral. She not only saw the play, but
she stayed until it was over and she applauded vigorously." The production
went on in Philadelphia as scheduled and no one in the audience seemed
to be particularly demoralized by the experience. Indeed, the *Record* noted
that the audience "sat, looked and laughed themselves silly."

A problem of a different sort arose in Jackson, Mississippi, where the
situation was precisely the reverse of the one the Lunts had faced in Little
Rock. The stage in Jackson's high-school auditorium was so small that the

set could not be accommodated at all and *Idiot's Delight* had to be given in front of black drapes.

Lunt himself was responsible for a mishap during one of the performances in Kansas City. As Renée Orsell tells the story:

> Mr. Lunt had been feeling very frisky that night and had added a few inventive steps to his "shuffle off" routine. The chorus girls were supposed to catch him as he fell, but dropped him. When the curtain came down, Mr. Lunt was furious, swore at the girls and carried on like mad until one of the chorus girls interrupted him with, "You god-damned son of a bitch, if you'd been where you should have been, we wouldn't have dropped you." Mr. Lunt's mouth fell open in astonishment. There was a moment of silence. And then he closed his mouth, looked directly at the chorus girl and said, "You're quite right. I apologize."

Lunt's interest in the business aspects of the tour was nearly as great as his artistic concern. After several trips to Pittsburgh in different plays over the years, the Lunts were convinced that their performances in that city were jinxed. For one reason or another—floods, snowstorms, public apathy—they never seemed to do as well at the box office in Pittsburgh as they did elsewhere. Lunt maintained that the company manager simply did not do a very good job of publicizing the productions and managing the money that was taken in. He often said that he himself could guarantee a profitable week in Pittsburgh if he were company manager, and during the 1938–39 tour he decided to give it a try. After the week, he proudly exhibited the company's books, demonstrating that a substantial profit had been made in Pittsburgh at last. It was pointed out that he had omitted one expensive item, however: he had forgotten to pay the sizable salaries of Alfred Lunt and Lynn Fontanne.

The tour was tiring for everyone, but the company was sustained by the Lunts' zest for the undertaking. Morton Eustis, who accompanied them for a time, wrote in *Theatre Arts Monthly:*

> Players like the Lunts, who would rather troupe than eat, would be the last to stress . . . the difficulties rather than the delights of trouping. For the difficulties to them are part of the delight. They like nothing better than to meet and surmount them. Each one is a challenge. Each one teaches them something new. Playing in a vast hall, like that at Wichita, Kansas—"which looked like Madison Square Garden"—they can learn how to project an intimate comedy into a huge space without losing the intimacy, or seeming to shout. Forced to play without scenery, they can discover how it is possible for the actor to supply the scenery. Acting every night in a different-sized theatre, without rehearsal, they can learn how to judge the "pitch" of a house so

that they know instantly, by second sight or sound, when to raise or lower the volume of their speech.

The tour over at last, the Lunts retreated, pleased but exhausted, to Genesee Depot for the summer. They needed to shore up their energies, for they planned to take to the road again in the fall with a new version of *The Taming of the Shrew.* Alexander Woollcott came to visit and recorded his stay by taking home movies. The Lunts must have fed him well. He wrote to thank them, saying, "After considerable gastric meditation I have come to the conclusion that you set the best table I know in America."

Prior to the tour of *The Taming of the Shrew* in 1939–40, the Lunts held auditions for four roles that would not be cast with the usual members of their company. The audition, scheduled to begin at 1:00 on a September afternoon at the Guild Theatre, was intended only for actors who had appointments. It was thus not publicly announced, but word of it obviously got out. When a young actor named William Le Massena arrived shortly before 1:00, he found that "the entire street—all of 52nd Street between 7th and 8th Avenues—was mobbed. It was like a street scene in a movie, with the crowds rioting." So many hundreds of actors had crowded around the theatre that Le Massena was unable to get near it.

A taxi arrived carrying Lunt, Richard Whorf and Sydney Greenstreet, and the crowd parted to let them through.* Lunt stepped out and shouted to the mob, "Ladies and gentlemen, I deeply regret this, but there are only four parts that Miss Fontanne and I are auditioning. There are two women's parts and there are two men's parts." Another producer might have dispersed the crowd by insisting that he would see only those actors who had appointments, but Lunt was far too sympathetic to the actor's plight. Instead he said, "I will see all the men on the stage level and Miss Fontanne will see all the women up in the big rehearsal hall above the theatre."

As Lunt walked through the crowd toward the theatre, Le Massena pushed his way up to him and said, "Can I audition too? I'm not a member of Equity." Normally, a nonprofessional would not even be considered, but Lunt, although he began with, "Oh, I don't know," ended by saying, "Certainly, certainly."

When everyone was inside the theatre, Lunt spoke to the actors. Only the roles of the pedant and the tailor were available, he said, plus a few nonspeaking parts. He had not anticipated that so many actors would be interested, he said, but he was willing to audition every one of them.

Le Massena, who was nineteen, told the stage manager he wanted to read for the pedant, but was told, "He's an old man. Go away." Finally, at around 5:00, Le Massena grabbed the script, stepped forward on stage and announced to Lunt, Whorf and Greenstreet, "Now you're going to hear

* According to Le Massena, Fontanne was not in the car. Presumably, she had arrived at the theatre earlier.

me read this." His initial reading interested all three of them. After a hasty conference, Lunt said, "We want Miss Fontanne to hear you. Will you come back tomorrow?"

Le Massena did return the next day—and the next as well—and eventually was cast in the role of the pedant. Meanwhile, Lunt and Fontanne auditioned every man and woman who attended the tryout, in an act of kindness and generosity almost unprecedented on Broadway.

The touring production of *The Taming of the Shrew* was not simply a revival of the work the Lunts had presented in 1935. Although the production was still based upon the original concept and a good deal of the original business was repeated, Lunt did not hesitate to redirect the play, adding business and new line readings. One significant change was to bring Fontanne on stage in a spectacular entrance. Amid offstage shouts from the actors and the sounds of Kate's whip cracking, she entered wearing a hunting outfit and carrying a blunderbuss. Circling the stage, she ended upstage center, where she aimed and "fired" the gun straight overhead. A large bird fell at her feet with a thud. The effect left the audience rocking with laughter.*

While the new version was being rehearsed, the Guild's Board members were kept away. During rehearsals, which were held in the Guild Theatre, William Le Massena recalled:

> There was a pass door at the top of the balcony from the office section of the theatre. And I remember once the pass door opened and the darkness was slit a couple of inches, and Alfred knew that somebody was up there watching. . . . I can remember him going down to the foot lights and calling up 'way to the back of the balcony, where there was this slit of light. He said, "I know you're up there! Now you can just go!" And *boom*—that little slit of light disappeared.

The *Taming of the Shrew* tour began early in October 1939 in Washington, D.C., then set out for the Midwest. After playing in that region for a month, the company worked their way to the west coast. By mid-December they were in the South and a month later headed north, giving performances along the eastern seaboard. The tour ended abruptly in Baltimore in late January 1940 when Fontanne came down with a bad cold. The scheduled final week of the tour was canceled, after which the play went to New York.

The touring production "played theatres that had been dark since Lotta Crabtree came out of the mining camps," said Robert Downing, an actor on the tour who later became the Lunts' stage manager. "They visited

* Harry Wagstaff Gribble's services were evidently not needed for the touring production. William Le Massena cannot recall Gribble's presence at any rehearsals. Lunt was in charge of the direction, with Fontanne closely watching the progress of the production and offering suggestions and comments to Lunt. Still, program credit for direction went to Gribble, as it had in 1935.

towns that had not seen a company of strolling players since Minnie Maddern Fiske took Ibsen to the sticks."

At some stops during the *Shrew* tour, the actors were not even provided with dressing rooms. In the Ryman Auditorium in Nashville, a converted tabernacle, everyone but the Lunts dressed in church pews; in another city Lunt had to duck into the alley behind the theatre to make quick
changes. In Austin, Texas, the actors made up in the theatre's boiler room.
Often, men and women were placed in the same large dressing room, at
which times Fontanne oversaw the hanging of bedsheets or curtains to
segregate the sexes.

Transportation problems also wreaked havoc during the tour, Alan
Hewitt recalled:

> Train delays often turned the crews' (and Mr. Lunt's) hair grey.
> In the fall of 1939, after two weeks in San Francisco, and a 1-
> nighter in Oakland, "The Shrew" was scheduled to play matinee
> and evening in Sacramento, but the baggage cars were late. The
> doors to the theater were opened to the public at 2 p.m., and
> they were allowed to watch the stage being set, with the curtain
> up. . . . The performance might have begun about 4 p.m. Later
> that same week, our train was delayed arriving at San Diego. We
> did not reach there until about 3:30 p.m. But the heroic crew
> got the show up in time for the announced 8:30 p.m. curtain.

Most performances were played before large, enthusiastic audiences,
who invariably delighted in the tarantella danced by the entire company
during curtain calls. On more than one occasion, the applause was so prolonged that the production was given more than twenty calls, leaving the
cast to hobble off stage gasping for breath.

The tour was extended in November 1939 to include additional performances in San Francisco. "It has been ever such an oasis in the desert,"
Fontanne wrote to Woollcott. "Will you believe it? We are selling out, and
with the *Shrew*, of all things. I'll never quite get over the wonder of a play
written three hundred years ago being a box-office wow. Thrilling,
isn't it?"

Christmas of 1939 saw the company in Fort Worth, Texas. Mary Martin, whose home was in Texas, joined the company for a holiday party at
the invitation of the Lunts, and was persuaded to sing for them. After a
large dinner, everyone in the group joined in song and danced together.
Later still, Robert Downing recalled, "Miss Fontanne gathered some of
her youngsters around her. She was radiant. She was with her company.
She was 'home for Christmas.' She looked into the shining faces. 'Isn't it
wonderful,' she said in that miraculous, liquid voice, 'when your dreams
come true?' " Downing thought at first that she was referring to the young
actors' dreams, but he later wondered if she weren't speaking of herself,
"the dreams of the stage-struck London girl who managed to audition for

Ellen Terry and to become, in her time, the greatest actress in the world."

Between matinee and evening performances on the tour, Fontanne would often return to her hotel room for a rest. Lunt, however, would generally go to see an early burlesque show. On one occasion, when all the men of the company planned to take in a burlesque show, the women argued that they should be included in the group. Fontanne was horrified and refused to permit it. Instead, she gave a tea party for the actresses while the men set off for their evening of burlesque.*

Lunt generally regarded himself as "one of the boys," although he did draw the line occasionally. During an evening in New Orleans, when most of the men went to a whorehouse to see "a circus"—two women and a man having sex on a large, circular, revolving bed—Lunt did not accompany them. But he was eager to hear the details from those who did attend.

In late 1939, Robert Downing began to write and edit a weekly company newsletter called *The Luntanne Tatler,* which he distributed to members of the company. The gratitude and warmth that most of the performers felt toward the Lunts was well expressed by Downing in the last issue of the *Tatler* in 1939:

> Many of us have enjoyed previous seasons with the Lunts. Like Moliere's company, the troupe of Alfred Lunt and Lynn Fontanne has become famous for retaining a group of players and presenting them in a series of productions. The soundness of their repertory policy is proven in the success of two fine artists, surrounded by the people they have especially chosen to support them. And those of us enjoying first seasons with the Lunts have learned what a magnificent experience it is to work with a company in which the spirit of professional cooperation is so strong, and the mutual estimation, one player for his fellow, is so justly and firmly established. Only the inspiration of people like our brilliant and sympathetic actor-managers could make all this possible.
>
> Any year with Alfred Lunt and Lynn Fontanne is certain to be rich and valuable and memorable to an actor, particularly a young actor, who discovers within the bounds of his small contributions to the perfected whole of a Lunt-Fontanne production, the existence of a school for self-training through the development of his faculties of observation and his capacities for learning and appreciation. 1939 was such a year for many of us, and . . . we trust that we may always be able to serve as best we can these people to whom we all owe so much.

*Fontanne always believed that a good cup of tea could help to make life more enjoyable. When the Lunts toured in *The Great Sebastians* in the 1950s, each of the actresses in the production was assigned to serve tea (with caviar) at 4:00 on a rotating basis. Peg Murray recalled that it was difficult to heat the tea to just the proper temperature and to find the right kind of caviar.

*   *   *

During their two seasons of touring, the Lunts traveled more than 34,000 miles and played to more than half a million people in more than sixty cities. By the end of the *Shrew* tour, the Lunts had played in nearly every state in America.

Lunt wrote a newspaper article in 1951 about his experiences on tour. Although "trains may be late, stages crowded, hotel rooms not up to promise," he said, the tours were "a glorious experience." Despite the discomforts, there was "the benefit to the actor in playing nightly to different types of audiences. What may be received with laughter and applause in Boston may find a different reception in Denver. All this makes for mental alertness, speedy adjustment of performance and creative clarity."

The Lunts felt an obligation to tour. As Donald Seawell explained, they felt obligated "to the playwright, to the play itself [and] to the investors to play on Broadway as long as it would run profitably and to tour America and to take it to London. If they didn't do that, they felt that they let their side down." But they also found it rewarding. Fontanne attributed much of the popularity of the Lunt-Fontanne team to their road tours. She felt that the stage, with its immediacy and reality, made audiences feel personally close to them. In 1978, shortly after Lunt died, she said to George Schaefer, "Do you know that when Alfred died, I had letters from almost everyone in America? Because we had been on the road and they had seen us."

It may not be too extravagant to say that the Lunts and a handful of other performers kept the legitimate theatre alive outside New York. In the late 1930s the American theatre was in serious decline in every big city except New York. Chicago's theatres, which had numbered sixteen before the onset of the Depression, had been reduced to four, Boston's from eight to three, Cincinnati's from three to one. Theatres everywhere were being converted to movie houses. Many of those that remained open were in use fewer than one hundred days a year, because of the shortage of road companies. In some large cities there were no legitimate theatres at all. Millions of people throughout the country had never seen a professional production of a play.

If the Lunts' tours did not reverse this trend, at least they helped to prevent it from worsening. When the Lunts or Helen Hayes or Katharine Cornell toured, it didn't matter whether they were playing in legitimate theatres, schoolhouses, municipal auditoriums or movie houses. People who otherwise would never have thought of seeing a play became avid theatregoers. Interest in the theatre was thus maintained, even if it could only occasionally be satisfied; and in the 1960s and '70s the regional theatre movement rekindled the interest that these performers had kept alive.

The Lunts' eventual goal was to establish their repertory theatre in New York as well as on tour. They had long been advocates of a permanent ensemble company playing in repertory. As early as 1930, Lunt wrote in an article for the New York *Times,*

> The present efforts in the theatre to create permanent and repertory companies are, it seems to me, splendid. . . . The opportunity to play continuously with the same group in a permanent company brings much harmony into a performance. A fine ensemble can be developed which will heighten the play's values and the author's intentions. It also eliminates, I think, the necessity which so many actors feel—that they must act their parts not for the good of the play but for the good of themselves. Under the system by which actors cast about for engagement after engagement they may instinctively work with the idea of making themselves conspicuous in order to obtain another part at the termination of the present play. Under the permanent company plan, with its attendant economic security, an actor can afford to act his part for the good of the play. Best of all, however, is the point that playing a variety of roles an actor must, of necessity, broaden, mature and purify whatever talent he may possess. . . .
>
> True repertory nurtures and encourages budding talent. It offers opportunities and a perpetual freshness which your young player will never find under the long-run system. It keeps a freshness in its performances, for although it isn't really necessary that a good performance should go stale, it often does. You can't say a rosary every night for seventy weeks and have it sound the same as it did the first time. Another great point in favor of a repertory company is that it acquaints players with many major items of dramatic literature. It brings them into a dazzling succession of new contacts and new roles, and if they are able and receptive, it is superb development.

In New York in the spring of 1940, the Lunts wanted to offer their "Festival of Comedy," including *Reunion in Vienna* as well as the four plays they had been giving on tour. Moreover, they hoped the project would continue in the years following, with plays to be added to the repertory annually. In 1939 they proposed a five-year plan to the Theatre Guild, suggesting that the organization be called the Lunt and Fontanne Repertory Company, its offerings to be sponsored by the Guild. The document they submitted stated, "The present plan is based upon the proposition that there is a fundamental artistic principle involved in repertory, but the experiences had by the various managements with repertory indicate that this can only be successful if it is based upon outstanding acting performances. The Guild, Lunt and Fontanne have been working for years in the development of a repertory, and it is believed that the splendid results achieved in all these years could be realized both artistically and financially by the formation of a Lunt-Fontanne Repertory Company managed by the Theatre Guild."

The second year of the repertory company would require additional plays. The Lunts suggested reviving *Arms and the Man, The Guardsman, Pygmalion, The Doctor's Dilemma* and *Strange Interlude.* In addition, they wanted to add productions of *He Who Gets Slapped, Much Ado About Nothing* (using Robert Edmond Jones's costumes but discarding his concept), *Macbeth* and *Hamlet.* The actors would be selected jointly by the Guild and the Lunts. The profits from the enterprise would be divided sixty percent to the Lunts and forty percent to the Guild.

Here was an opportunity to establish an American version of the Moscow Art Theatre or the Comédie Française: an organization in which many of the nation's best actors would be assembled to perform a repertory of the world's greatest plays.* Here, too, was the chance for the Lunts to appear in plays considered not commercially viable but perfectly appropriate in a repertory theatre.

The Guild studied the plan carefully, but its business manager, Warren Munsell, concluded that repertory could not survive in New York. The system would be prohibitively expensive, he pointed out. Playing in repertory necessitates hiring a sufficient number of actors to cover every role in the play with the largest cast. It also requires a theatre with an enormous amount of room backstage to store sets, props and costumes. Even if such a theatre were available in New York, the huge expenditures required by the system would have to be compensated by an extremely large seating capacity. Munsell concluded that no New York theatre combined the requisite seating capacity with the necessary backstage space, so the plan would have to be scrapped.

There can be fewer sadder moments in American cultural history than the failure to establish the Lunt and Fontanne Repertory Company. Such an organization might well have become the basis for an American national theatre. And Alfred Lunt would have been ideally suited to lead such a company by virtue of his extensive knowledge of acting, directing and theatrical management. Today, nearly fifty years later, there is still no national theatre in the United States, which stands alone among industrialized nations in its failure to establish such an institution. As a result, the finest American plays of the past are seldom performed by America's leading actors and directors, whereas the best plays of other nations are kept perpetually alive by the national theatres of those countries.

The Lunts' mistake was to recommend the establishment of a repertory theatre that would be self-supporting. As Warren Munsell pointed out, repertory is a hugely expensive venture. In order to sustain a repertory theatre, a generous subsidy would have to be provided, either by philan-

---

*The same basic plan is at the heart of England's National Theatre and Royal Shakespeare Company, but those companies did not exist in 1939.

thropists or (as in other nations) by the government in the form of funds raised by taxes. Perhaps the Lunts might have realized their goal had they been willing to lobby members of Congress and other elected officials to throw their support behind a federally funded national theatre. But that would have required all their energies, perhaps effectively ending their careers as performers, and they would almost certainly have been unwilling to make that sacrifice in 1939.

Then, too, 1939 was hardly the right time to appeal to Congress for financial support of a large-scale theatrical venture. The Federal Theatre, one of several projects established by the Works Progress Administration to reduce unemployment during the Depression, had been created in 1935 and had immediately been plunged into political controversy. The accusations leveled against the Federal Theatre—that it was mismanaged, Communist-oriented and staffed by incompetents—were almost totally untrue and unfair, but they took their political toll, and Congress withdrew its support of the project in 1939.

The notion of establishing a repertory company remained in the forefront of the Lunts' thinking, however. Several years later they broached the subject (on a somewhat smaller scale) to Robert E. Sherwood, hoping that the Playwrights' Company, of which he was a member, would be willing to underwrite the project. In 1942, Lunt wrote to Sherwood:

> Lynn has a very fine idea for next year and I think you should know of it—but please keep it under your hat because if you're not interested, we'll haul the idea around somewhere else—
>
> We would like to keep this company together (our seventh year!) and at the same time be able to present an entertainment both suitable for a big town or a training camp—and so Miss Lynnie suggests we do a series of one-act plays—with and without music. We've been reading "old ones" but I think we should do something new as well—one for Lynn, one for Dickie [Whorf], one for Sydney, one for me (all for one & one for all, you know) each actor eventually supporting the other—A repertory—in time—of say seven or eight plays—
>
> Would you and Elmer [Rice] and Berrie [S. N. Behrman] and Max [Anderson] be interested?* Maybe Moss [Hart] would do one or George [S. Kaufman] maybe—or Lindsay & Crouse—

Probably for the same reason the Theatre Guild declined to fund a repertory theatre, the Playwrights' Company was also forced to decline.

In later years the Lunts continued to hope that a permanent ensemble repertory theatre could be created. But after World War II the hope became more and more a futile dream. The actors who had performed with the

* Rice, Behrman and Anderson were Sherwood's partners in the Playwrights' Company.

Lunts for seven years had gone separate ways, the political system in America was as resistant as ever to providing tax support for the professional theatre, and the prospect of finding private funding was no better than before. Unfortunately, the real losers were not the Lunts but the American theatregoing public.

Chapter Eleven

THE WAR YEARS

Acting in *There Shall Be No Night* is "something like playing in *Uncle Tom's Cabin* before the Civil War."

Alfred Lunt

"We could not be at peace when they [the British] were fighting for their lives."

Lynn Fontanne

1940–43: The United States and Canada

The tour at an end, the Lunts had no plans or commitments beyond bringing their revival of *Taming of the Shrew* to the Alvin Theatre in New York, where it was scheduled to open on February 5, 1940, for a one-week run. For more than a year they had been discussing the possibility of appearing in a new play by the critic-turned-playwright Stark Young, but after the hectic schedule of the past several years they wanted nothing so much as a long rest. The next few years, however, turned out to be among the busiest and most eventful of their lives.

Until 1940 the Lunts generally maintained a studiously apolitical position.* Lunt strongly believed that actors should take no public political

---

*In 1933, George S. Kaufman used the example of Fontanne's life and career to make a political point when the House of Representatives passed a bill prohibiting American producers from "importing alien actors unless of distinguished merit and ability." On the surface, the bill's purpose was to protect American actors from foreign competition. Underneath, however, lay the real, xenophobic purpose of its sponsors: to add another restrictive measure to the immigration laws in order to keep America "pure."

When the Senate Immigration Subcommittee held hearings on the bill, Kaufman testified in opposition. He cited the example of Lynn Fontanne, "a timid, frightened girl who had not yet reached stardom when she came to this country from England," but who became one of the great actresses of the world. If the proposed law had been in effect in 1916, Kaufman pointed out, Fontanne would not have been able to perform in the United States.

stance, for their stature as performers tended to give undue—and therefore unreasonable—weight to their opinions.

The event that was to modify their view occurred in 1939, when Finland was invaded by the Soviets. By 1940, Lunt's "second home" was fighting desperately for its survival. Helen Hayes, chairman of the amusement division of the Finnish War Relief Fund, proposed to Lawrence Langner that the receipts from one performance of *Taming of the Shrew* be donated to the fund. Langner passed the proposal on to the Lunts, who said they wished to donate all the income from the entire *week's* engagement to Finnish War Relief. The Theatre Guild, the officers of Transatlantic Productions, the management of the Alvin Theatre and the other actors in the company all supported the gesture, and the Lunts, as well as other actors who could afford to do so, offered to waive their salaries.

Hayes also requested that other managements turn over the proceeds of a night's performance to Finnish War Relief. Her request—and the Lunts' acceptance of her suggestion—turned out to be unexpectedly controversial. Several Broadway producers categorically refused to consider the idea. Herman Shumlin, producer of two of the most successful plays in New York, *The Little Foxes* and *The Male Animal,* and Oscar Serlin, producer of the even more successful *Life with Father,* argued that charity should begin at home. If benefit performances were given, they said, the money should go to needy Americans rather than to Finns. Moreover, they contended that the benefits proposed by the Lunts were evidence of "war hysteria" and an "unneutral attitude."

Will Geer, who was playing Jeeter Lester in *Tobacco Road,* said he would refuse to perform if any of the money raised by his performance were to go to Finnish relief. Seven of the twenty-two actors in *The Time of Your Life* felt the same way, but said they would consent to play a benefit if the proceeds were given to American charities rather than to Finland.

Politics was obviously behind the uproar. Helen Hayes chose to couch her response strictly in terms of charity, however. "When you get in the habit of helping your fellow man," she said, "you don't stop to ask where he lives."

The growing menace of totalitarian oppression brought about the Lunts' greater participation in the political scene (but only in the broad sense; they still refused to endorse particular candidates). The invasion of Finland, they felt, could not be ignored. Despite their long-standing resistance to expressing political opinions, they could not turn away when asked to come to the aid of a small democratic nation under the threat of destruction by a totalitarian power.

In general, however, they still tended to keep their political views to themselves, a habit that led, in September 1940, to an acrimonious ex-

Kaufman's testimony helped to persuade the Senate committee to reject the bill. Fontanne herself never appeared before the committee.

change. The novelist and playwright Edna Ferber, certain that America would be involved in the war within six months, was trying to enlist celebrities to declare themselves Roosevelt supporters. She invited the Lunts to attend a lunch at Hyde Park and to endorse Roosevelt on a radio broadcast. Lunt replied that actors had no place in politics. Ferber responded, "Dear boy, it can't be done. There are no small quiet rooms without a view any more, except those intended for a last and permanent resting place." Still, the Lunts refused to take the public position that would, Ferber hoped, sway "the hundreds of thousands of people who have been stirred by you in your capacity as actors [and] would be impressed . . . by your names attached to any statement . . . that has to do with the support of Roosevelt." Lunt's opposition to Ferber's request became more determined, her irritation became more profound, until eventually they were barely speaking to one another.

Even as late as 1965, Fontanne publicly insisted, "I don't have any politics. I'm neither Republican nor a Democrat." In fact, however, the Lunts were committed Democrats who enthusiastically supported Franklin Roosevelt's policies. Fontanne's allegiance to the Democratic Party was expressed in 1940 during the tour of *There Shall Be No Night*, when there was a possibility that the company would be playing in Canada on the date of the American election. As Renée Orsell told the story, "A group of us, all very eager to vote, were discussing the problem and how to cope with it. Miss Fontanne turned to Mr. Lunt and said, 'Alfred, we could hire a bus to drive us down that day.' Then, with a wicked gleam in her eye, she glanced at Bill [Le Massena] and Charva Chester and me and added, 'We wouldn't have to take the Republicans.' "

Fontanne's naïveté was as evident as her partisanship. As Le Massena pointed out, "She didn't know anything about registration. She thought you'd just go over and pull a straw or drop a marble into a box or something." At any rate, the bus turned out to be unnecessary: the company was still playing on American soil on election day.

Fontanne's political views seem to have been based more on intuition and emotion than upon intellectual conviction or philosophical consistency. She supported the Conservatives in England with the same fervor with which she endorsed the Democrats in the United States. One reason she supported Roosevelt was loyalty to her friend Robert E. Sherwood, who functioned as a speechwriter in the Roosevelt administration. As Le Massena said, she "was interested in politics, but I don't think she knew too much about it. She was firmly committed to the idea of voting and democracy—as long as you voted for the right person."

The Lunts exchanged correspondence with the Roosevelts. After the 1940 election, in answer to the Lunts' letter of congratulations, the President sent them a personal reply, thanking them for "your thoughtfulness in sending us that nice message." They were even invited to attend the inauguration as representatives of the American theatre. Fontanne said, "We did intend to go because I am told, though I don't know how true it is, that it is the first time the theatre has been asked to be represented at an inauguration." But the Lunts were on tour with *There Shall Be No Night* at the time, and even so rare an invitation as this could not be allowed to take precedence over their commitment to a performance. "Unfortunately," Fontanne said, "we could not make connections from Chicago and back to Madison, where we were playing on Monday, and so had to refuse."

After they turned over the week's income from *The Taming of the Shrew* to Finnish War Relief, the Lunts evidenced the same generosity in connection with other causes. In September 1940 they donated a sizable check to the New York Guild for the Jewish Blind; in October they worked as volunteers at the Bundles for Britain warehouse, assisting in the preparation of a shipment of refugee clothing; in November they gave their salaries and the profits from a week's run of *There Shall Be No Night* to the Canadian Minister of Munitions and Transport, to be used toward the purchase of a Spitfire plane; and in December they contributed $900 to the British Ministry of Aircraft Production toward the purchase of military airplanes to aid Britain's fight against the Nazis. Their contribution was given on behalf of "the actors of the United States," they said. They also made substantial donations to the American Theatre Wing War Service, the English-Speaking Union (for war relief), the British Actors' Equity War Relief Fund, the USO and other organizations. And they made numerous speeches exhorting Americans to buy war bonds.

Beginning in 1940, Fontanne's letters regularly included political references. "You cannot be anti-British and anti-Roosevelt at this moment and still be pro-American," she wrote to Stark Young in December 1940, adding, "That belief is not derived from the place of my birth, but out of my true love for this country." Two years later she wrote, "I am a little tired of the griping and criticism" about Roosevelt's performance in office.

In March 1941, Fontanne became more directly involved in the political process. She wrote to Lunt's old mentor Margaret Anglin about Senator Gerald Nye, a prominent isolationist who supported a Neutrality Act that would embargo arms and munitions to countries engaged in war, thus harming the Allied cause. Her letter said, "If you disagree with Senator Nye, please telegraph your senator to that effect and get all those in sympathy to do the same. I read in his speech that he would like some telegrams and I think it would be nice to let him have some."

The Lunts' active support of the war effort led to their expressing their feelings on other issues as well. They supported critic Richard L. Coe of the Washington *Post*, for example, in his attempt to integrate the theatres of the nation's capital. As Coe said, "We wanted all Americans to be able to go to the theatre. We wanted more theatre and better theatre. It was a very simple matter, so we had no trouble agreeing about it."

In the 1950s they were confronted with the specter of McCarthyism when Lunt received a letter from a boyhood friend who had seen the Lunts perform in *I Know My Love*. A passionate anti-Communist, the former friend had given a speech in Los Angeles in which he spoke out against "the fifth column that operates within our borders, even in high places within the government [and who] needs to be uncovered and replaced." He asked Lunt to enlist in the ranks of those who were exposing the "betrayal" of the United States and to use his skill as a performer to portray heroic, God-fearing figures who might serve as role models for the American public. But Lunt had no sympathy for the anti-Communist hysteria that gripped the United States in the late 1940s and throughout the '50s.

On the contrary, the Lunts, although they did not express their views publicly, were firmly opposed to the practice of blacklisting in the entertainment world. During the run of *O Mistress Mine*, when an Equity meeting was called specifically to discuss the blacklisting issue, the Lunts declined to attend. Quietly, however, they did act upon their convictions. They hired John Randolph, a blacklisted actor, for their production of *The Visit* in 1958.

In New York the Lunts' revival of *Taming of the Shrew* was even more highly praised than their original production had been in 1935. "One of the most remarkable things about [the Lunts] is the enthusiasm they preserve about their work in the theatre," Brooks Atkinson said in his review. "They are never finished with anything they are doing. And their *Shrew* antic is a case in point. . . . [They] have raised the curtain with as much eagerness as though they had never staged *The Shrew* before."

Richard Lockridge, who said he had found the original production "a shade laborious," called the revival "quick, ribald and delightfully casual." Sidney J. Whipple's enthusiasm was unbounded; the production was "assuredly the most riotously funny performance of the venerable farce since the days of Shakespeare," he said.

Lunt gave a curtain speech following the opening performance, announcing that all of the evening's receipts, which amounted to $3,032, would go to the Finnish War Relief Fund. By the end of the week's engagement, that sum had grown to $23,287, with money from the sale of souvenir programs (sold by well-known performers in the lobby of the Alvin Theatre) and other donations bringing the total to more than $25,000. In addition to selling every seat throughout the engagement, each performance averaged more than one hundred standees. So great was the demand that the fire department had to limit the sale of standing-room tickets for the Saturday afternoon and evening performances.

The week's engagement over, the Lunts prepared to head home to

Genesee Depot for the long rest they had been looking forward to for months. Lunt had resigned from the Board of the Theatre Guild, primarily in order to divest himself of responsibilities so that he and Fontanne could devote themselves entirely to a lengthy vacation. "I feel I have not the time or energy to give it what I should," he wrote in his letter of resignation.

He told Maurice Zolotow that he had joined the Board in order "to find out about the financial side of the theatre," but his performing schedule prevented him from being present when finances were discussed.

> . . . the meetings would be called at half past four. I had to leave at a quarter of six. Well, they never came to a financial discussion until six o'clock, so I never did get to hear one bloody word of the financial side of the theatre except [that] which I just managed to pick up here and there and look over statements. I've always been interested in that side of the theatre, because I think it should always make money, and I always thought a production should never cost more than it [could] bring in. It's a cash business. . . . It's not that money is more important than the play, but I don't believe in a play going on unless it's sensibly financed. I see no reason for trim made out of oak, when if it were painted to look like oak, it would look like oak to the audience anyway. . . . A play that costs too much is something to be ashamed of. It's bad management, it's bad business.

One wonders if Lunt was aware of the irony in his complaint. Before he had become financially involved in the productions of the Theatre Guild, he had insisted that the Guild pay for the Lunts' elaborate costumes, regardless of the cost. But the perspective of the actor was clearly not that of the actor-manager.

Now free of responsibility to the Theatre Guild, the Lunts saw no impediment to their plan for an extended period of relaxation. Unbeknownst to them, however, Robert E. Sherwood had just completed a play that would change their plans completely.

The play derived from Sherwood's wish to write a drama about Finland's resistance to the invasion by Russia. From the beginning, he had the Lunts in mind for the leading roles, although he did not inform them that he was working on a new play for them. During the writing of the play, he often wrote letters to his wife in which he spoke of scenes and dialogue written "for Lynn and Alfred." He also asked Lunt to give him detailed information about Finland, a country whose history and customs Sherwood knew only superficially.

Sherwood set himself a deadline of February 10, 1940, to complete the second draft of his play, then called *Revelation*, because that was the day the Lunts' run in *The Taming of the Shrew* would end. He met his deadline precisely. At 5:15 he entered the Alvin Theatre, script in hand. When he gave the play to the Lunts, they made it clear they could not think of performing in a new play until they had had a long rest. Nevertheless, they agreed to take it with them on the train to Wisconsin and read it when they could.

Revelation deals with a Nobel Prize–winning Finnish scientist and pacifist, Kaarlo Valkonen, and his American wife, Miranda. During the course of the play, Finland is invaded by Russia and Dr. Valkonen's pacifism is put to the test. He comes to believe that the invaders must be forcibly resisted; that his pacifist principles must be suspended. Ultimately, Valkonen loses his life in defense of his country. For Sherwood, who had written *Idiot's Delight* as a plea for pacifism, the new play expressed the understanding that pacifism was of no use in resisting a determined and ruthless aggressor.

Moments after the train ride began, Lunt went to sleep and Fontanne began to leaf through Sherwood's play. Soon she was completely engrossed in it. She woke up her husband, insisting he read the play immediately. Suddenly, her weariness, her determination to rest, her longed-for vacation were forgotten.

At 3:00 a.m. the train stopped at Harrisburg, Pennsylvania, where Fontanne sent a telegram to Sherwood saying she was "wild" about the play and was ready to begin rehearsals immediately. "This half of the combination returns in two weeks for rehearsals," she said. Meanwhile, Lunt was becoming as excited as Fontanne. Later, in Chicago, he also sent a message to Sherwood. "So does this half," it said.

For the Lunts, whose concern for friends and relatives in Finland and in England was profound, and who believed that freedom in Europe could only be won if America joined the war on the side of the Allies, the play represented an opportunity to express their belief as they thought actors should express social convictions: through the characters and dialogue conceived by a first-rate playwright.

Two days later Lunt spoke to Sherwood by telephone from Genesee Depot. Not only did he and Fontanne wish to appear in the play, he said, he also wanted to direct it. He had even taken the liberty of asking Richard Whorf to design the sets. Whorf was on his way to Genesee Depot so that discussions could begin. Moreover, Lunt felt it important to open the play as soon as possible and proposed to do so in a mere five weeks' time, under the cosponsorship of the Theatre Guild and the Playwrights' Company.

Sherwood assented unhesitatingly. He made two trips to the Lunts' farm, during the second of which he was shown Whorf's preliminary sketches—some of them using the house at Genesee Depot as a model—which he and the Lunts agreed were excellent.

The Lunts reassembled many members of their acting company for the play, now retitled *There Shall Be No Night*. Whorf was featured in a prominent role, Sydney Greenstreet was asked to play Lunt's uncle, and William Le Massena, Thomas Gomez and Robert Downing were hired for supporting parts.

Several of the roles called for very young actors, which necessitated going outside the regular company. Nineteen-year-old Montgomery Clift played the pivotal role of the Valkonens' son. Phyllis Thaxter was told that she was cast in the role of the son's girl friend, Kaatri, but soon afterward an actress named Elisabeth Fraser, heading for an audition for another play, accidentally entered the theatre in which the Lunts were holding tryouts. Intrigued by her appearance, Lunt suggested that she read for *There Shall Be No Night*. He was so taken by her reading that he decided to give her the role of Kaatri and switch Thaxter to the smaller role of a maid. Realizing that Thaxter would be deeply upset, he offered to let her out of her contract when she arrived for the first rehearsal. "I was devastated," Thaxter said. "I went off to lunch by myself, crying over my chocolate milk, but, fortunately, when I came back I was smart enough to say yes, I would stay on." Thaxter elected to remain because of the benefits she would derive from observing the Lunts as they rehearsed the play. An added benefit, which she could not have foreseen, came the following year when Fontanne helped her win the leading role in the touring production of *Claudia*—the role that led directly to Thaxter's successful film career.*

One actor cast in *There Shall Be No Night* was fired by Lunt when he showed insensitivity to another performer, an attitude that Lunt could not abide. The actor was teasing Edward Raquello, who was playing the role of Major Rutkowski. During an early rehearsal the actor giggled and tittered whenever Raquello appeared on stage. Lunt flew into a rage, furious that any actor should make another's job more difficult. "Don't ever come in my view again!" he screamed. "I never want to see you again. Go away!" Lunt left the theatre to work off his fury by himself. Fontanne gathered the cast together, saying, "Now, we'll just go on with the rehearsal. We'll just take it from where we were, and Alfred will be back." He did return, of course, but only after suffering a bout of vomiting and a painful headache.

The first rehearsal demonstrated to Sherwood just how much still needed to be done, and he confided his feelings about the play to his diary:

---

*In August 1941, Thaxter was understudying Dorothy McGuire in *Claudia* in New York. The producer, John Golden, was considering casting Thaxter in the role for the road company, but was apprehensive because of her inexperience. When Fontanne learned that Thaxter was under consideration she called Golden to ask if she could be present when the audition was held. Golden replied that the reading was to be that very afternoon, and he invited Fontanne to watch. Thaxter did not know that Fontanne was out front until someone came backstage to prepare tea with honey, Fontanne's favorite drink. The reading went well, and Golden was encouraged, but still not persuaded that Thaxter should be given the role. Consequently, he arranged for her to play the next day's matinee in place of McGuire. Before that performance Fontanne invited Thaxter to the Lunts' apartment, where the two of them went over the role together, Fontanne offering several ideas that Thaxter said were "invaluable." At the matinee, Fontanne wrote to William Le Massena, "On one of her exits, she got a round of applause that the other Claudia never got." Golden then turned to Fontanne and said, "She plays the part. I'll let her have it." Fontanne told Le Massena, "I was terribly pleased and Phyllis, of course, ecstatic. Alfred and I are both so happy about it all. We feel as if we are running a preparatory school for the stage."

"Very sloppy. This is the first time I have heard it through or even read through. Awful repetition." He added, "Lynn wonderful, & Alfred." Two days later he noted, more optimistically, "Alfred is directing it exquisitely. It looks really lovely."

Fontanne had recommended changes to be incorporated into *Idiot's Delight,* and now she did so again, suggesting the ending of the third scene of *There Shall Be No Night.* Her idea was to include some dialogue about the coffee Mrs. Valkonen had made and which had cooled off. The dialogue that resulted from her suggestion seems unimpressive, almost superfluous, but Sherwood wrote it because, as John F. Wharton, the counsel to the Playwrights' Company, put it, "he knew that the Lunts would somehow make a discussion of coffee the climax of a moving reconciliation of husband and wife. It did."

As was so often the case with Lunt, he began work on his role by basing the characterization on a specific individual. Lunt took Thomas Mann, the German novelist, as his model for Dr. Valkonen. He had never met Mann, but, Fontanne explained, "Mann is a family man and a sort of scientist, and Alfred thinks he is probably very . . . like Dr. Valkonen." Later, however, after thousands of details had been added to the characterization and irrelevancies stripped away, the final product often bore little resemblance to the initial image, except in terms of Lunt's makeup. Four photographs of Mann were placed in Lunt's dressing room and the actor studied them each night as he applied his makeup, parting his hair and combing his mustache as Mann did. He also persuaded Sydney Greenstreet to make up to resemble Lunt's uncle, "except," he said, "my uncle had a beard and Sydney had an allergy to hair makeup and wouldn't wear a wig."

Now forty-seven and fifty-two respectively, Lunt and Fontanne more than ever assumed the roles of surrogate parents to the young members of the cast. Clift, Thaxter and Fraser were all in awe of the Lunts, who took special interest in their development as actors and as individuals. Clift, in fact, assumed many of Lunt's vocal and physical mannerisms during rehearsals and early performances. Eventually, Clift developed a distinctive manner of his own, but his early career was marked by a continual tendency to return to an imitation of Lunt's acting style.

The Lunts became so fond of Clift that they gave him a picture of themselves, inscribing it, "From your *real* mother and father." They often invited him to their apartment for dinner; Clift accompanied Lunt to his favorite burlesque shows; the Lunts selected plays for Clift to read in order to broaden his knowledge of dramatic literature; and they encouraged him to devote his career not to money or to fame, but to performing in work of the highest quality, as they had done.*

* In later years Clift always acknowledged his debt to the Lunts and their influence upon his acting. "Alfred taught me how to select," he was quoted as saying. "Acting is an accu-

The production opened in Providence on March 29, 1940, then moved on to Boston, Baltimore and Washington. Everywhere the verdict was the same: the play was stirring, the performances magnificent.

The New York opening was equally successful, the audience rewarding the company by calling them back for twenty curtain calls. Atkinson was correct when he said Sherwood's play was "no masterpiece," a ramshackle work that "does not hang together particularly well." But the Lunts' performances infused it with majesty and heartbreaking poignancy. As John Anderson pointed out, "The coherence of the whole performance and the sensitiveness of the acting throughout contribute greatly to the emotional value of the play, and give it a direct impact which the script does not always create."

For many years the Lunts had been regarded as great artists, but their performances in Sherwood's play moved observers to new heights of praise. Rosamond Gilder, writing in *Theatre Arts,* said, "Alfred Lunt and Lynn Fontanne as Dr. and Mrs. Valkonen give the most deeply moving performances of their joint career. Stripping away all superficial mannerisms, they play with a simplicity and directness that cuts to the heart of the issues they present."

Eleanor Roosevelt saw a performance and was deeply moved, calling it "an experience I shall never forget." She wrote in her newspaper column, "My Day":

> Robert E. Sherwood has written a remarkable play in *There Shall Be No Night*. Of course, Alfred Lunt and Lynn Fontanne give a performance so perfect that I felt I was living in this portrayal on the stage. The rest of the cast is so good that we finished the evening feeling that we had actually been through every experience in that Finnish family's existence, which tragically enough, is now part of the life of so many other people. May God grant that if such dark hours should ever come to us, we may acquit ourselves as well!

The theme of *There Shall Be No Night*—that one cannot remain uninvolved when threatened by oppression—was enormously controversial in 1940. Many Americans believed their country should become an active participant in the war in Europe, but millions wanted to avoid thinking about the problem in hopes that it would disappear. To see *There Shall Be No Night* was such a searing emotional experience, however, that it forced the issue into the open. It served to persuade some that aggression must be countered with active resistance.

For others, however, the play was anathema. The Communist *Daily Worker* called Sherwood "the stooge of the imperialist war mongers." A

---

mulation of subtle details. And the details of Alfred Lunt's performances were like the observations of a great novelist. . . ."

nationally syndicated columnist accused the playwright of cynically trying to exploit the attitude of American citizens sympathetic to Finland by turning it into militaristic fervor. A Washington columnist named Raymond Clapper branded the play "a rank, inflammatory job, pleading for intervention." The New York *Daily Mirror* vilified Sherwood's drama. An organization called the Theatre Arts Committee picketed the play, passing out leaflets headlined, "Warmongers Capture Alvin Theatre," and calling the drama "a weapon pointed straight at the hearts of the American people." The Committee asked audience members to sign peace petitions addressed to President Roosevelt. In the columns of the New York *Times,* Sherwood replied to the controversy his play had aroused:

> When I started to write this play, I had come to the conclusion that the isolationists were leading us into a position of really awful peril for this country. I certainly do not say in this play or anywhere else that we should plunge into this war with full force. . . . We should renounce neutrality or rather take the view that we are not neutral but that we are also not at war. I believe we have the power to shorten this war and save incalculable wastage of lives and money for ourselves and others, Germany included, if we will now express our obviously partisan interests in terms of definite action. And I don't mean military intervention . . . I mean joining the economic blockade, East and West. . . .
>
> If we wait until the Allies are obviously losing, and Russia, Japan and Italy jump in with full force, then this country will be in an appallingly perilous situation.

During the six-month run of *There Shall Be No Night,* Lunt gave a number of curtain speeches supporting the ideas expressed in the play. In July 1940 the Lunts further broke their own rule against taking public social positions by participating in a radio broadcast for the benefit of the Red Cross. They read a scene from the play, followed by Lunt's statement, "Giving these performances isn't just a generous gesture. It's something that we can't help doing."

The play received the Pulitzer Prize in May 1941, and Lunt was given the New York Drama Critics' Award (shared with Barry Fitzgerald in *Juno and the Paycock*) for the best male performance of the year. Fontanne said as late as 1978 that she regarded *There Shall Be No Night* as the high point of her career.

While Sherwood's play was running in New York, Germany invaded France, Holland and Belgium. The drama's message seemed to gain in significance with each passing day. As Brooks Atkinson said, what might once have seemed alarmist had become "an understatement of realities now." Sherwood told the Lunts and the coproducers he believed the play should be toured throughout the country despite the fact that it was still selling out in New York.

The Lunts thus set out in November 1940 on a tour that covered 12,000 miles, visiting forty-six cities in nineteen states, plus two Canadian provinces, always playing to capacity houses.

When the Lunts' train was passing through Vermont on its way to Canada, Alexander Woollcott met it at the railroad station near Bomoseen, bringing cider and doughnuts for the entire company. But, he told Graham Robertson, "if there is a troupe in the world that doesn't need feeding it's that one. Nor cheering, either. At least Lynn and Alfred feel as never before that they are engaged in something worth doing. This play lets them say every night what is in their hearts so that nightly they are refreshed and renewed."

Woollcott recalled that when he saw the Lunts' production of *The Sea Gull* before its first costume rehearsal, he had believed he would never again be so moved by a performance. But "There is that in the Sherwood play and the way they feel about it that somehow maintains that quality week after week, month after month, city after city," he wrote to Robertson. Woollcott did not see *There Shall Be No Night* until late in its New York run. "I had thought myself quite safe emotionally as it went along," he said, "and was the more unprepared, on my way backstage, for the sudden and violent need of privacy. I bolted for the nearest covert which turned out to be Lynn's dressing-room. She tactfully shooed people out so that I might have a little decent quiet for a good cry."

The mail the Lunts received during the tour indicated how deeply the play spoke to its audiences. "Nobody could come out of that theatre and still be afraid," said one letter. Another claimed, "I walked out of the theatre feeling somehow braver and stronger." Still another said, "You have given us something to hope for in these frightening times." Lawrence Langner wrote, "Wherever it was played, it stirred the audiences to an affirmative belief in democracy, and a determination to maintain what they had against totalitarian tyranny."

Some efforts were made by those who favored American neutrality to sabotage the play. One newspaper, opposed to the drama's expressed views, gave the play the silent treatment, refusing to accept advertisements for the production and not allowing the name of the play to appear in its pages. This led to a problem when the paper had to cover a story about Robert E. Sherwood in a completely different context. The newspaper's "solution" was to refer to Sherwood as "the author of *Idiot's Delight.*"

There Shall Be No Night was picketed in Philadelphia, but the controversy swelled the size of the audience rather than reducing it. The entire company was energized by the excitement. Lunt told the Philadelphia *Record*, "Lynn never used to read the papers. Now she reads them all—every word. The whole company's infected. . . . [The play], they say, gives them a definite sense of taking part in world events. It's something like playing in *Uncle Tom's Cabin* before the Civil War."

In Chicago, which Lunt told Sherwood was "notoriously anti-war, and I believe to a great extent anti-British," some of the reviews were less than enthusiastic. Again, however, attendance was not affected.

A more serious effort to disrupt the tour occurred when letters were sent to the drama critics of the Washington *Post* and the *Evening Star,* ostensibly from Genesee Depot. The letters read,

> My dear friend,
> I find that I must ask a favor of you, and, if you can do this favor, it would help all of us.
> When our show "There Shall Be No Night" comes to Washington, would it be asking too much to just forget writing a review? Or if you can't do that, just give us a very small notice—an unfavorable one. Of course, I would want you to consult your managing editor about this.
> I trust that you will understand my feelings in this matter as we are not at all eager to continue in this play. There are certain obligations which I cannot explain, and I am truly sorry that I cannot offer them to you, as this play will not do for us.
> If you can do this favor it will mean so much, and I thought it kinder to give you my honest opinion. I shall be very grateful.
> Yours sincerely,
> Lynn Fontanne

Fortunately, no one at either newspaper was taken in. Richard L. Coe, the critic for the *Post,* sent a telegram to Fontanne asking if she had written the letter. Harry MacArthur of the *Evening Star* also wired, asking, "IS THIS LETTER OSTENSIBLY FROM YOU REALLY [sic] OR IS IT SABOTAGE?" The Lunts replied, of course, that Fontanne had not written the letters.

Such efforts, aimed at maintaining American neutrality, failed largely because public opinion in the United States was inclining strongly toward the Allies. This growing sympathy could be seen in the response to Fontanne's several readings of Alice Duer Miller's *The White Cliffs.* In October 1940 she was persuaded to read the poem on the radio, and her reading was repeated by popular demand two weeks later. Then, during an off day in *There Shall Be No Night*'s Chicago engagement in January 1941, the Lunts traveled to Cleveland so that Fontanne could read the poem with the Cleveland Orchestra. The event raised $5,000 for the British War Relief Society. Still again the reading was repeated, this time for Canadian audiences when the Lunts were in Vancouver in February. The broadcast was considered to be of such importance that all other radio programming was suspended during the half-hour reading. In that same year a three-record set of Fontanne's reading, accompanied by music written by Frank Black and conducted by Arthur Lang, was issued by Victor Records. Fontanne gave all the money earned by the recording to the British War Relief Society.*

* Phyllis Thaxter vividly recalls the evening after a performance when she and Mont-

In Canada the Lunts also broadcast a scene from *There Shall Be No Night* at the request of the Director of Public Information, G. H. Lash, who asked them to help "awaken our people to what the threat . . . of a possible victory by the totalitarian powers . . . means to our democratic way of living." The Lunts were invited to visit with the speaker of the Canadian House of Commons, were given a reception by the lieutenant governor and, most rewarding of all, Premier Mackenzie King told them privately that the production of *There Shall Be No Night* marked a turning point in Canadian-American relations. The play had given him the courage to initiate a serious dialogue with Washington concerning the likelihood of war, he said. In Fontanne's words, "He wanted to say exactly what he thought about how [the United States and Canada] could cooperate in the crisis. But he was using the guarded terms of diplomacy which means so little or so much according to what one wishes to make of them. When he saw *There Shall Be No Night* he decided to give up these phrases and come down to the statements that anybody could understand. He told us this himself."

The tour took a hiatus on May 3, 1941. The Lunts originally planned to make a film of *There Shall Be No Night* during the summer, but, as Fontanne wrote to Alexander Woollcott, "we have been thinking a great deal about that and came to the conclusion about the same time as Bob [Sherwood] that the movie would in all probability be cut to pieces like his 'Abe Lincoln in Illinois' was and so render the purpose of our doing it useless." Instead, they decided to close the production for the summer* and begin another tour in the fall, primarily playing one-night stands in the South and the Midwest. The intention was to tour the play until February 7, 1942, then to reopen it on Broadway.

---

gomery Clift were leaving the theatre together, "and all of a sudden we heard, 'I have loved England dearly and deeply,' and there was Miss Fontanne on stage, and Mr. Lunt was sitting there. They were sitting at a work table with a worklight overhead. And I remember she had a big black hat with quite a wide brim and this gorgeous face underneath it. . . . And we sat up on the fire escape stairs and listened to her rehearse *The White Cliffs*. We heard it all right there and we were thrilled."

*The Lunts' vacation was much briefer than that of the other members of their company, however. Lunt directed *Candle in the Wind* by Maxwell Anderson, an anti-Fascist play set in occupied France. Starring Helen Hayes, the play was rehearsed during the summer and opened in New York on October 22, 1941. Lunt was unable to bring a weak script to life, and the play went on tour after only ninety-five performances. It marked the first occasion that Lunt directed a play in which he and Fontanne did not appear. He contributed fifty percent of his earnings ($1,000 plus two percent of the gross box-office receipts during the run of the play) to the Actors' Fund. Fontanne summed up the reasons for the play's failure from her perspective in a letter she wrote to Noël Coward. She said bitterly that *Candle in the Wind* had "flopped and the awful part of it is that it need not have. It was an excellent script. It needed a little toning down here and there. . . .Alfred made various suggestions to Max and I made one that everybody thought was good, but Max simply could not write it. He seemed plunged into a sort of elephantine lethargy—nearly drove Alfred insane—and then finally did nothing at all. The minute Alfred's back was turned . . . they [the managers of the Theatre Guild and the Playwrights' Company, who coproduced the play] did some rearranging to his direction, took themselves into New York and had a terrible flop and served them damned well right."

Before leaving Genesee Depot, the Lunts observed their nineteenth wedding anniversary. As Fontanne wrote to Woollcott:

we are quite worn out with celebrating. . . . First of all, Alfred made a mistake and got it three days earlier. He planned a surprise dinner for me, and I planned a surprise bottle of Château Yquem. We drank it all and woke up the next day with rather a headache (had been on the wagon for three weeks) when we heard, to our surprise, over the radio that it was our nineteenth wedding day again, so we celebrated again that night, and the next day old Louise's [their former cook's] letter came . . . to say that everyone was mistaken and it was that day, the twenty-sixth. So we celebrated again that night and God knows, I hope we were right as I have no more strength left.

The tour of *There Shall Be No Night* resumed in October, but it came to an abrupt conclusion before the year was out. The political situation had undergone a drastic change when Hitler attacked the Soviet Union in June 1941 and the Soviets entered the war on the Allied side. Another international development that stunned the world occurred when Finland became a Nazi ally that same year. The turn of events seemed to render the play meaningless, and the Playwrights' Company issued a statement saying, "In view of the current world situation that finds Finland enrolled, reluctantly enrolled in all likelihood, but nevertheless enlisted as an ally of the Axis powers, the best interests of this country would be served through the termination of the tour." Sherwood asked the Lunts to end the tour in mid-December, soon after the bombing of Pearl Harbor. Fontanne was not surprised. She had written to a friend, "I am afraid [the play's] day is over now . . . but it did a magnificent job while it lasted." The last performance in America was given on December 18, 1941, in Rochester, Minnesota.

The Lunts were determined to continue supporting the Allied war effort. Before there was any hint that *There Shall Be No Night* would close prematurely, Lunt had written to Robert E. Sherwood asking, "Would it be possible do you think to troupe this through some of the army camps when we close? Jo Mielziner might rig up some trick platform & curtains & we could go by truck & bus—Soldiers are nuts about this play & they're getting such lousy entertainment—it might be nice if we could help out —" That plan did not materialize, but the Lunts continued to look for a vehicle that would be suitable for touring to army camps. Fontanne told Noël Coward that she and her husband "want to do an hilarious comedy next but, even better, a musical—a revue. We could do all the sketches, *talk* the songs—take it on a grand tour (if this one doesn't kill us— 16 weeks of one night stands!), spot all the camps and naval bases. It's a good idea, isn't it?"

That comedy turned out to be *The Pirate,* a play with music that was not quite a musical, but was eventually turned into an MGM musical film with Judy Garland and Gene Kelly and songs by Cole Porter. In the Lunts' version there were no songs, but music was integral to the production, establishing the mood for each scene and providing several dances. It was twenty-five years since Lunt had played in Ludwig Fulda's original version of *The Pirate* in summer stock in Milwaukee. Early in 1942 he asked S. N. Behrman to revise the play for a new production, to feature color, romance and spectacle. Behrman, always pleased to write for the Lunts, began work immediately.

Behrman's version was not ready to go into rehearsal until August, but the Lunts were hardly idle. They were featured on several radio programs in 1942, including "The Cavalcade of America," on which Lunt appeared in *The Gentleman from the Islands,* a drama about the last days of Alexander Hamilton. More significant than any performance, however, was the opening by the American Theatre Wing of the Stage Door Canteen on March 1, 1942.

The Canteen, located in the basement of the 44th Street Theatre, was established to provide free food and entertainment for servicemen of all Allied countries. Most of the New York theatrical community was involved in the venture. Scene designers decorated the Canteen, actresses volunteered to serve as hostesses, food and coffee were donated by bakers, caterers and restaurant owners. Entertainers of all kinds, including Al Jolson, Ethel Merman, Ethel Waters and Gracie Fields, performed without charge. The menial jobs—washing trays, sweeping the floors—were taken over by actors, stagehands, directors and musicians—1,700 in all—who worked on a rotating basis. The Canteen was open from 6:00 until midnight every night of the week until the end of the war.

The expectation of the American Theatre Wing had been that some 500 servicemen per night would patronize the Stage Door Canteen. But the average turned out to be 3,000 to 4,000 nightly, keeping the unpaid staff hopping. Of all the menial workers, none worked harder than Alfred Lunt and Lynn Fontanne, whose jobs ranged from talking to servicemen to making sandwiches and washing trays, and—Lunt's specialty—emptying garbage cans. "He's the only man who succeeded in putting glamour into garbage," Katharine Cornell said.* The Lunts' activities at the Canteen were parodied in a sketch in Irving Berlin's *This Is the Army.* When the couple went to see the show, Fontanne told Woollcott, "That darling Irving was nice enough to come out during the first interval [intermission] and find us to warn us about the imitation and hoping that we wouldn't mind. *Mind, Mind*—we have naturally never been so honored in our lives."

* Alexander Woollcott called Lunt "the chief cook and bottle washer of the American Theatre Wing" and asked him, "Why 'Wing,' by the way?" The answer was that the word had a double meaning, referring both to the backstage space in a theatre and to the tactical unit of the Army Air Force. Lunt regarded his participation in the activities of the American Theatre Wing as the next best thing to joining the service. He wanted to join, he said, "and Lynn was all for it, but there is my age." Lunt turned fifty in August 1942.

Lunt was already recognized among his friends as an accomplished gourmet cook. Thus, the Theatre Wing asked him to conduct a series of cooking classes—six lessons for ten dollars—for the benefit of the Stage Door Canteen. The emphasis was to be on the preparation of simple meals, since many ingredients were not available during wartime. Lunt was terrified. He had always cooked "by ear," he said, and he wasn't at all sure he could teach his method to anyone in an organized way. Nevertheless, he was willing to try.

Fontanne maintained that Lunt was more nervous about his cooking classes than he was before an opening night. He lay awake the night before each class, she said, going over and over his recipes and his plan of instruction.

The first class was offered in April 1942 in the offices of the Theatre Wing at 730 Fifth Avenue. Lunt wore a white chef's apron and cap while teaching his forty-seven students, among whom were Antoinette Perry, Mrs. William Randolph Hearst, Armina Marshall, Peggy Wood, John Mason Brown, Mrs. Somerset Maugham, Nedda Harrigan and Lunt's sister Karin Bugbee. He demonstrated his skill at preparing Sunday breakfast, including scrambled eggs, fish, bacon, potatoes and fruit. The coffee was an unexpected disaster, however. Although Lunt was proudest of his recipe for coffee and always insisted that the cooks who worked for him make coffee to his precise specifications, something went drastically wrong that morning. Taking a sip, he announced, "This is the lousiest coffee I've ever tasted." But he offered a handy excuse. Pointing to the small stove provided for his use in the class, he said that the fire under the coffee had gone out right in the middle of the brewing process.*

After the first class, a number of the "students" remained to sample Lunt's cooking, eagerly devouring the Sunday breakfast. "The food was delicious," said Nedda Harrigan.

The cooking classes—two per week for five weeks—monopolized Lunt's time so completely that he was forced to give up his duties at the Stage Door Canteen temporarily. For Fontanne, however, "The Canteen is my pride and joy and the center of my life," as she told Woollcott on April 24.

*Lunt's recipe for coffee, courtesy of Carolyn Every, who cooked for him in the early 1930s: "Hills Brothers regular grind coffee and a granite open coffee pot. For 8 cups of coffee, in a bowl put 8 large tablespoons of coffee, plus one for the pot. Break a fresh egg into the coffee grounds, add cold water to moisten, mix well. Measure 8 cups cold tap water into coffee pot, bring to full boil. As soon as water boils, put coffee-egg mixture into pot and immediately stir with a long-handled spoon. The mixture will foam up; you are to continue stirring while you remove pot from the heat until foam is stirred down. Let it remain at very low simmer for 7 minutes. Put cover on pot, plug the spout with paper so as not to lose any fragrance. *Never let it boil!* The coffee you pour from the pot into your cup should be clear, and as Hattie [Sederholm] said, the same brown color as a new saddle." Fontanne's recipe for tea was equally precise. She told Alexander Woollcott, "It must be strong enough, and the way to do it is to warm the pot first, then fill an ordinary strainer, flat level, with tea, then pour boiling water, practically drip-by-drip—anyway, a very thin stream should run through, let it play all over the tea until the pot is about three-quarters full."

Lunt's fascination with cooking, begun when he tried to entice Fontanne to put on some weight at the time of their marriage, became his greatest passion outside the theatre and the building and decoration of his home in Genesee Depot. He loved to plan a meal, from first course to last, and to spend a full day in the kitchen preparing it. As he served the food, he carefully watched the faces of his guests for their reactions. "Eating one of Alfred's dishes in front of him is like writing a piece with an editor looking over your shoulder," said S. N. Behrman. Compliments elated him as much as if he had given a brilliant performance, but the merest hint that any dish was less than excellent sank him into the deepest depression.

His specialties included fiskeboller (Norwegian fish balls); creamed baked potatoes; cardamom coffee bread; clam chowder; And the Priest Fainted (an English adaptation of a Turkish dish, Imam Bayildi, containing a blend of eggplant, celery, onions and "a tremendous amount of garlic"); scrambled eggs (combined with tomatoes, onions, chili sauce and Madeira); chicken livers with curry; broiled filet of sole; turkey with a dry, simple stuffing made of a mixture of bread crumbs and butter, onion and sage; an elaborate dessert made of French ice cream in a coating of raspberry ice, under a sauce comprised of fresh crushed strawberries, Cointreau, grated orange peel and sugar; and Robert E. Sherwood's favorite, a combination of lamb, rice, mushrooms and bacon. Lunt was particularly knowledgeable about Scandinavian and German cooking—to which he added a familiarity with French cuisine when he studied at the Cordon Bleu in Paris in 1958.

There was no stopping Lunt when he wanted to acquire a recipe. It was not unusual for him to excuse himself in the midst of a dinner party at someone's home. After fifteen minutes or so, the host or hostess would remark on his extended absence. "Have you looked in the kitchen?" Fontanne would ask. Invariably, that is where Lunt would be found, writing down recipes as quickly as the cook could provide them.

He was equally persistent in tracking down ingredients. When a visitor from New York was invited to Genesee Depot, he was likely to be asked to pick up some spices before beginning the trip. "Can you bring me a *very small* amount of *powdered* fennel & a tiny amount of annis *(powdered)*," he wrote to William Le Massena before one visit.

Members of the Lunts' acting company always looked forward to playing in Milwaukee, for they often received an invitation to dine at Genesee Depot, where Lunt would spend the day preparing an elaborate meal.

Lunt was asked by publishers to write a cookbook comprised of the recipes he had collected. After many years of agonizing, he did assemble the book, intending to give the proceeds to the American Theatre Wing, but he was not satisfied with the result and he and Fontanne eventually decided not to publish it. Many of his recipes were printed, however, in such magazines as *Vogue, Collier's, McCall's, Ladies' Home Journal* and *Better Homes and Gardens*.

Lunt also took pride in his wife's cooking, although her range was far more limited than his. Visitors to Genesee Depot might be discussing the arts or another subject far removed from cooking when Lunt would suddenly ask, "Do you care for trifle?" If anyone answered "Yes," Lunt's face would crease in an enormous grin. "There you are, Lynn, this is your moment," his friend Peter Daubeny quoted him as saying. "All my life I've failed to make a decent trifle. But Lynn's—ah, there's a masterpiece!" Fontanne, smiling beatifically, would then take out her pencil and schedule book and ask her guests when they would like to sample her trifle.

The war brought out the Lunts' most generous instincts, and their generosity was already legendary. When Richard Whorf needed $500 to join the scene designers' union, Fontanne gave him the entire amount one Christmas. When the Lunts' maid married their chauffeur, the Lunts gave them an all-expenses-paid honeymoon including the use of their New York apartment for two weeks.

Their generosity extended to nonfinancial matters, as well. In 1940, Laurence Olivier and Vivien Leigh performed together in *Romeo and Juliet*. They were also living together despite being still married to others, a circumstance many regarded as outrageous. Their stay in New York was painful: the critics savaged *Romeo and Juliet,* and many old friends ignored them socially. During their New York visit, said Olivier, "We were not asked out to supper except by, of all people, the Lunts—just the four of us, rather a grand do with a white tie; it was kindly calculated to keep us looking *persona grata*." The Lunts kept up a flow of conversation throughout the meal, never mentioning or referring to Olivier's and Leigh's personal life. "I have never known such a supreme example of beautiful manners," said Olivier. "I would never know anyone within light-years of their generosity."

Cathleen Nesbitt, who visited the Lunts at Genesee Depot one Christmas, had no formal clothes to wear when the Lunts decided to dress to the teeth for dinner. Fontanne solved the problem by lending her a beautiful coral-colored designer gown. The next day, when Nesbitt tried to return the dress, Fontanne refused to take it, saying, "Alfred and I have decided that it suits you so well that you *must* have it."

Fontanne was friendly with the British actress Madge Titheradge, who was forced to retire from the stage when she developed severe rheumatoid arthritis. Some years afterward the hormone ACTH was discovered to ameliorate the symptoms of arthritis. Fontanne called her doctor, Edward Bigg, and asked if she could purchase some of the hormone for her friend. She was told that ACTH was still experimental, very difficult to obtain and extremely expensive. Fontanne told him she would pay any price if he could send ACTH to Titheradge's physician in England. A quantity of the hormone was subsequently obtained and sent to the stricken actress.

The Lunts were often equally generous to those outside their circle of close friends. Cathleen Nesbitt told of an actor who had performed minor roles with the Lunts, but who had been ill and down on his luck. "I was shuffling along Madison Avenue, feeling kind of sorry for myself," she quoted him as saying, "and suddenly there was Miss Lynnie tapping me on the arm and saying 'You don't look too well' and I said I didn't *feel* too well, and it ended up with her saying 'we are just going back to Genesee, come and stay there for a week.' I just couldn't believe it, it seemed like a beautiful dream. And all the time I was there, I was treated like I *was* somebody . . . they were like that with all of us in the company—big featured players—bit parts, stage managers, just all one family. You know I got back to New York and I was walking on air and singing, 'Everything's going my way.' "

Many actors who had worked with the Lunts found that they were regarded as members of the family forever after. Often when one of them was in financial distress the Lunts would lend him money and then forgive the loan. They were equally loyal to stagehands with whom they established a good working relationship. When Donald Seawell was producing plays for the Lunts, he was always reminded by Lunt to "be sure and hire so-and-so as the head carpenter and so-and-so as the electrician."

When *Amphitryon 38* was touring in 1938–39, the Lunts divided their share of the profits with the members of their company. They did so again with the profits of *There Shall Be No Night* in 1940. A number of the actors in their companies told me that no other management in their experience had shared the profits of a production with the performers.

During and immediately after World War II, the Lunts seemed to take it upon themselves to try to feed and clothe all their friends in Europe. To Jane and Wilfred de Glehn, for whom Fontanne had posed many years earlier as an aspiring actress in London, they sent canned chicken, "packages with beef drippings and lard and cooking things for the kitchen which I know you so sadly need." They sent stockings and a box of watercolors and brushes for Lady Juliet Duff, bedsheets for Terence Rattigan, clam chowder for Fryn Harwood. They sent the money for plane fare to and from America to Fontanne's sister Antoinette Keith in 1946, adding a pressure cooker, liver pills, a thermos and a hot-water bag for good measure.

To her other sister, Mai Potiki, who was living in New Zealand, Fontanne sent money so that Mai could mail hampers of foodstuffs to the Lunts' friends in England. She also sent Mai a miscellany of gifts: four pounds of tea, a comb-and-brush set, bedsheets—and she asked Antoinette to find out "if Mai wears an uplift brassiere. She ought to, as it will pop her bosom out, which will belittle her waist and produce a very nice line. If she hasn't got a good one, I will send her one."

The Lunts themselves, it should be noted, were hardly living in luxury during the period when they were sending food and clothing elsewhere.

As Fontanne told her British friend Habetrot Dewhurst, "Everyone here is very starving Europe conscious and the nicest ones are quite sincerely trying not to spend too much on themselves."

Throughout the run of *There Shall Be No Night,* Fontanne requested that cast members and stagehands bring in used magazines and books so that she could turn them over to agencies for distribution to Allied soldiers.

Peculiarly, Lunt could be as frugal at times as he was generous at others. These periodic outbreaks of stinginess can probably be attributed to his early years, when he grew up having to support his entire family. He might be willing to spend great amounts of money to build a swimming pool or buy a magnificent car, but the price of small items often drove him to distraction. A friend of his told me that Lunt's conception of the value of money dated from his boyhood and never really changed. "When he went to the grocery store and bought a dozen eggs, he remembered he used to be able to buy eggs for twenty cents and now they were a dollar forty cents a dozen. He just couldn't believe this. The same is true as far as paying somebody. He'd have a boy in to cut the grass or trim the trees and so forth, and he remembered when thirty cents an hour was a lot of money for some high-school boy to get." This would bring forth a good deal of grumbling about the cost of hired help.

Donald Seawell also noted Lunt's obsessive frugality. "Alfred would personally go shopping at the supermarket to save money rather than picking up the phone and ordering from Gristede's. And in his later years [in retirement in Genesee Depot] he wouldn't buy a new washing machine and dryer [until Fontanne finally persuaded him to do so]; he figured out how much it would cost and how long he thought they had to live and he said it would be cheaper for him to drive over to the town laundry."

But Lunt's occasional stingy impulse was an aberration. He more often surprised others with his thoughtfulness. When the George Schaefers stayed at Genesee Depot, for example, not only were they wined and dined for the length of their stay, but "on the day we left, Alfred got up early, went to the hen house and got a dozen fresh eggs; he made sure you never left without a dozen eggs in your hand."

In more significant ways, too, the Lunts "were unbelievably generous," as Donald Seawell remarked. "They felt their responsibility to Jules [Johnson, their longtime cook and dresser], for instance, when he retired and went to California; and to Benny [Perkins, the caretaker on their farm]; they didn't have to keep them on pensions for the rest of their lives, but they did."

Another aspect of the Lunts' kindness and generosity was the auditions they began to hold for promising young actors in the late 1930s and continued for a decade. During that time they were regarded as the most significant force on Broadway for promoting young talent. Night after

As Petruchio and Katharine in *The Taming of the Shrew*

One of Lunt's silent films: *Backbone*, 1923

Quadrille, 1954

The Lunts enjoying the role of simple farmers:
Three variations on a favorite pose over a fourteen-year period

With Montgomery Clift in *There Shall Be No Night*

With the USO in Germany at the end of World War II

Lunt posing with some of his prized
toy theatres; and (below) in the
kitchen at Genesee Depot; (right)
some of the murals that cover the
walls and ceilings at Ten Chimneys

Lunt and Fontanne as they appeared in *The Visit*

A portrait of the Lunts in their later years

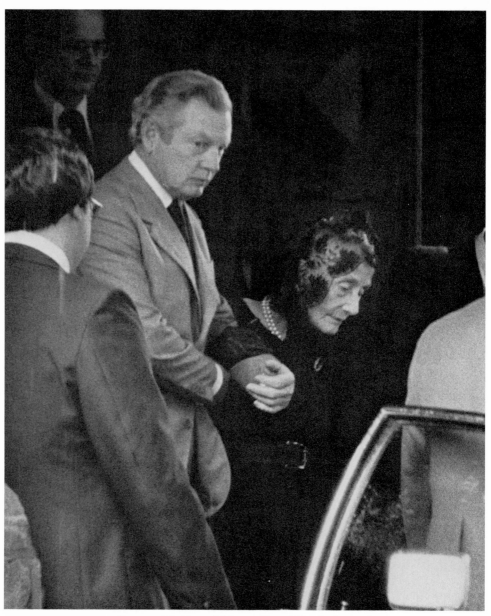

Lynn with Donald Seawell at Alfred's funeral

night, during the run of their productions, Lunt and Fontanne—or Fontanne alone—stayed after the performance to watch auditions.

Fontanne was asked why she took the time to watch the scenes when most managers simply interviewed the actors in whom they were interested. She told Helen Ormsbee in January 1938:

> I started the procedure when I realized that a five-minute interview with a girl wouldn't tell me as much about her as three minutes of watching her on the stage. In acting, very commonplace people often light up. So I tried having each person act two brief scenes for me—one comedy, one serious—doing anything she chose. My only stipulation was that it should be something she had not seen anyone else play.
>
> Novices have faults—bad ones. But I think one can detect people's underlying qualities. They may be frightened, and yet something is discernible. In a way, it is like an actor's performance on an opening night.
>
> . . . It doesn't interest me to see a girl give a nice imitation of a standard ingenue. I would rather discover some evidence of that instinct for knowing what is false and what is true.

When Fontanne conducted an audition without Lunt, four actors per night were scheduled to perform. As they entered, they gave their names to the company manager, who passed them on to a secretary. Fontanne preferred not to know the names of the candidates. As the scenes progressed, the secretary took down Fontanne's comments. Later, when the Lunts were casting a play, Fontanne would look through her files for the notes on the actors she had seen.

Occasionally, the actors, if found sufficiently promising, would receive the benefit of the Lunts' advice. Once in a great while, the Lunts would work with them on the intricacies of the scenes they chose. A few of the actors were rewarded with roles in the Lunt-Fontanne company (as Uta Hagen was in *The Sea Gull*).* Most often, however, the Lunts recommended the most promising youngsters to other managements. And just as Ellen Terry had given some money to Lynn Fontanne during Fontanne's lean days in England, so the Lunts occasionally contributed to the support of the young actors in whom they took an interest.

Typical, perhaps, was the experience of Jean Stapleton in 1946. Stapleton wrote to Fontanne asking for an audition. Renée Orsell, Fontanne's

---

* While Uta Hagen was participating in the readings of *The Sea Gull,* she mentioned to Lunt that she had considerable time on her hands. Lunt told her, "Well, there are all these young people doing these auditions—why don't you help them?" So she began helping the aspirants to select their material and coaching them for several hours each. This practice continued only for two weeks, however, for Lunt discovered that Hagen's energies for rehearsals were being sapped by the time she was spending on the audition scenes. But the coaching gave Hagen her first taste of teaching and marked the beginning of a long career as one of the most successful acting teachers in New York.

secretary, responded that Fontanne was too busy to hold an audition at that time. Stapleton, knowing that other actors who had persevered had eventually been seen, bided her time. Five months later she was informed that Fontanne would be able to watch her scene. As a direct result of the audition, Fontanne introduced Stapleton to John C. Wilson, who cast her in a summer-stock production.

In addition, the actors in the Lunts' companies sometimes asked them to watch scenes they had prepared. These were intended simply to sharpen the actors' skills, but, as William Le Massena pointed out, "the more you could prove to them that you could act, the better off you were because they were the most powerful people in the theatre at that time." After the scenes were performed, the Lunts would give comments and suggestions to the actors, who were then encouraged to rework the scenes with the recommended alterations.

The Lunts' reputation for generosity was so widespread that some tried to take advantage of it. Lunt was known in show business as a soft touch. Whether it was actors down on their luck who approached him for a loan or vagrants pleading for a handout, Lunt found it difficult to turn them down. The steady stream of letters asking him to give or lend money were placed in a file he and Fontanne called "Touch Letters." One of the people to whom Lunt gave some money in 1925 was a twenty-seven-year-old man who then wrote an effusive letter of introduction to which he forged Lunt's signature. The letter, referring to the man as "a charming person" and "a friend of mine," was presented by the forger to various actors in New York. Once the letter established his supposed relationship with Lunt, he asked the actors—among whom were Humphrey Bogart, Fanny Brice, Walter Huston and Roland Young—for a loan, and some of them gave him small sums.

The deception was soon discovered, but Lunt feared he would be unable to prevent the forger's continued use of the letter unless he informed every actor in America that his name was being used illegally. He was saved from that necessity when one night in Grand Central Station he saw the man passing by. Lunt intercepted him, held on to him when he tried to run away, and shouted for a policeman, who took the forger into custody.

He was arraigned on April 30, 1925, pleaded guilty in mid-May, and was sentenced to jail on May 28. On the day before sentence was handed down, he wrote to Lunt from jail, apologizing for the inconvenience and embarrassment he had caused, and promising to "go straight" in the future. In fact, he said, even before his arrest he had determined to sin no more.

Perhaps in an effort to ensure that his signature would never again be used in such a way, Lunt thereafter used two signatures—one for signing autographs, the other for signing checks.

*   *   *

In the spring of 1942 the Lunts participated in the making of a film entitled *Stage Door Canteen,* based upon the activities of the actual Canteen. Twentieth Century–Fox built a replica of the Canteen in Hollywood, where most of the film was shot, but the sequences that featured the Lunts, Katharine Cornell, Tallulah Bankhead, Helen Hayes and other Broadway luminaries were shot in Manhattan. More than eighty prominent Broadway and Hollywood performers played themselves in the film. The Lunts' contribution was a single short scene, completed in one day. They agreed to perform in *Stage Door Canteen* because all the profit from the picture was pledged to the American Theatre Wing and other Allied charities. Stage Door Canteens in Washington, Philadelphia, Cleveland, Los Angeles, San Francisco, Boston and Newark would receive funds, as would the Canteen in New York. The film itself turned out to be thoroughly pedestrian, but its contribution to the American Theatre Wing came to more than a million dollars.

In May 1942, preparations for the production of *The Pirate* were in full swing. The Theatre Guild, the Playwrights' Company and Transatlantic Productions all had a share in the production. Given the Lunts' irritation with the Theatre Guild, which had grown to monumental proportions, it seems remarkable that the couple would have consented to work with the Guild once again, but the partnership remained in force.*

The Pirate was codirected by Lunt and John C. Wilson, who—along with Fontanne—also helped Behrman shape the play. The four of them met in Genesee Depot in May 1942. Fontanne told Woollcott, "We have tea every afternoon in the studio and altogether it's a very happy family. We discuss nothing but scenic designers, casting, costuming and composers. . . . We wanted Kurt Weill for the music but, even before signing the contract, he has exhibited such signs of trouble that we have decided not to make the difficult days of production still more difficult by having him."

---

*The reasons for the Lunts' anger were explained by Fontanne to Woollcott in a letter written in 1941: "I thought you might be interested, although not surprised, to hear a small saga of Guild perfidy. Did we ever tell you that we had a completed plan for a way of doing 'Twelfth Night' which the Guild knew about? Without saying a word to us, we read in the papers that they are going to do it with Helen Hayes.

"They have known for a long time, as I daresay you have too, that we have an even more complete idea for a way of doing 'Macbeth,' with sets already designed by Dickie. Some of them are even in this month's Theatre Arts. Terry [Helburn], telephoning about something else, said quite casually to Alfred, didn't we want to do 'Macbeth' next season. Alfred replied that it was quite possible, but he couldn't say off hand.

"I said to Alfred, 'She is going to invite Maurice Evans to do it.' And the next morning we had a letter saying that Maurice Evans was pestering them to let him do it. . . .

"I really have come to the conclusion that they should be more pitied than anything else because all this seems like downright stupidity. Not, naturally, that they should do those two plays with other people, but that they should risk offending us, who are at the moment their only golden egg.

"However, if we wanted to do 'Macbeth,' they wouldn't deter us, naturally. In fact it would give me fiendish pleasure to take the risk of playing in the theatre next door to their 'Macbeth' and praying the gods to be kind."

Eventually, Herbert Kingsley was selected to compose the music. In June, Kingsley and the scene designer, Lemuel Ayers, joined the others at Genesee Depot.

Cast members included such newcomers to the Lunts' productions as Estelle Winwood, Robert Emhardt and Clarence Derwent. Sydney Greenstreet, after having spent years with Lunt and Fontanne, had achieved great success in John Huston's 1941 film *The Maltese Falcon* and remained in Hollywood. Richard Whorf and Thomas Gomez had also succumbed to the lure of the movies.

Set in Santo Domingo in the early nineteenth century, *The Pirate* tells of a former buccaneer who has settled into a life of respectability and taken a beautiful young wife, Manuela. But Serafin, a strolling player, falls in love with Manuela and, by means of trickery, exposes the supposedly honorable merchant as the scourge of the Caribbean. Manuela (played by Fontanne), her eyes open at last, returns the love of Serafin (played by Lunt) and joins his wandering troupe.

The Pirate went into rehearsal on August 1, 1942, and its premiere performance was given at the University Theatre in Madison, Wisconsin, on September 13. The production was spectacular, calling for seven changes of scenery, and flashy, colorful costumes. "The entertainment looks good," Fontanne reported to Woollcott. "We have put everything we have into it and Alfred has damned near killed himself, what with playing a great part, learning a dance, a few magic tricks, tight rope walking (not really), and directing the whole thing. It is all cued in with the music and, unlike a musical comedy where the dancing can be rehearsed in one place, the music in another, this all had to be done together and it has been quite the toughest thing we have ever bitten off."

After the opening in Madison, *The Pirate* set out on a two-month tour. When the production reached Chicago, the *Tribune* critic waxed enthusiastic, saying, "Both the play and the performance made excellent impressions. *The Pirate* turns out to be a bright little piece based on an enormously clever idea and equipped with enough surprises and odd twists to outwit half a dozen run of the mill plays." The *Sun* said, "Both Lunt and Miss Fontanne are at their very peak. . . . The company they have gathered around them is brilliant."

The Lunts' reason for selecting *The Pirate* was specifically to offer a light, amusing frolic that would be suitable for performances in military camps. "We want to entertain and amuse and if the play is a success we shall attain our wish," said Fontanne. Even before the production reached Broadway, however, there were mutterings that the play was too trivial and too escapist to be worth the Lunts' while. During a time of crisis, the dissenters argued, the Lunts and S. N. Behrman should be involved with more socially significant drama. There can be no question but that *The Pirate* was one of the less momentous occasions in the Lunts' careers, but as a lightweight diversion it succeeded admirably.

Despite the production's enthusiastic reception in Madison and Chicago, the Playwrights' Company was skeptical about its chances for success in New York. One of its members telephoned to Lawrence Langner of the Theatre Guild, asking that the Guild agree to close the play before it reached Broadway. Langner promptly went to Washington, D.C., where *The Pirate* was then running. According to Langner, he found the Lunts depressed and unhappy. Their spirits improved, however, after Langner watched a performance and told them that in his opinion the play needed only some fine tuning to be a first-rate entertainment. Behrman set to work on a sizable rewriting job, which included an entirely new second act. The strengthened production then went on to Boston and Philadelphia.

Elinor Hughes, writing in the Boston *Herald,* did not care for the play—"the lightest of puff balls," she called it—but acknowledged that it served as "a featherweight excuse for some of the most enchanting and fanciful goings on in a long time and for the most unbelievable and brilliant costumes [designed by Miles White] and settings imaginable. . . . Lynn Fontanne has never looked lovelier. . . . Alfred Lunt plays with a mannered romanticism that is most beguiling."

The Pirate opened at the Martin Beck Theatre in New York on November 27. Fontanne, who at almost fifty-five might have been thought far too old for her character, pulled off the role of the naïve young woman expertly and convincingly. Lunt's dancing, feats of magic and—especially—his "tightrope walk" from one balcony to another were all achieved with aplomb. Lewis Nichols reviewed the production for the New York *Times.* "Anything that serves to return the Lunts to Broadway is an occasion for rejoicing," he said, "for they are the theatre's greatest pair of actors. [*The Pirate*] is flamboyant and bizarre, and it gives the Lunts an opportunity for burlesque thus far unparalleled in their combined career."

Consistent with their notion that *The Pirate* should contribute to the war effort, the Lunts donated a substantial portion of their profits to the Stage Door Canteen.

In May they were given awards by the Drama League of New York for the best performances of the season. Lunt was also the winner of the best performance by an actor in *Variety*'s annual poll of the New York drama critics, who recognized Tallulah Bankhead's performance in *The Skin of Our Teeth* as the best by an actress.

As had become customary, the Lunts intended to offer *The Pirate* for one season on Broadway and to follow that engagement with a road tour, this one to include service camps. But the tour was canceled when Fontanne fell ill. A more substantial reason for its cancellation, however, had to do with a new idea Fontanne had conceived, an idea that would greatly alter the course of the Lunts' lives.

The Lunts could take satisfaction from their activities on behalf of the Allies in World War II. Their efforts had helped to raise millions of dollars as well as the spirits of thousands of Americans and Canadians. Still, Fontanne in particular felt that to remain in America when her sister and her friends in Britain were in constant danger from German bombing raids was somehow an evasion of responsibility. She had been informed by Jane de Glehn, she told Woollcott, "that the house in London is now a heap of dust. The studio that I posed for Wilfred in all my growing years. That lovely old house with its apple green door. . . . It was opposite Battersea Bridge and my best beau used to stand on the bridge looking over at the boats going underneath, waiting for me to finish my day's work. He was killed in the last war and the house he used to watch for me is now gone. . . ."*

Fontanne proposed to Lunt that, for the duration of the war, they emigrate to England, where they would offer performances in London, the provinces and at Allied bases on the Continent. Lunt agreed, and they asked Robert E. Sherwood to revise *There Shall Be No Night* so that they could offer it in London. Sherwood, who at the time was serving as the head of the Office of War Information, changed the situation of his play to reflect current political reality. In its transformed state, it dealt with the Nazi invasion of Greece, and the identities of the protagonists were changed from Finnish to Greek.

Fontanne wrote to Air Marshal Bishop of the Canadian Wartime Information Board asking for his assistance in shipping the costumes for *There Shall Be No Night* and *The Pirate* (which they also planned to offer) to London, since they would be performed "for the English and American troops, after which we are very anxious to come back and play [them] all over for American and Canadian troops." Wartime limitations restricted each passenger to forty pounds of luggage and, Fontanne pointed out, "the costumes for the second play are very rich, luxurious and showy and I am afraid I could not find the materials for them in England, so I am having them made here." Her hope was that the Air Marshal could "put the costumes for the play on a bomber going to England sometime, to be held for me when I arrive." The Wartime Information Board answered that it would do its best to cooperate, but its assistance became unnecessary when the Lunts decided not to present *The Pirate* in London after all. *There Shall Be No Night* would offer fewer production problems, and, more importantly, its theme seemed far more appropriate to a war-torn nation.

Securing passports for the journey was no easy task, but the Lunts' persistence finally convinced the officials in the Passport Division of the State Department to grant their request. The trip to England was long and arduous. In Philadelphia they boarded a small Portuguese boat "feeling that our adventure had really begun" (in Fontanne's words). One hundred twenty-five British children were also aboard, being returned home from

---

*This was one of the last occasions on which Fontanne corresponded with Woollcott, who died early in 1943. Woollcott's portrait continued to be prominently displayed in the library at Ten Chimneys until after Fontanne's death.

Canada. "The sea was a little choppy," Fontanne said, "but the next day it got worse and that night developed into a full cyclone. After going for a whole day in this the Captain realized that we were going around in a circle and that we were headed for the middle of it, pitching and tossing end to end." The storm continued for three days, but the next morning broke sunny and calm. The ship, back on course at last, proceeded to the Azores, where 200 troops were taken on board.

It took twenty days for the ship to reach Lisbon, and from there the Lunts took a plane to England, arriving in October 1943. Lunt wrote to Richard and Tinx Whorf, "The trip by air from Lisbon wasn't bad but we don't like flying & never will, Lynn is terrified & though I'm not so frightened I get awful ear ache (and sinus) & can't bear the whole thing." He did not mention that the plane had been flying the same route on which Leslie Howard's aircraft had been shot down by German guns three weeks earlier.

1943–45: Great Britain and Europe

"We're here at last and have loved every minute since the moment we stepped foot in England," Lunt wrote to the Whorfs. He told Robert E. Sherwood, "Our lives have been so enriched by the experience of coming here that we thank God, and you, every day that we have been given this glorious opportunity." Fontanne had no misgivings either, saying, "We are both blissful to be here."

The Lunts quickly adapted to the bombing raids that German aircraft regularly made over London. "We've had eight days of alerts and alarums," he told the Whorfs on October 24, "and bless my soul if they aren't at it again this very minute—guns booming like anything—you see how quickly you can accustom yourself to almost anything—Little did I think I could ever be writing a letter under such conditions. . . . We were at a play the other evening during a raid—the actors continued without a tremor or a moment's hesitation—the audience never budged—not a soul moved, not a head turned—Wonderful—I know now why we'll win—no doubt about it—"

In another letter Fontanne told of her impressions of wartime London:

> London on the surface is the same, but you will turn a corner suddenly and find two whole blocks wiped out, then long streets of lovely Regency houses with their facades completely untouched but with nothing behind them. Other houses are just a shell, empty of everything inside. Some lovely churches are made hideous with the ruins, others are strangely beautified. The spirit

of the people, which is really an important thing, is wonderful beyond words to describe.

We have been in several air raids now. One in particular was terrifically exciting and awful to watch. . . . The searchlights (about five of them) met in a "V" and coned what looked like a helpless silver butterfly. The ack-acks started blasting away in a shower of stars, a big red glow ensued on the plane, just a glow like a little red moon. The searchlights withdrew, guns stopped firing, evidently they knew they had received a mortal wound because she came down in flames outside London. . . . I think the most gratifying thing about human nature is that in spite of everyone here having suffered through a year of blitzes, some lost whole families as well as all they had, they can still find it in their hearts to be sorry for the boys in that little silver butterfly.

The Lunts stayed in a two-room suite at the Savoy Hotel in London. Their longtime dresser and cook, Jules Johnson, had remained in Genesee Depot, unable to accompany the Lunts to England because of wartime restrictions. Domestic help was impossible to find and, for the first time in many years, the Lunts discovered what it was like to shop and run errands of the kind they had long delegated to hired help.

Even if servants had been available, however, the Lunts had no intention of living in England as remote visiting celebrities. Both of them applied to serve (and were accepted) as air-raid wardens. Lunt also volunteered to work as an orderly for St. George's Hospital. Using the name Karilo Vlachos (the name of the character he played in Sherwood's revised version of *There Shall Be No Night*), Lunt emptied bedpans, made beds and performed all the menial jobs an orderly was expected to perform.

The Lunts' volunteer work was of great importance to them, but so was the theatrical aspect of their return to Britain. They began to cast *There Shall Be No Night* "the moment we arrived in London—literally," Lunt told the Whorfs. "Some of the cast have never acted before but are coming along splendidly.* How the *play* will go God only knows." Fontanne was confident of the reception. She said that "the cast and the new version are better than New York, I think. . . . The boys are played by American and Canadian discharged soldiers and Dickie's part is being done as well as he played it."

Lunt reported to Sherwood on the progress of rehearsals. "We have had great luck with the company so far," he said. "Our rehearsals proceeding beyond our wildest expectations." He also continued to implore Sherwood to make changes in the script, writing to ask the playwright on one occasion to allow him to restore a speech that had been cut from the play, and to send his answer by wire.

* Most professional actors below the age of forty were serving in one branch or another of the armed forces.

There Shall Be No Night opened in Liverpool on November 1, then played in Oxford, Newcastle and Edinburgh before beginning a run at the Aldwych Theatre in London on December 15, 1943. The house was packed with servicemen and -women as well as with civilians. The audience "refused to leave their seats until Alfred Lunt and Lynn Fontanne and the entire cast took ten curtain calls and Mr. Lunt made a brief speech of appreciation," noted an observer.

Audiences were deeply moved by Sherwood's play. The British "seemed to weep more than anyone had ever wept at *There Shall Be No Night*," Lunt said, to which Fontanne added, "And the Lord knows we drenched many a theatre with that play all over America and Canada."

"We found the British people had a special reason for liking *There Shall Be No Night*," Lunt astutely observed. "It gave them a chance to come and cry. In the darkened house, alone or in couples, they could weep, whereas they couldn't at home or in daily contacts with the world."

German bombers had resumed making regular raids over London shortly after the play opened. In a curious way, however, the sounds of destruction outside the theatre helped to reinforce the reality of the play, which called for offstage sound effects of bombs and guns. The audience knew that the attack was real—the shaking of the theatre convinced them of that—but the eerie combination of onstage and offstage reality conspired to make the play more moving than ever. In one scene Lunt spoke the line, "The enemy is not very far away." More than once the sounds outside the theatre gave his words a heightened reality and the audience, thinking Lunt had improvised the line, broke into cheers and applause.

But the most memorable occasion began with Lunt offstage. As Fontanne described it:

> A buzz bomb hit very near. I was on the stage and he was in the wings waiting for his cue when the smash came. I found myself somehow on the other side of the stage. The scenery was buckling like sails in a high wind, things were falling. I looked for Alfred. There he was, pushing a canvas wall up with one hand and starting to make his entrance. Then I saw the fire curtain coming down and heard him shout in that metallic voice he gets when he is excited, "Take it up! Take it!"
>
> Like a shot it went up and then he turned to me and curious as it may seem, the precise line he had to speak in the script at that moment was, "Are you all right, darling?"
>
> Well, neither of us ever had such applause as came up when he finished saying that. The audience, which had sat as silent as the grave all during the crashing—audiences never walk, much less run, for exits during blasts—burst right out in cheers and stood up and kept on and on, really holding up the play much longer than the buzz bomb. . . .

At the end of the scene when we went off, I said to Alfred, "From now on, you'll really know how to read that line." Really, I never heard a line read so well on any stage.

The bombing continued throughout the performance. With the theatre rattling from the explosions outside, Lunt's speech in his final scene was particularly appropriate. "Listen," he said. "What you hear now—this terrible sound that fills the earth—it is the death rattle. One may say easily and dramatically that it is the death rattle of civilization. But—I choose to believe differently. I believe it is the long deferred death rattle of the primordial beast. We have within ourselves the power to conquer bestiality, not with our muscles and our swords, but with the power of the light that is in our minds."

The audience was again uncertain whether Lunt was speaking in character or as himself, whether he was addressing the other characters or speaking directly to the assembled gathering. The occasion was deeply moving. Members of the audience cried openly. "The play was a catharsis," Fontanne said later, echoing her husband. "The English would never allow themselves to cry over their personal or national misfortunes or despairs. However, it was permissible to become so involved in a play that you wept for the characters, and, through them, for all decency and humanity. . . . That play afforded them such a blessed release."

The Lunts said they were not frightened by the sounds of devastation outside the theatre. "An actor doesn't think of death when a performance is going well," Fontanne told Maurice Zolotow. Lunt added, "I don't think I was heroic. An actor trains himself to give a performance any time— when he's feeling tired, sick, unhappy, whatever troubles he's having in his personal life. The fact that a bomb might have hit the theatre didn't change it."

The Dean of Windsor, an old friend, informed the Lunts he deeply regretted that his age and ill health would not permit him to travel to London to see *There Shall Be No Night.* Consequently, the Lunts and their company journeyed to Windsor Castle, where, after being served lunch, they performed the play in the drawing room for the Dean and the other members of the castle's household, an audience of forty or fifty people. There was no scenery; the Lunts simply used available furniture and presented the play without costumes, makeup or lighting. The audience was seated so close to the performers that the actors had to be careful not to stumble over the spectators' feet. At first the performance required no vocal projection whatever. However, when some of the spectators began sobbing audibly, it became necessary for the actors to raise their voices. "We couldn't act," Lunt said, "we had to be absolutely real. . . . It was the best performance of it we ever gave or ever will give. They wept. It was almost unbearably real."

The Lunts had an uncomfortably close brush with death on their return to London. Alighting from the train they had taken from Windsor, they were greeted with the sight of a flying bomb. As the bomb's motor cut out, there was a dreadful moment of silence just before it landed terrifyingly near the train station.

The return to their hotel was equally frightening. During their journey to Windsor, a bomb had crashed just outside the Savoy. The devastation was apparent as the Lunts neared the hotel. But they did not realize how fortunate they were until they entered their suite. Every window was shattered and the floors covered with broken glass.

The threat of death was constant. In 1943 and 1944, German bombing raids over London were at their height. "We were afraid of the bombs," Lunt admitted. But, he said, "it wasn't fear of death but fear of separation. There was the terror of being apart when something happened."

The Lunts were often amazed that, despite the havoc wrought by bombing raids, Londoners in considerable numbers continued to attend those theatres that remained open. Nor were theatregoers daunted by other circumstances. One day in February 1944, an impenetrable fog covered London, causing buses to cease operations. Even one of the subway lines shut down. The Lunts assumed that hardly anyone would be in the audience for either the matinee or evening performance, but they decided to play for the few who might attend. In the event, the theatre was full for both performances. "How on earth they got there and how they got home we will never know," Lunt marveled.

The Lunts received a letter written by a secretary to the King of England on February 7, 1944, conveying "his congratulations and grateful thanks for the magnificent way in which you are rendering every day from the scene of the Aldwych Theatre Mr. Sherwood's work on Greece 'There Shall be No Night.' I am to add," said the writer on behalf of the King, "that the Greek nation's unbending and courageous attitude towards the Fascist and Nazi aggressors and their fortitude in the face of cruel ordeals could not have found worthier or more sincere and convincing interpreters."*

The run at the Aldwych continued, but only until June 30, 1944, when buzz bombs damaged the theatre, killing an airman who was buying a ticket at the box office. The company took to the provinces, where audiences proved to be as eager and as responsive as spectators had been in London. The tour took the Lunts "from Bournemouth to Aberdeen, from

---

*Before the Lunts went to England in 1943, the King became aware of Fontanne's contribution to Allied morale. In a letter to an American friend, Fontanne said, "Hugh Beaumont (the man who is presenting us [in *There Shall Be No Night*] here) was in Africa with a troupe of entertainers and met the King, who told him that he and the Queen were crazy about a poem called 'The White Cliffs,' and that they always carried the little book around with them. Hugh asked him if they had heard the recording and the King said he didn't know there was one, so Hugh offered to send him it and the King asked him please to not forget to do so, as he wanted it above all things. So my sister's set of records are now on their way to Buckingham Palace."

Bristol to Newcastle," as Lunt wrote to William Le Massena. They often spent the nights in people's homes rather than in hotels, and while in Northampton for a stay of several days, the Lunts spent considerable time with the local inhabitants. "Sometimes Alfred would be the only man at dinner," Fontanne said, "and it was touching to me to see the reaction of the women whose men were all away from home, how much they enjoyed having someone from the outside to bring a change into their lives."

The Lunts' schedule was a hectic one. Eight performances per week was the maximum number professional actors were customarily permitted to give, but additional performances were scheduled for *There Shall Be No Night*. For example, a special matinee for the benefit of the Greek Red Cross was given on April 3, 1944, and once every other week an extra presentation was scheduled for Allied troops. On matinee days there was no time for a meal or a rest between performances. The matinee ended just before 5:30, and the curtain rose again at 6:00 (due to blackout restrictions) for the evening performance. At least, Lunt concluded philosophically, they were able to get to bed early.

There Shall Be No Night closed in Blackpool in July 1944. Appropriately enough, the last performance was given on the day the last German was driven from Greece. The Lunts then spent several weeks with the English playwright, composer and actor Ivor Novello at his home in the country, not far from Maidenhead. "We are safe & well & having a pleasanter time than you might suppose possible," Lunt told the Whorfs. Despite the strict rationing, he said, the food Novello served was excellent. Lunt was able to do some gardening and Fontanne a great deal of reading, so both were "more than happy and everlastingly grateful."

The Theatre Guild hoped that after their tour the Lunts would return to the United States to revive *The Guardsman* on the twentieth anniversary of its original production. But the war was still in progress, and the Lunts would have felt irresponsible had they returned home to safety at that moment. "We do not wish to go back to America now," Lunt stated categorically.

In fact, they had already begun working on a new project, one that Ivor Novello had suggested to them. Novello had introduced Lunt to a young British Air Force officer named Terence Rattigan, who had already written three plays that had enjoyed successful London runs. Rattigan's new play, *Love in Idleness,* was a drawing-room comedy of the sort the Lunts had so often appeared in, and Novello thought it might interest them.

He was right. They read the play, liked it and agreed to perform in it (with Lunt as director) if Rattigan would agree to make a few alterations. Not realizing that "a few alterations" would turn out to be a monumental job of rewriting, Rattigan eagerly accepted the Lunts' offer. He returned to his typewriter, writing when he could find time (he was still on active military duty), trying to solve the problems the Lunts perceived in his play.*

The British theatre was relatively inactive during the war because so many young actors and playwrights were in uniform. The few new plays offered were almost exclusively comedies. With the war winding down and victory in sight, British audiences expressed a clear preference for laughter over tears. Having faced tragedy every day for years, they wanted their theatrical entertainment to be of the escapist variety. This was apparent even during the run of *There Shall Be No Night*, when lines of dialogue that were intended to be wryly humorous elicited enormous bursts of laughter from the audience.†

The Lunts' new play, *Love in Idleness*, was calculated to give the British public what it so ardently craved. This light and inconsequential comedy was about a cabinet minister (Lunt) whose affair with an elegant widow (Fontanne) is interrupted when her seventeen-year-old son returns unexpectedly from Canada. The Lunts were eager to get to work on the new play immediately, but the opening had to wait several months until the scenery, props and costumes could be obtained.‡

An old friend appeared when S. N. Behrman, researching an article on wartime London for the *New Yorker*, arrived in 1944. Behrman visited the Lunts in the Savoy while the ominous sounds of warfare rumbled in the distance. As he ascended in the elevator to their rooms, he thought how foolish he had been to come to London at such a dangerous time. After exchanging greetings and sharing lunch, the Lunts asked Behrman's indulgence while they rehearsed their lines from *Love in Idleness*. The effect on the playwright was remarkably soothing and reassuring. "While I was with them I forgot I was in London, I forgot that there was a war on. The bombs didn't matter, nothing mattered," said Behrman. "I hated to have to go home."

Love in Idleness opened in Liverpool on November 27, 1944, to critical derision. The play, the critics said, was not worthy of the Lunts' time

---

*One problem was that the play had been conceived as a vehicle for Gertrude Lawrence. Although there was an important male character, his role was inferior to that of the leading woman. Lunt had no hesitation in agreeing to perform a play in which Fontanne's role would be slightly better, but he understandably wanted the play revised so that his performance could make a distinctive contribution as well.

†Nearly every play in London running concurrently with *There Shall Be No Night* was a light comedy or a musical. In addition to the Christmas pantomimes (*Cinderella, Humpty Dumpty*, etc.), there were *Sweet and Low, The Dancing Years, Blithe Spirit, This Time It's Love, Pink String and Sealing Wax, She Follows Me About, While the Sun Shines* and revivals of *Love for Love* and *The Admirable Crichton*.

‡Understandably, food that was rationed could not be consumed on the stage. This led to some ingenious fakery during one scene in *Love in Idleness*, in which the boy was supposed to eat an omelet and canned fruit while drinking a glass of milk. The omelet was made of potatoes and carrots, the fruit of sugarless stewed apples, the milk of milk powder and water. Clothing was also rationed, but there was simply no way to circumvent that problem. The actors adapted, using fewer costumes than were called for in the play.

and efforts, and the same comment was made the following week in Leeds. Rattigan was fearful Lunt would decide to close the play without taking it to London. His fear increased when Noël Coward saw a performance in Leeds and afterward told the Lunts and Rattigan quite candidly that the play was so poorly written and so unfunny that it could not possibly be salvaged. He recommended that the closing notice be posted immediately.

As Coward continued to list the play's inadequacies for Lunt, Fontanne signaled to Rattigan to follow her into another room. She assured the young playwright that although Lunt would be sunk in despair as a result of hearing Coward's opinion, she believed the play could be successful. "Don't worry," she told Rattigan, "I shall talk Alfred around."

Later that evening, while Coward was still holding forth on the deficiencies of the play, Lunt motioned Rattigan to accompany him into the next room. There he told him to pay no attention to Coward's criticisms. Neither should he be disturbed if Fontanne suggested closing the play, Lunt said. "Leave it to me to talk Lynn around to my way of thinking."

On the opening night in London, December 20, a dense fog descended over the city. Recalling the capacity audiences that had turned out for *There Shall Be No Night* despite the fog, the Lunts gave no thought to postponing the opening. Indeed, every seat was filled and the number of standees was limited only by the fire laws.

The evening was a great success, the Lunts felt. The audience remained to cheer and applaud long after the final curtain call had been taken. "It is a great huge walloping smash hit," Lunt wrote to William Le Massena. "We always loved playing in London but never more than now. Despite a few warnings and a couple of clumps . . . there they are in the theatre . . . and *on time*—so warm, so friendly—a 'gala' each performance."

The response of the London critics was not quite so enthusiastic. The *Times*'s notice said that playwright Rattigan had "been insufficiently inventive, and perhaps insufficiently witty" and that "Mr. Lunt is the chief sufferer." Rattigan's attempt to build up Lunt's role had not been successful, in the anonymous critic's opinion. But if Lunt's performance could not overcome the uninspired quality of his dialogue, the critic had no such reservations about Fontanne. "Miss Fontanne is in her element," he said, exhibiting "a genuine grace of spirit which can turn stage commonplaces to glittering comedy." The review was typical of most for *Love in Idleness*, both in Britain and the United States: praise for one or both of the Lunts, tolerance for a mildly amusing play.

The Lunts would hear that criticism echoed again and again for the next thirteen years, as each successive play in which they appeared was condemned as being unworthy of their talents. However, audiences both in England and in America tended to pay little attention to the critics' judgments regarding the Lunts' plays. If Alfred Lunt and Lynn Fontanne were appearing, the play seemed to make no difference.

One indication of the audiences' devotion was that they continued to attend *Love in Idleness* during the coldest days of winter, even though most theatres were unheated in wartime Britain. On December 26, 1944, when *Love in Idleness* was playing at the Lyric Theatre in London, the temperature on stage was a frigid 4° Celsius (about 39° Fahrenheit). The audience remained wrapped in overcoats during the performance, but the actors did not have that option. Fontanne's bare arms turned light blue by the end of the first act.

Early in 1945 the Lunts were feeling terribly homesick for the United States but still determined to remain in Europe until the war was over. Asked if they intended to go home, Lunt replied, "We don't see how we can do it. There's a curious enjoyment you take in living in England now, in spite of all the anxieties of war and its ugliness. Through it all, you feel a strong glow—a glow of vitality. You feel a terrific responsibility, too—responsibility to see the war through. You would feel a little bit like a deserter to be leaving just now."

The Lunts entertained several distinguished visitors after their performances, among them Generals George S. Patton and Alexander M. Patch and two members of the British cabinet, who approved of Lunt's portrayal of a cabinet minister. Winston Churchill had sent a giant cigar backstage for Lunt after he saw a performance of *There Shall Be No Night*. Lunt had carefully preserved it in cellophane, and he used it as a prop in *Love in Idleness*. During the play Lunt spoke the line, "I left Number Ten [Downing Street] only half an hour ago." Fontanne asked, "Was he nice about it?" Lunt brought the cigar from his pocket and replied, "Very."

When Churchill attended *Love in Idleness*, the Lunts heard cheering in the street before the curtain went up, and the Prime Minister walked down the aisle to his seat in the front row, waving to the applauding audience. "He sat there smoking during the performance, everybody watching him more than us," Lunt said. "When at the regular time I pulled out the cigar, such a cheering started as I'd never earned before by any stretch of the imagination. For five minutes, I suppose, they cheered and cheered and Churchill got right up, turned around and stood there waving and waving back to them."

On January 12, 1945, the Lunts were asked to give a special performance for 150 civilian munitions workers who had been working on a secret project in an underground section of the Houses of Parliament. The company was taken to the Royal Palace of Westminster, where the actors gave a performance similar to the one given at Windsor. The secretary of the House of Commons thanked them in a confidential letter, saying, "The almost complete absence of stage lighting and effects, which might well have made any less generous company refuse to appear, only enabled us to appreciate the more the unsurpassable brilliance of the acting." The performance marked the first occasion on which actors had played in Westminster Hall since the reign of Richard II, and special permission had to be sought from the King's representative, the Lord Great Chamberlain.

Before closing in London, *Love in Idleness* played in several American military hospitals and then began a tour of England and Scotland. Then, in April 1945, the Lunts arranged with the United Service Organizations– Camp Shows to make a tour of American military bases on the Continent, giving performances of *Love in Idleness*. The tour of "the Foxhole Circuit," as it was known, carried them into France and deep into Germany. The Lunts were the first prominent American stage actors to play in Germany since the outbreak of war. They hoped to be able to visit bases near the fighting front, but by the time the tour began—on June 24, 1945—the Germans had already conceded defeat.

The first stop was Paris, where *Love in Idleness* opened for an audience of Allied soldiers at the Théâtre Sarah Bernhardt on June 28. The play had been scheduled to open the night before, but the performance had to be canceled when Brian Nissen, the young British actor playing Fontanne's son, was recalled to London because he had failed to get an exit permit. Normally, the understudy, Robert Raines, would have gone on in Nissen's place, but Raines also had neglected to apply for a permit.

The Lunts feared the actors would still be absent on the 28th, so they pressed an American soldier, Sergeant Ellis Eringer, into service. Eringer, a native of the Bronx, had never acted before, but volunteered to learn the role in case he was needed. Meanwhile, Major Paul Warburg, assistant military attaché at the American Embassy, telephoned to Duff Cooper, the British Ambassador to France, asking him to help cut the red tape preventing Raines's and Nissen's return. The actors were put on a plane for Paris, arrived at Orly Airport at 7:25 p.m. on the 28th and rushed to the theatre just in time for Nissen to play his role. A weary Sergeant Eringer, who had been memorizing and rehearsing since the night before, concluded his professional theatrical career before ever stepping onto the stage.

The Foxhole Circuit tour lasted for six weeks. A performance in Nuremberg was given before an audience made up largely of GIs who had never heard of the Lunts and who had been told only that they were to see a free show. Few of them could have expected a drawing-room comedy performed by actors well into middle age. The skeptical attitude of the audience was apparent, as a steady hum of conversation could be heard in the auditorium during the first scene. But after only a few minutes the soldiers began to focus their attention on the stage, and after their initial antagonism was overcome, they were won over by the Lunts' performances. In the words of one spectator, "The temper of the audience changed from one of noisy skepticism and irreverence to one of silent, fascinated attention."

In August 1945, Fontanne received a letter from General Patton in answer to one she had written expressing the Lunts' gratitude for being allowed to perform for American troops. "I feel," he said, "that you should not thank me but that I, on behalf of the Third Army, should thank you,

Mr. Lunt and the others of your cast for the great pleasure which we derived from your unparalleled performances."

The Lunts returned to the United States on August 8, 1945, arriving at La Guardia airfield on an American Transport Command C-54 and wearing military uniforms with Camp Shows insignias.

Their first response to being back in America was incredulity at the abundance of food and the lack of shortages. Choosing a vegetable from a selection on a restaurant menu proved to be deliciously agonizing, and Lunt said that he and Fontanne hesitated for half an hour before making their decision.

Looking back on their experience in Europe, the Lunts dismissed the notion that they had exhibited great courage. "Why, it was the greatest opportunity a ham actor could ever have," Lunt assured a New York *Times* reporter. "To have your lives interrupted by a crash outside the theatre, to stand there while the echoes of falling buildings rumble and the sirens and the guns rip the air, and then, as soon as you can be heard, go on speaking some calm, impersonal line as if nothing had happened—that calls out all the ham in an actor, a chance like that.

"You take courage—you take your cue from the audience in that kind of situation. They are sitting there all through the storm, quiet, intense, bending forward—not a back touching a seat—readier with applause and laughs than any other audiences ever were. That's the opportunity of a lifetime for an actor."

Chapter Twelve

A LOSS OF PERSPECTIVE?
(1945–57)

"If their present policy continues, we may
never see the Lunts in a really good play
again."

W. A. Darlington

"The Lunts are so expert that they make
whatever they do seem like something to
watch even when there is very little."

Harold Clurman

". . . golly, what they could do if they selected a script as subtle and skillful as
they are! For instance, something written with literary distinction."

Brooks Atkinson

"The critics have been nice to us, but
they're always saying 'it isn't worthy of
them.' Well, you know, I'm getting kind
of sick and tired of that."

Alfred Lunt

Once known for appearing in several plays each season, the Lunts by
1945 had settled into a much more leisurely theatrical schedule.
Since 1935 they had appeared in only seven plays (although all of them
except *The Pirate* had been toured extensively). From 1945 until they retired from the stage in 1960, they acted in only four. Their fascination with
and love for the theatre did not diminish, but their emphasis shifted.
Rather than appearing in a variety of plays that would test their abilities
to jump from one sort of characterization to another, they chose their productions so that each play and each role would be tailored to their particular talents.

Their reasons for doing so are both understandable and reasonable. They were no longer young, no longer able to withstand routinely the strains and tensions that attend the birth of every new Broadway production. Moreover, their reputations as actors of the first rank may have influenced them to place caution ahead of adventurousness. It was one thing to experiment with an obscure, challenging drama like *Goat Song* in 1926; if the experiment failed, there were several other productions scheduled for the same season. But it was quite different in the 1940s and '50s. If they were going to appear in one play every two years, that play simply *had* to be shrewdly chosen to project the Lunts' strengths as performers.

If the significance of each production created insidious pressures to select only plays that *could not fail*, plays that were tailor-made to the Lunts' patented style of high comic playing, their choices, unfortunately, tended to emphasize the nature of their roles rather than the inherent quality of the play. Most of the plays they appeared in after their return to America in 1945 were written expressly as vehicles for them. Such plays, by their very nature, do not focus on the author's deepest concerns, expressed in his or her idiosyncratic manner. Rather, they focus on the leading roles and the opportunities they offer to demonstrate the skills of the actors who will play them. A well-written theatrical vehicle may produce a memorable evening, one in which the leading actors dazzle the audience with their skill; but it will seldom produce a memorable *dramatic* experience in which the audience is moved to tears or laughter by the originality and brilliance of the playwright's vision.

Even though the Lunts had offers to appear in plays and films of every kind (in the late 1940s and the 1950s, they turned down opportunities to appear in such plays as *A Month in the Country* and *Tartuffe,* Robert E. Sherwood's *The Twilight,** Maxwell Anderson's *The Masque of Queens* (a

---

*Their rejection of *The Twilight* was particularly painful to Sherwood, one of their closest friends, who had written three of their greatest successes, and who perhaps felt that that record entitled him to expect them to respond affirmatively when he submitted *The Twilight* in 1947.

Sherwood's best plays were written in the 1930s. By the time he gave *The Twilight* to the Lunts, he was no longer regarded as one of America's foremost dramatists. His theatrical career needed a boost and he felt that the Lunts' presence in his latest play would give it to him. But they found *The Twilight* unsatisfactory from the beginning. For months they told him so in the gentlest terms. But he continued to press the Lunts, imploring them to reconsider. In April 1947, during a discussion of the play, Sherwood was clearly hurt by Fontanne's criticisms. In June she sent him a note of apology. "Alfred and I do know the blood, sweat and tears that go into a play," she said, "and remembering you had said you would have thrown *There Shall Be No Night* into the wastebasket if we had not liked it, we felt and still feel doubly responsible." Then, however, she proceeded inadvertently to sting Sherwood once again with the frankness of her opinion. She wrote, "I have been thinking ever since, and cannot find anything wrong, except the most important, and the thing that makes or breaks—and that is, no story, no situations, no drama, no tears, and not enough laughter to cover. For my particular taste, I must have some of all. One cannot say [Noël Coward's] *Present Laughter* was not funny or witty, but it was all one color, and I did not like it at all, and for the same reason I did not care much for [Coward's play] *Private Lives,* but that is my personal taste."

Sherwood read the letter aloud to his partners in The Playwrights' Company, his bitter-

sequel to Anderson's earlier play, *The Masque of Kings*), Jean-Paul Sartre's *No Exit*, James Bridie's *The Cockpit* and an adaptation of Arnold Bennett's *Buried Alive*), most of the plays they chose were vehicles of the conservative, unadventurous variety. To ensure that the plays would give them every opportunity to display their skills, they worked closely with the playwrights, offering the advantage of their taste and experience, but also imposing upon them the sometimes unfortunate necessity of having to tailor each scene, each line of dialogue to the desires of the star performers.

1945–48

The Lunts returned to Genesee Depot in August 1945 for a short rest before returning to New York for the American premiere of *O Mistress Mine,* as *Love in Idleness* had been retitled. They still clung to the hope that they could form the sort of acting company they had maintained during the prewar years, one that was composed of seasoned performers and talented youngsters whose careers and attitudes they could help to shape. But the dream was dead. Even the Theatre Guild was having trouble finding audiences to support its noncommercial plays and was being driven more and more to offer standard Broadway fare. As a result of the vastly increased costs of production and the postwar appetite for escapism, the spirit of commercialism had triumphed on Broadway.

Perhaps it was this realization, coming to them immediately after their experience in England, where their friends Laurence Olivier, John Gielgud and Ralph Richardson were all active in repertory companies, that was

ness and anger apparent. But when he responded to the Lunts in July, he had either come to terms with Fontanne's criticism or had decided to mask his feelings. "What the hell?" he said in his letter. "We have been through all manner of experience together. You turned down 'The Road to Rome' (and, I think, rightly). You were very dubious about 'Reunion in Vienna' at first, but finally accepted it. You were, as I remember, immediately enthusiastic about 'Idiot's Delight' and 'There Shall Be No Night' (again rightly, as it turned out). So, the record is pretty damned good, and I can't feel very depressed about it, even if I have struck out completely on this latest effort. . . . You both did me the honor of being supremely honest and candid with me, and, believe me, I am very grateful for that. Any soft soap would have been patronizing and insulting. I know I can count on you always to be like that for I confidently expect to be trying again and again to write plays for you in the future. . . . Anyway, I love you both, very dearly, and no mere manuscript can interfere with that. . . ."

Lunt, afraid that their friendship might not survive, wrote to Sherwood in August: "I can only tell you that it is sickening to us both that we have doubts of 'The Twilight.' We talk about it almost constantly, but cannot for the life of us think of anything that will straighten it out for us. . . ."

Sherwood wrote another play for the Lunts, *Small War on Murray Hill,* in the 1950s, but again they declined, telling the playwright they didn't wish to appear in another light comedy at the time. Lunt suggested a vague idea for a play he and Fontanne might like to appear in. "Put us in a covered wagon," he said. That sort of hazy notion had served as an inspiration for Sherwood twenty years earlier, resulting in *Idiot's Delight;* in 1955, however, he was unable to turn the idea into a play.

responsible for altering the Lunts' theatrical priorities. The awareness that they would be unable to realize their dream could not have been easy for them to accept. Whatever the cause, the evidence suggests that their attitudes toward the theatre underwent a significant change that lasted for more than a decade—and it was not a change for the better.

Reconciling themselves to the new Broadway realities, the Lunts presented *O Mistress Mine* under the joint sponsorship of Transatlantic Productions and the Theatre Guild, but the Guild's involvement was purely a financial one. The managers were not asked (and they did not offer) to contribute creatively to the production process. Although the Lunts certainly did not feel so at the time, this decision may have been a mistake. For all their arguments with the Board members through the years, the Guild had been a positive force, encouraging the best in the American theatre. The tension that had long existed between the Lunts and the Guild was irritating, occasionally even infuriating to the Lunts, but it was a *creative* tension, resulting in a series of fine plays featuring brilliant performances. With the Guild removed from the possibility of influencing the Lunts' work in any but a financial way, that positive force—insisting that every play have something original and worthwhile to say—was stilled.

Following a one-month tryout tour, *O Mistress Mine* opened in New York at the Empire Theatre on January 23, 1946. The advance sale for the Broadway run was $100,000, the largest in the history of the Empire. The Lunts' return to Broadway after a three-year absence was the occasion for the most lavish first night New York had seen in years. It was as if the austerity of the war years was swept aside in that one night. Although the Lunts did nothing to encourage it, the opening was an event of major proportions in social circles, and subsequent productions in which they appeared duplicated the gala atmosphere of the first night of *O Mistress Mine*. For many of the actors appearing in those productions, opening nights were terrifying experiences. The almost palpable emanation of wealth and social standing, the feeling that the spectators had assembled to see one another rather than the play, were intimidating to the actors, who felt it would be impossible for them to hold the attention of such a crowd.

But the first night of *O Mistress Mine* was an unqualified success with the audience, perhaps because, having come to the theatre to be amused rather than challenged, they were not disappointed. After the final curtain, Lunt stepped forward to deliver a brief speech, which offered a rationale for the play. He and his wife hoped, he said, that their play would help to keep alive a spirit of laughter and good humor in "an angry and suspicious world."

As the house lights came up, Fontanne returned to her dressing room to find it choked with so many flowers that she was literally unable to close the door. She would not have been able to use the room in any case, however. So many well-wishers had descended upon the Lunts that it seemed the entire audience had come backstage. Not until hours later were the couple able to return to their apartment, where, too exhausted to cook, Lunt served a supper of two bowls of cornflakes.

Were the Lunts being showered with too much adulation? Possibly so. Their achievement in bringing a tepid comedy to theatrical life was considerable, but their decision to appear in such a play was questionable. To be sure, their options were limited by Broadway's disdain for either drama or comedy that strayed too far from the conventional, but *O Mistress Mine* was a particularly unadventurous choice. Some of the other successful plays running on Broadway in the 1945–46 season—Tennessee Williams's *The Glass Menagerie,* Lindsay and Crouse's *State of the Union,* as well as revivals of *Pygmalion* (with Raymond Massey and Gertrude Lawrence) and *Hamlet* (with Maurice Evans)—indicate that there was an audience for more substantial fare.

The next morning's reviews tended to characterize the play as inconsequential, but offered unanimous praise for the Lunts. "The theatre is cheerful again. The Lunts are back," said Lewis Nichols in the New York *Times*. Despite the thinness of Rattigan's play, Nichols added, the Lunts "make *O Mistress Mine* one of the season's most engaging evenings."

Seldom in history have actors achieved such independence from the quality of their material. Brooks Atkinson wrote, "There is hardly a witty line in the dialogue." Nevertheless, "the Lunts' performance must be the most accomplished piece of drollery in the theatre." Critical appraisals such as this one were not an unmixed blessing, however, as they seemed to eliminate the necessity for the Lunts to search for plays of distinction.

As had become their habit, the Lunts rewrote the play as the run progressed, in an effort to refine and sharpen it. They let Terence Rattigan know of the changes they made, always preceding the news by saying, "I do hope you don't mind, but . . ." The tone of their letters, nevertheless, would seem to indicate that they were not seeking the playwright's permission to alter his dialogue, but simply informing him of the changes they were making. For some observers, at least, the changes had no visible effect on the play. Brooks Atkinson, who saw *O Mistress Mine* in its second year,* lamented that the Lunts were "squandering subtleties of speech and movement on rubbish."

Ignoring their critics, the Lunts seemed to enjoy their success as much as if they had been beginners. There is no evidence to suggest that they questioned their decision to offer Rattigan's play in New York, or to tamper with his dialogue. Rather, the success of *O Mistress Mine* confirmed their belief that the play was a good one and that their changes improved it still further. Fontanne wrote to her sister Antoinette on March 23 that the production "is sold out all through June . . . and already they are selling seats for September and October. We are just a couple of hot cakes."

---

*Atkinson was in the army when *O Mistress Mine* opened. When he returned to the *Times* the following season, he reviewed all the plays then running on Broadway.

Lunt was prevented from enjoying their triumph, however, when he began to suffer severe abdominal pain in December. At first his physician was unable to determine the source of the pain, but told him that he must curtail his activities. If he would not agree to stop performing in *O Mistress Mine,* he would at least have to give up all other professional activities, such as the radio plays in which he was then acting. And on no account could he consider any of the several offers he had received to direct on Broadway. Lunt agreed to follow the doctor's advice, but the pain grew worse. In January 1947 he entered St. Luke's Hospital in New York for an emergency operation to remove a stone from his one remaining kidney.

Performances were suspended until he could return six weeks later. The canceled performances resulted in a loss of $100,000 in box-office income, but the Theatre Guild and Transatlantic Productions agreed that since the Lunt-Fontanne team was thought of by the public as inseparable and indivisible, it would be unthinkable to present one without the other.

The production resumed in late February, but Lunt was still weak. "I am getting on," he told the Whorfs, "though I take to my bed whenever I feel a curious fatigue coming on." And he developed other ailments, including gout. In March his doctor ordered him to take a long rest.

From then until the end of his life, Lunt's physical ailments became progressively more acute. During the long period in which he was playing in *O Mistress Mine,* he suffered continually from a painful bleeding ulcer and his diet had to be severely restricted—not an easy sacrifice for a man who delighted in good food. He was also told to give up alcohol, which was less of a sacrifice for him. In order not to make a public show of his abstinence, Lunt often filled a martini glass with water during social occasions. With an olive floating on the water, Lunt sipped periodically from his glass.

Because of Lunt's illness, the New York run of *O Mistress Mine* came to an end on May 31, 1947, after 452 performances (the longest Broadway run of the Lunts' careers). Afterward they headed immediately to Genesee Depot for the rest Lunt's doctors had instructed him to take. But the couple had no intention of postponing the national tour arranged for the 1947–48 season. Although they had given more than 700 performances of the play by that time, "we are not tired of it yet," Lunt told the Whorfs, adding, "It's a very pleasant show to be in."

As the summer progressed, however, they were more and more reluctant to end their vacation, although, characteristically, Lunt rested less than he worked at Genesee Depot. That summer he labored to build a greenhouse and a dairy. By early October, with only two weeks' vacation remaining, he told the Whorfs, "I am sick at the thought of leaving. It has been a wonderful summer, but has passed much, much too quickly." If this was one of the first times that either of the Lunts expressed a reluctance to leave Genesee Depot, it was by no means the last. They looked forward to their vacations with a greater eagerness each year, and had difficulty generating the enthusiasm for returning to the theatre that they had always felt in the past. Although both of them vociferously denied any plan to retire, they were clearly drawn more and more to the quiet life of rural Wisconsin and away from the excitement—and the tensions—of the theatre. Even so, once they were involved in a production, they were as passionate in their devotion to it as they had ever been. Fontanne, then nearing sixty, and Lunt, fifty-five, seemed uncertain what course to take. They would not permit themselves to contemplate retirement, but they craved the peace that only retirement could bring. For the next fourteen years they remained uncertain, continuing to perform each season but expressing an ever growing reluctance to leave home.

They toured *O Mistress Mine* until the middle of 1948—a run of three and a half years when one includes the performances in Europe. No other play in which they appeared, singly or together, ran for nearly as long. It is ironic that the Lunts, who had acted in some of the world's most distinguished plays, achieved their greatest commercial success in a trivial, if well-crafted, comedy.

However, both professed to believe that *O Mistress Mine* was not in any sense an inadequate play. On the contrary, Lunt said, "The plot line was so strong you couldn't budge it. You never had any trouble keeping the interest of the audience. You could be tired and sick, but you always held the audience." He found it puzzling that the play, which was so thoroughly enjoyed by the public, was so derided by the critics, but he had no doubt that the critics were at fault. "*O Mistress Mine* was the biggest money-maker we ever were in," he said. "We never played to an empty seat, and we never got a good notice on it, either."

The tour of *O Mistress Mine* eventually came to an end, as had the Broadway run, because of Lunt's ill health. He contracted a particularly virulent form of influenza, his temperature rising to 104°, accompanied by fits of shivering. Several days later an examination discovered that he had developed still another kidney infection. A shot of penicillin restored him to good health, but left him weak and groggy. The Lunts, who had planned to finish the tour with a series of one-night stands leading them back to the Midwest, decided instead to close the production prematurely in June 1948.

Lunt's doctors told him he must not perform again for at least a year. He followed half their advice, remaining professionally inactive for six months. A vacation of a month and a half in Genesee Depot was followed by a trip to England in July. Still, the Lunts refused to consider the possibility of retirement. They committed themselves to return home in order to begin rehearsals in January 1949 for a new play adapted by S. N. Behrman.

The great success of *O Mistress Mine* helped to make the Lunts rich. They had been financially comfortable for some time, but their income was greatly increased in the late 1940s, when it averaged about $200,000 per year. They had never invested their money in a systematic way, spending most of it on vacations, additions to their estate in Wisconsin and improvements to their apartment in New York, expensive cars and gifts to one another.

Lunt was a remarkably shrewd money manager when it came to the theatre. He knew, to the dollar, just how much money should be spent on a production to make it a worthwhile investment. He could recite the weekly grosses for any of the productions he appeared in; he remembered how much money a touring performance had brought in in Biloxi or Omaha years after the event. His personal money management was, however, far less skillful.

The Lunts might have accumulated far more money if they had not turned down one proposition after another that could have made them wealthy. In addition to the million-dollar film contract they rejected in 1931, they spurned many other lucrative offers to appear in movies such as *Marie Antoinette* in 1938. In 1933, Fleischmann's Yeast offered them an eighteen-week radio contract for one twenty-minute broadcast each week at $3,000 per episode. The Lunts declined, preferring to take *Reunion in Vienna* to England.

For many years they gave little thought to the future, unconcerned about saving for retirement, both because they rarely admitted that retirement was a possibility, and because their attitude toward money seems to have been—more or less simply—that it was meant to enable them to live as graceful and elegant an existence as possible.

The expense of sustaining that existence was considerable. When they gave a dinner party, the wonderfully prepared food was served by an impeccable butler; the china, silver and glassware were exquisite; the wines were perfectly chosen to accompany each course. Dinner at the Lunts' was a ceremonial event.

While Fontanne designed and sewed many of her own clothes, a hobby that saved a good deal of money, she also purchased gowns designed for her by Molyneux, Valentina and others, which were not inexpensive. Regardless of the origin of her clothes, however, they were invariably elegant and striking.*

In the late 1940s the Lunts finally realized that their ability to produce the sort of income they needed might be jeopardized by advancing age. Fontanne told her sister Antoinette, "I have just discovered that we haven't saved one cent in the last five years and what we have saved [previously] is

---

*Lunt showed much less interest in clothing, but he, too, radiated a sense of immaculate taste. Julie Harris auditioned for their production of *I Know My Love*, and, although she was not cast, she never forgot the occasion. "He was so beautiful," she said. "And she wore a pale mink coat with a mink turban and little ivory Harlequin glasses. They were the personification of glamour. 'They were two of the most beautiful people I've ever seen' is a line from *The Member of the Wedding*, but it was really true about them. They were just perfection."

about one fourth of what I thought it would be, so as we are now no longer young and our future is mostly behind us, we are going to start [saving] like mad so that we can live in comfort more or less when we are old."

The Lunts asked Donald Seawell to counsel them on investments. At the time all their money was tied up in United States "E" Bonds. "You could hardly think of a worse investment," the lawyer told them. Seawell, who said that the booming postwar economy made it difficult *not* to make money if one had considerable capital to invest, very quickly amassed a fortune for the Lunts. When he determined that their total worth exceeded a million dollars, he flew to Genesee Depot to tell them so. Lunt was overwhelmed and a trifle befuddled. "I don't understand numbers like that," he said. Fontanne, however, had less difficulty grasping the fact of her new wealth. "We want you to have a nice long stay with us, Donny," she told Seawell, "then go back and turn it into two million."

After learning of their status as millionaires, the Lunts decided to give one another presents. Fontanne planned to give Lunt a Rolls Royce, but he found it not roomy enough for his long legs. The first time he sat in a Mercedes-Benz, he announced that his search for the right car was over. When Seawell asked if he didn't wish to look at the motor, Lunt replied, "I don't care if it has a squirrel cage going around in there as long as it's big enough for me to stretch my legs." Lunt got his Mercedes and, in return, gave Fontanne a sable coat.

One investment the Lunts had made on their own was in the Theatre Guild's production of *Oklahoma!* in 1943. Although *Oklahoma!* is now firmly established as a classic of the musical theatre, it was thought at the time to be an extremely risky proposition, as it violated so many of the accepted conventions of musical comedy. The Guild feared it would lose money and Lawrence Langner tried to dissuade the Lunts from investing in it. Nevertheless, they insisted, and their judgment was rewarded for years afterward. *Oklahoma!* paid fifty dollars for every dollar invested.*

Surely no one could begrudge the Lunts their decision to accumulate as much money as possible for their retirement. Still, it seems unfortunate that the Lunts' financial concern led them away from plays that might challenge an audience's expectations.

In 1947, while *O Mistress Mine* was still playing on Broadway, tributes to the Lunts were commonplace. They found themselves honored as the "first couple" of the American theatre. One occasion that was particularly meaningful to Lunt, because it came from his peers in the theatre, was an

---

*Their investment in *Gentlemen Prefer Blondes* (they owned five percent of the production) also paid a handsome dividend. But they were less fortunate with investments in such productions as *Bless You All* and *Out of This World*.

evening in his honor (known as a "Pipe Night") given by the Players Club, of which he was a longtime member. The Players Club was closed to women, so Fontanne was not included in that tribute.*

The Lunts were further honored on several occasions in 1950. On June 3 they participated in commencement ceremonies at New York University, where they were awarded an honorary Doctorate of Humane Letters. It was the first time the University had ever conferred a joint degree, and their citation read, "Alfred Lunt and Lynn Fontanne, whom love, labor, and universal acclaim have joined together, let no mere university tradition put asunder; wherefore we cite them for academic honors not singly and separately but jointly and simultaneously." And Fontanne was honored that same month by Russell Sage College in Troy, New York, which awarded her an honorary Doctor of Letters degree.

Their new status as national treasures may also have contributed to the Lunts' conservative approach to the selection of plays and to their determination to fight through to success at all costs. Perhaps, too, the pressures of maintaining that status contributed to the unprecedented difficulties they experienced with their old friend S. N. Behrman, the author of their next play.

1949–51

As he had done with *Amphitryon 38,* Behrman went to the French theatre for the inspiration of *I Know My Love,* an adaptation of Marcel Achard's *Auprès de ma blonde.* Behrman's new work appealed to the Lunts both because they had been lucky with his plays in the past and because *I Know My Love* would give them the opportunity to portray the same characters at different periods of their lives, from adolescence to old age, in the portrait of a fifty-year marriage. The story would be told out of chronological order, beginning in 1939 (when the couple was celebrating their fiftieth wedding anniversary), then returning to 1888 (when they were courting) and then moving forward in time from 1902 to 1920. Behrman believed that the Lunts "saw in it a parable of their own marriage."

Perhaps this loss of objectivity toward the characters led to their taking a proprietary interest in *I Know My Love* that surpassed anything they

---

*However, in 1963 the Players violated its own rule by inviting Fontanne to a Pipe Night honoring both the Lunts. She thus became the third woman to be recognized by the Players; the others had been Sarah Bernhardt and Mary Garden, many years before. In later years Lunt took pleasure in the belief that he had been a member of the Players longer than any other living actor (he was accepted for membership in 1920). But he then discovered, to his chagrin, that Sidney Blackmer had a longer tenure in the organization than he.

had demonstrated previously. Whatever the reason, their intense interest, bordering on obsession, created a crisis in their relationship with S. N. Behrman.

Generally, the Lunts agreed to appear in a play only after they had read the finished script. They might suggest alterations before the play went into rehearsal, but those rarely necessitated wholesale revisions. They often restructured their own dialogue to suit their own rhythms, but generally with the consent of the playwright (unless, as in the case of Terence Rattigan, the playwright was an ocean away). *I Know My Love* was different. They demanded, politely but firmly, that each scene and each line of dialogue meet with their approval, forcing Behrman to make many changes he preferred not to make. Eventually, the tensions became so palpable that Behrman could barely contain his anger. The Lunts, focusing as always upon the theatrical effectiveness of the play, seemed to be almost unaware of Behrman's irritation—which only increased it.

Initially, the Theatre Guild had wanted Helen Hayes to play the leading female role in *I Know My Love*. But when the Lunts heard about the new play, they made it clear they wanted it for themselves. Fontanne wrote to Behrman in March 1948, "We had read your play and had talked wildly and excitedly about it. . . . Then we came home and were filled with a terrible depression and apprehension . . . about the Guild having something so perfect for us and allowing somebody else to have it—that old vendetta . . . Oh, darling, don't let anybody but us do it. I promise you that we shall be doing it for years."

Lunt also weighed in, telling Behrman, "We love this play of yours . . . Lynn likes it better than any play she's ever read—told me so last night." He did not overstate her enthusiasm. She told her sister Antoinette, "It is very moving and very interesting. . . . Behrman has made a really lovely job of it. Personally, I think it is better than the original French."

Behrman, the Guild and Helen Hayes evidently decided they could not withstand the natural force that was the Lunts determined to appear in a play. In May 1948, Fontanne wrote to Behrman from Seattle, where the *O Mistress Mine* tour was nearing its end, telling him how happy she was that Hayes was willing to bow out gracefully. She also began to apply pressure for script changes:

> I spoke to Terry [Helburn] on the telephone and she said you would telephone us, as you had two or three approaches to the last scene that you would like to discuss. We have one or two suggestions—not about the writing of the scene, but about the staging, to give us the best possible chance for the dreamiest of dreamy lighting so that poor old Lynnie and Alfred may be given every chance to what is known as "get away with it"—and these suggestions may or may not affect your approach to the scene. So do telephone us, darling.

Behrman suggested he visit the Lunts at Genesee Depot, where they could work on the play together. Fontanne replied that they would welcome a visit, but Behrman must plan to stay no longer than a week because "Alfred is *very, very* tired, and I am anxious for him. . . . The excitement of working with you for a longer period would, I know, be bad for Alfred at this time." She offered her opinion that the play would need little work in any case, as "it is in better shape than any script I have ever seen, including Shakespeare."

As had been his custom for most of the last fifteen years, Lunt directed as well as acted in *I Know My Love.* In his early directorial assignments, he had delegated a great deal of authority to his assistant, who received program credit as the director of the play. By 1948, however, that was no longer remotely true. As he made clear to Behrman, he expected to have total control of casting, the selection of designers and the conduct of rehearsals.

As director, coproducer and leading actor, Lunt also expected the playwright to accept unquestioningly his suggestions for revisions. But it must have seemed to Behrman that Lunt had wrested the play from his hands, and that he was functioning as little more than Lunt's subordinate. "The scene should have cacophony but Lynn's long drawn out melody must be innocent & sweet," Lunt wrote on one occasion. "Do make some nice cuts in Act II won't you and in Act III," he said in another letter. Every conceivable aspect of the play, from its basic structure to the most minor details, was covered in the notes Lunt sent to Behrman.

It may be that Lunt feared his career would soon be over and he wanted *I Know My Love* to be a monument to his lifetime in the theatre. A physical examination in October left Lunt feeling depressed. The doctor, he told Behrman, "is anxious over my ever acting again, not because I'm a poor actor he *swears,* but because the result of the constant strain may pull me back into a long and painful existence—It is a chance & a decision I have to take & make—and I have decided—to continue on the stage—" He added, "I do not know whether you should mention 'my state' to the Guild or not."*

* His state of health did not improve materially during the early performances of the pre-Broadway tour. Fontanne wrote to Lady Juliet Duff in March 1949, "We started the play in Wisconsin, then had a week in the Twin Cities, Minneapolis and St. Paul. At the end of the week Alfred complained bitterly of a pain in his stomach. We had him X-rayed, and they discovered an ulcer—very large and acute. We came down from St. Paul by the night train and arrived in Genesee to find our doctor waiting. The Milwaukee week, which was to follow, was cancelled and Alfred was taken immediately into Chicago and installed in hospital.

"He had a most intensive and careful treatment and at the end of the week the ulcer had been reduced to a pinpoint. . . . Now we are in St. Louis, having opened last night. He is keeping up the half-hourly dosage of alternate milk and medicine and resting in bed all day, then going down to the theatre only for the performance at night."

During the week Lunt was in the hospital, rehearsals continued under Fontanne's direction. She also worked with Behrman to create two entirely new scenes and to revise others. These scenes were then painstakingly rehearsed so that they were fully integrated into the performance by the time Lunt returned to the company.

Lunt wanted Richard Whorf to play the important supporting role of Lunt's brother and offered him the part without consulting Behrman. Whorf turned it down, citing financial reasons, and Henry Barnard was contracted to play the role. But Lunt's failure to consult Behrman about casting was just the first in a series of decisions that showed a lack of consideration for the playwright. Lunt asked a friend, Dr. Gustav Eckstein, a professor of physiology at the University of Cincinnati, to read Behrman's script and offer his opinion. Eckstein made various recommendations for alterations, which Lunt passed on to Behrman, who—although he did not say so—may well have been irritated by Lunt's seeking the detailed opinion of a man whose relationship with literature and the theatre, however well informed, was entirely nonprofessional.

Perhaps the Lunts pushed Behrman so hard because they felt his reluctance to make needed alterations during the rehearsals of *The Pirate* had harmed that play's chances for success. During that experience, Fontanne wrote to Noël Coward saying that the Lunts and John C. Wilson had finally managed to pry "a good many big words" out of the play—but "mostly over Behrman's dead body."

While tensions with Behrman were increasing, the Lunts were honored by the Theatre Guild. *I Know My Love* was the twenty-fifth play in which they appeared for the Guild, which commemorated the occasion by adding the name of the play to the silver plaque given them four years earlier engraved with the names of all the Guild's plays in which they had acted. The year the play opened, 1949, was also the twenty-fifth anniversary of the Lunts' acting partnership, begun in 1924 with *The Guardsman.* * Lunt and Fontanne had been performing together longer than any other team in theatrical history: longer than Julia Marlowe and E. H. Sothern; longer even than the legendary Henry Irving and Ellen Terry.

They elected to open their new play at the campus theatre of the University of Wisconsin. The first performance of *I Know My Love* in February 1949 was similar to the Broadway opening of *O Mistress Mine:* as much a social as an esthetic occasion. In fact, the evening may have been more successful socially than esthetically. The play was not a strong one, observers generally agreed, although it seemed to have the potential for success. The student newspaper panned Behrman's play unmercifully, calling it "largely tedious and occasionally quite bad." Lunt responded, "The babblings of child reporters." Andrew Weaver, the brother of Lunt's boyhood friend Ray Weaver and, in 1949, president of the University, apologized to Behrman for the critic's notice, saying the review was grossly unfair to the play and should not be taken seriously.

But the critic for the St. Louis *Post-Dispatch,* Myles Standish, was no more enthusiastic about the play, although he praised the Lunts' performances. And Standish's verdict was echoed by other reviewers as the pro-

---

*The Lunts estimated that they had given more than 8,000 performances together by 1949, for audiences that totaled more than 1,250,000 people.

duction worked its way first to the west coast and then to New York.

Increasingly frustrated by the Lunts' tendency to wrest control of his play from him, Behrman was feeling bitter when he wrote to his friend Carl Hovey on May 2. Hovey had seen the production in Pasadena, and although he claimed to have enjoyed it, he suggested some changes, including making Lunt's character "richer and deeper, more manic and dangerous." Behrman replied:

> Your letter . . . meant so much to me. I read it aloud to the Langners and Alfred Lunt in Fresno. It made a deep impression on the Langners but how much Alfred retained I don't know. . . . I would love to do everything you suggest and it needs badly to be done and I think I could do it but the gross trouble is that Lynn and Alfred have a kind of psychological block toward letting me come to grips with things in this play. Wonderful actors though they are, they are like all other actors in this respect: they wish to be at all costs, what they consider to be "sympathetic." In ordinary cases a manager can make actors do what he wants but in this case the Lunts are the managers and I really can't think what can be done.
>
> I left it in San Francisco, flying here Saturday night. I did quite a bit of work [on rewriting the play]. . . . They don't mind how much you do in the way of elaborating individual scenes but the major thing . . . [i.e., adding depth to the characters] which I am only too anxious to do they will not allow me to do. It is very frustrating and by the time I got on the plane I felt ill. . . . It makes me rather sick even to tell you about these things but that is what the theatre is when you get people like Lynn and Alfred whom the public adores and whom they come to see in droves willy-nilly.

As the months wore on, Behrman continued to feel ill-used. In August, during their summer vacation in Genesee Depot, the Lunts asked Joshua Logan, the prominent Broadway director, to read and comment on the play. Fontanne wrote Behrman, "He suggested two things. . . . Would you let him come and see you and tell you about it? Now don't be frightened, darling, the things we have thought of in no way change the play, they will only clarify and bring out your own meaning. . . . Do see him, darling."

A few weeks later Fontanne sent Behrman a scene she had rewritten. "Here is the last scene with a few things added," she said, "not much really. If you like what we have done would you write it in your own words and let us have it at once so that we can learn it and get it off our minds."

By September, Behrman was threatening to quit if the Lunts would not permit him to perform the playwright's function. His frustration was clear when he wrote to Theresa Helburn that he had rewritten one line of dialogue that "is tremendously important to put in. I have tried in various ways to do it so far without success," he said. "But I will hold firm to its going in now or tell Lynn and Alfred that I can do no more."

He drafted a letter to Lunt in October that strongly expressed his bitterness. "You change your own part practically at will," Behrman wrote. "I miss very much the cut you made about the war and I think it makes a hole in the play but I do not wish you to change other people's parts. I am writing you because I really haven't the strength to argue with you endlessly about it." But before having the letter typed, Behrman decided he had been tactless. The letter he sent read, "I miss very much the cut you made about the war and I think it makes a hole in the play. I am writing to you because I really haven't the strength now to discuss this personally with you."

Throughout the process Lunt bombarded Behrman with telegrams, requesting changes in the title (he lobbied for *My Beloved Is Mine*), "the division of scenes," the number of acts (he wanted Behrman to compress three acts into two), "the quarrel scene between Emily and Tom in Act Two Scene Two" which "I think . . . is a pretty weak spot" and recommending various revisions. He gently accused Behrman of losing interest in *I Know My Love* and turning his attention to other projects (to which Behrman responded, "Quite shocked by your wire. . . . I do have other commitments but you should know that I would not undertake anything which would interfere with our project").

I Know My Love opened at the Shubert Theatre on Broadway on November 2, 1949, to a chorus of praise for the Lunts' performances and derision for Behrman's effort ("a pretty flimsy play," said Ward Morehouse in the *Sun;* "Although the Lunts are dazzling actors, it is difficult not to look at what they are playing," commented Brooks Atkinson in the *Times,* adding that the play "has nothing to say and very little to contribute to entertainment . . . untidy in construction, cluttered with clichés and nonentities and deficient in wit"; "a sprawling and uncertain play . . . frankly a vehicle rather than a play," said Richard Watts, Jr., in the *Post*). Watts's comment must have particularly annoyed Behrman, since all his efforts had been to make the play less a vehicle for the leading actors and more an honest portrayal of the vicissitudes of the married couple in the comedy.

Another view was offered by John Mason Brown, writing in the *Saturday Review.* Brown suggested that the quality of the performances transcended the deficiencies of the play, saying, "What matters is not what the play is like as a play but what it becomes as a delectable theatrical experience because of the Lunts." He went on:

> No one needs to be reminded that, much as the theatre benefits from dramatic literature, it can thrive without it. Fine acting is capable of creating a satisfactory substitute for good writing. Actors of the Lunts' perfection endow shallow scenes with depth and make tarnished situations sparkle. Their faces do the work

of words. Their voices, gestures, expressions, stance, make-up and costumes supply a self-sufficient vocabulary of their own; a vocabulary which can be eloquent, witty, moving, simple or sophisticated, and altogether enjoyable.

None of the critical reservations mattered to the Lunts' loyal fans. *I Know My Love* enjoyed a successful Broadway run of 246 performances, during which the play continued to undergo minor revisions. The production was "a smash hit," Fontanne wrote to her sister Mai. "We have had almost nothing else, it seems to me, all our lives and I really quite expected to have a flop this time."

To be sure, the production achieved immense popularity with the Lunts' devotees. But in a Broadway season that offered *The Cocktail Party* and *The Member of the Wedding* (as well as productions of *Death of a Salesman, A Streetcar Named Desire* and *The Madwoman of Chaillot* that were still running from previous seasons), the thinness of *I Know My Love* was evident to discriminating theatregoers.

Shortly after the Broadway opening, Lunt had a thorough physical. To his relief and to Fontanne's, the examination showed him to be in good health, "which," Fontanne said in a letter to Mai, "considering that he is hopping along on one kidney and that not doing one hundred percent of its job, is very good indeed."

The Broadway run ended on June 3, 1950. When rehearsals for the tour commenced early in October, the Lunts asked Behrman for additional changes, which he seems to have made willingly. Indeed, when he saw one of the performances early in the tour, he told Lunt he believed the production had improved considerably since the Broadway opening. Furthermore, he added, either in acknowledgment that the Lunts' insistence on script changes had been justified or in an attempt to preserve their long-standing friendship, "I am happy about the changes which I made."* He even offered to rewrite a scene in the second act that had been singled out by many critics as particularly ineffectual. "This complaint has come to me so often," Behrman said, "and they say it is my fault to such an extent, that I felt I wanted to write to you and if you want me to, I will make one additional try at getting the scene for you and Lynn that will really be worthy of what you two bring to it. . . . I hate to be the recipient of constant statements that I am treating your and Lynn's talents . . . so cavalierly."

Reactions to the Lunts' touring performances were overwhelmingly favorable, as usual. But a few theatregoers began to register dissatisfaction with them as well as their play. One such was Kenneth Tynan, who told an entertaining but almost certainly fictional story about the Lunts' inability

---

*However, in the published edition of the play Behrman revised the sequence of the scenes, so that the first scene was set in 1888 and the play then moved in chronological order to its conclusion in 1939.

to keep their performances vital and spontaneous while playing *I Know My Love* on tour. In the midst of a rapid-fire exchange of dialogue, Tynan said, both Lunt and Fontanne suddenly dried up completely. Neither could recall the next line or think of a word to improvise. Instead, both stopped cold until they could be prompted. The stage manager found the line and whispered it to the actors, frozen in place on the stage. They didn't respond, so he gave the line again, slightly louder this time. When there was again no acknowledgment, he called the line still louder. At last Lunt turned his head toward the wings and whispered, "We know the line, dear boy, but we don't know which of us says it."

Whether or not Tynan's anecdote had any basis in fact—and it is impossible to believe that it is anything but an amusing invention—the story reveals the way some people were beginning to regard the Lunts.

Years before, Lunt had told Robert E. Sherwood that his only reason for being an actor and a director was to serve as a conduit from the playwright to the audience. There can be no question that he held that belief firmly and sincerely. But in *I Know My Love* he and his wife insisted that the play be wrenched out of shape only so that it would serve their purposes as star performers. Furthermore, the Lunts had exerted pressure on the Guild and Behrman to remove Helen Hayes from the play in order to get it for themselves—an action they would surely have called reprehensible had it been done to them.

Accusations were made that the Lunts were more interested in personal triumph than in the production of outstanding drama. More than a few theatregoers began to view them as an anachronism, a carry-over from a bygone era, appealing only to that portion of the theatrical public whose tastes were simple, whose intellectual and emotional horizons were limited, whose appetite for innovation was nonexistent. Perhaps the sort of audience the Lunts seemed to attract—the socialites, the pseudo-sophisticated—was what they deserved after all, some voices were heard to imply.

But the Lunts' loyal fans remained as devoted as ever. The tour continued until the late spring of 1951, playing to sold-out houses at each stop, and the box-office receipts helped to increase the Lunts' fortune.

Their concern with finances was evident in a letter Lunt wrote to Theresa Helburn, Lawrence Langner and Armina Marshall of the Theatre Guild. "I found out at the beginning of this tour that we have been charged half the salary of the wig man," he wrote. "Why? I told you before we started out two years ago that it would be cheaper to have a man do the wigs than to send them out locally. There are thirteen wigs in this play and because of the quick changes they must be dressed after every performance and the expense of sending them to local hairdressers would have been colossal, but by having our own man we save at least fifty dollars a week. I remember saying that if you couldn't get one I would have to, but we made no agreement to that effect and I must say, after fifty-three weeks of playing, it comes as something of a shock that we have been charged for this. In our checks I noticed we were each always short some thirty dollars. . . ."

Years before, the Lunts had deeply resented the Theatre Guild's refusal to reimburse them for costume expenses. Although they never said so publicly, perhaps it was this trivial matter—the Guild's charging them for the services of the wig man—that led them to sever their connection with the organization. After the tour of *I Know My Love*, the Lunts appeared in some radio and television productions presented by the Theatre Guild, but never acted in a stage play for the Guild again.

1951–53

When the Lunts went home to Genesee Depot in 1951, they had no definite plans for the future. Yet they still gave no indication that they were contemplating retirement.

Noël Coward came to visit that spring, and as the three old friends were talking one evening the Lunts idly suggested that it was about time he wrote another play for them. Coward needed no further prompting. He was well aware of the benefits of having the Lunts appear in one of his plays—or, for that matter, in the work of any playwright. Perhaps their presence was not an automatic guarantee of success, but it was surely the nearest thing to it. Their ability to turn any play into a commercial success had been commemorated as early as 1929 by Ring Lardner in a poem published in the New York *Morning Telegraph:*

> *Rhyme Without Treason*
>
> There was a man who wrote a play;
> One week it ran, then died away,
> Though critics said 'twould be a hit
> And even Ervine lauded it.*
> 'Twas not too pure or too obscene;
> The plot was hot, the satire keen.
> "It lacked two things," observed the man;
> "Just Alfred Lunt and Lynn Fontanne."
>
> A play that millions didn't see
> Was one by Mr. C'on and me;
> The star was Walter Huston and
> He acted absolutely grand.
> The piece's failure to endure

* St. John Ervine was the guest critic for the New York *World* when Lardner's poem was written.

Was not his fault, yet I am sure
We could have lasted out the mont'
With Lynn Fontanne and Alfred Lunt.*

The Theatre Guild takes Mother Goose,
A postcard from Anita Loos,
Professor Bore on Patent Law
An epigram by Harry Thaw,
Or some Hungarian goulash,
Adapted by Joe Balderdash,
And has a play you just can't pan
With Alfred Lunt and Lynn Fontanne.

I watched a crowd one recent night
Go into spasms of delight
About a play† whose claim to wit
Rests on one oft-repeated bit:
The swilling, by a profligate,
Of sodium bicarbonate.
They loved this subtly comic stunt
(With Lynn Fontanne and Alfred Lunt).

You want to pack 'em in out front?
Hire Lynn Fontanne and Alfred Lunt.
Is wounding Joe LeBlang your plan?‡
Hire Alfred Lunt and Lynn Fontanne.
Wouldst have a smash, not just a bunt?
Sign Lynn Fontanne and Alfred Lunt.
The madam craves a Rolls sedan?
Get Alfred Lunt and Lynn Fontanne.

To hell with story and with plot,
Love interest, passion, cold or hot,
With traffic meliorations which
End one-night stands in a one-way ditch!
To hell with competition from
The rasping pictures or the dumb!
Show business needs and needs at once
More Lynn Fontannes and Alfred Lunts.

The Lunts and Coward came up with the idea for a play to be set in 1873—possibly because Coward had been reading nineteenth-century novelists during his stay in Genesee Depot. Lunt was to play a wealthy Midwestern businessman, a railroad magnate. The idea struck Lunt's fancy

* Lardner and George M. Cohan collaborated on *Elmer the Great,* which lasted slightly more than a "mont'" (five weeks) in the 1928–29 season.

† *Caprice.*

‡ Joe LeBlang ran an office which sold cut-rate tickets to plays that were not selling out at box-office prices.

immediately, and he thought of his father as the model for the character. Together, Coward and the Lunts sketched out a plot, with each of them adding details of characterization and action. By the time Coward's visit was over, the play—to be called *Quadrille*—had taken on a reasonably firm structure in everyone's mind.

Less than ten months later, Coward brought the finished play to the Lunts in New York. He had reworked the original plot line considerably so that it now bore some resemblance to *Private Lives,* with the stories of two married couples intertwining. Lunt's character, Axel Diensen, has been deserted by his wife, who has run off with the Marquess of Heronden. Axel calls upon the Marchioness, Serena, the character to be played by Fontanne, at her home in Belgrave Square. They determine to win back their spouses by following them to France. They succeed, but both of them come to realize that the effort was hardly worth the trouble because, in the process of getting to know one another, Axel and Serena have fallen in love. Finally, in a reversal of the play's initial situation, it is Axel and Serena who leave their spouses and set off together for France, after which they plan to go to America.

The Lunts approved of Coward's work and agreed at once to perform in *Quadrille*. Before dinner the three of them not only discussed the casting of the other roles but also decided when and where they would like to open the production: in London in September. Two reasons governed this decision. After an absence of seven years, the Lunts longed to return to Fontanne's home country, and Coward had commitments in England he could not break, so that, had the rehearsals been held in America, he would not have been present to do whatever rewriting might become necessary.

The Lunts traveled to England five months before the scheduled opening in order to assist Coward—whom they had asked to direct—with the casting. When all the actors had been signed to contracts, the performers were told that rehearsals would begin on June 16, and that they would be expected to have their lines memorized at the first rehearsal. Meanwhile, they were free to do as they wished.

The Lunts rented a tiny apartment at 27 Kylestrome House in order to be close to Coward, who lived practically across the road. After working with him on minor revisions, the Lunts took a brief holiday in Paris. On May 15 Lunt wrote to William Le Massena, "We've been here ten days & for the first time I really love Paris. It's incredibly beautiful at this time of year & equally expensive—But the food is superb so what can one do but eat & pay—"

In early June they returned to London. The rehearsal process was smooth and uneventful. No rewriting was found to be necessary and only a few minor cuts were made. Everyone concerned believed the play would be successful, and that belief seemed to be confirmed when the production opened in Manchester on July 16. Despite the fact that Fontanne's wig fell off during one of her scenes, *Quadrille* was generally well received, although certain weaknesses became evident in the light of audience reaction. Coward was kept busy writing new scenes, which were handed out to the actors after each performance. The performers learned their new lines overnight, the scenes were rehearsed the following afternoon and added to the production in the evening. The necessity to learn and assimilate so much new material so quickly was a burden for the actors, and especially for Fontanne, who was then sixty-four. It was "like three months of opening nights," she said.

The reaction to *Quadrille* in Edinburgh was gratifying. The jagged edges were being smoothed, it seemed, and everyone connected with the production was encouraged. Lunt wrote to Le Massena on August 2, "We love the play & acting in it and the company are all dears—so we hope & pray London will like it—Five more weeks on tour—Glasgow & Liverpool after here—"

On September 12, *Quadrille* opened in London. As always, first-night nerves were in evidence; one member of the supporting cast was astonished to find Lunt and Fontanne less than majestic and serene, saying of them: "They were shimmering like a hot road!" But the audience was appreciative and a triumphant party was held at Hugh (Binkie) Beaumont's.

When the reviews came out the next morning, however, Coward was shocked and disappointed. He wrote in his diary: "Woke up after last night's [opening] to find that the Press were unanimous in abusing the play. The Lunts were praised, but the play viciously torn to pieces." The review in the London *Times* was typical. "Each [of the Lunts] acts brilliantly, or perhaps it would be more exact to say that the single performance into which their individual contributions coalesce has many shining passages," said the critic. But "it is an evening of hesitant laughter and of imperfect sentimental sympathies between author and audience. . . ." The critic for the *Daily Express* concurred. "Without the Lunts," he said, "*Quadrille* would be a dull dance indeed." Still, the critics noted that the play was likely to be a popular success. Indeed, box-office sales were brisk, and *Quadrille* settled down to an extended London run. Lunt wrote to Le Massena on September 27, "Quadrille is selling out but of course our pleasure has been dimmed by the cruelty of the press to Noel—He seems not to mind but it gets *me* down. However the play's a joy to act in & we look forward to each performance with renewed excitement—"

But even the Lunts came in for their share of criticism. Some observers expressed weariness at seeing the Lunts wasting their talents in such plays. W. A. Darlington noted that each of their last three plays—*Love in Idleness, I Know My Love* and now *Quadrille*—"had an air of being written to order; each was far below its author's standard. . . . It is disturbing to think that if their present policy continues, we may never see the Lunts in a really good play again. They are falling into a habit, which is apt to beset very great stars, of looking not for plays but for parts which may serve as vehicles for their personalities."

Kenneth Tynan agreed. "I wish the Lunts would test themselves in better plays," he said. "I wish I even felt sure that they knew a good script when they saw one. As things are, they have become a sort of grandiose circus act; instead of climbing mountains, they are content to jump through hoops."

As time went on, Coward began to be upset by Lunt's performance. "Alfred overplaying a little bit," he noted on November 6. On March 28, 1953, his diary entry says, "Alfred was overplaying a bit but Lynn was superb." And by September 13 of that year Coward was convinced that Lunt's "overplaying" had gotten completely out of hand. He wrote:

> I attended the last performance of *Quadrille* at Streatham. It was a fairly gruesome evening. Lynn was wonderful. . . . The real horror was Alfred, who overplayed badly. He crouched and wriggled and camped about like a massive *antiquaire* on heat [*sic*]. It is so depressing that such a really beautiful actor can go so far wrong. . . . When I think of Alfred's original performance and compare it with what I saw last night, I feel the clammy touch of despair. There is nothing to be done. I shall tell him later on when he is less tired, but the effect of what I say will soon evaporate and he will begin again to rearrange, re-rehearse and change everything about. It is really very tiresome. As far as the American production is concerned, there are only two alternatives: one is for me to be there virtually at every rehearsal and at least twice a week after they have opened. The other is to let them do as they like. I need hardly say I will choose the latter course because life is short. . . .

The charge that Lunt was rearranging and changing Coward's play and his direction was undoubtedly accurate. But this can be seen from a different perspective. Lunt rearranged and re-rehearsed each long-running production he was in, but his primary motivation was to ensure against the play's becoming stale through repetition.

While the run of *Quadrille* was in progress, Lunt found that he was failing to get a laugh he thought he should have been getting. He said:

> I was playing a Middlewest railroad man in an English drawing room and I suddenly ask [the Marchioness, played by Fontanne] for a cup of tea. Well, to me it was slightly amusing, because of all the men in the world, he wouldn't have asked for a cup of tea. He would have asked for a drink. Well, I said to her, "That has never amused the audience." You can always feel when an audience is amused, whether they laugh aloud or not, they don't have to guffaw all over the place. You know that they're amused. At least they aren't coughing. And she said, "Well, I know why it doesn't get a laugh. You're not asking for a cup of tea. You're

asking for a laugh." Well, it's a kind of thing in a reading—you understand, you can push something, and it isn't *true*.

It was precisely through this process of discussion leading to re-rehearsal, leading to fresher and more genuine methods of expression, that the Lunts' productions were so often observed to improve with time.

Coward made an interesting comment in an interview about his direction of the Lunts in *Quadrille;* interesting because it can be taken either as a compliment or as veiled derision. "Direct the Lunts?" he asked. "When you do a play with the Lunts, nobody directs them. Oh, they have a delusion that they listen to a director, but they don't. *Quadrille,* it was said, was directed by Noël Coward. Noël Coward refused the honor." In the program, Coward inserted the sentence: "Directed by the author with grateful acknowledgment to Miss Fontanne and Mr. Lunt."

Plans for an American presentation of *Quadrille* were taking concrete shape in the fall of 1953. By that time Coward felt that he had lost all control over his play, and he clearly resented it. His diary entries record descriptions of the Lunts' personalities that vary from laudatory to insulting. Fontanne, for example, is described as "mentally slow with flashes of brilliant swiftness," while Lunt is said to be "quick as a knife with flashes of dreadful obtuseness." He calls them "gay and sweet and warm and friendly" in one sentence while accusing them of being utterly selfish in the next. The only things that mattered to them, Coward said, were "themselves, the theatre (in so far as it concerns themselves), and food—good, hot food." Coward claimed to "love and admire them both so much," and he said that Lunt "has tremendous charm, great humor and is, or can be, an actor of genius"; but he also said that Lunt "is weak, hysterical and not to be trusted on stage."

If the Lunts had any inkling of Coward's ambivalent feelings, they kept the knowledge to themselves. Both in interviews and in private conversation, they always referred to Coward in the most complimentary and friendly terms.

After the year-long British run of *Quadrille* came to an end, the Lunts delayed the New York opening so that they could get some rest. They returned to the United States late in 1953.

1954–57

Since the American production of *Quadrille* was not scheduled to open until October 1954, the Lunts had the opportunity to take almost a full year's vacation at Genesee Depot. But for at least forty years both of them had been accustomed to returning to the theatre each autumn, and habit dies hard. So when the Playwrights' Company approached Lunt in the fall of 1953 asking him to direct the American premiere of Jean Giraudoux's *Ondine,* he agreed to do so.*

The summer of 1954 was a busy one at Genesee Depot. Ben Perkins, the farm's caretaker, was ill, so Lunt was driven to do Perkins's work as well as his own. "My hands are so sore I can hardly write," he said in a letter to Richard Whorf. His ulcer continued to plague him, as well, and that interfered with his farm work. Again, he must have been haunted by the possibility that he might be forced into an unwilling retirement.

The process of assembling a cast for *Quadrille* started in August, and rehearsals began in mid-September, with Lunt serving as director. Among the actors selected to be in the company were Edna Best and Brian Aherne, both of whom gave expert performances. *Quadrille* opened in Boston on October 14, with Lunt even more than usually tense. "Being director of the play, I had to watch the other actors. I stood in the wings during the first scene watching them, and watching made me nervous," he said.

"He certainly was," agreed Fontanne. "When he came onstage in his first scene, his hand was as cold as ice. He put his hand out and I took it. It was just as if someone had put a cold fish in my hand."

Despite Lunt's apprehensions, the production was greeted enthusiastically by the Boston critics. Lunt wrote to Noël Coward in England, enclosing the favorable notices, and told him he had put back many of the original lines that had been deleted while the play was in Great Britain. Coward replied, "It is all very exciting and I am terribly thrilled."

But Coward was beginning to suspect that the hostility he had felt toward the Lunts in England had not been concealed as thoroughly as he had believed. He detected a coolness in their letters. "The only thing, of course, that saddens me a little is the inside feeling I have of stiffness between you and Lynnie and me," he said in a letter to Lunt on October 25. "Lynn's tart little note which started 'Dear Noël' and finished 'Love Lynn' was rather chilling which I presume it was intended to be. None of this can be explained satisfactorily until we meet but it certainly must be then. It naturally makes me unhappy that my motives should be misunderstood by you two who I have loved so much for so many years.

"I shall come and see the play the night I arrive," he continued, "and will expect to be asked to supper after the performance. No place cards will be necessary and if conversation should be a little stilted during the first part of the soiree I hope by the end of the evening Lynnie might be induced to call me 'Noëlie' on leaving and even perhaps to let me kiss her hand. Failing this, I shall be forced to goose you both thoroughly as I always have and always will."

The production came to the Coronet Theatre in New York on November 3. As in London, the critical response tended to be rapturously enthusiastic with regard to the Lunts, but tepid about the play. Brooks

* A discussion of *Ondine* will be found in the next chapter.

Atkinson's review in the *Times* was representative: "This is what acting should be in an artificial though sentimental comedy, quick, resilient, charming, gallant, enormously expert. They play together even when they are listening." He further observed, "Ideally, they should devote these skills to Congreve or Wycherley. But, in devoting them to a pleasant charade by Mr. Coward, they are going to make a lot of people happy." They obviously made the voters for the Antoinette Perry Awards happy; Lunt was honored with a Tony for the best performance of the season.

When Noël Coward saw his play in New York at the end of November, he noted in his diary, "It is very well done, mostly better than in London. Lynn and Alfred are superb." The bitterness he had felt in England seemed to have vanished. When the published version of *Quadrille* was issued in America, the dedication read, "For Lynn and Alfred, with more than thirty years of love and admiration."

But Coward was less than pleased with the Lunts' decision to close the play on March 12 and not to tour with it to Philadelphia and Chicago. He claimed that the company pleaded with them to keep *Quadrille* going, but the Lunts' decision remained firm. "Whether this is because they are old or cross or tired or just stubborn I don't know," Coward said in a diary entry. "I think, for the sake of the company, the management and me, they should make the effort but I don't know what is really going on in their minds. They have, after all, played it a long time and I don't think either of them is very well. I have said nothing one way or the other. . . ."

Coward must have had a short memory. The decision to close the play—a decision in which he had been involved—was based on economic considerations. Earlier in the run of *Quadrille,* Coward and the Lunts had approached Donald Seawell, asking him to take over the management of the production from John C. Wilson. Coward, Wilson and the Lunts had been partners in Transatlantic Productions for more than two decades, but the relationship had become strained. Both Coward and the Lunts told Seawell that Wilson's drinking had begun to affect his professional judgment. For example, they said, he had budgeted *Quadrille* in such a way that even when the Coronet Theatre was filled to capacity, it was losing in excess of $5,000 each week. To rectify that situation, all agreed to Wilson's suggestion that they each accept five percent of the gross receipts rather than their customary ten percent. Now they wanted Seawell to dissolve Transatlantic Productions and assume the producer's responsibilities.

It must have been particularly frustrating to the Lunts that Brian Aherne was receiving more money than they were. Aherne had signed for a salary of $1,200 per week which was automatically to be raised to $1,500 in early February 1955. By that time the weekly grosses had fallen off to about $24,000, so that each of the Lunts was receiving $300 per week less than Aherne, whose contribution to the production was surely less significant than that of Lunt, the leading player, director and coproducer.

According to Donald Seawell, the Lunts told him when he agreed to take over the production, "You let us know the minute the investors are paid back in full, and we're closing this play." When he notified the Lunts that the investments had been repaid, they immediately told him to post the closing notice.

As for the decision not to take the play on tour, there are at least two different versions. Lunt told Alan Hewitt he "could not bear to read any more bad notices for Coward, although they liked the play, and enjoyed performing it." On the other hand, Lunt had written to Maxwell Anderson on March 30, 1954 (months before *Quadrille* opened in New York), "We can't take it on tour (even if it should happen to be a success) as the production is too heavy."

That summer the pair turned their energies to a new play being written for them by Howard Lindsay and Russel Crouse, to be called *The Great Sebastians*. Lindsay's friendship with the Lunts predated 1920, and Crouse's began in the 1930s when he was the press agent for the Theatre Guild. Lindsay and Crouse had begun writing together during that period, achieving considerable success with their book for the musical *Anything Goes* in 1934. When Crouse decided to pursue his writing career full-time, the Lunts threw an elaborate party for him on the stage of the Shubert Theatre, where *Idiot's Delight* was then running. When the party finally came to an end at 5:00 in the morning and Crouse was on his way out the door, Lunt stopped him and said, "Now that you're a playwright, go home and write a play for us."

Lindsay and Crouse never forgot that suggestion. They wrote several plays with the Lunts in mind, but one circumstance or another always prevented the Lunts from appearing in them. The playwrights believed that they could persuade them to play the leads in *Life with Father*, but while Lunt was enthusiastic about the play, Fontanne declined. "I've been seducing you in the theatre for twenty years," Lunt said to her. "Here's a chance to marry, settle down and have children. Don't you think it's about time?" Fontanne was unmoved. "I don't think I'd want to spend every night worrying about getting you baptized," she said laconically.

In the summer of 1954, Lunt had suggested to Lindsay and Crouse that they write a comedy about two mind-readers. Fontanne added that the characters might become involved in a dangerous situation from which they could extricate themselves by using their mind-reading skills. The playwrights devised a plot that would feature Lunt and Fontanne as a European mind-reading act caught up in a flurry of political intrigue. The Lunts had appeared in plays of many kinds, but never in a melodrama. The opportunity to act in such a play appealed to them, as did the fact that Fontanne's character was to be a Cockney. Moreover, Lindsay and Crouse intended to use the personalities of the Lunts as models for the fictional characters they would portray. They even included a characteristic bit of repartee that the Lunts had used in interviews and on occasions when they were being honored:

HE: In all our years together there has never been one thought
  of divorce.
SHE: Oh, no, never.
HE: Murder, yes!
SHE: Yes!
HE: But never divorce.

But all of these elements might not have persuaded the Lunts to do
the play if the main characters had not been performers in a vaudeville-like
setting. Lunt was a lifelong admirer of vaudeville, and his enthusiasm for
the form amounted to a passion.*

Perhaps the vaudeville act Lunt admired more than any other was the
mind-reading team of Harry and Emma Sharrock, who served as the pro-
totypes for the characters in *The Great Sebastians*. Lunt first saw the Sharrocks on the Orpheum Circuit in 1916. Their mind-reading system was
based on an elaborate code, a portion of which they taught to the fascinated young actor who was performing on the same bill as Lillie Langtry's
leading man in *Ashes*. They gave him a photograph of themselves in-
scribed, "To Al, our legit friend," which he retained as a treasured posses-
sion for the rest of his life. In an article for *Billboard*, he wrote, "I remember, with shivers still ascending and descending along my spine, the mind-
reading act of Harry and Emma Sharrock . . . the only word for which is
great. They were so good that when I was on the same bill with them I
was actually afraid to think, so sure I was that they could read my mind
right thru the dressing-room walls."

Lunt's affection for the Sharrocks and for vaudeville helped to interest
him in *The Great Sebastians*. Nor did it hurt when the playwrights sug-

---

*That enthusiasm dated from the time when, as a child in Milwaukee, he was taken to
see vaudeville shows by his mother, and was heightened when he was a young actor performing in one-act plays in vaudeville in 1916–17. Lunt invariably stood enraptured in the wings
as the other acts on the bill did their turns. "In fact," he said, "I was seldom out of the wings
except for the fifteen minutes when I had to be on stage myself."

After he had become established as an actor in New York, he never missed a Monday
matinee at the Palace, and when he was on tour he would always seek out the local vaudeville
houses. Vaudeville performers "were, intrinsically, the truest artists I have ever known," he
said later. "Vaudeville was real show business. I never saw any phase of the theatre in which
everything counted so much. Vaudeville actors never let down for a minute. They fought to
score each individual point and if they failed to do it they took the act apart to find out what
was the matter and worked until it was right. I have never known any group in the theatre
who, day after day and night after night, gave better performances."

The impact these performers made on him was enormous. He, too, was famous for
"never letting down for a minute." And there can be no doubt that his desire for perfection
was strongly influenced by his early vaudeville experiences.

Lunt's favorites among the vaudeville acts he saw included Fink's Mules, Burns and
Allen ("The thing of which I am proudest in the theatre," he said, "is that years ago, before
Broadway ever heard of them, I spotted Burns and Allen in vaudeville and predicted a sensational future for them"), Sophie Tucker, James Barton's mad-dog routine and Sliding Billy
Watson. His interest extended to burlesque, carnivals and the circus. He was an avid reader
of *Billboard*, the theatrical trade paper, because in its pages he could find news about the
variety performers whose fortunes he loved to follow.

gested the Lunts coproduce the play with full approval of the script, the casting, the director and the designers. Rather than having to fight for it, the Lunts were being offered near-total control of the production from the outset.

By early 1955 Lindsay and Crouse were taking scenes to the Coronet Theatre (where *Quadrille* was playing) for the Lunts' approval. After the Lunts returned to Genesee Depot, the playwrights sent more scenes as they were completed. The Lunts took an active hand in reshaping the material. Lunt, in particular, made notes on each segment of the play and sent his comments to Lindsay and Crouse. "We realize how enormously helpful you two are going to be," the playwrights said in a letter of June 15, and added: "We expect a great deal from you in the rounding out of the characters."

On several occasions Lindsay and Crouse visited the Lunts in Wisconsin for face-to-face discussions of the play and plans for its production. One idea, which came to fruition, was to approach CBS about supplying all the financing, with the understanding that the Lunts would perform the play on television at the conclusion of the Broadway run and the road tour. The expectation was that CBS would be especially enthusiastic because the program would represent the Lunts' television debut as a team.*

Rewrites continued throughout July and August, with the Lunts never quite satisfied. Invariably, as each new version arrived, they had more changes to recommend. There is no evidence to suggest that Lindsay and Crouse were offended by the Lunts' persistence, but at last, in late August, the playwrights suggested, "It is time for us to put the script into mimeograph and have parts made." Then Lindsay and Crouse began to interview prospective actors and wrote to the Lunts: "We hope to have quite a few lined up for you to look at when you arrive."**

Rehearsals began early in October under Bretaigne Windust's direction, and the production was ready for its out-of-town tryout on November 3, when the first performance was given in Wilmington, Delaware.

From the beginning, *The Great Sebastians* was popular with the public. Critics found little to praise about the play, but the Lunts reveled in their roles as mind-readers and seldom failed to astonish audiences. Walking in the theatre aisles, exchanging banter with the customers, Lunt would throw questions at Fontanne in her role as the "medium." She,

---

*In late 1951, Lunt had appeared twice on the "Ed Sullivan Show" on CBS. On November 18, he, Helen Hayes, Raymond Massey, Humphrey Bogart, James Mason and others were featured in a program that paid tribute to Robert E. Sherwood. On December 31, Lunt and Hayes appeared once again, and were joined on the telecast by Sherwood himself.

† Shortly before the Lunts left Genesee Depot, the playwrights sent a separate playful letter to each of them. To Fontanne, they said, "Dear Lynn: Would you read this play and consider playing the part of Essie? We are trying to interest Mr. Lunt in the part of Rudi." Fontanne wired back her equally playful answer: "YES, BUT NOT WITH ALFRED LUNT." The letter to Lunt read: "Dear Alfred: Would you read this play? We are hoping you will like the part of Rudi. We are also hoping Miss Fontanne will consider playing Essie." Lunt's telegram contained the message: "YES, BUT NOT WITH LYNN FONTANNE."

standing blindfolded on stage, would answer with accurate personal information about the members of the audience. The code they mastered, which enabled them to communicate "telepathically," involved approximately 150 cues, each one consisting of a phrase that corresponded to a number from one to nine. Each number signaled an object—a hat, a coat, a handkerchief, a glove, a pair of eyeglasses. For example, Lunt might ask, "Can you tell me, Madam, just what object this lady is showing me?" "Can you tell me" would translate to the number 2, "Madam" to the number 5, "this lady" to the number 8; and 258 would mean an engagement ring. Fontanne would call out the correct object, and the audience would invariably burst into applause.

Part of the fun, of course, was that Lunt actually walked into the auditorium and spoke directly to members of the audience. Lunt observed that the technique had its drawbacks, however. Certain people, he found, "just go rigid; they freeze. And if I try to look them in the face, they freeze up and turn away."

The Great Sebastians gave "out-of-town" performances for nine weeks before opening in New York. Each performance was used to examine the flaws in the play and the production, and the results were applied to the rehearsal that preceded the next evening's performance. In all, then, the production was rehearsed for thirteen weeks before its official opening, a much more extensive preparation period than any production would be likely to receive in the 1980s. The play itself never became a significant work, but the performance was polished until it shone brightly. Russel Crouse said, "The Lunts are perfectionists. Rehearsals are long and repetitious. They are tireless, they must go over and over it until it is perfect, and then they keep it the same way night after night after night."

The Lunts' enthusiasm for hard work had been their trademark for decades. But even if they had been inclined to give anything less than maximum effort in *The Great Sebastians,* there would have been little opportunity to do so. The play called for them to be on stage for all but seven minutes of the performance, during which they were making a costume change.

The Great Sebastians opened at the ANTA Theatre in New York (the scene of so many of the Lunts' past triumphs when it had been called the Guild before undergoing renovation) on January 4, 1956. As the performance began, Fontanne stood on stage, blindfolded, in a flowing white chiffon robe and a jeweled turban. Lunt roamed the audience, looking for items for his clairvoyant partner to identify. One of the "items" he found was Richard Watts, Jr., the New York Post's drama critic. Fontanne identified Watts and then proceeded to read his mind.

One of Lunt's standard lines when speaking to members of the audience was "Have we ever met before?" On opening night he asked this question of a man seated on the aisle, and the man answered, "Oh, hundreds of times! I've seen you hundreds of times!" Lunt was flabbergasted; the play could hardly proceed unless he could reestablish his persona as Rudi Sebastian, so he improvised: "Not in Prague! You must be thinking of my brother, who is much older than I am." The audience roared and the play was able to continue.

In a pattern that had become familiar, the critics' notices praised the Lunts and the production while expressing reservations about the play itself. Brooks Atkinson of the *Times* was especially critical. "As usual the Lunts are giving a bright performance in a dullish play," Atkinson's review began. "Being the most gifted comedy actors we have, they naturally love to imitate vaudeville hams and revel in the most elementary buncombe of the business—florid gestures, cocky strutting, shrewd behavior at the wings when they are milking the audience for applause. . . . For the next hour they struggle manfully with an inert drama."

There was some "merchantable melodrama" in the last act, Atkinson conceded, but it hardly made up for "the heavy boredom" of the earlier scenes. But if the play was a disappointment, the Lunts' performances once more compensated for it: "Mr. Lunt gives a gay and droll performance that is full of amusing details. And Miss Fontanne, reverting to the accent of Eliza Doolittle in *Pygmalion,* complements her husband's performance with some vaudeville mummery that is equally ironic and entertaining. Everything they do is meticulous, pertinent, fluent and funny.

". . . golly," Atkinson's review concluded, "what they could do if they selected a script as subtle and skillful as they are! For instance, something written with literary distinction."

This sort of notice might please many actors, but it left the Lunts dissatisfied. "The critics have been nice to us," Lunt said, "but they're always saying 'it isn't worthy of them.' Well, you know, I'm getting kind of sick and tired of that."

Fontanne claimed that the play "got the best notices we have had for many many years, almost 100%, only one dissenting voice, wonderful notices." And she was able to work in a sly bit of revenge against the "one dissenting voice" a few nights after the opening. When, in the first scene, Lunt asked her to name the newspaper a customer had in his pocket, she correctly identified it as the New York *Times* and then asked, innocently, "Is there such a paper?"

The Lunts were convinced—or pretended to be convinced—that *The Great Sebastians* was a good play, regardless of critical opinion. "All the time we played it we never once heard a cough," Lunt said. "Never. Now during the coughing season, all during the winter, viruses on the chests, nobody coughed at *The Sebastians,* and every line that was meant to get a laugh got a laugh. It's an extremely well-made play." Fontanne added that Noël Coward agreed with them; she said Coward had told her, "You know, this play is really brilliantly built, it's a very well-made play."

But, in fact, Atkinson's opinion was shared by many critics. Harold Clurman, writing in the *Nation,* said that when the play ended, "one remembers almost nothing of it, except that one was rather amused. The Lunts are so expert that they make whatever they do seem like something to watch even when there is very little." Clurman had often written that the Lunts' choice of plays was their weakest attribute, and had pleaded with them to select more substantial dramas. But he viewed *The Great Sebastians* with resigned acceptance. "The Lunts want to be just what they are," he lamented.

After a run of 174 performances on Broadway, the Lunts took their play on the road. There, as in New York, many of the critics dismissed *The Great Sebastians* as negligible. And again Lunt was irritated. He wrote to Crouse from Chicago on November 1, 1956, "the reviews were so dreary—might all have been written by one tired, shabby hack—so routine—so dusty." But, he said, "the audiences couldn't be more satisfactory."

Following their familiar pattern, the Lunts continued to strive for improvement with each performance. On January 14, 1957, when *The Great Sebastians* was playing in San Francisco, Lunt wrote excitedly to Crouse: "We have *3 new sure fire laughs* in Act I, Scene II." And the continuing hard work paid off in audience responses. "You should have been out front—at the Curran on Saturday," Lunt told Crouse; "laughs from start to finish & thunderous curtain calls—it would have done your heart & soul good. . . . We just pray it will keep up."

Even after forty-five years in the professional theatre, Lunt remained as enthusiastic as a beginner. And even after an extensive run in *The Great Sebastians,* he was still unable to control his stage fright. On one occasion he wrote to Crouse from Chicago: "Good audience last night, Lynn was wonderful, but I was jumpy—much too nervous."

As soon as the road tour ended, the television production of the play went into rehearsal. *The Great Sebastians* was transmitted live on April 2, 1957, and almost everything about the production seems to have been a disaster. The play was edited clumsily, so its contrivances seemed more awkward and unconvincing than they had on stage; there was no audience to provide a response to the broad humor of the play; and the Lunts' bravura performances, so skillful and ironic on the stage, seemed grotesquely exaggerated when seen in television close-up.* "To make matters worse,"

---

*Or perhaps it was simply an extension of the performances the Lunts gave on tour. At least two observers described the Lunts' performances at the end of *The Great Sebastians* tour as highly theatricalized—exaggerated to such an extent that the humanity of the characters was neglected.

Twelve years earlier, one writer commented that both the Lunts were overplaying when *Love in Idleness* was being given for army camps in France and Germany. Noël Coward found Lunt's portrayal becoming broader and less disciplined during the touring performances of *Quadrille* in England. The New York production of *Quadrille* demonstrated that the Lunts were capable of restoring discipline to performances that had become overblown (at least in the opinion of some), but it may be that from 1945 to 1957 the Lunts were guilty of progressively broadening their performances when they were appearing outside New York and London. If so, this would only be another example of their "loss of perspective" during these years.

Regardless of how broadly or subtly the Lunts were playing, they still aimed for perfec-

as Jack Gould said in the *Times,* the Lunts "had to race the clock to accommodate the plot. Accordingly, the familiar niceties of their interplay had to be sacrificed in deference to the play's narrative hokum." All in all, Gould, an admirer of the Lunts, was forced to report that the television production was "a painful embarrassment."

Not all the reviews were quite so critical. The *Herald Tribune* and the *World Telegram and Sun* expressed mild approbation, but the verdict expressed by *Variety* was shared by most observers—"one of the most abysmal productions yet to hit the television spec trail."

One person who was particularly happy to see *The Great Sebastians* come to an end was Noël Coward. "With the Lunts," he commented, "the play comes first. Right or wrong, the play comes first. . . . When they are working on a play they do have a tendency to concentrate on it to the exclusion of everything else. Every time I saw the Lunts they would start talking about *The Great Sebastians* until I said, 'If I hear this damned play mentioned once more, I'm going to get up and knock your damned heads together until your brains start rattling.'"

The allegation that so irritated the Lunts—that they had wasted their talents by acting in trivial plays—was not new. As early as 1934, Hiram Motherwell had taken the Lunts to task in the pages of *Stage* magazine for continuing to perform in *Reunion in Vienna* when more substantial plays could have been chosen instead. Motherwell had been told that Fontanne wished to appear in *Antony and Cleopatra,* and he wondered what had become of her intention. He was careful not to belittle Sherwood's play, calling it "a thing of wit and grace," but meanwhile, he said, "*Antony and Cleopatra* waits; and *The School for Scandal* and Ibsen and revivals of American classics like *The Great Divide* and in general all those plays which, if supremely well performed, make a nation's theatrical history." And, Motherwell added, Fontanne's hesitation to perform in great plays was particularly unfortunate because "she is . . . indisputably great. . . . Her ability is comparable to that of the best actors of any age." And "great ability should be applied to great tasks." Motherwell lamented that Fontanne's genius had been devoted instead to "merchandizing current entertainment."

Motherwell's charge was repeated, with variations, by one critic after

tion at every performance. Their commitment to continual improvement never wavered. But it is more difficult to act a mediocre play brilliantly than to shine in a good play because the lesser work does not provide the actor with the depth of character or the skillful dialogue of first-rate comedy or drama. Perhaps the Lunts were not achieving the results they hoped for in *Love in Idleness* and the plays that followed, with the result that they pushed slightly harder in every performance to win laughs that the playwrights had not provided. Over a period of months this slight daily adjustment can transform what began as a subtle portrayal into a broad one.

Thus, the tendency toward exaggerated performances may have been a sign that the Lunts—perhaps unconsciously—agreed with those who questioned the quality of the plays in which they appeared during this period. They might have been giving bigger, more blatant portrayals under the false impression that the additional energy with which they invested their performances would compensate for the weakness of the plays.

another, but the criticism reached a crescendo in the late 1940s and 1950s, when the Lunts performed successively in four undistinguished comedies: *O Mistress Mine, I Know My Love, Quadrille* and *The Great Sebastians*. A writer in the English magazine *Plays and Players* upbraided them for never having played Restoration Comedy. "One would have thought she would have made a delightful Millamant and he a perfect Mirabell," he said. J. B. Priestley contended that the Lunts shied away from masterpieces, "works that would test them right to the bone. What they brought close to perfection were too often dramatic toys, light-comedy playthings." Lee Strasberg sneered, "A man like Alfred Lunt has more equipment as an actor and director than Laurence Olivier. But what do the Lunts do? Fool around with tired Noël Coward . . . make nice nostalgic pictures in the Sunday supplement."

Were these attacks justified? It depends entirely on the way in which the evidence is interpreted. To put the case for the Lunts first:

When one looks over the full repertory of plays in which they appeared, the idea that they avoided acting in the best plays seems rather hollow, if not ludicrous. One or both of the Lunts appeared in *Pygmalion, The Doctor's Dilemma* and *Arms and the Man* by Bernard Shaw, *Goat Song* and *Juarez and Maximilian* by Franz Werfel, *The Brothers Karamazov*, adapted by Copeau and Croué from Dostoevsky's novel, Molnár's *The Guardsman*, Ben Jonson's *Volpone*, Giraudoux's *Amphitryon 38*, Chekhov's *The Sea Gull* and Shakespeare's *Taming of the Shrew*. It would be absurd to characterize any of those plays as a mere vehicle chosen to display the talents of the star performers. On the contrary, every play in that list represents a significant challenge to actors and a considerable commercial risk as well. One could add to the list *Much Ado About Nothing*, which failed to come to fruition through no fault of the Lunts. Then, too, they evolved production schemes for *Macbeth* and *Twelfth Night* although neither play was produced.

Lunt said, "The list of authors whose works we have used is not exactly undistinguished. . . . We were acting in George Bernard Shaw's plays before he had become a classic, but people were saying the same thing then that they say now."

When the tour of *O Mistress Mine* was over, in 1948, Lunt was fifty-six and Fontanne sixty-one. Every actress of that age has discovered that she must accept certain limitations if she wishes to continue performing. For one thing, there are fewer roles for sixty-one-year-old actresses than for actresses of thirty-one or forty-one. And an actress cannot ordinarily play roles written for a much younger woman for two reasons: audiences will not accept it and the physical demands on her energy may be too great. The Lunts were thus in the position of having to accept the best plays from among those submitted to them. They might have preferred to act in an occasional serious drama, but the serious dramas they read were unsuited to their abilities or their tastes for one reason or another. They did indicate they would like to appear in a play by Tennessee Williams, but Williams never submitted a play to them. They told Alan Hewitt they would have liked to play Willy and Linda in *Death of a Salesman,* but they were not offered the roles.

Then, too, the Lunts—having decided many years before to appear on the stage only together—required two roles of relatively equal size and strength. Plays of high quality that met that requirement were extraordinarily difficult to find. One option for the Lunts would have been retirement, but that was not an option they wished to consider. Another might have been simply to wait until a first-rate play meeting their special requirements came along, but that might have taken years and the Lunts knew there were not many active seasons remaining for them. A third—the one they chose—was to select the best plays from among those submitted to them even if those plays did not measure up to the highest standards, and then to restructure the plays until they achieved respectability if not distinction.

One may also reasonably ask how many plays it is possible for two actors to perform in their lifetimes. To be sure, the Lunts could have chosen to maintain the frantic pace of 1926–27, when she appeared in three large and challenging roles for the Theatre Guild and he appeared in four. But such a pace would have burned them out in very short order. They were both on the edge of exhaustion throughout that season as well as the ones that immediately preceded and followed it. Surely one cannot begrudge them the impulse to slow their pace as they grew older.

But a case can also be made that the Lunts' course from 1945 to 1957 was chosen for less defensible reasons, that they willingly decided to follow the line of least resistance because it was less likely to damage their reputations as actors who invariably played in successes and was more likely to bring them continued public adulation. One might ask why, if they were determined to perform in comedies, they insisted upon playing in comedies as tedious as *Quadrille* and as vacuous and clumsily crafted as *The Great Sebastians*. One finds it difficult to escape the conclusion that the Lunts chose those plays largely because they felt they could persuade the playwrights, who were personal friends, to alter the material to suit their own particular requirements.

Theresa Helburn described this situation as an awkward one "because it involved two clashing points of view: that of the actors and that of the playwright. Was it to be a good play or a good vehicle? The two are not necessarily the same thing. Frequently, the author's intention was altered completely by the Lunts' insistence on the kinds of parts they wanted to play."

One wonders, too, if the Lunts' uncharacteristic behavior during this period—coming from two people who had earned reputations as decent, generous, thoughtful human beings—did not have its origin in a feeling that they were, to a degree, betraying both their great abilities and the principles for which they had stood for so long a time.

Even if the Lunts were able to ignore the criticism of Atkinson, Clurman, Strasberg and others, such comments had an effect upon their reputations as great American actors. There was a definite tendency among a growing number of theatregoers and theatre practitioners in 1957, the year *The Great Sebastians* closed, to think of the Lunts as brilliant but shallow technicians who neither recognized the difference between superficial plays and meaningful drama nor wished to acknowledge that such a difference existed. The manner in which future generations would view the Lunts' contributions to the American theatre was in no little jeopardy.

Chapter Thirteen

ANOTHER PERSPECTIVE (1945–57)

> Performing with and observing the Lunts "was great discipline. . . . They were perfection. . . . I feel I learned everything from them."
>
> *Dick Van Patten*

A lthough the Lunts may have temporarily lost their perspective on certain aspects of their work during the years 1945–57, they continued to function in other areas as effectively as ever. The qualities for which they had always been noted—honesty, loyalty, compassion, consideration, generosity—were much in evidence.

1945–51

Despite their increased concern for financial security, there are many illustrations of the Lunts' continuing generosity during their years in *O Mistress Mine*. They continued to offer benefit performances for causes such as the Youth Conservation Service and the Turtle Bay Music School, which they considered to be worthy of support.

Lunt also volunteered to teach a class in the American Theatre Wing's actor-training program for returning service men and women, most of whom had had theatrical backgrounds and wished to resume their careers in the theatre.

Most telling of all, however, was the Lunts' eagerness to help promote the careers of young actors. Casting the role of Fontanne's son in *O Mistress*

Mine was the Lunts' major preproduction concern. They had thought of using the actor who had played the role in England, but decided that his pronounced British accent would not be appropriate for a young man who was supposed to have grown up in Canada. Finding another actor, they knew, would be no easy task. Not only was the role of great importance to the play, and secondary in size only to the roles played by Lunt and Fontanne, but it was a flashy part that could elevate a young actor to stardom. "It could easily turn out to be a disaster for the young actor who plays it," Fontanne said. "It could convince him, at the start of his career, that he knew all there was about acting, and he'd never learn another thing. There is a great responsibility in giving a sure-fire role to an unseasoned player. We must pick someone who will hold his head."

When auditions were held at the Shubert Theatre, the role of the boy attracted many fine young actors, among them Marlon Brando, who had achieved his first important success in *I Remember Mama* the season before. Lunt and John C. Wilson felt that Brando looked too old for the role, and called in the next applicant: Dick Van Patten. After watching Van Patten's audition, Lunt climbed the stairs to the stage and asked, "Would you come back in an hour and read again for Miss Fontanne?"*

Fontanne arrived at the Shubert ninety minutes later. She looked "like a queen—very grand," Van Patten felt. "She had an attitude like no one I'd ever seen before. When she came into a room, heads went up." Van Patten, a bit intimidated by her magisterial presence, read a scene with Lunt while Fontanne watched from the audience. Then Lunt, Fontanne and Wilson retired to the lobby while the young actor remained on stage. They returned in twenty minutes, Lunt saying (as Van Patten recalled it), "We like you very much. We recently worked with another young boy, Montgomery Clift, who was wonderful, and we hope we can have the same results with you. Do you have any objection to coming to our farm and working with us up there?"

The Lunts indicated to Van Patten that he would be needed at Genesee Depot for a week or ten days, but that time was eventually extended to three weeks, as the play was intensively rehearsed and the Lunts trained Van Patten in their methods. They taught him their technique of overlapping lines, which he was able to duplicate after repeated attempts.

Fontanne told her English friend Habetrot Dewhurst, "The American cast is, on the whole, an improvement on the English one. . . . The part of the boy is taken by a young American. He is really very wonderful. Only 17 and a brilliant young actor. We are very pleased and excited about him."

Van Patten joined a chorus of other voices in praising the Lunts' dedication and mastery of craft. His memories are valuable for an understand-

---

*Lunt always referred to his wife as "Miss Fontanne" when he spoke about her in public. Only with close friends did she become "Lynn" or "Lynnie." On the other hand, Fontanne generally referred to Lunt as "Alfred."

ing of how artists of their caliber worked to maintain their high standards.

To keep the production fresh, Lunt called a rehearsal once every two months to completely change the actors' patterns of movement—the blocking. That simple expedient eliminated any tendency on the part of the actors to become too set in their performances.

As Lunt well knew, the attitude of one person toward another tends to be influenced by their physical proximity. If one is standing inches away while a conversation is in progress, his attitude will be quite different from what it would be if he were seated and the other person standing over him. Van Patten said, by way of illustration, "Let's say I had a line, sitting in a chair: 'Oh, yes, I smoke—four or five cigarettes a day.' That was one of my big laugh lines in the show. So he'd change it so that I'm standing over here instead. It's amazing. When you say a line that you've been saying for months in one position and all of a sudden you're saying it from somewhere else, the line comes out differently. It works. It keeps it fresh. Absolutely."

The Lunts needed no reblocking to keep their own performances fresh. Van Patten was astounded to discover them rehearsing their lines throughout the tour. He was even more astonished when, after performing in the play for three and a half years, Lunt called a rehearsal in Seattle during the final week of the tour to thoroughly reblock the production.

Van Patten was also surprised to see how nervous Lunt became before and during every performance, even after the production had been running for years. "He was a nervous wreck. He would pace back and forth before he went on stage. And in between scenes when he was off stage and he'd have to go on again, he'd keep pacing and going over his lines. I think she was nervous, too, but she didn't show it as much. But I think that's what keyed them up. I think that's why they were so good."

One of Van Patten's most vivid recollections was of a performance in Washington, D.C., in early January 1946. The company, arriving in Washington after a long train ride from Madison, Wisconsin, discovered that their baggage car with the scenery was still in the Midwest.

Lunt did not for a moment consider canceling the opening; rather, the opportunity to perform without scenery delighted him. It was "the dream of a lifetime come true," he told Richard and Tinx Whorf. Van Patten remembered how excited Lunt was when he heard that the trucks which had hastily been contracted to bring the scenery east would be unlikely to arrive in time for the performance. He nearly danced with joy, exulting, "I don't think the trucks are going to get here in time."

As Lunt had hoped, the trucks did not arrive and the performance was given on a bare stage. Although he offered to refund the money of any patron who did not wish to see the play without scenery, no one accepted his offer. He was pleased that the audience seemed to enjoy the performance thoroughly, evidencing no disappointment in the lack of sets.

Van Patten also found the Lunts to be incredible disciplinarians.

They got to the theatre at 6:00 at night for an 8:30 curtain. No one was allowed to talk to them backstage. And they didn't talk to anyone—and I mean anyone. She stayed in her dressing room and got prepared and he stayed in his dressing room. And every actor had to stay in his dressing room until five minutes before he made his entrance. There was no walking around backstage or visiting in the dressing rooms or talking in the wings.

There were three co-stage managers with the production. And at 8:30, when they called places, two of the stage managers would stand on either side of Miss Fontanne's dressing room and shout, "Clear—clear—clear!" And she would come out of her dressing room and they'd escort her to the stage.

William Le Massena, who often appeared in the Lunts' productions, confirms Fontanne's need for solitude before every performance. "Her dressing room was always closed, and she would play Solitaire until the stage manager told her maid, Alma, to go get Miss Fontanne on for her entrance. Then Alma would go and tell Miss Fontanne that it was time, and then they'd get the gown on, or whatever it was. She would go quickly to the entrance. The less time she had to spend before entering the stage, I think, the better she liked it. She wanted it timed out pretty well so that nothing could distract her."

According to Van Patten, the Lunts enforced absolute silence backstage. As soon as the curtain went up, he said, all the stagehands who were not needed to shift scenery were ordered down to the basement. "And," he added, "they weren't allowed to leave that basement until five minutes before the curtain was going to come down."

Asked if he felt the backstage atmosphere was too solemn, too repressive, Van Patten shook his head. "It was great discipline," he said. "And even now I can't stand it when people are talking when there's a scene going on—because it was drilled into me so much. They just drilled it into you. You were never late. If you walked into that theatre at 8:05 instead of 8:00, I tell you, they'd give you one warning, and if you did it again, you were fired. That was it. They had no tolerance for lack of discipline."

Le Massena's memory of Lunt's backstage habits contrasts sharply with Van Patten's. Lunt "would mingle with everybody—stagehands, actors—anybody he could lay his hands on, to talk to and chat with and laugh with and tell jokes with, or fuss with the lights and check out the positioning of the lights on the rails."

Other actors who played with the Lunts—Alan Hewitt and Eugenia Rawls, to name two—also recalled the backstage atmosphere as being far more relaxed and sociable than Van Patten's recollection. Rawls said she and Fontanne often played Scrabble in Fontanne's dressing room after both had gotten into makeup and costume, and Hewitt remembers spending a good deal of time in Lunt's dressing room, where Richard Whorf was also a frequent visitor. Nor does Hewitt recall the Lunts' insistence on the actors' early arrival at the theatre. Perhaps Van Patten's youth and impressionability at the time he played with the Lunts accounts for his sense of their absolute, iron-handed discipline. Perhaps, too, the backstage environment of *O Mistress Mine* was relatively solemn because only seven actors were in the cast—a much smaller cast than usual for a Lunt-Fontanne production.

To the end of the *O Mistress Mine* tour, Van Patten found Fontanne's grandeur intimidating. "She was always very nice, but I never really felt that I knew her," he said. "I got to know him much better. He was very down to earth." Indeed, most of those who worked with or knew them found Lunt the more friendly and approachable. Fontanne tended to be more reserved, more guarded, often a bit remote. She could—and did—unwind with close friends (Carol Channing said of her, "What a warm person she was; warm, affectionate, very tender"), but she normally maintained an emotional distance.

On occasion, she was capable of playing the *grande dame*. In 1961, when John E. Booth and Lewis Funke interviewed the Lunts about their approaches to acting, the writers were invited to their house in Gracie Square, which they found "decorated to a jewel-like perfection." It was, they said, reminiscent of a setting for one of the Lunts' sophisticated comedies. Booth and Funke were a few minutes early for their appointment, which was set for 1:30. Lunt greeted them hospitably when they arrived, but Fontanne did not make her appearance until the dot of 1:30. It was "an entrance worthy of the setting," they said. "Her appearance is one of stylish perfection: the faultless coiffure of her brown hair; the elegance of her afternoon dress. . . . No moment is left to chance here."

When she first moved to Genesee Depot, some of the town's residents also felt that Fontanne assumed something of the attitude of the great actress, looking down upon them as "country hicks." But Fontanne did not strike everyone as aloof on first acquaintance. Peter Daubeny, a British impresario who met the Lunts in 1944, was invited to dine with them and several friends in their suite at the Savoy Hotel. He had anticipated a remoteness from Fontanne, but found instead that "her transparent goodness shone forth from candid eyes, a lovely smile and an unexpected schoolgirl laugh." He was also confounded by Lunt, whom he had expected to be much like the worldly sophisticates he so often played. His impression, however, "was of a huge, handsome collie who at any moment might sweep some delicate piece of Meissen off the table with his shaggy, faithful tail."

Perhaps Fontanne's occasional assumptions of artificial grandeur were a mask to cover her shyness. Certainly she did not affect the great lady with those who knew her well. Noël Coward said of both the Lunts, "They are incapable of being grand or pretentious. They are not snobbish or show-offs; no French poodles or French maids, they are very simple-hearted and true." And Charlotte Hughes, who wrote an article about Fontanne for the New York *Times* in 1942, found the actress "gracious and easy to talk to, [exuding] friendly warmth," as well as "level-headed, stable, benevolent [and] serene."

Alan Hewitt has described Lunt as "a cheerful man, a man who loved funny stories, loved to tell them, loved to hear them, and was a delightful companion." Harriet Owens, who worked as a secretary to the Lunts during their retirement, found him "very down to earth and very interested in other people," whereas Fontanne was "more reserved."

If Lunt was the more accessible, he was also the more emotional of the pair. When a performance failed to go well for him, he tried "as much as possible to keep it to myself," he said. But there were times, he admitted, when "I don't—and it is not such a pleasant home life." Theresa Helburn thought of him as possessing the quintessential actor's temperament, "suicidal and desperate." Having observed his work process in every play he did for the Theatre Guild, she said, "I can't remember a single play in which, sometime during the rehearsal period, he did not surrender his part and decide to abandon the stage forever."

On the other hand, Fontanne "never lacked confidence for a second," Helburn said, describing her as "strong" and "sure," often exerting a soothing influence on her husband. Her greater confidence was expressed by her composure. She could sit calmly for hours, talking, sewing or reading, while Lunt tended to move frequently about a room, emptying ashtrays or straightening up pillows.

Lunt's temper could be volcanic, and he would fly into a rage when he felt that a member of his company had committed a preventable blunder. On those occasions Fontanne would invariably step in, saying, "Now, Alfred, calm yourself, darling. Life's too short." After only a moment his fury would pass, to be supplanted by guilt at having hurt someone's feelings.

On at least one occasion, his anger sought its outlet in physical violence. For a scene in *The Pirate* he had to stand on a large crate which was wheeled across the stage by the crew. An artfully created set conveyed the illusion that Lunt was walking on a tightrope. During one performance, however, the curtain concealing the stagehands and the crate fell to the floor while the scene was in progress. Lunt stormed offstage and threw his boots at the stage manager. Fortunately, his aim was poor. At the end of the performance, he apologized for his outburst.

Lunt used prodigious displays of temper for effect, at times. Those who were close to him felt that some of his outbursts were carefully contrived. His brother-in-law, George Bugbee, said Lunt "used losing his temper as a management tool. It frightened people, but they certainly remembered what he said after one of those tirades."

But Lunt also showed fondness easily. He developed considerable af-fection for Dick Van Patten during the years they played in *O Mistress Mine* and often took him to rehearsals of the circus, which Lunt enjoyed more than the actual performances.

Van Patten also shared Lunt's enthusiasm for burlesque comedians, and while *O Mistress Mine* was on the road, Lunt would send the young actor to burlesque shows as a sort of advance scout. When Van Patten found a good comic, he would report his discovery to Lunt. Then the two of them would see the show together. Van Patten recalled a "crummy little theatre" in Detroit where he and Lunt went to watch a comic named Irving Harmon perform before a handful of people. They sat in the front row and roared with laughter at the comic's routine.

Many years later, when Van Patten was making a movie in Boston in the late 1970s, he was introduced to Irving Harmon. "He was an old man then," Van Patten said, "but I told him that I took Alfred Lunt to see him and Lunt loved him. Harmon got tears in his eyes. He said, 'Did Alfred Lunt see me?' And I said, 'Yes, he loved you.' He was thrilled. He said, 'My God, if I had known Alfred Lunt was sitting out there in that audi-ence . . .' Harmon died about a year later. It was just like I was meant to see him and tell him that."

Because Lunt severely restricted his diet, he developed the habit of using Van Patten's palate as a substitute for his own. Each night before the performance, Lunt would ask Van Patten what he had had for dinner. "Maybe I'd really only had a hamburger," Van Patten said to me, "but I didn't want to disillusion him, so I'd make up these fantastic dishes. And he'd sit there with his mouth watering while I described them."

Fontanne may have felt that her husband was being too indulgent and that she was needed to fill the role of disciplinarian, because she wrote to a friend, "I am afraid this little boy is too wild. He thinks only of gambling. He comes to the theatre with his left hand, as it were."* In any case, her relationship with the young performer remained friendly but distant. Afterward the Lunts did not see Van Patten for nearly twenty-five years. When they did meet him again and were introduced to his wife, the first thing Fontanne said to her was, "Is he still as mischievous as he used to be?"

Nor did Lunt entirely abdicate his role as disciplinarian. His perfec-tionism, both as an actor and as a director, would not allow him to be tolerant of Van Patten's inexperience. "He would yell at me," Van Patten said:

* According to Larry Farrell, the company manager, Van Patten's enthusiasm for horse racing was so great that he would often be at Belmont Park at 6:00 a. m. to watch the horses being exercised. But his gambling took other forms, too, and he was invariably in debt. To supplement his income on the road tour of *O Mistress Mine,* he occasionally ran hotel elevators after the evening performances. If Farrell's account was correct, it is no wonder that Van Patten was often tired for performances and that Fontanne would lose patience with him.

I remember one day I said a line I'd been getting a laugh on for months and I said it one night and it didn't get a laugh. He was fine during the scene, so I forgot about it. But when the curtain came down, all of a sudden he says, "God damn, you lost that laugh. And do you know why you lost it? You're pushing it. You're trying to be funny. God damn it, you're trying to be funny." And he scared the hell out of me. And then, the next night, I didn't push at all and the laugh came back. But he could be pretty stern.

As he looked back upon his experience of acting with the Lunts, Dick Van Patten seemed still to be in awe of their brilliance as performers. Of Lunt, he said, "He was the best actor I've ever worked with, and I've worked with the best. Nobody else came close to him." And of the Lunts together, "They were perfection—from the beginning. Even in the rehearsals, before we opened, you couldn't take your eyes off them. They were talking at the same time, yet every word was heard. It was such a pleasure to sit in the theatre and watch them work. I feel I learned everything from them."

Van Patten's admiration was echoed by Peg Murray, who, as a young actress in *The Great Sebastians,* was appearing in her first Broadway production. In awe of the Lunts, she soon discovered that all the members of the cast felt as she did. "Everybody was so deferential," she said, "but that was because everybody respected and loved them."

After the out-of-town performances began, Murray found that one of her scenes was not going well, and the more she tried to correct it, the worse it became. She felt she was letting the Lunts down because an important laugh that she had always gotten and that set up a laugh for them suddenly became impossible for her to achieve. The director was no longer traveling with the production, so she asked the stage manager what she was doing wrong; he suggested a change, but it didn't restore the laugh. She discussed the problem with other actors in the company, but they were unable to help. At last, in tears, she went to Lunt.

And I said, "I just feel so terrible. I don't know what to do." And he said, "Oh, darling, it happens, it happens all the time. You're too young, you don't know that, but it happens; it just goes. It'll come back. You mustn't think about it. And if you have any more trouble, we'll ask Miss Lynnie." Anyway, it didn't come back and we did ask Miss Lynnie, and she said, "Oh, I didn't know you were having any difficulty." Which wasn't true, of course, because, of all people, she knew exactly where and when every laugh should come. But she was just being so sweet. Well, now the stage manager, the other actors, Miss Fontanne and Mr. Lunt are all worried about this laugh. And I was so frightened by this time I could barely say the line. Then one

night, when it came time for the line, before I could get the
words out, Miss Fontanne said my line! I think *she* was nervous
about it, too, by that time. Yes, she said my line, and it didn't
make any sense at all. Well, I was so upset that now I *really*
wanted to die. I was in the prop room, crying, when Miss Fontanne came in and said grandly, "Miss Murray, I apologize. I
don't know what possessed me. I'm so sorry." But that's an indication of how caring they were, how marvelous.

Although the Lunts' enthusiasm for the theatre did not diminish in
the postwar years, it no longer dominated their lives to the exclusion of all
other activities. One project in which Lunt invested a great deal of time
and energy was a display of toy theatres at the Museum of the City of New
York. The theatres were like those Lunt had used as a small child to present
the plays he wrote and "staged" for his neighborhood friends. First sold
in England around 1820, they consisted of sheets of reinforced cardboard
with elaborate plain or colored drawings of all the elements of the theatre—proscenium arch, backdrops, side wings, actors in costume—that
were to be cut out and assembled to create a model, about a foot and a half
square, of a miniature stage. Known as "Penny Plain and Tuppence Colored" (because each sheet of heavy paper originally cost either a penny or
two pennies, depending upon whether it was tinted), the model theatres
fascinated Lunt throughout his life.* Their cost had escalated far beyond
one or two pennies by the time Lunt began to collect them in the 1940s.
Designed by some of the finest artists of their period, including William
Blake, and George and Robert Cruikshank, each model cost Lunt between
$50 and $200.

The ones he displayed in 1946 had all been collected while the Lunts
were in England during the war. Because performances during wartime
began at 6:00, he found himself with considerable free time in the evenings. To pass the time enjoyably, he bought more than twenty-five of
the nineteenth-century theatre replicas and painted many of them himself.

The idea for an exhibition was Lunt's. Looking at the windows of
jewelry stores on Fifth Avenue one day, he thought how much more dramatically the jewelry could be displayed if each piece were presented in a
carefully designed and skillfully lighted setting. That thought led him to
contemplate an exhibit of the models he had accumulated, an idea which
he then suggested to the Museum of the City of New York.

Lunt did much more than simply turn his models over to the curator.
For several weeks he appeared at the museum each morning and set to

---

*The name "Penny Plain and Tuppence Colored" is also applied to nineteenth-century
theatrical prints of actors in costume from various plays. Lunt also delighted in collecting
these prints, many of which are still on the walls of the main house at Genesee Depot.

work making a case to display each setting, then meticulously gluing together, painting and arranging each model in its glass-fronted case. He also whittled some of the tiny furniture and miniature props used in the models. The curator of the theatre and music collection at the museum, May Davenport Seymour, was astounded by his industry. "He's worked like a day laborer with hammers and saws and has been on the floor and up the ladders, and all over the place," she said.

Lunt was assisted by other members of the *O Mistress Mine* company, who volunteered to help construct the models. Another who helped—and who contributed some models of his own—was the great British actor Ralph Richardson.

The exhibition opened on December 17, 1946, billed as "the most comprehensive private collection of juvenile drama ever brought together." Twenty-five models were set up, lighted and outfitted with furniture, actors and props as if they were real stages. The cardboard actors represented characters from various plays, most of them nineteenth-century melodramas such as *Mazeppa* (the scene showed the hero tied to a horse crossing a bridge over a waterfall), *Robinson Crusoe* (a parrot perched upon Crusoe's umbrella while Friday stood nearby), *Three Fingered Jack or the Terror of Jamaica, The Maid and the Magpie* and *Timour the Tartar.* The scene from *The Corsican Brothers* showed the dying brother's spirit ascending to heaven. A few of Shakespeare's plays—*Othello* and *Richard III* among them—were also represented, as were some Christmas pantomimes. One of them, *Jack and the Beanstalk,* came complete with remarkable stage effects such as a flying ballet and an actor in the process of magically appearing (through a trap door in the stage floor).

The single most intriguing exhibit was "A New Serio-Comic, Operatic, Melo Dramatic, Cabalistic, Grand Christmas pantomime entitled *Uncle Tom's Cabin or Harlequin and Lucy Neal.*" Judging by the inclusion of Harlequin, not to mention numerous fairies and demons, the pantomime must have borne little resemblance to the Harriet Beecher Stowe novel.

More than a decade later, in June 1957, the Museum revived the exhibit, with the addition of the original toy theatre Lunt had used when giving neighborhood entertainments in Milwaukee in 1901, and the sets he had devised for *Julius Caesar* and *A Midsummer Night's Dream.*

When the exhibit closed in January 1958, Lunt was unsure what to do with the models. There were far too many of them, taking up too much space, to be taken home to Genesee Depot. Perhaps, Lunt thought, he would donate them to the University of Wisconsin. But in 1984 they were still in storage at the Museum of the City of New York, dissassembled and gathering dust.

The single offstage activity that was most important to the Lunts during this period reflected their determination to establish a home for themselves away from Genesee Depot. For years they had wanted to move out of their rented apartment and into a permanent New York home. At last, in 1949, they found an old red brick house, located between 86th and 87th streets, facing Gracie Square and the mayor's mansion, that seemed ideal.

They had the house entirely remodeled so that, although not large (the house was only sixteen feet wide), it offered the illusion of spaciousness. One device they used was to cover an entire wall of the living room with a mirror; another was Fontanne's ingenious solution to the problem of the boiler, which took up considerable room on the ground floor. "We'll fly it," she said, and, like a piece of scenery, the boiler was attached to cables and permanently lifted overhead to provide additional floor space.

Four stories high, the house had kitchen and dining room on the ground floor, living room on the second, bedroom and dressing room on the third, two servants' rooms and a guest room on the fourth, and a fireplace in nearly every room. At the back of the house was a small garden (sixteen feet by ten feet). Overhead was a roof garden, equipped with potted plants, deck chairs and canopies, where in warm weather the Lunts ate many of their meals. During the New York run of *I Know My Love,* they found themselves in "a frenzy of remodeling the house, auctions, buying materials, reupholstering, new curtains, more furniture and all the delirious joys of decorating a house," Fontanne wrote to Lady Juliet Duff.

Lunt supervised the decorating and remodeling, which included removing the high stoop so the house could be entered at sidewalk level. He designed and supervised the building of Fontanne's dressing room, with its complex arrangement of drawers for gloves, shoes, stockings, handkerchiefs and other accessories. He bought a good deal of new furniture, including two Louis XIV armchairs, a Louis XVI dressing table and a late eighteenth-century mahogany French table trimmed in brass. Stewart Chaney, who designed the scenery for *I Know My Love,* decorated the dining room and furnished it with white, wooden palm trees.

Knowing the Lunts' passion for elegant living and Alfred's enthusiasm for cooking, the *Ladies' Home Journal* offered to furnish the kitchen at the magazine's expense with "all kinds of modern and . . . very useful gadgets," in Fontanne's words, in exchange for photographs and an interview. Since Lunt had earlier complained, "You have never seen such a horrible kitchen in your whole life—it is unbelievably terrible," they accepted at once, and the *Journal* used every square inch of the tiny room—only eleven feet six inches by nine feet four—to create an ideal kitchen.

Lunt also worked out an elaborate scheme for moving in the furnishings and appliances, complete with scale drawings and models of the house and every piece to be moved. He carefully listed the order in which each piece should be carried; "it was all as thoroughly coordinated and arranged as if it had been a theatrical production," said Donald Seawell. Lunt's plan was so thorough and meticulous that the job was completed in a single day. He and Fontanne moved into the house in April 1950, and it remained their New York home until 1972.

The new house gave the Lunts an outlet for their skills and pleasure in interior decoration—"Offering us a room without furniture and bare walls is like offering a dog a bone," said Fontanne—but their greatest triumph of decoration was at Genesee Depot, which they always regarded as their true home.

The Lunts adored the haven they had created at Genesee Depot, glorying in it when they were there and longing for it when they were away. Fontanne often noticed how the tension drained visibly from Lunt's body when they finished a theatrical engagement and returned to Wisconsin, and she was affected the same way. "Theatre people live on their nerves, especially when the part is a demanding one," she said. "For days when I get [to Genesee Depot] after a show, I just sit and stare. Days later, I love to walk for hours over those fields."

After the original purchase of three acres in 1913, the living quarters grew in stages. Cathleen Nesbitt, an early visitor to Genesee Depot, described the original house as "one enormous room with staircases leading up to a gallery which had doors leading to bedrooms."

Later, after Lunt was married, he worked closely with the architect Charles (Karl) Dornbusch to convert what had been a chicken coop into a cottage for himself and his new wife. A bedroom, bathroom and kitchen were added to the main house, as well as three fireplaces, but, Lunt said later, no one remembered the need for closets. "You see, we had so few clothes."

The Lunts spent the summer of 1922 in the converted chicken house. Soon, however, they purchased another forty acres of land, and the estate began to grow. When they decided to spend as much time as possible at Genesee Depot, arrangements were made for Lunt's mother to move into the Cottage (as the refurbished chicken house became known) and for the Lunts to move to the main house. Again, Karl Dornbusch was put in charge of the architectural arrangements. This time a number of large closets were included, along with additional rooms and bathrooms.

Claggett Wilson, an artist who doubled as a scene designer, was asked by the Lunts to do the decoration. He received the following instruction from Lunt: "We don't want a house that looks like it's been decorated, but one that seems to have been lived in for years." Fontanne added, "I think being in a modern house all the rest of my life would be just like sitting nude forever in the center of a huge white dinner plate."

If Wilson thought the job would be relatively easy, he hadn't counted on the Lunts' passion for adding a room here or there as the mood struck them. Lunt was eager to work with the designer on every detail. Not only must every room be equipped with a fireplace, but murals must be painted on all the walls. Wilson's job lasted a full year, during which time he took up residence in Ten Chimneys, so christened after the Lunts made a count of the fireplaces.

Although Lunt once told an interviewer, "the whole house is Swedish ... It's all in the old Swedish style—some real, the rest copied," it is perhaps more accurate to say that the design is eclectic. It is essentially Swedish, but there are Finnish influences. Some of the house is decorated in the French Restoration style; furnishings came from Spain, Italy, Sweden, Hungary and from antique shops in New York. All five bedrooms were equipped with porcelain Swedish stoves, which were brought from Stockholm. Bright colors, mirrors and many chandeliers were used to create an atmosphere of gaiety.

The murals, some painted by Wilson and some by Lunt, cover nearly every wall in the house and even some of the ceilings. Several of the murals are biblical. Fontanne said that if Adam and Eve looked alike in Lunt's mural—and they do—it was because she posed for both figures. Others depict birds and flowers. Some of Lunt's murals are painted in a primitive style, others are meticulously detailed.

Incredible care was lavished on the house and grounds. Most of the furniture was selected by Lunt, all chosen on the basis of its esthetic appeal, never for comfort or utility. The piece might be virtually falling apart, but that made no difference as long as it was beautiful.

A good deal of the furniture had to be reupholstered, which was Fontanne's job. Among the furniture in the living room alone were a black-and-gold Queen Anne table, two American Regency chairs, a sapphire-blue velvet sofa, two white Hepplewhite chairs and two Victorian coral-velvet chairs, all set against an off-white background.

Another of Fontanne's responsibilities was to make the draperies for the house, which precipitated a domestic clash of modest proportions. Lunt believed it extravagant to buy enough material to cover each window fully because the drapes, rather than being drawn together, would be pulled back and tied off (esthetics again being more important than utility). He insisted, therefore, that she buy only enough material to create the desired illusion. The family, amused by Lunt's frugality, gave him the sobriquet "Split Curtain Alf."

The many decorative touches in Ten Chimneys—the murals, the scrolled carpets, the antique mirrors, the antique rock-crystal Swedish chandelier, the Delft pottery, the Chinese pewter figures, the dining-room chairs with seats embroidered in petit point (by the women in the family) in the signs of the Zodiac, the canopied beds (canopies designed and made by Fontanne)—were somehow integrated by Wilson and the Lunts so that, although no two rooms may have been done in the same style, each had its own unified, particular look. When Richard Whorf saw Ten Chimneys for the first time, he wandered through the house and remarked in astonishment, "My God! Every room's a stage set."

The kitchen was probably the most important room in the house. As an accomplished gourmet cook, Lunt no doubt insisted on a large, well-equipped and esthetically pleasing kitchen, and that is precisely how the room can be described.

Most of the structures at Genesee Depot were given names. The Studio, a single room with a large fireplace and small sleeping loft, was added to serve as a guesthouse or a rehearsal area. Like the main house and the Cottage, the Studio was decorated in Scandinavian style. Even the woodshed had a name: it was called Guarantee Trust because of its promise of comfort in the winter months.

As time went on and as the Lunts' financial situation improved, they continued to increase the size of their property; eventually the estate comprised about 160 acres. The L-shaped swimming pool, added in 1933, immediately became a topic of conversation among the citizens of Genesee Depot. Not many Wisconsinites built swimming pools during the Depression, and this one, located between the main house and the cottage, was particularly large and imposing.

Another addition came in 1952, when the Lunts built a dam and, as Fontanne said, "made a tremendous lake, five or six blocks long, and stocked it with perch and bass, but," she observed sadly in 1954, "the lake is disappearing. We went off happily to England [for *Quadrille*], thinking we had a lake, and then it began to disappear. We don't know why." The Lunts asked the state geologist of the Wisconsin Geological Survey to examine their vanished lake and tell them what could be done. He reported in November 1954: "I am afraid that the prospects for its recovery are not good. . . . If one looks at the origin of your lake from a geological standpoint, it was dead before it was exhumed. . . . The only permanent solution would be to clean out the accumulated peat and return to the original postglacial status-quo; however this would be extremely expensive and the dredged material would destroy the beauty of the area if the dredging was extensive." The Lunts decided to maintain the beauty of the area and forgo the pleasures of the lake.

Ten Chimneys was more than a residence for the Lunts: it was also a working farm in which they took a great deal of delight. The farm in 1954 contained a small barn, a hen house (to replace the chicken house that had been converted to a residence), a greenhouse and a dairy (both added in 1947), a deep-freeze room and a small house for the farm's superintendent, Ben Perkins.

Whenever the Lunts were in residence—and that meant nearly every summer—Lunt took pride in working the farm himself. "There's endless excitement, in a quiet way," he said about his farming. Typically, he would awake every morning at 5:30 or 6:00 and set to work. Perhaps his favorite job was working in the vegetable garden, which was enormous. Lunt described the crops: "Carrots, turnips, beets, cauliflower, tomatoes, squash, eggplant, the best corn I ever ate, and all sorts of greens—collards, mustard, kale, and okra. The most beautiful cucumbers! Delicious!" So passionate was he about his garden that no one else invaded his territory. "Mr. Lunt cares for the truck garden alone," Ben Perkins said in 1945. "When he is through with his day's work, it looks as though he had gone through it with a vacuum cleaner."

Lunt told an interviewer, "After I finish working in the garden, I'm quite content to sit and stare at it. Crazy, isn't it? . . . I like doing physical things, and I like a clean weedless garden. Then I sit and watch it for hours. I suppose I enjoy it because it's a kind of showing off, like acting."

He also spent hours in the greenhouse, where he did all the potting when he was home. "Hundreds and hundreds of pots!" he said. "I have a passion for menial work. I love to shovel gravel, clean out the barn. Everything I do is by hand. I don't even use a cultivator on the garden," he told the *New Yorker* in 1954; "I do it by hand, with a hoe."

When he wasn't busy in garden or greenhouse, Lunt found other chores to do. There were always logs to chop and walls to build. "We have so many small round boulders that the ridiculous walls look like cupids' bottoms," he said. And the buildings could always be improved. In 1950, Lunt decided to remodel the hen house, installing enormous plate-glass windows on the theory that his 200 Leghorn chickens would lay more eggs if they had more light. He claimed that the grateful hens responded to his thoughtfulness by laying twice as many eggs as before, and that his discovery might well revolutionize the poultry business.

Lunt's pride in his chicken flock grew with the years. Although he complained about them—they were too tough to make good stew, he said—and often threatened to get rid of them, he remained oddly devoted to them. During the Lunts' retirement, Donald Seawell gave him a tape recorder and pleaded with him to record some of his reminiscences. Instead, Lunt took the machine into the hen house and recorded the clucking of his chickens.

The dairy, where he churned the butter, separated the milk and made cottage cheese and buttermilk, also claimed much of his time. "We're drowning in milk these days," he told an interviewer in 1942. "I make very good butter, but I'm feeling my way with cheese." Fontanne told her sister Antoinette, "Alfred makes the butter himself and he puts on the oddest costume to do it in—a clean but old pair of blue linen slacks, a white coat and white apron—all very hygienic. One morning, unfortunately, the slacks got torn in the seat, of which he was quite unaware, and every time he passed through the kitchen he couldn't think why there were subdued giggles when he turned his back." When Lunt finally discovered the cause of the laughter, he told Ben Perkins to make an addition to that morning's marketing list: one fig leaf.

Lunt also attended to the pigpen, which he cleaned out each week with a hose. Four pigs inhabited the pen most of the time. In the 1950s the Lunts kept a horse named Franklin (after Franklin D. Roosevelt) and four Jersey cows. One of the cows, named Belle, was given to them in

1941. Racked with guilt when they contemplated Belle's loneliness in the winter to come, they purchased a second cow and named her Lily (after the Jersey Lily, Lillie Langtry). Still, Lunt said, "we found our barn was not warm enough. So we had to buy a third cow as a radiator to help keep them warm." This one was christened Sugar, which was Langtry's pet name for her husband, Hugo de Bathe. When Belle had a calf in 1942, Fontanne named her Little Ellen for her mentor, Ellen Terry. In June of that year, Fontanne wrote to Antoinette: "The cows are out of the barn for the first time and in the pasture and Baby Ellen has a little enclosure of her own. She is so sweet and as strong and as wild as a bull. The cows have given the whole place such a lovely domestic, warm touch and it's wonderful having our own butter and milk and cream." But the Lunts sold their cows in 1953 because, said Lunt, "I found they were too expensive when I wasn't there."

On one occasion Lunt arranged for Ellen to be artificially inseminated. But he had not taken into account his wife's affection for the cow. Fontanne discovered Lunt's intention and, accompanied by her pet goose Walter, she set out to put an end to the enterprise. She told the artificial insemination technician to remove his equipment, saying to her husband, "I will not have this, Alfred. A cow gets little enough pleasure out of life." To insure that Ellen was not entirely deprived of enjoyment, Fontanne saw to it that she and the local bull were united for a weekend of pleasure. Her ruse seems to have worked, for the Lunts received word months later that Ellen had given birth to a healthy calf.

Fontanne did not share her husband's passion for backbreaking work, but she had responsibilities on the estate as well. These included cutting flowers each day and arranging them for the house, designing and sewing her own hats and dresses, and making curtains and bedspreads.

Some of the Lunts' theatre friends found it hard to believe that the sophisticated actor and actress they knew could be genuinely devoted to their farm. A few suspected that all the work was really done by hired employees. Others refused to acknowledge the reality of the farm even when they saw it for themselves. S. N. Behrman, for example, after a visit to Genesee Depot in 1942, claimed that the only animals on the farm were four or five poorly fed, thoroughly miserable cows.

On the other hand, James Gray, a visitor in 1945, saw all the animals and was astonished by the care they received. "Never have there been farm animals more handsome, better cared for, better groomed," he said. "The coat of the Jersey cows shows a tawny gloss . . . the Plymouth Rocks have a satiny luster of feather. . . . Unlike the cows they are not washed every day, yet such is the effect of proper food on their general look of well-being that they seem just to have been removed from the tissue paper of the dry-cleaner's box."

A flock of sheep joined the menagerie for a while, as did a small collection of carrier pigeons. To these must be added the many pets that were always welcome at Ten Chimneys. At one time or another, the Lunts owned the dachshunds Elsa and Rudolph, who had a daily diet of fresh-ground lean beef, were taken to New York and on tour, and even accompanied the Lunts to the theatre; Walter, the white goose, who, Fontanne said in 1967, "lets me stroke him and nibbles at my fingers. He welcomes me vociferously, and he cries piteously when I go." Walter followed Fontanne docilely wherever she wandered at Ten Chimneys, but threatened to bite everyone else; he was "cruelly murdered by something—we think a fox," Lunt told his friend and fellow actor Romney Brent in 1970; then there was a Doberman pinscher named Nebuchadnezzar; Winnie, a black poodle, who was Fontanne's favorite in her last years; and Fontanne's most remarkable conquests: two squirrels named Lovey and Cup-Cake and a chipmunk named Joey, all of whom she tamed and trained to eat from her hand.

Fontanne's favorite pet was a little dachshund given to her by the company of *O Mistress Mine* on opening night in 1946. Fontanne described her to Molly Humphrey on May 14 of that year as "enchanting," but said, "I might just as well have had a baby. She was not house trained, kennel bred, utterly unaccustomed to people. I was never off the floor, cleaning up hastily. But I have got her in much better shape now. She never leaves my side and won't speak to anybody else except perhaps to growl or bark. Her name is Lisa and in spite of the fact that she is more trouble than ten children, I adore her."

Fontanne told her sister on September 6, "Lisa is at last house trained—a model of beautiful behavior. Sometimes in the morning when she first gets up she dances when she sees Alfred, but that is a great concession and doesn't happen very often. He was so good to her and patient and sweet with her even when she peed all over the carpets, which he *hated*."

By September 12 the situation had improved even further. Fontanne wrote to her British friend Graham Robertson, "Lisa is now perfectly behaved. She still will not make friends with anyone but Alfred and me and Alma, my maid. But she does not shrink as from a blow any more when someone reaches out to pat her and she will go and kiss the hand of anyone I tell her to—cost her what it may. She also has a strong theatrical instinct. When she thinks she deserves a tidbit, she goes out of the room and comes dancing in to attract attention as though she had just come in from a walk."

Lisa inadvertently gave her mistress a ringing headache on September 25. As Fontanne described the incident to Terence Rattigan, "Alfred and I had rather a bad night last night, caused by the following. I woke up and thought the room was getting rather chilly and leant far out of bed to put a small blanket on my little dog. Alfred awoke at the same time and heard the rustle in the dog's bed and thought she was getting into our bed. Seeing something black on the edge of the bed, he hauled off and gave it a whack. The 'something black' was not the dog—it was my head. It was all a great surprise to both of us—whereupon ensued a free-for-all, and we didn't get much sleep."

Fontanne was so devoted to Lisa that she couldn't bear to part with her when the Lunts were planning a trip to England in 1950. She wrote to Sibyl Colefax, "There is one thing that rather haunts me about coming to England and that is my little dog. She lives and breathes only for me and I am so afraid she will die of grief if I go away. I know that the law forbidding dogs except after quarantine has stamped out rabies, but I was wondering if they couldn't amend the law, inasmuch as anyone staying in England for any length of time and wishing to bring their dog could take the dog to a well accredited doctor *here* (not a veterinarian), chosen by the English government and have blood tests taken of the dog for over a period of three or six months, whatever time necessary, and with the certificate in hand be permitted to come into England. I do feel that while this government is making all these uncomfortable laws they could make one that could give aid and comfort to a little dog."

Fontanne must have swelled with pride on the night that Lisa was awarded the Blue Ribbon of Merit by the *O Mistress Mine* company. Typed on a sheet of paper with a blue ribbon attached was the following message:

> On this eighth day of January in the Year of our Lord, 1947, MISS LISA LUNT has merited the praise of all members of the 'O Mistress Mine' Company, indeed, all occupants of the Empire Theatre.
>
> At her post on this night she sprang quietly and quickly into action, above and beyond the line of duty, and single-handed and unarmed, met and conquered the Invading Enemy in the form of a Very Large Mouse.
>
> For this great achievement and for her glorious service to mankind, it is hereby authorized that MISS LISA LUNT be decorated with the Blue Ribbon of Merit.

Both the Lunts felt almost parental toward their pets, whose illnesses were taken as seriously as if they had indeed been their children. When Lisa became ill one night in 1961, Lunt promised he would find a veterinarian in nearby Waukesha to minister to the dog. The veterinarian's office was closed when he arrived, but, undeterred, he carried Lisa down the street until he saw the shingle of Dr. E. B. Davies, who was about to close his office for the night. Lunt asked the physician to examine Lisa. When Dr. Davies explained he was not a veterinarian, Lunt replied that the veterinarian's office was closed, that a doctor was a doctor, and surely no medical practitioner would refuse to provide help in an emergency. Dr. Davies could only repeat his explanation, adding that he was not trained to treat animals and had no license to do so. The two of them continued to argue the issue for a time, but Dr. Davies was powerless to help. At last, as Gwen Davies, the doctor's sister, put it, "a very disgruntled, defeated, inconvenienced Alfred Lunt walked angrily out of the office with the sick dog in his arms."

The Lunts enjoyed having guests stay at Genesee Depot. Helen Hayes, Noël Coward, S. N. Behrman, Howard Lindsay, Russel Crouse, Clifton Webb, Alexander Woollcott, Edna Ferber, Gustav Eckstein, Enid Bagnold and Carol Channing came to visit, as did William Le Massena, George Schaefer, Cathleen Nesbitt, John C. Wilson, Katharine Cornell, Thornton Wilder, Margalo Gillmore, Robert La Follette, Laurence Olivier, Alan Hewitt and a great many others. Often, when the Lunts were on tour in the Midwest during the Christmas season, the entire cast would be invited to Genesee Depot for a grand dinner. However, the Lunts also enjoyed their solitude, and many of their happiest times were spent alone together on the farm.

On a typical summer day Lunt would have his breakfast an hour or so before his wife did so that he could get to work in the vegetable garden. Fontanne always ate her breakfast on a card table in the living room. After their morning's work in the house and on the farm, the Lunts would spend the afternoons in and around the swimming pool, or take a picnic basket into the woods and have a leisurely lunch. Dinner might be casual, or the Lunts might dress for the occasion, but in either case it nearly always featured vegetables from the garden. Lunt sometimes did the cooking himself, but even when the meal was prepared by a cook, it was done according to Lunt's recipes and under his watchful eye. This was especially true when there were guests in the house. Both the Lunts took great pleasure in good food and were suspicious of anyone who felt differently. Those who didn't eat a great deal risked being crossed off their guest list.

Until Lunt's mother died in 1955, they would often visit her in the Cottage after dinner and play a game of bridge. Other favorite pursuits included listening to symphonic and operatic music on the phonograph and playing Scrabble. Fontanne was a devoted Solitaire player (she always used the British term, Patience), claiming to know hundreds of varieties of the game, many of which were taught to her by Noël Coward.

Both Lunt and Fontanne were avid readers. Lunt's favorite novelist was probably Dickens; Fontanne read every sort of fiction, from the most serious works to the romances of Barbara Cartland. Both of them enjoyed mystery novels, especially those of Dorothy L. Sayers and Agatha Christie. Lunt also read a daily newspaper, a habit Fontanne did not share.

Bedtime came early at Genesee Depot. Eight-thirty was customary; 9:00 was shockingly late. How the Lunts were able to adjust their schedules from one season to another is something of a mystery—during the months they were working, they rarely got to bed before 2:00 or 3:00 a.m., and generally awoke at noon—but this was only one of many habits that changed when they returned to Genesee Depot.

They frequently hired local high-school boys to act as waiters and butlers during the summer. George Schaefer told me that Fontanne "loved training the young boys up there. She would love to be around them and to talk about them. She'd make it a point to know their families and to know what they were studying in school and where they were planning to go to college. And she'd give them little approving looks at the table if they did something right. It was charming." As Lunt got older, he used the local boys to help him with the heavy work on the farm. But he complained in 1973 that "they don't like to work in the garden because they don't like vegetables. They don't like to chop wood or saw wood because they don't like fireplaces. They don't mind mowing the lawn as long as they can ride the mower. And they never speak. I ask them, 'What are you going to do when you finish high school?' and they say 'I dunno.' 'Well, what do you like to do?' 'I dunno.' Well, where do you go from there?" But beneath Lunt's curmudgeon-like grouchiness there was genuine affection. The "summer boys" were the Lunts' link to the world of adolescents, and one they both seem to have enjoyed.

As the Lunts' fame increased, sightseers stopped in Genesee Depot hoping to catch a glimpse of the famous stars and any guests who might be staying with them. But the townspeople took it upon themselves to protect the Lunts' privacy, often denying to outsiders that the couple was in town, or intentionally misdirecting them to some remote spot. If one or both of the Lunts happened to be in a store or a restaurant when sightseers were present, the townspeople would acknowledge them with a barely perceptible nod or a blink of the eyes. Names would never be used so that the sightseers would not be aware of the Lunts' presence.

Carol Channing told of an occasion when she and her husband were visiting the Lunts after their retirement. "We would sit in the kitchen and just talk and talk and talk," she said. "There is a peculiar feeling for actors or anybody in the theatre that when you went to Ten Chimneys it meant you must have done something right. You had died and gone to heaven. You were home."

While Channing was staying in Genesee Depot, she experienced a remarkable example of the townspeople's devotion to their famous neighbors. Because she was a health-food addict, she had brought her own food with her and had put it in the refrigerator. One morning at about 4:00, she got hungry and decided "to tiptoe downstairs and get an apple. Charles [Lowe, her husband] said, 'Bring me an apple, too. So I tiptoed down and when I got to the refrigerator an alarm went off—the most terrible screech and siren you ever heard.

"By the time I got to the refrigerator, the whole house was alive," Channing said; "lights were on and everything. Then suddenly there were sirens *outside!* The police were coming, and the townspeople with rifles, and the fire department! Everything was blasting and blaring. I was scared to death and I dropped to the floor because I thought, 'I'm going to be shot.' So I fell flat on the floor in my pajamas. I could hear Lynnie at the top of the stairs. There she stood in a white nightgown—a Shakespearean-looking nightgown—all white with a ruffle around the neck, and ruffles around the sleeves, an English white flannel country nightgown. And she had a nightcap with a point on the top on her head. And in those beautiful clarion tones, she said: 'Alfred, to your post! Benny, to your post! Cook, to your post! Everyone to his post!' Lynnie gave the orders and Alfred went exactly where he was told to go. Finally, I said, 'Lynnie, it's me, it's me.' Everybody was coming at me, and I stood up in my pajamas and she stopped short, said, 'Oh!' and began to laugh." Then Fontanne explained that ever since the burglar alarm had been installed, the household had been rehearsing the proper drill, but this was the first time they had had a chance to put it to the test.

"Well, it shows you how the Genesee Depot people felt," said Channing. "This was their White House. It was as if they lived in Washington, D.C., and the White House was being invaded. They came because these were the deities of Genesee Depot. They loved them as dearly as they loved the President of the United States. They protected them."

The Lunts' enthusiasm for the farm was so great that when they were in New York or on tour, they telephoned Ben Perkins, often on a daily basis, to keep up with events at home. Perkins wrote to them as well, detailing the daily activities on the farm.

As the years went on, the Lunts became fonder and fonder of the restful life in Wisconsin. When they were leaving home for longer than normal—when they were going to England, for instance—the leave-taking was "positively Russian," as Fontanne said. And, indeed, her description does sound reminiscent of a scene in a play by Chekhov: "We cried," she said, "all the maids cried. We waved and they all waved. Somebody tried to give us a pie to eat on the train. It was extremely harrowing."

On several occasions during performances of *I Know My Love,* different aspects of the Lunts' characters were revealed. For example, Fontanne's amazing ability to shut out all reality except that of the play was illustrated by an incident that occurred during the New York run. During a matinee, in an early scene in which the members of the play's family were assembled on stage, something went wrong and Lunt muttered a profanity under his breath. At least he thought the word was muttered, but the reaction of the spectators in the first several rows indicated that his profanity had been clearly heard. Throughout the remainder of the performance, he was thoroughly ashamed of himself and upset by his momentary outburst. Fontanne was not told of Lunt's depression until after the final curtain. As she heard the story in her dressing room, she became puzzled. "Why does Alfred mind?" she asked. "There was nobody in the drawing room but the family."

There was never any possibility, however, that she would forget she was giving a performance. Once, as she stood in the wings waiting for her entrance cue, she asked the stage manager to deliver a message to her husband. "Please tell Alfred to come down the stairs in the last scene more quickly, as he holds up my line," she said. When the message was delivered, Lunt responded, "Please tell Miss Fontanne if she wants me to come downstairs faster, she should have married a younger man."

Fontanne displayed her dedication to theatrical discipline once again when she broke her wrist during the tour of *I Know My Love*, but that was only one of a series of "strange accidents," as she put it, that occurred on the tour. In Springfield, Massachusetts, Esther Mitchell, who played an important supporting role, "was putting her make-up case in the big prop box in which all the make-up of the company is carried. The lid of the prop box fell and hit her on the head and she went into hospital with a brain concussion," Fontanne wrote. In Chicago the company manager "slipped on the ice and fell, knocking his head against a hydrant," she reported. "We feared concussion but the X-ray found it was not and he is all right now."

Fontanne, however, was not so fortunate. On November 3, 1950, as she was leaving the hotel in Portland, Maine, on her way to the theatre for the evening's performance, she caught her heel in the hem of her skirt, slipped and fell down a staircase. She was taken immediately to a hospital,* where the physician on duty told her that her wrist was broken and would have to be set at once, making it impossible for her to give a performance that night. Fontanne coolly insisted that she would perform. Even though the wrist was badly swollen and misshapen, she refused to permit the doctor to put her wrist in a cast or to administer any pain-killer for fear it would make her drowsy and take the edge off her performance. She did allow the doctor to set the wrist in a temporary cast and to give her a shot of novocaine. While he was doing so, Fontanne instructed the stage manager, Charva Chester, to call the wardrobe mistress and tell her to make several slings: one to match each of the costumes Fontanne wore in the production.

The performance that night began only twenty minutes late. Chester informed the audience of what had happened and told them, "Miss Fontanne hopes you will ignore the cast and enjoy the play." Renée Orsell, writing to Fontanne's sister Antoinette, reported, "Her appearance, after the announcement was made . . . was sensational. Naturally, at the end of the performance everyone cheered and even the grumpiest of the old stage-hands applauded and wept. She was magnificent. I can't tell you what courage she has nor how much she is adored and admired—in fact, worshipped by everyone in the company."

The arm remained temporarily set throughout the next day, a Saturday. A matinee and an evening performance were scheduled, and Fontanne would not think of undergoing surgery until afterward. After the evening

---

*Lunt did not accompany her. "He probably would have fainted," Fontanne said.

show, she finally entered a hospital, was given an injection of pentathol, which put her instantly to sleep, and had the arm reset in a plaster cast that extended from her fingers almost to her shoulder. On Sunday the tour progressed to Montreal, where Fontanne played with her arm in the cast, as she continued to do for months afterward.

The condition grew progressively more painful as the bones began to join together, and, combined with arthritis in her shoulder, the pain prevented her from getting to sleep without the aid of sleeping pills. Lunt told Antoinette, "She doesn't complain at all but now and then she goes awfully white. . . . If she would only yell and go into tantrums and complain, I would find it—curiously enough—a little easier to take." Weeks later, when the cast was removed, Renée Orsell was present as Fontanne looked at her limp arm and said, "Oh dear! It looks like a dead calla lily."

In Pittsburgh—the Lunts' "jinx city"—the two Saturday performances were nearly canceled because of the worst blizzard in twenty-five years, "thirty inches of snow, completely immobilizing the city," Fontanne reported. Until the final day, the company had broken all house records at the new Nixon Theatre, "but on that deadly white Saturday" they had to refund $11,000, playing to only seventy-three people at the matinee and one hundred in the evening.

Leaving Pittsburgh was nearly as difficult for the Lunts as enduring the pain of having to return so much money. Their train left the city seven hours late, then took twenty-two hours for a journey that normally lasted seven. The train had no dining car, so the company arrived in Detroit cold, exhausted and very hungry—and without their scenery, costumes, props and makeup, all of which were snowbound in Pittsburgh.

Once again Lunt realized his dream of being able to give a performance without scenery. This occasion was even more to his liking than the performance of *O Mistress Mine* given under similar circumstances, for the missing costumes, props and makeup would even more severely test his theory about the purity of the dramatic experience. Lunt went before the curtain in an approximation of his costume to announce that the performance would proceed despite the lack of accouterments. If anyone did not wish to remain, the price of his ticket, Lunt said, would be "refunded promptly, but with some reluctance." Only one patron took advantage of the offer: a student had come to the performance because she had been assigned to write a paper on the production, and her teacher had stressed the importance of evaluating the contribution made by costumes and scenery. Otherwise, the audience remained to watch the actors, wearing street clothes, perform on a stage enclosed by velvet drapes. A ladder was set up where the staircase would have been. At one point Fontanne was obliged to speak a line referring to "this lovely room, this beautiful staircase," which brought an appreciative laugh. At times Lunt stepped to the footlights to tell the audience that the characters at that moment would have been made up to appear youthful or elderly if makeup were available. The spectators seemed not to miss the scenery and costumes in the slightest. Lunt was gleeful. .

1951–56

Lunt directed two productions in the 1950s, both of which were highly successful and both very different from the kinds of plays he had directed in the past, representing significant challenges to him and to Fontanne, who contributed greatly to the productions. Thus, although the Lunts chose to perform in second-rate comedies during this period, the works they directed were distinctly more adventurous.

Lunt, a lifelong devotee of opera, was asked in 1951 to direct the first production of Mozart's *Così fan tutte* that the Metropolitan Opera had given since 1928. His first reaction was to decline Rudolf Bing's offer, which was made while Lunt was touring in *I Know My Love*. He was tired, he said, and he had promised his doctors he would take a long rest. Besides, he was unfamiliar with the opera. Bing refused to accept Lunt's answer and continued to telephone him until Lunt at last decided to accept the challenge. But he had misgivings, as indicated in a letter he wrote to Laurence Olivier in August 1951, regretting his "childish mistake."

Several days after Lunt accepted Bing's offer, the conductor, Fritz Stiedry, showed up in Buffalo, where the Lunts were performing. The conductor played the score of the first act, and, as Lunt wrote to Bing, "tried to instill in me some Mozartian feeling. He gave me the impression that I might be capable of doing the directorial job and I sincerely hope I can as it is truly fascinating."

Three days after their tour ended, Lunt returned to New York to sign a contract with the Metropolitan Opera and to meet with Rolf Gérard, who had been hired to design the production, and discuss their attitudes toward the visual statement they wished to create. Lunt had already formulated specific ideas, as he informed Bing in a letter:

> Much depends upon the set and I have a very definite idea of what it should be and hope you will approve. I think we should establish the fact that the opera is being sung by a troupe of singers in a little pavilion in a park beside a lake. The pavilion, of course, must be raised up at least three steps and on it can the scene changes be made very simply and with no stage waits. . . . Not only can the little pavilion stage be used, but also the stage around it, which would naturally be done if we were doing the opera in a park. I think the dark woods and the little rococo

baroque stage and the shimmering lake behind gives much of the feeling of "Così Fan Tutte." And, of course, you could at the end use chandeliers and a considerable amount of glitter.

When Lunt left New York for Genesee Depot, he took with him a score, a recording of the opera and an English translation of the libretto. In Wisconsin he listened to the recording again and again until he had committed every note to memory. He also read everything he could find that would familiarize him with eighteenth-century life and customs.

Bing's instructions had been terribly unnerving, he said. The impresario had asked only that the production "should be light, gay and elegant." But, as Lunt knew, achieving gaiety and elegance on the stage was no easy matter. "Do you think that I am Mme. Lazanga," he asked Bing, "who guarantees to teach ballet in six easy lessons?"

Although he had been reluctant to accept the job, Lunt threw himself into the work with relish. He sought out each of the six singers in his cast (Richard Tucker, Patrice Munsel, Eleanor Steber, Blanche Thebom, John Brownlee and Frank Guarrera), assuring them of his eagerness to work with them. He asked if they would mind his attending the musical rehearsals—something few directors did—and they assured him that he would be welcome. He wished to be present from the beginning because he believed the singers would be able to assimilate his directorial ideas more easily if they were communicated as early as possible in the rehearsal process.

His primary concern, he said, was simply to allow the opera to be heard. That is, he did not want to overwhelm Mozart's work with so much visual ornamentation that the audience would pay more attention to the staging than to the music. To that end, he said, "We are trying to make everything very clean, very fresh and clear. . . . It is not the story which is important but the music. It is a sort of celestial revue, sung by uninhibited angels, a string of jewels, flashing their colors on a slender thread of unimportant plot. Like the poetry of Keats and Shelley it sings to the heart. Each jewel is entirely different from the one next to it. Each scene is in absolute contrast from those before and after."

But a visual image of some sort would have to be projected to the audience, and Lunt believed it should be a stylized one, reflecting the manners of the period in which the opera was written. "You have to remember that the people you find in 'Così fan tutte' moved with leisurely grace in the eighteenth century," he said. "The story is about love, but making love in that period was a slow, artful affair. Each move was like a step in a minuet."

Before beginning rehearsals with his cast, Lunt invited six Broadway actors to his house on Gracie Square. There, for several days, he worked with them to devise patterns of movement that would convey the flavor he hoped to suggest. Thus, when he first met with his singers, the blocking as well as the overall conception had been thoroughly planned.

"Remember," he said to his cast, "you have to feel at home in those eighteenth-century, lace-frilled costumes." Elegance and lightness were the goals for which they should strive. Moreover, there would be no hiding behind the obscurities of a foreign language, since the opera would be sung in English. "If you beat your breast as they sometimes do in opera, I'll kill you," he warned them.

Breaking the singers of their bad habits (as he saw them) was no easy task. Lady Juliet Duff, who was visiting the Lunts while rehearsals were in progress, recalled him arriving home each night, moaning, "Oh, those singers can't act, they just can't act. What am I going to do?" But this was an observation he would never make in public. When asked by a reporter in 1965 if opera singers were difficult to work with, he shot back, "No! I would like to disillusion you about opera singers. They are not temperamental at all. They are all enchanting, hard working darlings. . . . You couldn't meet nicer or easier people to work with. They're really enchanting. And then the privilege, you know, of going to rehearsals and to hear extraordinary sounds from those great singers. What more do you want?"

Still, he privately wished that the performers in *Così fan tutte* had more acting ability. In a letter to William Le Massena, who was appearing with Carol Channing in *Gentlemen Prefer Blondes,* Lunt asked him to "tell Carol that I do so wish she could be in 'Così fan tutti' [*sic*]—she's just what it needs—and [the production] might, in that case, be more real fun—"

Eventually, Lunt was delighted by the work of some of the singers, particularly Patrice Munsel. Years later he told Le Massena how "bewitching" she had been in the production. "Never has 'Despina' been sung as well and certainly never acted as well," he said, "nor will it be again."

Munsel reciprocated Lunt's admiration. In an article she wrote for *Esquire,* she said that each of the singers voluntarily spent many additional hours with Lunt "so we'd have a really polished performance. . . . He worked even harder than we did. . . . He sat in with us on our purely musical rehearsals to see how we worked with our voice coaches. He had dozens of conferences with Dr. Fritz Stiedry, the conductor. And when he got us into the dramatic rehearsals he didn't waste a minute."

Munsel explained that Lunt had gone over every step of the opera with the singers, "planning all our key gestures with us, so we wouldn't ever have to improvise," and when something looked clumsy to him, "he took over the stage himself and showed us how he wanted to do it. Sometimes he showed us twice. Sometimes he showed us three times."

Lunt lamented that he did not have enough time to perform all the tasks for which an opera director is responsible. But he strove to overcome that limitation in various ways. *Così fan tutte* was not the only opera using the stage of the Metropolitan for rehearsal, and because the stage was often unavailable to him, he scheduled brief rehearsals when the performers from the other operas were at lunch or dinner. His six principal singers could not always be available at the same time, so Lunt would work with them individually or in pairs when necessary. "As it turned out," said Howard Taubman, who observed the rehearsal process, "these six put in more hours rehearsing their stage business than most opera singers devote to a new role."

In some respects Lunt was more comfortable directing an opera than he was directing a play. The conventions of staging in the dramatic theatre required a realism that was often at odds with his own imagination. Many years before, he had expressed his enthusiasm for Gordon Craig's dramatic theories, especially his belief that the realistic stage should give way to a theatre of poetry and imagination. But the audience for the dramatic theatre always seemed to crave a sense of realism, and Lunt, as director, found it unwise to shatter their expectations. The conventions of the opera permitted him far more directorial latitude. Characters might face front even while addressing one another; they might carry properties with them that were purely functional, having no realistic connotation;* the setting might do without walls and doors and still suggest an interior. Because he felt that audiences for opera did not expect realistic detail, he was liberated from the necessity of providing it.

Still, Lunt's artistic insecurities, formidable to begin with, were magnified by the fact that he was working in a new medium. He was frequently heard bemoaning his ignorance of the principles of operatic staging or predicting that his production would be a dreadful flop. *Così fan tutte* was, of all operas, the most difficult to direct satisfactorily, he decided, and he should never have given in to the temptation of Bing's offer.

The only solution was to press on in the hope that hard work and careful planning would overcome any deficiencies in his knowledge. Leaving nothing to chance, Lunt spent much time shopping for props. He bought inexpensive wine glasses and painted them himself. Fontanne, who felt that the handkerchiefs used by Eleanor Steber and Blanche Thebom looked altogether too modern, tore up one of her lace negligees, then sewed delicate handkerchiefs from the material.

Clearly, the effort was a labor of love. The Metropolitan paid Lunt only a fraction of his usual salary ($1,000 to direct and another $1,000 to cover expenses)—although Lunt joked to Bing, "You are paying me too much for a production that will be done a half dozen times." But the money he spent for props and costume accessories alone eroded his paycheck. As much as the job absorbed him, he maintained that he could not afford to do it again.

He felt that the production of *Così fan tutte* should begin with a stagehand, in a costume of scarlet and lace, lighting a row of candle-lit footlights with a long taper. This facsimile of eighteenth-century stage practice would immediately put the audience in the mood of the production. Bing agreed, but thought that the business would gain a special distinction if

---

*One example, from an *Opera News* article about Lunt's staging of *Così fan tutte:* "Why should a knapsack be large enough to contain everything which appears to come out of it?"

Lunt played the stagehand. The director agreed to do it for the first performance, but he enjoyed the assignment so much that he repeated it on each of the six occasions the opera was given that season. The program listed Alfred Lunt as "A Servant."*

The first performance of Lunt's production was given on December 28, 1951, and Olin Downes's review in the New York *Times* stated, "Last night's very brilliant presentation . . . was due primarily to the new stage direction of Alfred Lunt and the admirable sets and costumes of Rolf Gérard. There were highly meritorious features of the cast, and there was an excellent and spirited ensemble, musical and dramatic, but this is first of all a new, very witty and admirably stylized stage conception of Mozart's work. No such result had been attained in any previous production of *Così fan tutte* in this city."

Lunt's great achievement was to take opera singers whose acting abilities were marginal and mold them into a polished comic ensemble. The final result was not unlike that of a Lunt-Fontanne drawing-room comedy set to music—with the exception, as Howard Taubman noted, that "he did not forget that underneath the story's artifices Mozart had remembered the heart. He made sure that in her big second-act aria Fiordiligi ceased to be a charming puppet and became a vulnerable woman. No meaningless action was allowed to obtrude on the aria. With the uncommon sensitivity

---

*The impact of Lunt's brief performance on the production as a whole turned out to be sizable. John Mason Brown, writing in the *Saturday Review of Literature,* devoted most of his criticism of the production to a discussion of Lunt's walk-on:". . . Mr. Lunt's brief crossing is more than a personal appearance. It provides as vivid an illustration as can be found of the gifts he possesses which have enabled him to blend theatre with opera and hence light up the whole performance of 'Così fan tutte' at the Metropolitan.

"What makes Mr. Lunt's presence at the Met notable is that he appears there as an actor on a stage where singers are always plentiful and actors usually scarce. To watch him enter, cross and exit is to sample the kind of lesson in acting which as a director he must have given his singers when he transformed them into players.

"Mr. Lunt does not emerge; he makes an entrance, the sort of entrance only a real actor could make. The minute he steps into view the audience becomes a 'captive audience.' Plainly Mr. Lunt is not a person but a personage. Trying to behave as if he were nobody, he is beyond mistaking somebody. White-wigged, beruffled, wearing a smartly cut plum-colored coat, knee breeches, silk stockings, treading on high-heeled shoes, and flourishing a long taper in his right hand and a lace handkerchief in his left, he is the epitome of courtly elegance.

"His immediate domination of the stage and auditorium, however, is not a matter of costume but of personality and technique. No one can fail to recognize that Mr. Lunt is completely at home behind the footlights. He is a master of his craft whose authority is such that he can be relaxed. He knows exactly what he wants to do and how he wants to do it, and proceeds to do it in precisely that fashion.

"Does the importance of a part depend upon its length? Certainly not; a part, as Mr. Lunt proves, is as important as the actor who plays it. Can a silent man be witty? The answer is, of course, 'Yes,' if he happens to speak the language of pantomime with Mr. Lunt's eloquence. Without a word to say, Mr. Lunt converts the wavings of his taper into demonstrations of eighteenth-century decorum, the flourishes of his handkerchief into epigrams, and the grace of his movements into perfect patterns for the stance and stylization of Mozartian characters. Then, suddenly, the little that is so much is over, and Mr. Lunt is gone. But his spirit, his manner, and his wonderfully gay comic touch remain, brightening at every turn and in beguiling ways the performance of 'Così fan tutte' he has staged."

of an artist he knew that this moment of truth must be conveyed purely and simply through Mozart's genius and the singers' voices."

Lunt's staging remained in the Met's repertoire for twenty-five years and came to be regarded by many as the definitive approach. The production of *Così fan tutte* was given its final performance of the season on February 9, 1952, with Lunt vowing never again to direct an opera. The difficulties attendant to the birth of an operatic production exceeded those in the theatre, and although his work with the singers had proved to be enjoyable, he found the experience, as a whole, grueling. After *Così* opened, Lunt wrote the following lines to Margaret Webster, who had encountered great frustrations when she directed *Don Carlo* for the Met:

> My blood has gone, but not the tears,
> They will remain with me for years.
>
> As for the sweat, 'tis flowing yet.
> I hope some day 'twill drown the Met.

But Lunt's resolve did not hold. On two later occasions he returned to the Met: once to revive *Così*, and again to direct a new production of *La Traviata*. He did manage to turn down Rudolf Bing's request that he direct *The Barber of Seville* and *Don Giovanni*.

Lunt's reasons for agreeing to direct opera were perhaps a natural outgrowth of his view of the director's function in the theatre. He saw the director as the equivalent of the conductor of a symphony, whose job was to bring forth the purest sound of which each musician was capable and then to blend those sounds so that they became beautiful music. In his directorial work for the spoken theatre, Lunt also tried to create that "beautiful music"—working through his actors and designers to create a coherent and esthetically pleasing production that would serve the playwright in much the same way that inspired musicians would serve the composer. The analogy also held true in this respect: just as the conductor is not at liberty to alter the composer's score, the director, Lunt felt (except in the case of *I Know My Love*), must always remain faithful to the playwright's words and intentions.

As a director, Lunt tended to show infinite patience with his actors. Sensitive to the actor's need for self-discovery, he preferred not to tell or show a performer precisely what he wanted him to do. His method was, as Theresa Helburn said, to "suggest gently, hesitantly, with an actor's great sensitivity and a real humility." (Fontanne, on the other hand, tended to be more direct, communicating to each actor precisely what was wanted. She "senses the actor's weakness and her method is a strength-giving one," said Helburn.) Lunt's approach to directing was undoubtedly rewarding to the actors, but it was hard on him, perhaps contributing to his ulcer. When, for example, he worked with an actor in *Candle in the Wind* whose technical training was deficient, he betrayed no irritation at rehearsals. Afterward, however, he could not contain his frustration. On one occasion he shouted to John F. Wharton of the Playwrights' Company, "John, that man doesn't even know how to lift his ass off one chair and put it down on another." Still, Lunt continued to treat the actor with courtesy and respect, gradually drawing a respectable performance from him.

Perhaps the ultimate tribute to Lunt's directorial method was paid by one of the singers in *Così fan tutte,* who said, "He made us feel that we were doing it all ourselves."

But this should not suggest that Lunt played a passive role when he directed. When asked, he was always ready with a suggestion, which he sometimes found easier to demonstrate than to explain. As William Le Massena (who said, "Lunt was one of the two or three great directors I've ever worked with") put it, "He was a performer himself, so he must necessarily perform while showing you. But he was constantly apologizing because he knew that a lot of actors don't like to be given line readings. They don't like to imitate the director. So he would always say, 'You don't mind if I suggest a reading? Now, try it this way.' And he was always so right-on-the-nose with everything he gave you." Then, when the actor was still trying to absorb Lunt's recommendation, Le Massena said, "He'd move on to something else. He'd find another good idea and another one. Of course, it baffles some actors. A lot of actors just can't work that way because they're asked to absorb so much so quickly." But for those who were able to keep up with the outpourings of Lunt's creativity, the result was immensely gratifying. Each of the items Lunt worked upon—a reading, a gesture—may have been only a minor detail, but every suggestion gave added dimension to the character.

Lunt demanded—and received—total commitment from his actors. "A director must have absolute authority," he told Maurice Zolotow, "but it is authority that should stem from the director's more extensive knowledge of the play. The actor, naturally, tends to see only his microscopic segment of the play. The director must . . . see the play steadily and see it whole. So the actor must listen carefully to every word the director says and must obey him—even if the command contradicts the actor's conception."

Lunt directed few plays in which he did not himself appear, but his services as a director were very much in demand. Over the years, he turned down the opportunity to direct such plays as *Medea, Caligula, An Inspector Calls* and *Small War on Murray Hill.*

One play he was unable to turn down was Jean Giraudoux's *Ondine.* In 1939, while visiting Ten Chimneys, the playwright had asked the Lunts to play the leading roles in *Ondine,* but they believed the characters were too young for them. When the offer to direct the play came fourteen years later, it represented a chance to work on a play they had always admired.

Another attractive feature for Lunt was that Robert E. Sherwood had agreed to supervise the production for the Playwrights' Company. Lunt and Sherwood, who had worked together so often in the past, both looked forward to renewing their association.

Even before Lunt signed the contract to direct *Ondine,* he began to plan the sets and costumes. The leading roles were already cast: Audrey Hepburn, who had recently won an Academy Award for her role in *Roman Holiday,* was to play Ondine, and Mel Ferrer, a movie actor with whom she had fallen in love, would play opposite her.

Sherwood was particularly enthusiastic about the casting of Audrey Hepburn. "I think [she] is absolutely ideal for the part of Ondine," he told Lunt in a letter on November 4. "She has had ballet training and I think that is extremely important, as the whole play seems to have a ballet quality." And, Sherwood added: "It needs the 'Così Fan Tutte' treatment in direction, and I know of only one living individual who can supply that."

The casting of Mel Ferrer was regarded as a riskier proposition. Ferrer's reputation was less well established and his professional stage experience was not extensive. But the Playwrights' Company offered him the role in order to persuade Audrey Hepburn to play Ondine. As a member of the production team put it, "We bought Hepburn and the price was Ferrer," adding, "It turned out to be much too expensive."

Ondine is by no means typical Broadway fare. It is a fantasy, a fairy tale, based upon myth and legend, populated with sprites and knights-errant. As Lunt began conceiving a visual style he believed would capture the spirit of the play, he became more and more enthusiastic about the project. "I am beginning to find 'Ondine' almost too exciting to think about," he wrote Sherwood on November 11. "It has problems, far more difficult than any play I know—If we could just find the right man to do the scenery!" Lunt believed that only a combination of Cecil Beaton, Marc Chagall, Jo Mielziner, Oliver Messel, Rolf Gérard and Richard Whorf would be capable of doing the job with the proper combination of skill and imagination. "Isn't there some young budding genius?" he asked. "The actors of course must have their feet on the ground but the scenery must literally ebb and flow." Eventually, he chose Peter Larkin to heighten, modify and realize the visual ideas he had conceived. As this was one of Larkin's first Broadway assignments, Lunt was concerned about his youth and relative inexperience, but impressed by his talent. He was also pleased that Larkin did not hesitate when Lunt asked him to spend some time at Ten Chimneys in November so that they could work together in the tranquil surroundings in which Lunt felt most comfortable.

Lunt also told Sherwood that the production needed "music too, amplified—so that it comes from everywhere—a quartet like Ravel's Introduction for Harp & strings & wood instruments—and one trumpet & percussion. Five union musicians could do it—Anyway Music—*you must have*. Thomson could do a lovely score." On Lunt's recommendation, Virgil Thomson was commissioned to compose the music.

Once more Lunt was beset by artistic insecurities, as he confessed to Richard Whorf on November 25: "I've not been awfully well and am in bed until Monday—Nothing serious—no ulcer, nothing like that—but it is wisest I be quiet for a while—I never should have attempted the play in the first place but I'm so Goddam weak—Rehearsals start on December 28th. So little time—"

Not until about three weeks before the scheduled first rehearsal was the Maurice Valency adaptation of the play delivered to Lunt. He and Sherwood (acting on behalf of the Playwrights' Company) were pleased with Valency's work, but felt that the three-and-a-half-hour play needed considerable cutting for an American audience. Lunt said: "We didn't do big cuts—it was little snippets here and there with a manicure scissors so we wouldn't lose the texture of the play."

Casting for *Ondine* was complicated by the lack of classically trained American actors. Lunt auditioned hundreds of performers,* but was frustrated by the difficulty of finding actors who could speak poetic language with understanding and authority. Too many of those who auditioned tended to shout, or to slur their lines, or to recite them in singsong fashion. Both Lunt and Fontanne believed that the methods for training American actors that were in vogue in the 1950s were deficient in preparing them to perform in anything but modern realistic drama. Emphasizing the search for inner truth, such methods neglected the actor's need to deal with material that cannot be internalized effectively. Fontanne said she knew many young actors who could "throw a good fit of hysterics quite convincingly. . . . They could say, 'I feel as if I'm going out of my mind,' and start to scream and cry. It's something very young actors have a great gift for, but it doesn't last very long, emotion and hysteria." And what, Lunt asked, will the young actor do who "tries to play Congreve or Shakespeare or Wilde?" All too often he will speak "with no coloring at all; no accentuation or elegance."

The Lunts were certainly not opposed to the actor's quest for inner truth. Of all performers, they were among the foremost examples of those who went to great lengths to achieve a sense of internal reality. But they were skeptical of any training that emphasized inner truth to the exclusion of all else. The auditions for *Ondine* convinced Lunt that the American theatre was experiencing the inevitable result of a method for training actors that denied the necessity of mastering technical skills. In the end, he selected a number of actors with whom he had worked in the past (such as Edith King and William Le Massena), because he knew their performances would be sensitive to the play's language and imagery.

Ondine was to be in rehearsal for four weeks before its out-of-town opening, and Lunt was determined to use every moment profitably. Although most rehearsals did not begin until 1:00 p.m., Lunt awoke every morning at 8:00 so he could check on the progress of the scenery or costumes or work on his notes for the afternoon's rehearsal.

Lunt was the only credited director on the production, but Fontanne,

* He had already offered roles to some actors, such as Alan Hewitt.

on hand at all the rehearsals, was instrumental in shaping many of the individual performances. Le Massena said, "You never saw her walk up to
[Lunt] and whisper and say, 'Well, listen, if you did so and so . . .' At least
I can never remember anything of that kind. But I know they discussed
every phase of the theatre." Speaking specifically of her participation in
Ondine, Le Massena said, "She was working with Dickie Whorf on the
costumes, and she had a very active part in it." In a letter written on December 30, Fontanne substantiated Le Massena's assertion, saying, "we are
in N.Y. directing a play by Giraudoux called 'Ondine' . . . we have a lovely
cast."

Her role was generally restricted to that of a skilled observer, but
sometimes she participated directly. For example, when one actress had
difficulty with a formal bow and the lines that accompanied the movement,
Fontanne took her aside and worked with her until the bow and the line
readings had been finely polished.

But it was Lunt who generally communicated directly with the actors,
and he was anything but passive in his directorial role. Rather than sitting
in the auditorium and taking notes, he sat on the stage only a few feet away
from the actors. When he saw something that needed work, he immediately approached the actor with suggestions. Then he returned to his chair
downstage center, but only for a moment before dashing to one side of
the stage in order to check on the scene from another vantage point.

An actor in the *Ondine* company described Lunt's methods to a writer
for *Theatre Arts:*

> Lunt works us until we're ready to drop. The first week of
> rehearsal I think we all tried to see how much we could get away
> with. He wouldn't stand for it, wouldn't give way one inch. He
> made his authority stick the first week—I've heard he handed in
> his resignation twice. While I wouldn't exactly say he's a tyrant,
> he certainly is the boss and won't stand for any tricks or temper
> tantrums. . . .
>
> On the other hand, Lunt, though he can give you a raised
> eyebrow and a sharp reprimand that will make you wish you
> were dead, is just about the most wonderful audience an actor
> could want. He's a genuine appreciator. If you're having a good
> moment, he's so warm and generous in his praise that you forget
> all the times he's glared or made you feel like an ignorant slob by
> reading one of your speeches more beautifully than you know
> you could ever do it yourself.

In order to ensure that his actors would not internalize emotion but
fail to share it effectively with an audience, Lunt insisted they speak with
full projection from the earliest rehearsals. Although he sat on the edge of
the stage, where he could hear the faintest whisper, he always thought in
terms of the spectator seated in the last row of the balcony. Then, too,

Fontanne was seated out front, and she would inform him if there were any problems of projection or articulation. The following comment, or a minor variation of it, was made again and again to an actor or actress in the production: "It's no use; you're doing it beautifully—but it's no use because they won't be able to hear you." On the other hand, not wishing the performances to become artificial, he could frequently be heard advising an actor to "play it truly, play it truly."

The actors were clearly grateful for Lunt's suggestions and responsive to his direction—except for Mel Ferrer, who was convinced that Lunt's ideas were stale and his direction unimaginative. Furthermore, Ferrer resented Fontanne's presence at rehearsals and complained to the Playwrights' Company, insisting that the play should have only one director. Recognizing that Audrey Hepburn was clearly outshining him, he repeatedly asked the producers to revise the play so that her role would be lessened and his made more prominent. He also behaved temperamentally at rehearsals. He "got under Lunt's skin and made him very angry," said an observer, "and was a terrible nuisance."

One distinguished visitor at a late runthrough was Margaret Sullavan, who was so enthralled that she sent Lunt the following note:

> Until this afternoon I had always complained that I had never seen a really creative job of direction—one that made the play more exciting to watch than to read. The most one could hope for was that the director kept out of the way of the play, and arranged his actions and pace so that one was unaware of them.
>
> But at the run through of "Ondine" this afternoon I was lost in admiration for you. Your contribution was greater than Giraudoux' to me. I am still spellbound, and at your feet.

Maxwell Anderson, a member of the Playwrights' Company and an old friend and colleague of the Lunts, also came to see a late rehearsal of *Ondine*. He told Sherwood afterward that he was "happier about *Ondine* than anything else in the theatre for years." Sherwood passed the message along to Fontanne, and told her: "Max has been in a very despairing, defeated state of mind, for a long time. . . . But what he saw of one rehearsal of 'Ondine' has evidently revived his faith and his will to live and write. This should be tremendously pleasing to you and Alfred."

When *Ondine* opened in Boston on January 29, 1954, the members of the Playwrights' Company were confident the play would succeed. They had seen a dress rehearsal and were convinced that Lunt's direction was superb. For his part, Lunt was worried about various details of music and lighting, but he had long ago established his reputation as a chronic worrier. The Boston opening seemed to confirm the confidence of the producers, as everything went splendidly. Sherwood returned happily to New York.

But the tensions that had been building between Lunt and Ferrer spilled over immediately after the play's premiere. Ferrer openly expressed his contempt for Lunt's direction, and made clear that he would listen to him no longer. Moreover, Ferrer again demanded of the Playwrights' Company that his role be rewritten and expanded. "He wanted to use the play as a vehicle for himself and it griped the hell out of him that [Hepburn] was getting all the notices," said an observer at the rehearsals. Robert E. Sherwood instructed Maurice Valency not to alter a word, even if Ferrer threatened to quit the production and to pull Audrey Hepburn out of the cast as well.

Lunt telephoned Sherwood, offering to resign if that would prevent Hepburn's leaving. Sherwood, saying he would not hear of it, called Ferrer's agent in Hollywood; the agent, in turn, called Ferrer and reportedly warned him that he was jeopardizing his career. Ferrer then apologized to Lunt and promised to create no further difficulties.

A few days later Audrey Hepburn left Boston on an early plane and unexpectedly arrived at Sherwood's apartment. She was obviously in a delicate position. *Ondine* would be her first appearance in New York since her immense success in the film *Roman Holiday,* and as such it was enormously important to her career. She needed to have faith that she was doing well in *Ondine* and that the production as a whole was likely to succeed. Ferrer had undermined that faith. Moreover, she and Ferrer were engaged to be married, so she could hardly be expected to be neutral in the conflict between him and the director. To Sherwood she expressed the conviction that it might be better for all concerned if she were to withdraw from the production. After considerable discussion, Sherwood managed to restore her confidence, and she returned to Boston that night and continued to perform.

Sherwood cabled to Lunt: "DEAR ALFRED I HAVE HAD A VERY USEFUL AND SENSIBLE TALK WITH AUDREY HEPBURN AND AM GOING TO BOSTON TOMORROW SATURDAY AFTERNOON TO DISCUSS WITH YOU VALENCY AUDREY AND FERRER ANY POINTS THAT REMAIN IN DOUBT. . . . AUDREY SAID TO ME THAT SHE COULD ASK NOTHING BETTER FOR HER FUTURE CAREER THAN ALWAYS TO BE DIRECTED BY YOU AND I TAKE THAT STATEMENT LITERALLY AS EVIDENCE OF HER INTELLIGENCE."

Lunt was pleased by the response of the Boston critics. The reviews in the *Evening American,* the *Herald* and the *Post* can only be described as raves, with Audrey Hepburn being singled out for special praise. Perhaps the reviews, coupled with Sherwood's counsel, had calmed Hepburn's fears, for in an interview with the Boston *Sunday Globe* she said: "We are fortunate to have Mr. Lunt as director. I have never met a man whose encouragement, kindness and understanding does so much for an actress. Miss Fontanne, with her enormous experience, is always ready to give an actor advice, when we go to her."

Alan Hewitt was unhappy that Lunt had not been given sufficient credit by the critics. Consequently, he wrote to Elinor Hughes of the Boston *Herald:* "No critic writing about 'Ondine' has said enough, in my opinion, about Alfred Lunt. He is the star of the show. Sets and costumes were designed according to his notions. Actors took their impulses from him. Author abided by his textual cuts. To put it mildly, he's a genius."

Another who considered Lunt a genius was Maurice Valency, who was astonished by the imagination and thoroughness Lunt had brought to the production. "When he came to New York in November," Valency said, Lunt "had it all done in his head—sets, costumes, direction and, in a general way, cast. There was hardly any change in his conception thereafter. The play that opened in Boston was—scene for scene—almost exactly what was sketched out the day we went into rehearsal."

Ondine opened in New York on February 18 and was received with great enthusiasm by the first-night audience. Afterward, at the inevitable party, everyone was radiant. The mood changed, however, when one woman asked Lunt, in all innocence, "Did you learn anything from working with a movie star like Mel Ferrer?"

Lunt was staggered by the naïveté of the question, but managed to reply, "Yes, madam. I learned that you cannot make a knight-errant out of a horse's ass!"

In later years Lunt became philosophical about his conflict with Ferrer, but Fontanne could not suppress her anger whenever the subject came up. About Ferrer's refusal to take direction from Lunt, she said, "That wasn't jealousy, that was imbecility."

Ferrer's battle with Lunt continued throughout the run of the play, extending even to the curtain calls. Lunt had arranged that Audrey Hepburn would take the final call, but Ferrer insisted that he share in the final bow, and further demanded that she not be given *any* individual curtain call.

The New York critics were nearly unanimous in their praise for *Ondine*. Brooks Atkinson called it "ideal from every point of view. Ideal literature, ideal acting, ideal theatre." John McClain concurred, saying in the New York *Journal-American,* "This is quite the most enchanting evening I have spent out of this world since I can recall."

Richard Watts, Jr., of the New York *Post,* shared in the general approval, but said: "My only reservation has to do with the performance of Mel Ferrer as the knight-errant of the fable. . . . To my mind, his playing is curiously uninteresting. It lacks vividness, style and imagination almost completely, which is all the more distracting because these are the qualities that the production of *Ondine* otherwise possesses so winningly. I guess the American theatre, otherwise blessed in fine actors, lacks good romantic players. If Mr. Lunt were just a few years younger, how splendid he would have been in the part!"

There were some dissenters from the general attitude. Eric Bentley was captivated by Audrey Hepburn, but found the rest of the cast wanting. "The failure of Mel Ferrer would not, perhaps, have been fatal, even though his part is a big one," said Bentley, "were it not that the rest of the cast . . . seem to take their cue from him. Or did he and the others take their cue from the director, Alfred Lunt? One cannot but wonder if the latter didn't fall asleep at rehearsals. . . . How otherwise could he have permitted character work at the level of summer stock? And failed to find any 'line' of style or meaning?"

But the majority view was clearly stated by Atkinson: "As a work for the theatre, *Ondine* is perfect. It is all imagination, which is the genius of the stage. . . . Under Alfred Lunt's skimming direction, it emerges as a fully wrought work of art composed of dialogue, music, pantomime and spectacle."

The theatregoing public clearly agreed. Although *Ondine* had been scheduled from the beginning for a limited run of only twenty weeks, the production returned a profit of over $40,000. In all, *Ondine* played on Broadway for 156 performances, with rarely a vacant seat.

Later in the year, Audrey Hepburn was selected to receive the Antoinette Perry Award for the finest performance given by an actress in a nonmusical play. Lunt was also given a Tony for his direction of *Ondine*. He wrote to Richard Whorf from Genesee Depot on March 16, "Alas, I cannot come in to accept it & so I wonder if you would for me. . . . Should I see myself presented with an honour for 'Ondine' I'm afraid I'd merely be flabbergasted with surprise and astonishment—" Convinced that the award was undeserved, he wrote to Sherwood three months later, "All the medals & praise in the world will never convince me that beautiful play comes off. Of course people are disappointed in the love story—*She* jumps on the hero's lap & he holds her like a potted palm—he sits beside her at the table & treats her like a tired waitress at Child's—Listen! If he played his scenes on top of her you'd have the feeling he was laying a corner stone. Personally, I'd call the whole show a fucking failure—"

For the Lunts, their health and the health of their friends and relatives was a constant concern. In the late 1940s their advancing age and Lunt's various disabilities made it difficult for them to meet the physical demands of giving eight performances a week in *O Mistress Mine*. In May 1946, Fontanne wrote to Habetrot Dewhurst that she and Lunt were both looking forward to July with near-desperation. "We both need the vacation very badly, as we have worked like dogs this season," she said.

Fontanne, like her husband, was determined to continue her career despite declining stamina. Still, when Lunt entered the hospital for his kidney operation in January 1947, forcing *O Mistress Mine* to close for six weeks, she found herself unexpectedly enjoying the enforced rest. She spent the period of Lunt's convalescence very quietly, she wrote to Lady

Juliet Duff, "not going anywhere, but having long evenings at home alone and enjoyed them so tremendously. It seemed very queer and odd to be doing that in the middle of a New York season, but I grew so used to it that I felt rather elderly and retired. . . ." Weeks later, after performances were resumed, she said, "The routine of coming down to the theatre, having one's breakfast at noon and dinner at five, seems quite strange to me now."

When *O Mistress Mine* was on tour and Lunt's doctor, Edward Bigg, discovered that his ulcer was bleeding once again, Bigg told him that he would have to enter a hospital immediately. Lunt shouted, "No, no!" Bigg recalled. "And when he said *no*, you could hear him for blocks. As I went downstairs, Lynn was sitting in the drawing room." When told Lunt was adamant in his refusal to go to the hospital, she said, "Oh, Edward, you must talk with him. He'll listen to *you*." The argument continued for four or five hours, until at last Lunt reluctantly agreed.

Bigg drove the Lunts to Passavant Memorial Hospital in Chicago. Throughout the long ride, he remembered, "not a word was said from the moment we left Genesee until he got in the hospital [because] he was so depressed and angry." Lunt "really behaved himself very well" in the hospital, but he became progressively more irritated by the constant parade of nurses and orderlies entering his room, especially when he was trying to sleep. He took his revenge in small but satisfying ways. One morning, Bigg recalled, "He was fast asleep when he heard the door slowly being opened. He opened his eyes a crack and saw a young orderly coming in balancing a tray very gently. As he was putting it down, Alfred roared at the top of his lungs, 'Go away!' He could be heard throughout the hospital. The poor chap dropped his tray and ran out the door as fast he could."

Fontanne was deeply concerned about her husband's health, but she also demonstrated a motherly concern for the entire company. She told Binkie Beaumont in a letter, "We have had the whole company inoculated against [influenza], scene-shifters and all." She implored Beaumont to do the same with his British companies, "and certainly, darling, please do it yourself and make all my dear friends—Noel, Antoinette, Terry [Rattigan]—oh, you know—everybody—do the same. You will never be able to persuade Edith Evans [a Christian Scientist] to have it done, but perhaps somebody with a hypodermic could goose her just as she is making an entrance."

The fragility of their lives and of those they loved was brought home to them in especially poignant fashion when Lunt's mother's health began to fail in 1953. In November of that year, he wrote to Richard Whorf that his mother was in Chicago: "nearer to doctors, etc.—she's so frail—I doubt if she'll ever come to Genesee—again—" Eventually she did return to Genesee, but her condition continued to deteriorate. The Lunts' friend Dr. Gustav Eckstein went to visit her, and wrote, "Her body is in the country but her mind is on people, and she anticipates the time when you will come back." She clung to life until two months after the run of *Quadrille* ended, dying on May 16, 1955, in Genesee Depot, at the age of ninety-three, her son and daughter-in-law at her bedside.

Later that year the Lunts lost one of their closest friends. In mid-November, *The Great Sebastians* was playing in Philadelphia when word reached them that Robert E. Sherwood had died. Maxwell Anderson wrote a eulogy for Sherwood's funeral, and Lunt hastily arranged a trip to New York. He delivered Anderson's eulogy the following day at St. George's Protestant Episcopal Church in Stuyvesant Square.

Many married couples become more dependent upon one another as they grow older and their friends pass away, but the Lunts' mutual reliance dated from the beginning of their relationship. Seldom have two people been so interdependent, so genuinely in harmony. From the very beginning of their married life, they shared a mutual respect and affection that grew stronger throughout the years. At first their reliance on one another seems to have been related primarily to their work. Each realized that the other was his best critic, and each depended on the other for advice. "Over a long run," Fontanne said, "you lose your eye and you lose your ear. And I have to keep watch over him as he does over me. . . . And I think that is very possibly one of the reasons, if I might say so, for our success. I think that we are terrifically critical of each other. And we've learned, the both of us, to take it. . . . If [when I'm performing] I'm tired and it gets into my own voice—I hear about it from Alfred. Make no mistake, I hear about it."

And he heard about it from her as well, sometimes in unconventional ways. One night during a performance of *Quadrille,* the Lunts were seated on a sofa. Fontanne was positioned so that her face was to the audience. During a speech of Lunt's, she managed to whisper to him through a smile—without moving her lips even a fraction of an inch—"You're in my light!"

Soon the closeness of their relationship as performers came to be reflected in the closeness of their private life. They felt uncomfortable when they were apart, even for the briefest periods. In 1930, for example, Lunt went for a walk by himself one afternoon and decided to visit a friend for a half-hour or so. As it was nearly dinnertime, the friend suggested that he and Lunt go out together for a bite to eat. Lunt looked at him, astonished. "Without Lynn?" he exclaimed, picked up his hat and headed home.

A similar incident occurred many years later, in the mid-1960s. The Lunts were no longer active in the theatre, but they were visiting New York and staying at their house on East End Avenue. Alan Hewitt described the incident to me:

> Alfred called me around 6:30 or 7:00 in the evening and said, "Are you doing anything for dinner?" And I said, "Well, I was just about to fix something for myself here." He said,

"Would you do me a great favor? We've got so much food here, and I'd like you to help me with it. Lynn has fallen and broken her arm, you see, and I've taken her to Doctors' Hospital. So we have all of this perfectly good food here, and she's not here to eat it. Would you come up and share it with me?" So I said, "Of course." And so I went up to have dinner with him.

Alfred offered me a drink, and then he said, "Now, before we have dinner, if you don't mind, I'm just going to run over and see Lynn." So he went over to Doctors' Hospital, which was just a block away. When he came back the cook served dinner, and before dessert Alfred said, "I'm sorry, Alan, but I've got to make sure that Lynn's all right. You don't mind, do you?" And back he went to the hospital. Well, that evening he went there four times! And as I was leaving, he said, "Why don't I walk part of the way with you? It'll give me a chance to stop at the hospital and see how Lynn is doing."

William Le Massena watched Lunt try to cope without Fontanne one day in the 1940s. "He was just totally lost without her," said Le Massena. "He was just like a cat that had been put in a strange house. He was wandering around as if he was lost. All I could think of was, 'If one of them has to go before the other, I hope that Alfred isn't left without Lynn.' Everyone hoped that. Lynn was the silent, strong one, and she would be able to carry on without him. But Alfred . . . I believe that Lynn knew that and *willed* herself to live longer than he did so that he wouldn't be left alone."

On one occasion the Lunts went to see their lawyer and close friend Donald Seawell at his office in New York. Alfred said, "Donnie, we want you to draft our will." Seawell said, "Your wills, you mean." Lunt stared at him blankly. Seawell explained that they would be well advised to draw up separate wills. The Lunts looked at one another in disbelief. Lunt got up from his chair and put his arms around his wife. "Donnie," he said, "you'll have to forgive us. It just never occurred to us that one of us might have to go on without the other."

The Lunts' deep affection was based on the fact that each was endlessly fascinated by the other. When asked how he and his wife had managed to maintain so close a relationship for such a long time, Lunt said, "The answer is so simple, really, but no one believes me. I've never been bored by her. She is the most continually exciting and enchanting person I have ever known."

For her part, Fontanne relied upon Lunt as much as he did upon her, although she was less likely to reveal it to others. But in 1967, when she acted without Lunt in *Anastasia* for television and they were separated during the day for the first time since early in their married lives (he was busy directing *La Traviata* at the Metropolitan Opera while she was taping *An-*

astasia), she found that she missed him terribly. It wasn't only that she missed acting with him, she explained; she missed him "going to rehearsal and coming home. He's very attentive—always remembers my glasses and my script. And when we're working together, we bring a picnic basket and eat together. . . . Alfred and I are so used to each other's faces that playing a scene with a stranger now throws me off for a time."

Whether out of envy or simply because of an inability to conceive that any relationship could be as warm as theirs seemed to be, some people suspected that this picture of the Lunts' lives together was simply a product of expert press-agentry. Reporters, acquaintances, even some of their friends were on the lookout for behavior that would reveal the Lunts' relationship to be less close than it was portrayed. Rumors were rife: their union had begun as a "marriage of convenience"; they were said to argue furiously in private; they never shared the same bed; Lunt engaged in homosexual relationships; they saw as little as possible of each other offstage. If any of these rumors had been remotely true, however, some confirmation would surely have been found; they were married for fifty-five years— ample time for the dark underside of their marriage to be seen by *some*one, at *some* time, *some*where. But the simple, honest truth, disappointing no doubt to some, was that the rumors had no basis in fact.

Certainly the Lunts did quarrel or bicker on occasion. She would become testy about her memorization, which often came hard for her, and when she went up in her lines during a rehearsal, she would be apt to stare at him and insist that it was his fault. She claimed there was one thing that "really enrages me—and that is when Alfred tries to direct me at rehearsal when we are both working under another director. That is murder! I will not tolerate such interference, and it makes me furious even to think about it." And when they were working together on the intricacies of a scene, they could fight "angrily and embarrassingly and pretty ludicrously, about ways and means of solving little problems," as Robert E. Sherwood said of them. But Lunt was being perfectly accurate when he said, "It is nearly always about some detail connected with the theatre that we argue." And it is important to realize that these arguments were genuinely creative, that the two of them were trying to arrive—not always in the most temperate way—at the most effective acting of which they were capable. Even then, their disagreements rarely became personal or truly acrimonious. William Le Massena said, "I never saw a roaring fight between them. I've seen them disagree. But it seems to me that they would just cool themselves off right on the scene. They just realized that there was no point." No one seems to have noticed any significant discord between them that did not relate directly to their work.

Which does not mean they might not contradict one another. He might express his favorable opinion of a play while she looked fixedly at the ceiling, revealing her unspoken but unmistakable disagreement. She might begin to tell a story only to have him interrupt her because he insisted she was forgetting the most important incidents. She would correct him about his memory for details. But, as their friend George Schaefer said, these were always "loving, loving exchanges. It would be hard for me to picture them really at odds."

The notion that they were sexually incompatible is disputed by the fact that they *did* always sleep in the same bed, and they left no doubt with anyone who knew them well that they enjoyed it. Fontanne once mentioned to Arthur Marshall that when the Lunts were in England in the 1940s to perform *There Shall Be No Night*, "the sides of their double bed in their hotel was higher than the bit in the middle, which tended to roll them together and [Fontanne said] that this was much jollier than the converse. She added . . . that it is extremely difficult to keep up a squabble in a double bed."

Nearly every well-known figure in show business has been rumored to be homosexual. But if Lunt had any such tendencies, they were kept well-hidden from his family and friends. Not one person to whom I spoke could substantiate the rumors. As one actor who appeared in many of the Lunts' productions put it, "If Lunt was homosexual, I must have been very unattractive, because he never made a pass at me. And there would have been plenty of opportunity to be surreptitious about it, to invite me out, or to do something or other to indicate that he was interested—but it never happened. And if he was having a relationship with anyone else in the company at any time, he was awfully discreet about it. I certainly never heard anything to indicate that it might have been true."

The belief that the Lunts rarely spent time together offstage is contradicted by everyone who knew them. It was axiomatic among their friends that it was pointless to invite Lynn anywhere without Alfred or to invite Alfred without Lynn because they simply would refuse to be separated.

When the Lunts celebrated their twenty-eighth wedding anniversary in 1950, the Boston *Traveler* asked them how they had managed to remain happily married for so many years. They wrote, in part:

> We always have been careful to separate our personal and our professional lives. We are together practically all the time offstage; once we enter the stagedoor we are like polite strangers. There is no visiting between dressing rooms. We have work to do until the curtain falls at eleven o'clock. After that we always resume our other life and generally go straight home to a supper of cereal and milk. . . .
>
> When we spend our summer holidays on our farm in Wisconsin, we are careful to give each other plenty of time to be alone to devote to separate interests. On the other hand we are fortunate in liking the same things. We both enjoy reading, sometimes aloud. We like to take long walks, to work in our garden, to just sit and talk. We are fortunate also in liking the

same people, so that our friends are always mutually welcome. Neither of us is much of a partygoer. Many of our friends are outside the theatre as well as in it. We like nothing better than having a quiet dinner together and we never have come to that unfortunate state in which you "run out of conversation" which sometimes happens to people who have been married a quarter of a century.

Perhaps the aspect of their personalities that most attracted the Lunts to one another was their sense of humor. Noël Coward described an evening at their home in New York when he arrived before 6:00 and remained until 2:30 in the morning. "We just talk and talk and laugh and laugh," he said. "They are the most enchanting people to be with. They are unique. The interplay of one with the other is extraordinary, you know, utterly charming. They seem to know what each other is thinking. He'll start a sentence and she'll finish it." Carol Channing told me similar stories about evenings with the Lunts at Ten Chimneys. "They were having a disagreement or something," Channing said, "and then they suddenly stopped and started to laugh—right in the middle of the argument—all of a sudden they started to laugh. They couldn't stop it. And I thought, 'How wonderful. They're just like that. They really are.'"

The Lunts also used their histrionic abilities to amuse themselves. "They acted all the time," according to George Bugbee, Lunt's brother-in-law, who, with his wife, Karin, was closer to the Lunts than anyone else from 1940 on. Alfred and Lynn "tried to fool one another," he said, and occasionally succeeded. "I think it amused them to do it," he concluded; "it was a game they played."

Another game involved the creation of an imaginary child, "Winnie," to whom they often spoke aloud. One should hastily add that this was a playful rather than a neurotic pretense. Their "conversations" with the "child" were occasionally conducted for the amusement of Karin and George.

Of course, some people behave one way when they are among friends and another way when they are with employees or children, or think they are not being observed, but that was not the case with the Lunts. Carolyn Every, who worked for them as secretary and cook in the early 1930s, said, "I never heard them fight. And nobody I know of ever heard them fight. They were very much in love with each other." Dick Van Patten, who was only seventeen when he appeared with them in *O Mistress Mine,* used exactly the same words: "I never heard them fight," he said. "I never heard them make a scene or yell at one another. If she said something he disagreed with, he'd just laugh at her affectionately, and she'd laugh at him. And that would be the end of it." Suzanne Knapp, Lunt's niece, lived with her mother and father in the Cottage at Genesee Depot when the Lunts occupied the large house during their summer vacations. "When you're five or six years old, you sort of creep through the house," she said, "and I'm sure I was in the house often when they didn't realize I was around. And I *never* heard their voices raised to one another." George Bugbee agreed: "They didn't have arguments," he said. "I never heard them argue."

Fontanne was a much more reserved person than Lunt, and much less given to telling others how deeply she loved her husband. But several remarks, such as this statement to an interviewer, revealed her feelings: "I used to stand in the wings and be staggered by Alfred's acting, it was so beautiful." Several years after Lunt's death, an interviewer asked her: "With all the triumphs and accolades you've received through the decades, what was the real highlight of your life?"

"My marriage to Alfred," she answered. "I miss him every second of every day."

Chapter Fourteen

THE VISIT

"Directing Lunt is a revelation. You can't imagine the countless tiny details that Alfred puts into a performance. This may sound like finicky acting but these painstaking details make up an enormous conception. It is like one of Seurat's pointillist paintings. Each little dot is not art, but the whole is magnificent. Alfred and Lynn start by getting a broad outline of what they're going to do and then they fill in the details. It's absolutely like somebody making a mosaic. They work endlessly from one detail to the next— fine, fine points—one after another. They're deep and flexible people and they have lightning speed and great artistic glory."

Peter Brook

In 1957 it was clear that the Lunts would not be physically capable of performing on the stage for very much longer. Fontanne was in good health, but she was nearly seventy years old. Lunt was five years younger, but he had long been plagued with various illnesses, many of them serious. Their next play was very likely to be their last, and, as such (one can clearly see with hindsight), it needed to be the kind of play that would offer them depth, richness and an opportunity to display their histrionic abilities to the fullest—the kind of play their critics had long been challenging them to attempt. In short, although they could not have known it at the time, they needed Friedrich Duerrenmatt's mordant satire, *The Visit*.

1957–60

The television production of *The Great Sebastians* over, the Lunts returned to Genesee Depot for two months' rest. Their plan was to sail for England in June to present the Lindsay-Crouse comedy in London. During their vacation, however, the Theatre Guild sent a play called *The Old Lady Pays a Visit,* by the Swiss dramatist Friedrich Duerrenmatt (in an English adaptation by Maurice Valency), to Donald Seawell, upon whose counsel the Lunts had become increasingly dependent in theatrical as well as financial matters. Knowing that their careers on the stage were nearing an end, they were less eager to read every play submitted to them, so Seawell took over that function. Intrigued by the play, Seawell journeyed to Genesee Depot to pass the script on to the Lunts. They, too, were fascinated.

The play, a powerful, skillfully written indictment of the way people allow money to control their lives and alter their characters, focuses upon Claire Zachanassian, one of the wealthiest women in the world, who returns to the small, rundown town in Central Europe where she grew up. The townspeople, hoping the elderly Mme. Zachanassian will pay for refurbishing their depressed village, court her eagerly. She consents to give them a billion marks, but under one condition: they must agree to kill the grocer Alfred Ill, who had seduced Claire many years before and had refused to assist her when she was pregnant. The townspeople react to Mme. Zachanassian's demand with horror and outrage, but slowly, gradually, their attitudes change. What, they ask, is a single life compared to the well-being of an entire community? Why shouldn't Alfred Ill be punished for his past transgression? The play details the townspeople's inexorable passage from righteous indignation to equally righteous participation in the murder.

The Theatre Guild hoped that Fontanne would be willing to play Claire Zachanassian and that Lunt would wish to portray Alfred Ill. "We thought it an extraordinary, a fascinating play; original, superb 'theatre,' and important," Lunt told Theresa Helburn of the Guild. Despite their admiration for the play, however, "It simply wasn't right," Donald Seawell said. "In fact," he remembered, "I couldn't tell whether it was meant to be played for comedy or tragedy." Indeed, that is one of the most intriguing features of Duerrenmatt's play: it mingles gallows humor with horror in such a way that the play seems to reflect both a comic and a tragic view of life. In that respect, it was similar to the plays of several other dramatists who were coming to attention in the 1950s: Samuel Beckett *(Waiting for Godot, Endgame),* Harold Pinter *(The Birthday Party, The Room, The Caretaker)* and Eugène Ionesco *(The Chairs, The Lesson, The Killer).* All wrote with intense seriousness about such aspects of man's nature as brutality,

greed, malice and the drive to oppress, but their themes were often expressed in a form that had previously been more closely associated with
comedy than with serious drama. Their work was often misunderstood
and their sardonic treatment of tragic matter taken for confusion and lack
of discipline. Consequently, their plays were rarely produced in the United
States.

Seawell returned *The Old Lady Pays a Visit* to the Theatre Guild when
the Lunts decided that it was not for them. Upon hearing their decision,
the Guild elected not to buy *The Old Lady Pays a Visit* and the rights were
picked up by producer Roger Stevens, who soon afterward contacted the
Lunts. Again they declined the play, electing instead to go forward with
their plan to present *The Great Sebastians* under Binkie Beaumont's management in London. They sailed aboard the *Queen Elizabeth* on June 2,
1957, in the company of Donald Seawell, Howard Lindsay, Dorothy
Stickney (Lindsay's wife) and Noël Coward, who had forgotten his irritation with them during *Quadrille*. "The Lunts are as sweet as ever," he
noted in his diary.*

But during the voyage the subject of the Duerrenmatt play came up
again and again. The Lunts were not sure it could be produced successfully,
but they were fascinated by the characters, the plot and the playwright's
masterful handling of the townspeople's murderous change of heart.

In London the Lunts and Seawell had lunch with Binkie Beaumont
of H. M. Tennent, Ltd., to discuss arrangements for *The Great Sebastians,*
but the conversation kept shifting to *The Old Lady Pays a Visit*. Beaumont
mentioned that he had recently discussed Duerrenmatt's play with the
gifted British director Peter Brook. Brook thought the play too long and
occasionally lacking in focus, but he, like the Lunts, was fascinated by the
conception and thought the play potentially brilliant. Beaumont suggested
that the Lunts speak to Brook; perhaps, among the three of them, they
could decide whether or not an English-language production of the play
would be feasible. If so, Beaumont would seek Duerrenmatt's permission
to coproduce the play in Britain (with the Producers' Theatre, Roger Ste-

---

*Another passenger on the *Queen Elizabeth* was Madeline Sherwood, the widow of
Robert E. Sherwood. When she and the Lunts encountered one another, there was an awkward moment. The Lunts, who had appeared for so many years in *There Shall Be No Night*
that their names were inextricably associated with the leading roles, had been offended when
Madeline Sherwood permitted Katharine Cornell and Charles Boyer to do the play on television. For their part, they would not have thought of acting in *The Barretts of Wimpole Street,*
the play with which Cornell's name was most closely linked. They regarded this as a simple
courtesy among prominent actors.

In February 1957, after Madeline Sherwood had agreed to the Cornell production, she
wrote the Lunts apologizing for her action, stating that it had never occurred to her that
they might wish to appear in the televised version of the play. "Oh, why did nobody tell me!"
she lamented. "I wish I had had the sense to get in touch with you. . . . This is too awful. In
a way, 'There Shall Be No Night' belongs to you two. What can I do? I feel dreadful."

The Lunts were still upset about the matter when they met Sherwood aboard the *Queen
Elizabeth*. However, she apologized to them again, and by the end of the voyage they were
on friendly terms once more.

vens's organization) with the modifications Brook and the Lunts thought desirable.

Brook met with the Lunts, agreed with them about the play's virtues and its shortcomings, and said he would be eager to direct it if he could persuade Duerrenmatt to make some cuts and revisions. For their part, the Lunts were persuaded by their discussion with Brook that his directorial approach would be ideal in bringing the play to life. If Brook could succeed in his mission to Duerrenmatt, they said, they would be eager to perform in the play.

From that moment, all thoughts of *The Great Sebastians* were forgotten, and Donald Seawell was given the unenviable task of explaining to Howard Lindsay that the Lunts' enthusiasm for Duerrenmatt's play had become so passionate, so all-consuming, that the production of *The Great Sebastians* would have to be postponed and, possibly, canceled entirely.

Peter Brook, Friedrich Duerrenmatt and Maurice Valency all met in Paris in July 1957.* Valency's adaptation was a skillful one, calculated to appeal to American audiences by eliminating some of the grotesque elements and emphasizing the love-hate relationship of Claire Zachanassian and Alfred Ill.

Brook emerged from his meetings with Duerrenmatt and Valency with a significantly revised play, yet one that retained all the virtues of the original. At Brook's suggestion, Duerrenmatt and Valency introduced new characters, deepened the portrayals of the characters who already existed, and added telling details to the plot. Duerrenmatt, far from resenting Brook's suggestions, cooperated eagerly; the process of writing a play, he believed, should incorporate the ideas of the director and the actors, especially if they were of the caliber of Peter Brook, Alfred Lunt and Lynn Fontanne. It did not bother him in the slightest that two quite different versions of his play—one in German, one in English—would exist, for he maintained that the text of a play should only serve as a springboard for the production, and that each production had its own requirements.

Soon afterward Donald Seawell, back in the United States, received a telephone call from the Lunts asking him to return to London as soon as possible. The reason for his trip would become clear soon after he arrived, they told him.

Seawell described what happened when he reached their rented house. "They couldn't wait when I walked in," he said. "They sat me down on a sofa and they sat on the other side of the fireplace. Then they read *The Visit* aloud. Lynn took all of the women's parts and Alfred took all the

---

*The Lunts also journeyed to Paris, but, having complete confidence in Peter Brook's judgment, they rarely participated in the meetings. Instead, Lunt realized a lifelong dream when he enrolled at the Cordon Bleu school of cooking. Taking the six-week course alongside him was his friend and longtime dresser, Jules Johnson. Both passed the course—"with flying saucepans," in Fontanne's words—with Lunt finishing one mark ahead. His certificate, the *Diplome de Cuisine Bourgeoise et de Patisserie Courante,* was "the best one can get in six weeks," he said proudly.

men's parts. It was the finest performance of *The Visit* I've ever known. I was so shattered when they finished reading it that I couldn't move." The Lunts nodded to one another with satisfaction over Seawell's reaction, which convinced them that the new version was a great improvement.

In the course of the revision by Duerrenmatt, Valency and Brook, they retitled the play *Time and Again.** The name of the character whose life is threatened by Mme. Zachanassian's return was changed from Alfred Ill to Anton Schill. Finally, and perhaps most importantly, the physical characterization of Claire Zachanassian was thoroughly altered. In the original text she was grotesquely disfigured and severely crippled: she had an ivory hand and a wooden leg. The new version referred to accidents Claire had suffered in the past, but emphasized that she was a physically attractive woman.

Some critics later objected to this change, claiming that the Lunts had insisted upon it so that Fontanne would look her best; that the change had, in effect, been a concession to vanity. They were correct in their assumption that Fontanne would have refused to play the role had it not been rewritten. It is also true that she insisted the character's age be changed from sixty-five to fifty. However, Valency was convinced from the beginning that Claire's physical characterization must be altered. "I thought this was the key to a successful play, at least in America," he said. In fact, although Claire's disfigurement in the original script is a powerful metaphor for her emotional derangement, the alterations in her physical character worked to the benefit of the play. The horror of hearing Claire insist upon Schill's death in exchange for a billion marks was considerably greater when it came from a woman who apparently had everything a woman could wish for, including physical beauty. In Fontanne's interpretation, Claire's insanity was concealed from the townspeople by her grace and beauty, and Duerrenmatt himself later said that the play was improved by Claire's physical transformation.

Another advantage that resulted from changing Claire's physical characteristics was that the love Claire and Schill had once shared (and which is rekindled for a time during the events of the play) became much more believable.

Peter Brook had commitments that prevented him from beginning rehearsals for several months, which suited the Lunts, who were tired and welcomed the rest. When rehearsals began in November 1957, they were refreshed, reinvigorated and eager to get to work.

Lunt said he modeled his character "on a man in Genesee Depot, in looks, in clothes, in gestures. Miss Fontanne had many 'Claires' in mind, one in particular," but, for obvious reasons, neither of the Lunts ever gave any hint of her actual identity.

---

* As the British critics later pointed out, however, the title seemed to have no relevance to the play. Thus, even before the production came to America, an abbreviated version of the original title was used and the play came to be known as *The Visit*.

In keeping with the new physical characterization, Fontanne did not emphasize Claire's coarseness as previous actresses had done. Instead, she concentrated upon conveying a remote, goddess-like quality which removed her character effectively from the world the other characters—the townspeople of Güllen—inhabited.

The Lunts were concerned, as always, about their costumes. Fontanne, wanting to look her best, asked that Castillo be hired to design her gowns. Lunt felt strongly that his character would wear a worn-out, ill-fitting suit with an old hat, torn shirt and socks that were darned at the heel. (The audience would never see the socks, but they nevertheless were an integral part of the costume in Lunt's mind, serving as part of his "green umbrella.") Brook, who believed that the best actors are (and should be) determined to select their costumes as carefully as they select their gestures and tonalities, welcomed their interest.

Not content to purchase new clothes and rumple them, Lunt personally selected his suit from a stall in the Portobello Road.* To age it further, he left the jacket and trousers outdoors in the rain for several weeks. Then, he said, "I rolled around in them [and] dragged them across the stage [and] into the street. . . . And the shoes. They were old, old shoes of mine that I'd worn in the garden a lot." Lunt continued to wear the same suit—mended and remended again and again—throughout the run of the play in Britain and America. To add to his unflattering, unkempt appearance, Lunt cut his own hair.

Fontanne also changed her personal habits in order to play her character, smoking three cigars in the course of each performance, a duty she found most unpleasant.

Peter Brook, one of the most creative directors of the twentieth century, whose brilliant productions first came to the attention of London critics when he was still an undergraduate at Oxford, described his directorial method to Randolph Goodman, comparing it to "painting a picture in oils. First, I make a large free sketch, then I put in more and more details, but I keep changing and adding throughout the rehearsal period." Brook preferred never to tell an actor precisely what to do; instead, he responded to the actor's questions by encouraging him to try many alternative solutions until the right one was mutually discovered, perhaps several weeks later. Like Philip Moeller, he disliked planning "too precisely in advance," claiming that technique led him to become "parental, possessive and proprietary," whereas "if you don't plan, you don't mind scrapping what you've done. The danger in the latter technique, however," Brook added, "is that in continually revising you sometimes scrap something that is excellent and ought to be retained. The Lunts were able to hold me down. They would say, 'You've done something good, let's save it.'"

---

*The market in the Portobello Road is set up one morning each week. There, discriminating buyers may find occasional antiques, but most of the items on sale are secondhand pieces of little value.

From the beginning, the Lunts had enormous respect for Brook. Fontanne told John Randolph, an actor in the New York cast of *The Visit,* "Alfred and I have been directing each other for over thirty years. You know, we never really trusted anyone else, but he's the first person we really trust when it comes to taste. He appeals to the actor's imagination— the area where the actor is a specialist—and that's why we're so excited about him."

Brook reciprocated the Lunts' admiration. "Directing Lunt is a revelation," he said. "You can't imagine the countless tiny details that Alfred puts into a performance. This may sound like finicky acting but these painstaking details make up an enormous conception. It is like one of Seurat's pointillist paintings. Each little dot is not art, but the whole is magnificent. Alfred and Lynn start by getting a broad outline of what they're going to do and then they fill in the details. It's absolutely like somebody making a mosaic." On another occasion Brook was asked to name the finest living English-speaking actor. "There are three," he said: "Laurence Olivier, John Gielgud and Alfred Lunt. Take your pick."

The first week of *Time and Again* performances began in Brighton on December 24, 1957. Opening the play on Christmas Eve turned out to be a serious error in judgment, as did the decision of H. M. Tennent, Ltd., to advertise the play as a "high comedy." As Donald Seawell recalled, "All of the parents brought their little children to see a new drawing-room comedy with their beloved Lunts. People clawed their way up the aisles at intermission to get out of the theatre or to the bar." Those spectators who remained for the second act greeted the final curtain with total silence. The actors stood embarrassedly on stage during the single curtain call as the shocked and bewildered audience departed the theatre.

Critical reaction was no better, and the newspapers received letters from outraged theatregoers who said they felt degraded by the play and condemned the Lunts for appearing in it. The reaction was altogether so negative that it appeared the production might be forced to close prematurely.

The horror of the play's theme was mirrored by several incidents during the week in Brighton. At the Saturday matinee, during the climactic scene in which Schill is strangled to death by the townspeople of Güllen, an elderly woman seated close to the stage was heard to mimic the strange gurgling noises Lunt was making. Not until the end of the performance, when the house lights came on, did those seated near her discover that the sounds coming from her throat had been a death rattle. Later that week a spectator suffered a heart attack while the performance was in progress.

Some of the actors wondered whether the play was too strong for its audiences. An assistant stage manager insisted that the "wickedness" of the play was palpable, and an actress in the company predicted, "This is an evil play; it will never get to London."

The plan had been to open *Time and Again* in the English capital after the week in Brighton. But the owner of the London theatre where the production was to be given decided he would not permit his building to be used for such a revolting play. No other theatre was immediately available, so Beaumont and Stevens elected to tour the play in the English provinces, as well as in Scotland and Ireland, until they could secure a theatre in London.

Throughout the British tour, Peter Brook traveled with the company, holding daily rehearsals. Most productions go through changes before being brought to London or New York. In the case of *Time and Again*, however, those changes were far more sweeping than usual. In Stratford, where the company played in late January, Peter Brook said, "we introduced a completely new version of the play with much less text and more action; Lynn went on trembling, but came off convinced that the new version was better than the old." Many versions of the play were rehearsed and performed before the final one emerged. Friedrich Duerrenmatt and Maurice Valency (who had been given carte blanche by Duerrenmatt to make whatever changes he, Brook and the Lunts deemed necessary) wrote new scenes, eliminated old ones and revised existing ones. "The play is coming together slowly," Lunt wrote to his physician and friend Edward Bigg on January 29. "We are making changes that require constant rehearsing, but all that seems to be almost at an end. . . ." Before the production assumed its final shape, Lunt said, the company had rehearsed and played four distinct versions.

Years before, when the Lunts had acted in *I Know My Love*, S. N. Behrman had accused them of wishing, at all costs, to appear "sympathetic" to their audiences, and of having sacrificed his play in order to win that sympathy. After the response of the Brighton audiences to *Time and Again*, one might have expected them to make similar concessions in order to win audience approval, but they did not make the slightest attempt to modify their characterizations. Peter Brook was gratified by their determination and astonished at their audacity. "What would you expect two established stars to do?" he asked. "They would compromise, soften the characters, adulterate them, sweeten them, bring it closer to what audiences expected of them, what they'd always played. For thirty years the Lunts have been having a love affair on the stage, flirting with each other and with their audiences. They knew how to make audiences love them. They knew they were now playing with fire in *The Visit*. But they didn't retreat or ask me to tone down the play. They explored every aspect of evil in it."

In the English provinces, the play "continues to interest and shock people," Lunt told Dr. Bigg. Everywhere, reactions to the play reflected polar extremes. Those who responded favorably thought it a masterpiece, while those who were made uncomfortable by its ideas and its presentation rejected it completely.

In order to improve box-office sales, the production's press agent attempted to arrange interviews with the Lunts at each stop on the tour. They demurred, however, preferring to conserve their energies for rehearsals and performances. "Neither of us are very good subjects for publicity," Lunt explained. "Our own private lives are too phlegmatic for that purpose & we *never* have been good at interviews—and we *can't* do T.V. which completely disembowels us." Instead, Lunt suggested that the proper person to interview was Peter Brook, because, he said, "'The Visit' [as the play was renamed in February] is a real *ensemble* play. . . . It's his show & we like that."

In Dublin, where the play opened on February 22, the audience was attentive but unmistakably hostile. The performances there did nothing to change the growing opinion that *The Visit* was certain to be a failure in London.

The response in Edinburgh was heartening, however. "The press was mighty fine," Lunt wrote to press agent Barry Hyams; "the play is a true success here—10 curtain calls on Sat. eve—which will give you a rough idea of how they like it." Lunt was concerned, though, about an interview with Kenneth Tynan that would take place in Newcastle. He feared Tynan would write a negative review of the production for the London Sunday *Observer,* "which," Lunt said, "would be fatal."*

Everyone hoped the favorable reaction in Edinburgh had marked a change in the play's fortunes. But that was not to be. British critics and audiences continued to be deeply shocked by the harshness of *The Visit,* finding it impossible to believe that their adored Lunts were appearing in an uncompromising play depicting the most brutal side of human nature. Many spectators walked out; some were so outraged that they shouted epithets at the stage; most theatregoers simply stayed away. At one performance a grand total of three people purchased tickets, and the actors outnumbered the audience by a sizable margin.

Eventually, after performances in Newcastle-on-Tyne, Binkie Beaumont decided not to bring the play to London. The reaction had been so generally unfriendly that it was thought unwise to risk further hostility. Lunt wrote to Dr. Bigg, "I shall be glad to be home—it's been a long hard tour & the play is depressing—but fascinating too—"

The experience was sufficiently discouraging that, for the first time, the Lunts told their friends they were contemplating retirement. "I doubt very much if I shall ever do another job in the theatre," Lunt told Bigg; "it just doesn't seem worth it—I'd rather go out & cook special dinners." Lunt's depression was particularly severe because neither he nor Fontanne had lost faith in the play or in Peter Brook's production.

The story of *The Visit* might have ended at that point had not Roger Stevens flown to Dublin to see a performance the month before. Despite the small audience's cool response, Stevens was fascinated. He found the

---

*Tynan did review *The Visit* for the *Observer* in March. To Lunt's relief, the notice was not at all unfavorable.

production magnificent and the Lunts' performances unforgettable. Backstage, he told them he was as enthusiastic as ever about bringing *The Visit* to New York. And, he said, if his partners in the Producers' Theatre did not wish to join him, he would present it by himself.

Normally, a New York engagement of a Lunt-Fontanne play was preceded by reports of the production's success elsewhere. Since that would be impossible in the case of *The Visit,* Stevens needed another way to whet the interest of theatregoers. Fortunately, the way was at hand. In May 1957, Stevens's organization had purchased the Globe Theatre on West 46th Street in New York. The Globe, built in 1910, had housed many Broadway productions, but had been converted to a movie theatre in 1931. Stevens and his partners, Robert Whitehead and Robert Dowling, had already begun the process of reconverting it to a legitimate theatre. Their intention was to fashion the Globe into the most beautiful and comfortable theatre in New York.

Stevens's idea was to give the refurbished theatre a new name. It would be called the Lunt-Fontanne Theatre,* and its first production would feature the Lunts in the New York premiere of *The Visit.* Dowling agreed with Stevens's idea immediately. Whitehead, who initially wished to retain the name of the Globe Theatre, needed only slight persuasion to change his mind.

In order to secure the maximum publicity, the Producers' Theatre called a press conference on February 16, 1958, in the unfinished basement of the theatre to announce its new name. Then, over a two-way radio hook-up from Dublin, where *The Visit* was about to open, the press interviewed the Lunts about the play and about their reactions to having a theatre named in their honor, a distinction few living actors had ever known.

Work on the theatre would be complete within a month, the press was told, and *The Visit* would open there on April 14. Later it proved impossible to have the theatre ready by that date, and the opening was postponed until May 5.

To the press the Lunts expressed optimism about the fate of *The Visit,* but privately they were not so certain. Pleased that the production would be given another chance and delighted that a theatre would bear their name, they were nonetheless concerned that *The Visit* might be greeted by New York's playgoers with the same scorn it had encountered in Britain. "It seems completely mad, but Roger Stevens is determined," Lunt wrote to Alan Hewitt. "I wonder if this is the play to open a grand new theatre?

*The original suggestion to rename the theatre had come from Charles Bowden, a producer who had acted with the Lunts' companies, served as their stage manager and taken on some of the directorial responsibilities for the scenes in which Lunt appeared in *I Know My Love.* At a party in New York, Roger Stevens mentioned to Bowden that he wished to buy the Lunts a gift—a Georgian antique tea service—to express his gratitude for their work in *The Visit.* Bowden replied, "Listen, the last thing in the world they need is another antique tea service. The closets in Genesee are groaning with them." When Stevens asked what gift would be distinctive, Bowden answered, "Give them a theatre." Two months later Stevens did exactly that.

It's so sordid—half the audience hates it, and they will feel the same in New York. . . . We continue to get the most violent letters protesting against our acting two such frightful people in this bitter play."

Lunt, of course, was always skeptical about the chances for success of any play in which he appeared. In the case of *The Visit*, the controversial nature of the play only exaggerated his customary fears. But Roger Stevens had no doubt. "I thought the play would be a great success in America for a number of reasons," he said in 1985, "the most important of which was that the New York critics had for years been asking the Lunts to act in a serious play. Also it happened to be a very important play and, in my opinion, one of the best of this century. . . . I was so enthusiastic about it that I persuaded them to bring it to the U.S. because I was convinced it would be a big success."

The Lunts sailed to New York on March 20, along with several members of the company who had been playing *The Visit* in Britain. Eric Porter as the Burgomaster and Peter Woodthorpe as the Teacher were among those who were retained. But more than twenty-five roles were to be recast with American actors.

Adding to the pressures of wondering how the play would be received in New York, Lunt was taken ill again just prior to the first American rehearsals, this time with a severe sinus infection that forced him into a hospital. Even after he was released, he suffered continually from pain in his chest and stomach.

One of the new actors cast in the production was John Randolph, who played the town's Police Chief. Rehearsals, held in the New Amsterdam Roof Theatre on 42nd Street, began immediately to integrate Randolph, William Hansen and other new members into the cast. For those who had been performing in Britain, however, the rehearsals represented far more than simply marking time, as Peter Brook continued to refine the play's structure and staging.

The Lunts brought sandwiches in a picnic basket to rehearsals. During the lunch breaks, they would generally retire to a dressing room and share their sandwiches with Brook while the three of them discussed the play and the progress of rehearsals. Throughout the process, the Lunts remained deeply impressed by their director's perception and sensitivity, deferring to him in all matters pertaining to the production. "They worshiped him," said William Le Massena.

Final rehearsals were held in Boston, just prior to the out-of-town opening at the Shubert Theatre on April 9. John Randolph wrote frequently to his wife about his observations and experiences during the rehearsal process. On April 6, he told her, the rehearsal was called for 8:00 p.m. The theatre was in chaos as stagehands milled around, tinkering with the lights and making last-minute additions to the set. The Lunts were not scheduled to arrive until later. At about 8:30, Randolph wrote, "Peter

Brook called me over and said Alfred Lunt wanted me to go up to his room at the Ritz-Carlton to run lines."

When Randolph was asked to see the Lunts, he told me, "I felt myself tighten up inside." As he crossed the Common in a driving rain, he tried to concentrate on his character's lines, but he found it difficult to do so because he believed he was about to be fired. He began to compose imaginary letters to his agent and his wife, explaining why he was no longer going to be in the production. He disliked the Lunts, he would say; he "wasn't their kind of actor"; he had concluded that they were too rough on young performers; so he had decided to quit.

When he arrived at the Ritz-Carlton, he was surprised to discover that "Alfred greeted me quite warmly." Fontanne excused herself so that Lunt and Randolph could work together. "Well, we didn't work right away," Randolph's letter to his wife continued. "He asked me all sorts of questions about the state of the stage, etc.—like a nervous mother." Lunt apologized to Randolph for having gotten testy during a scene he and another actor had repeated fifteen times, attributing it to his illness. "You know," he told Randolph, "I'm never really bored on stage working. I love rehearsal. Doing the play at night isn't as exciting to me as the rehearsal period."

Lunt then proceeded to demonstrate how exciting a rehearsal could be. Randolph told his wife:

> After a little more small talk we began to work on the scene—just talking it—Well, ol' Sal, it was the most exciting hour I've had yet. It was all the purity, all the honesty, all the maturity of working at a craft the way they—the Lunts—must have worked for 30 years in their own private way. It was not a one-way street. We went through the scene several times. Then we went back. There was something wrong in the way the line, "You're not elected Burgomaster yet as far as I know" hit him. He tried it several ways. He decided it was badly written & difficult to say. Then we talked about other ways it could be done. Then I told him why I felt it should be done my way. Then we discussed other reasons the Police Chief might have in saying it. Then I tried something I had done before a while back that hit his ear. And he said, "Well, if you feel that it should be that way, with a slight laugh, then try it really full." I did—and it sounded right. So then we went back to the scene from the beginning and we came up to *that* line and it sounded right. But now to do it even more fully he suggested that it should begin with "My what?" laughing, & then more so on "You're not elected Burgomaster yet." I tried it & it struck a chord. "You see," he said, "that's closer to your personality & it's more you—it rings true."
>
> Well Sarah we went on like that until we got things done beautifully & he called Lynn in to hear it. He said, "Now, Lynn,

we'll just do it for you quietly, not acting, but I think it's right."
To me he said, "You know it's good to do it for someone else.
She's a good critic and you can test it with a third person." She
said, "No, Alfred, do it fully. You act it quietly and naturally in a
small room and it sounds beautiful to you and then you go on
the stage and have to project and it all seems destroyed. So really
act it up—fully."

We did—and well, too, and she was quite pleased. But there
were a few points she had some ideas on and we spent ¾ of an
hour talking over one point. It was in relation to the play, to my
character, to *his* character, what we were trying to do in the
scene, what it had to do with Peter Brook's ideas of the second
act, etc., etc. We hit on a compromise that should work out
beautifully. Once more the process of distillation, simplicity,
truth, but all in relation to the *specific* play!

. . . I wish I could go on & on—or had a tape recorder to
tell you how excited I was when I left about 10:45 to go back to
the theatre.

Randolph was so invigorated by the session that he was barely conscious of the rainstorm as he walked back to the Shubert. Eric Porter, who
also had thought Lunt's summons meant Randolph would be fired, met
him as he entered the theatre and began to commiserate about his bad
fortune. Randolph replied that he had just enjoyed the most rewarding
experience in his career. That night he stayed awake until 3:00 a.m. to
record his observations.

The belief Randolph had once held that the Lunts were not committed to theatrical truth was revealed to him as entirely mistaken. Moreover,
he came to believe that the Lunts' approach to the theatre produced a
greater sense of truth than was provided by many of those who purported
to follow Stanislavski's method to the letter. As Randolph told me, when
he had been directed years before by Lee Strasberg in a production of *Peer
Gynt,* all the actors were instructed to speak their lines quietly in rehearsal—so quietly they could barely be heard—so that they could concentrate on their feelings and inner reactions. "He was trying to get the truth,"
Randolph said. "Well, I've never gone through so much bullshit in my life.
If anything was a mockery of the Method, it was Lee Strasberg directing
Peer Gynt. Everything was supposed to be real—but everything to me was
just deadly." In contrast, he said:

The Lunts were just the opposite. Their scenes were always done
with a constant energy, constant vitality from the very first rehearsal. They never saved themselves. Whereas, with Strasberg,
you thought you were doing it truthfully, but you weren't using
much energy, and then when you went on the stage the projection was nil. So then you worked to get the projection and the

truth disappeared. But working with the Lunts—from the very first day they were totally and completely full stage voice, full energy, even when they experimented. That doesn't mean that they weren't realistic or truthful. So there was no different performance on the opening night than the performance you gave in rehearsal.

The opening in Boston seemed to elicit from its audience precisely the response that was most appropriate for the play. The applause was enthusiastic during the curtain calls, Randolph recalled, but there were "no bravos or cheers to speak of . . . it was as if the audience was applauding with their mind in another world. It was the weirdest sensation." He conjectured the audience might have felt depressed as they contemplated the issues raised by the play.

That night Randolph wrote to his wife about Lunt's intensity on stage during the performance, a greater intensity than he had experienced from any other actor. "Playing with him under performance conditions is like playing a crushing game of football opposite a pile driving tackle," he said. "You feel bruised all over."

Randolph had already gotten a hint of Lunt's intensity on stage during rehearsals. The first time the play was run through with the new cast, he expected little energy from Lunt, who had just emerged from the hospital. "I thought it was going to be just a sick old man," he said. "But in the scene with me he came on with enormous energy, and near bowled me over." In the middle of the scene, Lunt stopped, dissatisfied, and asked Peter Brook if he could approach it differently. This time, he suggested, he would like to try it with his back to the audience. Brook responded, "No, no, we've had enough of the famous Lunt back," Randolph recalled. Lunt then asked to replay the scene with the actors improvising their own blocking rather than using the movements previously worked out by the director. Randolph discovered that this was a routine rehearsal device for the Lunts. "They always improvised," he said, "changing the blocking and the interpretation, but never changing the lines."

Randolph also discovered how determined Lunt was never to allow any aspect of a performance to fall below the highest standard. During one scene in which the Police Chief and Schill confront one another, the production called for Lunt, as Schill, to open John Randolph's mouth and say, "You have a new gold tooth," the implication being that Schill realized the Policeman had already begun to spend the money he anticipated receiving from Claire. Lunt would always perform the business gently, taking care not to hurt Randolph. At one performance, however, Randolph realized that something was wrong. "He was shooting cues at me very fast. He never did that before. And then when he said the line about the tooth to me, he grabbed hold of my nose with one hand and pulled my jaw down *hard* with the other. He practically ripped me apart. Well, I got angry. I was supposed to push him away and pound him on the back and say, 'Go home, Schill.' So I pounded him on the back—man, I tell you, I really smacked the shit out of him. But then when I got off stage, I got scared. I thought, 'I'm going to be fired.' So later I went up to him and I apologized, but I said, 'You were hurting me.' And he said, 'You were reading the lines in a different way and it was upsetting me. You were doing it wonderfully before. Do it exactly the same way you were doing it before.'" Randolph, astonished that Lunt was neither injured nor disturbed, then began to worry about Fontanne's reaction. But he later learned that she had watched the scene closely, then turned to another actor, and said, "My, the dear boys are having a fight. How interesting."

The most terrifying scene of the drama takes place at the end of the play, at the railroad station. During this scene Anton Schill fails to board the train that will take him to safety and realizes that the people of Güllen are going to kill him. As the scene was played in England, only a few men crowded around Schill, but the physical intimidation they projected was sufficient to make the scene highly effective. In the American production, however, Brook staged the scene with many more townspeople converging slowly and ominously on Schill, threatening him with the implication of death rather than with fists upraised.

Lunt played the reaction to the threat no differently than he had in England until shortly after the Boston opening. Then, during one performance, Lunt had an inspiration. To interviewers Lewis Funke and John E. Booth he described the way he had earlier played the scene:

> At first I sort of used to lie there on the floor. I just lay there on the floor and did nothing. And then one night in Boston it occurred to me that a man like Schill—all sorts of men, in fact, if they were dreadfully frightened, if they knew that in short order they would face being murdered—would be frightened out of his wits. In this condition Schill would either vomit or mess his pants. So, one night, I leaned over and retched. Peter—my back was to the audience, I had turned away—came up afterward and said, "Did you vomit?" and I said, "Yes." And he said, "Oh, I like it."

The idea originated during Lunt's stay in the hospital just before rehearsals began in New York. He had heard a man vomiting in the room next to his, and, as actors are wont to do, he filed the sound in a compartment of his mind. When the inspiration occurred to him during the Boston performance, he attempted to duplicate the sound he had heard in the hospital.

Lunt's retching, which was retained in the production, was unforgettable for all who saw it. The business delineated Schill's fear so graphically and so intensely that it was almost unbearably moving.

Lunt's death scene was painfully vivid for him. He recalled that his mother had murmured, "Oh God . . . oh God!" just before she died, and he used the same words (which were not in the script) and the same intonation as his killers closed in on him.

Fontanne, who watched every rehearsal and performance from the wings (and, during one long sequence, from a balcony, where as Claire Zachanassian she sat smoking a cigar), noted afterward, "This is Alfred's Actors' Studio moment." But John Randolph, who had attended many sessions at the Studio, said, "It outdid anything I ever saw in the Actors' Studio, and I've seen the most incredible things. But this was remarkable. He really threw up, spit and stuff coming out of him when he was so panicky kicking at these people with his back on the ground—kicking like a wounded animal trying to fend off the attacking dogs."

After Schill was strangled, each of the townspeople lit a cigarette. The effect of matches being lit everywhere on stage immediately after Schill's life had been extinguished was one of Peter Brook's most stunning—and chilling—conceptions.

At a later performance in Boston, Lunt accidentally bumped into one of the actors as he was backing away from his murderers. Thoroughly in character, Lunt produced what Randolph described as "the most blood-curdling scream I've ever heard on a stage. I mean, I've never heard *anything* like it. It was frightening. Everybody on stage almost died. And then when we came off stage, after the throwing-up scene, I asked Alfred about it. I said, 'Are you going to keep that scream in?' He said, 'I don't know. I don't think so. It was wonderful, but I think it took away from the climax at the end of the scene.' So he never put it back in." Lunt's ability to be so fully absorbed in the moment and in his character that he could spontaneously react to and intensify a small mishap while simultaneously evaluating the contribution his unplanned scream made to the shape of the production as a whole surely qualifies as a remarkable feat of balancing subjectivity and objectivity.

Fontanne continued to watch the play carefully during the scenes in which she sat on the balcony. In effect, she became a second director, once saying to John Randolph after a performance in Boston, "I'm glad you've stopped using your hands so much."

The Boston tryout gave early indications that *The Visit* would win greater acceptance in the United States than it had in Great Britain. Backstage visitors told the actors how moved they had been by the play's vigor and theatricality. Audrey Wood, Tennessee Williams's agent, who was known to be sparing with her compliments, simply said, "Now you're back in the theatre of style and magnificence." After Boston, *The Visit* moved to New Haven, where it was greeted with equal acclaim.

On the Friday before the New York opening, a dedication ceremony for the press and distinguished guests was held in the mezzanine lobby of the Lunt-Fontanne theatre. Helen Hayes, the only other current performer to have had a Broadway theatre named in her honor, gave the Lunts a

"housewarming" gift, a drawing by Don Freeman depicting Hayes, standing at a window of "her" theatre, tossing a bouquet of flowers across 46th
Street to the Lunts, who were leaning out a window of "their" theatre.
Hayes spoke briefly at the ceremony, saying the event "commemorates the
moment when the two most beautiful people in the world become the
most beautiful theatre in the world." Indeed, no effort had been spared to
make the auditorium the last word in comfort and elegance.*

Opening night was a gala occasion seldom matched in the New York
theatre. That a beautifully refurbished theatre was opening its doors for
the first time was in itself a significant occasion. That the Lunts were returning to New York after an absence of two years was a reason for cele-
bration. But that Lunt and Fontanne should be opening their new play in
the new Lunt-Fontanne Theatre was a once-in-a-lifetime event.

Traditions of all kinds were broken. Champagne was served before the
opening curtain and between the acts. Smoking was permitted in the mezzanine. The audience, which had been asked to dress formally, was composed largely of well-known figures from the worlds of society, the theatre
and politics. Among those in attendance were Ambassador and Mrs.
Henry Cabot Lodge, Jr., Mr. and Mrs. John D. Rockefeller III, Mr. and
Mrs. William Zeckendorf, Mary Martin, Anita Loos, Beatrice Lillie, Pau-
lette Goddard, George Schaefer, Spyros Skouras, Bette Davis, Helen Menken and Ginger Rogers.

The assembled crowd marveled at the new theatre. The marquee
alone, 130 feet long and 14 feet wide, adorned with a scalloped Plexiglas
curtain, was worthy of comment. The design of the theatre was in the baroque style. Elaborate ceiling murals depicted the muses of the theatre and
the Four Winds. Crystal chandeliers of Maria Theresa design decorated the
lobbies. The carpeting was thick and elegant, the orchestra seats luxuri-
ously upholstered. In the loge boxes, the custom-made seats were covered
in rich blue damask. Cushions and footstools were also provided in the
loges, which were the most expensive seats in the theatre, costing all of
$8.80.

John Randolph described the reactions of the actors backstage to the
hubbub in the auditorium before the performance began:

> The audience was noisy. Now, you as an actor can hear them over
> the backstage speakers. And we knew that they were drinking
> champagne in the lobby and that people had come from dinner

---

*However, workmen had not had sufficient time to ready the stage and backstage areas
properly. The dressing rooms were unfinished, the backstage carpeting was incomplete, the
stage—which must always be made of wood so that flats can be screwed into the floor—was
simply a slab of concrete over which layers of wood had to be placed. The set of *The Visit*
had to be cut down in size, as it was too large for the stage space, and even then it covered
every inch of the stage area, making it impossible for actors to cross behind it. Instead,
whenever actors needed to cross, unseen by the audience, from one side of the stage to the
other, they had to go outside—holding umbrellas if it was raining—and around the rear of
the building.

parties to the opening of the Lunts. Now, the opening of the Lunts is something that I never experienced before—the limousines and the Cadillacs and the famous people from Washington, the politicians and the top-notch producers . . . I mean the whole atmosphere was incredible. And all the actors could hear were these loud noises, and you said to yourself, "Oh, Jesus, they're drunk, what's going to happen?"

When the curtain went up, the actors first came on the stage—not the Lunts, but the townspeople—and the noise was really, I think, indecent. The audience was talking. You could hear them, mumbling, talking and laughing, and the actors were trying to talk over it. The feeling we got is that the audience had come to see a comedy—a Noël Coward comedy—and they had no idea what kind of a play *The Visit* was. I'm sure they didn't read the out-of-town notices, didn't know who Duerrenmatt was, thought it was going to be a funny play in the Lunts' tradition, in the way they were known.

The moment Alfred appeared, not in a dress suit or a tuxedo but in this shabby outfit, what you heard was as if the sound suddenly began to go out of the audience. From that time on, the silence was deafening. The audience started listening. And the Lunts acted on that opening night exactly with the kind of concentration and energy that we had in Boston.

When the final curtain descended, there was a long moment of silence. The actors were uncertain what to make of it. Was the audience disappointed? Were they resentful that the Lunts were not giving them what they had expected to see? Not until the curtain rose for the curtain calls did the actors discover how absorbed the audience had been in the play, how deeply they had been affected by the theme, how appreciative they were of the brilliance of the production. A roar of approval arose from the auditorium; wave upon wave of cheers greeted the actors, many of whom were stunned by the reaction.

Afterward, appreciative members of the audience came backstage, as was customary, to congratulate the actors, but, as John Randolph said, "No one talked about what they ate for dinner, how's your mother, I liked the show, that sort of thing. *Everybody* who came backstage wanted to talk about the play, about Duerrenmatt and his ideas. And if you went out after the show to Sardi's or anywhere else, the conversation was not small talk. It was large talk."

Immediately after the performance, a lavish party in honor of the Lunts was held in the Grand Ballroom of the Astor Hotel. The guests of honor danced together and shook hands with the partygoers, who included Katharine Cornell, Laurence Olivier and Henry Fonda. Mary Martin sang a tribute to the Lunts as the guests drank a champagne toast.

Mayor Robert Wagner presented them with a City of New York Citation.

The reviews the next morning were, for the most part, enthusiastic "beyond our wildest dreams—we are stunned," Fontanne told her sister Antoinette. Brooks Atkinson, who had so often chided the Lunts on their choice of plays, wasted no time in offering congratulations on this occasion. "After squandering their time on polite trivialities for a number of years, Alfred Lunt and Lynn Fontanne are appearing in a devastating drama," he began. "Whether *The Visit* suits them or they suit *The Visit* is beside the point. For . . . our two most gifted comic actors look like our most gifted dramatic actors. Under Peter Brook's ingenious direction, they give an unforgettable performance." Several days later Atkinson added these comments in his Sunday piece:

> When Miss Fontanne makes her entrance . . . in the first scene, her familiar combination of irony and grandeur promises another evening of witty entertainment. But that is not what she has in mind. The grandeur becomes power. The coolness disguises ferocity. Reserved, detached, elegant, responsive, intelligent, Miss Fontanne gives a superb performance that is meticulously planned but marvelously spontaneous on the stage.
>
> As the aging, limp, helpless grocer, Mr. Lunt gives a brilliant performance, particularly in the scenes in which the author does not give him much to say. For Mr. Lunt is the master of wordless eloquence. When the grocer is trying to leave town Mr. Lunt vividly describes his lonely terror in a memorable pantomime at the railroad station. . . . The grocer's silent submission, his inner pride revealed against the final act of outward obedience are infinitely moving in the theatre, not because the author has stated them, but because Mr. Lunt has imagined them and knows how to transfer them to the imagination of the audience.

Richard Watts, Jr., spoke of Fontanne's "haunting and enigmatic power," of Lunt's "sensitive and deeply touching poignancy." Frank Aston in the *World-Telegram and Sun* called the Lunts "beyond comparison." John McClain said, "This is easily their most notable contribution in the past 10 years." And, for the first time in many seasons, the critics praised the play as lavishly as they praised the Lunts.

As in Great Britain, some theatregoers found the play too strong, too upsetting. Robert Coleman, whose review appeared in the *Daily Mirror,* spoke for those in New York who were offended by the play. "It is difficult to understand how the Producers Theatre persuaded the wonderful Lunts to dull their sparkle in such dreary, unrelievedly sardonic fare," he said, "but it has, and more's the pity."

Originally, *The Visit* was scheduled for a New York run of only nine weeks, as the Producers' Theatre believed the play would have limited appeal. The morning after the opening, however, long lines formed at the box office and every ticket for the nine-week run was soon sold. Week after week the income for the production exceeded $52,000, yielding a greater profit than anyone had believed possible. The producers thus arranged to rent the Morosco Theatre (the Lunt-Fontanne having been previously booked) so that the production could reopen after a summer vacation.

During the New York run, Lunt added an effective piece of business that resulted from an accident. John Randolph as the Police Chief was seated on a bench during the scene just before Schill's execution. He had a line, "Schill, come here," after which Lunt normally sat beside him and played with Randolph's lapel before asking, "Must it be now?" One night, however, Lunt stumbled as he reached the bench and banged his knee against it. Randolph, turning at the sound to see Lunt falling, held out his arms to break the fall. Rather than trying to rise, Lunt remained slumped in Randolph's arms and whispered, "Must it be now?" The effect—of one of Schill's executioners holding the grocer in his arms while he pleaded for his life—was deeply moving. From that night on, the business was re-peated.

Lunt's health was precarious throughout the run of *The Visit,* and on more than one occasion his stomach pain became so great that he was forced to improvise a momentary exit. He would work his way toward the wings, then invent a line to justify Schill's momentary departure.

In late June 1958 an acute stomach spasm forced him into New York Hospital. John Wyse, Lunt's understudy, went on in his place, although Fontanne feared most of the audience would demand their money back when it was announced Lunt would not perform that night. For nearly thirty years she had acted only with her husband. As she peeked through the curtain to see how many people would leave after the announcement, she said to no one in particular, "I really believe people come to see Alfred, not me." When fewer people departed than she had anticipated, she was elated.*

Since World War II, if either Lunt or Fontanne was too ill to go on in a play, the performance had been canceled. The fact that *The Visit* was continued during Lunt's hospitalization represented a tacit admission on the part of the Lunts that, once again, the *play* had assumed its rightful place as the center of the theatrical experience. *The Visit,* unlike the vehicles in which they had been appearing for more than a decade, was not a flimsy structure that would collapse upon the loss of one of its star performers. Nevertheless, the box-office income dipped considerably (from $50,000 to $38,300) during the week Lunt was hospitalized, causing him to miss five performances.

Lunt's eyes also began to fail him during *The Visit.* He was unable to control the pupil in one eye, which often rolled to one side. He had suf-

*After Lunt returned to the production, however, she told Robert Whitehead of the Producers' Theatre that she could not bring herself to appear without him again.

fered the same problem (exotropia) since birth, but it became worse with advancing age. During the next fifteen years, his vision in that eye gradually deteriorated until it was lost completely.

Fontanne's health remained good despite her age (she was seventy when *The Visit* opened in New York), but she began to have difficulty remembering her lines, occasionally going blank in the middle of a performance. Lunt protected her as often as possible, improvising dialogue to cover her lapse of memory.

After the run at the Lunt-Fontanne Theatre, the Lunts returned to Ten Chimneys. Lunt was "damned exhausted," he told Dr. Bigg. "This just is not quite as easy as I thought it would be," he added. His stomach problems—perhaps complicated by the nightly retching he voluntarily included in the performances—had left him weak and unsteady.

The Visit reopened at the Morosco Theatre on August 20, ran until November 29, and was as successful as it had been the previous season. Lunt told Whitney Bolton in an interview that he was astonished by the demand for matinee tickets. "Rows of women watching this macabre play about a rich widow willing to pay for the murder of her girlhood betrayer. I have wondered: is the matinee business so sensational because secretly most women yearn to be rich enough to buy the murder of some man they detest? It's possible. Women can harbor dark thoughts and yearnings, I know."

"There isn't a woman who wishes she hadn't the immunity and courage to do the same thing to some man in her past who has wronged her," Ina Claire told Lunt. Fontanne agreed. "Of course they do," she said. "Women are the most cruel and remorseless of all breathing creatures."

The Morosco was a considerably smaller theatre than the enormous Lunt-Fontanne, and in that sense more suited to a nonmusical production, but it required some adjustment on the part of the actors. During a scene early in the play when Schill and Mme. Zachanassian were seated downstage on a bench, Lunt was distressed to hear a woman in the front row whisper to her companion, "Well, she certainly looks years younger than he does."

Broadway productions may be required to offer one special performance within fifteen weeks of the New York opening, with all proceeds going to the Actors' Fund of America. Unless *The Visit* gave such a performance, other actors performing on Broadway would be unable to see it. Consequently, Iggie Wolfington, then appearing in *The Music Man,* tacked up a petition backstage at his theatre, asking for the signatures of those performers who would buy tickets if a special presentation of *The Visit* was offered. Every actor in the company signed the petition. Wolfington then contacted every theatrical company on Broadway to see how many other actors wanted to see a special performance. The response was overwhelming: nearly every actor in New York hoped the Lunts would schedule a presentation they would be able to see. Wolfington sent his petition and the results of his survey to the Lunts, who immediately agreed to give a performance. Initially scheduled for June 29, it had to be postponed when Lunt required hospitalization, but the benefit was given at a Thursday matinee on August 21.

Again, the Producers' Theatre posted a closing date, November 29, despite the fact that *The Visit* was selling out. The Lunts wished to continue the run and were puzzled by the producers' haste. Others in the cast were equally perplexed. John Randolph wrote to Brooks Atkinson expressing his dismay "that the Lunts, with a great play, production and notices, critically hailed as being their best in years should have their shortest run." The producers' answer was that the Morosco was booked for another production and no other Broadway theatre could be found. In fact, they were evicting *The Visit* in order to bring in another Producers' Theatre production, *The Cold Wind and the Warm.* In any case, one of the great productions of modern times was forced to close because of a temporary shortage of real estate.

The Lunts wanted to tour, but they believed that a skeptical management feared audiences outside New York would reject the play, finding its content too grim. "Our phantom management is very vague indeed," Lunt wrote to William Le Massena. "We still don't know why we closed—as there was never a losing week & we were willing to stay on or take to the road so your guess is as good as ours."*

Fontanne told her sister Antoinette that she and her husband were particularly eager to tour "because the play is not yet paid for—as we have never been in a play that has not made money . . . we are anxious not to spoil our record." Fontanne's recollection was not entirely accurate, but if one omits such productions as *Goat Song, The Brothers Karamazov* and *Point Valaine,* her statement was substantially correct.

The Visit was chosen to receive the Drama Critics' Circle Award as the best foreign play on Broadway that season. Perhaps that honor helped persuade the American Theatre Society (an offshoot of the Theatre Guild), the Council of the Living Theatre and the Producers' Theatre to send the play on tour. Still, nearly ten months passed after the closing at the Morosco before the Lunts took *The Visit* on the road, beginning in Wilmington, Delaware, on September 16, 1959. The tour, lasting nearly six months, covered seventeen cities in the United States and Canada, with Lunt serving as director of the touring production.†

---

* In 1985, Robert Whitehead maintained that the Producers' Theatre had never been reluctant to send the play on tour. Roger Stevens recalled that the organization was eager to sponsor a tour. Perhaps the difficulties of securing theatres and arranging an itinerary at a time when touring had become prohibitively expensive accounted for the delay the Lunts impatiently misinterpreted as lack of interest on the part of the producers.

† As director, Lunt insisted that the actors follow precisely the blocking Peter Brook had conceived. Actors were free to experiment with line readings, but Brook's "choreography" was sacrosanct.

When the tour began, John Randolph was unable to join it, having been cast in another production. He has summarized his experience with the Lunts by saying:

> They were people that I did not ever go to see on the stage because they were supposed to be decadent, conservative, old-fashioned. I was young, radical, working-class. I identified with the Stanislavski method and the left-wing movement, and who wanted to see these reactionary actors who did Noël Coward and *The Great Sebastians?* The actors I identified with did working-class plays that reflected the turbulence of our time, and were realistic, and so on. And then, when I got to work with the Lunts, I realized how much I had missed. They were closer to the work that Stanislavski talked about than the actors in the Actors' Studio were. I saw a lot of very good actors, but I never saw the kind of hard work and analysis of a part that they did. When they worked with me in that hotel room in Boston, he talked about the town, where the characters came from, what they did. She talked about the town, the period, her background, the situation when she was kicked out. Then they asked me a million questions about the Police Chief. I had never seen that kind of intensive work. They were true craftspeople in the finest sense of the word.

The long wait between the Broadway engagement and the tour allowed the Lunts to spend their first full winter at Genesee Depot. As eager as they were to get back on stage again, they also delighted in being home. Early in February 1959, Lunt wrote to Edward Bigg, "I've never been here at seed planting time and am most excited that my petunias & peppers & parsley & dill and thyme are just coming up—"

As spring arrived, Lunt found himself torn between the delights of home and his enthusiasm for *The Visit*. "The thought of going back to the theatre is revolting," he wrote to Richard and Tinx Whorf on April 4, "but we start a tour in September—if the caste [*sic*] can be found. . . . How it will 'go' on the road—God knows—as it's really a shocker."

Still, when September came, the Lunts set off eagerly. If they were concerned about making the arduous tour at their ages, they gave no indication of it. Indeed, Fontanne said, "In the theatre in which we were raised, it was taken for granted that one toured. To ask us if we like touring is like asking us if we like to eat. It is sad that younger actors have not had the experience of playing before different audiences in theatres of different sizes. It is part of the job of being an actor."

Fortunately, the tour of *The Visit* was less fraught with hardships than their earlier tours had been. The weather was pleasant everywhere except in Salt Lake City, where the temperature was well below freezing. Unlike the other members of the company, who rode trains, the Lunts traveled from city to city by air. Fontanne had always detested flying, but her fear soon evaporated and she welcomed the additional leisure time.

In line with Lunt's belief that "When there are cast changes [for a touring production], they should be made better, not worse than in the original production," two outstanding performers, Glenn Anders and Thomas Gomez, were hired to play the Schoolmaster and the Burgomaster.

The Visit turned out to be a surprising commercial success. The New York and touring productions took in more than two million dollars. In Washington, San Francisco, Philadelphia and Los Angeles, it broke box-office records for a nonmusical play. Indeed, in Los Angeles the balcony of the Biltmore Theatre was reopened after many years in order to accommodate the requests for tickets.

The production was such a large one that actors' salaries alone made it impossible for the tour to show more than a small profit. Nevertheless, it demonstrated how hungry audiences were for fine drama given an outstanding production. "If we could have played one-night stands, we could have stayed out for years and years with this play," said Lunt.

Those who believed *The Visit* would arouse controversy on the tour were correct. One woman in Cleveland sent a note to the Lunts immediately after she returned home from the theatre. The note read, "Dear Mr. and Mrs. Lunt: I saw your play. It was well acted, as is always the case with you. But it made me quite ill and I am going straight to bed."

In Washington there was a near-riot. A woman seated at the back of the orchestra began screaming, "If you're going to kill him, bring down the curtain!" during the climactic scene. That provoked yelling from other members of the audience. After a brief scuffle, ushers took the woman from the theatre and the play limped to its conclusion.

The tour of *The Visit** concluded with a two-week engagement at the

* During the Los Angeles run, Carol Channing arranged to have the Lunts invited to a dinner party at the home of George Burns and Gracie Allen. She knew they all admired one another's work but that they had never met. Both couples were as afflicted with nerves as if it had been an opening night. To Fontanne and especially to Lunt, Burns and Allen represented the finest in vaudeville entertainment. To Burns and Allen, the Lunts represented the American theatre at its most distinguished. Channing and her husband, Charles Lowe, picked up the Lunts at the Biltmore Hotel. As she told the story, "They were so nervous that Alfred said, 'I swear, Lynnie started at 3:00 this afternoon to get her makeup on and to get herself together for tonight.' And Lynnie kept saying, 'Alfred, I've got too much rouge on.' Then she'd take it off. Then she'd go back and put it on. So, finally, Alfred said, 'Lynnie, Lynnie, just relax. Now, relax. We'll have one little jigger of scotch—just one little jigger.' So Lynnie had a jigger of scotch and it gave her the courage to forget whether she looked all right and whether she was going to say the right thing."

Meanwhile, the atmosphere was equally tense at the Burns house in Beverly Hills. Burns had a double martini while Gracie changed her dress several times. When the Lunts arrived, Gracie opened the door. She and Burns were astonished when the first thing out of Lunt's mouth was a line from a Burns-and-Allen vaudeville act of thirty-six years before: "I'm glad I'm dizzy boys like dizzy girls and I like boys and you must be glad I'm dizzy because you're

New York City Center, where it played to sold-out houses (breaking another house record). Lewis Funke's review in the New York *Times* tells why. "Incredible as it may seem to say so," Funke began, "Alfred Lunt and Lynn Fontanne are better in it now than when first the curtain rose . . . in May, 1958.

"They, of course, do endow their roles with their accustomed perfection. Not a detail that is helpful in the construction of their characters seems to have gone unnoticed or unpracticed. But somehow they also have succeeded in deepening the essences of their characters. The poignancy is sharper now, and, consequently, stronger is the effect upon the emotion."

Now that the production was a certified American success, London theatres suddenly became available. The Lunts were invited to perform *The Visit* there and at the International drama festival in Paris. The Paris visit did not take place,* but the Lunts opened a new theatre, the Royalty—the first theatre built in central London in nearly thirty years—when they began a scheduled eight-week run in the English capital on June 23, 1960. The opening night was so successful, however (Lunt wrote to Edward Bigg, "The audience cheered & screamed & all was very thrilling not to say touching"), that the run was eventually extended to twenty weeks. Most of London's critics were as impressed by *The Visit* as their American counterparts had been, although some were repelled by the play's portrait of unbridled greed.

As the London run neared its end, the Lunts began to think more seriously about retiring from the stage. Both were deeply weary. Fontanne said she was so exhausted on the night of the closing performance, "I stood in the wings and said to myself, this is serious, you can't go on. Even my lips were shaking." And when at last the engagement was over, she admitted, "You can't know how wonderful it feels not to have a performance to give in the evening." The Lunts then journeyed to Switzerland for a well-deserved rest at the home of Noël Coward.

---

a boy and I like boys!" Gracie threw her arms around Lunt and said, "I forgot that line. I forgot it myself."

Everyone "had a marvelous evening," George Burns said, "until it was time for dinner." He went on, "In the excitement Gracie had forgotten to tell our help that there would be two more place settings at the table. So when we all walked into the dining room, there we were, twelve people with only ten chairs. It got pretty confusing—no matter how Gracie arranged the seating, there were always two people left standing. Finally Gracie realized what had happened. "Oh, my goodness," she said, 'I'm so embarrassed. I forgot the Lunts!'

"The Lunts laughed, and Alfred said, 'Don't worry about it, Gracie, we can always eat standing up.'

"And Lynn added, 'Relax, Gracie. I've been married to Alfred long enough to know he likes dizzy girls.' So we got two more chairs, and it was a very memorable evening."

*The State Department, which had initially offered to pay the cost of a week's performance at the Théâtre des Nations, ultimately claimed that its budget was too limited to support cultural projects. Whether or not the State Department objected to the play's content is open to question. Also, Lunt objected to presenting the play as an example of American theatre, since the author was Swiss, the director and some of the actors British.

The chronicle of *The Visit* ends with the several unsuccessful attempts to televise the production. As early as May 1960, "The Play of the Week" expressed interest in a two-hour special, but nothing came of it. According to George Schaefer, the Lunts very much wanted to televise the play, thereby making a permanent record of it. They grew even more interested after a film version was released with Ingrid Bergman and Anthony Quinn which the Lunts felt had trivialized and adulterated the play. Schaefer secured the television rights and proposed to direct a production for the "Hallmark Hall of Fame." The owners of the Hallmark company were enthusiastic, but, according to Schaefer, "then other voices came in—the business end of the agency—and they reversed themselves a week later, saying, 'We can't sell Mother's Day cards showing *The Visit,* so we won't do it.'

"So then I went to Mike Dann, who was running CBS at the time," Schaefer continued, "and I said, 'Look, I've got the Lunts in *The Visit.* You've got to do it.' He said, 'My God, yes, absolutely, we'll do it.' But then he called back a week later and told me that his board of directors said they lost so much money doing *Death of a Salesman* the year before, they wouldn't let him do another artistic thing. So it never happened. The performance was gone."

But the stage performance will never be forgotten by those who were fortunate enough to have seen it. Moreover, its importance to the Lunts cannot be overstated. Their decision to appear in *The Visit* was an act of great artistic daring. But the gamble paid off handsomely. The production salvaged the Lunts' reputations as truly great performers and silenced their critics once and for all.

Still claiming they had not retired, insisting they would continue to read plays submitted to them as eagerly as before, the Lunts returned to Genesee Depot in the winter of 1960–61. They had often denied rumors of retirement in the past, but this time the rumors turned out to be true. *The Visit* proved to be their last appearance on any stage.

Chapter Fifteen

SEMI-RETIREMENT

"We're not going to retire. If we find a
script, we'll beat it right back into a theatre."

Alfred Lunt, 1965

"Can't find a play we like . . . but we are
happy here [in Genesee Depot], and until something comes up, we shall stay
put."

Alfred Lunt, 1966

The Lunts undoubtedly planned to return to the stage as soon as they could find a good play. Throughout the 1960s they continued to read scripts, but many factors took precedence over their selection of a new play.

First, there was their delight in spending long periods of time in Genesee Depot. The winter spent at home in 1959–60 had whetted their appetites for more of the same. They were able to invite such old friends as Enid Bagnold, Katharine Cornell, Laurence Olivier, Helen Hayes and Cathleen Nesbitt to Ten Chimneys for long visits without the pressure of worrying about when they would have to return to a theatrical engagement.

In New York, too, they were often able to give and attend get-togethers with their friends ("at least 3 parties a week," Lunt told William Le Massena in 1965, "& it's been highly enjoyable"). Had they been working in November 1961, as they usually were at that time of year, they would not have been able to spend a delightful evening with Noël Coward. "We started [dinner] at a quarter to eight and finished at a quarter past one," Coward said, "during which time we never drew breath. We wandered back and forth happily over the forty-one years we have known and loved one another and it was altogether enchanting and, above all, comforting. Lynn looks marvellous and Alfred much better than he has looked for years. They are a fabulous couple."

And then, there was the increased opportunity for travel. They journeyed to Mexico in February 1962. In 1965 they visited old friends in London and took the opportunity to spend two weeks in the château country of France. They went fishing on Martha's Vineyard in 1968, spent several months wintering in Florida in 1970–71 and visited Katharine Cornell there in 1973, then traveled to the Orient the following year.* They returned to Mexico in 1975; later that year they took a fishing trip to Canada, then visited England once again.

Another consideration that kept the Lunts off the stage after 1960 was the chance to spend considerable time in their New York townhouse and enjoy a pleasure they had had too little time for in the past: theatregoing. Lunt's declining health and Fontanne's increasingly unreliable memory were additional factors.

Certainly there was no shortage of plays submitted to them. They were sorely tempted to appear in a musical version of Jean Giraudoux's *The Madwoman of Chaillot,* in which Fontanne would play the Countess and Lunt the Ragpicker. Had they gone through with it, the project would have marked their debuts as musical performers. Lunt was apprehensive about his singing voice, but plans called for him to speak his songs rhythmically in the manner of Rex Harrison in *My Fair Lady.* But even though producers Robert Whitehead and Bob Fosse acquired the rights, with Stephen Sondheim contracted to write the score and Fosse prepared to choreograph, the production did not come about. The main stumbling block seems to have been the disparity in the size and quality of the roles the Lunts were asked to play. Despite the best efforts of Sondheim and the producers, the role of the Ragpicker remained a relatively minor part. Whitehead suggested that the Lunts' contribution could be made equal if Lunt were to direct, but the couple disagreed and the project was abandoned.†

Other possible projects fell through as well. In 1962, Donald Seawell's production company, Bonard Productions, announced that the couple was considering an appearance in Enid Bagnold's *The Chinese Prime Minister,* a play about a seventy-year-old English actress, which Lunt would also direct. Bagnold had the Lunts in mind for her play from the beginning. She wrote many drafts, including numerous revisions suggested by the Lunts during a summer Bagnold spent at Genesee Depot, but she was unable to fashion a version that appealed to them sufficiently.

---

*"We didn't like Japan," Lunt wrote to Romney Brent. "It was cold, drizzly, dirty—and the trip from Kobe to Kyoto was the ugliest we have taken in all our lives. It beat Pittsburgh, the old towns in England, and Birmingham, Alabama for filth and ugliness. Kyoto had been so modernized and the highways widened to such an extent that many of the temples are closed in with a high wall. We loved Hong Kong and Singapore."

†Several years later Jerry Herman, Jerome Lawrence and Robert E. Lee created their own musical adaptation of *The Madwoman of Chaillot,* calling it *Dear World.* It played on Broadway during the 1968–69 season, with Angela Lansbury in the leading role.

"It's a fine play," said Lunt, "but there's no part for me and Lynn won't do it alone."

A similar problem prevented them from acting in *Film of Memory.* Lunt found the part of the husband "not awfully good," he told Cheryl Crawford in a letter rejecting the play, adding that his wife "doesn't want to isolate herself in the theatre away from me—not after all these years—'Most of my life is gone,' she says—'practically all of it in plays and we must have more fun together. There isn't so damned much time left.'" That same year the Lunts also turned down *The Marriner Method* by Otis Bigelow and *Bashful Genius,* a play about Bernard Shaw and his wife Charlotte.

The Lunts asked Noël Coward to write a "farewell play" for them in 1962, and the three of them concocted a plot about two elderly actors, reunited after a separation of thirty years, who were rehearsing their last production. But Coward's play, tentatively titled *Rehearsal Period* or *Swan Song,* was never written.

In 1963 the Theatre Guild thought they would return to the organization to appear in *Buried Alive,* Leonard Spigelgass's dramatization of Arnold Bennett's novel. The couple, who had appeared in radio adaptations of Bennett's story in 1947 and 1949, approved of Spigelgass's second and third acts, but concluded that the first act needed considerable work. The production was postponed until the following season, and eventually canceled when succeeding revisions were found wanting.*

Jean Dalrymple wrote to the Lunts in 1963, asking them to perform a scene from *The Visit* in the New York City Center's 20th Anniversary Showcase. Lunt replied that, although he and Fontanne regarded their two weeks' engagement at the City Center in 1960 as "about the most exciting & satisfying experience we have ever had," they would have to decline the invitation.

By 1964 the Lunts were admitting to their friends that their stage careers were over. "The thought of acting makes me sick," Lunt wrote to Richard Whorf. "Wouldn't mind a quick T.V. maybe, but that's about all—" To William Le Massena he wrote in 1965, "We have no plans, theatrically or otherwise, and we are settled down and are having the time of our lives here."

But Lunt was unwilling to make the same concession in public. He told the New York *Times* in 1965, "We're not going to retire. If we find a script, we'll beat it right back into a theatre." However, Fontanne said, "We cannot find a script we both like." She added, perhaps in reference to *The Chinese Prime Minister,* "I have a beautiful play. It's a big play for me, but it has nothing for Alfred. I cannot at this late date go into a theatre by myself. We've been together 40 years. It would be too dismal." She also made clear that any play in which they decided to appear would have to be substantive, saying, "When you're getting on, you have to be increas-

---

*In 1968, Spigelgass's script was used as the basis of an unsuccessful musical, *Darling of the Day.*

ingly cautious. Authors are kind enough to send us scripts. But you don't want your last play to be something that shouldn't be remembered."

David Merrick attempted to persuade the Lunts to act in Eugène Ionesco's *Exit the King* in 1965. They found the play "most interesting," Lunt said, "but we can't do it—one reason being that I'm not anxious to act again—"

In 1966, Lunt wrote to Ward Morehouse from Genesee Depot saying that he and Fontanne "can't find a play we like . . . but we are happy here, and until something comes up, we shall stay put."

Several producers believed that the Lunts could be induced to return to the stage in a presentation that would incorporate scenes from plays in which they had earlier appeared as well as moments from other classics. But Lunt told Donald Seawell, "There is no such thing as a great moment in a play standing by itself. Every great scene has had the rest of the play to build on. If you take it out of its context, it's no longer a great scene. Besides, we'd be foolish to challenge people's remembrance of us; we might not be able to measure up to their recollections. Unlike Hills Brothers coffee, we are not so unbeatable as to be reheatable."

Although reluctant to act in plays, the Lunts were eager to see as many productions as they could, an activity they had rarely had time for in the past.* Early in 1963 they saw *Oliver* in the company of Noël Coward. "They were thrilled," he reported. "They go to the theatre so seldom, it was like taking the kiddies to the panto."

American theatre went through a phase in the 1960s that could be described as either adventurous or vulgar, depending upon one's point of view. Many plays featured nudity, profanity and an emphasis on the sordid. In some cases those elements took the place of plot and character. Lunt did not reject the plays of the '60s out of hand, but Fontanne often did. "Lately I find the theatre—on the whole—rather dull," she said in 1967. "I go in, and I feel exactly the same when I come out—neither amused, nor moved, nor *anything*. I saw a play in London which was an enormous success there. In the course of it we were not told who the characters were, what their backgrounds were, what the story was—indeed, there didn't seem to *be* any story. Finally, at the end of the second act, one character got up and explained himself from birth. He was exactly a whole act too late. I'd been *bored* until then."

Dan Sullivan of the New York *Times* asked the Lunts in 1968 what they thought of the contemporary theatre and reported their answer as follows:

---

*They had thoroughly enjoyed theatregoing whenever they had been able to fit it into their schedules. Dick Van Patten recalled the Lunts taking him to a performance of Oscar Wilde's *The Importance of Being Earnest* (with John Gielgud) in 1947. They laughed loudly and applauded enthusiastically, Van Patten remembered. Indeed, Fontanne wrote to Binkie Beaumont, "We loved the play and him [Gielgud] and some of it made me laugh louder and longer than I have laughed in the theatre for years."

SHE: Dull!

HE: What do you mean, dull?

SHE: I go in cold, and I come out colder. I haven't been thrilled in the theatre since, what . . . ?

HE: Well, you liked *Becket*.

SHE: Yes, and *Man for All Seasons*.

HE: And the first two acts of, what was it?

SHE: *Tiny Alice*. But the third act did not exist. The author hadn't finished the play. We were left high and dry!

HE: Well, Lynnie . . .

SHE: No, wait a minute!

HE: . . . We liked Helen [Hayes] in *The Show Off*.

SHE: I haven't quite finished with this! I came out of that theatre so annoyed and cross that I really might have hit Mr. Albee. I knew that he had sold John [Gielgud] on the basis of two acts, and then he let him down!

HE: Now *Marat/Sade* was my cup of tea.

SHE: I found it deadly. I knew Charlotte Corday would kill him and I kept wishing she would.

HE: Oh, but what Peter Brook did with it!

SHE: It's not enough, Alfred.

HE: It was just enough.

SHE: It wasn't a bit. I didn't like it.

At other times Lunt was less enthusiastic about the course the New York theatre was taking. In 1967 he said, "The theatre's very sad these days; so little in it to make you think life is worth living, so little that is really literate or about civilization's triumphs." When he saw *The Man in the Glass Booth* in 1969, he confessed, "I haven't the slightest idea of what some of it was about—" Perhaps Fontanne's aversion (and Lunt's perplexed reaction) to much of the drama of the '60s helps to account for their rejection of so many opportunities to appear on the stage after *The Visit*.

Lunt saw hope in the growth of the regional resident-professional-theatre movement, which he called "wonderfully exciting," to some degree because it was largely dedicated to reviving the great plays of the past. However, he wondered how long the movement could survive if it did not stimulate the writing of new plays.

William Le Massena learned Fontanne's emphatic opinion of nudity in the theatre when he was cast in a play called *Grin and Bare It* in the 1960s. "It was a comedy," he told me,

> written in England in 1928. Until the nude thing came along in the '60s, you couldn't do it, so it was called an unplayable play. I wondered if I'd be able to go through a nude audition. Well, by God, you know, I'm like millions of other actors—you give me a job, I'll do anything. So they offered me the part and I went

ahead and did it. Well, Alfred was intrigued with this, and he got me on the phone. I can remember he'd call up from Genesee Depot and he'd say, "What happens if you have to sneeze? Suppose you need a pocket handkerchief? What would you do?" But Lynn felt it was degrading to the profession and degrading to myself. She really was deeply upset by it. She'd be on the upstairs phone at Genesee Depot while he was on the downstairs phone and she'd say, "I think it's disgraceful—disgraceful!" And I stood a very good chance of losing her friendship from that.

Both the Lunts felt strongly about the "new breed" of actors in America who demanded that the director provide them with a "motivation" for every impulse. Fontanne said she and Lunt "cannot abide the young actor who is relentlessly probing into a character and pestering the director with 'Why.' You have a certain part to play in a larger whole. [Alfred] once replied to an actor asking 'Why,' 'Because I tell you to, that's why.' "

Fontanne had little patience with actors who could not respond immediately to a director's instructions. "That realistic business of working themselves into a flood of tears before they come on by thinking of something terribly sad in their past lives and then coming on all emotionalized—you know, they're doing that just because they're amateurs and emotion doesn't rise quickly for an amateur and he has to work it up. But a good seasoned actor can call up a flood of tears like that," she said, snapping her fingers, "in two seconds. Any good actor can turn anything on, like turning on a tap.

"When I was very young," she continued, "one of the hallmarks of an actor who was inexperienced was that he answered the director back, or that he stopped rehearsal or took too much of rehearsal time talking about himself and his difficulties . . . the hallmark of a greenhorn. The hallmark of an experienced actor is that he does implicitly what the director says. Now, if he's a fine actor and the director has told him to do something which he doesn't think is very good, he does it, but he does it his own way, and he makes it real and vivid, but he must do what the director says and he must follow him, because the director knows the whole play and you know only your one part, and he may have reasons for telling you to do something that does not appear [evident] to you. But you never hold up a rehearsal. Only amateurs do that."

Brook Seawell, the daughter of Donald Seawell and Eugenia Rawls, made her Broadway debut when she was seven, appearing in *Traveling Lady*. "Alfred and Lynn were very afraid because she might be too much subjected to 'Method' direction and 'Method' acting," Donald Seawell told me, "so they asked me to bring her around for tea. I brought her to their house and Alfred said, 'Now, Brooky, I want you to know that you don't have to get sick in the wings in order to feel emotion.' He said, 'Cry, Lynnie,' and Lynnie just started great tears running down her cheeks. And he said, 'Laugh, Lynnie.' The tears dried up and Lynnie started laughing; and he said to this little girl, 'See what I mean?' "

Perhaps, however, Fontanne was overstating the case when she claimed that actors should make no attempt to use their own emotional lives as the basis for the emotions of their characters. George Schaefer told me that he often observed the Lunts using their personal experiences as the basis for their acting: "They would constantly, in rehearsals, be relating to something personal—or to something that happened in their lives, which is what most actors and actresses do. They'd say, 'Oh, I see what you mean because one time when my father did this to me, I remember I was so angry. Let me see if I can recall that.' They were very observant and very intuitive."

Although the Lunts did not make conscious use of Stanislavski's "method," they did not insist that the approach they used was a superior one. They believed—as Stanislavski himself would surely have agreed—that every actor must find the technique that works best for him. Lunt summarized his feelings in an anecdote. "Some years ago Miss Fontanne had a maid who was going to join us in the country for a weekend," he related. "I said to her, 'Will you want to go to church on Sunday?' And she said, 'Yes, I'd like to go to church.' And I said, 'You're a Methodist, aren't you? You know there is only one church here, and it is a Catholic church.' And she said, 'Oh, that doesn't bother me. We're all heading for the same place.' I often think of that in connection with acting. We're all just heading for the same place. . . . How we get [there] may vary maybe. What counts is the end product."

The Lunts did express disdain for gifted actors who deserted the stage for the lure of Hollywood. They regarded Judith Anderson as a supremely talented actress and could not reconcile themselves to the fact that she had left the theatre. "How dare she go to Hollywood and do movies like *Lady Scarface?*" Fontanne asked angrily. On the other hand, they continued their close friendships with Sydney Greenstreet and Richard Whorf after they left the Lunts' company to perform in films.

Their attitude stemmed from their conviction that the theatre was a more satisfactory medium *for audiences* than was television or the movies. "A live person walking around [on stage] radiates something," Fontanne said. "I think there are chemicals there that don't come through on television."

When the Lunts attended the theatre, they were invariably—sometimes remarkably—polite. The Denver *Post* reported that a steady rain fell while they watched an outdoor performance of *The Sound of Music* by the Denver Opera Foundation. Although they had no umbrellas, they remained stoically in their seats until the end.

When it became apparent the Lunts would not act again on the New York stage, their appearances as spectators took on an added dimension. In 1970, for example, when they saw *Home* on Broadway, the audience rose and cheered as the Lunts walked down the aisle to their seats. Lunt turned to Fontanne, saying, "Lynnie, there must be someone important here—they're all standing." Not until this scene was repeated the next time the Lunts attended the theatre did they realize the ovation was intended for them.

When in Wisconsin, they journeyed to Milwaukee periodically to see the productions of the Milwaukee Repertory Theatre. In 1967, Lunt said, "The best [production] we've seen was recently in Milwaukee, of all places. It was splendidly, expertly acted, far better than anything I've seen in New York lately." When an official of the theatre mentioned that several period plays were scheduled for production, the Lunts volunteered to search their closets for items that might be used as costumes. Lunt personally delivered a package to the theatre in late 1965, containing suits, dresses, ballgowns and vividly colored Spanish shawls, some from their personal wardrobe, others from a collection of costumes they had worn in past productions.

The actors who most impressed the Lunts in the 1960s included several young performers as well as those of their own generation. Among them were Julie Harris, Sydney Greenstreet, Helen Hayes, Edward G. Robinson, Richard Whorf (all of whom played with one or both of the Lunts), John Gielgud, Laurence Olivier, Katharine Cornell, Ralph Richardson, Paul Scofield, Maggie Smith, Albert Finney, Edith Evans and Richard Burton. "I saw Richard Burton only once, years ago," said Lunt, "acting, not saying a word. He was scrubbing a floor in John Gielgud's production of *The Lady's Not for Burning* by Christopher Fry. Burton lifted that scrubbing brush with such authority! He scrubbed the floor with truth! Greatness was in him, so early in his career."

During their active years, the Lunts had offered intriguing opinions about the art of acting, but often seemed reluctant to go into detail. As they neared retirement, they felt no such reticence, adding to and elaborating on comments they had made in the past, such as Lunt's insistence that there were no "rules" an actor should be made to observe. Indeed, the Lunts may be best remembered as actors who created their own rules. "People used to talk about our tricks in the theatre," said Lunt. "You know, they weren't tricks at all. On the contrary, we never did tricks. We just did things the way they weren't supposed to be done. For instance, you weren't supposed to talk through your fingers with your head down because it wouldn't be heard, it wouldn't get a laugh. But it did."

Comic acting was considerably more demanding than any other kind, Lunt believed. "Anyone who says comedy isn't harder to act than tragedy doesn't know what he's talking about," he said. "Timing in comedy is so much more difficult. Waiting for the laughs. Not waiting for them when they don't come, which is even more important. And then if the laugh comes, you have to cut it off before it dies out. Comedy—you really have to have that ear out and that eye on yourself. You really do. You have to be very up and very brilliant and faster, much faster than you are when you play tragedy. And that, of course, is very tiring, very exhausting. And no emotional undercurrent to sustain the interest."

Lunt believed not all actors were cut out to play comedy. "I don't think you can train comedians, teach an actor how to say lines just that certain way unless they have humor," he said, "and then you've got to be willing to be ridiculous. You must be willing to be laughed at as well as to be laughed with. Some persons have an ego that is so, I don't know, weak, perhaps, and they fight against it [being laughed at]."

Fontanne argued that technical mastery of voice and movement did not necessarily make a fine actor. "I don't think technique is the art of acting," she said. "I think the art of acting is . . . an imaginary thing. You imagine yourself the person that the author has written, and you sink yourself into that. Then out of your throat comes, perhaps, quite a different voice. And you don't think it out. But it is a mental thing, it is done with your mentality and your imagination."

Beyond imagination, Fontanne stressed the importance of the actor's maintaining a critical view of his performance even in the midst of the production. "A very good actor has to have [an outside eye], or acquire it," she told Lewis Funke and John E. Booth.

> How you do, I can't possibly tell you. You can look at yourself.
> For instance, you know exactly where your arm is, so that it is
> graceful, you know. And anything like that, you learn. You have
> to have an outside eye, and you also have to have an outside ear,
> so that when you say something, your outside ear tells you that
> it is the wrong inflection, just as you, yourself, in life, if you say
> something irritably and you are not at all irritable, but it comes
> out irritably, you say to yourself, "Now that sounds as if I were
> cross," and you explain to the person you are talking to, "I am
> not cross." You see? Well, that's it. Same thing, exactly. And that
> ear also guides your timing, which is vital in comedy, in speaking
> the lines of, say, Shaw or Coward or S. N. Behrman. But the
> timing must not be methodical or deliberate. Too much preci-
> sion is worse than none. Better to be offbeat a bit than too delib-
> erate. A good actor cannot be so self-conscious, or so shy or so
> nervous and tightened, that he can't hear. A good actor hears,
> and a good actor sees.

Most important of all, however, was a strong sense of discipline, which, the Lunts believed, evidenced a respect for the theatre. The worst possible breach of discipline occurred when an actor drank before or during a performance. Consequently, Charles Bowden, the Lunts' stage manager, often warned actors who were known to drink occasionally, "Look, we really don't care what you do after eleven o'clock, but please don't have a drink before the performance." If this advice was ignored, the actor would be fired on the spot. Bowden explained to me, "The smell of alcohol, particularly to Lynn—even if it had only been a mouthful and spit out afterwards—would freeze her. She had had rather unfortunate experiences with drunken actors early in her career and she would not put up with it."

Fontanne's belief in discipline was clearly conveyed to the young actors she auditioned in the 1930s and 1940s. Bowden recalled her admonition (reminiscent of the advice Ellen Terry had given her many years earlier) to talented actresses: "You're very, very good, and I will do whatever I can to make your path easier, but I do want you to understand one thing: that if you succeed in the theatre, it will be a job of work. There are no flowers at the stage door, no stage-door Johnnies—that has nothing to do with it. You have to know that it's a job of work and that any other kind of work you choose would be easier. Now, if you understand that— and you must think about it—I'll arrange with Mr. Bowden to assist you in any way we can."

That the Lunts were not forgotten during their years of semi-retirement is evident from the steady stream of awards they received, including the Fashion Forum Award given to Fontanne "for the most distinguished contribution to the world of fashion by a Wisconsinite" (which, she said graciously in her acceptance speech, "means more to me than an acting award. I have always been interested in apparel and have been proud to be named in lists of the ten best-dressed women"), the Rodale Creative Arts Award from Brandeis University, honorary doctorates from Yale University and the Goodman School of Drama, and the Presidential Medal of Freedom, the nation's highest civilian award, given to them jointly in 1964.*

The thirty Americans who received the Medal of Freedom that year included John Steinbeck, Aaron Copland, T. S. Eliot, Carl Sandburg, Helen Keller, Willem De Kooning, Walt Disney, civil-rights leader A. Philip Randolph and scientist Detlev W. Bronk. The Lunts, who found it difficult to understand why they were being honored ("Perhaps it merely comes under the heading of longevity," Lunt said), tried to stay out of camera range when photographs were taken. President Lyndon Johnson took them by the arms, however, and pulled them toward him.

Johnson saluted the medal winners, saying, "Collectively, they have made man's world safe, his physical body more durable, his mind broader, his leisure more delightful, his standard of living higher and his dignity important. They are the creators; we are the beneficiaries."

The Lunts gave as well as they received. In the 1960s they established the Lunt-Fontanne Foundation, Inc., in order to provide donations of

*The award, created in 1945 to honor civilians who had helped to win the war, was extended in 1952 to cover citizens who made important contributions to national security. Not until February 1963 did President Kennedy alter the nature of the award so that those who had contributed most significantly to the quality of American life in any field might be recognized. The Lunts were included in the second group chosen to receive the expanded award.

money and *objets d'art* to various theatre-related organizations. At a meeting of the foundation in 1966, for example, they donated more than $15,000 worth of paintings, sculptured medallions, porcelain figures and miniature stages to the American Academy of Dramatic Arts and the Actors' Fund, as well as to the University of Wisconsin and to the New York Public Library's Theatre Collection. Ultimately, the foundation was liquidated after the passage of the Tax Reform Act of 1969, one of whose consequences was to withdraw tax privileges from private foundations.

The Lunts presented a special gift to the Players when that organization honored them jointly in 1963: the reading desk of Sarah Siddons, the eighteenth-century English performer who has often been called the finest actress in British history. They also contributed some original Robert Edmond Jones set designs to the State Historical Society of Wisconsin in 1975.

Although they elected not to act on the stage any longer, the Lunts' careers were hardly over. Both appeared several times on television, and Lunt directed three stage productions in the 1960s.

Late in 1961 he undertook to direct Samuel Taylor's *First Love* on Broadway. The play, adapted from Romain Gary's novel *Promise at Dawn,* opened at the Morosco Theatre on Christmas Day. Although Lunt's direction was praised as "expert" by Howard Taubman of the *Times,* the play, which contained forty-one scenes, was too loosely structured to maintain the audience's interest, and it closed after 24 performances.

Taylor's working relationship with Lunt was valuable to him, however. "Doing a play with Alfred Lunt is like taking a refresher course in the arts and humanities," he said. "We spent a week working on the play at his place in Genesee Depot, Wis., and I would go to bed at night so stimulated by the swarm of ideas that bubbled endlessly from him that I would lie awake half the night. I told him before I left that I was going to call it through the streets and cry it from the rooftops that Alfred Lunt doth murder sleep."

In January 1965, Lunt revived his production of *Così fan tutte* at the Metropolitan Opera. Two of the singers, Donald Gramm and Leontyne Price, were new to the production, which was assigned a full rehearsal period. Lunt faced the same difficulties he had encountered in 1951 and was so nervous about getting the production in shape for the opening that he and Fontanne declined an invitation to attend Lyndon Johnson's inauguration rather than miss any rehearsals.

The revival of *Così fan tutte* did not, however, return Lunt to the stage. He turned down the opportunity to reprise his small role as the candle-lighter during the overture.

Two seasons later he staged a production of *La Traviata,* which opened during the inaugural week of the new Metropolitan Opera House in September 1966. Lunt wished to present a more sensual Violetta than had generally been seen. When Anna Moffo was cast in the role (Lunt originally preferred Joan Sutherland, but Rudolf Bing persuaded him that Moffo would be a better choice), he explained his concept to her. Their Violetta, he said, should neither look nor act like Harriet Beecher Stowe. "After all, she's a Parisian whore, and the person she was based on, Alphonsine Plessis, had so many lovers . . . that she died of overwork at the age of twenty-three." He was further determined that the party scene in the first act give an impression of sensuality rather than being "as sedate as a reception at Buckingham Palace."

However, he found that some of his plans had to be discarded because of the demands of Verdi's music. "You don't really direct an opera, it directs you," he told Maurice Zolotow. "The music comes first. Oh, I had so many charming ideas for Anna Moffo in the first act—some romantic sighs and lovely pauses—but, you see, I couldn't do them because one has to follow the music. The music doesn't stop, and by the time Miss Moffo was doing all those nice pieces of business I'd invented for her, the music would have been in the middle of the next aria."

Ultimately, the production reflected Lunt's conception without neglecting the work of the composer. Moffo said:

> Lunt is a good director in opera because he respects the music and knows that it comes first. I can't explain how he directs. He doesn't talk a lot. He directs by casting a spell. . . . He sort of shrugs, or smiles in a strange way at you, and then maybe stands or sits to illustrate something, and he doesn't expect you to copy it, but in some mysterious way he gets across to you how he thinks you should do it. The most important thing he did for me was to show me that in certain passages I was moving around too much—my hands, my body—for no reason. He showed me it was like an unconscious, nervous reaction when I was singing a difficult passage, and convinced me that if I stood perfectly still, this would be strong. I never realized before how strong, how very strong it is to stand still like a statue, and that you can act even when standing still.

The production received mixed notices, although many who saw it felt it illuminated the work as few previous presentations had done. Harold C. Schonberg, writing in the *Times,* found it "a very fine production."

The Lunts' first foray into television since the disastrous production of *The Great Sebastians* occurred when they agreed to participate in a program about the ancient Greek theatre entitled *Athens, Where the Theatre Began*. CBS made the offer early in 1963, proposing to tape the production in April. The Lunts had no other projects and were still not fully committed to retirement. Moreover, the job meant an all-expenses-paid trip to Athens at the most congenial time of year. "I thought, why not?" Lunt said. "Greece is a lovely place." The Lunts' assignment was to describe the development of the Greek theatre while others performed scenes from the plays of Aeschylus, Sophocles and Aristophanes.

At the first rehearsal, one of the actors arrived ten minutes late. Neither the Lunts nor the director, Tom Donovan, said anything about it. Weeks later, however, Fontanne said to Donovan, "I will never understand how anyone who is supposed to be an actor could do anything like that."

One evening when the Lunts were studying the script in their Athens hotel room, the telephone rang. It was Paul I, the King of Greece, asking them to join him for dinner. "That's very kind of you," Lunt replied, "but we can't tonight as we're going over our lines for tomorrow. I'm sure you'll understand." Evidently the King did understand, for the invitation was repeated after the program had been taped, and the Lunts were happy to accept.

The program taxed their energies very little, giving them plenty of time to enjoy sightseeing in Greece. "We loved it and Delphi in particular," Lunt wrote to Richard Whorf later in 1963.

Before the program was shown, the Lunts went to work on another television production.* They agreed to perform in a one-act play by J. M. Barrie, *The Old Lady Shows Her Medals*, in June 1963. "The United States Steel Hour," the television arm of the Theatre Guild, had begun presenting dramas for television ten years earlier, and *The Old Lady Shows Her Medals* was to be its final production. In order to give the finale a special distinction, the Guild asked Lunt and Fontanne to participate.†

The play featured Fontanne as a Cockney charwoman who is adopted as a mother by a Scottish soldier during World War I. Lunt went along for the ride, as it were, serving as the on-screen narrator of the play. He was seen only for about four minutes, although he claimed it seemed more like fifteen hours. "I'm sure it will seem that long to the viewers, too," he complained as rehearsals were in progress. "I stand there and talk to a big black box, but it does not respond. At least I'd like to see a couple of eyes." In some respects, television was a kinder medium than the stage for Lunt; it made him less nervous, since a scene could always be retaped and there was no audience present. In other ways, however, he was clearly uncomfortable without the presence of the audience.

The play, like much of Barrie's work, is sentimental in the extreme,

---

*Three months later, *Athens, Where the Theatre Began* aired on CBS. The Lunts' portion of the program was pedestrian in its writing but capably presented, critics agreed. However, the scenes performed to illustrate the narrative—scenes in which the Lunts did not appear—were poorly acted and directed. Calling the effort a "solemn and portentous disaster," John Horn of the New York *Herald Tribune* said the "dull exposition" of the narrative was "little alleviated by dramatics that looked and sounded like a high-school rehearsal."

†Although this was the only time the Lunts performed for the Theatre Guild on television, they had acted together in ten radio plays for "The Theatre Guild on the Air" between 1945 and 1952. On three occasions Lunt appeared without Fontanne, and once—when she played in *Strange Interlude*—Fontanne acted without Lunt. Their last radio broadcast for "The Theatre Guild on the Air" was *The Old Lady Shows Her Medals*, on February 3, 1952.

but Fontanne believed that a different approach to the charwoman could make the play more palatable. Besides, she felt, "They're not sentimental, that class of people. They're very hard, very hard going, very hard lives and they wouldn't be sentimental."

Tom Donovan, who had directed *Athens, Where the Theatre Began,* was engaged to direct *The Old Lady Shows Her Medals*. Again he was impressed with the Lunts' drive and dedication. During the first rehearsals, held in a dingy hall on Second Avenue, Donovan noted that they arrived early each morning, eager to begin work. "They brought their lunch with them and they seemed anxious to get back to work before the lunch period ended," Donovan said. "They didn't want to take the regular five-minute breaks each hour, either. Once, when I announced a break, Mr. Lunt asked me, 'Do we have to?' I told him it was a union regulation. He replied, 'Oh, well, if we have to, we will.'" Donovan expressed the wish that "every young actor should be forced to watch the Lunts work. They can teach an awful lot in the way of discipline."

During the taping, Fontanne surprised Donovan by unexpectedly singing a Cockney song in the middle of a scene. Because the production was not transmitted live, Donovan had the option of cutting the song out, but he realized that it added dimension to the character and variety to the play.

The Old Lady Shows Her Medals was greeted with acclaim. Jack Gould's review in the New York *Times* spoke of his pleasure at watching "skilled and disciplined hands transform a drama of marked sentimentality into a believable occasion of warmth and sincerity." The play, he said, "is unabashedly corny. . . . But to make a judgment by that perfunctory criterion of sophistication fails entirely to reckon with the magic of Miss Fontanne. By nothing more than a lovely smile, she made the years fade away from the spinster's face and totally involved the spectator in the woman's joy of having a lifelong dream come true."

Lunt did a smooth, professional job of narration, but he was convinced his performance was poor. "I'm sorry you missed Lynn," he told Richard Whorf. "She was truly marvelous—I was not so good. . . . I hate trying to be myself (& with reason) & talking to that great black machine sends me higher than a kite."

An equally happy experience was *The Magnificent Yankee,* by Emmet Lavery, in which the Lunts appeared for the "Hallmark Hall of Fame" on January 28, 1965. George Schaefer, who often directed for Hallmark, had been trying for years to persuade the Lunts to appear on the program. He discussed the possibility of directing them in *The Sea Gull,* but that project fell through. Several other plays were also considered and rejected. Then he read *The Magnificent Yankee* and believed it would be ideal for them. Fontanne was equally enthusiastic about the script, which focuses on the last thirty years in the lives of Oliver Wendell Holmes, Jr., and his wife, Fanny, beginning with their arrival in Washington when Holmes was sixty-two and about to begin his tenure on the Supreme Court. She suggested to Lunt that they agree to Schaefer's proposal.

They began working on the play long before the production went into rehearsal. During the summer of 1964 they learned and rehearsed their dialogue, arranging the balance of each scene as meticulously as they had done in their days in the theatre. They also let it be known that they expected all the other actors in the production to be word-perfect at the first rehearsal in New York.

Schaefer was uncertain how the Lunts would respond to his direction. On the day they met, however, the Lunts reassured him. "Please remember one thing—you *can't* give us enough direction."

Schaefer had a reputation as a hard-working and demanding director, but the Lunts' energy and passion for work took him by surprise. The rehearsal each morning began at 10:30. When Schaefer arrived, he said, "I would find the Lunts had been there for an hour, running through their scenes, polishing little bits and pieces to surprise me with." If the rehearsal was a particularly good one, Schaefer customarily let the actors go at 5:20, ten minutes before the work day was scheduled to end. Whenever he did that, however, "Sure enough, one of the two would come over and say, 'We've got a few minutes. Let's do that scene over again.'"

The Lunts were favorably impressed by Schaefer. If Peter Brook represented their ideal stage director, Schaefer became the television director for whom they had the most respect and in whom they most trusted. "He's the most beautiful, superb director of acting," Lunt said. Fontanne added that Schaefer was always ready with a helpful suggestion whenever a problem of interpretation or delivery arose.

The Lunts considered themselves novices in television. On the first rehearsal day in the television studio for *The Magnificent Yankee*, Fontanne noticed that the seasoned performers were delivering their lines in low, conversational tones. In contrast, she thought, her voice was booming as if she were trying to fill a large theatre. She determined to try the other actors' technique.

When Lunt began playing the next scene with Fontanne, he was surprised at how quietly she spoke. "I can't hear a word you're saying," he said to her. As she began to explain, George Schaefer came out of the control room with a small microphone. He brought the device to Fontanne and asked, "Do you think you could put this under your dress somehow?" When she gave him a puzzled look and asked why, he answered, "Well, you see, we can't quite hear you."

Fontanne, only momentarily embarrassed, said, "You go back to your little box and see if you can hear me now." She played the next scene at such ear-splitting volume, she said, "I nearly broke the mike."

Whereas Lunt's forays into television may not have lessened his customary nervousness, Fontanne seemed able to relax during a television taping in ways she would never have permitted herself on the stage. Eugenia

Rawls, the Lunts' longtime friend and the wife of Donald Seawell, asked Schaefer if she could be involved in the television production in some way. She was cast in two small roles: a maid and the wife of a senator. One scene—a banquet at the White House—included both Rawls and Fontanne. As the banquet guests got up from the table, ostensibly to go into the next room, Fontanne—off camera and off microphone—playfully whispered to Rawls, "Shall we join the ladies and get pissed?"

Still, she made it clear that she felt more comfortable on the stage. Among the advantages of the theatre, Fontanne said, one of the greatest was that "you can't see yourself." When she saw the tape of *The Magnificent Yankee,* she was disappointed in her performance. "I didn't like myself," she said.

Nevertheless, the taping, in December 1964, was accomplished with such smoothness and speed that author Lavery was astonished. "One day for blocking, three days for taping, and through it all a sense of style and joy," he said.

Critical reaction to the production was overwhelmingly favorable. And to millions of television viewers the Lunts showed why they were legendary theatrical figures. Noël Coward's response was typical. "Absolutely superb," he recorded in his diary. "The best acting possible. They are both incredible."

Both the Lunts received Emmies for their performances, but they did not go to New York to pick up the awards, watching on television at Ten Chimneys as Joan Crawford and Melvyn Douglas accepted on their behalf. They were, however, "awfully damned pleased," Lunt said.

Although the taping of *The Magnificent Yankee* represented the last time the Lunts acted together in any medium, the production was seen once again when, by popular demand, the tape was shown for a second time in February 1966.

Other than a handful of radio dramas, the Lunts had not acted in separate plays since 1928. In 1966, however, when Lunt was to direct *La Traviata* for the Metropolitan Opera, he suggested to George Schaefer that Fontanne would be available to perform on television if a good role could be found for her. Schaefer asked her to appear with Julie Harris in a "Hallmark Hall of Fame" presentation of *Anastasia*. More than a little apprehensive at the thought of performing without Lunt, but excited by the challenge of portraying the Dowager Empress who alone could decide whether the woman claiming to be the Russian princess Anastasia was authentic, Fontanne decided to accept.

She was also motivated by a desire to play opposite Julie Harris, whom she called "a remarkable young woman. She's an important actress already," she said, "and I think her importance will grow because—besides being highly intelligent—she has no bad habits. She doesn't drink, or do anything to excess."

Harris was determined to maintain Fontanne's respect. Knowing that the older actress had the reputation of arriving early for rehearsals, Harris decided to get to the studio at 9:30 on the first day, half an hour before the call. Even so, she was too late. Fontanne had been there since 9:00.

The seventy-eight-year-old actress and the young star got along famously, although Harris was intimidated by Fontanne's aura. "I cannot call her Lynn, you know, although she calls me Julie," she said. "It would be unthinkable for me to address her as anything but Miss Fontanne. That sounds stiff, though, so I don't call her anything—I just say 'good morning' or 'good night.'"

Fontanne offered to share her lunch—a chicken sandwich Lunt had made for her—on the first day of rehearsal. Harris admired the dress Fontanne was wearing and thought, when Fontanne told her she had made it, "Look at this woman. There's nothing she can't do."

After six days of rehearsal, the cast was given a day off. Fontanne asked Harris what she was planning to do with her free time. "The laundry," Harris replied, "and I'm doing some shopping." Fontanne smiled and said that Harris's schedule would work out perfectly. One of the other actors was coming to the Lunts' home at 11:00, she said. "It would be nice if you came about one. We'll give you a little lunch." Harris was initially baffled, but quickly realized that Fontanne wished to go over their scenes together. Like so many others before her, Harris was struck by Fontanne's singlemindedness. "She was an actress who seemed to me completely taken up with her work," she said. "Nothing else for the time she was working. Of course she did all these other things—gardening, sewing and whatever she did at home—but while she was in the theatre or television [studio], that was the only thing that existed."

Despite Fontanne's age, she never wilted under the pressure of the six-day-per-week schedule. On the last day of shooting, Harris recalled, "We were still taping at midnight, and she seemed just as fresh then as when she started at nine in the morning. Her attitude was just, 'Well, when do we begin the next scene?'"

Indeed, Fontanne sometimes wore out the other actors with her requests for line rehearsals. "She and Julie Harris would sit in the corner and run their speeches over and over. Then she'd get the other actors to run lines—over and over and over again until everybody was groggy," George Schaefer said.

During the taping, Fontanne repaid Harris for the additional hours she had willingly rehearsed. One scene featured Harris lying on a couch, crying. As Fontanne leaned down to comfort her and stroke her hair, she noticed a black line of mascara running down the actress's cheek. The next shot was a close-up of Fontanne. During the few seconds Harris was off camera, Fontanne took a handkerchief and carefully wiped the smudge away while continuing to speak her dialogue. The next shot revealed an unmarked Anastasia. Fontanne knew exactly when to seize the moment. "I was watching for my opportunity. I had to wait . . . so it would be perfectly natural," she said, "and Julie knew something was wrong, so she kept perfectly still."

Anastasia was taped between August 8 and 23, 1966, and telecast on NBC on March 17, 1967. It was the last play in which either of the Lunts performed.

Jack Gould's review of the program concentrated primarily upon Fontanne's performance. His assessment reveals that she had lost none of her ability despite her age, her absence from the stage for six years, or the fact that she was acting without her husband (with the exception of some performances Lunt was forced to miss because of illness) for the first time in nearly four decades. She "registered a triumph of regal power, loneliness and realism," he said. "It was she who commanded the evening, a glowing matriarch around whom all other events revolved."

In 1970 the Lunts and Noël Coward appeared together on the "Dick Cavett Show" on ABC. The program was broadcast on February 10 and repeated on June 1. Cavett called it "the one show that people seem to recall with a slight catch in the throat and hush in the voice." Coward and the Lunts reminisced about old times and discussed the modern theatre in polished, often witty fashion.

Because of Lunt's deteriorating vision, an inspection of the studio prior to the interview was necessary. The Lunts arrived hours before the scheduled time in order to check the positioning of the chairs and rehearse their entrance. Walking down a ramp that had been especially constructed for their appearance, they "checked how many steps it took them to get to the bottom of the ramp, and decided when they would bow," said Cavett.

Characteristically, Lunt fretted that his contribution to the program would be unsatisfactory. When it was over, he apologized to Cavett for his inability to hold up his end of the conversation. But Cavett and the viewers agreed that he had been as charming and eloquent as the other guests. Jack Gould expressed his enthusiasm for a program "that combined the engaging qualities of lightly recalled nostalgia, the sophisticated stiletto, and a demonstration of genuine affection. . . . It was an enchanting show . . . and the badinage was warm and delightful."

The Lunts contemplated coming out of retirement in 1971 in order to appear in a television film called *The Royal Family of Broadway*. Leonard Spigelgass wrote a screenplay for Universal based upon the George S. Kaufman–Edna Ferber comedy *The Royal Family*. Fontanne was to star as the matriarch of the family; Lunt was to be the narrator. Other actors were to include Edward G. Robinson, Mia Farrow, Eva Marie Saint, Danny Kaye and, according to the Universal script, "four major stars yet to be announced." Fontanne prepared for the role diligently, covering two scripts with notes on her character. But the project, like so many other television possibilities, was shelved because Universal and NBC were unable to line up enough sponsors.

George Schaefer and Hallmark wanted the Lunts to appear in an original television play. Many writers were contacted and several ideas sent to the Lunts. Schaefer was certain he had found an ideal script in *Love Among the Ruins,* James Costigan's comedy about an actress and a lawyer. "The parts were tailor-made for them," Schaefer said. "They would have been magnificent." The Lunts loved the play, according to Schaefer, but were extremely reluctant to act again and eventually decided not to appear in it. Not until years later was the play produced, when Katharine Hepburn discovered the script and said she would like to act in it with Laurence Olivier. Together, they played *Love Among the Ruins* under George Cukor's direction. The Lunts watched the result and, Schaefer said, "they were glad they hadn't done it although they thought it pretty wonderful in some ways."

But the Lunts, apparently, had firmly decided never to act again. They retained a strong interest in the theatre, but only as onlookers. In 1972 they paid a visit to the American Academy of Dramatic Arts, watched attentively as scenes were performed and spoke with the students afterward. A letter from the AADA thanked them for the inspiration they had provided and detailed the progress of students in whom they had expressed particular interest.

Often asked what advice they would give to aspiring young actors, the Lunts invariably responded with three cardinal rules: (1) don't drink to excess; (2) don't tire yourself out with physical or mental activities on the day of a performance; and (3) always accept any offer to tour in a production, for in that way you can reach people who would not otherwise see you.

Beyond those somewhat superficial suggestions, Fontanne believed that an actor must "cultivate honesty. He must know the value of honesty. Honesty is tremendously important in acting his part." She felt that one could not become a good actor without first becoming a good person. "You have to cultivate strength of character," she said.

Lunt added that discipline and alertness were essential for an actor. "For instance, I don't understand anyone missing a cue," he said. "It drives me mad. I mean an entrance—late for an entrance. This, I have never understood—ever. I mean, they are paid to be there. Why should they be called?"

Both the Lunts felt it was dangerous for young actors to win success before they had become thoroughly seasoned performers. While it was understandable that a young actor would wish to reach the heights early in his career, they believed he would suffer the consequences later on. Still, they recognized that only an extraordinary individual would voluntarily delay his rise to stardom, that only one who possessed "an inward desire to be better" would turn down such an opportunity before his ability merited it.

Fontanne hoped that young actors would not be diverted by irrelevant details. "There are a few things that I find young actors are concerned with that I now know are not worth bothering about," she said. "When they sign their contract, it won't push them on any further in the world if they demand this kind of dressing room or that kind of dressing room, their name in this position and in that size on the billing. The only thing of importance is their performance when they get out on the stage."

Fontanne advised actresses not to reveal their ages. Eventually they would be regarded by the public or by producers as "too old," even if they were perfectly capable of playing characters younger than themselves. Actresses should follow her example, she felt, and conceal their ages until after they retired.

In September 1972 the Lunts decided to make their retirement complete. They elected to sell the New York town house they had owned for twenty-three years, along with most of its furnishings. (Books and a number of china tea sets were shipped to Genesee Depot.) The house was bought by Mr. and Mrs. Sidney Luria for $125,000.

"No regrets," Fontanne wrote to Tinx Whorf. "We were always working when we were there and used it since when we went to New York, which was seldom. When we were working we were nearly always tired, and the old friends that sometimes came on Sunday nights—some of them are dead and others going to be soon—so, no regrets."

In January of the following year, in an auction at Sotheby Parke Bernet, the Lunts sold their Louis XVI dressing table, their Italian eighteenth-century red lacquered bureau, the Meissen and Chinese porcelains, clocks and chandeliers. They were not the least bit nostalgic about the pieces. "For the people the things remind us of, yes we are—but not for the things themselves," Lunt said.

Unsentimentally and with determination, the Lunts had finally severed the last tie that bound them to New York and the professional theatre. They would spend the rest of their lives in a pleasant and fulfilling retirement.

Chapter Sixteen

SLOW CURTAIN

"The best thing in a way about our marriage was retirement: after all those years of work we had a long, marvellously peaceful time in the garden."

Lynn Fontanne

1962–77

Ten Chimneys occupied most of the Lunts' time during their years of retirement. "I'm busy in the greenhouse & fuss around trying to keep this place looking fairly respectable," Lunt wrote to Richard Whorf in April 1962. "It's too big & spread out & help is short but it keeps me well & I'm happy at it." Two years later he told William Le Massena he was "really up to my neck in all sorts of outdoor work. The greenhouse is a lovely sight and I have done over 400 pots in the last two weeks. It has been great fun." On his seventy-sixth birthday in 1968, he was hard at work cleaning out the garage and building a storage box for the guest-house.

During their retirement, the Lunts became more involved in the activities of Genesee Depot. In earlier years they had attended local dances, the Waukesha fair (sometimes selling food Lunt had prepared—cookies, currant jelly, vichyssoise, Swedish meat pastries, veal-and-ham pie—to benefit the local symphony orchestra) and other functions, but they stepped up their participation in the 1960s. Fontanne left Ten Chimneys less frequently than her husband, but Lunt often went into the village to shop and pick up the day's mail. Together, they occasionally visited the local tavern—only a few hundred yards from their front gate—where they were greeted with affection by the villagers as fellow Wisconsinites rather than theatrical luminaries.

They attended town meetings, sent a condolence card to the town clerk when her husband died in 1973, shopped at the local butcher and enthusiastically approved when the town chairman proposed to renovate the older buildings in Genesee Depot.

Lunt also made frequent trips to Waukesha, a few miles to the east. On one occasion Lunt had his shirts washed and ironed at a laundry in Waukesha and, when he went to pick them up, told the boy behind the counter, "I'm Alfred Lunt." The boy regarded him skeptically. "Sure," he said, "and I'm Clark Gable."

Lunt was characteristically involved in the most minute details of the running of Ten Chimneys. Once he scolded a housekeeper for working too hard. When she answered that she would have more than enough time to rest in the next life, he said, "Oh, no, you won't. You'll probably walk around heaven with a cloth in one hand and a can of polish in the other, calling, 'Come here, little angels. Your wings are dirty.' "

But Lunt ran the house according to Fontanne's wishes. One autumn she went to New York to have surgery performed and was absent from home for a week. She left meticulous instructions with Lunt and the housekeeper concerning every aspect of the daily routine. Helen Hayes and Evelyn Varden were houseguests, and one of her directives was to keep fires going in their bedrooms. The weather turned unexpectedly warm and the guests told Lunt their rooms were terribly hot. Couldn't they do without fires? they asked. He answered good-naturedly, "Lynn says you must have a fire in the fireplace and you're going to have it whether you like it or not." He added, "You know, I thought I ran this house. I thought I was really in charge. But I've discovered, with Lynn away, that she's the one who's in charge."

In fact, however, he was firmly in control, planning the daily menus and often doing the shopping. At one point he agreed to turn the menu planning over to Fontanne, at her request. For a few weeks she assumed the responsibility, but, a relative said, her menus "were so complicated and so unrelated to the capabilities of the kitchen—and of Alfred's household budget—that he quickly took back the job."

Once the Lunts admitted to themselves that their theatrical careers were over, they took to retirement eagerly and without regret. "It is wonderful not to have to do a show at night," Fontanne said. "A working actor wakes up and says, hmm, what's that? A cough? How do I feel? Will I have enough vitality tonight? On the last night of a show, with these things facing you, a dreadful tiredness comes over you and you can hardly go on. Then you tell yourself that tomorrow you can go home! You feel there is this beautiful bright future opening before you, and you can hardly wait to begin it. I don't expect anyone who hasn't been in the theatre for a long time to understand this." Lunt went so far as to tell a reporter in 1965, "I like getting old. Does that surprise you? I do like it. As I get older, I have more memories, some good, some not so good, but they're all mine."

When the Lunts looked back over their careers, their view was not nostalgic as much as it was analytical. When Dan Sullivan interviewed them for the New York *Times* in 1968, he found Fontanne eager to demonstrate a facial expression she had borrowed from Ethel Barrymore when she played in *The Second Man* in 1927. Arthur Marshall, a friend who visited them in Wisconsin and in Florida in the 1970s, was surprised and charmed to find them arguing about a scene that had been cut from their production of *The Taming of the Shrew* in 1935. "Alfred, I could have got a laugh in that scene," Marshall quoted Fontanne as saying. "Oh, no, Lynnie, no, it was a dull scene and better out of the way," Lunt replied. As usual, Fontanne had the last word, insisting, "Alfred, there was a *laugh* there!"

In addition to their two daily games of Scrabble, reading and gardening, which both enjoyed, Lunt spent much of his time cooking and painting, while Fontanne continued to design and make clothes for herself. They were given a television set by one of the national networks, but for several years the set was rarely used. Fontanne found it "deadly, deadly, deadly dull," she told Maurice Zolotow. "You sit there and you think the next thing will be something good, and you wait for an hour and a half, and nothing, absolutely nothing." The only program Lunt enjoyed was a morning cooking class from Milwaukee. The set was banished to a small sitting room next to the kitchen. "We thought of putting one of those sets with a big screen in the Studio," Fontanne said. "Then I realized that all those lovely experiences, conversation and music would be dead while we turned off the lights and watched advertising on television. So," she concluded emphatically, "there'll be no television."

But as time went on, the set was used more regularly, and apparently without much discrimination. In 1977 they indicated that their favorite program was *Upstairs, Downstairs,* not an unexpected choice. But their other favorites—"Hollywood Squares" and "Policewoman" among them—seemed unlikely selections. Fontanne was an admirer of Telly Savalas, although she disliked his program, "Kojak" ("I never know how the stories end and I never know if they're over," she said when she was ninety-two), and Lunt enjoyed the acting of Betty White and Peter Falk. "Yes," he told Zolotow, "we've changed our minds about TV—completely."

Fontanne, in fact, sometimes became so engrossed in watching television that, if she started watching a program before dinner, "it was impossible to get her to go to the table, and the only alternative was to serve her in the Yellow Room, where the television was located," according to George Bugbee.

Lunt's affection for his garden and his dairy remained as great as ever. "We're very busy indeed what with separating & washing up & churning & making cottage cheese (& cake—cheese cake)," he wrote to William Le Massena in 1972, signing the letter "Old Farmer Lunt." He shared some of the fruits of his labors with the villagers—for a small price. Although no sign was posted, the Lunts' friends in Genesee Depot knew that good values in eggs could be had at Ten Chimneys. The downstairs door was open, said Mary Sargent, the Lunts' neighbor in the early 1960s. "The eggs were there, and you could just leave your thirty-five cents and take your eggs if no one was there."

Lunt gave away more food and flowers than he sold, however, and Sargent remembered him calling to ask if she would like some red geraniums, of which she was particularly fond.

The Lunts ate as well as ever. Their food was as rich and fattening as before, but the portions were far smaller to compensate for their relative lack of exercise. Suzanne Knapp, Lunt's niece, recalled their eating habits:

> I remember tea for 4 would be accompanied by 6 Brownies—one each and then for "seconds" Lynn would *carefully* divide the remaining two into equal halves. There were always two vegetables at dinner, so their servings of meat and potatoes were smallish. And then they would eat a moderate portion of some sweet with a lovely blob of whipped cream on top.
>
> First courses were small servings. If Alfred made a rich soup it would usually be served at noon, and the rest of the luncheon would be just a little cold meat on a piece of lettuce. Except for strawberries, raspberries and tomatoes from the garden here, I don't remember that they ever ate raw fruits or vegetables.
>
> Alfred was an early riser, and his favorite breakfast was a thin slice of rye bread with sweet (unsalted) butter, a couple of *thin* slices of summer sausage, a thin slice of Swiss cheese. Lynn usually had a soft boiled egg, 1½ slices of buttered toast with orange marmalade. Alfred drank coffee, Lynn tea.
>
> After they retired dinner was always served promptly at 7 p.m. They were never "snackers." That style of eating certainly kept Lynn and Alfred going for a long time.

When Lunt was working, he dressed comfortably in an old pair of jeans, a battered straw hat and a red bandana tied around his neck. When he saw sightseers approach the gate to Ten Chimneys and peer inside, he would stroll toward them and, in a Midwestern drawl, ask what they were looking for. If they said they were trying to catch a glimpse of the Lunts, he identified himself as a farmhand and said, "Now, what do you want to see those people fer? They're not worth waitin' around fer." That was usually sufficient to send the gawkers on their way.

Mary Sargent received a phone call one morning from Fontanne, who had been told by Lunt's half-sister Louise that Sargent liked to sew. Lunt was still wearing the same pair of Russian pajamas he had worn for decades, Fontanne said. "He only likes one kind and he can't buy them anymore. I said, 'I'm not going to sleep with that bundle of rags any longer, Alfred.' If I brought them over, could you try to copy them?" Sargent not only created a duplicate pair, she also monogrammed the pockets. Later she volunteered to monogram the nightshirts he liked to use in warm weather.

Sargent recalled Fontanne as youthful and buoyant in the '60s. She "would bound up our front steps in a pink play suit," Sargent said, "looking like a child." Lunt, too, retained remarkable vitality. A television reporter who visited Ten Chimneys to interview Lunt was astonished to find him perched high on a stepladder painting murals in a stairwell.

Mary Sargent loved to receive telephone calls from Lunt. "You could hold the phone away from you," she said, "and this marvelous voice would just roll out like brown velvet." He also enjoyed teasing her, it seems, for he told her that the murals in Ten Chimneys—which he and Claggett Wilson had painted—had been done by Walt Disney.

For several years the Lunts were annoyed by trespassers on their land. Particularly irritating was the influx of hunters every fall. "People come out from the city, you know," Lunt said. "They think [the land] is theirs. All the signs we put up are all shot down. So we don't walk in the fall." In 1970 they considered establishing a state refuge on their property to protect its wildlife, but were turned down by the state of Wisconsin on two grounds: refuges of less than sixty acres were not effective in preserving game, they were told, and the conservation wardens would be hard put to enforce laws against trespassing if many small refuges were established throughout the state.

In September 1972 the town of Genesee Depot arranged to purchase twenty-seven acres adjoining the Lunts' estate, proposing to turn them into a park. Initially opposed to the purchase because of the possibility that the park would increase the likelihood of trespassers on their land, the Lunts soon reversed themselves, offering to give the town a twenty-five-acre wooded tract across the road from the proposed park land. But a group of angry citizens, who considered the price of the original twenty-seven acres exorbitant, challenged the town's plan. Although their ire was directed at the Genesee Town Board, the Lunts evidently felt their proposed gift was not appreciated and withdrew the offer.

In that same year the Lunts attended a concert performance given by Carol Channing at the Wisconsin State Fair in Milwaukee. "They came for the matinee" and sat in a steady rain, Channing said. She continued:

> They sat there in the rain and they doggedly watched the entire show. I was wearing a blonde wig and it got drenched. Afterwards they rushed backstage, and Lynnie said, "Your wig is drenched and your costumes are probably ruined. Let me take over." So she took over. She got an iron and ironed the costumes. She set my wig and dried it on the radiator. I started to help with the wig, but she said, "No, no, you must get your makeup repaired. You must get your tights on. Get yourself ready for the next show. You only have an hour. I'll take care of the costumes

and the wig." She gave Alfred jobs to do—he fastidiously took rain spots off the costumes. They pitched in and got my show together. I said to my husband, "I feel guilty. The Lunts are doing all the work." And he said, "Don't worry about it. They're very happy. They're delighted." And he was right. I looked at them carefully and I saw that they were in heaven—back in the theatre again.*

In 1975 the Lunts, no longer irritated at the citizens of Genesee Depot, gave eighteen acres of their estate to the town. As they had always used the land for picnics, they asked that Genesee Depot restrict its use to strolling in the woods and picnicking. The gift was donated at a ceremony held before 250 residents, at which Fontanne said that Genesee Depot was a mirror of the good life and the good people of the United States. "Here when a woman takes ill," she said, "a neighbor woman comes in to fix breakfast, while another comes in to do the house." Lunt recalled that he and his family had picnicked on the donated land as much as seventy-five years before. He remembered having carried pails of beer to the picnickers and one of the men having told him, "Alfred, when you grow up, don't you never take a woman who can't take in a good load of wash."

In 1977 the Lunts increased the gift by another twenty acres, leasing the land to the town for one dollar a year, with the agreement that it would be used as a nature-study area.

In 1970 the Lunts' lifetime contribution to the theatre was recognized with a special Tony award. Two years later, in honor of their fiftieth wedding anniversary,† the American National Theatre and Academy (ANTA) held a gala at the Beverly Hilton Hotel in Los Angeles. The Lunts were

---

*The Lunts' friendship with Channing began when *Gentlemen Prefer Blondes* was being cast in 1949. Anita Loos, the author of the original novel on which the musical was based, had already settled on Channing as her choice for the leading role. But Channing was not well known and she did not at all match the physical description of the character in the story. Rather than being blue-eyed and five feet two, Channing was over six feet tall with brown eyes. As a result, investors expressed their displeasure about giving her the role. Anita Loos asked the Lunts for their opinion. They went to see Channing in *Lend an Ear,* the revue in which she was playing. Afterward they asked to speak to her. Fontanne began a conversation that lasted an hour by saying, "Tell me about Lorelei." After Channing's response, she proceeded to ask such questions as, "Where did she come from?" and "Who were her mother and father?" and "Tell me how she became rich."

"Instead of auditioning me," Channing said, "we talked. Alfred asked questions. Lynn asked questions. As we talked, I talked like Lorelei because I couldn't help it. Alfred listened to me talk and I heard him laugh to himself. Then after almost an hour Alfred looked at Anita and said, 'We would like to put money into this show.' After that, everybody wanted to invest, naturally; they trusted the Lunts. For me, the whole experience was like being knighted in St. James's Court or being blessed by the Pope."

† Asked to explain the secret of fifty happy years of marriage, Fontanne replied, "Perhaps it's that we would be ourselves in the daytime and then go to the theatre and be two other people at night." Lunt was more prosaic. "She gets a salary," he said. "I get a salary. She pays for her things. I pay for mine. We share expenses. There's none of that stupid haggling about money."

presented with the first National Artist award by Donald Seawell, their longtime friend and lawyer, who also served as the president of ANTA.

The California visit was marked by one celebratory occasion after another. The Actors' Fund of America gave the Lunts a certificate of appreciation for their many benefit performances for the Fund over the years; UCLA awarded them special degrees. And on the day before the ANTA festivities, the Lunts attended a party at the Bel Air home of producer Martin Manulis (who had worked for John C. Wilson) and his wife, Katharine Bard (who had appeared in *I Know My Love*).

The party began before noon and lasted all day. Everyone who was invited had had some professional connection with the Lunts, and nearly fifty of the guests had acted in one of their companies.

Each guest was introduced during an elaborate luncheon, several of them responding with a brief speech of gratitude to the Lunts. William Le Massena reminded everyone that the guests of honor were the most severe taskmasters in the theatre. He had been in the army, he said, and he could assure everyone that the discipline there was not nearly as rigorous as that which existed in the Lunts' companies. Lunt answered that he found it difficult to understand how the assembled actors could have such fond memories when they had been treated like inmates in a concentration camp. The affection of their former colleagues was evident throughout the afternoon, as was the Lunts' depth of feeling. "You are our life," Lunt said in a brief speech.

Years before, Robert E. Sherwood, writing of his "love and respect" for the Lunts, had claimed that the same attitude prevailed among all who had worked with them. "You have only to consult any actor or actress, however humble, who has played in one of their companies," he said. "Ask the hind legs of the horse in *The Taming of the Shrew* or the unseen fellow who cast Pan's shadow in *Goat Song* . . . and you will get the same kind of fatuous admiration you are getting out of me." The unabashed emotion felt by those at the Manulises' party demonstrated the truth of Sherwood's assessment.

On the next evening—June 11, 1972—Donald Seawell presented ANTA's award to the Lunts. As he did so, he quoted Noël Coward (who was too ill to attend), who referred to the couple as "the greatest monsters in the history of show business because they demanded from everyone a degree above perfection that only they could achieve."

More than six hundred guests were present for the ceremonies and the champagne supper. Performers such as John Gielgud, George Burns, Edward G. Robinson and Henry Fonda participated in the ceremonies, which included a revue, film clips from *The Guardsman* and the Lunts' silent pictures, as well as home movies taken at Genesee Depot. Ring Lardner's poetic tribute was read aloud, as was a portion of *The White Cliffs*. Jack Benny recalled that the Lunts had had to borrow two dollars at City Hall on the day they got married. Claiming to have been a bystander who lent them the money, Benny said he would be willing to forgive the interest but he would like to receive his two dollars back.

Fontanne spoke, saying how touched she was at the outpouring of affection, and Lunt added a few thoughts of his own, including his assessment of marriage based on his fifty years with Fontanne. "Try it," he said, "you'll like it."

Later, Fontanne wrote to Tinx Whorf from Genesee Depot. Although the parties and award ceremonies were exhausting for Lunt and herself, she said, "The whole thing was an experience we will never forget."

A penalty for living a long life is that one tends to lose one's friends and relatives with increasing frequency. The Lunts suffered several particularly devastating losses during their retirement.

Lunt's sister Karin underwent heart surgery in October 1970. Initially the surgery appeared to have been successful, but, suddenly and unexpectedly, she went into a coma and died twenty-four hours afterward. Both the Lunts deeply mourned their favorite relative. Karin and her husband, George Bugbee, had often traveled with the Lunts—to England in 1953, to France two years later, and afterward journeyed together to the Scandinavian countries, the Netherlands and Belgium. After Lunt's mother died in 1955, George and Karin had moved into the Cottage, where Bugbee continues to live as of this writing.

In 1972, Jules Johnson, who had been with the Lunts for thirty-four years and was "as close to being a member of the family as you can imagine," according to Donald Seawell, suffered a diabetic stroke. After many weeks in a hospital, he was told by the doctors he could no longer continue working. He moved with his sister to Los Angeles, where he received a monthly stipend from the Lunts until he died.

Even more distressing, perhaps, was the loss of the Lunts' closest friend, Noël Coward, in 1973.

The Lunts' health, like that of their friends and relatives, became increasingly precarious. Lunt contracted pneumonia in 1965 and spent nearly a month in Passavant Memorial Hospital in Chicago. Fontanne broke her arm on a trip to New York in 1968 and the recovery period was slow. She suffered continuous pain for four months.

An operation that same year temporarily halted the deterioration in Lunt's vision, but the glaucoma could not be stopped altogether. Again in 1969 the doctors "had a go at my eye," Lunt told Margaret Webster. "I am able to see much better than I have in years, but still am unable to write by hand." The following year he had a cataract removed, delaying the onset of blindness.

Lunt's progressive loss of vision was painful and inconvenient. Fontanne had to read to him ("I can hardly complain," he said, "since my reader is the world's greatest actress"). When Paul Myers, curator of the Theatre Collection of the Library and Museum of the Performing Arts in

New York, asked him to make an appearance on behalf of the Library in 1972, Lunt answered, "I am obliged to wear heavy dark glasses, and I don't think any audience would be enchanted by the spectacle of an old actor being led about like a performing dog. It would be embarrassing for the audience and, certainly, embarrassing for me."

Lunt found it more difficult to see in the winter. He wrote to George Oppenheimer in 1975, "My eyes are off these days because of the snow which is so white and bright, it is blinding. It seems at times it comes right into the room."

Despite his impaired vision, Lunt spent many hours painting. He also continued his cooking, but noted good-humoredly in 1972, "Do you know, last night I made a sauce Béarnaise and for the first time in my life it curdled. It's pretty hard to cook by ear."

Earlier, when the Lunts visited Noël Coward at his home, White Cliffs, they had spent an evening in the company of Katharine Hepburn, Spencer Tracy and Constance Collier. Coward asked Collier, who was nearly blind, if she could see the food she was served. "Yes, darling," she answered, "but please don't give me white fish on a white plate." Lunt went her one better. "Why, that's nothing," he said. "*I've* had to eat white fish on a white plate on a white tablecloth!"

Ultimately, he could barely see at all. Any strong light was painful to him. He was unable to watch television or be outside in the sunlight. Rather than bemoan the fact, however, Lunt took his blindness as an opportunity to live more fully in the world of imagination and memory. For example, he put through a telephone call to Helen Hayes one day in the mid-1970s, beginning the conversation by saying, "I can't see anymore, I can't watch the television, I can't read, so I just sit and remember. And I had a long session of remembering you." He reminded her of the time they had played together in *Clarence* more than fifty years before. Once, he recalled, she had forgotten her lines in the middle of a scene and he had had to improvise some dialogue to cover for her.

In 1973, Lunt returned to the hospital when X-rays revealed "something the doctors don't like," as he told William Le Massena. "Not surprising in a way," he added, "as for seventy years my innards have been stripped and yanked, and tossed about. How I have managed to live this long still puzzles the medical profession."

An operation was successful—"saved my life," he wrote to Romney Brent—but left him extremely weak and unable to leave Genesee Depot for months afterward. "I have the most terrible scar you ever saw running right down the front of me . . . and now that it is stitched, I must say it looks as though I've got on a pair of corsets of Lillian Russell's." In a later letter, he added that his recovery was "surprising to everyone as they thought I was too old to survive such complicated surgery. I am tough—"

Despite the never ending series of illnesses and operations, Lunt retained his zest for life. Having many years earlier accepted the prediction of one physician that he was unlikely to live beyond his forties, he told George Schaefer, "You know, I had a long, happy life on borrowed time. How can I complain?" "Thanks to Edward [Bigg]," he wrote in August 1975, "we have been able to spend 15 hours a day in the kitchen. The house is normal, once again—and so will I be, hopefully, soon!" Even in June 1977, after he was admitted to a hospital with the cancer that would take his life within six weeks, he could write to Le Massena with apparent cheerfulness, "I have been involved in some hi-jinx in the hospital."

Fontanne's health had never been as fragile as Lunt's. She did suffer digestive problems, however. For the last forty years of her life, she followed a regimen of exercise and a low-fiber diet, to which she adhered zealously. But she was more susceptible to illness and accidents in her old age. In the fall of 1975, Fontanne, then eighty-seven years old, injured her shin. Even after ten weeks, the wound would not heal and she required a skin graft. Two months after her surgery, Lunt told Le Massena, "Lynn's wound is still behaving rather badly & she may have to return to hospital again! The damned thing refuses to heal properly." By February 1976, however, the wound had finally closed and she was able to move about freely once more.

Whenever she could, she took daily exercise, walking about the farm for two miles each day during warm weather, and pedaling an indoor bicycle in her bedroom when the climate prevented her going outside. She often managed to read a book while riding the bicycle.

In the mid-1970s, Lunt's favorite pastime, gardening, was severely limited by his physical condition. So many of his stomach muscles had been removed and those that remained were so weak that he was no longer able to perform many of the functions he had previously taken for granted. One day he bent over to pick some vegetables and found he could not straighten up. He fell to his knees as the cane on which he was leaning sank slowly into the sodden ground. Unable to rise, he lay down and remained in that position for two hours until he was discovered.

When he knew the end of his life was approaching, Lunt spoke to Donald Seawell about his premonition that he would not survive another operation. He asked Seawell to make preparations for Fontanne's care in the event of his death.

George Bugbee wrote to Alan Hewitt on July 11, 1977, "Alfred currently is very uncomfortable with pain most of the time. He is to go back to the hospital about the first of August. Just what is ahead is not clear." A few days later Lunt wrote to Helen Hayes, speaking frankly of his condition. "This great hulk of mine is not easy to turn around," he said, adding, "This convalescence seems endless."

His declining health would not permit him to wait for the scheduled August visit to the hospital. On July 21, 1977, the day after he wrote to Hayes, he complained to Fontanne of intense pain. She telephoned Dr.

Bigg, who instructed her to call for an ambulance at once. Lunt did not want to leave Ten Chimneys, but Fontanne insisted. He was taken to Northwestern Memorial Hospital in Chicago.

A diagnosis of prostatic cancer was established and surgery recommended. Carol Channing called Lunt before the operation and, during a conversation that lasted nearly two hours, found him apparently as cheerful as ever. "Of course, they all know me at this hospital," she recalled him saying. "I left my liver on the second floor, my aorta on the fourth floor, my kidneys on the fifth floor. Now here I am back in the same old room and I feel right at home. After all, most of me is here."

Channing said, "Alfred, I'm not going to worry about you because you still have such a sense of humor." Then, she said, "he stayed silent. He knew very well what was happening to him."

Earlier he had said, "I've been so near death so many times that the prospect of dying doesn't bother me at all. The only thing that I do mind is a long, painful, boring illness." Mercifully, he was spared that ordeal. After undergoing two operations within a week, he was placed in an intensive-care unit and, though conscious, remained in critical condition. The cancer continued to advance at an alarming rate, and on August 1 he underwent still another operation.

Fontanne, who had initially remained at Ten Chimneys because Dr. Bigg thought her too frail to travel, was driven to Chicago by George Bugbee the following day. The two of them remained in Lunt's hospital room for several hours, Fontanne holding the hand of her unconscious husband. She and Bugbee then returned to Genesee Depot, where they later received a telephone call informing them that the doctors were considering yet another operation. It was clear, however, that his life could be prolonged only briefly; recovery was impossible. Fontanne and Bugbee agreed that Lunt's request not to undergo the indignity of "a long, painful, boring illness" should be honored, and asked that no further surgery be performed. Several hours afterward, the telephone rang again. Lunt had died early that morning: at 4:05 a.m. on August 3, less than two weeks short of his eighty-fifth birthday.

1977–83

Alfred Lunt's funeral was held on Friday, August 5, at 2:30 p.m. at Forest Home Cemetery in Milwaukee. At Fontanne's request, only about thirty relatives and close friends were present. The day, rainy and dark, reflected the mourners' moods. The Reverend Michael Stolpman, chaplain and vicar to the Episcopal Bishop of Milwaukee, presided. As he began to speak, bolts of lightning were accompanied by loud thunderclaps—a theatrical touch that might have pleased the actor whose death was being mourned. As the thunder subsided, Donald Seawell spoke briefly. "Nothing I may say . . . can do justice to that noble spirit. How often . . . shall we recall, with happiness, Alfred's many-faceted genius, his gentle humor, his quiet dignity, his devotion to work and perfection."

Fontanne, attired in a black dress, hat and veil, maintained her composure throughout the ceremonies. After the service, but before the burial, she returned to Genesee Depot, followed by the other members of the funeral procession.

Lunt was buried in the family plot, with his mother, father, sister Inez and his half-brother and half-sister, Carl and Karin. His grave was marked with an unimposing granite slab one foot high.

Before leaving for Wisconsin to attend the funeral services, Alan Hewitt had arranged with Charles Bowden to organize a tribute to Lunt with the cooperation of the League of New York Theatres and Producers. At 7:55 on the evening of August 5, the lights of all Broadway theatre marquees but one were extinguished for one minute. The exception was the Lunt-Fontanne, whose lights continued to blaze. Numerous actors and actresses who had worked with the Lunts stood under the marquee, as did a number of old friends, including Helen Hayes, Lillian Gish and Marian Seldes.*

At the same moment Fontanne was presiding over a gathering of friends at Genesee Depot. Hewitt told the group that New York's theatres had just been darkened. The guests observed a moment of silence, broken when Fontanne raised her glass of champagne and proposed a simple toast: "To Alfred."

Throughout the evening she betrayed few signs of grief. Perhaps, indeed, her dominant reaction was one of gratitude. As she later said, "Toward the end he was in a lot of pain, so it was really a great relief." The flag in front of the post office in Genesee Depot was lowered to half-staff. A cigar box at the local grocery store was placed under a hand-lettered sign saying, "Alfred Lunt Flowers." The money that was collected—perhaps fifteen or twenty dollars—was used to buy a bouquet for Fontanne.

Telegrams and letters arrived at Ten Chimneys by the thousands. All the years that the Lunts had played in New York and toured throughout the country had made them seem to many like members of the family, and much of the mail Fontanne received indicated that the letter-writers, who were often complete strangers, felt a sense of real personal loss.

Lunt was mourned in England as well. John Gielgud's letter to the *Times* of London summed up the feelings of the British theatrical community. "Witty and modest, a perfectionist in anything he undertook," the letter said, "Alfred Lunt's generosity of spirit and creative skill was ever a

*The event marked only the third time the lights of Broadway had been extinguished. Gertrude Lawrence had been the first to be so honored, in 1952, and the death of Oscar Hammerstein 2nd was similarly observed in 1960.

wonder and a joy, both to the public and to his fellow players, and his devotion to his dazzling partner brought to their performances together a perfect combination which we can never hope to see again, but which all of us who had the privilege of seeing them will always remember with admiration and delight."

Fontanne returned to her native England later that August, escorted by Donald Seawell. They had planned to fly on the Concorde, but at the last minute their flight was canceled by a strike. Space was found on a 747, but the substitution meant they had to sit up all night. They had intended to see a play each night of their stay, but when they arrived early on the morning of the 25th, Seawell said, "I know you're too tired to go to a play tonight." "Nonsense," Fontanne answered, "pick one for me."

That night they watched Ralph Richardson and Celia Johnson in *The Kingfisher*. "What happened that night happened every night when we went to the theatre," Seawell said: the audience broke into cheers as they saw Fontanne. "She was treated as royalty," he said. "At every play we attended, she was recognized and the audience gave her a standing ovation. At the Drury Lane [Theatre], Prince Charles was there. He came down and insisted that she sit in the Royal Box." The theatre in which Lynn Fontanne had made her debut seventy-two years before as a frightened chorus girl rang with cheers in 1977 as she bowed, first to the balcony, then to the orchestra. It seems remarkably fitting that that first play had been *Cinderella*.

Although Fontanne had lived in America for many years and had come to love her adopted country, she continued to think of herself as British. She hoped that she would be given a title by the British government in recognition of her contributions to the English theatre. She told others she believed it unlikely she would be honored so late in her life, but it was clear to her friends that she felt hurt when each year's Honors List was issued without her name.*

During her visit Fontanne presented a copy of *King Lear* to the British Theatre Museum: the script, annotated with Ellen Terry's handwritten notes dating from the time Terry had played Cordelia with Henry Irving in 1892, which had been given by Terry to Fontanne so many years earlier. Fontanne, who had bound the script in brocade, presented it to Donald Sinden, who accepted on behalf of the Museum.

While in London, Fontanne found herself requiring constant personal attention. Consequently, Suzanne Knapp flew to England to be with her. They returned to Wisconsin in September. During Fontanne's absence, several of the Lunts' friends had been arranging memorial services for Lunt in New York, Los Angeles and elsewhere. Fontanne felt that the

---

*Fontanne's loyalties to the country of her birth and to the United States are graphically displayed at Ten Chimneys. Over a portrait of herself by Jane de Glehn, Fontanne hung three small flags: a British flag on the left and American flags in the center and on the right. Her decorative arrangement is still intact as of this writing.

services would prove to be too much of a strain, however, and asked that they be canceled. Besides, she wrote to Alan Hewitt, "it is time we stopped crying."

By November 1977 she had become sufficiently reconciled to Lunt's death to give away some of his clothes and effects. Hewitt received a solid gold cigarette case. She offered William Le Massena Lunt's pocket watch, adding, "I have some more things of Alfred's that I would like you to have. There is that lovely brown and white check suit and his evening clothes. What size shoe do you take? Because there are all kinds here. And how I would love you to be wearing them!" When Le Massena visited Genesee Depot, he was invited to select whatever he liked from Lunt's wardrobe.

If Fontanne was initially comforted by the belief that Lunt's death had spared him more pain, the thought did not console her forever. Six months later, in a quivering voice, she told an interviewer her life was empty without her husband: "We were together all the time, and I'm very lonely." Charles Bowden said that when Lunt died, "I think half of her life went with him." Le Massena added, "I think after he died she was just treading water until the time that was chosen for her to go."

She was never alone at Genesee Depot. George Bugbee spent most of his time at Ten Chimneys, living in the Cottage. As one aspect of running the estate after Lunt's death, he planned all the meals, and he and Fontanne always had dinner and tea together. Often, too, they would drink a glass of sherry at noon. Bugbee cared for Fontanne with affectionate diligence and, when he had to go to Chicago on business, always made sure a housekeeper was in attendance twenty-four hours a day. Most of the housekeepers he hired also had training as nurses and were thus able to monitor Fontanne's health.

Still, no one could take Lunt's place in her life. Although she continued reading, watching television and playing games of Solitaire, much of the zest she had always displayed seemed to be ebbing from her. Throughout her life she had been prompt and attentive in her correspondence, but in the years after Lunt's death she would often hand letters to her secretary, saying, "You answer them."

In an attempt to restore her *joie de vivre*, George Schaefer suggested to Fontanne that she might want to make one more professional appearance. Since the proposed film of *The Royal Family* had not come to fruition, he recommended that she act in the play on the London stage. He contacted a British production company and found "they would have leaped to have Lynn Fontanne." He called to tell her, "It's all set. It's just up to you to let me know when you want to do it." She asked if she could give him her answer within a week. "I don't know if I can learn words anymore," she told Schaefer. Later she said, "In three days I had learned only three lines, and not very well, so I told him, 'It's no good.'"

Instead, Schaefer spent several days at Genesee Depot in early 1978 taping a "conversation for television." Six hours of interviews were condensed into one for showing on the Public Broadcasting network in 1980.

In one respect, Fontanne told Schaefer, Lunt's death liberated her from the necessity of having to conceal her age. During their conversation, she finally admitted she was ninety years old. "I lied in the beginning," when she and Lunt first met, she said, "because I was afraid he wouldn't like me. And I lied and lied and lied. I lied to everybody. I lie very well, being an actress, naturally." But with Lunt no longer living, there was no reason to maintain the fiction. She believed to the end that Lunt had been convinced she was three months younger than he.

Fontanne traveled to New York in April 1978 for a three-week visit, staying in Dorothy Stickney's townhouse. Together they attended a performance of *Hello, Dolly!* with Carol Channing at the Lunt-Fontanne Theatre. Fontanne, Stickney and several friends also attended a small party given by Armina Marshall, the widow of Lawrence Langner of the Theatre Guild. Marshall was surprised at her appearance. "She had shrunk from this tall woman down to a small little lady," Marshall said. "It amazed me so, because I was always looking up at Lynn and suddenly she was tinier. And she said to me, 'Armina, all of us here have lost our husbands,' and I said, 'Yes, we have, we're survivors, for better or for worse.'"

Although she had passed her ninetieth birthday, she continued to walk two miles each day or to ride her stationary bicycle for three quarters of an hour. She spent most of her time in the library at Ten Chimneys, where her meals were often served. She read voraciously ("I read anything so long as it's well written," she said. "I can't bear badly written things"), but her taste inclined more and more to Barbara Cartland's romance novels.

Fontanne sent Cartland a fan letter at her house in Hertfordshire, England, asking her to visit Ten Chimneys. The novelist responded in May 1978, saying that she would treasure Fontanne's letter and appreciated the invitation, but could not spare the time for a visit, as she was kept busy writing a prodigious number of romances each year. She asked her publisher, Bantam Books, to send Fontanne complimentary copies of two of her latest books.

Fontanne continued to travel, undaunted by her years. In October 1978 she returned to England once again, accompanied by Suzanne Knapp, staying at the Dorchester Hotel in London. Early in 1980 she and George Bugbee journeyed to Denver so that Fontanne could present a National Artist Award to Henry Fonda on behalf of ANTA and dedicate the latest addition to the Denver Center for the Performing Arts. Fonda wept as he accepted the award, saying he never "dreamed that the reigning greatest lady of the theatre would lay this on me."

In one of her last interviews, given to a reporter for the Milwaukee *Journal* in 1980 in conjunction with the Public Television showing of the program she and George Schaefer had made, *The Lunts: A Life in the Theatre,* Fontanne was once again asked how she and her late husband had managed to live together so agreeably for fifty-five years. She attributed it to the roles they played, saying, "In the play, you see, we were always madly in love with each other, and that always put everything all right."

Reactions to Schaefer's televised interview with Fontanne poured in to Ten Chimneys. Hundreds of letters came from individuals throughout the United States who had no professional connection with the theatre but wanted Fontanne to know how favorably she had impressed them. Among the performers who wrote to congratulate Fontanne on her lucidity and charm were Ruth Gordon, Lynn Redgrave, Simon Oakland, Alan Hewitt and Efrem Zimbalist, Jr. Helen Hayes wrote, "Last night you gave me one more glorious experience to treasure. . . . You are an everlasting wonder."

But many were shocked by Fontanne's appearance and demeanor. She looked as if she had aged thirty years since Lunt's death, appearing frail and unsteady. Her memory was so shaky that Schaefer had to prompt her continually. Often she seemed in a world of her own.

On December 6, 1980, Fontanne celebrated her ninety-third birthday in especially festive style. As one of five recipients of honors bestowed by the John F. Kennedy Center for lifetime achievements in the performing arts, she attended a champagne reception at the White House, then sat in the Presidential Box next to Jimmy Carter at the Kennedy Center as Jason Robards, Jr., and Beverly Sills led an audience of more than two thousand in singing "Happy Birthday" to her. Robards said, in his speech, "Alfred Lunt and Lynn Fontanne worked together on the stage nearly every day for decades with a dedication to the theatre matched only by their devotion to one another."

Fontanne, along with James Cagney, Leontyne Price, Leonard Bernstein and Agnes de Mille, had been given a medal by the President at a State Department banquet the night before. Asked for her reaction to the ceremony and her award, she could only say, "I'm bedazzled."

The ceremony marked the culmination of the hundreds of honors she had received over the years. It was the zenith of her career. No greater height could be reached, no more significant recognition could be made of her lifetime in the theatre.

Gradually, the signs of old age became more noticeable. By 1981, Fontanne was no longer able to take her accustomed walk. She lost interest in inviting visitors to Genesee Depot and soon was unable to function without a nurse. Her ability to concentrate steadily diminished. Sometimes, Suzanne Knapp noticed, she would begin a game of Solitaire, then drift away and forget what she had been doing.

Fontanne collapsed one evening in 1983, falling to the floor as she was taking her medicine. She was driven to Waukesha Memorial Hospital, where X-rays were taken to determine if she had broken any bones. No serious damage was found, and she was sent home. But she never really recovered from the fall and the accompanying shock. Within a month she was unable to come downstairs. She spent the last six weeks of her life in her bed.

On a Friday evening in July 1983, it was apparent to George Bugbee that Fontanne was near death. He and the nurse in attendance made her as comfortable as possible and remained with her until she fell asleep. The following morning—Saturday, July 30—the nurse discovered that Fontanne had died during the night. She was ninety-five years old and clearly had been awaiting death for some time. Officially, she died of pneumonia and the "gradual slowing down of old age," as Edward Bigg put it, but those who loved her knew that at least an equal contribution to her death was loneliness for her husband of more than half a century.

Fontanne was buried two days later in Forest Home Cemetery, at her husband's side. The private funeral was attended by about twenty-five friends and relatives. Again, as he had at Lunt's memorial service, Donald Seawell spoke the eulogy. This time the weather was bright and sunny, in contrast to the lightning and thunder that had accompanied his eulogy for Lunt. "It made you think of an English June day," said Suzanne Knapp, who added that the weather on the days of their respective funerals "was so like their personalities."

A Milwaukee newspaper ran an editorial cartoon showing Fontanne entering the gates of heaven. Overhead, a sign on a marquee reads, "Lunt, Fontanne—Together Again." An angel, reading a copy of *Variety*, watches her going through the gates and calls, "Break a leg, Miss Fontanne."

Epilogue

Fontanne left an estate worth nearly two million dollars, primarily the value of the land and the buildings. After inheritance taxes totaling approximately $900,000 were paid, very little cash remained. Ten Chimneys was given to George Bugbee, with a provision that it go to his daughter, Suzanne Knapp, after his death. They briefly considered the possibility of turning the house into either a theatrical museum or a home for elderly actors. But its location militated against both possibilities. Genesee Depot was too far off the conventional theatrical path to serve as a good location for a museum; and actors, regardless of how old they become and how long it has been since they were last employed, always believe that the next telephone call will bring the offer of a job. Consequently, most elderly actors want to remain in or near New York so they can begin work immediately.

The town chairman of Genesee Depot spoke of building a memorial of some sort to the Lunts, but the suggestion did not become reality.

Many of Fontanne's gowns were given to a Catholic girls' school. The remainder of her wardrobe (as well as many of Lunt's clothes and personal effects) was sold at auction in Milwaukee. About ninety people attended, bidding on thousands of hats, dresses, suits, costume jewelry and other items. The winning bids "were not lavish," an article in the Milwaukee *Journal* reported, ranging from $10 to $120. Even if one accepts the idea that the items sold were not of great intrinsic value, one would have expected more interest from a public in the grip of the nostalgia wave of the 1980s, especially as it concerned theatrical figures. How to explain such an apparent lack of interest in owning an item that had belonged to the Lunts and was therefore a fragment of theatrical history?

The answer is that the Lunts had been largely forgotten by 1983. Television anchorpeople who had obviously never heard of her reported the death of "Lynn *Fontaine*" on various stations throughout the country. But the public's knowledge of the Lunts' place in history had faded at least a decade earlier. In the late 1970s, Harold Clurman wrote that half the graduate students in his theatre class at Hunter College looked at him blankly when he included Alfred Lunt as one of America's foremost twentieth-century actors.

In large part, this was understandable. The Lunts had not appeared on stage since 1960. Their appearances on television had been few, their film work almost nil. *The Guardsman* was rarely shown, either theatrically or on television. It is not surprising that most people under thirty-five were unaware of their careers.

But the ignorance of the Lunts included more than the youngest generation of Americans. Many in their forties and fifties had only the vaguest recollections of their names and none whatever of their significance. Some people dimly recalled that they might have been a dance team. Were they a nineteenth-century vaudeville act? some wondered. One middle-aged woman with a self-proclaimed interest in the theatrical world hazarded the guess that they had been well-known acrobats.

Late in 1983 the Theatre Guild organized a tribute to the Lunts. Although the event was held in New York, where the Lunts' names might have been thought still to be widely recognized, and although it was known that such famous personalities as Helen Hayes, Carol Channing and Douglas Fairbanks, Jr., would speak, hundreds of seats at the Lunt-Fontanne Theatre were not filled for the event.

To those who know of the Lunts' almost unbroken string of successes over a period of nearly forty years, of their enormous appeal to audiences throughout the country, of their direct and indirect influence on many of the finest actors of stage and screen, it is the profoundest irony that these most versatile and accomplished of American actors should have so quickly faded into relative obscurity.

In their time, no performers were more influential or more highly respected. Few theatrical personalities practiced their professions over as long a period. Lunt's career as an actor spanned fifty-two years; Fontanne was active for a remarkable sixty-one. She began in the theatre when England's most prominent nineteenth-century actress, Ellen Terry, was nearing the end of her career, and was fortunate enough to receive personal instruction from the legendary performer. When Lunt first acted professionally, America's leading performers included Mrs. Fiske, William Gillette, Julia Marlowe and E. H. Sothern, George M. Cohan, George Arliss, Maude Adams, Otis Skinner and Billie Burke—names that have long since receded into the cobwebs of memory. Lunt and Fontanne both began their careers on Broadway before John F. Kennedy was born. They were regarded as America's greatest acting couple before *The Jazz Singer* became the first talking picture.

The Lunts retained that position of eminence during the Depression, an era in which the serious theatre was dominated by dramas of social protest. Their stars remained as bright as ever following the Second World War, when a roster of great new theatrical names, such as Marlon Brando, Montgomery Clift and Julie Harris, came into prominence. They directly affected Clift and Harris by performing with them and serving as exemplars of all that was superior in America's theatrical tradition. Uta Hagen, whose attitude toward her profession was profoundly affected when she appeared in *The Sea Gull,* continues at this writing to be one of the foremost teachers of acting in New York, passing on to her students the sense of discipline and craft she learned from the Lunts. Thus, Alfred Lunt's and Lynn Fontanne's techniques continue in use today, although few young actors are aware of their origins. One has only to watch a Robert Altman film to see how fully accepted their use of overlapping dialogue has become.

Those who knew and worked with the Lunts were privileged to observe their achievements at first hand. As I interviewed many of those actors, directors and producers, I was intrigued to hear the same observation repeated again and again, almost in the same words: the Lunts' methods were well in advance of those of other artists in the American theatre, and today's actors and directors still have much to learn from their example.

The Lunts kept alive the tradition of the actor-manager, a tradition that dates back at least to the sixteenth century, when wandering troupes of *commedia dell'arte* performers in Italy were generally headed by the troupes' foremost actors. These individuals served not only as the companies' leading players, they also assembled the members of the companies, saw to their economic well-being, selected the dramatic materials they would play, and, because they had attained positions of such power and importance, were able to exert artistic control over the productions.

The roster of actor-managers includes such historic names as Molière, David Garrick, John Philip Kemble, Sarah Bernhardt, Eleonora Duse, Edwin Booth, Constantin Stanislavski and Henry Irving. All of them are revered for their many contributions to shaping the theatrical milieux of their time. Lunt and Fontanne were in the same tradition and, in their time, called forth the same reverence. Their eminence as actors had the almost inevitable result of leading them into directing: other actors, admiring the Lunts' achievements, eager to listen to and learn from them, willingly accepted their authority in all artistic matters. And as the Lunts extended their concern from their own performances to the performances of all the actors with whom they were working, they became eager to assume the producer's function as well: to select the members of their companies, choose the plays in which they would appear and determine where, when and under what conditions they would perform.

When the Lunts died, the tradition of the actor-manager in America died with them. Perhaps never again will it be possible for performers to influence the American theatre as profoundly as did the Lunts.

Alfred Lunt and Lynn Fontanne fought valiantly but vainly to reestablish repertory as a viable theatrical system in New York, believing it to be more conducive to the production of first-rate works of art than the long-run system. They maintained an ensemble company for years despite the financial disadvantages it entailed. They struggled successfully to maintain the interest of audiences outside New York City in the legitimate theatre. It may reasonably be argued that the decentralization of American theatre today, with the establishment of fine professional companies throughout the country (most of which offer plays in repertory and employ actors on a long-term ensemble basis) owes much to the efforts of the Lunts and a handful of other actors who refused to limit their appearances to New York when it would have been far easier (and far more profitable) to do so. If not for the dedication of these actors, interest in the legitimate theatre outside New York might have been extinguished forever.

With a determination bordering upon fanaticism, the Lunts devoted themselves to the pursuit of perfection in the theatre. No effort was too great, no rehearsal too long, no detail too small for them in their unceasing attempts to give the finest possible performance on every occasion, in New York, in London or on tour. Perhaps no other performers before or since have so deservedly earned reputations as actors who brought an undiminished enthusiasm to every performance of every play, with the result that (excepting their work in the plays they appeared in from 1945–57) their productions consistently improved rather than deteriorated the longer they ran.

The Lunts brought wit, style and grace to every production with which they were associated. They brightened even the most somber dramas with moments of humor and invested the most frivolous comedies with a depth that could not have been suspected from a reading of the script.

Can any other American twentieth-century theatrical figures be said to have influenced their theatre so profoundly?

Finally, one remembers the fundamental decency of Alfred Lunt and

Lynn Fontanne: their fidelity and devotion to one another, their loyalty to friends, their compassion, their dignity in the face of adversity and serious illness, their humor, their integrity, their warmth, their charm. They embodied a goodness rarely seen in any walk of life. In the theatre, they demonstrated that success is possible in that volatile world without undue temperament or ambition so great that it overrides all human considerations. The Lunts' character and behavior, as well as their brilliance as artists, combined to set them apart from so many other leading figures in theatrical history. Their example serves as a beacon for all who would enter the profession.

Bibliography

I. BOOKS

Abbott, George, *Mister Abbott*. New York: Random House, 1963.

Adams, Samuel Hopkins, *Alexander Woollcott: His Life and His World*. Freeport, N.Y.: Books for Libraries Press, 1946.

Anonymous, *Current Biography, 1941*. New York: The H. W. Wilson Company, 1941.

Anonymous, "To Architects: Stop! Look! Listen!" in *Theatre Arts Anthology,* Rosamond Gilder, ed. New York: Theatre Arts Books, 1950.

Atkinson, Brooks, *Broadway*. New York: The Macmillan Co., 1970.

Baxter, John, *Hollywood in the Thirties*. London: Tantivy Press, 1968.

Beaton, Cecil, and Kenneth Tynan, *Persona Grata*. New York: G. P. Putnam's Sons, 1954.

Behrman, S. N., *People in a Diary*. Boston: Little, Brown and Company, 1972.

Bentley, Eric, *The Dramatic Event: An American Chronicle*. New York: Horizon Press, 1954.

Blum, Daniel, *Great Stars of the American Stage: A Pictorial Record*. New York: Greenburg Publisher, 1952.

Bogard, Travis, Richard Moody and Walter J. Meserve, *The Revels History of the Drama in English,* Volume VIII: *American Drama*. London: Methuen & Co., 1977.

Bosworth, Patricia, *Montgomery Clift*. New York: Harcourt Brace Jovanovich, 1978.

Brown, John Mason, *The Ordeal of a Playwright: Robert E. Sherwood and the Challenge of War*. New York: Harper & Row, 1970.

Brown, John Mason, *Seeing More Things*. New York: McGraw-Hill, 1948.

Brown, John Mason, *The Worlds of Robert E. Sherwood*. New York: Harper & Row, 1962.

Burke, Billie (with Cameron Shipp), *With a Feather on My Nose*. New York: Appleton-Century-Crofts, 1948.

Burns, George, *Living It Up, or, They Still Love Me in Altoona*. New York: G. P. Putnam's Sons, 1976.

Cavett, Dick, and Christopher Porterfield, *Cavett*. New York: Harcourt Brace Jovanovich, 1974.

Churchill, Allen, *The Theatrical 20s*. New York: McGraw-Hill Book Company, 1975.

Clurman, Harold, *All People Are Famous (Instead of an Autobiography)*. New York: Harcourt Brace Jovanovich, 1974.

Clurman, Harold, *Lies Like Truth*. New York: Grove Press, 1958.

Cocroft, Thoda, *Great Names and How They Are Made*. Chicago: The Dartnell Press, 1941.

Cole, Toby, and Helen Krich Chinoy, eds., *Actors on Acting*. New Revised Edition. New York: Crown Publishers, 1970.

Courtney, Marguerite, *Laurette*. New York: Rinehart & Company, 1955.

Coward, Noël, *Future Indefinite*. Garden City, N.Y.: Doubleday and Company, 1954.

Coward, Noël, *The Noël Coward Diaries*, edited by Graham Payn and Sheridan Morley. Boston: Little, Brown and Company, 1982.

Coward, Noël, *Play Parade*. Garden City, N.Y.: Doubleday, Doran and Company, 1933.

Coward, Noël, *Present Indicative*. Garden City, N.Y.: Doubleday, Doran and Company, 1937.

Crawford, Cheryl, *One Naked Individual*. New York: The Bobbs-Merrill Company, 1977.

Crow, William L., *Wisconsin Lives of National Interest*. Appleton, Wis.: C. C. Nelson Publishing Company, 1937.

Daubeny, Peter, *My World of Theatre*. London: Jonathan Cape, 1971.

Eaton, Walter Pritchard, *The Theatre Guild: The First Ten Years*. Freeport, N.Y.: Books for Libraries Press, 1929 (reprinted 1970).

Eustis, Morton, "On the Road with the Lunts" in *Theatre Arts Anthology*, Rosamond Gilder, ed. New York: Theatre Arts Books, 1950.

Eustis, Morton, *Players at Work: Acting According to the Actors*. New York: Theatre Arts Books, 1937.

Forsee, Aylesa, *My Love and I Together: The Story of Six Famous Marriages*. Philadelphia: Macrae Smith Company, 1961.

Freedley, George, *The Lunts*. New York: The Macmillan Company, 1958.

Funke, Lewis, and John E. Booth, eds., *Actors Talk About Acting*. New York: Avon Books, 1961.

Gelb, Barbara and Arthur, *O'Neill*. New York: A Delta Book, 1960.

Goodman, Randolph, *Drama on Stage*. New York: Holt, Rinehart and Winston, 1961.

Gordon, Max (with Lewis Funke), *Max Gordon Presents*. New York: Bernard Geis Associates, 1963.

Gray, James, *Pine, Stream & Prairie*. New York: Alfred A. Knopf, 1945.

Hagen, Uta (with Haskel Frankel), *Respect for Acting*. New York: Macmillan Publishing Co., 1973.

Hagen, Uta, *Sources: A Memoir*. New York: Performing Arts Journal Publications, 1983.

Hayes, Helen, *On Reflection*. New York: M. Evans and Company, 1968.

Helburn, Theresa, *A Wayward Quest*. Boston: Little, Brown and Company, 1960.

Hewitt, Alan, "Repertory to Residuals" in *The American Theatre: A Sum of Its Parts*, Henry B. Williams, ed. New York: Samuel French, 1971.

Houseman, John, *Run-Through*. New York: Simon and Schuster, 1972.

Langill, Ellen, *Carroll College: The First Century*. Waukesha, Wis.: Carroll College Press, 1980.

Langner, Lawrence, *The Magic Curtain*. New York: E. P. Dutton & Co., 1951.

Laufe, Abe, *The Wicked Stage*. New York: Frederick Ungar Publishing Co., 1978.

Le Gallienne, Eva, *With a Quiet Heart*. New York: The Viking Press, 1953.

Lesley, Cole, *Remembered Laughter: The Life of Noel Coward*. New York: Alfred A. Knopf, 1976.

Lesley, Cole, Graham Payn and Sheridan Morley, *Noël Coward and His Friends*. New York: William Morrow and Company, 1979.

Mander, Raymond, and Joe Mitchenson, *Theatrical Companion to Coward*. London: Rockliff, 1957.

Maney, Richard, *Fanfare*. New York: Harper & Brothers, 1957.

Maney, Richard, "To Err Is Human" in *The Passionate Playgoer*, George Oppenheimer, ed. New York: The Viking Press, 1958.

Manvell, Roger, *Ellen Terry*. New York: G. P. Putnam's Sons, 1968.

Marion, Frances, *Off with Their Heads! A Serio-Comic Tale of Hollywood*. New York: The Macmillan Company, 1972.

McClintic, Guthrie, *Me and Kit*. Boston: Little, Brown and Company, 1955.

Meredith, Scott, *George S. Kaufman and His Friends*. Garden City, N.Y.: Doubleday & Co., 1974.

Meserve, Walter J., *Robert E. Sherwood: Reluctant Moralist*. New York: Pegasus, 1970.

Morehouse, Ward, *Matinee Tomorrow: Fifty Years of Our Theater*. New York: McGraw-Hill Book Co., 1949.

Morley, Sheridan, *A Talent to Amuse: A Biography of Noël Coward*. Garden City, N.Y.: Doubleday & Company, 1969.

Morris, Lloyd, *Curtain Time*. New York: Random House, 1953.

Mosel, Tad, with Gertrude Macy, *Leading Lady: The World and Theatre of Katharine Cornell*. Boston: Little, Brown and Company, 1978.

Nadel, Norman, *A Pictorial History of the Theatre Guild*. New York: Crown Publishers, 1969.

Nathan, George Jean, *Encyclopedia of the Theatre*. Rutherford, N.J.: Fairleigh Dickinson Press, 1940 (reprinted 1970).

Nathan, George Jean, *The Establishment of a Nation, or Three-Sheets in the Wind*. New York: Alfred A. Knopf, 1942.

Nathan, George Jean, *The Theatre of the Moment*. New York: Alfred A. Knopf, 1936.

Nesbitt, Cathleen, *A Little Love and Good Company*. London: Faber & Faber, 1975.

Olivier, Laurence, *Confessions of an Actor*. New York: Simon and Schuster, 1982.

Oppenheimer, George, "The Great Days of Broadway" in *The Rise and Fall of the Matinee Idol*, Anthony Curtis, ed. London: Weidenfeld and Nicolson, 1974.

Ormsbee, Helen, *Backstage with Actors*. New York/London: Benjamin Blom, 1938 (reissued 1969).

Parker, H. T., "*Reunion in Vienna* in Boston" in *The American Theatre as Seen by Its Critics, 1752–1934*, Montrose J. Moses and John Mason Brown, eds. New York: W. W. Norton & Company, 1934.

Priestley, J. B., *Particular Pleasures*. New York: Stein and Day, 1975.

Runkel, Phillip M., *Alfred Lunt and Lynn Fontanne: A Bibliography*. Waukesha, Wis.: Carroll College Press, 1978.

Sheaffer, Louis, *O'Neill: Son and Artist*. Boston: Little, Brown and Company, 1973.

Sherwood, Robert E., "The Lunts" in *The Passionate Playgoer*, George Oppenheimer, ed. New York: The Viking Press, 1958.

Sichel, Pierre, *The Jersey Lily*. Englewood Cliffs, N.J.: Prentice-Hall, 1958.

Skinner, Cornelia Otis, *Life with Lindsay & Crouse*. Boston: Houghton Mifflin Company, 1976.

Skinner, R. Dana, *Our Changing Theatre*. New York: Dial Press, 1931.

Skolsky, Sidney, *Times Square Tintypes*. New York: Ives Washburn, 1930.

Stern, G. B., *And Did He Stop and Speak to You?* Chicago: Henry Regnery Company, 1958.

Stevens, Ashton, *Actorviews*. Chicago: Covici-McGee Co., 1923.

Tarkington, Booth, *On Plays, Playwrights and Playgoers: Selections from the Letters of Booth Tarkington to George C. Tyler and John Peter Toohey, 1918–1925*, edited by Alan S. Downer. Princeton: Princeton University Library, 1959.

Taubman, Howard, *The Making of the American Theatre*. New York: Coward-McCann, 1965.

Teichmann, Howard, *Smart Aleck*. New York: William Morrow and Company, 1976.

Terry, Ellen, *Ellen Terry's Memoirs,* with notes and additional biographical chapters by Edith Craig and Christopher St. John. New York: G. P. Putnam's Sons, 1932.

Thomas, Bob, *Thalberg: Life and Legend*. Garden City, N.Y.: Doubleday and Company, 1969.

Wagner, Frederick, and Barbara Brady, *Famous American Actors and Actresses*. New York: Dodd, Mead & Company, 1961.

Waldau, Roy S., *Vintage Years of the Theatre Guild: 1928–1939*. Cleveland: Case Western Reserve University, 1972.

Webster, Margaret, *Don't Put Your Daughter on the Stage*. New York: Alfred A. Knopf, 1972.

Wharton, John F., *Life Among the Playwrights: Being Mostly the Story of the Playwrights Producing Company, Inc*. New York: Quadrangle/The New York Times Book Company, 1974.

Wilson, Garff, *A History of American Acting*. Bloomington: Indiana University Press, 1966.

Woodress, James, *Booth Tarkington, Gentleman from Indiana*. Philadelphia: J. B. Lippincott, 1954.

Woollcott, Alexander, *The Letters of Alexander Woollcott,* edited by Beatrice Kaufman and Joseph Hennessey. New York: The Viking Press, 1944.

Yurka, Blanche, *Bohemian Girl: Blanche Yurka's Theatrical Life*. Athens: The Ohio University Press, 1970.

Zolotow, Maurice, *Stagestruck: The Romance of Alfred Lunt and Lynn Fontanne*. New York: Harcourt, Brace and World, 1964.

II. PERIODICALS

Anderson, John, "Sketches: Lynn Fontanne—Paul Muni—Jed Harris." *Theatre Arts Monthly,* January 1931.

Anonymous, "Alfred Lunt Presents: Penny Plain and Tuppence Colored." *Theatre Arts,* January 1947.

Anonymous, "At Home with the Lunts." *Theatre Arts,* April 1961.

Anonymous, "Behind the Scenes at 'Clarence.'" the New York *Times,* September 28, 1919.

Anonymous, "Celestial Reviewer: Alfred Lunt." *Opera News,* January 7, 1952.

Anonymous, "Country Cousins." *The New Yorker,* December 4, 1954.

Anonymous, "Fontanne Without Lunt." *TV Guide,* December 31, 1966.

Anonymous, "He Likes to Cook." *Better Homes and Gardens,* August 1962.

Anonymous, "In the Spotlight." *Theatre,* January 1917.

Anonymous, "The Lunts at Ten Chimneys." *Country Beautiful,* October 1962.

Anonymous, "The Lunts Celebrate 25 Triumphant Years." *Life,* November 7, 1949.

Anonymous, "The Lunts, World's Greatest Acting Team, Again Make Fun of Married Love." *Life,* November 1, 1937.

Anonymous, "Mr. and Mrs." *Time,* November 8, 1937.

Anonymous, "Mr. Lunt in a New Role." *Vogue,* April 1, 1932.

Anonymous, "On the Farm with the Lunts." *Christian Science Monitor Magazine Section,* October 28, 1950.

Anonymous, "Opening in Wisconsin." *Time,* March 7, 1949.

Anonymous, "The Talk of the Town." *The New Yorker,* January 11, 1947.

Anonymous, "They Glory in a Rustic, High-Style Hideaway." *Life,* July 26, 1963.

Anonymous, "Value Is a Family Affair." *House and Garden,* October 1959.

Anonymous, "Vignettes." *Landmark* (a publication of the Waukesha County Historical Society), Autumn 1981.

Anonymous, "Visit with the Lunts." *Theatre Arts,* April 1958.

Atkinson, Brooks, "The Lunts Celebrate Their Silver Jubilee." *The New York Times Magazine,* October 30, 1949.

Beaton, Cecil, "Diary of a Designer: Setting the Stage for *Quadrille.*" *Theatre Arts,* November 1954.

Boeth, Richard, "Alfred the Great." *Newsweek,* August 15, 1977.

Brady, Susan Elizabeth, "For Which Wise Men Pray." *Motion Picture Classic,* January 1925.

Brown, John Mason, "Reunion in New York." *The Saturday Review of Literature,* February 16, 1946.

Brown, John Mason, "Seeing Things." *The Saturday Review of Literature,* January 19, 1952.

Clurman, Harold, "Theatre." *The Nation,* September 10, 1977.

Corathiel, Elizabeth, "How They Began." *Theatre World,* March 1934.

Courtney, Marguerite Taylor, "Lynn Fontanne: A Memory and a Tribute," Los Angeles Music Center Program, 1983.

Daniel, Clifton, "With the Lunts on the (Buzz-Bombed) Road." *The New York Times Magazine,* February 4, 1945.

Downing, Robert, "The Movie That Changed a Life." *Films in Review,* August–September 1952.

Eustis, Morton, "A Play in the Making: The Lunts Rehearse *Amphitryon 38.*" *Theatre Arts,* December 1937.

Every, Carolyn, "Friday Night in Genesee Depot." *Heartland Journal,* Fall/Winter 1983.

Every, Carolyn N., "Home Life of the Lunts." *Wisconsin Magazine of History,* Spring 1983.

Fontanne, Lynn, "Making the Most of Your Looks." *Ladies' Home Journal,* September 1927.

Freedley, George, "A Profile of the Lunts." *The Theatre,* February 1959.

Giannini, Paula Nordland, "Lunt and Fontanne: Theater's Royal Couple." *Fine Tuning,* December 1983.

Hackett, Francis, "After the Play." *The New Republic,* August 31, 1921.

Hall, Jane, "Lunt at Carroll." *Landmark,* Autumn 1981.

Hughes, Charlotte, "Leading—and Vibrant—Ladies." *The New York Times Magazine,* January 4, 1942.

Hunt, George P., "Editor's Note." *Life,* July 26, 1963.

Johns, Eric, "The Lunt Legend." *Theatre World,* November 1952.

Johns, Eric, "The Lunts and Peter Brook." *Stage,* June 9, 1960.

Kowalski, Jan, "The Critics' Choice." *Landmark,* Autumn 1981.

Lader, Lawrence, "Lunt and Fontanne: First Family of the Theater." *Coronet,* June 1948.

Laurence, Paula, "Alfred Lunt and Lynn Fontanne . . . Their Most Memorable Theatrical Experience." *Playbill,* November 1972.

Lewis, Lloyd, "With the Lunts It's Time for Comedy." *The New York Times Magazine,* November 11, 1945.

Lewis, Therese, "Ten on the Isle." *Town and Country,* August 1938.

Lindsay, Howard, "Lindsay and Crouse and the Fabulous Lunts." *Good Housekeeping,* February 1956.

Lunt, Alfred, "An Editorial." *Theatre Arts,* February 1950.

Lunt, Alfred, "Mr. Lunt Writes of Actors and Acting." the New York *Times,* November 16, 1930.

Lunt, Alfred, "Twenty-Six Weeks in Vaudeville—Learning Things I Have Never Forgotten." *The Billboard,* December 26, 1936.

Lunt, Alfred, "Why Make Up?" *Theatre Guild Magazine,* November 1928.

Marshall, Arthur, "The Tall Gentleman." *The New Statesman,* August 12, 1977.

Maxwell, Elsa, "Alfred Lunt . . . Cook." *Vogue,* June 15, 1942.

Moats, Alice-Leone, "Mr. and Mrs. Alfred Lunt." *Ladies' Home Journal,* December 1940.

Morehouse, Ward, "Lynn Fontanne and Alfred Lunt, of Genesee, Wisconsin." *Vogue,* April 1, 1940.

Motherwell, Hiram, "The High Art of Comedy Acting." *Theatre Guild Magazine,* March 1932.

Motherwell, Hiram, "When Great Acting?" *Stage,* April 1934.

Mullett, Mary B., "Jealous? We Should Say Not!" *American Magazine,* December 1928.

Munsel, Patrice, "Alfred Goes to the Met." *Esquire,* September 1952.

Nathan, George Jean, "Theater." *Scribner's,* October 1939.

Nolan, Libbie, "Lunt-Fontanne: Magic Names in American Theatre." *Landmark,* Autumn 1981.

Nolan, Libbie, "So Many Talents . . ." *Landmark,* Autumn 1981.

Norton, Elliot, "What Ever Happened to Elegance?" *The Christian Science Monitor,* November 21, 1983.

Patterson, Ada, "The Gentleman and His Wife." *Theatre Magazine,* March 1925.

Phillips, Charlie, "One-Hundred Sittings." *Landmark,* Autumn 1981.

Pringle, Henry, "The Husband-Wife Act." *Collier's,* June 4, 1932.

Pringle, Henry and Helena, "Why Don't They Fight?" *Ladies' Home Journal,* July 1936.

Ray, Marie Benyon, "Chef's Role." *Collier's,* October 21, 1933.

Ray, Marie Benyon, "The Lunts on Their Farm." *McCall's,* April 1935.

Roberts, Peter, "Truth, Tricks or Technique?" *Plays and Players,* August 1960.

Robinson, Clarke, "Silhouettes of Celebrities." *World Digest,* July 1941.

Savage, Richard, "'Creating' a Part." *Theatre Magazine,* February 1927.

Sedgwick, Ruth Woodbury, "Stage Awards the Palm." *Stage,* June 1938.

Service, Faith, "A Happy Young Man." *Motion Picture Classic,* December 1923.

Straus, Dorothea, "There Go the Lunts." *Vogue,* May 1974.

Taber, Gladys, "Star Performance." *Ladies' Home Journal,* October 1950.

Taubman, Howard, "Inescapable Stamp of the Lunt Style." *The New York Times Magazine,* January 27, 1952.

Taylor, Laurette, "Lynn Fontanne." *Town and Country,* August 1942.

Vane, Timothy [Alexander Woollcott], "General Utility." *The New Yorker,* April 28, 1928.

Woollcott, Alexander, "The Actor from Genesee Depot." *McCall's,* April 1929.

Woollcott, Alexander, "The Haunted House of Lunt." *Vanity Fair,* March 1929.

Woollcott, Alexander, "Luck and Mr. Lunt." *Hearst's International combined with Cosmopolitan,* April 1933.

Young, Stark, "Important Variety." *The New Republic,* June 17, 1936.

Zolotow, Maurice, "Alfred Lunt, Director." *Theatre Arts,* April 1954.

Zolotow, Maurice, "Design for Gracious Living." *Woman's Home Companion,* November 1956.

III. NEWSPAPERS MOST FREQUENTLY CONSULTED

Milwaukee *Journal*   *Times* of London
Milwaukee *Sentinel*   Waukesha *Freeman*
New York *Times*

IV. CORRESPONDENCE

LETTERS FROM THE LUNTS TO:

Anderson, Maxwell (Harry Ransom Humanities Research Center, The University
    of Texas at Austin)
Anglin, Margaret (Billy Rose Theatre Collection, Performing Arts Research Cen-
    ter, New York Public Library)
Atkinson, Brooks (Billy Rose Theatre Collection, Performing Arts Research Cen-
    ter, New York Public Library)
Bagnold, Enid (State Historical Society of Wisconsin)
Barnouw, Erik (Rare Book and Manuscript Library, Columbia University)
Beaumont, Hugh [Binkie] (State Historical Society of Wisconsin)
Behrman, S. N. (State Historical Society of Wisconsin)
Belmont, Mrs. August [Eleanor Robson] (Rare Book and Manuscript Library,
    Columbia University)
Bigg, Edward (by special permission)
Bing, Rudolf (State Historical Society of Wisconsin)
Bishop, Air Marshal William Avery (State Historical Society of Wisconsin)
Brent, Romney (Billy Rose Theatre Collection, Performing Arts Research Center,
    New York Public Library)
Brent, Romney (The Players Club)
Brown, Chamberlain (Billy Rose Theatre Collection, Performing Arts Research
    Center, New York Public Library)
Carson, William G. B. (William G. B. Carson Papers, Washington University Li-
    braries, St. Louis, Missouri)
Clift, Montgomery (Billy Rose Theatre Collection, Performing Arts Research
    Center, New York Public Library)
Colbourne, Maurice (State Historical Society of Wisconsin)
Colefax, Sibyl (State Historical Society of Wisconsin)
Connelly, Marc (State Historical Society of Wisconsin)
Coward, Noël (State Historical Society of Wisconsin)
Crawford, Cheryl (Billy Rose Theatre Collection, Performing Arts Research Cen-
    ter, New York Public Library)
Dalrymple, Jean (Billy Rose Theatre Collection, Performing Arts Research Cen-
    ter, New York Public Library)
Davis, Fitzroy (Billy Rose Theatre Collection, Performing Arts Research Center,
    New York Public Library)
De Glehn, Jane and Wilfred (State Historical Society of Wisconsin)
Dewhurst, Habetrot (State Historical Society of Wisconsin)
Duff, Lady Juliet (State Historical Society of Wisconsin)
Evans, Mrs. Walter Ream (State Historical Society of Wisconsin)
Fields, William (Billy Rose Theatre Collection, Performing Arts Research Center,
    New York Public Library)
Franken, Rose (Rare Book and Manuscript Library, Columbia University)

Freedley, George (Billy Rose Theatre Collection, Performing Arts Research Center, New York Public Library)

Golden, John (Billy Rose Theatre Collection, Performing Arts Research Center, New York Public Library)

Gordon, Ruth (State Historical Society of Wisconsin)

Harwood, Fryn (State Historical Society of Wisconsin)

Hayes, Helen (Billy Rose Theatre Collection, Performing Arts Research Center, New York Public Library)

Helburn, Theresa, Lawrence Langner and Armina Marshall (State Historical Society of Wisconsin)

Hewitt, Alan (by special permission)

Humphrey, Molly (State Historical Society of Wisconsin)

Hyams, Barry (Billy Rose Theatre Collection, Performing Arts Research Center, New York Public Library)

Johnson, Arnold (State Historical Society of Wisconsin)

Keith, Antoinette [née Fontanne] (State Historical Society of Wisconsin)

Kesselring, Joseph (Billy Rose Theatre Collection, Performing Arts Research Center, New York Public Library)

King, Edith (Billy Rose Theatre Collection, Performing Arts Research Center, New York Public Library)

King, S. (State Historical Society of Wisconsin)

Kippen, Manart (New York Public Library)

Le Massena, William (by special permission)

Lindsay, Howard, and Russel Crouse (State Historical Society of Wisconsin)

Mamoulian, Rouben (Billy Rose Theatre Collection, Performing Arts Research Center, New York Public Library)

McIlwaine, Betty (State Historical Society of Wisconsin)

Morehouse, Ward (Billy Rose Theatre Collection, Performing Arts Research Center, New York Public Library)

Myers, Paul (Billy Rose Theatre Collection, Performing Arts Research Center, New York Public Library)

Office of Patents and Copyrights (Rare Books and Special Collections, The University of Michigan)

Oppenheimer, George (Billy Rose Theatre Collection, Performing Arts Research Center, New York Public Library)

Potiki, Mai [née Fontanne] (State Historical Society of Wisconsin)

Rankin, May N. (State Historical Society of Wisconsin)

Rattigan, Terence (State Historical Society of Wisconsin)

Rice, Vernon (Billy Rose Theatre Collection, Performing Arts Research Center, New York Public Library)

Robertson, Graham (State Historical Society of Wisconsin)

Robertson, Graham (Billy Rose Theatre Collection, Performing Arts Research Center, New York Public Library)

Salisbury, Leah (Rare Book and Manuscript Library, Columbia University)

Sederholm, Harriet (Rare Books and Special Collections, The University of Michigan)

Sederholm, Harriet (State Historical Society of Wisconsin)

Sherwood, Robert E. (State Historical Society of Wisconsin)

Van Druten, John (Billy Rose Theatre Collection, Performing Arts Research Center, New York Public Library)

Weaver, R. [Ray] Bennett (Rare Books and Special Collections, The University of Michigan)

Webster, Margaret (Library of Congress, Manuscript Division)

Whorf, Richard and Tinx (by special permission)

Wilson, Antoinette [née Fontanne] (Billy Rose Theatre Collection, Performing Arts Research Center, New York Public Library)
Woollcott, Alexander (Billy Rose Theatre Collection, Performing Arts Research Center, New York Public Library)
Woollcott, Alexander (State Historical Society of Wisconsin)
Wright, Lee (Rare Book and Manuscript Library, Columbia University)
Young, Stark (Harry Ransom Humanities Research Center, The University of Texas at Austin)
Zolotow, Maurice (Billy Rose Theatre Collection, Performing Arts Research Center, New York Public Library)

AND

Anderson, Maxwell, to Alfred Lunt and Lynn Fontanne (State Historical Society of Wisconsin)
Anonymous letter to "Dramatic Critic, Washington Post" (State Historical Society of Wisconsin)
Bardsley, Doris O., to Maurice Zolotow (Billy Rose Theatre Collection, Performing Arts Research Center, New York Public Library)
Beale, John A., to Alfred Lunt (State Historical Society of Wisconsin)
Behrman, S. N., to Theresa Helburn (State Historical Society of Wisconsin)
Behrman, S. N., to Carl Hovey (State Historical Society of Wisconsin)
Behrman, S. N., to Alfred Lunt and Lynn Fontanne (State Historical Society of Wisconsin)
Bennett, Dorothy C., to Lynn Fontanne (Rare Book and Manuscript Library, Columbia University)
Bing, Rudolf, to Alfred Lunt (State Historical Society of Wisconsin)
Bugbee, George, to William Le Massena (by special permission)
Cartland, Barbara, to Lynn Fontanne (State Historical Society of Wisconsin)
Cocks, T. G. B., Secretary of the House of Commons, to Alfred Lunt and Lynn Fontanne (State Historical Society of Wisconsin)
Coe, Richard L., to Lynn Fontanne (State Historical Society of Wisconsin)
Coward, Noël, to Alfred Lunt and Lynn Fontanne (State Historical Society of Wisconsin)
Eckstein, Gustav, to Lynn Fontanne (State Historical Society of Wisconsin)
Ferber, Edna, to Alfred Lunt and Lynn Fontanne (State Historical Society of Wisconsin)
Haake, Alfred P., to Alfred Lunt (State Historical Society of Wisconsin)
Hayes, Helen, to Lynn Fontanne (State Historical Society of Wisconsin)
Lash, G. H., to Alfred Lunt (State Historical Society of Wisconsin)
Lindsay, Howard, and Russel Crouse, to Alfred Lunt and Lynn Fontanne (State Historical Society of Wisconsin)
Lunt, Alfred, Sr., to his family (State Historical Society of Wisconsin)
Merrill, Robert, to Alfred Lunt (State Historical Society of Wisconsin)
Munsell, Warren, to Alfred Lunt and Lynn Fontanne (State Historical Society of Wisconsin)
Orsell, Renée, to Antoinette Wilson (Billy Rose Theatre Collection, Performing Arts Research Center, New York Public Library)
Pappy, Earle B., to Alfred Lunt (State Historical Society of Wisconsin)
Patton, George S., Jr., to Lynn Fontanne (State Historical Society of Wisconsin)
Roosevelt, Eleanor, to Alfred Lunt and Lynn Fontanne (State Historical Society of Wisconsin)

Roosevelt, Franklin, to Alfred Lunt and Lynn Fontanne (State Historical Society of Wisconsin)

Scott, Louise, to Alfred Lunt and Lynn Fontanne (State Historical Society of Wisconsin)

Seawell, Donald, to Alfred Lunt (State Historical Society of Wisconsin)

Sherwood, Madeline, to Alfred Lunt and Lynn Fontanne (State Historical Society of Wisconsin)

Sherwood, Robert E., to Alfred Lunt and Lynn Fontanne (State Historical Society of Wisconsin)

Stapleton, Jean, to Lynn Fontanne (State Historical Society of Wisconsin)

State Geologist of the Wisconsin Geological Survey to Alfred Lunt and Lynn Fontanne (State Historical Society of Wisconsin)

Sullavan, Margaret, to Alfred Lunt (State Historical Society of Wisconsin)

Tyler, George C., to Alfred Lunt (State Historical Society of Wisconsin)

Weaver, A. T., to S. N. Behrman (State Historical Society of Wisconsin)

Windust, Bretaigne, to S. N. Behrman (State Historical Society of Wisconsin)

Woollcott, Alexander, to Alfred Lunt and Lynn Fontanne (State Historical Society of Wisconsin)

V. INTERVIEWS

(All interviews were conducted between October 1983 and November 1985)

Berg, Anna Jane
Bigg, Edward
Bowden, Charles
Bugbee, George
Burns, George
Channing, Carol
Davies, Gwen
Every, Carolyn
Hagen, Uta
Harris, Julie

Hewitt, Alan
Hoag, Adaline
Knapp, Suzanne
Le Massena, William
Lowe, Charles
Marshall, Armina
Murray, Peg
Orsell, Renée
Owens, Harriet

Randolph, John
Rawls, Eugenia
Sargent, Mary
Schaefer, George
Seawell, Donald
Stevens, Roger
Thaxter, Phyllis
Valency, Maurice
Van Patten, Dick

VI. OTHER SOURCES

"American National Theatre and Academy and the Antans (Women's Auxiliary of A.N.T.A.) Dinner Dance and An All Star Tribute to Alfred Lunt and Lynn Fontanne on the occasion of their Golden Wedding Anniversary, International Ballroom, Beverly Hilton Hotel, Sunday, June 11, 1972." Souvenir Booklet (includes Alan Hewitt's "Two Careers Become One: Lunt and Fontanne Chronology Revised and Updated")

Birth Certificate, Alfred David Lunt, Jr.

Birth Certificate, Lillie Louise Fontanne

Bugbee, George: tape-recorded interview with Alfred Lunt, 1972 [?]

Carroll Echo (Carroll College Newspaper)

Castle Square Theatre programs, 1912–1915

Closed-circuit interview with Alfred Lunt and Lynn Fontanne, conducted by George Schaefer, 1965

Columbia Oral History interview with May Massee
Contracts, The Metropolitan Opera–Alfred Lunt
Contracts, The Playwrights' Company–Alfred Lunt
Contracts, The Theatre Guild–Alfred Lunt and Lynn Fontanne
"The Dick Cavett Show" (telecast on ABC Network, February 10, 1970; repeated
    June 1, 1970)
Hannum, Charles Ray, "A Study of Alfred Lunt's Approach to the Role," unpub-
    lished Ph.D. dissertation, Wayne State University, 1974
Hewitt, Alan: unpublished reminiscences
Hinakaga (Carroll College Yearbook)
Linley, Marilyn Williams, "History of Educational Theatre in Waukesha," unpub-
    lished M.A. Thesis, Marquette University, Milwaukee, 1969
Lunt, Alfred: videotaped interview following his receipt of the First Carroll Col-
    lege Distinguished Alumnus Award, 1973
Lunt, Alfred, and Lynn Fontanne: tape-recorded interview conducted by Anna
    Crouse and Dorothy Stickney (Lunt-Fontanne Collection, State Historical
    Society of Wisconsin)
Lunt, Alfred, Andrew Weaver and Ray Weaver, *The Greater Love,* unpublished
    play (Rare Books and Special Collections, The University of Michigan)
Lunt, Alfred, Andrew Weaver and Ray Weaver, *The White Cowl,* unpublished play
    (Rare Books and Special Collections, The University of Michigan)
"The Luntanne Tatler" (newsletter circulated among Lunt-Fontanne company
    members)
"The Lunts: A Remembrance" (television production, WTMJ, Milwaukee; tele-
    cast 1984)
Metropolitan Opera Broadcasts, February 20, 1965, and March 31, 1984
Pipe Night at the Players (recording), February 10, 1963
Press release from American Theatre Society, 1960
Press release from the Museum of the City of New York, June 17, 1957
Press release from NBC, 1965
Press release from Producers' Theatre, Inc., 1958
Programs of numerous Alfred Lunt–Lynn Fontanne productions
Randolph, John, diary of *The Visit* in the form of letters to Sarah Randolph, letter
    to Brooks Atkinson and miscellaneous notes
Rawls, Eugenia, "For the Lunts" (unpublished poem)
Rawls, Eugenia, "My Best Friend" (unpublished memoir)
Scrapbooks (Carroll College Library; Billy Rose Theatre Collection, Performing
    Arts Research Center, The New York Public Library)
Seawell, Donald, Eulogies for Alfred Lunt and Lynn Fontanne
Spector, Susan, "Uta Hagen: The Early Years: 1919–1951." Unpublished Ph.D.
    dissertation, New York University, June 1982
TAC News (publication of the Theatre Arts Committee), June 1, 1940
Theatre Guild tribute to Alfred Lunt and Lynn Fontanne, November 16, 1983
Unedited videotapes, George Schaefer–Lynn Fontanne, 1978 (in preparation for
    The Lunts: A Life in the Theatre, telecast by PBS in 1980)
Unpublished paper: "Project for Lunt-Fontanne Repertory Company Managed
    by the Theatre Guild"
Wedding certificate, Jules Pierre Antoine Fontanne and Frances Ellen Thornley
    Barnett
Zolotow, Maurice: tape-recorded interviews with Alfred Lunt, Lynn Fontanne,
    S. N. Behrman, Noël Coward and others in preparation for his biography,
    Stagestruck: The Romance of Alfred Lunt and Lynn Fontanne, 1964

Notes

Throughout the biography I have quoted freely from the tape-recorded interviews made by Maurice Zolotow with Alfred Lunt, Lynn Fontanne, S. N. Behrman, Noël Coward and others. Quotations from these tapes are used by permission of Maurice Zolotow. (Abbreviated as ZT)

The sources for each chapter are given below. Abbreviations used in notes:

AL = Alfred Lunt

LF = Lynn Fontanne

ACDS = tape-recorded interview with AL and LF conducted by Anna Crouse and Dorothy Stickney

NYT = New York *Times*

SHSW = State Historical Society of Wisconsin

BRTC = Billy Rose Theatre Collection, Performing Arts Research Center, New York Public Library

UVGS = Unedited videotapes, George Schaefer-Lynn Fontanne, 1978 (in preparation for *The Lunts: A Life in the Theatre,* telecast by PBS in 1980)

Chapter One: GETTING STARTED

Much of the information on Lynn Fontanne's girlhood and her early years in the theatre came from interviews with Lynn Fontanne and Antoinette Keith recorded on ZT. Mary B. Mullett's article "Jealous? We Should Say Not!" provided useful material. Miscellaneous important information was provided by the wedding certificate of LF's parents and LF's birth certificate. LF spoke of her childhood in the closed-circuit interview conducted by George Schaefer and on UVGS.

Those tapes also provided information about LF's studies with Ellen Terry, as did Roger Manvell's *Ellen Terry; Ellen Terry's Memoirs; NYT,* December 24, 1916 (which tells of LF playing scenes opposite Terry); *Times* of London, October 31, 1978; Milwaukee *Sentinel,* December 17, 1980; Helen Ormsbee's *Backstage with Actors;* Elizabeth Corathiel's "How They Began"; and Peter Roberts's "Truth, Tricks or Technique?"

LF's experiences in *Cinderella* were related in UVGS and George Freedley, "A Profile of the Lunts."

Interviews with George Bugbee and Suzanne Knapp helped to fill in details about LF's early years, as did *Current Biography,* 1941.

Material on Alfred Lunt's family, birth and childhood came primarily from several interviews with George Bugbee; the taped interview Bugbee made with AL; ZT; AL's birth certificate; clippings and documents in the Lunt-Fontanne files in SHSW and BRTC; ACDS; Timothy Vane [Alexander Woollcott]'s "General Utility"; and "The Talk of The Town" in the *New Yorker,* January 11, 1947. AL's childhood scrapbooks are in BRTC.

AL provided information about his early years in letters to Maurice Zolotow, Ray Weaver and Mrs. Warren Ream Evans. Interviews with George Bugbee, Anna Jane Berg, Adaline Hoag and Donald Seawell helped to provide meaningful details, as did May Massee's Columbia Oral History interview. Mary B. Mullett's article was also helpful in this section, as were clippings from Milwaukee newspapers in the Carroll College archives; *NYT,* March 15, 1942, May 29, 1958, and August 4, 1977.

The history of Carroll College is recounted in Ellen Langill's *Carroll College,* which includes a section on AL's activities at Carroll. His work at Carroll College is also covered in the *Hinakaga,* the Carroll yearbook, and the *Carroll Echo,* the school newspaper. AL discussed his recollections of Carroll College in Marilyn Linley Williams's "History of Educational Theatre in Waukesha," from which his comparison of May Rankin to Stanislavski was taken. I found pertinent information about his years at Carroll in the Carroll College Catalogues, 1906–10; clippings, theatre programs and scrapbooks in the Carroll College Archives (including clippings, a handbill and programs, 1908–12); a program of Carroll College Interpretive Recitals at the Department of Special Collections, the University of Michigan; AL's interview at Carroll College upon receipt of an honorary degree; and a discussion with the registrar about AL's academic record at Carroll College. The article by Jane Hall, "Lunt at Carroll," was helpful. AL's letter to the Office of Patents and Copyrights (November 10, 1909) concerned his plays *The Greater Love* and *The White Cowl* (draft and final versions); those handwritten scripts were perused as well. The handbill AL distributed is in the Carroll College archives.

The description of Waukesha in 1891 appeared in the Waukesha *Journal;* the clipping is in the Lunt-Fontanne file, SHSW.

AL's trip abroad is detailed in his letters to R. (Ray) Bennett Weaver. These letters also include AL's description of the glee-club tours, his move to Boston and his encounter with John Craig and George Henry Trader of the Castle Square Theatre.

The story of AL's destroying his scene designs was told to me by Donald Seawell.

Miscellaneous additional information came from AL's letter to May Rankin, August 16, 1910; New York *Post,* January 17, 1931; Boston *Sunday Globe,* January 9, 1921; Waukesha *Freeman,* February 14, 1973, and August 3, 1977; Milwaukee *Journal,* February 15, 1973; clippings from Milwaukee *Journal,* 1910, and Waukesha *Freeman,* 1910 and 1912; "The Lunts at Ten Chimneys" in *Country Beautiful;* Alexander Woollcott's "The Actor from Genesee Depot"; and Maurice Zolotow's *Stagestruck.*

Chapter Two: THE FONTANNE OF YOUTH

The quotation beginning, "While acting with . . ." is from "Lynn Fontanne" by Laurette Taylor.

LF's search for work in England is discussed in ZT; UVGS; and the closed-circuit interview with AL and LF conducted by George Schaefer. The excerpt of the review of *My Lady's Dress* is taken from George Freedley's *The Lunts. Milestones* was reviewed in the *Times* of London, November 2, 1914. LF's work process in *Milestones* was described on UVGS.

LF's meeting with Laurette Taylor and J. Hartley Manners and the events that followed are chronicled in Marguerite Courtney's *Laurette* and her article "Lynn Fontanne: A Memory and a Tribute"; Ashton Stevens's *Actorviews;* Laurette Taylor's "Lynn Fontanne"; Mary B. Mullett's "Jealous? We Should Say Not!"; George Freedley's "A Profile of the Lunts"; Maurice Zolotow's *Stagestruck;* ZT; and UVGS.

LF's relationship with Edmund Byrne is discussed in *Stagestruck;* ZT; and UVGS.

LF's arrival in America is discussed in the *Times* of London, October 31, 1978; and UVGS.

The various productions in which LF appeared in America are discussed and/or reviewed in the following:

The Wooing of Eve: NYT, November 10, 1917 (which also tells of the necessity to dim the lights on Broadway); New York *World,* November 10, 1917; Maurice Zolotow, *Stagestruck.*

The Harp of Life: New York *World,* November 28, 1916; New York *Sun,* December 10, 1916; *NYT,* November 28, 1916; Guthrie McClintic, *Me and Kit.*

Out There: Town Topics, March 29, 1917; *NYT,* March 28, 1917.

Happiness: NYT, January 1, 1918; *Christian Science Monitor,* January 8, 1918; *Vanity Fair,* March 1918; Marguerite Courtney, *Laurette.*

Laurette Taylor's Shakespeare Scenes: Helen Hayes, *On Reflection;* Marguerite Courtney, *Laurette;* Burns Mantle and Garrison P. Sherwood, eds., *The Best Plays of 1909–19,* New York: Dodd, Mead and Company, 1933.

Evidence of LF's advancing career is in the articles written about her in *Theatre Magazine,* January 1917; and the *Dramatic Mirror,* January 27, 1917.

LF's decision to conceal her age is discussed in UVGS; *NYT,* April 24, 1978; New York *Herald Tribune,* November 16, 1935; interviews with William Le Massena, George Bugbee and Donald Seawell.

The stories concerning George S. Kaufman's work on *Someone in the House* are taken from Scott Meredith's *George S. Kaufman and His Friends* and Ward Morehouse's *Matinee Tomorrow.* Reviews of *Someone in the House: Town Topics,* September 12, 1918; New York *Star,* September 18, 1918; *Vanity Fair,* November 1918; *NYT,* September 10 and September 15, 1918. AL's comment about the production was taken from ACDS.

Chapter Three: AN ONION IS AN ONION

The quotation beginning, "Make no mistake . . ." is from Howard Lindsay's "Lindsay and Crouse and the Fabulous Lunts."

A great deal of the material in this chapter is taken from AL's letters to R. (Ray) Bennett Weaver. Other sources describing AL's three seasons with the Castle Square Theatre are: AL's letter to his mother, December 26, 1912; letter to May Rankin, December 16, 1913; programs from Castle Square Theatre productions; review from the Boston *Globe* (clipping in Rare Books and Special Collections, the University of Michigan); Brooks Atkinson, *Broadway;* Ward Morehouse, *Matinee Tomorrow; NYT,* September 28, 1919; New York *Sun,* January 20, 1930; letter from Doris O. Bardsley to Maurice Zolotow, March 20, 1961; ZT; reviews from Boston newspapers (clippings in AL-LF file in SHSW); letter to the author from William Morris Hunt, May 15, 1985.

Howard Lindsay's article "Lindsay and Crouse and the Fabulous Lunts" details AL's audition for Margaret Anglin and his subsequent work under her guidance. Also useful in describing the relationship between AL and Anglin were Cornelia Otis Skinner, *Life with Lindsay and Crouse; NYT,* September 28, 1919; ZT; ACDS.

AL's love for vaudeville is described in his article "Twenty-Six Weeks in Vaudeville."

AL described his meeting with Lillie Langtry in Pierre Sichel's *The Jersey Lily,* which also includes AL's poem about Langtry.

The various productions in which AL appeared are discussed and/or reviewed in the following:

Beverly's Balance: Christian Science Monitor (clipping in BRTC); *Argonaut,* September 18, 1915.

Medea, Iphigenia in Aulis and *Electra:* Howard Lindsay's article; Thoda Cocroft, *Great Names and How They Are Made;* ZT; letter from AL to Arnold Johnson, February 22, 1971; *Californian* (clipping in BRTC); *Argonaut,* August 21, 1915; articles in *NYT,* March 2, 1915–August 29, 1915; programs in BRTC; ACDS.

As You Like It: Articles in *NYT,* January 20, 1916–June 8, 1916; Thoda Cocroft, *Great Names and How They Are Made.*

Her Husband's Wife: ZT; clippings in AL-LF collection, SHSW.

Ashes: Argonaut, September 16, 1916; ZT; clippings by Carlton W. Miles and others in AL-LF collection, SHSW; clipping from Denver newspaper in BRTC.

Green Stockings: Howard Lindsay, "Lindsay and Crouse and the Fabulous Lunts"; Atlantic City *Gazette-Review,* May 11, 1917; Atlantic City *Daily Press* (clipping in SHSW).

The Pirate: Cathleen Nesbitt, *A Little Love and Good Company;* Milwaukee *Free Press,* August 21, 1917; H. H. Ryan's review from a clipping in SHSW.

Romance and Arabella: NYT, October 18, 1917; clippings in AL-LF file, SHSW.

The Country Cousin: George C. Tyler and Alexandra Carlisle were quoted by AL in ZT. The St. Paul *Daily News,* October 14, 1918; *NYT,* September 28, 1919; clippings in AL-LF file in BRTC; James Woodress, *Booth Tarkington;* Booth Tarkington, *On Plays, Playwrights and Playgoers.*

Woodress's and Downer's books also discuss Tarkington's decision to write a play for AL.

AL's description of the onset of war in Finland appeared in a Boston newspaper. A clipping exists in Rare Books and Special Collections, the University of Michigan.

AL's attention to detail (his use of the "green umbrella") in *Pygmalion* and *The Visit* are discussed in Charles Ray Hannum's "A Study of Alfred Lunt's Approach to the Role" and S. N. Behrman's *People in a Diary.*

Chapter Four: TRIUMPH AND FRUSTRATION

Noël Coward's quotation beginning, "From these shabby . . ." is taken from his *Present Indicative.*

The first meeting of AL and LF is discussed in Lawrence Lader, "Lunt and Fontanne"; Mary B. Mullett, "Jealous? We Should Say Not!"; *Current Biography,* 1941; Ada Patterson, "The Guardsman and His Wife"; Alice-Leone Moats, "Mr. and Mrs. Alfred Lunt"; clippings in SHSW; UVGS; the *Times* of London, October 31, 1978. The subsequent romance is detailed in Laurette Taylor's "Lynn Fontanne"; John Mason Brown's *The Worlds of Robert E. Sherwood;* and *NYT,* January 27, 1952. AL and LF's meeting at Genesee Depot, the coolness between LF and Hattie Sederholm, the decision to become engaged, and the subsequent difficulties in AL and LF's romantic relationship are discussed in Taylor's "Lynn Fontanne"; my interview with George Bugbee; Ada Patterson's "The Guardsman and His Wife"; a letter from AL to Maurice Zolotow, December 1963; Maurice Zolotow's *Stagestruck;* and ZT.

LF's attempt to get George C. Tyler to raise her salary, followed by her meek reaction, is told by Helen Hayes in *On Reflection* and Scott Meredith in *George S. Kaufman and His Friends.* Both authors also described Tyler's importance and his relationship to the actors with whom he worked. AL's attempt to effect a break with Tyler was countered by a letter from Tyler to AL dated February 5, 1921.

The Actors' Equity strike is discussed in Brooks Atkinson's *Broadway* and in Burns Mantle's *The Best Plays of 1919-20*. Helen Hayes's affiliation with the "Fidos" is described in her book *On Reflection*.

The incidents that took place in Dr. Rounds's boardinghouse are described in ZT; Noël Coward's *Present Indicative;* Allen Churchill's *The Theatrical 20s;* a letter from AL to Maurice Zolotow, December 1963; and a note from LF to Zolotow.

LF's backstage visits to *Clarence* and the hostility she felt from the actresses were described in UVGS and in Helen Hayes's *On Reflection*. Thoda Cocroft told of LF being stranded in Chicago in *Great Names and How They Are Made*. Theresa Helburn's description of LF is from her book, *A Wayward Quest*.

Robert E. Sherwood's view of AL and LF in 1920 is taken from his "The Lunts."

AL's intimation that his real name was not Lunt but Ecklunt or Erklund appeared in Ada Patterson, "The Guardsman and His Wife"; *Zit's Weekly,* December 21, 1921; *NYT,* May 27, 1922.

The story of AL's and LF's wedding was told in *NYT,* May 26 and May 27, 1922; George Freedley's "A Profile of the Lunts"; Allen Churchill's *The Theatrical 20s;* UVGS; "The Dick Cavett Show." The "second wedding" was described by Billie Burke (with Cameron Shipp) in *With a Feather on My Nose* and repeated in a newspaper (clipping in SHSW). The Lunts' small New York apartment is described in ZT.

Information on LF's friendship with Noël Coward is taken from Sheridan Morley's *A Talent to Amuse;* UVGS; "The Dick Cavett Show"; and the *Times* of London, October 31, 1978.

LF's careful cultivation of her appearance is discussed in LF's "Making the Most of Your Looks"; LF is quoted in Cathleen Nesbitt's *A Little Love and Good Company;* also useful in this section were Daniel Blum's *Great Stars of the American Stage;* Howard Lindsay's "Lindsay and Crouse and the Fabulous Lunts"; Lawrence Lader's "Lunt and Fontanne"; Thoda Cocroft's *Great Names and How They are Made;* Noël Coward, *The Noël Coward Diaries; NYT,* July 31, 1983; Laurette Taylor's "Lynn Fontanne"; interviews with Renée Orsell, Peg Murray, William Le Massena and Edward Bigg; Antoinette Keith's remarks on ZT; and the closed-circuit interview with AL and LF conducted by George Schaefer. LF's toothbrush ritual was described by Dick Van Patten in an interview, and in Ward Morehouse's "Lynn Fontanne and Alfred Lunt, of Genesee, Wisconsin." The story about LF's hands and arms is from Alice-Leone Moats's "Mr. and Mrs. Alfred Lunt."

The conflict between LF and Laurette Taylor is described in Marguerite Courtney's *Laurette;* AL's letter to Maurice Zolotow, December 1963; Zolotow's *Stagestruck;* and Marguerite Taylor Courtney's "Lynn Fontanne: A Memory and a Tribute."

Articles and reviews and accounts of specific plays and films include the following:

Made of Money: clipping in BRTC; Washington *Post,* June 8, 1919; *Christian Science Monitor,* June 17, 1919.

A Young Man's Fancy: The advertisement giving LF and AL star billing is in BRTC; Tyler's apology to LF for casting other actors in the Broadway production is taken from a note from LF to Maurice Zolotow; a clipping of a review is in BRTC.

Clarence: Booth Tarkington is quoted in *On Plays, Playwrights and Playgoers*. The letter from Tarkington to the cast of *Clarence* is quoted in *NYT,* September 28, 1919. AL's aversion to "hokum" is told in the *Christian Science Monitor,* February 8, 1921; the story regarding Robert McLaughlin's signing of AL to play *Clarence* for $100 week less than his usual salary was told in the New York *World-Telegram,* October 30, 1937, and in clippings and documents in SHSW. AL's determination to learn the saxophone and the piano are chronicled in ZT. Reviews of *Clarence: NYT,* New York *World,* New York *American,* New York *Herald* and New York *Sun,* all September 22, 1919. Also: Philadelphia *Inquirer,* July 13, 1919; *Christian Science Monitor,* October 28, 1919; *NYT,* September 28, 1919; *Variety,* July 9, 1919.

Chris: Barbara and Arthur Gelb, *O'Neill;* Louis Sheaffer, *O'Neill;* ZT.

One Night in Rome: The incidents surrounding this production are detailed in the *Times* of London (April 15–May 4, 1920); *NYT* (April 30–May 4, 1920); and Marguerite Courtney's *Laurette.*

Dulcy: Scott Meredith's *George S. Kaufman and His Friends:* George Abbott's *Mister Abbott;* Howard Lindsay's "Lindsay and Crouse and the Fabulous Lunts." AL's and Coward's apprehensiveness are detailed in Coward's *Present Indicative* and repeated on "The Dick Cavett Show." Reviews: Chicago *Post* and Chicago *Journal,* both February 21, 1921; New York *Telegraph* and *NYT,* both August 15, 1921. *NYT* also discussed the play on August 21 and November 6, 1921. The *New Republic*'s review appeared on August 31, 1921.

The Intimate Strangers: Billie Burke (with Cameron Shipp), *With a Feather on My Nose;* LF's reaction to AL's performance (and the couple's ability to criticize one another without rancor) appeared in an interview in the Los Angeles *Times,* June 11, 1972. Reviews: Washington *Star,* November 1, 1921; *NYT,* November 8, 1921.

Banco: George Tyler's letter to AL was written on August 12, 1922. S. N. Behrman wrote about the play in *People in a Diary* and spoke about it on ZT. Reviews: *Variety,* September 15, 1922; New York *Telegram,* New York *World,* New York *Globe,* and *NYT,* all September 21, 1922.

Backbone: James Dean is quoted in the Milwaukee *Journal,* May 11, 1923; AL's account of his own performance is from the same article. Review: *NYT,* April 30, 1923.

Sweet Nell of Old Drury: Laurette Taylor, "Lynn Fontanne"; Marguerite Courtney, *Laurette;* ACDS. Reviews: *NYT,* New York *World,* New York *Herald,* New York *Sun* and New York *Globe,* all May 19, 1923. A clipping from the New York *Post* is in BRTC. A brief account of the production appeared in *Time,* November 8, 1937.

The Ragged Edge: The story about the "scandalous" advertising campaign appeared in the New York *Morning Telegraph,* June 8, 1923. *NYT* reviewed the film on June 5, 1923.

Second Youth: AL was quoted in *Motion Picture Classic.* A review appeared in *NYT,* April 22, 1924.

In Love with Love: Noël Coward claimed AL had coached LF in sex appeal in *Present Indicative;* LF responded in a letter to him, May 19, 1949. Reviews: *NYT* and New York *Morning World,* both August 7, 1923; New York *World,* August 29, 1923; Philadelphia *Ledger,* January 29, 1924; Boston *Transcript* and Boston *Traveler,* both March 18, 1924.

Robert E. Lee: An account of the Confederate organizations' opposition to the play appeared in *NYT,* November 7, 1923. Reviews: *NYT,* New York *Tribune,* New York *World* and New York *Herald,* all November 21, 1923.

Outward Bound: A discussion of the play's reception in Atlantic City appears in several *NYT* articles: December 30, 1923; January 6, 1924; January 13, 1924. The newspaper reviewed the play on January 8, 1924. May Massee's reaction to seeing AL is in her Columbia Oral History Interview.

Chapter Five: THE GUARDSMAN

Accounts of the production of *Where Ignorance Is Bliss* are from Theresa Helburn's article in *NYT,* November 30, 1924; Walter Pritchard Eaton's *The Theatre Guild;* interview with Armina Marshall; and Lawrence Langner's *The Magic Curtain.* The agent's insistence on casting *The Guardsman* with established stars is told in Langner's book and in Theresa Helburn's *A Wayward Quest,* in which she also reveals her satisfaction at having thought to cast AL and LF.

The Lunts' view of the Theatre Guild and its "sense of mission" is from ZT, which was also the source for Helburn's offer of $500 to the Lunts, LF's insistence on elegant costumes and the Guild's refusal to pay more than $50 per costume, LF's assertion "I've never been in a failure . . ." and the Lunts' trip to Europe for costumes (which is also detailed in AL's interview at Carroll College in 1973).

AL's visit to the grocery store in the makeup of the Guardsman is told by Uta Hagen in *Respect for Acting.*

The Theatre Guild's system of "managers' rehearsals" is detailed in Brooks Atkinson's *Broadway;* Lawrence Langner's *The Magic Curtain;* and by Theresa Helburn in a chapter she wrote for Walter Pritchard Eaton's *The Theatre Guild.* The characterization of Philip Moeller and his directorial methods is derived from S. N. Behrman's *People in a Diary;* Louis Sheaffer's *O'Neill;* and Roy S. Waldau's *Vintage Years of the Theatre Guild.* AL's comments about Moeller are from Lewis Funke and John E. Booth, eds., *Actors Talk About Acting.* Moeller's insistence that "you can't play comedy in black" and Lunt's rejoinder is also told in *Actors Talk About Acting;* Lunt repeated the story in ZT and in his 1973 interview at Carroll College. Those sources provided accounts of the stormy rehearsal process of *The Guardsman,* as did Allen Churchill's *The Theatrical 20s* and LF on ACDS.

Theresa Helburn's description of LF's performance is from an article in *NYT,* November 30, 1924. AL spoke of his and LF's work on the overlapping technique in Funke and Booth's *Actors Talk About Acting,* and LF amplified his remarks in ZT.

The quotation "Tell me I'm rotten . . ." is from Henry Pringle, "The Husband-Wife Act." AL's insecurities are detailed in Lawrence Lader's "Lunt and Fontanne"; Arthur Marshall's "The Tall Gentleman"; "Mr. and Mrs." in *Time,* November 8, 1937; Noël Coward on "The Dick Cavett Show"; and in an interview with Dick Van Patten. AL's revulsion at seeing his image on television was told to Dan Sullivan in *NYT,* August 19, 1968. LF's letter to Woollcott about AL's uneasiness when he was cheered by the audience in London is dated June 23, 1938.

AL's statement that he cried after the managers' rehearsal is from ZT. Howard Lindsay's advice to the Lunts and their response is from Lindsay's "Lindsay and Crouse and the Fabulous Lunts." The story is repeated in Cornelia Otis Skinner's *Life with Lindsay and Crouse.* The opening-night ordeal is described by LF in UVGS and by Brooks Atkinson in "The Lunts Celebrate Their Silver Jubilee."

All the quoted reviews of *The Guardsman* were printed on October 14, 1924.

The Lunts' refusal to take curtain calls between acts is told in ZT. Their insistence on sharing calls with the other members of their casts is from an interview with Armina Marshall, and from ZT.

The Lunts' plans to revive *The Guardsman* can be found in the *NYT Magazine,* November 11, 1945; *NYT,* September 29, 1943; Roy S. Waldau, *Vintage Years of the Theatre Guild;* and in a letter from AL to Richard and Tinx Whorf, July 8, 1944.

AL's retort to the Theatre Guild Board ("like feeding a soufflé to a horse") was taken from ZT and from Arthur Marshall, "The Tall Gentleman."

Chapter Six: ART THEATRE—OR SWEATSHOP?

The quotation beginning, "Was the cruelest" was derived from ZT. The Lunts' salaries are from contracts with the Theatre Guild in the L-F collection at SHSW.

Information about the Lunts' attempts to conserve their energies so that performances would not suffer was taken from interviews with Edward Bigg, William Le Massena, Peg Murray and Dick Van Patten; Helen Ormsbee's *Backstage with Actors;* LF, quoted in Morton Eustis's *Players at Work;* Mary B. Mullett, "Jealous? We Should Say Not!"; Helen Hayes, speaking at a tribute to the Lunts in 1983; LF, quoted in the Los Angeles *Times,* June 11, 1972; AL, quoted on the closed-circuit interview with George Schaefer; and LF on UVGS.

The story of Tallulah Bankhead and her marijuana party was told by LF on UVGS.

The Lunts' attitudes toward having children came from the following: interviews with Edward Bigg, Peg Murray, Armina Marshall, George Bugbee, George Schaefer, Dick Van Patten and Donald Seawell; *NYT,* April 24, 1978.

Fontanne's illness, causing her to miss performances of *The Second Man* and *Pygmalion,* is documented in *NYT,* April 17, 18, 19 and 21, May 2, 3 and 29, 1927. The salaries of Ed Wynn and Marilyn Miller were printed in Allen Churchill's *The Theatrical 20s.* Robert E. Sherwood said that the Lunts rejected *The Road to Rome* in a letter he wrote to them on July 26, 1947. Helen Westley's view of the Theatre Guild's function appears in Walter Pritchard Eaton's *The Theatre Guild.* The award to Lunt as the finest stage actor of 1926–27 is mentioned in the New York *Daily News,* June 12, 1927, and *NYT,* June 22, 1927. *NYT*'s shift of emphasis from LF to AL and LF together can be seen in an article of September 3, 1927.

AL and LF's views of the actor's job are taken from Morton Eustis's *Players at Work* and ZT. The Lunts' ambivalent view of the Theatre Guild is taken from ZT, as is their conflict with the Guild over star billing. LF's reference to Katharine Cornell's proposed production of *The Doctor's Dilemma* is from a letter dated February 1, 1941. The Lunts' meeting with (and attitude toward) George Bernard Shaw is derived from an interview with Armina Marshall; LF on UVGS; and the San Francisco *Chronicle,* April 18, 1948. AL's description of what Shaw's plays require of actors comes from ZT.

AL's recommendation that Noël Coward play *The Second Man* in London is from Sheridan Morley's *A Talent to Amuse.* Material on the symposium on censorship came from *NYT,* February 5, 1927. The visits of the moral guardians to *Strange Interlude* and *Volpone* (and the events leading up to the visit) were reported in *NYT,* April 25–May 2, 1928. AL's comments on Eugene O'Neill appear in Barbara and Arthur Gelb's *O'Neill.* AL's quip about "suing Lynn for desertion" is taken from Jan Kowalski's "The Critics' Choice."

Notes and comments about individual plays and films appear below. *All* of the plays discussed in this chapter are covered in Roy S. Waldau's *Vintage Years of the Theatre Guild;* Lawrence Langner's *The Magic Curtain;* and Walter Pritchard Eaton's *The Theatre Guild.*

Sally of the Sawdust: AL's comments about D. W. Griffith and W. C. Fields appear in a letter he wrote to Maurice Zolotow in 1963. A review of the film appears in *NYT,* August 3, 1925.

The Man Who Found Himself: NYT, August 24, 1925 (review).

Lovers in Quarantine: NYT, October 13, 1925.

Arms and the Man: Lunt's attempts to make Bluntschli sympathetic to the audience are detailed in his interview at Carroll College in 1973. LF spoke of her drying up on opening night on UVGS. Reviews: *NYT,* September 15 and

October 4, 1925; New York *Tribune,* New York *World,* New York *Evening World,* all September 15, 1925.

Goat Song: Blanche Yurka's *Bohemian Girl;* Laurette Taylor's comment to the Lunts was quoted by AL on ACDS. Reviews: *NYT,* New York *Tribune,* New York *Post,* New York *Telegram,* all January 26, 1926.

At Mrs. Beam's: AL's insistence on having LF genuinely hit him was taken from a quotation in Mary B. Mullett, "Jealous? We Should Say Not!" Reviews: *NYT* and New York *Tribune,* April 26, 1926.

Juarez and Maximilian: The quotation by Lawrence Langner is taken from *The Magic Curtain.* Reviews: *NYT,* New York *World,* New York *Post,* all October 12, 1926.

Pygmalion: LF's hunt for costume accessories is told by Timothy Vane [Alexander Woollcott] in "General Utility." Mrs. Patrick Campbell's visit to LF was related by LF on UVGS. LF's relationship with Cheryl Crawford is detailed in Crawford's *One Naked Individual.* Reviews and comments came from Brooks Atkinson, *Broadway; NYT,* New York *Sun,* New York *World,* all November 16, 1926.

Ned McCobb's Daughter: Theresa Helburn's *A Wayward Quest* and Allen Churchill's *The Theatrical 20s.* AL was quoted in the Los Angeles *Times,* June 11, 1972, concerning his request not to allow anyone else to use a gold tooth. Reviews: *NYT,* November 30 and December 5, 1926; New York *Tribune,* New York *Post,* New York *Telegram,* all November 30, 1926; New York *Evening World,* December 1, 1926; New York *American,* December 3, 1926.

The Brothers Karamazov: The rehearsal process was described by Harold Clurman in *All People Are Famous* and in "Theatre," the *Nation,* September 10, 1977. Lawrence Langner in *The Magic Curtain* tells of the incident of the scar. Reviews: *NYT,* New York *Post,* New York *Telegram,* New York *World,* all January 4, 1927.

The Second Man: The rehearsal process was described by S. N. Behrman in *People in a Diary* and on ZT. Clurman also discusses the process in "Theatre," the *Nation,* September 10, 1977. Reviews: *Women's Wear Daily,* New York *Herald Tribune,* New York *Telegram, NYT,* New York *World,* New York *Evening Post,* all April 12, 1927; the *Nation,* April 27, 1927; the *New Yorker,* April 23, 1927.

The Doctor's Dilemma: AL calls Dubedat "the easiest and most satisfactory part" in Lewis Funke and John E. Booth, eds., *Actors Talk About Acting.* The Granville-Barker production of the play is described in *NYT,* November 20, 1927. S. N. Behrman spoke of LF's performance on ZT. Reviews: *NYT,* New York *Post,* New York *Sun,* New York *World,* all November 22, 1927; Boston *Transcript,* January 6, 1928.

Marco Millions: Louis Sheaffer discusses the play in *O'Neill.* An article in *NYT,* January 8, 1928, does the same. Mamoulian's idea for ending the play is described by Roy S. Waldau in *Vintage Years of the Theatre Guild.* Reviews: *NYT,* New York *Evening World,* New York *Telegram,* New York *Post,* all January 10, 1928.

Strange Interlude: Lawrence Langner discusses the difficulties in casting the role of Nina in *The Magic Curtain* and in Norman Nadel's *A Pictorial History of the Theatre Guild.* Philip Moeller's solution to the problems of staging the play appears in an article he wrote for *NYT,* February 26, 1928. Other aspects of the play and production are discussed in Louis Sheaffer's *O'Neill;* Barbara and Arthur Gelb's *O'Neill;* Lloyd Morris's *Curtain Time.* The Lunts' attitude toward the play is discussed in Maurice Zolotow's *Stagestruck.* LF's comment to O'Neill that he should write a play about possessive mothers is taken from

"The Lunts at Ten Chimneys" in *Country Beautiful* and from Zolotow's biography; LF's story of cutting dialogue from the play is told on UVGS and
in Sheaffer's *O'Neill*. Noël Coward's critical comment to LF which necessitated his return to see the production once again was taken from ZT. Reviews: *NYT,* January 31 and February 5, 1928; New York *Evening World* and
New York *World,* January 31, 1928.

Volpone: AL was quoted about the physical difficulties he had playing Mosca in
Mary B. Mullett's "Jealous? We Should Say Not!" AL's leap into bed with
Dudley Digges was described by Cheryl Crawford in *One Naked Individual.*
The story of LF's plea to the Theatre Guild to give AL a rest and his volun-
teering to play Mosca is told in Timothy Vane [Alexander Woollcott]'s "Gen-
eral Utility." Reviews: *NYT,* April 10 and April 22, 1928; New York *Post* and
New York *World,* both April 10, 1928.

Chapter Seven: TEAMWORK

The quotation "Isn't it nice . . ." is taken from John Mason Brown's *The Worlds of
Robert E. Sherwood.* A slightly different wording is given in Lawrence Lader's
"Lunt and Fontanne."

The Lunts' decision to act only together was discussed by LF on UVGS; by
George Schaefer on *The Lunts: A Life in the Theatre;* and in interviews with Schaefer and with Donald Seawell.

Accounts of an earlier scheduled production of *Caprice* (prior to the Lunts'
production) came from *NYT,* December 23 and December 30, 1928; from Roy
S. Waldau's *Vintage Years of the Theatre Guild;* and from ZT. Walter Pritchard
Eaton tells of the Theatre Guild sending the production of *Caprice* to London as
a reward to the Lunts in *The Theatre Guild.*

LF's opinion of Philip Moeller's directorial ability was taken from UVGS.
The account of the Lunts at the St. James's Theatre in London appeared in Wilson
McCarty's "The Lunts Meet the 'Gods,'" *NYT,* June 30, 1929.

The Lunts' experiments with theatrical technique are recounted in ZT (the
"white handkerchief" story) and in AL's interview at Carroll College in 1973 (the
variations in *O Mistress Mine*). AL told Morton Eustis in *Players at Work* that "No
good actor is bound by any rules." Lunt often told the story about teaching a class
at the American Theatre Wing and asking LF to define technique; it appears in
the *Times* of London, June 20, 1960; AL told it to Marilyn Williams Linley (she
quotes him in her "History of Educational Theatre in Waukesha") and repeated it
at Carroll College in 1973.

Cheryl Crawford spoke of the Lunts' misbehavior in *Caprice* in *One Naked
Individual.* The steamy love scene in *Reunion in Vienna* was described by Alexan-
der Woollcott in a letter to Paul Bonner, December 30, 1931. The story concern-
ing the Lunts' performance in *Love in Idleness* in an unheated theatre was told by
George Freedley in *The Lunts.* AL spoke about the business in *O Mistress Mine* on
"The Dick Cavett Show." AL's comments on sex in the theatre are taken from ZT.

Accounts of the intense work the Lunts did at home prior to (and between)
rehearsals are numerous. Their method of memorization was discussed by Richard
Boeth in "Alfred the Great." Charles Ray Hannum in "A Study of Alfred Lunt's
Approach to the Role" speaks of AL's penchant for improvisation, as does Morton
Eustis in "A Play in the Making." Additional sources were Lewis Funke and John
E. Booth, eds., *Actors Talk About Acting,* and Morton Eustis's *Players at Work.*

The quotation from George Schaefer is taken from an interview with the
author. Alexander Woollcott ("It is easy to tell . . .") is quoted in *Current Biography,* 1941 and in *NYT,* August 4, 1977. Noël Coward's remark "To see the Lunts

. . ." is from ZT. AL said, "You stumble along . . ." to Lewis Funke and John E. Booth, eds., *Actors Talk About Acting*. LF ("Falling off a hill") is quoted by Richard Savage in "'Creating' a Part." Her answer about "long and arduous training" was given to Funke and Booth, as was AL's response when asked if LF let him know if his performances were flawed.

R. Dana Skinner discusses AL's versatility in *Our Changing Theatre*. LF described her work process ("I have discovered . . .") to Toby Cole and Helen Krich Chinoy, eds., in their *Actors on Acting*. S. N. Behrman tells of the Lunts' rehearsing lines in the streets of Boston in *People in a Diary*. Lawrence Langner quotes the actress who was jealous of the Lunts' closeness in *The Magic Curtain*. Arthur Marshall reported on the rehearsal of *Love in Idleness* in "The Tall Gentleman." S. N. Behrman said on ZT that AL modeled his makeup for *Meteor* on Jed Harris. The anecdote about LF and Charva Chester was told to me by Renée Orsell.

AL's neuritis in 1929 was reported by the New York *Evening World,* January 8, 1930, and *NYT,* January 3, January 20 and February 15, 1930. The story of the Lunts' loss of their money to a dishonest broker was told to me by George Bugbee. The story of AL moving into the living room rather than calling a doctor was told by Noël Coward on ZT.

The section on AL's state of health was derived from an interview with Dr. Edward Bigg. The Lunts' attitude toward accidents during performances was recounted in Arthur Marshall's "The Tall Gentleman"; by LF in Lewis Funke and John E. Booth, eds, *Actors Talk About Acting;* and by AL in Helen Ormsbee's *Backstage with Actors* (from which his statement "I take my job . . .") is taken. The Lunts' attitudes toward Shakespeare is discussed in "The Lunts at Ten Chimneys" and on ZT; Alan Hewitt told me that Lunt refused to use a British accent; LF was quoted in *The Lunts: A Remembrance;* AL's joke about playing in *Romeo and Juliet* is from the closed-circuit interview with George Schaefer.

Offers from Carl Laemmle and Irving Thalberg to make more films after *The Guardsman* are discussed on ZT and in Lawrence Lader's "Lunt and Fontanne." Robert E. Sherwood is quoted ("I suppose every playwright . . .") in John Mason Brown's *The Worlds of Robert E. Sherwood*. AL's detailed knowledge of the critics' verdicts on *Reunion in Vienna* is from Robert E. Sherwood's "The Lunts." Woollcott's letter to the Lunts ("When your grandchildren . . .") was written on December 14, 1931; his letter to Paul Bonner about *Reunion in Vienna* is dated December 30, 1931.

The Theatre Guild's negotiations with the Lunts in 1931 and 1932 are detailed in Roy S. Waldau's *Vintage Years of the Theatre Guild*. The story of the Guild's refusal to replace AL's uniform jacket on tour was told in *Variety,* August 3, 1983. George Schaefer quoted AL's attitude toward the Guild in an interview with the author. AL said, "They handled authors very badly" on ZT. The Lunts told Ray Weaver in a letter (May 5, 1932) that their next project would be a play with Noël Coward. Waldau also discusses their "association for a season" in *Vintage Years of the Theatre Guild*.

Notes and comments about individual plays (and the film of *The Guardsman*) appear below:

Reviews of the New York production of *Caprice:* New York *Evening World* and New York *Post,* both January 2, 1929; New York *World,* January 1, 1929; *NYT,* January 1 and January 13, 1929. Reviews in the Boston *Globe* and the Boston *Herald* are quoted by Roy S. Waldau in *Vintage Years of the Theatre Guild*.

The London production of *Caprice* was reviewed by the *Times* of London on June 5, 1929; by *Punch* on June 12, 1929; and by *NYT* on June 23, 1929. J. B. Priestley discusses the performance in *Particular Pleasures*.

Meteor: The rehearsal process is described in Lawrence Langner's *The Magic Cur-*

tain. Reviews: Boston *Herald,* December 8, 1929; *NYT,* New York *Telegram,* New York *Sun,* all December 24, 1929; the *Outlook,* January 8, 1930; Springfield (Mass.) *Union,* January 9, 1930.

Elizabeth the Queen: Maxwell Anderson's rewriting process is discussed by Lawrence Langner in *The Magic Curtain.* Jan Kowalski discusses the production in "The Critics' Choice." Reviews: Baltimore *News,* October 14, 1930; *NYT,* November 4 and November 9, 1930; New York *Sun,* New York *Tribune,* and New York *Post,* all November 4, 1930; Washington *Post,* March 24, 1931. A feature story appeared in *NYT* on January 18, 1931.

Much Ado About Nothing: The "nonproduction" is described by LF on ZT; in Theresa Helburn's *A Wayward Quest;* Roy S. Waldau's *Vintage Years of the Theatre Guild;* and Alan Hewitt's "Repertory to Residuals." The production was announced in *NYT* on June 8, 1930, and announcements of its cancellation were carried on January 14 and 15, 1931.

The Guardsman (film): accounts of the filmmaking process are derived from Frances Marion's *Off with Their Heads!;* Bob Thomas's *Thalberg;* John Baxter's *Hollywood in the Thirties;* LF's comments on ZT; the *Times* of London, June 20, 1960; New York *Daily News,* August 2, 1983; and an interview with Donald Seawell. AL was interviewed in *NYT* about his experiences in Hollywood. There are many versions of the "no lips" story. One was told by LF in a note to Maurice Zolotow; another was told by LF on UVGS. Robert Downing's comments about the film appeared in "The Movie That Changed a Life." The Lunts' viewing of the film in the 1970s is described in the San Diego *Union,* January 9, 1977. The Lunts' contractual arrangements with MGM are set forth in their contract, now at SHSW. Reviews are quoted from *NYT,* September 10 and September 20, 1931; and *Liberty,* October 1931.

Reunion in Vienna: Sherwood's conflict with Lee Simonson is detailed in John Mason Brown's *The Worlds of Robert E. Sherwood* (which also describes Sherwood's working with the Lunts in Hollywood as well as Sherwood's impressions of the Lunts) and in Lawrence Langner's *The Magic Curtain.* Reviews: *NYT,* New York *Sun* and New York *American,* all November 17, 1931; Boston *Evening Transcript,* September 20, 1932.

Chapter Eight: NOW APPEARING UNDER NEW MANAGEMENT . . .

The quotation beginning, "The actor is as much . . ." is from AL's article "Mr. Lunt Writes of Actors and Acting." LF's comment ". . . forget 'the play is the thing' . . ." was quoted in *NYT,* July 4, 1934.

Books that contributed significantly to this chapter include: Noël Coward, *Play Parade;* Max Gordon (with Lewis Funke), *Max Gordon Presents;* Roy S. Waldau, *Vintage Years of the Theatre Guild;* Cole Lesley, Graham Payn and Sheridan Morley, *Noël Coward and His Friends;* Sheridan Morley, *A Talent to Amuse.* Miscellaneous sources include Noël Coward on "The Dick Cavett Show"; LF on UVGS; AL being interviewed at Carroll College in 1973; AL on ZT; Maurice Zolotow's notes from an interview with R. (Ray) Bennett Weaver. The author's interviews with Carol Channing, George Schaefer, Alan Hewitt and John Randolph were also useful.

LF said that Noël Coward was the first truly creative director she had worked with on ACDS. The argument between AL and LF during *Design for Living* rehearsals was described by Noël Coward on ZT. The story of Lunt and Coward exchanging lines in *Design for Living* has been told often. Three sources are Morton Eustis, *Players at Work;* Noël Coward on "The Dick Cavett Show"; LF on UVGS. The aftermath—AL and Coward discovering one another in a movie theatre—was described to me by Donald Seawell. The "less elaborate version" was told by AL to Alan Hewitt.

LF's perfectionism in *Design for Living* has been detailed by Noël Coward on ZT; AL on the closed-circuit interview with George Schaefer; G. B. Stern in *And Did He Stop and Speak to You?;* and Sheridan Morley in *A Talent to Amuse.*

AL's desire to make the play the focus of his work is discussed in his article "Mr. Lunt Writes of Actors and Acting." His letter to Robert E. Sherwood is dated January 7 [1934].

The Lunts' difficulties getting passports: New York *Tribune,* September 14, 1933; New York *Sun,* September 16, 1933. The trip to Russia: Noël Coward, *Future Indefinite;* ZT; New York *Herald Tribune,* December 3, 1933; *NYT,* July 4, 1934; the *Times* of London, June 20, 1960. The Lunts' mode of travel in Egypt: New York *World-Telegram,* January 10, 1934. The visit to the circus by AL, LF and Noël Coward: *NYT,* April 10, 1933. LF's accidents in the summer of 1933: *NYT,* July 24, 1933; letter from LF to Alexander Woollcott, August 25, 1933.

Lunt's restaging of *Reunion in Vienna* for its London production is described by Elizabeth Corathiel in "How They Began." AL's letter to Robert E. Sherwood expressing irritation with the response to the play is dated January 7 [1934].

The formation of Transatlantic Productions is detailed in an interview with Donald Seawell; Sheridan Morley, *A Talent to Amuse* (in which he also speaks of the production of *Biography* in London); letter from LF to Alexander Woollcott, March 31, 1934.

The Lunts' reluctance to appear in *Point Valaine* is made clear by LF on UVGS. AL learning to play the accordion: New York *Herald Tribune,* January 27, 1935.

Reviews and descriptions of specific productions were taken from the following:

Design for Living: Cole Lesley, *Remembered Laughter.* Reviews: Cleveland *Plain Dealer,* quoted in *NYT,* January 8, 1933; Washington *Post,* January 17, 1933; *NYT,* January 25 and January 29, 1933; New York *Sun* and New York *American,* both January 25, 1933.

Reunion in Vienna in London: AL's account of LF turning blue on the unheated stage appears in a letter to Vernon Rice, January 29, 1946. Reviews: London *Observer,* the *Times* of London, London *Star,* London *Daily Telegraph,* London *Evening Standard,* all January 4, 1934; the *London Stage,* January 11, 1934; *NYT,* January 4 and January 28, 1934.

Point Valaine: Noël Coward in *Future Indefinite* described the rehearsal process as well as his evaluation of the play. Cole Lesley in *Remembered Laughter* tells of AL's embarrassment when stranded on the rock and his subsequent decision to quit the theatre. Sheridan Morley in *A Talent to Amuse* speaks of the production's technical difficulties. Reviews included reports from Boston in *NYT,* December 26 and December 30, 1934. The New York production was reviewed in *NYT* on January 17 and February 3, 1935.

Chapter Nine: RETURN TO THE THEATRE GUILD

The chief sources for this chapter included interviews with Uta Hagen, Alan Hewitt, Carolyn Every, William Le Massena, George Bugbee, Charles Bowden, Donald Seawell and Carol Channing; the books that were used throughout the chapter were: Roy S. Waldau, *Vintage Years of the Theatre Guild;* John Mason Brown, *The Worlds of Robert E. Sherwood;* Lawrence Langner, *The Magic Curtain;* Thoda Cocroft, *Great Names and How They Are Made.*

AL told Helen Ormsbee in *Backstage with Actors* about his attitude regarding playing in Shakespeare. John Mason Brown in *The Worlds of Robert E. Sherwood* tells of the Lunts turning down *Tovarich* to play in *The Taming of the Shrew*. The Lunts' performing as extras in *The Scoundrel* is detailed by Sheridan Morley in *A Talent to Amuse*. AL told Maxwell Anderson in an undated letter about Richard Whorf's eagerness to read for every role in *Shrew*.

The section on Woollcott used the following sources: LF on UVGS; "Vignettes," *Landmark;* letter from LF to Antoinette Wilson, February 27, [?]; Scott Meredith, *George S. Kaufman and His Friends;* Carolyn Every, "Home Life of the Lunts." The story of Woollcott's attempts to adopt the Lunts' techniques in *Brief Moment* is chronicled in Howard Teichmann's *Smart Aleck* and in Maurice Zolotow's *Stagestruck*.

Thoda Cocroft tells the story of "Uncle Billy" in *Great Names and How They Are Made*. The same source yielded the stories of the Lunts' acceptance speeches at the conference of club presidents and program chairmen.

The Los Angeles *Times* of December 23, 1983, revealed that *Kiss Me, Kate* had been derived from the Lunts' version of *The Taming of the Shrew*. The description of the Lunts' apartment at 130 East 75th Street is taken from a letter from LF to Graham Robertson, April 17, 1936. The Lunts' "parental feelings" were described in a letter from Bretaigne Windust to S. N. Behrman, February 2, 1937. The same letter tells of the Lunts' reaction to Tommaso Tittoni's death and of the decision not to employ Igor Stravinsky to write a score for *Amphitryon 38*.

Helen Deutsch's comment about critical expectations for *Amphitryon 38* appeared in the New York *Tribune*, October 31, 1937. The quotation of G. B. Stern's is from *And Did He Stop and Speak to You?* The Lunts' desire to form a permanent company can be found in AL's article "Mr. Lunt Writes of Actors and Acting"; Lloyd Lewis's "With the Lunts It's Time for Comedy"; and the San Francisco *Chronicle*, June 24, 1937. George Jean Nathan claimed that the Lunts were personality actors in *Encyclopedia of the Theatre*. *Stage* magazine's tribute to the Lunts appeared in "Stage Awards the Palm," *Stage*, June 1938.

Sources for specific plays are given below:

The Taming of the Shrew: Contract, Theatre Guild–John C. Wilson. The production concept is discussed in *NYT*, September 29, 1935; and in Thoda Cocroft's *Great Names and How They Are Made*. G. B. Stern's comment about Petruchio's real feelings for Kate is from *And Did He Stop and Speak to You?* LF's remarks about the difficulties involved in playing Kate appear in Morton Eustis's *Players at Work*. Reviews: *NYT*, April 23, 1935 (report from Pittsburgh); September 22, 1935 and September 29, 1935 (reports from Philadelphia); October 1 and October 20, 1935 (New York). Also: New York *Evening Journal*, October 1, 1935.

Idiot's Delight: Alan Hewitt's unpublished reminiscences supplied much of the information about the production of this play. John Mason Brown's *The Worlds of Robert E. Sherwood* contained considerable detail about the rehearsal process and the difficulties Sherwood had with the Theatre Guild's Board of Directors; Brown's book also includes Sherwood's invaluable diary for this period. AL's letter to Sherwood (speaking of "that old flapdoodle farce") is quoted in the same book. Sherwood's letter to AL was written on February 3, 1936. LF's letters to Graham Robertson are dated January 24, March 11 and April 17, 1936. LF told of her initial reading of the play in Lewis Funke and John E. Booth's *Actors Talk About Acting*. AL's preparations to play Harry are described in the same book, and are further discussed by AL on ACDS and in his article "Twenty-Six Weeks in Vaudeville"; in Morton Eustis's *Players at Work;* and in the New York *Evening Journal*, May 15, 1936. John F. Wharton in *Life Among the Playwrights* told about the contention between AL and

Sherwood on one side and the Theatre Guild's Board on the other. LF's contribution to the writing of the play can be found in letters she wrote to Sherwood dated July 1 and September 1, 1936; in a letter from AL to Sherwood, September 2, 1936; in a note from LF to Maurice Zolotow; in Morton Eustis's *Players at Work* (Eustis also refers to the production as one in which the actors' contribution was intended to outweigh that of the director); Lawrence Langner's *The Magic Curtain;* and Norman Nadel's *A Pictorial History of the Theatre Guild*. Reviews: *NYT,* March 10, 1936 (report from Washington), March 25 and April 12, 1936 (New York). The controversy in Omaha: undated letter from Alexander Woollcott to Gustav Eckstein; *NYT,* May 19, 1937; LF's note to Maurice Zolotow; letter from LF to Alexander Woollcott, June 1937; LF on UVGS; S. N. Behrman on ZT. Sherwood expressed his unhappiness that LF did not get enough credit for the success of the production in a letter to Alexander Woollcott, quoted by Walter J. Meserve in *Robert E. Sherwood*. Scott Meredith tells of the sound effects of *Idiot's Delight* interfering with *You Can't Take It with You* in *George S. Kaufman and His Friends*.

Amphitryon 38: Morton Eustis's "A Play in the Making" contains a detailed discussion of the rehearsal process. Other important sources include letters from LF to S. N. Behrman, April 5 and April 6, 1937; letter from AL to S. N. Behrman, April 5, 1937; letters from Bretaigne Windust to Behrman, February 2, April 7, April 20 and June [?], 1937; George Schaefer on *The Lunts: A Life in the Theatre*. AL's idea for the prologue is described in a letter from Bretaigne Windust to S. N. Behrman, February 2, 1937, and further discussed by AL on ZT; in a letter from S. N. Behrman dated April 23, 1953; and by Behrman on ZT. George Freedley in *The Lunts* tells the story of AL's inability to find his "green umbrella." S. N. Behrman's discussion in *People in a Diary* provided details. The story of LF's concentration preventing her from realizing that her breast was exposed to the audience was told by Renée Orsell in an interview and by Maurice Zolotow in *Stagestruck*. LF's letter to Alexander Woollcott from San Francisco is dated "June 25th on, 1937." John Hobart's account appeared in the San Francisco *Chronicle,* June 24, 1937. LF's letter to Woollcott about the performance in Baltimore was written on October 14, 1937. Reviews: Cleveland *Plain Dealer,* October 26, 1937; San Francisco *Chronicle,* June 24, 1937; Los Angeles *Daily News,* July 6, 1937; Washington *Post,* October 19, 1937; *NYT,* June 24, 1937 (report from San Francisco), November 2 and 7, 1937; New York *Journal and American,* November 2, 1937; *New Republic,* November 17, 1937.

The Sea Gull: The rehearsal process was described in interviews with Uta Hagen and Alan Hewitt, as well as in Susan Spector's "Uta Hagen" and Margaret Webster's *Don't Put Your Daughter on the Stage*. Harold Clurman says in "Theatre," the *Nation,* September 10, 1977, that he heard AL say, "Perhaps we're not . . ." AL's speech to the audience ending "Heaven help us" appears in a newspaper clipping in SHSW. AL spoke of the difficulty of the play in the New York *Journal and American,* March 27, 1938. Woollcott's reaction to the rehearsal in Baltimore is told in a letter he wrote to Graham Robertson, March [?], 1938. Fontanne spoke about her decision to wear a red wig in the New York *World-Telegram,* April 23, 1938. AL's comments to Wilella Waldorf appear in a newspaper clipping in BRTC. LF's comment "We got better as we went along" is from the *Times* of London, June 20, 1960; Harold Clurman's unfavorable verdict regarding Robert Milton's direction is from *All People Are Famous*. Reviews: Boston *Globe,* March 22, 1938; *NYT,* March 17, 1938 (report from Baltimore), March 29 and April 3, 1938 (New York);

New York *Tribune,* New York *World Telegram,* New York *Daily Mirror,* all March 29, 1938; clippings in BRTC. E. F. Harkins of the Boston *Daily Record* is quoted in Roy S. Waldau's *Vintage Years of the Theatre Guild.*

Chapter Ten: TOURING IN REPERTORY

The quotations at the head of the chapter: AL's "Why the word 'touring' . . ." is from AL's "An Editorial" in *Theatre Arts,* February 1950. LF's "I hope to be like Mrs. Fiske . . ." is from a letter she wrote to Alexander Woollcott, November 1, 1941.

The Lunts' love of touring, the difficulties they cheerfully encountered, and their activities while on tour are detailed in the following: Lewis Funke and John E. Booth, eds., *Actors Talk About Acting;* AL, "An Editorial," *Theatre Arts;* Lawrence Lader, "Lunt and Fontanne"; Carolyn N. Every, "Home Life of the Lunts"; "That Road Tour of the Lunts," *NYT,* March 26, 1939; Alice-Leone Moats, "Mr. and Mrs. Alfred Lunt"; George Freedley, "A Profile of the Lunts"; *NYT,* March 6, 1960; Robert Downing, "Perfection, Top Casts and Scripts Add to Lunts' Genius," Denver *Post,* June 20, 1971; AL in Carroll College interview, 1973; LF on UVGS; closed-circuit interview with George Schaefer, 1965; clippings in SHSW.

Particularly useful for the material in this chapter were Morton Eustis's "On the Road with the Lunts"; Alan Hewitt's reminiscences (including several interviews with Hewitt) and his "Repertory to Residuals"; *The Luntanne Tatler,* edited by Robert Downing; interviews with Uta Hagen, Wiliam Le Massena, Renée Orsell, Donald Seawell and Peg Murray.

AL said that there was progressively less movement by the actors in the production of *Amphitryon 38* on ZT; the London production was discussed and reviewed in *NYT,* May 18, 1938. Charles Morgan's review expressing his belief that LF was a more limited actor than AL appeared in *NYT,* June 5, 1938. Morgan also reviewed the play for the *Times* of London, May 18, 1938. George Jean Nathan's view of LF's limited abilities was expressed in two of his books: *The Theatre of the Moment* and *The Entertainment of a Nation.* LF's dissatisfaction with her own work appears in Morton Eustis's "Players at Work."

LF's letter to Alexander Woollcott about the success of *Amphitryon 38* is dated June 23, 1938. In that same letter she tells of her meeting with Anthony Eden. The Lunts' report about the imminent war in Europe was carried by *NYT,* September 13, 1938. LF's letter to Woollcott about the death of the Theatre Guild's electrician was written on November 7, 1938. In her letter to Woollcott of January 18, 1939, she speaks of the family Christmas and of the Lunts' determination to produce *The Sea Gull* regardless of the response. Eva Le Gallienne told of the Lunts' request that she work with them on the touring production of *The Sea Gull* in her book *With a Quiet Heart.*

AL's feud with Phil Baker is discussed in two letters he wrote to Robert E. Sherwood, dated November 13 and December 13, 1938. In the latter AL tells Sherwood that the company will be playing one-night stands for twelve weeks. In another letter to Sherwood (December 28, 1938) AL claims that the touring cast of *Idiot's Delight* will be better than the original. Alexander Woollcott's letter to AL ("After considerable gastric . . .") is dated June 6, 1939. LF reported that San Francisco was "an oasis in the desert" and that *The Taming of the Shrew* was selling out in a letter to Robert E. Sherwood, November 22, 1939.

The story of AL's taking over as company manager during the stopover in Pittsburgh was told in the Toledo *Blade,* February 4, 1951, and in other newspapers. The account of new business in the 1939–40 production of *The Taming of the Shrew* is from Travis Bogard, Richard Moody and Walter J. Meserve, *The Revels History of the Drama in English* and from an interview with Alan Hewitt. AL's report on touring ("Trains may be late . . .") is from the Columbus *Dispatch,* January 14, 1951. His article advocating a permanent ensemble company playing in repertory, entitled "Mr. Lunt Writes of Actors and Acting," appeared in *NYT,* November 16, 1930.

A document in SHSW, headed "Project for Lunt-Fontanne Repertory Company Managed by the Theatre Guild," is attached to correspondence from Warren Munsell and was probably prepared by him. The document details the plans for the proposed company. AL proposed a less ambitious repertory to Robert E. Sherwood in a 1942 letter (no specific date given).

Chapter Eleven: THE WAR YEARS

The quotations at the beginning of the chapter are from the Philadelphia *Record,* April 13, 1941 (". . . something like playing . . .") and from Maurice Zolotow's *Stagestruck* ("We could not be at peace . . .").

George S. Kaufman's testimony before the Senate Immigration Subcommittee is detailed in Scott Meredith's *George S. Kaufman and His Friends.* The letter from LF to Margaret Anglin is dated March 6, 1941. The controversy about the benefits for the Finnish Relief Fund is discussed in *NYT,* January 19, 1940. Letters from Edna Ferber to AL are dated September 18 and September 21, 1940.

Information about the Lunts' political philosophy came from interviews with Renée Orsell, Donald Seawell, William Le Massena, George Bugbee and George Schaefer. LF told of her political impartiality on the closed-circuit interview with George Schaefer in 1965. LF's support of the Conservatives in England is clear from a letter she wrote to Lady Juliet Duff on March 16, 1950. Franklin Roosevelt's letter to the Lunts was written on November 28, 1940. The Lunts' inability to attend Roosevelt's inauguration is told in a letter from LF to Stark Young, February 1, 1941. The Lunts' contributions to Allied causes are detailed in documents in SHSW and in *NYT,* September 24 and 26, October 22, November 11 and December 7, 1940.

LF's letter to Stark Young ("You cannot be . . .") was written on December 31, 1940. Her letter from which "I am a little tired . . ." was taken is dated December 3, 1942. Richard Coe spoke of the Lunts' assistance in his effort to integrate Washington's theatres at the Theatre Guild tribute to the Lunts in 1983. The letter from AL's boyhood friend is in the Lunts' file at SHSW.

AL's letter resigning from the Theatre Guild board is dated May 25, 1940. His efforts to learn about the financial side of the theatre were described on ZT.

The most significant sources detailing the production of *There Shall Be No Night* are: John Mason Brown, *The Ordeal of a Playwright;* interviews with Phyllis Thaxter and William Le Massena (the story about LF's helping Thaxter get the leading role in the touring production of *Claudia* is from a letter of LF's to Le Massena, August 22, 1941); John F. Wharton, *Life Among the Playwrights;* Patricia Bosworth, *Montgomery Clift;* Brooks Atkinson, "The Lunts Celebrate Their Silver Jubilee"; *Current Biography,* 1941; and LF on UVGS.

Reviews and comments about *There Shall Be No Night: NYT,* March 30, 1940 (report from Providence), April 30 (New York) and May 5, 1940. New York *Journal-American,* May 1, 1940; New York *Herald Tribune,* April 30, 1940; Eleanor Roosevelt in "My Day" (clipping in BRTC). A story in *NYT,* June 30, 1940, discusses the production and includes the detail that AL based his makeup on Thomas Mann. Information (including the story about LF asking actors to contribute books and magazines for distribution to Allied soldiers) was taken from *The Luntanne Tatler.* The difficulties with the Theatre Arts Committee are detailed in *NYT,* May 31, 1940, and *TAC News,* June 1, 1940.

Robert E. Sherwood's article about his intentions in writing the play appeared in *NYT,* May 5, 1940. AL's statement ("Giving these performances . . .") is taken from *Current Biography,* 1941. Alexander Woollcott's letter to Graham Robertson is dated November 20, 1940; the same letter contains his description of his emotional reaction to *There Shall Be No Night.* An account of the tour is provided in *NYT,* March 30, 1941 (Maurice Colbourne, "Note from the Tour of the Lunts"), which tells of the newspaper calling Sherwood "the author of *Idiot's Delight*" and quotes letters sent to the Lunts by spectators.

AL's statement "Lynn never used to read . . ." is from the Philadelphia *Record,* April 13, 1941. AL told Sherwood that Chicago was "notoriously anti-war" in a letter, December 27, 1940. The forged letters to Washington newspapers are in the Lunts' file in SHSW, as are the responses of Richard L. Coe and Henry MacArthur.

LF's readings of *The White Cliffs* are described in letters from LF (February 1 and 8, 1941), the latter to Ruth Gordon; *NYT,* August 31, 1942; and George Freedley's "A Profile of the Lunts."

The impact of *There Shall Be No Night* on Mackenzie King was told in the Boston *Globe,* November 1, 1942. G. H. Lash's letter to the Lunts is dated July 25, 1940. The Lunts' decision not to film *There Shall Be No Night* is revealed in a letter from LF to Alexander Woollcott, March 19, 1941.

The production of *Candle in the Wind* is detailed in many letters AL wrote to Maxwell Anderson; all are undated and are collected at the University of Texas. John F. Wharton's *Life Among the Playwrights* provided meaningful information, as did an article in *NYT,* June 17, 1942; a letter from AL to Helen Hayes, June 24, 1941; letters from LF to Alexander Woollcott, June 17, 1941 and August 20, 1941; and the contract AL signed with the Playwrights' Company. LF's letter to Noël Coward is dated October 25, 1941. The review in *NYT* appeared on October 23, 1941.

LF's letter to Alexander Woollcott about the Lunts' anniversary was written on May 28, 1941. The decision to cut short the tour of *There Shall Be No Night* is detailed in *NYT,* December 15, 1941. AL wrote to Robert E. Sherwood about touring plays to army camps on November 15, 1941.

Information about the Stage Door Canteen came from Brooks Atkinson's *Broadway; Leading Lady* by Tad Mosel, with Gertrude Macy; *NYT,* August 17, 1942; and an interview with Alan Hewitt. Woollcott called AL "the chief cook" in a letter dated May 26, 1942. The letter from LF to Woollcott about *This Is the Army* was written on July 13, 1942.

AL's cooking classes were described by Elsa Maxwell in "Alfred Lunt . . . Cook"; *NYT,* April 15, 1942 ("Lunt Shows His Skill as a Wartime Chef [Coffee Excepted] for a Theatre Wing Class"); and in a letter from LF to Woollcott, April 24, 1942.

AL's skill at cooking and love of good food are discussed in the following: Carolyn Every, "Home Life of the Lunts"; interviews with Carolyn Every, Peg Murray, Suzanne Knapp, Dick Van Patten and Harriet Owens; Peter Daubeny, *My World of Theatre;* "He Likes to Cook" in *Better Homes and Gardens;* Lawrence Lader's "Lunt and Fontanne"; "Mr. Lunt in a New Role" in *Vogue; NYT,* March 15, 1942, November 22, 1942, and May 29, 1958; Marie Benyon Ray's "Chef's Role"; Milwaukee *Journal* (n.d.; clipping in SHSW); Libbie Nolan's "So Many Talents . . ."; letters from AL to: Maurice Zolotow (July 9, 1959); William Fields (August 12, 1951); Lee Wright (June 26, 1962); William Le Massena (November 12, 1972). Also: S. N. Behrman on ZT; letter from LF to Antoinette Keith, June

11, 1942; AL on the closed-circuit interview with George Schaefer, 1965; LF on UVGS. AL's unpublished cookbook is in the Lunt-Fontanne file at SHSW. LF's recipe for tea is from a letter she wrote to Alexander Woollcott, January 12, 1942.

The Lunts' generosity is described by Laurence Olivier in *Confessions of an Actor;* Cathleen Nesbitt's *A Little Love and Good Company;* interviews with Dr. Edward Bigg, Donald Seawell, William Le Massena, George Schaefer, Carol Channing and Alan Hewitt; Charlotte Hughes, "Leading—and Vibrant—Ladies"; Clarke Robinson, "Silhouettes of Celebrities." The Lunts' commitment to sending gifts of food and clothing to friends in Europe during and after the war are documented in many letters expressing thanks in the Lunt-Fontanne file, SHSW; letters from LF to: Bessie Porter (June 1, 1942); Jane and Wilfred de Glehn (September 28, 1946); Habetrot Dewhurst (May 30, 1946); Lady Juliet Duff (January 5, 1946, and February 25, 1947); Antoinette Keith (April 18, September 6 and December 23, 1946); Fryn Harwood (January 30, 1947); Mai Potiki (August 31, 1946); Terence Rattigan (June 22 and September 26, 1946); Binkie Beaumont (November 9, 1946). Also: a clipping from the Louisville *Times* (n.d.) in SHSW; New York *World-Telegram,* February 3, 1943.

Information about the audition scenes the Lunts held for young actors was derived from interviews with Uta Hagen, William Le Massena, Donald Seawell, George Bugbee, Charles Bowden and Alan Hewitt; Charlotte Hughes, "Leading—and Vibrant—Ladies"; letters from Jean Stapleton to LF, February 17 and June 13, 1946; LF, quoted by Helen Ormsbee in a newspaper clipping in BRTC; *NYT,* July 31, 1983.

The "Touch Letters" file is in SHSW. The story of the twenty-seven-year-old forger is told in *NYT,* May 1, 1925.

The film *Stage Door Canteen* is discussed in the New York *Evening Star,* October 22, 1942; *NYT,* January 10, May 13, June 25 (review) and November 28, 1943.

LF's angry letter to Alexander Woollcott about the Theatre Guild is dated March 8, 1946.

The production of *The Pirate* is discussed by Lawrence Langner in *The Magic Curtain;* S. N. Behrman in ZT; a letter from LF to Woollcott, May 28, 1942; and an interview with Renée Orsell. Reviews appeared in the Chicago *Tribune* (clipping in SHSW); Chicago *Sun,* September 16, 1942; Boston *Herald,* October 27, 1942; *NYT,* September 15, 1942 (report from Madison), November 26, 1942 (New York), December 6, 1942; New York *Sun,* November 27, 1942.

The Lunts' decision to go to England during the war is told in LF's letter to Noël Coward, December 8, 1942, and in an interview with Donald Seawell. LF's letter to Air Marshal Bishop is dated April 19, 1943. Her description of the trip to Lisbon comes from an undated letter (written in 1943) at SHSW; the same letter contains her impressions of wartime London; AL described the flight to London in a letter to Richard and Tinx Whorf on October 24, 1943; AL's volunteer work in London is described by Maurice Zolotow in *Stagestruck;* AL told the Whorfs about casting *There Shall Be No Night* in London in a letter dated October 24, 1943; LF expressed her belief that the London cast was better than the New York cast in an undated letter in SHSW; AL reported to Robert E. Sherwood on the progress of rehearsals in a letter on October 19, 1943. The critical reaction to the London production appears in the *Times* of London and *NYT,* December 16, 1943.

Details of the Lunts' performances in England were taken primarily from Clifton Daniel's "With the Lunts on the (Buzz-Bombed) Road" and Lloyd Lewis's "With the Lunts It's Time for Comedy." AL's comments about the British audiences' response to *There Shall Be No Night* appear in Lewis's article. LF is quoted on the same subject in Paula Laurence's "Alfred Lunt and Lynn Fontanne . . .

Their Most Memorable Theatrical Experience"; Lewis and Laurence both discuss the near-miss of the buzz bomb during a performance. AL expresses his lack of fear ("I don't think I was heroic . . .") in Maurice Zolotow's *Stagestruck*. The account of the performance at Windsor Castle is taken from ZT, Daniel's article and the *Times* of London, June 20, 1960. The return to the Lunts' hotel is also described in the last two sources. AL's comments ("We were afraid of . . ." and "How on earth . . .") both appear in Daniel's article.

The letter from the secretary of the King of England to the Lunts is dated February 7, 1944. LF's letter telling of the King's interest in *The White Cliffs* is undated; it can be found in the Lunt-Fontanne file, SHSW. AL's letter to William Le Massena about the tour of the British provinces was written on January 4, 1945. The Lunts told Richard and Tinx Whorf of their stay with Ivor Novello in a letter, July 8, 1944. In that same letter AL said, "We do not wish to go back to America now."

The writing, rehearsal process and production of *Love in Idleness* are discussed in Maurice Zolotow's *Stagestruck*; ZT; LF on UVGS; and in Clifton Daniel's "With the Lunts on the (Buzz-Bombed) Road." Daniel quotes Lunt saying, "We don't see how. . . ." AL tells about Winston Churchill's attending a performance of *Love in Idleness* in Lloyd Lewis's "With the Lunts It's Time for Comedy." The Lunts were thanked for their performance in the Royal Palace of Westminster by T. G. B. Cocks, Secretary of the House of Commons, in a letter dated January 15, 1945. That performance is discussed in "The Lunts at Ten Chimneys," *Country Beautiful*, October 1962.

Love in Idleness on the "Foxhole Circuit" is described in *NYT*, April 20, 1945, and May 26, 1947; and in a clipping from an unidentified newspaper in SHSW. George S. Patton's letter to LF was written on August 15, 1945. *NYT*, August 9, 1945, described the Lunts' return to the United States. Lunt's comment "Why, it was the greatest . . ." is taken from Lloyd Lewis's "With the Lunts It's Time for Comedy."

Chapter Twelve: A LOSS OF PERSPECTIVE? (1945–57)

The four quotations at the beginning of the chapter: W. A. Darlington, "London Letter," *NYT*, October 12, 1952; Harold Clurman, *Lies Like Truth;* Brooks Atkinson, *NYT*, January 5, 1956; AL, ZT.

The Lunts' rejection of *The Twilight* is detailed in LF's letter to Robert E. Sherwood, April [?], 1947; Sherwood's letter to the Lunts, July 26, 1947; AL's letter to Sherwood, August 2, 1947; and in John F. Wharton's *Life Among the Playwrights*. AL told of his suggestion, "Put us in a covered wagon," in ZT. Sherwood's response is in a letter to AL, March 20, 1955.

O Mistress Mine is discussed in Lawrence Lader's "Lunt and Fontanne" (for an account of opening night) and John Mason Brown's "Reunion in New York" (quoting AL's curtain speech). Reviews of the production appeared in *NYT*, January 24 and February 3, 1946 (Nichols), September 1, 1946 (Atkinson); and the New York *Morning Telegraph*, January 25, 1946. *NYT* (January 12 and 27, February 24, March 28, 1947) details AL's ailments forcing a suspension of the production. Helen Ormsbee spoke of the pre-sale in a newspaper clipping in the AL-LF file, BRTC.

Evidence that LF was rewriting *O Mistress Mine* during the run appears in a letter she wrote to Terence Rattigan, September 26, 1946. A clipping from the New York *Post* in SHSW tells about AL giving up alcohol and carrying a water-filled martini glass. AL said "We are not tired of it . . ." in a letter to Richard and

Tinx Whorf, April 22, 1947. AL insisted the play was a satisfactory one ("The plot line . . .") on ZT.

The section on the Lunts' wealth is derived from interviews with Donald Seawell, George Bugbee, Edward Bigg and Julie Harris. Alan Hewitt told me AL turned down *Marie Antoinette;* LF told Alexander Woollcott about the offer from Fleischmann's Yeast in a letter dated July 26, 1933. The story of the Lunts' investment in *Oklahoma!* is told by Richard Maney in *Fanfare.* Profit distribution sheets from that musical are on file at SHSW. LF told Binkie Beaumont of the investment in *Gentlemen Prefer Blondes* in a letter, December 12, 1949. The investments in *Bless You All* and *Out of This World* are authenticated in documents in the Lunts' file, SHSW.

Tributes from the Players Club: *NYT,* April 30, 1947; "Pipe Night at the Players" (recording); interview with Alan Hewitt; documents in the Players Club library. The honorary doctorate awarded the Lunts by NYU is discussed in *NYT,* June 15, 1950; LF's doctorate from Russell Sage College is described in *NYT,* July 31, 1983.

The most significant sources for the production of *I Know My Love* are: letters and a telegram from S. N. Behrman to AL, May 1948 through October 1950; letters from LF to Behrman, March 1948 through September 1949; letters and a telegram from AL to Behrman, April 1948 through September 1949; a letter from Behrman to Carl Hovey, May 2, 1949; a letter from Behrman to Theresa Helburn, September 7, 1949; and a letter (March 17, 1948) and a telegram from Helen Hayes to Behrman. All of this material is in the S. N. Berhman file, SHSW.

Other sources include: S. N. Behrman, *People in a Diary;* Norman Nadel, *A Pictorial History of the Theatre Guild;* letter from A. T. Weaver to Behrman, February 23, 1949; letter from LF to Mai Potiki, December 8, 1949 (describing *I Know My Love* as "a smash hit" and telling of AL's state of health). LF says she likes Behrman's version better than the French in a letter to Antoinette Keith, May 13, 1948; she told Lady Juliet Duff in a letter of March 16, 1949, and Noël Coward in a letter of October 23, 1950, of AL's illnesses on the pre-Broadway tour. The problems the Lunts had with the "wig man" are detailed by AL in a letter he wrote to Theresa Helburn, Lawrence Langner and Armina Marshall, November 3, 1950.

Reviews of *I Know My Love: Time,* March 7, 1949 (Madison); St. Louis *Post-Dispatch* (clipping in S. N. Behrman file, SHSW); Milwaukee *Sentinel,* February 23, 1949; Orgeon *Journal,* May 18, 1949; Kansas City *Times,* March 23, 1949; New York *Sun* and New York *Post,* November 3, 1949; *NYT,* February 24, 1949 (Madison), October 14, 1949 (Boston), November 3 and 20, 1949 (New York); John Mason Brown's notice is in the *Saturday Review,* December 3, 1949. Kenneth Tynan's account of the Lunts' touring performance appears in Cecil Beaton and Kenneth Tynan's *Persona Grata.*

Material discussing *Quadrille* includes: AL's letters to William Le Massena; AL, LF and Noël Coward on "The Dick Cavett Show"; an article by Elliot Norton in the Boston *Post* (clipping in the Lunts' file, SHSW); G. B. Stern, *And Did He Stop and Speak to You?;* Cecil Beaton, "Diary of a Designer: Setting the Stage for *Quadrille*"; Eric Johns's "The Lunt Legend"; and Sheridan Morley's *A Talent to Amuse.*

Rehearsals and performances of *Quadrille* in England are described in Elliot Norton's article in the Boston *Post* (clipping in SHSW), which includes the quotation "They were shimmering. . . ." Reviews in England: the *Times* of London, September 13, 1952; *NYT,* September 13, 1952 (quotes reviews from the following London newspapers: *Daily Telegraph, Daily Express, Daily Mail* and *News Chronicle*), October 12, 1952, April 5, 1953; London *Morning Advertiser,* September 13, 1952. Kenneth Tynan's verdict is in Cecil Beaton and Kenneth Tynan's *Persona Grata*.

Noël Coward's diary entry "I have seldom read . . ." is dated September 19, 1952. All diary entries used in this chapter are taken from Noël Coward, *The Noël Coward Diaries*, September 13, 1952–March 10, 1955.

The quotation about AL not getting the laugh he wanted in *Quadrille* is from his interview at Carroll College in 1973; he told the same story in different words on ZT and on "The Dick Cavett Show." Noël Coward's statement about directing the Lunts is from ZT. AL's letter to Richard Whorf ("My hands are so sore . . .") is dated September 1, 1954. AL is quoted on the Boston opening of *Quadrille* ("Being director . . .") by Elliot Norton in the Boston *Post* (clipping in SHSW). Coward's letter to AL ("It is all very exciting . . .") is dated October 25, 1954. New York reviews of *Quadrille: NYT,* November 4 and 14, 1954; New York *Journal-American,* November 4, 1954.

Information about the Lunts' decision to close *Quadrille* comes from interviews with Donald Seawell and Alan Hewitt; a letter from Donald Seawell to AL, August 30, 1954; AL's letter to Maxwell Anderson, March 30, 1954.

The story of LF's reluctance to play in *Life with Father* is taken from Richard Maney's "To Err Is Human." The story has been told in many other articles and books.

Material about the production of *The Great Sebastians* came primarily from letters from Howard Lindsay and Russel Crouse to AL and LF, April 1955 through September 1955; and letters from AL to Lindsay and Crouse from April 1955 through January 1957; these letters are housed in the Lindsay-Crouse file at SHSW. Also: AL and LF on ACDS; interviews with Peg Murray, Eugenia Rawls and Donald Seawell; ZT; *NYT,* January 1 and 7, 1956; Cornelia Otis Skinner's *Life with Lindsay and Crouse*.

AL's love of vaudeville is told in his article "Twenty-Six Weeks in Vaudeville"; and in the New York *Daily News*, April 25, 1933; *NYT,* March 22, 1936.

Reviews of *The Great Sebastians:* Harold Clurman in *The Nation* (reprinted in *Lies Like Truth*); *NYT,* January 5 and 15, 1956; and the Detroit *Free Press,* October 2, 1956.

AL on the difficulty of conversing with the audience: interview at Carroll College, 1973. AL's letter to Russel Crouse: "The reviews were so dreary . . ." is dated November 1, 1956; "We have *3 new sure-fire laughs* . . ." is dated January 14, 1957; and "Good audience last night . . ." is dated November 6, 1956.

Television production and reviews: interview with Donald Seawell; ZT; *NYT,* April 2 and 7, 1957; New York *World-Telegram,* New York *Herald Tribune* and *Variety,* all April 2, 1957. Noël Coward's comment about *The Great Sebastians* appears on ZT.

The section concerning the Lunts' "wasted talents" quotes Hiram Motherwell in "When Great Acting?"; Peter Roberts in "Truth, Tricks or Technique?"; J. B. Priestley in *Particular Pleasures;* Lee Strasberg in Toby Cole and Helen Krich Chinoy's *Actors on Acting;* and AL ("The list of authors . . .") in a newspaper article by William Glover of the Associated Press (the clipping is in the Lunts' file at SHSW). Theresa Helburn's comments are from *A Wayward Quest*.

Chapter Thirteen: ANOTHER PERSPECTIVE (1945–57)

The quotation at the beginning of the chapter is from an interview with Dick Van Patten, who also served as the primary source for the material dealing with the production and tour of *O Mistress Mine*.

Theresa Helburn in *A Wayward Quest* described AL's reaction to the missing scenery. LF's views on casting the role of the boy were quoted by Lloyd Lewis in "With the Lunts It's Time for Comedy"; an account of various production details was given in the Milwaukee *Journal,* July 24, 1977; AL's last-minute attempts to improve the play were described by Lawrence Langner in *The Magic Curtain; NYT* (February 10, 1946) spoke of the benefit performances given; LF discussed her opinion of the American cast and of Dick Van Patten in a letter to Habetrot Dewhurst, May 30, 1946. Other sources include AL's letter to Richard Whorf, January 8, 1946; interviews with William Le Massena, Eugenia Rawls and Alan Hewitt (who recalled the backstage atmosphere during the Lunts' productions).

The Lunts' personalities were explored by Lewis Funke and John E. Booth in *Actors Talk About Acting* (which also quotes AL: "As much as possible . . ."); Peter Daubeny in *My World of Theatre;* Alan Hewitt, George Bugbee, Anna Jane Berg, Eugenia Rawls, Renée Orsell, Dick Van Patten, William Le Massena and Peg Murray in interviews; Noël Coward on ZT ("They are incapable . . ."); Charlotte Hughes in "Leading—and Vibrant—Ladies"; Theresa Helburn in *A Wayward Quest;* Frederick Wagner and Barbara Brady in *Famous American Actors and Actresses;* Lawrence Lader in "Lunt and Fontanne"; Henry and Helena Pringle in "Why Don't They Fight?"; *NYT,* August 4, 1977.

AL's toy-theatre collection and the exhibition at the Museum of the City of New York: a poster issued by the Museum, 1946; a press release from the Museum, June 17, 1957; interview with Wendy Warnken, Assistant Curator of the Museum, 1983; "The Talk of the Town," *New Yorker,* January 11, 1947; John Mason Brown, *Seeing More Things;* "Alfred Lunt Presents: Penny Plain and Tuppence Colored," *Theatre Arts,* January 1947; Lawrence Lader, "Lunt and Fontanne"; Cincinnati *Enquirer,* December 17, 1946; Ward Morehouse, "Lunt's Toy Theatres," clipping in SHSW (quotes May Davenport Seymour); letters from LF to Graham Robertson, September 12, 1946, and to Jane and Wilfred de Glehn, September 28, 1946.

The Lunts' New York house was described in interviews with George Schaefer, Donald Seawell (who told about LF's solution to the problem with the boiler); Gladys Taber, "Star Performance" (quotes AL, "You have never seen . . ."); New York *Morning Telegraph,* September 17, 1958 (article by Whitney Bolton); the Louisville *Courier-Journal,* January 27, 1951. LF wrote to Lady Juliet Duff about the house on March 16, 1950 ("A frenzy of remodeling . . ." and "All kinds of modern . . .") and to Binkie Beaumont on December 12, 1949. She is quoted saying, "Offering us a room . . ." in "Value Is a Family Affair," *House and Garden,* October 1959.

Ten Chimneys, the Lunts' activities there, their farming and the village of Genesee Depot are discussed in: Peter Daubeny, *My World of Theatre;* Lloyd Lewis, "With the Lunts It's Time for Comedy"; "Mr. and Mrs.," *Time,* November 8, 1937; "Country Cousins," *New Yorker,* December 4, 1954 (quotes AL about his garden, the farm animals, the dairy; quotes LF about AL's passion for back-breaking work and about the disappearing lake); "They Glory in a Rustic, High-Style Hideaway," *Life,* July 26, 1963 (quotes AL about his stone wall looking "like cupids' bottoms" and his enthusiasm for hard work); "Value Is a Family Affair," *House and Garden,* October 1959; Lawrence Lader, "Lunt and Fontanne"; Carolyn Every, "Home Life of the Lunts"; Dan Sullivan, "Alfred Lunt, Actor and Farmer, is 76 Today," *NYT,* August 19, 1968; "On the Farm with the Lunts," *Christian Science Monitor* Magazine Section, October 28, 1950; John F. Wharton, *Life Among the Playwrights* (tells of S. N. Behrman's report that only a few cows inhabited the farm); "Reunion in Genesee," *Vogue,* November 1, 1933 (tells that LF posed for both Adam and Eve); Ward Morehouse, "Lynn Fontanne and Alfred Lunt, of Genesee, Wisconsin" (quotes AL's instructions to Claggett Wilson and LF's comment; also describes the furnishings in the house); interviews with Mary

Sargent, Carol Channing, Charles Bowden, Gwen Davies, Carolyn Every, Edward Bigg, George Bugbee, Suzanne Knapp and George Schaefer; Waukesha *Freeman,* August 3, 1977, and August 20, 1983; *NYT,* June 30, 1940, and March 15, 1942 (quotes AL, "You see, we had so few clothes"); Milwaukee *Sentinel,* September 15, 1972; James Gray, *Pine, Stream & Prairie;* Marie Benyon Ray, "The Lunts on Their Farm"; Alice-Leone Moats, "Mr. and Mrs. Alfred Lunt"; clippings in SHSW and BRTC; letter from LF to Antoinette Keith, June 11, 1942 (about the tear in AL's slacks); Libbie Nolan, "Lunt-Fontanne"; Aylesa Forsee, *My Love and I Together* ("Guarantee Trust"); New York *World-Telegram,* February 3, 1943 (buying a third cow "as a radiator"); Clarke Robinson, "Silhouettes of Celebrities"; letters from AL to William Le Massena, Richard and Tinx Whorf, Edward Bigg; Maurice Zolotow, "Design for Graceful Living"; AL at Carroll College interview, 1973 ("They don't like to work . . ."); Milwaukee *Journal,* May 15, 1954; letter from the State Geologist of the Wisconsin Geological Survey to the Lunts, November 30, 1954; "The Lunts at Ten Chimneys," *Country Beautiful,* October 1962 (quotes LF; "Theatre people live on their nerves" and AL: "After I finish working . . ."); AL and LF on closed-circuit interview with George Schaefer, 1965; LF on UVGS.

Additional information about the Lunts' pets and animals was furnished by Cathleen Nesbitt in *A Little Love and Good Company;* "Vignettes," *Landmark,* Autumn 1981; a letter from LF to William Le Massena, June 30, 1967 (about Walter the goose); a letter from AL to Romney Brent, February 4, 1970 (about the death of Walter the goose); New York *Post,* February 26, 1938; New York *World-Telegram*—clipping in BRTC (tells of squirrels and a chipmunk eating from LF's hand); Boston *Globe,* November 1, 1942; letters from LF to Molly Humphrey, May 14, 1946 (about the *O Mistress Mine* company giving Lisa to LF as an opening-night gift), to Sibyl Colefax, April 20, 1950 (about bringing Lisa to England), to Graham Robertson, September 12, 1946 (about Lisa's progress), to Jane and Wilfred de Glehn, September 28, 1946, and to Terence Rattigan, September 26, 1946 ("Alfred and I had . . ."); Blue Ribbon of Merit award to "Miss Lisa Lunt" given by *O Mistress Mine* company, January 8, 1947 (SHSW); Los Angeles *Times,* June 11, 1972; Chicago *Sun-Times,* August 10, 1983.

The tour of *I Know My Love* was discussed in *NYT,* November 4, 1950 (LF breaking her arm), and November 28, 1950 (about the performance without scenery or costumes). LF's letter to Maurice Zolotow, January 2, 1951, told of the series of accidents on the tour and about the missing scenery. More information about LF's broken arm came from an interview with Renée Orsell, a letter from Renée Orsell to Antoinette Keith, November 4, 1950, and LF on UVGS.

The anecdote ending "Why does Alfred mind?" appeared in the Boston *Evening American,* October 23, 1950; LF's message to AL, delivered by the stage manager, is described in the Toledo *Blade,* February 4, 1951; AL said the touring cast of *I Know My Love* was better than the original in a letter to Ray Weaver, October 5, 1950. Elliot Norton's notice appears in a clipping in the AL-LF file, SHSW.

Così fan tutte is discussed on ZT; "Celestial Reviewer: Alfred Lunt," *Opera News* (quotes AL: "We are trying . . ." and describes his feeling of freedom to dispense with realism in the staging of operas); *NYT,* December 23, 1951 (article by Howard Taubman about AL's staging which includes several quotations from AL); Howard Taubman, *The Making of the American Theatre;* Howard Taubman, "Inescapable Stamp of the Lunt Style" (discusses AL's private expenditure of money and his comment "You are paying . . ."); *NYT Magazine,* January 27, 1952 (quotes a singer, "He made us feel . . ."). *NYT,* December 28, 1951; December 29, 1951, and January 6, 1952 (reviews); letters from AL to William Le Massena, June 17, 1951, and August 21, 1962; letter from Rudolf Bing to AL, April 5,

1951 (stipulates contractual arrangements); letter from AL to Bing, March 28, 1951 ("Much depends on . . ." and "tried to instill . . ."); Patrice Munsel, "Alfred Goes to the Met" (quotes AL: "If you beat your breasts . . ."); Metropolitan Opera broadcasts, February 20, 1965, and March 31, 1984; AL on closed-circuit interview with George Schaefer, 1965 ("No! I would like . . ."); Eric Bentley, *The Dramatic Event* (review). John Mason Brown's description of AL's performance is in the *Saturday Review of Literature*, January 19, 1952.

The contrast between the directorial styles of AL and LF is told by Theresa Helburn in *A Wayward Quest*. AL's statement while directing *Candle in the Wind*, "John, that man . . . ," is from John F. Wharton's *Life Among the Playwrights*. William Le Massena provided insights into Lunt's directorial style in an interview. Maurice Zolotow quotes AL, "A director must have . . ." in "Alfred Lunt, Director." Evidence that Lunt turned down the opportunities to direct *Medea, Caligula, An Inspector Calls* and *Small War on Murray Hill* is found in documents in the Lunts' file, SHSW; a letter from AL to John Golden, December 18, 1946; and letters from Robert E. Sherwood to AL, April 12 and May 2, 1955.

Important sources for the section on *Ondine* included AL's letters to Richard and Tinx Whorf, and interviews with Alan Hewitt and Maurice Valency. The New York *World-Telegram*, February 18, 1954, told of Giraudoux's asking the Lunts to act in *Ondine;* AL's letter to Robert E. Sherwood ("Music too . . .") is dated November 11, 1953; the difficulty of casting *Ondine* was told by AL and LF on ZT; An unidentified actor is quoted saying, "Lunt works us . . ." in Maurice Zolotow's "Alfred Lunt, Director," which also includes AL's comment "It's no use. . . ." Margaret Sullavan's appreciative letter to AL is undated.

Robert E. Sherwood wrote to LF about Maxwell Anderson on February 10, 1954; the story of Audrey Hepburn's trip to New York to visit Sherwood is told in John F. Wharton's *Life Among the Playwrights*. Sherwood's cable to Lunt is dated February 5, 1954.

The Boston reviews of *Ondine* appeared in the Boston *Evening American, Herald* and *Post*, all on January 30, 1954. Audrey Hepburn was quoted in the Boston *Sunday Globe*, January 31, 1954. Alan Hewitt was quoted in the Boston *Herald*, February 8, 1954. The opening-night party is described by John F. Wharton in *Life Among the Playwrights*. LF's comment on Mel Ferrer ("That wasn't jealousy . . .") is taken from ZT; the battle over curtain calls is described in a clipping in SHSW (probably the New York *Journal-American*, February 27, 1954).

New York reviews of *Ondine: NYT,* New York *Journal-American,* New York *Post,* New York *Herald Tribune,* New York *Daily Mirror,* Long Island *Evening News,* all February 19, 1954. Also, *NYT,* February 28, 1954, New York *Post,* February 28, 1954, Eric Bentley, *The Dramatic Event*. The letter from AL to Sherwood ("All the medals . . .") is dated June 2, 1954. The box-office returns for *Ondine* were detailed in the Long Island *Star Journal,* July 10, 1954.

The section on the Lunts' health is derived from an interview with Dr. Edward Bigg, letters from LF to Lady Juliet Duff, Binkie Beaumont and Habetrot Dewhurst. Hattie Sederholm's death: AL's letter to Richard Whorf, November 25, 1953; Gustav Eckstein's letter to the Lunts, November 23, 1952; *NYT,* May 17, 1955. The death of Robert E. Sherwood: Alan Hewitt, unpublished reminiscences; ZT; *NYT,* November 17, 1955.

The section dealing with the Lunts' relationship and their interdependence was derived largely from interviews with Edward Bigg, William Le Massena, Alan Hewitt, George Bugbee, Suzanne Knapp, Mary Sargent, Peg Murray, Phyllis Thaxter, Donald Seawell, George Schaefer, Carol Channing and Dick Van Patten; also from the eulogy to the Lunts by Donald Seawell; LF on UVGS; and LF and AL on "The Dick Cavett Show."

Specific sources in this section included the following: LF, quoted in Lewis Funke and John E. Booth's *Actors Talk About Acting* ("Over a long run . . ."); Washington *Post,* August 10, 1976 ("You're in my light!"); Henry Pringle in "The Husband-Wife Act" (quoting AL: "Without Lynn?"); ZT (on which AL says, "The answer is so simple . . ." and Noël Coward says, "We just talk . . ."); Milwaukee *Journal,* March 12, 1967 (quoting LF, ". . . going to rehearsal . . ."); Eric Johns, "The Lunts and Peter Brook" (quoting LF, ". . . really enrages me . . ."); Robert E. Sherwood, "The Lunts" (". . . angrily and embarrassingly . . ."); Arthur Marshall, quoting LF in "The Tall Gentleman." AL and LF wrote about their twenty-eighth anniversary in the Boston *Traveler,* October 10, 1950; LF was quoted saying, "I used to stand . . ." in the San Diego *Union,* January 9, 1977; she answered, "My marriage to Alfred . . ." in Libbie Nolan's "Lunt-Fontanne."

Chapter Fourteen: THE VISIT

The single most important source in this chapter was John Randolph's account of *The Visit* in America, recorded in letters he wrote to his wife, Sarah, and in several interviews with the author.

The quotation at the beginning of the chapter by Peter Brook is taken from Randolph Goodman's *Drama on Stage,* which also served as the basis for much of the material in this chapter.

Interviews with Donald Seawell, Roger Stevens, Maurice Valency, Charles Bowden and William Le Massena also contributed significantly to the writing of this chapter.

AL's comment "We thought it . . ." was contained in a letter from AL to Randolph Goodman, published in Goodman's *Drama on Stage.* Madeline Sherwood's letter to the Lunts is dated February 4, 1957. LF's letter (". . . with flying saucepans . . .") was written to Edward Bigg, October 6, 1957. An article by Craig Claiborne in *NYT,* May 29, 1958, discusses AL's cooking class. AL is quoted having modeled Schill "on a man in Genesee Depot . . ." in Randolph Goodman's *Drama on Stage.* AL also made the same claim to Lewis Funke and John E. Booth, eds., in *Actors on Acting.*

AL spoke about aging his costumes ("I rolled around in them . . .") in the interview he gave at Carroll College in 1973. Peter Brook's comment ("Painting a picture . . .") is from Randolph Goodman's *Drama on Stage.* Brook's view of AL as one of the three greatest living English-speaking actors in 1958 was quoted in the Newark *Star-Ledger,* May 16, 1958.

Reaction to *The Visit* in England was described in interviews with Donald Seawell and Maurice Valency; and in Kenneth Tynan's review in *The Observer,* March 23, 1958. The actress's comment "This is an evil . . ." is from Goodman's *Drama on Stage,* as is Brook's "We introduced a . . ." Maurice Zolotow, in *Stagestruck,* quoted Brook's statement, "What would you expect . . ."

AL wrote a series of letters which are quoted in the text. ". . . continues to interest" was written to Edward Bigg, January 20, 1958; "Neither of us . . ." was written to Barry Hyams, February 22, 1958; Hyams also received the letter saying, "The press was . . ." on March 3, 1958. Letters to Edward Bigg (February 25 and February 20, 1958) contained the comments "I shall be glad . . ." and "I doubt very much . . ."

The section on renaming the Globe Theatre the Lunt-Fontanne was derived from interviews with Roger Stevens, Charles Bowden and Robert Whitehead; "Visit with the Lunts," *Theatre Arts,* April 1958; *NYT,* February 17 and May 2, 1958 (the latter article quotes Helen Hayes); and Randolph Goodman's *Drama on Stage.* AL's description of his playing of the scene in *The Visit* ("At first I sort of . . .") is quoted in Lewis Funke and John E. Booth's *Actors Talk About Acting.* Audrey Wood was quoted by John Randolph in an interview. Descriptions of the Lunt-Fontanne Theatre came from *NYT,* May 6, 1958, and a press release from the Producers' Theatre, Inc. LF on smoking cigars in the play: *NYT,* May 9, 1958.

New York reviews of *The Visit: NYT,* May 6, May 18, September 7, 1958, and March 9, 1960. The following New York newspapers: *Post, Daily News, World-Telegram, Sun, Journal-American, Herald Tribune, Daily Mirror* all printed reviews on May 6, 1958. The party at the Hotel Astor is described by Randolph Goodman in *Drama on Stage;* and by LF on UVGS. Accounts of AL being forced into the hospital and an understudy going on in his place appeared in *NYT,* June 26, 1958; clipping in the Lunts' file, BRTC; and in Robert Whitehead's speech at the Theatre Guild tribute to the Lunts in 1983.

Alan Hewitt told me about LF's lapses of memory and AL's attempts to cover for her. AL wrote "damned exhausted" in a letter to Edward Bigg, June 20, 1958. He spoke to Whitney Bolton ("Rows of women . . .") in the New York *Morning Telegraph,* September 17, 1958. Ina Claire's comment ("There isn't a woman . . .") appeared on ZT. LF's "Of course they do . . ." was quoted in the New York *Morning Telegraph,* September 17, 1958. The audience member's whisper "Well, she certainly . . ." is from AL at the Carroll College interview, 1973.

Accounts of the Actors' Fund performance came from an interview with Alan Hewitt and an article in the New York *Herald Tribune,* June 9, 1958. AL's comment to William Le Massena ("Our phantom management . . .") appears in a letter dated January 31, 1959. LF wrote to Antoinette Keith Wilson on February 27, 1959, saying ". . . because the play . . ." AL's letter to Edward Bigg ("I've never been here . . .") is dated February 2, 1959. LF is quoted ("In the theatre in which we were raised . . .") in *NYT,* March 6, 1960. AL said, "When there are cast changes . . ." in Randolph Goodman's *Drama on Stage.* The commercial success of the tour was detailed in a press release from the American Theatre Society, 1960.

AL's comment "If we could have played . . ." is quoted by Randolph Goodman in *Drama on Stage.* Goodman also quotes AL about the woman's remark in Cleveland, a story that AL repeated in a letter to William G. B. Carson, October 30, 1959. The interrupted performance in Washington was described by AL in his interview at Carroll College in 1973. The account of the Lunts' visit to the home of George Burns and Gracie Allen was told in an interview with George Burns; in Burns's *Living It Up;* and in an interview with Carol Channing.

The scheduled visit to Paris and its subsequent cancellation was discussed in *NYT,* March 4, 1960, and in a clipping from *Variety* in BRTC. Reviews of the London production appeared in the following London newspapers: *Daily Express, Daily Mail, News Chronicle, Times* and *Financial Times,* all June 24, 1960. *NYT* also carried a London review on July 24, 1960. AL wrote, "The audience cheered . . ." to Edward Bigg on July 17, 1960. LF's comment "I stood in the wings . . ." was quoted by Dan Sullivan in *NYT,* August 19, 1968. Accounts of the attempts to televise *The Visit* came from an interview with George Schaefer and *NYT,* May 4, 1960.

Chapter Fifteen: SEMI-RETIREMENT

The quotations at the beginning of the chapter are reproduced in the text. Significant sources for this chapter were interviews with Donald Seawell, Charles Bowden, George Schaefer, Julie Harris, Carol Channing and William Le Massena.

The Lunts' social life was described by AL in a letter to William Le Massena

("At least 3 parties . . ."), February 9, 1960; by Noël Coward in *The Noël Coward Diaries* ("We started [dinner] . . ."). AL's letter to Romney Brent ("We didn't like Japan . . .") was written October 22, 1974.

The Lunts' search for new plays: AL's "It's a fine play . . ." was quoted in *NYT,* September 16, 1962. AL's letter to Cheryl Crawford ("not awfully good") was written October 29, 1959. He called the engagement at the City Center "about the most exciting . . ." in a letter to Jean Dalrymple, September 14, 1963. His letter to Richard Whorf ("The thought of acting . . .") is dated March 6, 1964. He told William Le Massena, "We have no plans . . ." in a letter of June 29, 1965. His comment "We're not going to retire . . ." was quoted in *NYT,* January 20, 1965, as was LF saying, "We cannot find a script . . ." AL's comment about *Exit the King* ("most interesting") appeared in an undated letter to Leah Salisbury. He told Ward Morehouse, "Can't find a play . . ." in a letter dated January 28, 1966. Samuel Taylor compiled a script of "great moments" entitled *Things We've Never Done;* AL's comments to Donald Seawell were reported to me in an interview with Seawell.

The Lunts' theatregoing: Noël Coward recorded his observation "They were thrilled . . ." in his diary (Graham Payn and Sheridan Morley, eds.); LF's comment "Lately I find the theatre . . ." was quoted in *NYT,* March 12, 1967. She told Binkie Beaumont, "We loved [*The Importance of Being Earnest*] . . ." in a letter, February 22, 1951. The sequence of dialogue beginning, "She: Dull!" is quoted by Dan Sullivan in *NYT,* August 19, 1968 (combined with material in the *International Herald Tribune,* June 23, 1972). Richard Coe quoted AL saying, "The theatre's very sad . . ." in the Washington *Post,* January 20, 1967. AL told William Le Massena, "I haven't the slightest . . ." in a letter dated February 9, 1969. Le Massena's account of *Grin and Bare It* is from an interview.

LF's comments ("cannot abide the young actor . . ." and "That realistic business . . .") are from ZT; AL's anecdote "Some years ago . . ." was told on the closed-circuit interview with George Schaefer, 1965, as was LF's comment "A live person . . ."; the Lunts' attitude toward Judith Anderson deserting the theatre for films was quoted by Dick Van Patten in an interview. Donald Seawell told me about the ovation the Lunts received when they attended *Home.* AL's comments about the Milwaukee Repertory Theatre were quoted by Richard L. Coe in the Washington *Post,* January 20, 1967. The Lunts' donation of clothing and costumes is described in the Milwaukee *Journal,* November 21, 1965. His evaluation of Richard Burton was quoted in "The Lunts at Ten Chimneys," *Country Beautiful,* October 1962.

AL's observations "People used to talk . . ." and "I don't think you can train . . ." are both from ZT; his statement "Anyone who says . . ." is from Morton Eustis's *Players at Work.* LF told Lewis Funke and John E. Booth, "I don't think technique . . ." and "A very good actor . . ." in *Actors Talk About Acting.* Charles Bowden described LF's attitude toward drinking and discipline in the theatre in an interview.

LF's speech to the Fashion Forum was quoted in the Milwaukee *Journal,* May 14, 1961. The Medal of Freedom ceremonies were described in *NYT,* July 4, 1964; AL said, "Perhaps it merely comes . . ." to Maurice Zolotow in a letter dated July 17, 1964. The activities of the Lunt-Fontanne Foundation, Inc., were described in an interview with Donald Seawell. Documents detailing its activities are in the Lunts' file at SHSW. Samuel Taylor's comments were quoted in *NYT,* December 17, 1961.

The section on the revival of *Così fan tutte* and the production of *La Traviata* was derived primarily from Maurice Zolotow's "When a Broadway Star Stages an Opera," *NYT,* October 9, 1966, including the quotations from AL and Anna Moffo. The *NYT* review appeared September 26, 1966.

Athens, Where the Theatre Began: Material came from *NYT,* May 17, 1963 ("I thought, why not?"), and June 9, 1963 ("I will never understand . . ."); AL's response to the King of Greece was quoted by Donald Seawell in an interview; his letter to Richard Whorf ("We loved it . . .") was written on August 6, 1963. John Horn's review appeared in the New York *Herald Tribune,* September 12, 1963.

The Old Lady Shows Her Medals: AL was quoted ("I'm sure it will seem . . .") in *NYT,* May 17, 1963. LF said, "They're not sentimental . . ." on UVGS. Tom Donovan's comments about the Lunts' enthusiasm on the set appeared in *NYT,* June 9, 1963. Jack Gould's *NYT* review appeared on June 13, 1963. AL told Richard Whorf, "I'm sorry you missed . . ." in a letter dated August 6, 1963.

The Magnificent Yankee: George Schaefer told me of his various attempts to persuade the Lunts to appear on television. AL was quoted in a 1965 NBC press release saying, "Please remember one thing . . ." Schaefer said, "I would find the Lunts . . ." on the closed-circuit interview with the Lunts, 1965. On the same occasion AL said, "He's the most beautiful . . ." and LF told about her attempts to temper her vocal projection. Eugenia Rawls told me about Fontanne's off-camera comment in an interview. LF's comment "You can't see yourself" appeared in *NYT,* January 20, 1965. Emmet Lavery summed up the rehearsal and taping process in "Some Notes on Two-Piano Music," ANTA Souvenir Booklet, 1972.

Anastasia: An article by Joanne Stang in *NYT* (March 12, 1967) quoted LF ("a remarkable young woman") and Julie Harris ("I cannot call her Lynn . . ."); Julie Harris described the rehearsal process to me in an interview. George Schaefer told of LF running lines "until everybody was groggy" in an interview. LF's statement "I was watching for . . ." is a combined quotation from UVGS and *NYT,* March 12, 1967. Jack Gould's review appeared in *NYT,* March 18, 1967.

"The Dick Cavett Show": Quotations from Cavett came from *Cavett* by Dick Cavett and Christopher Porterfield. Jack Gould's verdict appeared in *NYT,* February 12, 1970.

The unproduced television film *The Royal Family of Broadway* was described in interviews with Alan Hewitt and Donald Seawell. LF's annotated scripts are in the Lunts' file, SHSW. George Schaefer told me about the proposed production of *Love Among the Ruins* in an interview.

Advice to aspiring actors: LF ("Cultivate honesty") and AL ("For instance, I don't . . .") were quoted in Lewis Funke and John E. Booth's *Actors Talk About Acting.* AL spoke of "an inward desire . . ." in "Mr. Lunt Writes of Actors and Acting." LF is quoted by Toby Cole and Helen Krich Chinoy in *Actors on Acting* ("There are a few things . . .").

The Lunts' sale of their New York house was described in *NYT,* January 19, 1973, which quoted LF ("For the people . . ."). LF's letter to Tinx Whorf ("No regrets") is dated December 16, 1972.

Chapter Sixteen: SLOW CURTAIN

The quotation beginning the chapter ("The best thing . . .") is from Sheridan Morley's "Lynn Fontanne's Happy Memories," the *Times* of London, October 31, 1978.

The following individuals provided information about the Lunts' activities during their retirement: George Bugbee, Suzanne Knapp, George Schaefer, William Le Massena, Edward Bigg, Donald Seawell, Mary Sargent, Carol Channing, Alan Hewitt.

AL's letter to Richard Whorf ("I'm busy in . . .") is dated April 4, 1962; his letter to William Le Massena ("really up to . . .") was written April 18, 1964. Dan Sullivan, interviewing AL for *NYT,* found him hard at work on his seventy-sixth birthday. Suzanne Knapp described the Lunts' eating habits in retirement to me; a slightly modified version of her remarks was originally given to Richard L. Coe in a letter, November 3, 1984.

AL's jest to the housekeeper ("Oh no, you won't") was quoted in the Chicago *Tribune,* August 8, 1977. His insistence upon keeping fires burning while LF was away was told to me by Alan Hewitt. LF's comment "It is wonderful not to . . ." came from an article by Dan Sullivan that appeared in several newspapers, among them the *Capital Times* (Madison, Wisconsin), August 6, 1983, and the Chicago *Sun-Times,* August 10, 1983. Arthur Marshall quotes the Lunts arguing about *The Taming of the Shrew* in "The Tall Gentleman." The Lunts' attitudes regarding television were taken from ZT; an interview with George Bugbee; AL's remarks at Carroll College, 1973; and from AL's notes to Maurice Zolotow, 1963. AL's letter to William Le Massena ("We're very busy . . .") was written January 12, 1972.

The Lunts' contribution of acreage to Genesee Depot for a park is detailed in the Milwaukee *Sentinel,* September 14, 15 and 28, 1972; the Milwaukee *Journal* (clippings); the Waukesha *Freeman,* September 9, 13, 22, 23 and 26, 1972; February 13, 1973.

The ANTA tribute and associated events were described in interviews with Dick Van Patten, Donald Seawell, Alan Hewitt and William Le Massena. Robert Downing's article "Lunts Honored with 'Party of Century' for 50th Anniversary," which appeared in the Denver *Post* (clipping) in 1972, quotes AL ("You are our life") and tells about Jack Benny's speech.

Robert E. Sherwood wrote of his "love and respect" for the Lunts in "The Lunts." LF's letter to Tinx Whorf ("The whole thing . . .") is dated December 16, 1972. Information about Karin Bugbee's death came from a letter from LF to Romney Brent, October 17, 1970. LF and AL commented on fifty years of married life ("Perhaps it's that . . ." and "She gets a salary . . .") in *NYT,* May 27, 1972.

The Lunts' deteriorating health was described to me by Dr. Edward Bigg. AL's letter to Margaret Webster ("had a go . . .") was written on December 12, 1969. AL was quoted saying, "I can hardly complain . . ." in *Variety,* August 10, 1977. His letter to Paul Myers is dated March 16, 1972; the letter to George Oppenheimer ("My eyes are off . . .") is dated December 13, 1975. His remark about sauce Béarnaise was quoted in the Milwaukee *Journal* (clipping), 1972. The story of AL's comment to Constance Collier is told by Cole Lesley, Graham Payn and Sheridan Morley in *Noël Coward and His Friends.*

AL wrote to William Le Massena ("something the doctors don't like . . .") on September 20, 1973; his letters to Romney Brent ("saved my life" and "surprising to everyone . . .") are dated November 10, 1973, and May 4, 1974. The letter including the phrase "Thanks to Edward [Bigg] . . ." was written to Jerry [?], August 3, 1975. AL's letters to William Le Massena ("I have been involved . . ." and "Lynn's wound is still . . .") were written June 23, 1977, and January 12, 1976. The incident of his having to remain lying in his garden for two hours was described in the New York *Post,* August 3, 1977; it was also described to me by George Schaefer. AL's remark to Helen Hayes ("This great hulk . . .") was quoted in the Milwaukee *Sentinel,* August 4, 1977. His comment "I've been so near death . . ." is from ZT.

AL's funeral is described by Alan Hewitt in his unpublished reminiscences; information also came from the Milwaukee *Sentinel*, August 4, 1977, and the Waukesha *Freeman*, August 6, 1977. Donald Seawell gave me copies of the eulogies he delivered for the Lunts. Alan Hewitt and Charles Bowden described the circumstances surrounding the dimming of the lights on Broadway's theatre marquees in interviews; information also came from *NYT*, August 6, 1977, and *Variety*, August 24, 1977.

LF ("Toward the end . . .") was quoted in the *Times* of London, October 31, 1978. Material on the aftermath of AL's death came from the Chicago *Tribune*, August 8, 1977. John Gielgud's letter to the *Times* of London appeared in August 1977 (clipping). LF's presentation of Ellen Terry's script to the British Theatre Museum was discussed on UVGS; and in the *Times* of London, September 23, 1977. LF also described her trip to England on UVGS; further information was gleaned in interviews with Donald Seawell and George Bugbee. LF's remark to Alan Hewitt ("It is time . . .") appeared in a letter she wrote to him, November 10, 1977. LF is quoted saying, "We were together all the time . . ." in *NYT*, April 24, 1978.

LF's answer to George Schaefer ("I don't know if . . .") about appearing in *The Royal Family* was quoted in *NYT*, April 24, 1978. George Schaefer also described her reaction to me. Similar stories appear in the Milwaukee *Journal*, June 15, 1980, and the Milwaukee *Sentinel*, December 17, 1980. LF said, "I lied in the beginning . . ." on UVGS.

Information on LF's trip to New York in 1978 came from an interview with Armina Marshall and from *NYT*, May 4, 1978. LF spoke of her reading habits in stories appearing in *NYT*, April 24, 1978, and the Waukesha *Freeman*, December 5, 1980. Barbara Cartland wrote to LF on May 25, 1978. LF's trip to Denver to present an award to Henry Fonda is described in *NYT*, January 4, 1980. She is quoted ("In the play, you see . . .") in the Milwaukee *Journal*, June 15, 1980.

LF's receipt of the award for career achievement in the performing arts was described in *NYT*, December 8, 1980. Helen Hayes's letter to LF ("Last night you gave me . . .") is dated June 26, 1980.

The circumstances of LF's final days and her death were described to me by George Bugbee, Suzanne Knapp and Dr. Edward Bigg. Additional information came from the Waukesha *Freeman*, December 5, 1980. The *Freeman* also told of the possibility of a memorial to the Lunts in Genesee Depot in the issue of August 20, 1983. The auction of the Lunts' effects was described in the Milwaukee *Sentinel*, October 19, 1983; and in the Milwaukee *Journal* (clipping), 1983. Harold Clurman wrote about his students' inability to identify AL in "Theatre," the *Nation*, September 10, 1977.

Index

JARED BROWN, born in New York City and raised in Los Angeles, was educated at Ithaca College, San Francisco State College, and the University of Minnesota. He is currently professor of theatre at Western Illinois University, where he directs the programs in theatre history, directing, and playwriting. He has contributed articles—among them a series comprising a comprehensive study of the theatre in America during the Revolution—to many leading theatrical and historical journals, written eight plays, directed more than fifty, and, for a brief time, acted professionally. *The Fabulous Lunts* is his first book.